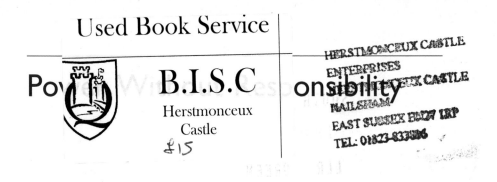

Power Without Responsibility

Press, broadcasting and the internet in Britain

Seventh edition

James Curran and Jean Seaton

Routledge
Taylor & Francis Group

LONDON AND NEW YORK

First edition published 1981 by Fontana
Second edition published 1985 by Methuen & Co. Ltd
Third, fourth, fifth and sixth editions published 1988, 1991, 1997 and 2003
respectively by Routledge
This edition published 2010 by Routledge
2 Park Square, Milton Park, Abingdon, Oxon, OX14 4RN

Simultaneously published in the USA and Canada by Routledge
270 Madison Ave, New York, NY 10016

Reprinted 2010

Routledge is an imprint of the Taylor & Francis Group, an informa business

© 1981, 1985, 1988, 1991, 1997, 2003, 2010 James Curran and Jean Seaton

Typeset in Garamond by Taylor & Francis Books

Printed and bound in Great Britain by
CPI Antony Rowe, Chippenham, Wiltshire

British Library Cataloguing in Publication Data
A catalogue record for this book is available from the British Library

Library of Congress Cataloging in Publication Data
Curran, James.
Power without responsibility : the press, broadcasting, and the internet in
Britain / James Curran and Jean Seaton. – 7th ed.
p. cm.

ISBN 978-0-415-46698-1 (hardback : alk. paper) – ISBN 978-0-415-46699-8
(pbk. : alk. paper) – ISBN 978-0-203-87140-9 (e-book) 1. Press – Great
Britain. 2. Broadcasting – Great Britain. 3. Digital media – Great Britain. I.
Seaton, Jean. II. Title.
PN5114.C84 2009
072 – dc22
2009008954

ISBN10: 0-415-46698-9 (hbk)
ISBN10: 0-415-46699-7 (pbk)
ISBN10: 0-203-87140-5 (ebk)

ISBN13: 978-0-415-46698-1 (hbk)
ISBN13: 978-0-415-46699-8 (pbk)
ISBN13: 978-0-203-87140-9 (ebk)

Contents

About the authors

James Curran is Professor of Communications at Goldsmiths College, University of London, and Director of the Goldsmiths Leverhulme Media Research Centre. He is the author or editor (some jointly) of *Mass Communication and Society*; *The British Press*; *Newspaper History*; *Culture, Society and the Media*; *British Cinema History*; *Media, Culture and Society: A Critical Reader*; *Bending Reality*; *Impacts and Influences*; *Mass Media and Society*; *Cultural Studies and Communications*; *Media, Ritual and Identity*; *Media Organisations in Society*; *De-Westernizing Media Studies*; *Media* and *Power*; *Contesting Media Power* and *Media and Cultural Theory*. He has been an amateur journalist, as a weekly columnist for *The Times* and editor of *New Socialist*, and a Visiting Professor at the Universities of California, Oslo, Stockholm, Stanford and Pennsylvania.

Jean Seaton is Professor of Media History at the University of Westminster and Official Historian of the BBC. She is director of the Orwell Prize for political writing and journalism (theorwellprize.co.uk). She is author, editor or joint editor of *Carnage and the Media: the Making and Breaking of News about Violence*; *The Media in British Politics*; *The Media of Conflict*; *The Prerogative of the Harlot: Politics and the Media*; and *What is to be done? Making the Media and Politics Better*. She is an editor of *Political Quarterly*; has written widely on the media, wars and disasters, and their impact on children and women; media policy, and on the role of the BBC nationally and internationally. She broadcasts regularly. Her next book will be *The BBC Under Siege*.

Acknowledgements

This book has been more like a project that has arched over our lives than a simple volume. When we started it, we were young and various editions have punctuated our private and public existence. Our children were born and grew up during its lifetime. The media landscape has been transformed since the first edition: in 1981, the personal computer had only just been invented, and the World Wide Web existed in embryonic form only as a science fiction fantasy. Blogging had not been invented, but reporting and comment (which it is related to) had. Governments of the left and right have come and gone. Yet the compulsion to write and rewrite this book has remained constant because the media matter. Democracies depend on informed electorates; institutions become corrupt unless they are examined in public; individuals find their emotions and wants moulded in ways that can enhance or diminish their lives; all these things are influenced by the media.

We started with the history of the press and broadcasting because history is a very good way of undermining fables about the past, and because we believed that without understanding the past it is difficult to be sensible about the present. We also believed that policy is important – that getting the right policies has a tremendous impact on how the media perform. Thus the destruction of the fairness doctrine in America in 1987 that had obliged broadcasters to be fair and balanced in their political reporting powerfully influenced America for a generation.

On the way, over the years, many people have helped with the book (all acknowledged in previous editions). James Curran's wife, friends, colleagues and students have all contributed very directly to its development (most notably, in this edition, Goldsmiths postgraduate student Joanna Reddern who provided key information for chapter 16). But none contributed more than the late Ben Pimlott, who suggested the title of the book and made many valued suggestions. As the husband of Jean Seaton and close friend of James Curran, he is much missed. This edition is dedicated to him.

Preface to the seventh edition

This book has evolved, and also expanded, since it was first published. This new edition introduces a new Chapter 19, Metabolising Britishness, and drops a previous chapter (former Chapter 20). It extensively revises Chapter 20, which has a new title, Global Understanding. In addition, so much has changed since the last edition was published that it has been necessary to substantially rewrite Chapter 16 on New Media in Britain, and also Chapter 24, which has been given the new title of Media Reform: Democratic Choices. Many other chapters have been revised and updated to take account of changes in the media, and in media research.

To the memory of Ben Pimlott

Part I

Press history

Chapter 1

Whig press history as political mythology

The orthodox interpretation of the development of the British press has remained unchanged for over a century. 'The British press,' writes David Chaney, 'is generally agreed to have attained its freedom around the middle of the nineteenth century.'[1] This view, first advanced in pioneer Victorian histories of journalism, has been repeated uncritically ever since.

The winning of press freedom is attributed in part to a heroic struggle against state repression. The key events in this struggle are generally said to be the abolition of the Court of Star Chamber in 1641, the ending of press licensing in 1694, Fox's Libel Act, 1792, and the repeal of press taxation – the so-called 'taxes on knowledge' – in the period 1853–61. Only with the last of these reforms, it is claimed, did the press become fully free.

It is also argued that the market development of the press contributed to its emancipation. Indeed, some researchers place greater emphasis on this than on the fight against restrictive laws. 'The true censorship,' John Roach writes of the late Georgian press, 'lay in the fact that the newspaper had not yet reached financial independence, and consequently depended on the administration or the parties.' The growth of newspaper profits, largely from advertising, supposedly rescued the press from its compromising dependence on state or party subsidies. This view of advertising as the midwife of press freedom is restated succinctly by Ivon Asquith in a scholarly study of the early nineteenth-century press. 'Since sales were inadequate to cover the costs of producing a paper,' he writes,

> it was the growing income from advertising which provided the material base for the change of attitude from subservience to independence. It is perhaps no exaggeration to say that the growth of advertising revenue was the most important single factor in enabling the press to emerge as the Fourth Estate of the realm.

Orthodox histories of the press, with their stress on the free market and legal emancipation as the foundation of press freedom,[2] provide a powerful, mythological account with a political moral. Thus, Lord Francis-Williams, Labour Prime Minister Clement Atlee's spin doctor, invoked press history to defend advertisers' funding of the press. 'The dangerous dependence of newspapers on advertising,' he wrote,

> has often been the theme of newspaper reformers – usually from outside its ranks. But the daily press would never have come into existence as a force in public and social life if it had not been for the need of men of commerce to advertise. Only through the growth of advertising did the press achieve independence.

Similarly, journalists have cited the historic struggle against state repression as grounds for opposing any state-sponsored reform of the press. For instance, former *Sunday Times* journalist John Whale concluded a brief historical account of state censorship with the warning that politicians are still seeking 'indirect ways of bringing state power to bear on unsympathetic journalism'. The principal way that this is being manifested, he cautioned, is in proposals to curb concentration of press ownership.

However, while Whig history is invoked to oppose change in the press, it is summoned as an ally to justify the fundamental reorganization of broadcasting. Thus, the Peacock Committee – appointed by the Thatcher government to investigate the funding of the BBC – retold the history of the dismantling of press censorship[3] as a prelude to arguing for the eventual removal of all broadcasting regulation (which it equated with 'censorship'). In effect, it deployed a particular view of newspaper history to advocate the reconstruction of television along the free market lines of the press.

Orthodox accounts of press history thus have policy implications for the present day. The ideological resonance of this standard approach is reinforced by the eloquent way in which a supposedly independent press is portrayed as empowering the people. According to the *New Cambridge Modern History*, free newspapers became 'great organs of the public mind' during the nineteenth century: they relayed public opinion to authority, and rendered governments accountable. The free press contributed, it is also argued, to the maturing of Britain's democracy by becoming more responsible, and less partisan. This establishment view has gained surprising adherents. Even a Marxist such as Raymond Williams noted with approval that after 1855 'most newspapers were able to drop their frantic pamphleteering',[4] while the radical historian Alan Lee portrayed the later Victorian period as the 'golden age' of British journalism.

Agreement among historians is not total. There is a continuing debate about when newspapers became fully independent of political parties. A number of historians also express misgivings about the growing 'commercialization' of the press, and are sharply critical of the first generation of press lords. But few contest the conventional wisdom, embalmed in a much-acclaimed two-volume study by Stephen Koss, that the capitalist development of the press contributed to its 'transition from official to popular control'.

What follows is a long-overdue attempt to reappraise this standard inter-pretation of press history.[5] It will indicate the need not merely to re-examine critically the accepted view of the historical emergence of a 'free' press but to stand it on its head. The period around the mid-nineteenth century, it will be argued, did not inaugurate a new era of press freedom and liberty; it established instead a new system of press censorship more effective than anything that had gone before. Market forces succeeded where legal repression had failed in conscripting the press to the social order in mid-Victorian Britain.

However, the press market evolved subsequently in a way that created new openings, while the political climate of Britain changed in a way that made possible the development of new progressive newspapers. If the radical jour-nalism of the early nineteenth century was stifled, its place was taken by a reformist press that contributed to the building of the welfare state.

Notes

1. Notes for each chapter have been limited, although their number has tended to grow with each new edition. An extensive bibliography is provided at the end of the book.
2. For a restatement of this position in a standard textbook, see H. Barker, *Newspapers, Politics, and English Society, 1695–1855* (Edinburgh, Longman, 2000).
3. The Peacock Committee's historical account is extremely simplistic, and ignores revisionist interpretations by historians of the seventeenth- and eighteenth-century press.
4. R. Williams, *The Long Revolution* (Harmondsworth, Pelican, 1965), p. 218. He later modified his view in R. Williams, 'The press and popular culture: an historical perspective', in G. Boyce, J. Curran and P. Wingate (eds), *Newspaper History* (London, Constable, 1978).
5. A number of important studies of early nineteenth-century working-class politics – notably by the Thompsons, Hollis, Wiener and Epstein – provide evidence that, by implication at least, casts doubt on the conventional Whig thesis of the triumphant rise of a free press in mid-Victorian Britain. The wider implications of these studies for reinterpreting press history have been buried, however, because they focused on early working-class struggles rather than on the long-term development of journalism.

Chapter 2

The struggle for a free press

The remarkably resilient Whig interpretation of press history is sustained by focusing attention upon mainstream commercial newspapers, while ignoring or downplaying the development of the radical press. Only if this selective perspective is maintained does the conventional view of the rise of a free press appear plausible.

During the second half of the eighteenth century and in the early nineteenth century, a section of the commercial press did indeed become more politically independent, partly as a consequence of the growth of advertising. This additional revenue reduced dependence on political subsidies; encouraged papers to reject covert secret service grants (the last English newspaper to receive a clandestine government grant was the *Observer* in 1840); improved the wages and security of employment of journalists so that they became less biddable; and, above all, financed greater expenditure on news gathering so that newspapers became less reliant on official sources and more reluctant to trade their independence in return for obtaining 'prior intelligence' from the government. This shift was symbolized by *The Times*'s magisterial declaration on Boxing Day 1834 that it would no longer accept early information from government offices since this was inconsistent with 'the pride and independence of our journal', and anyway its 'own information was earlier and surer'.

However, the growth of advertising did not transform the commercial press into an 'independent fourth estate'. On the contrary, the development of modern political parties from the 1860s onward encouraged a closer interpenetration of party politics and commercial journalism. A number of leading proprietors in Victorian and Edwardian Britain were Members of Parliament, while some national newspapers were subsidized by party loyalists or from party funds until well into the twentieth century. This continuing party involvement belied the often-repeated claim that the press was an *independent* check on Parliament and the executive; in reality, newspapers long remained an extension of the party system.[1]

The conventional portrayal of advertising as the midwife of press independence is also directly contradicted by the emergence of the radical press as a political force in the early nineteenth century. As we shall see, pioneer radical papers did not obtain significant advertising support; yet they were independent both of government and the opposition in Parliament. Their rise demonstrated that newspapers could – and did – become autonomous from the state and party through financial support other than advertising.

The rise of the radical press as an extra-parliamentary force also revealed the limitations of official censorship. Successive governments sought to curb the radical press through restrictive laws. But although seditious and blasphemous libel law was framed in a catch-all form that made any kind of fundamental criticism of the social order a legal offence, it was not always easy to enforce. Juries, empowered by Fox's Libel Act (1792) to determine guilt or innocence, were often reluctant to convict. This was brought home to the authorities by the sensational acquittals of Eaton, Hardy and Tooke in the 1790s, Wooler and Hone in 1817, and Cobbett in 1831. The sharp edge of the law was further blunted in 1843 when Lord Campbell's Libel Act made the statement of truth in the public interest a legitimate defence against the charge of seditious libel.

Even before the 1843 Act was passed, the authorities had come round reluctantly to the view that libel prosecutions were often counter-productive. When the editor of *The Republican* was prosecuted in 1819, the paper's circulation rose by over 50 per cent. Similarly disillusioning experiences prompted the Attorney-General to conclude in 1843 that 'a libeller thirsted for nothing more than the valuable advertisement of a public trial in a Court of Justice'. This disenchantment was reflected in a shift of government policy: there were only sixteen prosecutions for seditious and blasphemous libel in the period 1825–34, compared with 167 prosecutions during the preceding eight years.

Instead, the authorities came to rely increasingly on the newspaper stamp duty and taxes on paper and advertisements as a way of curbing the radical press. The intention of these press taxes was twofold: to restrict the readership of newspapers to the well-to-do by raising cover prices; and to limit the ownership of newspapers to the propertied class by increasing publishing costs. The belief was that substantial stakeholders in society would conduct newspapers 'in a more responsible manner than was likely to be the result of pauper management',[2] and that it was potentially dangerous to the social order to allow the lower ranks to read newspapers at all.

So, successive governments increased the burden and scope of press taxation in order to make it a more effective safeguard against subversion. The stamp duty was increased by 266 per cent between 1789 and 1815. Publications subject to the stamp duty were redefined in 1819 to include political periodicals. In the same year, a security system was introduced which required publishers of weeklies to register their papers and place financial bonds of between £200 and £300 with the authorities. Although the ostensible purpose of this requirement was to guarantee payment of libel fines, its real objective was to force up the cost of publishing and ensure, as Lord Castlereagh explained to the Commons, that 'persons exercising the power of the press should be men of some respectability and property'.[3] It is perhaps worth noting – in view of what happened later – that the opposition persuaded the government that £500 was too high a figure to set as a bond on the grounds that it would be an excessive constraint on the freedom to publish.

The government's reliance on taxes and securities as a way of containing the radical press worked for a time. The upsurge of radical journalism that occurred in the wake of the Napoleonic wars weakened in the 1820s. But with the revival of radical agitation in the early 1830s, the authorities faced a more formidable challenge – the systematic evasion of the stamp duty by an underground press, which had developed a well-organized distribution network and even set up a financial support system for the families of jailed newspaper sellers.

The government's first response was to seek to enforce the law more effectively. Printers of unstamped newspapers were rounded up; supplies of paper were intercepted; sellers of underground papers were gaoled. At least 1130 cases of selling unstamped newspapers were prosecuted in London alone during the period 1830–36. Yet, despite these measures, the radical press continued to flourish. 'Prosecutions, fines and imprisonments were alike failures', the minister in charge of the fight against the unstamped press later recalled.[4] By the summer of 1836 the government was forced to concede defeat. The Commons was informed on 20 June that the government 'had resorted to all means afforded by the existing law' but that it 'was altogether ineffectual to the purpose of putting an end to the unstamped papers'.

The government's strategy had failed. By 1836 the unstamped press published in London had an aggregate readership of at least two million. According to government estimates, its circulation even exceeded that of the respectable, stamped press. The whole system of press control seemed on the point of final collapse, since leading publishers of stamped papers warned the government that they would also evade the stamp duty unless more effective steps were taken to enforce it.

The Whig government responded to this crisis with a well-planned counter-offensive. New measures were passed which strengthened the government's search and confiscation powers. Penalties were also increased for being found in possession of an unstamped newspaper, and the stamp duty was reduced by 75 per cent in order to make 'smuggling' less attractive. Thus what has been seen as a landmark in the advance of press freedom was manifestly repressive both in intention and in effect. As Spring Rice, the Chancellor of the Exchequer, explained to the Commons, a strategic concession, combined with increased coercive powers, was necessary in order to enforce a system that had broken down. The aim of these new measures, he stated candidly, was to 'put down the unstamped papers'.[5]

The government's new strategy succeeded in its immediate objective. 'No unstamped papers can be attempted with success', declared Hetherington, a leading radical publisher, shortly after being released from prison, unless 'some means can be devised either to print the newspaper without types and presses, or render the premises ... inaccessible to armed force'.[6] By 1837 the clandestine radical press had disappeared.

Compliance with the law forced radical newspapers to raise their prices, even though the stamp duty was much reduced. Whereas most unstamped papers had sold at 1d in the early 1830s, most of their successors in the 1840s sold at 4d or 5d – a sum that was well beyond the means of individual workers. However, the government's aim of destroying the radical press was frustrated by organized consumer resistance. Informal groups of working people pooled their resources each week to purchase a radical paper. Union branches, clubs and political associations financed the collective purchase of newspapers. Even taverns were threatened with the withdrawal of custom unless they bought radical papers. Partly as a consequence of this concerted action, new radical papers emerged which gained even larger circulations than those reached by their best-selling unstamped predecessors.

Admittedly, after 1836 the radical press was not as strong in relation to the respectable press as it had been before. There was a substantial growth, between 1836 and 1855, in the number and circulation of commercial local weekly papers as well as in the readership of religious publications and of family and 'useful knowledge' magazines. However, since much of this expansion appears to have taken place among the middle and lower-middle classes,[7] it did not greatly diminish the radical press's influence within the working class.

The principal rivals to the radical press within the working class (of whom well over half were literate or semi-literate by the 1830s) were almanacs, printed ballads, gallowsheets and chapbooks. However, radical newspapers far outstripped rival *political* publications read by the working class.

Indeed, the radical press was the circulation pace setter for the nation's press throughout much of the period 1815–55. Cobbett's radical *Twopenny Trash* broke all circulation records in 1816–17. This record was probably beaten by the left-wing *Weekly Police Gazette* which, to judge from a government raid on its premises, had a circulation of over 40,000 in 1836 – well over double that of leading conservative weeklies such as the *Sunday Times* and *Bell's Life in London.* In 1838 the militant *Northern Star* gained the largest circulation of any newspaper published in the provinces and, in 1839, the largest national circulation of any paper apart from the liberal-radical *Weekly Dispatch.* The *Northern Star's* circulation was later exceeded by that of the militant *Reynolds News*, which in the early 1850s had the second-largest circulation in Britain. Along with the liberal-radical *Lloyds Weekly*, *Reynolds News* became the first newspaper to break through the 100,000 circulation barrier in 1856.[8]

While newspaper circulations during the first half of the nineteenth century are small by modern standards, circulation figures are not a constant index of consumption. The sharing of high-cost papers, together with the widespread practice of reading papers aloud for the benefit of the semi-literate and illiterate, resulted in a very high number of 'readers' for each newspaper sold. Hollis and Epstein estimate, respectively, that radical newspapers reached upward of twenty readers per copy in the 1830s and 1840s. This compares with an average of only two to three readers per copy of contemporary daily papers. Yet even if a cautious estimate of ten readers per copy is taken as the norm for radical papers in the early Victorian period, it still means that the *Northern Star* and its successor, *Reynolds News*, each reached at their peak, before the repeal of the stamp duty, half a million readers. This was at a time when the population of England and Wales over the age of 14 was little over ten million. The emergent radical press was thus a genuinely popular force, reaching a very large public.

The economic structure of the radical press

The rise of the radical press was a direct consequence of the growth of trade union and working-class political organizations. However, this rise was also enabled by the prevailing economic structure of the press industry. Since this is an important aspect of the central argument that follows, it is worth examining in some detail the finances of the early radical newspapers.

The initial capital required to set up a radical paper in the early part of the nineteenth century was extremely small. Most radical unstamped papers were printed not on a steam press, but on hand presses, which cost as little as £10 to acquire. Metal type was often hired by the hour and print workers paid on a piecework basis.

After 1836 leading stamped radical papers were printed on more sophisticated machinery. The *London Dispatch*, for instance, was printed on a Napier machine, bought with the help of a wealthy well-wisher and the profits from Hetherington's other publications. The *Northern Star* had a printing press specially constructed for it in London. Even so, launch costs were extremely small in comparison with the subsequent period. The *Northern Star*, for instance, was launched in 1837 with a total capital of £690, mostly raised by public subscription.

Financing a paper during its initial trading period could often cost more than setting it up. Even so, early losses were minimized by low operating costs. Radical unstamped papers paid no tax, relied heavily upon news reports filed by their readers on a voluntary basis, and had small newsprint costs because of their high readership per copy. Consequently they needed to attain only small circulations in order to be economically viable. For instance, the *Poor Man's Guardian*, a leading newspaper of the early 1830s, broke even as soon as its circulation reached 2500.

Even after 1836, when a penny stamp duty had to be paid on each copy, the running costs of the radical press remained relatively low. The influential

London Dispatch reported, for example (17 September 1836), that 'the whole expense allowed for editing, reporting, reviewing, literary contributions etc., in fact, the entire cost of what is technically called "making up" the paper, is only six pounds per week'. In the same issue it reported that, at its selling price of 3/d, it could break even with a circulation of 16,000. Similarly the *Northern Star* which, unlike its predecessors, developed a substantial network of paid correspondents, claimed to be spending little more than £9 10s a week on its reporting establishment in 1841. Selling at 4/d, it was able to break even with a weekly circulation of about 6200. This low break-even point meant that its run-in costs were very small. Indeed the *Northern Star* almost certainly moved into profit within its first month of publication.

Because publishing costs were low the ownership and control of newspapers could be in the hands of people committed, in the words of Joshua Hobson, an ex-handloom weaver and publisher of the *Voice of West Riding*, 'to support the rights and interests of the order and class to which it is my pride to belong'. Some newspapers, such as the *Voice of the People*, the *Liberator* and the *Trades Newspaper*, were owned by political or trade union organizations. Others were owned by individual proprietors such as Cleave, Watson and Hetherington, many of them people of humble origins who had risen to prominence through the working-class movement. While not lacking in ruthlessness or business acumen, the people they entrusted with the editing of their newspapers were all former manual workers like William Hill and Joshua Hobson, or middle-class activists like O'Brien and Lorymer, whose attitudes had been shaped by long involvement in working-class politics. A substantial section of the popular newspaper press reaching a working-class audience was thus controlled by those who were committed to the working-class movement.

This influenced the way in which journalists working for the radical press perceived their role. Unlike the institutionalized journalists of the later period, they tended to see themselves as activists rather than as professionals. Indeed many of the paid correspondents of the *Poor Man's Guardian*, *Northern Star* and the early *Reynolds News* were also political organizers for the National Union of the Working Classes or the Chartist Movement. They sought to describe and expose the dynamics of power and inequality rather than to report 'hard news' as a series of disconnected events. They saw themselves as class representatives rather than as disinterested intermediaries and attempted to establish a relationship of real reciprocity with their readers. As the editor of the *Northern Star* wrote in its fifth anniversary issue,

> I have ever sought to make it [the paper] rather a reflex of your minds than a medium through which to exhibit any supposed talent or intelligence of my own. This is precisely my conception of what a people's organ should be.

The second important feature of the economic structure of the radical press in the first half of the nineteenth century was that it was self-sufficient on the proceeds of sales alone. The radical unstamped press carried very little commercial advertising and the stamped radical press fared little better. The *London Dispatch* (17 September 1836) complained bitterly, for instance, of the 'prosecutions, fines and the like et ceteras with which a paper of our principles is sure to be more largely honoured than by the lucrative patronage of advertisers'. The grudge held against advertisers by the *London Dispatch* and other radical newspapers was fully justified. An examination of the official advertisement duty returns reveals a marked disparity in the amount of advertising duty per 1000 copies (an index that takes account of circulation difference) paid by the radical press compared with its more respectable rivals. For example, in 1840 two middle-class papers published in Leeds (the *Leeds Mercury* and *Leeds Intelligence*) and the four leading national daily papers (*The Times*, *Morning Post*, *Morning Chronicle* and *Morning Advertiser*) all paid over fifty times more advertisement duty per 1000 copies than the radical *Northern Star*, a Leeds-based paper with a national circulation.

A similar pattern emerges in the case of the other leading radical papers for which returns are available. In 1817, for instance, Cobbett's *Political Register* received only three advertisements: its advertisement duty per 1000 copies was less than one-hundredth of that of respectable rival periodicals, although this disparity was somewhat reduced by the 1830s. The *London Dispatch* in 1837 was only marginally better off: it paid per 1000 copies less than one twenty-fifth of the advertisement duty collected from each of its main respectable rivals in London, also with a national circulation.

This lack of advertising support meant that radical papers had limited money at their disposal for editorial development. Some were forced to close down, even though they had larger circulations than their respectable rivals better endowed with advertising. The radical press was thus put in a position of competitive disadvantage at a time when the high price of newspapers, inflated by the stamp duty, was already a major deterrent against buying papers among the working class.

Yet despite these substantial disadvantages, the absence of advertising did not prevent the radical press from flourishing. While fortunes were not easily made, radical newspapers – both stamped and unstamped – could be highly profitable. Hetherington, the publisher of the stamped *London Dispatch*, was reported to be making £1000 a year from his business in 1837. Similarly the stamped *Northern Star* was estimated to have produced a remarkable profit of £13,000 in 1839 and £6500 in 1840, which was generated very largely from sales revenue.

This independence from advertising was a liberating force. Radical papers were, by the 1830s, increasingly oriented towards a working-class audience, and became more uncompromising in their attacks on capitalism. They were not forced to temper their radicalism or to seek a more affluent readership by the need to attract advertising. Instead they were free to respond to the radicalization of the working-class movement: they relied on their readers rather than advertisers for their economic viability.

The impact of the radical press

The radical press did not merely reflect the growth of the working-class organizations; it also extended their influence. One of the most important, and least remarked on, aspects of the development of the radical press in the first half of the nineteenth century was that its leading publications developed a nationwide circulation. Even as early as the second decade, leading radical papers such as the *Twopenny Trash*, *Political Register* and *Republican* were read as far afield as Yorkshire, Lancashire, the Midlands and East Anglia, as well as in the south of England. By the early 1830s the principal circulation newspapers like the *Weekly Police Gazette*, the *Poor Man's Guardian* and *Dispatch* had a distribution network extending on a north–south axis from Glasgow to Truro, and on an east–west axis from Norwich to Carmarthen. Part of the impact of the radical press stemmed from this central fact – the extent of its geographical distribution.

The radical press was effective in reinforcing a growing consciousness of class and in unifying disparate elements of the working community, partly because its leading publications provided national coverage and reached a national working-class audience. It helped to extend the often highly exclusive occupational solidarity of early trade unionism to other sectors of the labour community by demonstrating the common predicament of union members in different trades throughout the country. Workers attempting to set up an extra-legal union read in the radical press in 1833–34, for instance, of similar struggles by glove workers in Yeovil, cabinet-makers and joiners in Glasgow and Carlisle, shoemakers and smiths in Northampton, and bricklayers and masons in London, as well as of working-class struggles in Belgium and Germany. Similarly the radical press helped to reduce geographical isolation by showing that local agitation – whether against Poor Law Commissioners, new machinery, long working hours or wage reductions – conformed to a common pattern throughout the country. The radical press further expanded its readers' field of social vision by publishing, particularly in the later phase from the 1830s onward, news that none of the respectable papers carried, and by interpreting this news within a radical framework of analysis. It was, in the words of the Chartist leader Feargus O'Connor, 'the link that binds the industrious classes together'.[9]

The radical press also helped to promote working-class organizations. Movements ranging from early trade unions to political organizations, such as the National Union of the Working Classes and the Chartist Movement, partly depended for their success on the publicity they obtained from the radical press. O'Connor recalled that before the emergence of Chartist newspapers, 'I found that the press was entirely mute, while I was working myself to death, and that a meeting in one town did nothing for another'. Press publicity stimulated people to attend meetings and to become involved in political and industrial organizations; it also brought the activist vanguard of the working-class movement into national prominence, helping, for example, to transform unknown farm workers victimized for joining a trade union in the remote village of Tolpuddle into national working-class heroes. No less important, it also contributed to the morale of activists in the working-class movement who were confronted by what must have seemed, at times, insuperable odds. Without the *Northern Star*, declared one speaker at a local Chartist meeting, 'their own sounds might echo through the wilderness'.[10]

Above all, the radical press was a major mobilizing force in its own right. We have become so accustomed to the individualized pattern of newspaper consumption amid a steady flow of information from a variety of media that it is difficult to understand the political significance of newspapers in the early nineteenth century. Newspapers were often the only readily available source of information about what was happening outside the local community and, in some cases, generated passionate loyalty among their readers. Fielden recalls, for instance, 'on the day the newspaper, the *Northern Star*, O'Connor's paper, was due, the people used to line the roadside waiting for its arrival, which was paramount to everything else for the time being'. The impact of the radical press was reinforced further by the discussions that followed the reading aloud of newspaper articles in taverns, workshops, homes and public meetings, vividly described in memoirs and reminiscences.[11] This social pattern of consumption (which continued on a diminished scale late into the nineteenth century) resulted in newspapers having a greater public impact than they do today.

The first wave of radical papers from the 1790s through to the late 1820s played an important part in the general reorientation that preceded the political mobilization of a section of the working class. They raised expectations both by invoking a mythical past in which plenty and natural justice had prevailed, and by proclaiming the possibility of a future in which poverty could be relieved through political means. It was this raising of hopes, combined with a direct assault on the Anglican 'morality' which sanctioned the social order, which most alarmed parliamentarians at the time. As Dr Philimore, MP, warned the Commons following official reports that servants and common soldiers had been seen reading radical newspapers,

> Those infamous publications ... inflame [working people's] passions and awaken their selfishness, contrasting their present conditions with what they contend to be their future condition – a condition incompatible with human nature, and with those immutable laws which Providence has established for the regulation of civil society.[12]

The radical press not only helped to weaken political passivity, based on fatalistic acceptance of the social system as 'natural' and 'providential', but also began to dispel the collective lack of confidence that had inhibited working-class resistance. The least valued section of the community was able to obtain a new understanding of its role in society through its own press. 'The real strength and all the resources of the country,' characteristically proclaimed Cobbett's *Political Register*, 'ever have sprung from the *labour* of its people.' This novel view of the world, popularized through the more radical journals, provided a means of reordering the entire ranking of status and moral worth in society. The highest in the land were degraded to the lowest place as idle parasites: working people, in contrast, were elevated to the top as the productive and useful section of the community. The early militant press thus fostered an alternative value system that symbolically turned the world upside down. It also repeatedly emphasized the potential power of working people to effect social change through the force of 'combination' and organized action.

The radical press played a part in radicalizing the emergent working-class movement by developing a more critical political analysis. The first generation of radical papers was trapped inside the intellectual categories of the eighteenth-century liberal attack on the aristocratic constitution. Conflict was generally portrayed in political terms as a struggle between the aristocracy and the 'productive classes' (usually defined to include working capitalists as well as the working classes), while criticism was focused mainly upon corruption in high places and repressive taxation that was said to impoverish the productive community. This critique implicitly promoted 'liberal' political reform rather than a far-reaching transformation of the reward structure of society.

By the 1830s the more militant papers had shifted their focus of attack from 'old corruption' to the economic process which enabled the capitalist class to appropriate in profits the wealth created by labour. Conflict was redefined as a class struggle between labour and capital, between the working classes and a coalition of aristocrats, 'millocrats' and 'shopocrats'. This more militant analysis signposted the way forward towards a far-reaching programme of social reconstruction in which, in the words of the *Poor Man's Guardian* (19 October 1833), workers will 'be at the top instead of at the bottom of society – or rather that there should be no bottom or top at all'.

This new analysis was often conflated with the old liberal analysis in an uncertain synthesis. There was, moreover, a basic continuity in the perspectives offered by the less militant wing of the radical press, which gained in influence during the 1840s. But such continuity should come as no surprise. It was only natural that the political complexion of the broad left press should reflect the ebb and flow of militancy. Nor is it at all surprising that traditional political beliefs should have persisted in view of what we now know about the enduring resilience of belief systems. But so long as the activist working class controlled its own popular press, it possessed the institutional means to explore more radical understandings of society. It also had a collective resource for defining, expressing and maintaining a radical public opinion different from that proclaimed by the capitalist press, as well as a defence against the ideological assault mounted on the working class through schools, churches, mechanics' institutes and useful knowledge magazines.

The militant press sustained a radical subculture, which represented a potential threat to the undemocratic social order. Indeed, in 1842 a General Strike was called to secure universal suffrage through the force of industrial action. It received extensive support in industrial Lancashire, much of Yorkshire and parts of the Midlands. While the strike was crushed, and some 1500 labour leaders were imprisoned, it was a sign of an increasingly unsettled society in which the radical press had become a significant force.

In short, the control system administered by the state had failed. Neither prosecutions for seditious libel nor a tax system designed to restrict newspaper readership had succeeded in preventing the rise of the radical press. As we shall see, this prompted thoughtful parliamentarians to consider whether there might be a better way of containing insurgent journalism.

Notes

1. Five researchers – George Boyce, Alan Lee, Stephen Koss, Colin Seymour-Ure and Lucy Brown – have documented the press's continuing involvement in party politics long after the press is supposed to have blossomed as an 'independent fourth estate'. Their studies have thus modified one aspect of the traditional Whig interpretation of press history. For more about this, see Chapter 5.
2. Pelham, *Parliamentary Debates*, 11 (1832), cols 491–92.
3. Castlereagh, *Parliamentary Debates*, 91 (1819), cols 1177ff.
4. Spring Rice, *Parliamentary Debates*, 138 (1855), col. 966.
5. Spring Rice, *Parliamentary Debates*, 34 (1836), cols 627–34; 37 (1837), col. 1165.
6. *London Dispatch* (17 September 1836).
7. Report of the Select Committee on Newspaper Stamps (SCNS), *Parliamentary Papers*, 17 (1851); Milner-Gibson, *Parliamentary Debates*, 135 (1853), col. 1136, among others.
8. P. Hollis, *The Pauper Press* (London, Oxford University Press, 1970), p. 95; *Parliamentary Debates*, 34 (1836), col. 627; SCNS Appendix 4; V. Berridge, 'Popular Sunday papers and mid-Victorian society', in G. Boyce, J. Curran and P. Wingate (eds), *Newspaper History* (London, Constable, 1978), p. 249.
9. *Northern Star* (16 January 1841).
10. *Northern Star* (26 August 1848).
11. For instance, W. E. Adams, *Memoirs of a Social Atom*, vol. 1 (London, Hutchinson, 1903), pp. 164–66; interview with Wesley Perrins, *Bulletin of the Society for the Study of Labour History* (1970), pp. 16–24.
12. Dr Philimore, *Parliamentary Debates*, 91 (1819), col. 1363.

Chapter 3

The ugly face of reform

The parliamentary campaign against 'the taxes on knowledge' is generally portrayed as a triumphant struggle for press freedom, sustained by an amalgam of special interests but motivated largely by libertarian ideals in opposition to the authoritarian legacy of the past.[1] The only discordant note in this inspiring account comes from the parliamentary campaigners celebrated in this historical legend. Their aims and, indeed, their public utterances are difficult to reconcile with the historic role assigned to them in liberal ideology.

Widespread evasion of the stamp duty in the early 1830s caused press regulation to become a major political issue. Traditionalists argued that the government should enforce the stamp duty with tougher measures, while a relatively small group of reformers in Parliament argued that the stamp duty had become unenforceable in the face of mass resistance and should be repealed. The two sides in the debate did not disagree over objectives so much as over tactics. As the Lord Chancellor succinctly put it in 1834,

> the only question to answer, and the only problem to solve, is how they [the people] shall read in the best manner; how they shall be instructed politically, and have political habits formed the most safe for the constitution of the country.

Traditionalists alleged that abolition of the stamp duty would result in the country being flooded with 'atrocious publications'. Reformers countered by arguing that the stamp duty merely suppressed 'the cheap reply' to seditious publications from responsible quarters. Radical publishers were not being silenced by inefficient controls; instead they were being given a clear field in which to indoctrinate the people with 'the most pernicious doctrines' without encountering effective competition.[2]

Underlying this difference over tactics were divergent approaches to social control. Supporters of press regulation tended to favour coercion. Reformers, on the other hand, generally stressed the importance of engineering social consent. As Bulwer Lytton argued when proposing the repeal of the stamp duty in 1832:

At this moment when throughout so many nations we see the people at war with their institutions, the world presents to us two great, may they be impressive examples. In Denmark, a despotism without discontent – in America, a republic without change. The cause is the same in both: in both the people are universally educated.

The parliamentary repeal lobby argued that the lifting of the stamp duty would encourage men of capital to invest in an expanding market and consequently enrol 'more temperate and disinterested friends of the people who would lend themselves to their real instruction'. In particular, many of the parliamentary campaigners of the 1830s believed that cheap newspapers, owned by business people, would become an educational weapon in the fight against trade unionism. Francis Place, the organizing secretary of the repeal campaign, even told a Parliamentary Select Committee in 1832 that 'there would not have been a single trades union either in England or Scotland' if the stamp duty had been repealed some years earlier. Similarly Roebuck informed the Commons that, if the stamp duty had been lifted, agricultural workers at Tolpuddle would probably not have been so ignorant as to have joined a trade union. Another leading campaigner, Grote, was even more sanguine about the benefits of an expanded, capitalist press: 'a great deal of the bad feeling that was at present abroad amongst the labouring classes on the subject of wages' was due, he believed, to 'the want of proper instruction and correct information as to their real interests' caused by taxes on the press.[3]

What these parliamentary campaigners for a 'free press' emphasized was not libertarian principle but the need for a more active approach to political socialization. However, their speeches occasionally betrayed anxiety that the time might not be right to lift controls on the press. This ambivalence perhaps explains why so few among the repeal lobby of MPs voted consistently against the government's counter-offensive in 1836 designed, as we have seen, to restore the stamp duty and destroy the radical press. In the revealing words of Collet, who was later to co-ordinate the campaign for a free press in Westminster, the government's attack on radical journalism was 'not a liberal, but it was in some respects, a statesman-like measure'.[4]

The new campaign

A new parliamentary lobby against 'the taxes on knowledge' was organized in 1848. Although it claimed to be a broadly based group, it had a narrow social base. As Cobden confided privately, 'exclusively almost, we comprise steady, sober middle-class reformers'. The driving force behind the campaign was Liberal industrialist MPs who saw in the repeal of press taxation a means of propagating the principles of free trade and competitive capitalism. In particular, they hoped that a reduction in newspaper prices, following the abolition of press taxes, would assist the growth of the local commercial press with which many of them were closely associated, and would undermine the dominant position of the 'unreliable' *Times* by exposing it to increased competition.

The campaign won the backing of politicians of all persuasions, as well as a variety of groups such as temperance campaigners, educationalists and publishers (though the latter were deeply divided over the stamp duty). While campaigners had different reasons for wanting to reach a wider public, they were united in believing that the social order would be rendered more secure if it was based on consent fostered by an expanded, capitalist press. 'The larger we open the field of general instruction,' declared Palmerston when speaking for the repeal of the stamp duty in the Commons, 'the firmer the foundations on which the order, the loyalty and good conduct of the lower classes will rest.' Repeal the taxes on knowledge, proclaimed the Irish politician Maguire, and 'you render the people better citizens, more obedient to the laws, more faithful and loyal subjects, and more determined to stand up for the honour of the country'. 'The freedom of the press,' argued Gladstone, 'was not merely to be permitted and tolerated, but to be highly prized, for it tended to bring closer together all the national interests and preserve the institutions of the country.' The new market-based press, in their view, would be a stabilising force.[5]

However, while the fundamental objectives of the campaign against press taxes were the same as before, its rhetoric changed in the early 1850s. Whig history was invoked more often to stigmatize supporters of press taxes as enemies of liberty and the heirs of court censorship. Opposition to press taxation was voiced more frequently in the form of abstract and elevated principle. Freedom of expression should not be taxed; truth will confound error in open debate; good publications will drive out the bad in fair competition; and truth will triumph in the free marketplace of ideas.

However, reformers sometimes combined libertarian and authoritarian arguments in ways that now seem incongruous. They seemed often to be unaware of any tension between the objectives of freedom and social control. Thus Alexander Andrews, editor of the first journalists' trade journal, argued that the great mission of a free press was to 'educate and enlighten those classes whose political knowledge has been hitherto so little, and by consequence so dangerous'. This theme of political indoctrination fused naturally and unselfconsciously with that of liberty. 'The list of our public journals,' Andrews continued, 'is a proud and noble list – the roll call of an army of liberty, with a rallying point in every town. It is a police of safety, and a sentinel of public morals.'[6] The facility with which these dissonant themes could be conflated reveals the ideological universe inhabited by reformers like Andrews. A tacit model of society which acknowledged no conflict of class interest, only a conflict between ignorance and enlightenment and between the individual and the state, provided the intellectual framework in which a free press could be perceived both as a watchdog of government and a guard dog of the people.

Indeed, the respectable campaign for press freedom was never simply about press freedom; it was also motivated by a desire to stabilize the social order in Britain at a time when mainland Europe was rocked by the 1848 revolutions and their aftermath. The campaign may also be viewed as being part of a reformist drive to restructure that social order. Commitment to the principle of free competition, and its extension to new spheres of economic and public life, was the central goal of middle-class reform. The material blessings of the free market had been extensively invoked in the 1830s and 1840s in the campaign against the corn laws, which imposed tariffs on cheap grain imports. The virtues of free competition were also widely aired in the 1850s in attacks on public appointments through social connection. This culminated in the 1870s in the overhaul of the civil service and armed forces, which widened middle-class access to influential and remunerative employment. The campaign against the 'taxes on knowledge' was thus part of a wider discourse deployed against protection of the landed interest and the unreformed, aristocratic state. It also reflected growing confidence among middle-class reformers (some of whom were involved in a parallel campaign to set up public libraries) that their version of enlightenment would prevail through the enlargement of 'public knowledge'.

The key members of the press freedom campaign were also under no illusion that a free market would be neutral. They had closer ties with the regional press than their predecessors in the 1830s, and a better understanding of how the press industry worked. The repeal of press taxes, declared Milner-Gibson, President of the Association for the Promotion of the Repeal of the Taxes on Knowledge, would create 'a cheap press in the hands of men of good moral character, of respectability, and of capital'. Aware of the rising costs of popular newspaper publishing in the USA, he believed that free market processes would favour entrepreneurs with substantial financial resources. Free trade, he stressed, in common with other leading campaigners, would 'give to men of capital and respectability the power of gaining access by newspapers, by faithful record of the facts, to the minds of the working classes'. The free market, argued Sir George Lewis, the Liberal Chancellor of the Exchequer, would promote papers 'enjoying the preference of the advertising public'. Furthermore, reformers argued, responsible control over a cheap press would educate public demand. As one campaigner put it, 'The appetite grows by what it feeds on.'[7]

Some reformers also believed that an expanding capitalist press would raise the pay, status and quality of journalists, with the clear implication that this would promote moderation and good sense. The establishment of a cheap press, explained Hickson, a leading campaigner, would create a new hier-archical system of communication in which journalists 'two or three degrees'

above the labouring classes would enlighten them. To Gladstone, the principal attraction of repeal was that it would lead to more men of 'quality'
working in the press, and consequently educating the people. 'A perfectly
free press,' wryly commented the journalist J. F. Stephen, 'is one of the
greatest safeguards of peace and order' since successful journalists belong to
'the comfortable part of society' and will 'err rather on the side of making
too much of their interests than on that of neglecting them'.[8]

Reinforcing this commitment to creating a cheap, unrestricted press was a
growing conviction that it was now safe to lift controls. The radical working-
class movement was on the retreat in the 1850s. There was, proclaimed
reformers, 'a great increase of intelligence among the people'.[9] Even those
who were uncertain whether the working class would 'become the glory, or
might prove greatly dangerous to the peace, of the country' agreed that it
was a good time to attempt an experiment. Significantly, only public figures
who remained convinced that the lower classes were wedded to 'radical prejudices' (and this group included not only entrenched traditionalists but also
some distinguished liberals committed to free market competition in other
spheres)[10] remained resolutely opposed to the repeal of the stamp duty.

The campaign against press taxes was conducted with remarkable skill
and tenacity. Reformers packed the Parliamentary Select Committee on the
stamp duty and largely determined the contents of its report. They attacked
poorly briefed ministers and won the support of officials in the Board of
Inland Revenue. They harassed the government through the law courts,
exposed the inconsistencies in the way the stamp duty was enforced, organized public meetings, petitions and deputations, and attacked press taxes in
sympathetic newspapers. Their political virtuosity was finally rewarded with
the abolition of the advertisement duty in 1853, the stamp duty in 1855,
the paper duty in 1861 and the security system in 1869.

However, the parliamentary campaign for a free press was never inspired
by a modern libertarian commitment to diversity of expression. Indeed, the
ruthless repression of the unstamped press in the mid-1830s had much the
same objective as the campaign which set the press 'free' twenty years later:
the subordination of the press to the social order. All that had changed was a
growing commitment to positive indoctrination of the lower orders through
a cheap press, and a growing conviction that free trade and normative controls were a morally preferable and more efficient control system than direct
controls administered by the state. Underlying this shift were the growing
power and confidence of the Victorian middle class, which dominated the
parliamentary campaign for repeal of press taxes and recognized in the
expanding press a powerful agency for the advancement of their interests.

The confidence of reformers in the outcome of free market competition
proved to be justified. The radical press was eclipsed in the period after the
repeal of press taxes. The reasons for this have never been adequately
explained.

Notes

1. For instance, G. A. Cranfield, *The Press and Society* (Harlow, Longman, 1978), p. 205. This view is contested in relation to the 1830s by P. Hollis, *The Pauper Press* (London, Oxford University Press, 1970) and J. H. Wiener, *The War of the Unstamped* (New York, Cornell University Press, 1969).

2. *Parliamentary Debates*, 13 (1832), cols 619–48; 23 (1834), cols 1193–1222; 30 (1835), cols 835–62; 34 (1836), cols 627ff.; 35 (1836), cols 566ff., 46 (1837), cols 1164–84. In actual fact the radical unstamped press did not have a 'clear field'. The authorities harassed radical unstamped papers, while regularly turning a blind eye to 'moderate' unstamped papers in the early 1830s.

3. Place, Select Committee on Drunkenness, *Parliamentary Papers*, 8 (1834), question 2054; Roebuck, *Parliamentary Debates*, 23 (1834) cols 1208–9; Grote, *ibid.*, col. 1221.

4. C. D. Collet, *History of the Taxes on Knowledge: Their Origin and Repeal*, vol. 1 (London, T. Fisher Unwin, 1899).

5. Palmerston, *Parliamentary Debates*, 127 (1854), col. 459; Maguire, *Parliamentary Debates*, 157 (1860), col. 383; Gladstone, cit. J. Grant, *The Newspaper Press: Its Origins, Progress and Present Position* (London, Tinsley Brothers, 1871–72).

6. A. Andrews, *The History of British Journalism to 1855* (London, Richard Bentley, 1859), vol. ii, p. 347.

7. Milner-Gibson, *Parliamentary Debates*, 137 (1855), col. 434, and *Parliamentary Debates*, 110 (1850), col. 378; Lewis, *Parliamentary Debates*, 137 (1855), col. 786; Whitty, Report of the Select Committee on Newspaper Stamps (SCNS), *Parliamentary Papers*, 17 (1851), para. 600.

8. Hickson, SCNS (1851), para. 3, 169; Gladstone, *Parliamentary Debates*, 137 (1855), col. 794: J. F. Stephen, 'Journalism', *Cornhill Magazine*, 6 (1862).

9. Bulwer Lytton, *Parliamentary Debates*, 137 (1855), col. 1118; Ingram, *Parliamentary Debates*, 151 (1858), col. 112; Digby Seymour, *Parliamentary Debates*, 125 (1853), col. 1166.

10. For instance, J. R. McCulloch, *Dictionary of Commerce and Commercial Navigation* (London, Longman, Brown & Green, 1854), p. 893.

Chapter 4

The industrialization of the press

During the half-century following the repeal of the 'taxes on knowledge', a number of radical newspapers closed down or were eventually incorporated into the mainstream of popular Liberal journalism. Militant journalism survived only in the etiolated form of small-circulation national periodicals[1] and struggling local weeklies. Yet this decline occurred during a period of rapid press expansion, when local daily papers were established in all the major urban centres of Britain and a new generation of predominantly right-wing national newspapers came into being. These included newspapers such as the *People* (1881), *Daily Mail* (1896), *Daily Express* (1900) and *Daily Mirror* (1903), which have played a prominent role in British journalism ever since.

Most historians, on the left as well as on the right, attribute the decline of radical journalism to a change in the climate of public opinion. The collapse of Chartism in the early 1850s produced a wave of disillusion. Some radical activists were absorbed into the Liberal Party, particularly after the upper strata of the working class gained the vote in 1867. Trade unions also became more inward looking, seeking to improve wages and working conditions rather than to restructure society. These changes were reinforced by the winning of significant social reforms and, above all, by the relative success of the British economy: most workers in employment became substantially better off during the second half of the nineteenth century. Intensive proselytization of the working class through schools, churches, youth clubs, and other socializing agencies such as the Volunteer Force also contributed to the spread of anti-socialist views.

These developments undoubtedly diminished the market for radical journalism. They also had another consequence, which has tended to be overlooked. The reduction of support for the left made it more difficult to raise money within the working-class movement for new publishing ventures. As the Trades Union Congress debates in the early part of the twentieth century make clear, many Liberal and Lib–Lab trade unionists were reluctant to invest their members' money in setting up new socialist publications, because they had become reconciled to the commercial press.

However, while this *Zeitgeist* interpretation partly accounts for the fall of the radical press it is an incomplete explanation. It is often based on the over-simplistic assumption that journalists are influenced by the prevailing political culture of the time, and are forced to respond in a competitive market to the demands of the sovereign consumer. Consequently the press ventriloquizes, it is claimed, the views of the public.

In fact the evidence shows that there was no close correspondence between the climate of opinion in the country and the political character of the press. What may be broadly defined as the radical press was still a force in popular journalism in 1860 when the working-class movement was divided and defeated. In sharp contrast, the radical press was dwarfed by its rivals fifty years later, when the radical movement was gathering momentum.[2] The steady growth of general trade unionism, the radicalization of skilled workers, the spread of socialist and Labourist ideas, the rise of the suffragette movement and the revival of industrial militancy did not give rise to a powerful radical press in the early twentieth century, although it produced a few notable publications. The absence of a close correlation between press and public opinion is underlined further by voting figures. In the 1918 general election, for instance, the Labour Party gained 22 per cent of the vote but did not win the unreserved support of a single national daily or Sunday newspaper.

Lucy Brown has advanced a supplementary explanation for the decline of 'critical vigour' in the Victorian press. She shows that the political élite devoted more time and skill to cultivating the press, and became increasingly dominant as sources and definers of news. However, while this helps to explain the rightward drift of part of the commercial press, it still does not account for the eclipse of radical journalism. The militant press's adversarial style effectively inoculated it against the gentler arts of press management described by Brown. The defeat of the radical press was more fundamental: it was eclipsed rather than seduced.

Virginia Berridge has advanced a more compelling, if also incomplete, explanation of the decline of committed journalism.[3] This was due, she argues, to the 'commercialization' of the popular press. New popular papers came into being which were primarily business ventures, relying on sensationalist manipulation of popular sentiment rather than on what she calls the 'genuine arousal' of militant journalism. In other words, they concentrated on entertainment rather than on taxing political analysis, and consequently secured a much larger audience than politically committed papers.

Berridge's pioneering analysis focuses attention upon a significant change within part of the radical press. Its circulation during the 1840s was swollen by the emergence of the *News of the World* and *Lloyds Weekly*, both commercial papers whose initial radicalism was the product more of commercial expediency than of political commitment. As the *News of the World* frankly stated in its first issue (1 October 1843). 'It is only by a very extensive circulation that the proprietors can be compensated for the outlay of a large capital in this novel and original undertaking.' Although the same issue contained an impassioned attack on conditions in some poor-houses, where inmates were forced to wear prison clothes, the paper also made clear that its general orientation was to please as many people as possible by serving 'the general utility of all classes'. This led to the adoption of consensual views, and the growth of entertainment at the expense of political news. Yet, not very surprisingly, Sunday papers in the *News of the World* mould, with a professionally processed combination of news, sport, human interest stories and political commentary, proved more appealing than the didactic journals that were the principal organs of the left in late Victorian Britain.

This explanation is persuasive as far as it goes. But it glosses over one striking feature of the development of the radical press. During the first half of the nineteenth century left-wing papers evolved from being journals of opinion, based on a quarto format, into broadsheet newspapers carrying news as well as commentary. This change was particularly marked during the 1830s, and was accompanied by a significant broadening of news content. Some of these radical papers began to develop a wide audience appeal by drawing upon the popular street literature tradition of chapbooks, broadsheets, gallowsheets and almanacs. Indeed, Cleave's *Weekly Police Gazette*, the *London Dispatch* and the early militant *Reynolds News* were important partly because they started to rework this popular tradition in ways that projected a radical ideology through human interest news and entertainment as well as through political coverage.

Why, then, did the committed radical press retreat increasingly in the second half of the nineteenth century into the ghetto of narrowly politicized journalism? Why did it leave the field of popular news coverage and entertainment to the commercial press? Thus the question that needs to be asked is not why Victorian working people should have preferred the *News of the World* to rather arid socialist journals such as *Justice* and *Commonweal*, but why the radical press should have failed to live up to its early promise (or, in Berridge's terms, to its early indications of debasement).

Her analysis is a historical version of a standard critique of mass culture. This assumes that communication processed commercially as a commodity for the mass market is inevitably impoverished because it relies on the manipulation of public tastes and attitudes for profit. This is based on fundamentalist assumptions that are open to question. In the context of Victorian Britain, it also obscures under the general heading of 'commercialization' the complex system of controls institutionalized by the industrialization of the Victorian press.

The freedom of capital

One of the central objectives of state economic controls on the press – to exclude pauper management – was attained only by its repeal. This was partly because a craft system of production was replaced by an industrial one.

The lifting of press taxes set up a chain reaction: lower prices, increased sales and the development of new print technology to service an expanding market. Rotary presses, fed by hand, were introduced in the 1860s and 1870s and were gradually replaced by web rotary machines of increasing size and sophistication in late Victorian and Edwardian England. 'Craft' composing was mechanized by Hattersley's machine in the 1860s, and this was replaced by the linotype machine in the 1880s and 1890s. Numerous innovations were also made in graphic reproduction. These developments led to a sharp rise in fixed capital costs. For example, Northcliffe estimated half a million pounds as 'the initial cost of machinery, buildings, ink factories and the like, and this was altogether apart from the capital required for daily working expenses' in setting up the *Daily Mail* in 1896.[4]

The rise in fixed costs made it more difficult for people with limited funds to break into mass publishing. It also generated a relationship of economic inequality, since leading publishers were able to obtain large economies of scale (through spreading their 'first copy' costs over a large print run). In addition, major publishers such as Edward Lloyd gained significant economies of scope by diversifying into paper manufacture in the 1870s and 1880s. However, while new technology raised the level of investment needed to start a paper, and tended to strengthen the position of major publishers, it did not in fact constitute an insuperable obstacle to the launch of new publications with limited capital, even in the national market. Newspapers such as the *Daily Herald*, launched in 1912, could be started with only a limited outlay by being printed on a contract basis by an independent printer.

A more important financial consequence of the repeal of press taxes was to force up the running costs of newspaper publishing. National newspapers became substantial enterprises, with growing newsprint bills and staff costs. They also cut their cover prices. The combination of rising expenditure and lower cover prices forced up the circulation levels that newspapers needed to achieve in order to be profitable. This raised, in turn, the run-in costs of new papers before they built their circulations to break-even point. New newspapers could be launched with limited funds and derelict newspapers could be bought relatively cheaply. It was increasingly the establishment of newspapers that required large financial resources.

Thus in 1855 Disraeli was advised by D. C. Coulton that a capital of about £20,000 was needed to start a London daily paper. In 1867 W. H. Smith estimated that about £50,000 was needed to fund a new London morning paper. By the 1870s Edward Lloyd needed to spend £150,000 to establish the *Daily Chronicle* (after buying it for £30,000). During the period 1906 to 1908 Thomasson spent about £300,000 attempting to establish the Liberal daily, *Tribune*. By the 1920s, however, Lord Cowdray spent about £750,000 attempting to convert the *Westminster Gazette* into a quality daily. Even more was spent on developing mass-circulation papers during the same period.

Indeed, the full extent of the material transformation of the press is per-haps most clearly revealed by comparing the launch and establishment costs of newspapers before and after the industrialization of the press. As we have seen, the total cost of establishing the *Northern Star*, a national weekly newspaper, on a profitable basis in 1837 was little more than £690. It was able to break even with a circulation of about 6200 copies, which was probably achieved in its first month. In contrast the *Sunday Express*, launched in 1918, expended over £2 million before it broke even, with a circulation of well over 250,000. Thus, while a public subscription in northern towns was sufficient to launch a national weekly in the 1830s, it required the resources of an international conglomerate controlled by Beaverbrook to do the same thing nearly a century later.[5]

These statistics illustrate the privileged position of capital in the creation of the modern press. Even when the costs of launching and establishing a popular paper were relatively low in the 1850s and 1860s, they still exceeded the resources readily available to the organized working class. The *Beehive*, for instance, was started in 1862 with capital of less than £250 raised by trade union organizations and a well-to-do sympathizer. Its inadequate funding crippled it. Although it set out to carry both news and features and to reach a wide audience, it lacked the finances to be anything other than a weekly journal of opinion. Despite a small amount of additional capital put up by unions and other contributors, it was also forced to sell at double the price of the large-circulation weeklies it had been intended to compete against. In effect, its under-capitalization condemned it to the margins of national publishing as a specialist, if influential, weekly paper.

As the resources of organized labour increased, so did the costs of establishing a national paper. It was not until 1912 that papers financed and controlled from within the working class made their first appearance in national daily journalism – long after most national daily papers had become well estab-lished. The brief career of the *Daily Citizen* and the early history of the *Daily Herald* illustrate the economic obstacles to setting up papers under working-class control. The *Daily Citizen*, launched in 1912 with a capital of only £30,000 (subscribed mainly by trade unions), reached a circulation of 250,000 at its peak within two years and was only 50,000 short of over-hauling the *Daily Express*. But although the *Daily Citizen* almost certainly acquired more working-class readers than any other daily, it still closed three years after its launch.

The more left-wing *Daily Herald*, started with only £300 and sustained by public donations, lurched from one crisis to another despite reaching a cir-culation of over 250,000 at its meridian before 1914. On one occasion it came out in pages of different sizes and shapes because someone 'found' old discarded paper supplies when the *Daily Herald* could no longer afford to pay for new paper. On another occasion it bought small quantities of paper under fictitious names from suppliers all over the country. Later it secured paper supplies without a guarantee by threatening to organize, through its trade union connections, industrial action against paper manufacturers. While the *Daily Citizen* closed, the *Daily Herald* survived by switching from being a daily to becoming a weekly during the period 1914–19. Lack of sufficient capital prevented its continuation in any other form.

The rise in publishing costs helps to explain why the committed left press in the late nineteenth century existed only as under-capitalized, low-budget, high-price specialist periodicals and as local community papers, an important but as yet relatively undocumented aspect of the residual survival of the radical press. The operation of the free market had raised the cost of press ownership beyond the readily available resources of the working class.

Market forces thus accomplished more than the most repressive measures of an aristocratic state. The security system introduced in 1819 to ensure that the press was controlled by 'men of some respectability and capital' had fixed the financial qualifications of press ownership at a mere £200 to £300. This financial hurdle was raised over a hundredfold by the market system between 1850 and 1920.[6]

However, although the heavy capitalization of the British press was an important factor inhibiting the launch of new radical papers, it still does not explain the ideological absorption of radical papers already in existence before the repeal of the press taxes. Nor does it fully explain why small-circulation radical papers could not develop into profitable mass-circulation papers and accumulate enough capital, through retained profits, to finance new publications. For an answer to these questions we need to look elsewhere.

The new licensing system: advertising

The crucial element of the new control system was the strategic role acquired by advertisers after the repeal of the advertisement duty in 1853. Before then, the advertisement tax had made certain forms of advertising uneconomic. As John Cassell, the publisher of popular useful knowledge publications, argued before the Parliamentary Select Committee on Newspaper Stamps, 'It [the advertisement duty] entirely prevents a certain class of advertisements from appearing: it is only such as costly books and property sales by auction that really afford an opportunity of advertising and for paying the duty.'

Cassell exaggerated the impact of the advertisement duty for political reasons. The growth of trade, and the halving of the advertisement duty in 1833, had led to a substantial increase in press advertising in the 1830s and 1840s. Even before that, most commercial newspapers – but not the radical press – had been reliant on advertising. But it was only with the abolition of the advertisement duty in 1853 that popular press advertising came fully into its own. Between 1854 and 1858, for instance, *Reynolds News* increased its advertising volume by over 50 per cent. This surge in advertising expenditure, combined with the repeal of the stamp and paper duties, transformed the economic structure of the popular press. The modal price of popular papers was halved in the 1850s and halved again in the 1860s. At the new prevailing price structure, nearly all newspapers – including those with very large circulations such as *Reynolds News* – depended on advertising for their profits since their reduced net cover prices no longer met their costs. Advertisers thus acquired a *de facto* licensing power because, without their support, newspapers ceased to be economically viable.

Rising circulations, decreasing print unit costs and, between 1875 and 1895, the sharp fall in the price of newsprint did not diminish the central role of advertising in the press. Advertising expenditure increased steadily in the Victorian and Edwardian period, rising to an estimated £20 million in 1907. This financed bigger papers, more staff and the introduction of sale-or-return arrangements with distributors. It also helped to underwrite a further halving of the price of most popular papers to $^1/_2$d in the late Victorian period.

The political implications of newspapers' economic dependence on advertising have been ignored largely because it is assumed that advertisers bought space in newspapers on the basis of market rather than political criteria. But political considerations played a significant part in some advertisers' calculations during the Victorian period. In 1856 the principal advertising handbook detailed the political views of most London and local newspapers with the proud boast that 'till this Directory was published, the advertiser had no means of accurately determining which journal *might be best adapted to his views*, and most likely to forward his interests' (emphasis added).[7] Even non-socialist newspapers found that controversial editorial policies led to the loss of commercial advertising. The *Pall Mall Gazette*'s advertising revenue dropped sharply in response to its 'Maiden Tribute' crusade in 1885 in which the editor 'procured' a 13-year-old girl as part of his paper's campaign to raise the legal age of consent to sex. The *Daily News* was boycotted by some advertisers in 1886 when it campaigned for Home Rule. Government advertising long continued to be allocated on a partisan basis. As late as 1893 the incoming Home Secretary, Herbert Asquith, was told that generally 'it is the custom to transfer advertisements according to the politics of governments'.

Political prejudice in advertising selection almost certainly declined during the latter part of the nineteenth century and early twentieth century. The rise of advertising agencies, the emergence of major, national advertisers and the increasing availability of circulation statistics encouraged the adoption of a more professional approach. Even so, the frequent remonstrations against 'mixing business and politics' in advertising manuals published between 1850 and 1930 suggest that political prejudice continued to influence some advertisers.

However, even when political partisanship played no part in advertising selection, left-wing publications still faced discrimination on commercial grounds. As the head of a well-known advertising agency wrote in 1856, 'Some of the most widely circulated journals in the Empire are the worst possible to advertise in. Their readers are not purchasers, and any money thrown upon them is so much thrown away.'[8] Newspapers read by the well-to-do were assessed differently. 'Character is of more importance than number,' advised an advertising handbook in 1851, adding that 'A journal that circulates a thousand among the upper or middle classes is a better medium than would be one circulating a hundred thousand among the lower classes.'[9] Similar, though usually more qualified, advice continued to be given for some time. For example, Sir Charles Higham, the head of a large advertising agency, wrote in 1925, 'A very limited circulation, but entirely among the wealthy ... may be more valuable than if the circulation were quadrupled.'[10]

Some advertisers also made a key distinction between the skilled and poor working class. Indeed, the latter were often excluded from the early market research surveys in the 1920s on the grounds that they were not worth bothering about. Once newspapers became identified with the poor, they found it difficult to attract advertising. As an advertising handbook cautioned in 1921, 'You cannot afford to place your advertisements in a paper which is read by the down-at-heels who buy it to see the "Situations Vacant" column.'[11]

This combination of economic and political discrimination by advertisers crucially influenced the development of left-wing journalism. In the first place, it exerted pressure on the radical press to move upmarket in order to survive. A number of radical newspapers redefined their target audience, and moderated their radicalism, in an attempt to attract the more affluent readers whom advertisers wanted to reach.

This process is well illustrated by the career of *Reynolds News*. It was founded in 1850 by George Reynolds, a member of the left-wing faction of the Chartist National Executive. Reynolds had urged a 'physical force' strategy in 1848 and opposed middle-class collaboration in the early 1850s. His paper was initially in the *Northern Star* tradition of class-conscious radicalism, and had close links with the working-class movement.

Yet despite its radical origins, *Reynolds News* changed under the impact of the new economic imperatives of newspaper publishing. The fact that it never provided, even at the outset, a consistent theoretical perspective doubtless made it vulnerable to ideological incorporation. Inevitably it was influenced by the decline of radicalism in the country during the 1850s and early 1860s, but an important factor in its absorption was also the need to attract advertising revenue. The change was symbolized by the inclusion of regular features on friendly societies in the year after the repeal of the advertisement duty, as a ploy to attract advertising. Thus enterprises which had been attacked in militant newspapers as 'a hoax' to persuade working-class people to identify with capitalism became a much-needed source of revenue for *Reynolds News*.

The paper continued to take a radical stand on most major events of the day, but it expressed increasingly the individualistic values of the more affluent readers whom it needed to attract. It adopted some of the tenets of liberal political economy that it had attacked during the 1850s, including the palliatives of 'prudent marriage' (i.e. sexual restraint) and emigration as solutions to unemployment. It became still more populist, focusing on the vices of the aristocracy, corruption in high places, and poverty as a source of melodrama (rather than as a condition to be overcome through socialist advance). Its early assault on the workings of industrial capital was modulated to criticism of monopoly and speculators, while criticism of shopkeepers as the exploitive agents of capital gave way to articles that tacitly accepted the market economy. *Reynolds News* became a paper that catered for the coalition of lower-middle-class and working-class readers necessary for its survival. Acquired by the Dicks family in 1879 and later by J. H. Dalziel, it gradually evolved into a conventional Liberal paper.

Reynolds was accused of commercial opportunism by contemporary critics (including Karl Marx); yet it is difficult to see what else he could have done if the paper was to survive the transition to an advertising-based system. Even the radical *People's Paper* boasted in 1857 of its appeal to 'high paid trades and shopkeepers' in its promotion to advertisers. Failing to attract affluent readers in sufficient numbers, the *People's Paper* was forced to close down with a circulation far larger than middle-class weeklies such as the *Spectator* and *John Bull*.

Radical newspapers could survive in the new economic environment only if they moved upmarket to attract an audience desired by advertisers or remained in a small working-class ghetto, with manageable losses that could be offset by donations. Once they moved out of that ghetto and sought a large working-class audience, they courted disaster. If they sold at the competitive prices charged by their rivals, they made a loss on each copy, due to lack of advertising. If they increased their sales, they merely incurred greater losses and moved more heavily into debt.

This fate befell the London *Evening Echo*, which was taken over by wealthy radicals in 1901 and relaunched as a socialist paper. A special number was issued, firmly committing the paper to 'the interests of labour as against the tyranny of organized capital'. In the period 1902 to 1904 its circulation rose by a remarkable 60 per cent, leading to its abrupt closure in 1905. The *Evening Echo*'s advertising had failed to keep pace with its growth of circulation, making its continuation impossible.[12]

The same thing almost happened to the *Daily Herald* when it was relaunched as a daily in 1919. It spent £10,000 on promotion – a small amount by comparison with its main rivals, but sufficient to ensure that it sharply increased its circulation. 'Our success in circulation,' recalled George Lansbury, 'was our undoing. The more copies we sold, the more money we lost.' The situation became increasingly desperate when, aided partly by the unexpected publicity of attacks on the *Daily Herald* by leading members of the government alleging that it was financed from Moscow, the *Daily Herald's* circulation continued to rise in 1920. 'Every copy we sold was sold at a loss,' mourned Lansbury. 'The rise in circulation, following the government's attacks, brought us nearer and nearer to disaster.'[13] The money raised from whist drives, dances, draws and collections was not enough to offset the shortfall of advertising. The desperate expedient of doubling the paper's price in 1920 was not enough to secure its future. Money from the miners and the railwaymen prevented the paper from closing. But the only way the paper could be saved, in the long term, was by its being taken over as the official organ of the Labour Party and TUC in 1922. A paper that had been a freewheeling vehicle of the left, an important channel for the dissemination of syndicalist and socialist ideas in the early part of the twentieth century, became the official mouthpiece of the moderate leadership of the labour movement.[14] Lack of advertising forced it to become subservient to a new form of control.

In short, one of four things happened to national radical papers that failed to meet the requirements of advertisers. Either they closed down; accommodated to advertising pressure by moving upmarket; stayed in a small-audience ghetto with manageable losses; or accepted an alternative source of institutional patronage.

Yet publications which conformed to the marketing requirements of advertisers obtained what were, in effect, large external subsidies which they could spend on increased editorial outlay and promotion in order to attract new readers. Rising advertising expenditure also provided a powerful inducement to entrepreneurs to launch publications directed at markets that advertisers particularly wanted to reach. Between 1866 and 1896 the number of magazines increased from an estimated 557 to 2097, many of which were trade, technical and professional journals aimed at specialized groups attractive to advertisers. The number of local dailies grew from only two in 1850 to 196 in 1900, falling to 169 by 1920, due mainly to the casualties caused by intense competition. There was also a substantial expansion in the number of local weekly papers from fewer than 400 in 1856 to an estimated 2072 in 1900, declining to an estimated 1700 by 1921. Above all, there was a substantial increase in the number of national daily and Sunday papers, mostly founded between 1880 and 1918, which catered for either mass, middle-market or small élite audiences.[15]

This growth in the number of publications was accompanied by an enormous expansion in newspaper consumption. Annual newspaper sales rose from 85 million in 1851 to 5604 million in 1920. Only part of this increase was due to rapid population growth: the number of newspapers purchased *per capita* over the age of 14 rose from six copies in 1850 to 182 copies in 1920.

Even allowing for a reduction in the number of readers per copy, due to a marked decline in the collective purchase and reading aloud from newspapers, this still constitutes a remarkable increase in the audience reached by the press. Sunday and local daily papers achieved aggregate circulations of 13.5 million and 9.2 million respectively by 1920. In contrast, the national daily press, with a predominantly middle-class public, had a circulation of only 5.4 million in 1920, while the local weekly press (which was particularly strong in rural areas) had 6.8 million circulation.[16]

This growth was facilitated by new print technology, rising advertising subsidy and lower cover prices. The rise of mass consumption was also a product of cumulative social and economic change. Adult literacy (as measured very imperfectly by the ability to sign one's name) rose from 69 per cent in 1850 to 97 per cent in 1900. The normal number of hours worked in many industries fell from sixty hours a week to fifty-four hours or fewer between 1850 and 1890, and average real wages rose by an estimated 84 per cent between 1850 and 1900.

In brief, the radical press suffered a double defeat. It lost its leading position in popular journalism, and was overtaken by new publications that built a much larger aggregate readership.

Impact of the industrialized press

At the turn of the nineteenth century, traditional educationalists such as Hannah More taught working-class children to read but not to write. Something like this division of labour was institutionalized through the industrialization of the press. The working class became consumers but not producers of newspapers.

Many of the new local dailies, founded after 1855, were started or bought by leading local industrialists. Both the *Northern Daily Express* and the *Northern Leader* were bought by colliery owners; the *South Shields Gazette* was acquired by Stevenson, a member of a local chemical manufacturing family; the *Bolton Evening News* belonged to local industrialists, the Tillotsons; the *Yorkshire Post*'s principal shareholder was the Leeds banker Beckett-Denison; the *Ipswich Express* was owned by Colman, the mustard manufacturer, and so on. These papers offered a very different view of the world from that of the early radical press they supplanted. Papers such as the *Northern Star* had amplified class conflicts in the local community ('to talk of reconciliation between the middle and working classes in Leicester will, henceforth, be a farce'[17] was a typical lead-in to one of its news reports). In contrast, the new local commercial press tended to block out conflict, minimize differences, and encourage positive identification with the local community and its middle-class leadership. Characteristic of this style of consensual journalism was a report in the *Leeds Mercury* (printed in the same city as the *Northern Star*) of a local dignitary addressing the annual public soirée of the Leeds Mechanics Institute on the subject of 'these popular institutions, sustained by the united efforts of all classes ... thereby to promote the virtue, happiness and peace of the community'.[18]

The early militant press had fuelled suspicion of middle-class reformists with a barrage of criticism against 'sham-radical humbugs' and 'the merciful middle-class converts to half Chartism at half past the eleventh hour'.[19] In contrast, the new local daily press encouraged its readers to identify with the political parties controlled by a reconstituted Establishment, based on a coalition of the old landed élite and new industrial and commercial interests. Ten of the new local dailies that emerged between 1855 and 1860 were affiliated to the Liberal Party; eighteen created between 1860 and 1870 were affiliated to the Conservative or Liberal parties, and forty-one of the local dailies created in the following decade were similarly aligned. The new party press helped to build a popular base, transforming what had been little more than aristocratic factions in Parliament into mass political movements. This reinforced the political division of the working class, and encouraged the assimilation of some working-class activists into a parliamentary system that, until 1918, was still only quasi-democratic.

The new Liberal press, in particular, played a significant role in re-routing radical politics. It adapted or diluted radical themes in ways that fundamentally changed its meaning. Co-operation based on shared ownership, proclaimed by the early radical press, was reincarnated as a new spirit of partnership between masters and men that would bring prosperity to all. The early radical stress on social reconstruction became transmuted into moral improvement through middle-class enlightenment, while a view of education as a tool of collective resistance gave way to one that emphasized individual advancement. Admittedly these transformations drew upon a radical tradition that had contained contradictions and ambiguities. However, by giving prominence to the liberal elements of this tradition, the new press weakened the radical movement.

There were of course politically meaningful differences between individual newspapers, not least in their reporting of trade unions, the emergent women's movement and state reform. But notwithstanding these differences, all national newspapers launched between 1855 and 1910, and the overwhelming majority of new local daily papers, encouraged positive identification with the social system in contrast to their radical predecessors. The shift that this represented is perhaps best illustrated by the way in which Queen Victoria was portrayed. The radical press in the period 1837 to 1855 was aggressively republican: the Queen was vilified as politically partisan and reactionary, the head of a system of organized corruption, the mother of a brood of royal cadgers, and the friend and relative of European tyrants. In contrast, the new press portrayed the Queen from the mid-1870s onward as a dutiful and benign matriarch who symbolized in an almost talismanic way the moral and material progress of her reign. Projecting her as the living embodiment of national unity, they also played a key role in converting the jubilee celebrations of 1887 and 1897 into popular, mobilizing rites of national communion.

Above all, the new popular press fostered the wave of imperialism that swept through all levels of society. Popular newspapers tended to portray Britain's colonial role as a civilizing mission to the heathen, underdeveloped world, and as an extended adventure story in which military triumphs were achieved through individual acts of courage rather than through superior military technology. Common to both themes was pride in Britain's ascendancy: as the *Daily Mail* (23 June 1897), the most popular daily of late Victorian Britain, enthused:

> We send out a boy here and a boy there, and the boy takes hold of the savages of the part he comes to and teaches them to march and shoot as he tells them, to obey him and believe in him and die for him and the Queen. A plain, stupid, uninspired people they call us, and yet we are doing this with every kind of savage man there is.

This celebration of Britain's dominion sometimes struck a more atavistic note, as in this report of the 1898 Sudan expedition in the *Westminster Gazette*:

> A large number of the Tommies had never been under fire before ... and there was a curious look of suppressed excitement in some of the faces ... Now and then I caught in a man's eye the curious gleam which, despite all the veneer of civilization, still holds its own in man's nature, whether he is killing rats with a terrier, rejoicing in a prize fight, playing a salmon or potting Dervishes. It was a fine day and we were out to kill something. Call it what you like, the experience is a big factor in the joy of living.

The paper which celebrated 'potting Dervishes' was, in terms of the narrow political arc represented by the contemporary national press, on 'the left'. It was, for example, one of the few papers not to be in favour of the Boer War. However, it subsequently joined other papers (apart from the *Herald*) in providing Hun-hating support for Britain's involvement in the First World War.

Conclusion

The radical press was defeated decisively after the abolition of the 'taxes on knowledge'. Its defeat cannot be attributed solely to the changed climate of opinion, following the collapse of the Chartist Movement. This *Zeitgeist* or 'sovereign consumer' interpretation, though often invoked, fails to explain why the press, taken as a whole, moved further to the right than public opinion; nor does it explain why the subsequent revival of the radical movement did not give rise to a stronger revival of radical journalism. Both the extent and permanence of the eclipse of the radical press as the dominant force in national popular journalism were due to structural changes in the press industry. The industrialization of the press, with its accompanying rise in publishing costs, led to a progressive transfer of ownership and control of the popular press from the working class to wealthy businessmen, while dependence on advertising encouraged the absorption or elimination of the early radical press and stunted its subsequent development before the First World War.

Notes

1. M. Tusan, *Women Making News* (Urbana, University of Illinois Press, 2005) provides an illuminating study of the feminist press (first emerging in the 1850s) during this period.
2. For the relative weakness of the radical press in 1910, see A. J. Lee, 'The radical press', in A. Morris (ed.), *Edwardian Radicalism, 1900–1914* (London, Routledge & Kegan Paul, 1974).
3. V. Berridge, 'Popular Sunday papers and mid-Victorian society', in G. Boyce, J. Curran and P. Wingate (eds), *Newspaper History* (London, Constable, 1978). This interpretation has since been developed further by J. Chalaby in *The Invention of Journalism* (London, Macmillan, 1998) and M. Conboy in *The Press and Popular Culture* (London, Sage, 2002).
4. R. Pound and G. Harmsworth, *Northcliffe* (London, Cassell, 1959), p. 206.
5. A. J. P. Taylor, *Beaverbrook* (London, Hamish Hamilton, 1972), p. 175.
6. The costs of market entry for mass publishing were particularly high in Britain, due to the dominant role of the national press. This explains partly why the radical press was much weaker in Britain than in some other European countries, where the press remained decentralized and entry costs were lower.
7. *Mitchell's Newspaper Press Directory* (Mitchell, 1856). It should be noted, however, that Mitchell himself cautioned advertisers against political bias.
8. *Mitchell's Newspaper Press Directory* (Mitchell, 1856).
9. Anon., *Guide to Advertisers* (1851).
10. C. Higham, *Advertising* (London, Williams & Norgate, 1925), p. 166.
11. C. Freer, *The Inner Side of Advertising: A Practical Handbook for Advertisers* (London, Library Press, 1921), p. 203.
12. F. W. Pethick-Lawrence, *Fate Has Been Kind* (London, Hutchinson, 1943), pp. 65ff.
13. G. Lansbury, *The Miracle of Fleet Street* (London, Victoria House, 1925), pp. 160ff.
14. H. Richards, *The Bloody Circus: The Daily Herald and the Left* (London, Pluto, 1997).
15. The figures for regional dailies relate to Britain and for other categories of publications to the UK, as reported in *Mitchell's Newspaper Press Directory*.
16. N. Kaldor and R. Silverman, *A Statistical Analysis of Advertising Expenditure and of the Revenue of the Press* (Cambridge, Cambridge University Press, 1948), p. 84.
17. *Northern Star*, 7 May 1842.
18. *Leeds Mercury*, 14 June 1851.
19. *Northern Star*, 26 February and 11 June 1842.

Chapter 5

The era of the press barons

The era of the press barons is often seen as a maverick interlude in the development of the press, when newspapers became subject to the whims and caprices of their owners. According to this view, the press barons built vast press empires and ruled them like personal fiefdoms. In the hands of men like Beaverbrook and Rothermere, newspapers became mere 'engines of propaganda', manipulated in order to further their political ambitions. As Stanley Baldwin declared in a memorable sentence (suggested to him by his cousin, Rudyard Kipling), 'What proprietorship of these papers is aiming at is power, and power without responsibility – the prerogative of the harlot throughout the ages.'

The despotic rule of the press barons is usually compared unfavourably with a preceding 'golden age' when proprietors played an inactive role and 'sovereign' editors conducted their papers in a responsible manner. In some accounts, too, the era of Northcliffe and Rothermere is contrasted with the period after the Second World War when journalists became more educated, independent and professional. The press barons have thus become favourite bogeymen: their indictment has become a way of celebrating the editorial integrity of newspapers, both past and present.

But in reality the reign of the press barons did not constitute an exceptional pathology in the evolution of the press, but merely a continuation of tendencies already present before. Indeed, insofar as the barons may be said to have been innovators, it is not for the reasons that are generally given. They did not break with tradition by using their papers for political propaganda; their distinctive contribution was rather that they downgraded propaganda in favour of entertainment. Nor did they subvert the role of the press as a fourth estate; on the contrary it was they who detached the commercial press from the political parties and, consequently, from the state. What actually happened is, in some ways, the exact opposite of historical mythology.[1]

The creation of press empires

The newspaper chains built by the press barons were not a new phenomenon. Multiple ownership of weekly newspapers had developed as early as the eighteenth century. Local daily chains had also emerged shortly after the regional daily press was established in the mid-nineteenth century. By 1884, for instance, a syndicate headed by the Scots-American steel magnate Carnegie controlled eight dailies and ten weeklies.

Although some papers controlled by the press barons gained a dominant market position, this too had happened before. *The Times*, for example, had dominated the respectable daily press during the early Victorian period. This recurring pattern arose from the unequal competitive relationship that developed between strong and weak papers. As soon as one paper gained a market lead, it was in a strong position to move further ahead because it had more money than its rivals from both sales and scale economies to invest in editorial development.

While the press barons reached a growing audience as a consequence of a rapid increase in circulation, this was also not new. There had been a sustained growth of newspaper consumption ever since the seventeenth century, and this growth was already accelerating before the press barons made their mark.

The large empires created by the press barons may thus be viewed as a continuation of three well-established trends – chain ownership, an expanding market and a tendency for a few papers to become dominant. All that happened was that some of these trends became more pronounced during the period of the press barons' ascendancy. In the first place, there was, between 1890 and 1920, a rapid growth of newspaper chains which incorporated national as well as regional papers. By 1921 the three Harmsworth brothers (Lords Northcliffe, Rothermere and Sir Lester Harmsworth) controlled newspapers with an aggregate circulation of over six million – probably the largest press group in the western world at the time.[2]

Between the wars, concentration of press ownership entered a new phase, with the spectacular consolidation of the regional chains. The percentage of provincial evening titles controlled by the five big chains rose from 8 to 40 per cent between 1921 and 1939; their ownership of the provincial morning titles also increased, from 12 to 44 per cent during the same period. The power of the chains was extended further by the elimination of local competition. Between 1921 and 1937, the number of towns with a choice of evening paper fell from twenty-four to ten, while towns with a choice of local morning paper declined from fifteen to seven.

The principal pace-setters in the expansion of the regional chains were the Berry brothers, Lords Camrose and Kemsley. Their group grew from four daily and Sunday papers in 1921 to twenty daily and Sunday papers in 1939. This was achieved only after a long-drawn-out and costly 'war' with Lord Rothermere, which was eventually resolved in a series of local treaties in which the three lords divided up different parts of the country between them.

There was also, during the inter-war period, an enormous increase in the sales of national dailies, which for the first time overtook those of local dailies. Between 1920 and 1939 the combined circulation of the national daily press rose from 5.4 million to 10.6 million, while that of the local daily and weekly press remained relatively static. This major expansion of the London-based press meant that some proprietors gained enormous audiences even when they owned relatively few papers. This applied in particular to Lord Beaverbrook, controller of the *Daily Express*, the leading popular daily of the late 1930s.

These changes meant that, after the death of Lord Northcliffe in 1922, four men – Lords Beaverbrook, Rothermere, Camrose and Kemsley – became the dominant figures in the inter-war press. In 1937, for instance, they owned nearly one in every two national and local daily papers sold in Britain, as well as one in every three Sunday papers that were sold. The combined circulation of all their newspapers amounted to over thirteen million.

However, their pre-eminence was not in fact as great as that of their less well-known predecessors. In 1937 the three leading Sunday papers' owners (Kemsley, Beaverbrook and Camrose) controlled 59 per cent of national Sunday newspaper circulation – significantly less than the 69 per cent share of national Sunday circulation controlled by three less power-hungry proprietors (Dalziel, Riddell and Lloyd) in 1910. Similarly, in 1937 Rothermere, Beaverbrook and Cadbury controlled 50 per cent of national daily circulation – again, much less than the 67 per cent share controlled by Pearson, Cadbury and Northcliffe in 1910.

This relative decline was due partly to the re-emergence of a significant Labour press. The Co-operative Movement bought *Reynolds News* in 1929; the TUC formed a partnership with Odhams to relaunch the *Daily Herald* in 1929; and the Communist Party established the *Daily Worker* in 1930. The rising capitalization of the press led also to an increased dispersal of shareholdings. Two important papers, the *Daily Mirror* and *Sunday Pictorial*, ceased to have a controlling shareholder in the mid-1930s. The press magnates' hegemony over the press was, in fact, waning during the period celebrated for their ascendancy.

Press barons and proprietorial control

Not all press proprietors were interventionist. For instance, Astor, joint owner of *The Times* after 1922, was teased by his friends for not reading his own paper. Even the quintessential press barons – Northcliffe, Rothermere, Beaverbrook and Kemsley – did not exercise a uniform degree of control. They tended to lavish attention on their favourite papers, while taking a lesser interest in others they controlled.

Thus, in the late 1930s Beaverbrook deluged the *Daily Express* with instructions to support appeasement ('No War Talk. NO WAR TALK' read one telegram of that period), but did not seem to mind that its sister paper, the *Sunday Express*, expressed growing disquiet about Germany's remilitarization, or that another of his papers, the *Evening Standard*, under the socialist editor Percy Cudlipp, urged a popular front against fascism. Similarly, Northcliffe was mainly concerned in his later years with the *Daily Mail*, a preoccupation that his brother Rothermere later shared.

The two archetypal press barons, Northcliffe and Beaverbrook, had very different personal styles. While Northcliffe was notorious for personally harassing his staff, Beaverbrook's remoteness was legendary. In *Scoop*, Evelyn Waugh satirized a visit to him:

> The carpets were thicker [as one approached Lord Copper's private office], the lights softer, the expressions of the inhabitants more care-worn. The typewriters were of a special kind: their keys made no more sound than the drumming of a bishop's finger-tips on an upholstered prie-dieu. The telephone buzzers were muffled and purred like warm cats. The personal private secretaries padded through the ante-chambers and led them nearer and nearer to the presence.

Yet despite their differences of personality, both men exercised detailed control over their favourite papers through a constant barrage of instructions. Beaverbrook sent 147 separate instructions to the *Daily Express* in one day. Northcliffe would sometimes phone his staff at six in the morning: 'Wake up! Have you seen the papers yet?' he would demand. One editor, who replied that you could not get the *Mail* in Northlake at 6 a.m., was woken at five the next morning by a copy delivered to his door by a pantechnicon.

The press barons maintained their personal domination with extreme ruthlessness. Northcliffe, in particular, had a brisk way of dismissing employees. 'Who is that?' Northcliffe said on the phone. 'Editor, *Weekly Dispatch*, Chief,' came the reply. 'You were the editor,' responded Northcliffe. When a luckless subeditor filled a lull in conversation over lunch with the information that he had been shipwrecked three times, Northcliffe said abruptly, 'Four times.' Beaverbrook also had a fearsome reputation. 'Fleet Street,' recalled one of his employees, 'was strewn with the corpses of *Express* editors.'[3]

The barons combined terror with generosity. Journalists' memoirs and official histories are full of anecdotes about the sudden gifts, holidays and salary rises which were showered on staff. As a genre these stories could be called 'courageous underling gets his reward'. They usually take the form of the plucky journalist standing up for himself (or, more rarely, for what he believes) in the face of the baron's fury. They are clearly intended to enhance both the baron, who is revealed as discriminating and fundamentally right-minded in his judgements, and the journalist, whose independence is demonstrated by his courage. But what they actually reveal is an almost continuous process of humiliation. Bernard Falk, usually rewarded with a cigar when he took down Northcliffe's dictated social column for the *Mail*, was once allowed to choose the one he wanted. 'What!' said Northcliffe,

'You have the nerve to pick on those cigars! Don't you know, young man, that they cost 3/6 each?' 'Yes,' said the fearless reporter, 'but they're worth every penny.' Another editor, who dared to disagree with Northcliffe, recorded gratefully the telegram he received: 'My dear Blackwood, you are grossly impertinent to your affectionate Chief.'

Losing a battle with a press baron hardly made such a good story. Buckle, the editor of *The Times* (whose editorial independence Northcliffe had promised to uphold), was eased out of the editorship when he failed to adapt to the political views and managerial strategy of the Chief, Lewis Macleod, literary editor of the *Daily Mail*, received a communiqué from Northcliffe: 'This is the last occasion on which I can tolerate Macleod's gross neglect and carelessness. He will read this message out to the editorial conference on Monday.' When Northcliffe was angered by what he thought were defects on the *Daily Mail*'s picture page, he lined up all those involved in its production and put the tallest man in charge. Feeling dissatisfied with the *Mail*'s advertising department, he appointed the commissionaire to vet advertisements. Beaverbrook was also unpredictable, though not on the scale of Northcliffe.[4] Yet behind both men's seemingly random acts of ferocity and generosity, there was often a careful regard for self-interest. Beaverbrook insisted, for instance, that some of his best journalists write under pseudonyms so that, if they left the *Express*, they could not take the goodwill generated by their copy with them.

Northcliffe and Beaverbrook shaped the entire content of their favourite papers, including their layout. Thus Northcliffe raged at an employee at *The Times*, 'What have you done with the moon? I said the moon – the *Moon*. Someone has moved the moon! ... Well, if it's moved again, whoever does it is fired!' (The position of the weather report had been changed.) Beaverbrook and Northcliffe constantly pestered journalists about the language and phrasing of their reports. 'To Eastbourne's balding, myopic, Edinburgh-trained physiotherapist, William John Snooks, 53, came the news that ... ' parodied Tom Driberg, a former *Express* journalist, in the approved Beaverbrook style. Both press barons also interfered in the choice of pictures. 'Alfonso' (King of Spain), complained Northcliffe, 'is always smiling. This smile is not news. If you get a picture of Alfonso weeping, *that* would be news!'

The barons' personal foibles influenced the selection of news stories, thereby helping to shape the news values of the national press. Northcliffe had a lifelong obsession with torture and death: he even kept an aquarium containing goldfish and a pike, with a dividing partition, which he would lift up when he was in need of diversion. His obsession was reflected in his first magazine, *Answers*, which dealt with such enquiries as: 'How long is a severed head conscious after decapitation?' The first feature article Northcliffe wrote for his first evening newspaper described the day he spent with a condemned murderer in Chelmsford Prison. He later briefed *Daily Mail* staff to find 'one murder a day'. Similarly Beaverbrook, a hypochondriac, told the editor of the *Daily Express* that 'the public like to know ... what diseases men die of – and women too'.

Proprietors' perceptions of their readers set the tone of their papers. The *Daily Express* aimed, in Beaverbrook's words, at 'the character and temperament which was bent on moving upwards and outward', reflecting Beaverbrook's North American admiration for self-made success. The *Daily Mail*, on the other hand, projected a more static, hierarchical world appealing, as Northcliffe put it patronizingly, to 'people who would like to think they earned £1,000 a year'.

The proprietorial control exercised by the press magnates did not represent, however, a decisive break with the past. Indeed, Lucy Brown's revisionist account of the Victorian commercial press even argues that 'what is an important and unvarying generalization is that the sovereign powers of decision were exercised by the proprietors and not by the editors'. Many of the Victorian editors celebrated for their independence, such as C. P. Scott of the *Manchester Guardian* (1877 to 1929), were either owner-editors or members of the proprietorial family. Other leading editors prove, on close examination, to have been less autonomous than has usually been claimed. Even Delane of *The Times*, often seen as a model of the sovereign editor, was repeatedly excluded from key corporate decisions affecting the development of his paper. Indeed, he was so convinced that he was going to be sacked at one stage that he started 'taking dinners' in order to become eligible to practise as a barrister. Others were less fortunate: Cook, Gardiner, Massingham, Greenwood, Annand, Watson and Donald were only some of the distinguished editors who were compelled to resign between 1880 and 1918 as a result of political disagreements with their proprietors.

The tradition of editorial sovereignty which the press magnates allegedly destroyed was, to a large extent, a myth. The press barons were no different from their immediate predecessors in involving themselves in the editorial conduct of their papers. What made them innovators, to some degree, was that they were heavily involved in the business side of their papers. Yet even this difference should not be overstated, since some of the earlier pioneers of 'popular' journalism, notably Edward Lawson and Edward Lloyd, were also active business managers.

Profits and politics

However, the press barons are usually portrayed as journalist-politicians – a view of themselves which they publicly cultivated. Beaverbrook, for instance, told the first Royal Commission on the Press that he ran the *Daily Express* 'merely for the purpose of making propaganda and with no other motive'. Yet this simple image of the propagandist has tended to obscure another, more important aspect of their dominion over the press – their demotion of politics.

Intense competition resulted in rising levels of paging, bigger editorial staffs and, above all, massive promotion. Northcliffe and Rothermere led the way by spending, up to 1928, approximately £1 million on the *Daily Mail*'s readers' insurance scheme in order to attract more readers. Rival press magnates fought back with competitions offering lavish prizes and their own readers' insurance schemes. After a legal judgment in 1928 outlawed newspaper competitions as lotteries, promotion shifted towards free gifts. Teams of canvassers moved through the countryside offering housewives anything from cameras and wristwatches to silk stockings and tea-kettles, in return for taking out a newspaper subscription. The promotion for the *Daily Herald* alone is estimated to have amounted to £1 per new reader between 1930 and 1932. Even in 1937, when the 'circulation war' had abated, a typical national daily newspaper employed five times as many canvassers as editorial staff.[5] The effect of this heavy promotion and rising editorial outlay was to force up costs, and therefore the circulations that popular newspapers needed to achieve in order to stay profitable.

Publishers were consequently under increasing pressure to give more space to material with a general appeal to less differentiated audiences. The editorial implications of this were spelt out in market research, which most leading publishers commissioned during the 1930s, into what people read in newspapers. A major survey, based on a national quota sample of over 20,000 people and commissioned by the *News Chronicle* in 1933, revealed, for instance, that the most-read news in popular daily papers were stories about accidents, crime, divorce and human interest. They had a near-universal appeal. In contrast, most categories of public affairs news had only an average or below-average readership rating. This was because, although some aspects of public affairs had an above-average readership among men and people over the age of 35, they had a weak appeal among women and the young. Public affairs content was thus, in marketing terms, a commodity with a sectional appeal. It lacked, moreover, the passionate following among a large minority commanded by sport, and it also lacked the appeal to advertisers possessed by some minority consumer features.

Pressure to maximize audiences consequently resulted in the cumulative downgrading of political coverage. By 1936 six out of our sample of seven papers devoted more space to human interest content than to public affairs – indeed, in some cases three or four times as much.[6] Among popular papers, the one exception to this trend towards depoliticization was the *Daily Herald*, which allocated 33 per cent of its editorial content to public affairs in 1936. This reflected the socialist priorities of the paper's TUC-nominated directors. To the press barons, by contrast, ultimately profits mattered more than politics.

This shift away from the traditional concept of a *news*paper was part of a long-term trend dating back to the mid-nineteenth century. It accelerated, however, during the inter-war period. Thus, between 1927 and 1937 home political, social and economic news almost halved as a proportion of total news in the *Daily Mail*.[7]

The quality press remained more faithful to the traditional concept of the newspaper, despite the fact that market research showed that the most-read news items in quality dailies were very similar to those in popular papers.[8] However, quality newspapers continued to give high priority to public affairs as a consequence of a felicitous conjunction between professional and commercial concerns. By the mid-1930s, over two-thirds of quality newspaper income came from advertising. This was generated by charging high rates to reach small but affluent audiences: diluting this select readership with working-class readers, attracted by a popular editorial strategy, would have been economically counter-productive.

The rise of the 'fourth estate'

The press barons are usually accused of using their papers as instruments of political power, but they were hardly unique in this. What actually made the more notorious press magnates fundamentally different from their immediate predecessors was that they sought to use their papers not as levers of power within the political parties, but as instruments of power against them. The basis of the Establishment's objection to men like Rothermere and Beaverbrook was not that they were politically ambitious, but that they were politically independent.

In the early twentieth century the majority of London-based daily papers were owned by wealthy individuals, families or syndicates closely linked to a political party. Between 1911 and 1915, for instance, funds from the Unionist Central Office were secretly paid through respectable nominees to the *Standard*, *Globe*, *Observer* and *Pall Mall Gazette*. A wealthy Conservative syndicate, headed by the Duke of Northumberland, bought the Tory *Morning Post* in 1924. Similarly, Lloyd George engineered the purchase of the *Daily News* in 1901 by the Cadbury family in the Liberal interest, and arranged the purchase of the *Daily Chronicle* in 1918 through a syndicate headed by Dalziel, with money accumulated through the sale of honours and laundered through the Lloyd George Fund.

This pattern of political control was undermined by the growth of advertising expenditure (mostly on the press) which nearly trebled from £20 million in 1907 to £59 million in 1938. This funded an escalating rise in editorial and promotional spending, and increasingly made papers too expensive for political parties and their supporters to sustain. Pearson refused to dig deeper into his pocket to keep the *Westminster Gazette* going in the Liberal cause after 1928; Lloyd George and his associates were forced to sell the *Daily Chronicle* in 1928; the TUC gave up financial control of the *Daily Herald* to the Odhams Group in 1929; no Tory syndicate could be found to prevent the *Daily Graphic* from closing in 1926 or the *Morning Post* from disappearing in 1937.

The enormous expansion of advertising weaned the national press from dependence on the political parties. Although mostly conservative, the major press barons were first and foremost newspapermen. With the exception of papers controlled by Beaverbrook in his early days, all their publications were free of party subsidy, and consequently were able to operate independently. The 'fourth estate' (in the limited sense of a press autonomous from government) – prematurely announced in the mid-nineteenth century – came closer to reality under the press barons.

Beaverbrook and Northcliffe played an important role in the political revolt that unseated Asquith as premier in 1916 and established Lloyd George in his place. After the war they adopted a more unconventional, outsider role. Between 1919 and 1922 Rothermere, aided by Northcliffe, launched a virulent campaign against 'squandermania'. When the Coalition government partly rejected its cost-cutting prescriptions, Rothermere appealed directly to the country by backing the Anti-Waste League (AWL). In 1921, AWL-backed independents won parliamentary by-elections in Dover, Westminster St George's and Hertford. Although these victories were not matched by by-election gains elsewhere, Rothermere had demonstrated the strength of grassroots Conservative opposition to government policies. Partly in response to this pressure, the government abolished three ministries, lifted a wide range of public controls, and sold off public assets.

The Anti-Waste Campaign petered out with the breakup of the Coalition government in 1922, and its replacement by a Conservative administration. Beaverbrook and Rothermere then took up the cause of imperial protectionism, believing that Britain's economic problems could be solved by converting the Empire into a free trade zone protected by a high tariff wall. Unable to persuade the Conservative Party leadership, they again made an independent foray into politics by backing the United Empire Party (UEP). In 1930 its candidate, Vice-Admiral Turner, won unexpectedly the safe Tory seat of Paddington. His success was followed by another by-election upset at East Islington, where Labour and UEP came respectively first and second, pushing the Conservative candidate into an ignominious third place. This led to an internal party revolt, prompting Sir Robert Topping, the chief Conservative agent, to call for the party leader, Stanley Baldwin, to resign. This call was endorsed by most leading Conservatives consulted by party chairman Neville Chamberlain. Baldwin agreed to go, saying angrily that 'the sooner, the better' suited him.

After further reflection, Stanley Baldwin decided to stay and fight, staking his political career on the outcome of the parliamentary by-election at Westminster St George's. Mounting a brilliant political campaign in which he shifted attention from empire free trade to the unaccountable power of the press barons, he helped the Conservative candidate, Duff Cooper, to win with a comfortable majority. Thereafter Baldwin's personal position was safe, though he was sufficiently shaken to make what was, in effect, a private peace treaty with Beaverbrook shortly after the by-election.

The political impetus behind the empire free trade campaign was broken by the 1931 crisis, the collapse of the Labour government and the landslide election victory won by the Coalition administration headed by Ramsay MacDonald. It was also weakened by lack of enthusiasm in the Dominions for the press barons' grand design. Nevertheless, Beaverbrook and Rother-mere succeeded in strengthening the imperialist wing of the Conservative Party, and getting significant imperial preference policies implemented during the 1930s. This last was more than Joseph Chamberlain, the great apostle of empire free trade, had accomplished despite the havoc he wrought inside the Conservative Party some thirty years earlier.

Rothermere subsequently came out in support of the British Union of Fascists (BUF) in 1934. His papers pumped out stirring calls such as 'Give the Blackshirts a Helping Hand' (*Daily Mirror*, 22 January 1934) and 'Hurrah for the Blackshirts' (*Daily Mail*, 15 January 1934). The *Evening News*, under his control, even ran a competition for the best letter on the theme of 'Why I like the Blackshirts'. This support from a mass-circulation press thrust a relatively obscure organization into the limelight and con-tributed to an increase in its membership. However, Rothermere withdrew his support after little more than five months, thereby helping to deny the BUF the legitimacy it needed in order to attract 'respectable' support.

Press barons and social order

Some historians have interpreted the relative failure of the press barons to sway governments as evidence that they exercised no significant political power. However, this implies mistakenly that the influence of the press barons can be assessed only in terms of winning support for a change in public policy, as if they were merely the equivalent of a pressure group. In reality, their main impact lay in the way in which their papers selectively represented the world. This tended to strengthen the mainly conservative prejudices of their readers, and reinforce opposition, particularly within the middle class, to progressive change.

Their papers projected imaginary folk devils, the most threatening and prominent of which were Marxists whose secret allegiance was to a foreign power. Even the moderate and ineffectual administration headed by Britain's first Labour Prime Minister, Ramsay MacDonald, was branded in 1924 as being subject to Marxist influence. In the subsequent general election battle, the 'red peril' campaign reached new heights. 'Civil War plot by Socialists' Masters' screamed the *Daily Mail*'s (25 October 1924) front-page banner headline, heading a report of a letter supposedly sent by Zinoviev (President of the Third Communist International in Moscow) to the British Communist Party. Although the letter was patently a forgery, it was given massive, largely uncritical publicity by all the press barons' papers, and was shame-lessly exploited to define the choice before the electorate as a simple one between moderation and Marxism, British civilization or alien domination. 'Vote British, not Bolshie', urged the *Daily Mirror* (29 October) in its front-page headline. Underneath it printed the question in heavy type: 'Do You Wish to Vote for the Leaders of Law, Order, Peace and Prosperity?' (with reassuring pictures of Lloyd George, Baldwin, Asquith and Austen Chamberlain), 'or to Vote for the Overthrow of Society and Pave the Way to Bolshevism?' (with sinister pictures of Russian leaders).

It is doubtful whether such crude propaganda deterred many would-be Labour voters – not least because the majority of working people did not read a daily paper in 1924 (unlike ten years later). Although the Labour Party lost forty seats, its share of the vote increased by 3.2 per cent, largely because it fielded sixty-four more candidates. But the effect of the sustained red scare in the press was to polarize the election between left and right. The centre vote collapsed, with the Liberal Party being reduced from 158 to 40 seats. The hysteria whipped up by the press also contributed to a massive increase in turn-out, which rose by over two million compared with the previous general election called only eleven months before. The combined effect of Liberal defections and higher turn-out increased the Conservative vote and resulted in a landslide Tory victory.

The press also tended to interpret conflict within a conservative framework. Most national newspapers portrayed retrospectively the 1926 General Strike, called by the TUC in support of coal-miners, as a contest between a minority and the majority. This representation concealed the class dynamics of the conflict. It also enabled trade unionists to be portrayed as being opposed to the 'rule of the majority', and therefore the democratically elected government. This justified, in turn, retribution against trade unionists as an act of collective self-defence. 'Trade unionists in this country,' declared the *Observer* (16 May 1926), 'are and always will be a minority, and if they seriously try to break the majority, they make it quite certain that the majority, if further provoked, will break them.' The portrayal of trade unionists as an unrepresentative minority also facilitated their identification with communist subversion. 'The defeat of the General Strike,' thundered the *Daily Mail* (14 May 1926), 'will end the danger of communist tyranny in Europe.' A similarly persuasive and traditionalist framework was deployed in explaining the Depression. It was portrayed widely as a 'natural catastrophe', comparable to a hurricane or flood. In this way, the appropriate response was defined as national unity in the face of a common calamity.

The press controlled by the barons helped to sustain the social order by stigmatizing its radical opponents. Thus, the communist-dominated Unemployed Workers' Movement received hostile coverage when it organized marches of unemployed workers from Scotland, Wales and the north of England, all converging on London early in 1929. The *Daily Mail* (24 February 1929) called the protest 'a weary tramp to advertise Reds', while *The Times* (11 January 1929) claimed it to be 'heartless, cruel and unnecessary'. In common with other papers, they defined the culminating march mainly in terms of its threat to law and order, thereby diverting attention from its central objective – the relief of mass unemployment. Significantly, the press provided much more sympathetic coverage of the 1936 Jarrow March, which had the support of both Conservative and Labour councillors and a more limited underlying agenda. The press thus helped to police the boundaries of legitimate dissent.

However, the central core of the conservatism expressed by papers under the barons' control was a deep and emotional attachment to Britain and her empire. This intense patriotism sometimes shaded off into open racism and, particularly in the case of the papers controlled by Rothermere, aggressive anti-Semitism. The *Daily Mail* (10 July 1933) interpreted Hitler's rise as a response to 'Israelite' provocation. As it patiently explained:

> The German nation was rapidly falling under the control of its alien elements. In the last days of the pre-Hitler regime there were twenty times as many Jewish government officials in Germany as had existed before the war. Israelites of international attachments were insinuating themselves into key positions in the German administrative machine.

The Rothermere press (along with some other papers) campaigned against giving sanctuary to large numbers of Jewish refugees fleeing from Nazi Germany. Opponents like a local magistrate who declared that 'the way that stateless Jews from Germany are pouring in from every port of this country is becoming an outrage' were assured prominent and sympathetic coverage (*Daily Mail*, 30 August 1938). This press campaign exerted pressure, in turn, on the authorities to deny refuge to people later slaughtered in the death camps. As many as ten times the number of European Jews were blocked, it is estimated, as were granted asylum in Britain during the later 1930s.[9]

But if the inter-war press supported the social order, it also cautiously embraced some forms of change. Most national popular dailies portrayed woman's increased freedom from confining social codes and dress in the 1920s as an advance, part of a generational shift that should be embraced as a necessary form of modernization. Successful women in public life were often portrayed in a favourable light. Most newspapers – though not those owned by Rothermere – also argued that young women should be allowed to vote (something that was introduced in 1928). Yet, this opening to change was full of contradictions. The women's movement tended to be ignored or presented as superfluous; women's pages were preoccupied with fashion, housewifery and motherhood; and women, unlike men, came to be presented in more overtly sexualized ways in the inter-war press.[10]

Modification of economic controls

Although the press became more independent of political parties and of government, it still operated within a framework of market censorship. Some aspects of this censorship remained little changed, while other aspects eased.

Thus, newspaper publishing remained a rich person's prerogative. Indeed, the rise of publishing costs was so great during the 1920s that it largely excluded new entrants into the national newspaper press. With one exception, no new national daily or Sunday paper was established during the inter-war period. The exception was the Communist *Sunday Worker*, launched in 1925 and converted into the *Daily Worker* in 1930. However, it was boycotted by distributors and existed only on the margins of publishing, with a small circulation and manageable losses.

The easiest way to break into national newspaper publishing was to buy an established newspaper. However, a substantial outlay was still necessary if the acquired title was in decline and needed to be revived. This was beyond the readily available resources of the Co-operative Movement when it took over *Reynolds News*. The *Daily Herald* only triumphed because Odhams, one of the country's largest publishing corporations, ploughed £3 million into the paper when it acquired a 51 per cent stake in 1929. Carrying twice as many pages as before, equipped with a northern as well as a London printing plant, and very heavily promoted, the *Daily Herald* increased its circulation from a little over 300,000 in 1929 to two million in 1933. Without this backing, Labour's official voice in the press probably would have been muzzled by under-investment.

Advertising discrimination against the left press also persisted for both economic and political reasons, and this continued to act as a brake on its development. *Reynolds News*, for instance, received only 0.82d gross advertising revenue per copy sold to the public in 1936, less than half that obtained by the *Sunday Express* (1.9d per copy) and less than one-eighth of that bestowed on the *Sunday Times* (6.4d per copy).[11] Left publications were also forced to close down with circulations far higher than some of their more right-wing rivals. Thus the *Clarion* closed in 1933 with a circulation of over 80,000 copies – more than four times that of the *Spectator* and ten times that of the *Economist*. Even massive circulations were not enough to overcome radical papers' advertising deficit. Thus, the very successful *Daily Herald* obtained in 1936 less than half the gross advertising revenue per copy of the smaller-circulation *Daily Mail*.

This said, advertising hostility towards the radical press during the inter-war period was not as great as it had been before. The standard advertising textbook of the 1930s advised that 'the first test that must always be applied to a press advertising medium is the cost of placing an advertisement of a given size before a given number of suitable readers'. This precept could be followed because the information became available on which to make such a calculation. Circulation figures became more reliable during the 1920s and this trend was consolidated by the establishment of the Audit Bureau of Circulation in 1931. More importantly, survey research into the size and social composition of newspaper readership was introduced on a commercial basis in 1924 and obtained official endorsement from the advertising industry in 1930.

This encouraged a more impersonal approach to advertising selection, based on quantifiable cost criteria, in which subjective judgements, sometimes coloured by ideology, played a less significant part. Readership research also caused advertisers to reassess stereotypical images of left publications as being read by the 'down at heel'. For instance, the 1934 official readership survey showed that the *Daily Herald* was read by more middle-class people than *The Times* (largely because the *Herald*'s readership, though predominantly working class, was so much bigger).

The development of market research in the 1920s also helped radical publications by underlining the economic importance of the working-class market. Typical of the shift of orientation among some advertisers during this period was Sun-Maid Raisins, which changed its advertising from high-class women's magazines to mass-market media in 1929 because research 'shows that 91.2 per cent of the families of Great Britain have incomes of under £400'.[12] The adoption of more sophisticated methods of analysis reinforced this more positive valorization of the working-class market. 'Inequalities of consumption,' concluded the principal marketing manual of the mid-1930s, 'are less than inequalities of income, and inequalities of income are less than inequalities of wealth.'[13] A similar message was put rather less abstractly in the trade promotion of Odhams, the publisher of the *Daily Herald, John Bull* and other working-class publications. As one of their advertisements proclaimed. 'If the housewives who read *John Bull* put their purses together next year, they could buy the Giaconda diamond or Da Vinci's "Mona Lisa" hundreds of times over, then they could spend the change on the richest treasures of Bond Street or the Rue de la Paix.'

Selling the working class to advertisers was also made easier by the growth of working-class purchasing power, and the related growth of consumption of mass-market goods. *Per capita* annual consumer expenditure at constant (1913) prices rose from £42 in 1921 to £54 in 1938, reflecting the increase of real wages among working people in employment during the Depression. This fuelled a very large increase in the purchase of heavily advertised, branded products such as cosmetics, medicines, bicycles and electrical appliances.

These cumulative changes were of crucial importance in enabling the *Daily Herald* to survive. Even in 1933, when the *Daily Herald* became the largest circulation daily in the western world, it still traded at a loss. However, its rise had not been stalled by economic exigencies, as before. By 1936, it obtained over £1.5 million in gross advertising receipts. The *Daily Herald* had ceased to be an advertising pariah, even if it attracted less advertising per copy than its direct competitors.

Changes in the orientation of advertisers, and also a dispersal of shareholdings, contributed to another important development in the press – the relaunch of the *Daily Mirror* and *Sunday Pictorial*. In the early 1930s the *Daily Mirror* seemed to be a dying paper. Its circulation was declining by about 70,000 a year. Yet, it was denied the usual advertising benefits of reaching an affluent audience because, as a tabloid, it was thought mistakenly to be scanned rather than read thoroughly. Faced with rising costs, and anticipating closure, Rothermere quietly sold his controlling shares in the paper.

This created an unusual situation in which there was no dominant proprietor. The paper was free to change and, under the editorship of Harry Bartholomew, it shifted downmarket. This was a commercially inspired move, since the working class market for dailies was growing, had been neglected by publishers, and was becoming more attractive to advertisers. The commercial orientation of the new régime was underscored by the way in which it involved a leading advertising agency, J. Walter Thompson (JWT), in the paper's relaunch. JWT carried out market research into readers' preferences; advised on layout; supplied staff to become key members of the new *Mirror* team; and, most important of all, encouraged clients to advertise in the rejuvenated paper. The market reorientation of the *Daily Mirror* encouraged a shift in its politics, away from Rothermere's neo-fascism. As Cecil King, the paper's advertising director, put it:

> Our best hope was, therefore, to appeal to young, working-class men and women ... If this was the aim, the politics had to be made to match. In the depression of the 1930s, there was no future in preaching right-wing politics to young people in the lowest income bracket.

However, the *Daily Mirror*'s make-over was actually more cautious than was remembered by those involved. The paper backed Stanley Baldwin in the 1935 general election, gradually adopted an anti-appeasement policy, but drew back from anything as provocative as outright support for the Labour Party. It also developed an ambivalent editorial identity, combining deferential coverage of the aristocracy with brash reporting of 'show business' stars.

This gradualism was dictated partly by a desire to recruit new readers without alienating old ones. It also reflected a concern not to be typecast as a working-class tabloid. The *Daily Mirror* continued to emphasize its appeal to middle-class readers in its self-presentation to the advertising industry. In 1938 it even paid for advertisements in the advertising trade press boasting of its upper-class 'A' readership (the top 5 per cent of the country). 'Only one of the six popular national papers,' the *Daily Mirror* proclaimed, 'can claim more "A" class readers.'

The really significant change represented by the *Daily Mirror*'s make-over, however, was not its crablike movement towards the centre-left, but its relegation of politics in favour of content with a wide appeal to the young and women. Between 1927 and 1937 the *Daily Mirror* cut by half the proportion of its news devoted to political, social, economic and industrial issues in favour of lighter articles.[14] The shift meant that, in 1936, the *Daily Mirror*'s coverage of domestic public affairs was less than half that of its sports coverage, and little over one-third of its coverage of crime, sex and other human interest content.[15] The *Daily Mirror*'s relaunch constituted a key moment in the incorporation of the press by the entertainment industry.

The *Daily Mirror*'s circulation rose to 1.5 million by 1939 and, after an initial period of difficulty, its advertising revenue increased substantially. The *Mirror*'s success inspired a similar make-over of its sister paper, the *Sunday Pictorial*, in 1937, under the aegis of Cecil King and Hugh Cudlipp. The *Sunday Pictorial*, also without a dominant shareholder, moved away from right-wing politics and cautiously downmarket.

In short, advertising patronage still inhibited the development of radical journalism. Yet the rise of working-class living standards, and changes in the way in which advertisers selected media, had encouraged part of the popular press to drift from its conservative moorings. The foundation had been laid for the development of a powerful social democratic press that would push for reform in the different social and economic context of the Second World War.

Notes

1. A useful assessment of the press barons, not mired in mythology, is provided in P. Catterall, C. Seymour-Ure and A. Smith (eds), *Northcliffe's Legacy* (Basingstoke, Macmillan, 2000).
2. Circulation figures for the inter-war period are not entirely reliable. The principal sources for circulations used in this chapter have been T. B. Browne's annual *Advertisers' ABC*; Royal Commission on the Press 1947–49 Report (London, HMSO, 1949); N. Kaldor and R. Silverman, *A Statistical Analysis of Advertising Expenditure and of the Revenue of the Press* (Cambridge, Cambridge University Press, 1948); W. Belson, *The British Press* (London, London Press Exchange, 1959); the Audit Bureau of Circulations; and individual publishers.
3. In fact most of Beaverbrook's senior editors kept their jobs for long periods of time, though this was less true of his more junior employees.
4. Northcliffe's unpredictability increased to the point of insanity, possibly induced by syphilis.
5. *Report on the British Press* (London, Political & Economic Planning, 1938), p. 132.
6. The relative proportion of space devoted to different categories of article is what is significant in discussing the evolution of the newspaper as a medium. For a different view, see Ralph Negrine, *Politics and the Mass Media in Britain* (2nd edn) (London, Routledge, 1994). Our content analysis was based on a sample of twelve issues of daily, and six issues of Sunday papers, in 1936. Public affairs is defined as political, social, economic, industrial, scientific and medical affairs. For a summary of the results, see Chapter 7, this volume.
7. *Royal Commission on the Press 1947–9 Report*, Appendix 7, p. 250.
8. *A Survey of Reader Interest* (*News Chronicle*, 1934).
9. L. London, *Whitehall and the Jews, 1933–48* (Cambridge, Cambridge University Press, 2000).
10. A. Bingham, *Gender, Modernity and the Popular Press in Inter-war Britain* (Oxford, Clarendon, 2004).
11. 'A statistical survey of press advertising during 1936' (London Press Exchange Ltd records). The figures exclude certain forms of classified advertising.
12. 'The Sun-Maid plan 1929–30' (J. Walter Thompson Ltd records).

13. G. Harrison and F. C. Mitchell, *The Home Market: A Handbook of Statistics* (London, Allen & Unwin, 1936), p. 6.
14. *Royal Commission on the Press 1947–9 Report*, Appendix 7, pp. 257–58.
15. This represented a reduction in real terms of its domestic public affairs during the period 1927 to 1937, notwithstanding the increase in the size of the *Daily Mirror* and the rise in the proportion of its editorial content devoted to news.

Chapter 6

The press under public regulation

Nostalgia has encouraged the belief that the British people closed ranks with bulldog determination under the unchallenged leadership of Churchill during the Second World War. This mythical view obscures the political and social crisis of the early war years, which led to a major confrontation between the government and the left press.

Many senior politicians and officials doubted the commitment of the British people to winning the war. A significantly named Home Morale Emergency Committee of the Ministry of Information reported in June 1940 on 'fear, confusion, suspicion, class feeling and defeatism'. Even the Ministry's parliamentary secretary, Harold Nicolson, confided in his diary during this period. 'It will now be almost impossible to beat the Germans.'[1] For at least the first two and a half years of the war, the relationship between the authorities and the press was dominated by a constant and probably misplaced concern about the state of public morale.

This anxiety was combined with growing concern among conservative politicians and civil servants about the growth of radicalism in Britain. In February 1942 the Home Intelligence Division reported a wave of admiration for Soviet Russia and a growing suspicion among sections of the working class that financial vested interests were hampering the war effort. A month later it commented on what was to become a familiar theme – the flowering of 'home-made Socialism' of which important elements were 'a revulsion against "vested interests", "privilege", and what is referred to as "the old gang"' and 'a general agreement that things were going to be different after the war'.[2] Left-wing press criticism, in these circumstances, appeared to some politicians to be especially damaging. It was strengthening political division at home when the country needed to be united against a common enemy. It was also undermining military discipline and impeding efficient arms production. The maintenance of public morale came close to being equated, in some quarters, with suppressing radical criticism of any kind.

Yet a succession of military defeats provoked mounting attacks on 'the old gang'. In 1940 Neville Chamberlain was forced to resign as Prime Minister. The new Coalition government under Churchill also came under growing attack as the military situation deteriorated. A cumulative political crisis developed which was only partly defused by changes in the Cabinet and leadership of the armed forces in 1940, 1941 and 1942. Press censorship thus became part of a beleaguered administration's battle for survival.

The Second World War was also different from previous wars in that the British people were in the front line for the first time. The strategic objective of the blitz was to both physically impede war production and destroy psychologically the will of the civilian population to service the war effort. Extensive censorship controls were needed, it was claimed, in order to combat the new, deadly technology of aerial warfare.

Censorship and resistance

Amid mounting fears of invasion in the summer of 1940, the government issued regulations which gave the Home Secretary sweeping powers to control the press. The most important of these was Regulation 2D, conferring on the Home Secretary the personal power to ban any publication which published material 'calculated to foment opposition to the prosecution to a successful issue of any war in which His Majesty is engaged'. The regulation also denied the offending publication any automatic right of appeal or recourse to the law courts. As one angry MP declared, 'Its effect will be to put the Ministry of Home Security in a position by no means inferior, as regards the scope of its powers over newspapers, to that occupied by the distinguished Dr Goebbels in Germany.'[3]

A major campaign was organized against these new measures. Leading members of the old political Establishment, including Lloyd George, were mobilized, and much of the press joined in the protest. Concerted opposition was mounted in the Commons, with the result that the government secured ratification of the regulations by only thirty-eight votes – the smallest majority on any issue gained by the new government. This opposition was important because it gave rise to two vital concessions that limited the way in which the regulations were implemented subsequently. First, Sir John Anderson, the Home Secretary, gave an undertaking that the regulations would not be amended without parliamentary consultation. Cabinet memoranda show that three months later this pledge was effective in blocking moves to ban publications which were deemed to 'disrupt the unity of effort' in the country.[4] Second, Sir John Anderson indicated in the Commons that the regulations would apply only to papers opposed to the continuance of the war. When government ministers later wanted to close down a pro-war paper, they felt it necessary to reinterpret the scope and purpose of the regulations. This created a delay which enabled effective opposition to be organized.

Silencing the communist press

The communist *Daily Worker* and the *Week* were closed on 21 January 1941. The *Daily Worker* had modified its anti-fascist editorial policy following the signing of the Nazi–Soviet pact in 1939, and attacked the war as a struggle between imperialist powers. The ostensible ground for banning the two publications was that they were impeding the war effort by setting people against the war. This was not borne out by research undertaken by the Ministry of Information, which indicated that they had little influence on public attitudes. The *Daily Worker* accounted for less than 1 per cent of total national daily circulation, while the *Week* had even smaller sales.

But if the two publications did not weaken public morale, they disturbed the peace of mind of some government ministers. The *Daily Worker* campaigned against a number of shortcomings, such as the lack of deep shelters, which the government was not in a position to rectify in the short term. The *Daily Worker* also published vituperative attacks – including a cartoon portraying Bevin, the Minister of Production, as being in the pay of capitalist bosses – which caused deep personal offence.

The ban on the two papers was also part of a wider government campaign against communism in Britain which was being organized by the interdepartmental Committee on Communist Activities, including representatives from the Foreign Office and MI5, strongly supported by leading right-wing ministers. That the ban was motivated, in part, by political prejudice – and not simply by a concern about the papers' impact on public morale – is confirmed by the unwillingness of the authorities to allow the *Daily Worker* to begin republication when the British Communist Party came round to full-hearted support of the war.

The government chose to close down the two communist papers by ministerial decree rather than prosecute them through the law courts. Summary execution was preferred, partly because the government feared that it might lose the case and partly because, as a private memorandum from the Home Secretary explained, a law suit would provide the *Daily Worker* with 'a good opportunity for propaganda against what it would describe as the government's effort to "gag" the press'.[5] Although the government's actions clearly amounted to an attack on freedom of expression, press 'watchdogs' were mostly silent or approving. When the Home Secretary informed the Newspaper Proprietors Association of the ban, only one person objected. In Parliament the more successful of the two motions opposing the government's actions attracted eleven votes.

Harassment of the left press

The assault on the communist press was part of a wider move to curb criticism from left papers. The *Daily Herald*, which had been outspokenly critical during the early stages of the war, moderated its tone when the Labour Party joined the coalition. Pressure was brought to bear upon the paper through its TUC-nominated directors. Appeals to loyalty also helped to subdue criticism of the government in *Reynolds News*, the paper of the Co-operative Movement. But the *Daily Mirror* and *Sunday Pictorial*, which moved sharply to the left during the war, were much more difficult to deal with. They were not controlled by the labour movement, nor were they answerable to a dominant shareholder (as the Cabinet discovered after authorizing an investigation into the share ownership of the two papers).

At first, pressure was exerted informally through a series of meetings between senior members of the government and directors of the two papers. When this failed, Churchill urged a more direct approach. Both papers, he argued in a Cabinet meeting on 7 October 1940, published articles that were subversive. He went on to suggest that a conspiracy lay behind this criticism. 'There was far more behind these articles,' Churchill warned, 'than disgruntlement or frayed nerves. They stood for something most dangerous and sinister, namely an attempt to bring about a situation in which the country would be ready for a surrender peace.'[6]

The new Home Secretary, Herbert Morrison, asked for time to consider the issue. The next day he circulated a sharply worded memorandum to his Cabinet colleagues in which he suggested that 'there is much in the papers [*Daily Mirror* and *Sunday Pictorial*] which is calculated to promote a war spirit. They seem to be clearly anxious for the defeat of Hitlerism'. After arguing that government action would be counter-productive, he concluded: 'It is a tradition of the British people that they still remain obedient to the constituted authorities while retaining their liberty to ridicule and denounce the individuals who are actually in authority.'[7]

An unlikely struggle developed in which Morrison, the archetypal machine politician, vigorously defended press freedom against Churchill, a former journalist who, on numerous occasions, had apostrophized on the subject of liberty. In the next Cabinet meeting, Churchill accused the *Daily Mirror* and *Sunday Pictorial* of 'trying to rock the boat', and demanded 'firm action to deal with this menace'. He was strongly supported by, among others, Sir John Anderson, who was in favour of issuing a warning to the two papers and then closing them down if they did not change. Morrison opposed this, arguing that such action would divide the Commons on party lines and amount to 'interference with the liberty of the press'.

In the end the Cabinet agreed, at Beaverbrook's suggestion, to exert pressure on the two papers through the Newspaper Proprietors Association (NPA). A meeting was arranged between Beaverbrook and Attlee, representing the government, and the NPA. The proprietors were warned that compulsory censorship might be introduced if the *Daily Mirror* and *Sunday Pictorial* were not more restrained. The proprietors protested strongly at the meeting, but subsequently urged the senior management of the *Daily Mirror* and *Sunday Pictorial* to exert a moderating influence on their staff. The effect of this intervention was limited. 'We shall pipe down for a few weeks,' Cecil King, a director of both papers, commented in his diary.

Churchill's allegations that the two papers were motivated by a desire to secure 'a surrender peace' were unjustified. Both papers were totally committed to winning the war. Indeed, they had opposed appeasement with Germany before anti-appeasement had become government policy; and they had backed Churchill for the premiership on the grounds that he would push for a more vigorous prosecution of the war. Indeed, at times, the *Daily Mirror* assumed almost the John Bull style of the Prime Minister: 'We appeal to every worker and every employer to play the man ... stick to your job unless it is foolhardy to do so' (30 September 1940). The *Sunday Pictorial* was no different. Pillorying Lloyd George as 'the Marshal of the weak and the terrorized' when he proposed a negotiated settlement, it had even less time for pacifists. 'Put the lot behind barbed wire,' it urged.

The real reason for the attack on the two papers was that they had become increasingly critical of the government. The *Sunday Pictorial* (29 September) called the reverse at Dakar 'another blunder' while the *Daily Mirror* referred pointedly to 'futile dashes at remote strategic points'. Both papers began also to urge for social reform at home. But they left no doubt in the minds of their readers that victory against Hilter was what mattered most. 'However bad the "pluto-democratic" world may be,' declared a *Daily Mirror* columnist, 'it is at least better than the depravity that would suppress all independent action and thought under the devilish way of life commended by Nazi fanatics.'

Clashes between the government and the *Mirror* and *Pictorial* recurred throughout 1941 and early 1942, largely because both sides had irreconcilable understandings of the national interest.[8] Leading Conservative ministers believed that criticism of officers in the *Daily Mirror* – including a reference to them as 'brassbuttoned boneheads, socially prejudiced, arrogant and fussy' – served to undermine the respect for rank that was the basis of good discipline in the army. They also felt that the *Daily Mirror*'s calls for post-war reconstruction were needlessly introducing political controversy and dividing the nation at a time of national emergency. The *Daily Mirror*, with an average circulation of 1,900,000, had become in their view a serious obstacle to winning the war.

Daily Mirror journalists, on the other hand, saw themselves as contributing to the war effort. They argued that Britain, in its hour of need, could not afford the incompetence that arose from snobbery and privilege: responsible jobs should go to those selected on the basis of ability rather than of birth. And plans for a new deal after the war were not divisive in a society already divided by class inequalities; on the contrary, a programme for 'winning the peace' would help win the war by motivating people to contribute even more to the war effort.

These differences flared up into a full-scale confrontation in March 1942. The occasion, though not the cause, of the confrontation was a cartoon published in the *Daily Mirror* by Zec which showed a torpedoed sailor adrift on a raft in the open sea, with the caption: 'The price of petrol has been increased by one penny – official.' This was interpreted by Churchill and

many of his Cabinet colleagues as an irresponsible attack upon the government for sanctioning oil company profiteering at the expense of people's
lives. Its real intention was quite different: Zec meant it as an attack upon
the needless waste of petrol by dramatizing the human sacrifice involved in
shipping oil to Britain. This was how it was understood by most people,
according to a Home Intelligence Report, as well as by most MPs who
commented on it in a subsequent Commons debate.[9]

Ministers' misunderstanding of the Zec cartoon was a symptom of their
growing demoralization. In the three months preceding the confrontation
with the *Daily Mirror*, the allies had suffered defeats at Guam, Wake, Hong
Kong, Manila, the Dutch East Indies, Rangoon, Benghazi and Singapore. In
the embattled atmosphere of Cabinet discussions, the paper came to be held
partly responsible for some of the things that were going wrong. Bevin, the
Labour Minister, demanded in a highly emotional state, 'How was he to
"press" people almost into the Merchant Navy if they were then to see the
suggestion [in the Zec cartoon] that they were being "pressed" in order to
put the price of petrol up for the owners?' The *Daily Mirror*'s staff had
become scapegoats for failure. 'We will flatten them,' Churchill told his
Information Minister, Brendan Bracken.[10]

The assault on the *Daily Mirror* was part of the government's struggle for
political survival. A *Daily Mirror* editorial on 16 February 1942 came very
close to demanding a new administration:

> The assumption that whatever blunders are committed, and whatever
> faults are plainly visible in organization, we must still go on applauding
> men who muddle our lives away, is a travesty of history and a rhetorical
> defiance of all the bitter lessons of past wars.

This indictment was published at a time when a number of insiders
believed that the government could be forced to resign. Churchill himself
believed that he might be ousted. 'My diary for 1942,' writes a member of
Churchill's personal entourage, 'has the same backcloth to every scene:
Winston's conviction that his life as Prime Minister could be saved only by
victory in the field.' Even the general public, previously more loyal to the
premier and his administration than the political élite, showed signs of
turning against Churchill in early 1942.[11]

The attack on the *Daily Mirror* was thus a pre-emptive strike against the
government's principal critic. Its purpose, as discussion among Cabinet
ministers made clear, was not only to silence the *Daily Mirror* but also to
intimidate the rest of the press into being less critical. Churchill demanded
the immediate closure of the *Daily Mirror*, in a full Cabinet meeting on 9
March 1942. The matter was referred to a Special Committee under the
chairmanship of Sir John Anderson. The committee was advised by the law
officers (rather surprisingly in view of the terms in which censorship

regulations had been introduced) that it was legal to close down the *Daily Mirror* because, although it supported the war, it impeded its 'successful prosecution'. Indeed, the Lord Chancellor urged immediate suspension of the paper since the experience of the last war suggested, in his view, that quick, decisive action would be effective. 'When the then Home Secretary quite illegally suppressed the *Globe* newspaper,' he recalled inaccurately, 'there was a row in the House in one debate in which the government received overwhelming support, and nothing was ever heard of the *Globe* newspaper again.'[12]

The committee did not, however, endorse this proposal although it agreed that 'it would be helpful if an example could be made' to curb press criticism. Those opposed to an immediate ban stressed that 'it was clear from the debates in parliament at the time when Regulation 2D had been enacted that it would be used to deal with Communist, Fascist or Pacifist Anti-War agitators' – but not, they pointed out, 'for the purposes now suggested'. There had to be a public redefinition of the government's censorship powers before anything could be done.[13]

At this stage a near consensus had been reached in favour of banning the *Daily Mirror*. The hawks, who wanted immediate suspension, had been strengthened by the recruitment of Bevin, the only trade union leader in the Cabinet. The opposition of the doves, on the other hand, had weakened. They stood out for giving the *Daily Mirror* one last chance in which to reform itself, while at the same time seemingly consenting to the paper's suppression if it did not 'improve'. Even Morrison, the principal dove and the minister who would be responsible for carrying out Cabinet policy, apparently agreed that if the *Daily Mirror* people 'did not amend I would suppress them'.[14]

Morrison announced that Defence Regulation 2D empowered the government to ban pro-war papers which undermined the war effort, even if the offence was not intentional but merely arose from a 'reckless and unpatriotic indifference' to the interests of the nation. He added that the *Daily Mirror* would be banned without further notice unless 'those concerned recognized their public responsibilities'. The same warning was given personally to the *Daily Mirror's* senior management, and a report of the meeting was released to the press.

Most members of the government clearly did not anticipate the storm of protest that followed. A large group of MPs demanded a special debate in the Commons. In a packed House a Liberal MP, Wilfred Roberts, aptly quoted an article published in the USA by the Minister of Information, Brendan Bracken. In this Bracken had argued that 'the savage censorship imposed on the French press played no small part in the fall of France. It encouraged defeatism, and bred complacency. A blindfolded democracy is more likely to fall than to fight'. A Labour MP, Frederick Bellenger, then cited an article written by Herbert Morrison during the First World War in which he had urged all soldiers not to fight 'your German brother' in an imperialist struggle. Morrison was pointedly asked why he was not now extending the same freedom of expression to others.

As the debate progressed, the government rather than the *Daily Mirror* was placed in the dock. While loyal Conservative MPs rallied to Morrison's defence, the great majority of Labour and Liberal MPs who spoke were sharply critical. The Coalition administration was confronted, as Morrison had feared, with an issue that divided the Commons along party political lines.

Newspaper proprietors and editors were also not as compliant as they had been over the closure of the *Daily Worker*. While many Sunday and local papers supported the government, the majority of national daily papers sided with the *Daily Mirror*. It thus became clear that closing the paper would lead to a major confrontation with a powerful section of the press.

The strength of opposition was such that, after March 1942, the *Daily Mirror* was never really in any danger of being banned. Thereafter official displeasure took the form of harassment, such as Churchill's personal request that Cecil King be conscripted into the armed forces.[15] However, the outcome was not entirely one sided. The *Daily Mirror*'s outspoken radicalism became more subdued and the paper's most controversial columnist, Cassandra (Connor), decided it was time to join the army.

The defence of the *Daily Mirror* overlapped with a major campaign to lift the ban on the *Daily Worker*. Mass rallies were organized in Trafalgar Square and in London's Central Hall. The Labour Party Annual Conference voted down its national executive's recommendation by backing the ending of the ban. The Cooperative Congress and the Scottish TUC followed suit. In the face of this escalating pressure from the organized working class, the government relented. The ban on the *Daily Worker* was lifted on 26 August 1942 – more than a year after the USSR had become one of Britain's closest allies.

The defeat of censorship

The *Daily Mirror* and *Daily Worker* campaigns were part of a wider victory. The government rejected general schemes for compulsory censorship of the press. It also turned down an insidious proposal for allocating rationed newsprint to publications according to their contribution to the war effort. The notorious Regulation 2D was never invoked again after the closure of the *Daily Worker*.

Admittedly, the government drew back from taking full advantage of its censorship powers partly because the press proved, on the whole, to be co-operative. Thus, the Chairman of the Newspaper Emergency Council told the Ministry of Information in 1939 that 'our respective tasks and duties are complementary'.[16] Some editors even took the Ministry of Information to task for being too permissive in its advisory guidelines. The press, including critical and independent-minded papers such as the *Daily Mirror*, consciously sought to bolster public morale at the expense of objective reporting. Coercive censorship was, to some extent, made unnecessary by self-censorship.

The authorities also refrained from exercising greater control over the press for purely pragmatic reasons. Military censorship of dispatches sent by war correspondents accompanying the armed forces provided a discreet means of filleting out bad news. A number of senior Ministry of Information officials also became convinced that compulsory censorship was unnecessary, once they came round to the view that public morale was holding up. Some also believed that the credibility of a largely co-operative press would be undermined if it was seen to be directly controlled by the government. These arguments from the Ministry of Information helped to deflect more authoritarian attempts to censor newspapers. When the military situation improved after the summer of 1942, and the position of Churchill's administration became secure, ministers also became notably less sensitive to criticism.

However, widespread commitment to the ideal of a free press also played an important role in preventing illiberal politicians such as Churchill and Anderson from silencing their press critics. Press freedom was one of the symbols of democracy that Britain was defending against Nazi Germany. This point was made repeatedly in anti-censorship campaigns, and was not something that the government could readily ignore. When a senior official in the Ministry of Information wrote that 'it would be improper to propose in this country either a moral or a political censorship of opinion, for that would be contrary to the last 300 years of English history', he added a significant postscript: 'It would also be perilous in view of the recent events surrounding the *Daily Mirror* and *Daily Worker* and the parliamentary and public attention that has been paid to them.'[17] In resisting the abuse of arbitrary censorship powers, relatively obscure politicians such as Bellenger and Roberts, along with a large number of now-forgotten labour movement activists, kept alive the tradition of an independent press. The political processes of a democratic society saved the government from itself.

Freedom from commercial controls

Ironically, it was partly the government's economic intervention in the press industry that caused leading politicians to be subject to such critical scrutiny. Newsprint was rationed, on a statutory basis, in 1940 in order to husband a scarce resource and ensure its equitable distribution. The unintended effect was to liberate the press from some of the economic pressures that had previously inhibited radical journalism.

The press voluntarily curtailed in 1940 the amount of advertising that was accepted, because newsprint rationing reduced papers to less than one-third of their pre-war size. This self-imposed rationing was formalized in 1942 by new regulations which restricted the proportion of newspaper space that could be allocated to advertising. As a consequence, the money that people paid for their papers once again made a substantial contribution to the finances of the press. London-based dailies, for instance, derived 69 per cent of their revenue from sales in 1943, compared with only 30 per cent in 1938.

Newsprint rationing also redistributed advertising expenditure. Newspapers which had difficulty attracting advertising before the war found agencies begging them to take their placements, due to the general shortage of advertising space. This meant that radical editorial policies and low-income readers no longer carried a financial penalty.

These changes did not in themselves account for the sharp move to the left made by some papers during the war. The experience of the war changed the outlook of some journalists and expanded consumer demand for radical journalism. As A. C. H. Smith has shown, a radicalizing rapport developed between the *Daily Mirror* and its audience. Readers' letters and documentary-style reporting influenced the tone and orientation of the whole paper, helping it to acquire a distinctively working-class voice. However, while economic controls did not cause the wartime transformation of the *Daily Mirror* and *Sunday Pictorial*, they provided the economic environment that made it possible.

Economic pressures had restrained both papers from moving further to the left in the late 1930s. But the wartime liberation from advertisers meant that they could aim exclusively at a working-class public. They could also develop clear political identities in keeping with the greater social homogeneity of their readers. Survey research shows that the *Sunday Pictorial* entered the war with a disproportionately middle-class readership and emerged after the war with a mainly working-class one. Similarly the *Daily Mirror* had the most cross-sectional readership of all national dailies in 1939, but its readers were solidly proletarian by 1947. The readers of both papers were overwhelmingly Labour immediately after the war.

Newsprint rationing also reduced the polarization between quality and popular papers. Popular papers were no longer under intense pressure to seek ever larger audiences, because circulation levels were 'pegged' during much of the war. By reducing costs and redistributing advertising, newsprint controls also increased the profitability of many newspapers. These changes coincided with a new interest not only in war news, but also in politics in general. As a consequence the proportion of space devoted to public affairs doubled in all wartime popular national dailies, save in the already public-affairs-oriented *Daily Herald.*

Wartime controls thus contributed to the development of a radical, repoliticized press. The aggregate circulation of the *Daily Mirror* and *Sunday Pictorial*, combined with that of the *Daily Herald*, *Reynolds News* and *Daily Worker*, amounted to nearly nine million copies in 1945. This formidable grouping of papers was supplemented by the progressive *Picture Post*, an illustrated weekly with a readership (as distinct from circulation) of well over four million people. Not since the mid-Victorian period had the left enjoyed so much press support.

These publications provided a strong impetus behind social democratic change in wartime Britain. This can be illustrated by the reception given to the Beveridge Report, published in 1942, which provided the basis of many of the reforms later implemented by the Attlee government. The Report was hailed by the left press with banner headlines, congratulatory editorials and detailed summaries of its recommendations. It 'will so much break the old order', proclaimed the *Sunday Pictorial* (6 December 1942), 'that it will rank as little short of a Magna Carta for the toiling masses in Britain'. The *Daily Herald* (2 December 1942) declared the Report to be a 'massive achievement'. The *Daily Mirror* (2 December 1942), while being no less enthusiastic, also published a sober article by Beveridge entitled, 'Britain Can Afford It'. The Report received sympathetic coverage from liberal papers such as the *News Chronicle* and *Manchester Guardian*, and also the conservative *Daily Mail*. As Cecil King noted at the time, 'The volume of press support is so great that it seems to be assumed in the House that it will be politically impossible to drop the Report.'

What might have been a relatively obscure official document (which the Minister of Information, Brendan Bracken, had initially wanted to be published quietly) was transformed by press publicity into a cornerstone of the new consensus. Indeed, a British Institute of Public Opinion survey in 1943 found that no fewer than 86 per cent of people wanted the Beveridge Report to be adopted. Radical newspapers were thus helping to lay the foundation for Labour's 1945 landslide victory more than two years before Labour's election campaign had even began.

In short, public regulation during the Second World War helped rather than hindered the growth of radical journalism. Government attempts to silence the radical press were eventually stopped by public protests, while official economic controls had the effect of making the press more responsive to changes in the public mood. State intervention proved to be, on balance, a liberating rather than a repressive influence.

Notes

1. Ministry of Information (INF) 1/250, Report to Policy Committee (June 1940); H. Nicolson, *Diaries and Letters 1930–45* (London, Collins, 1967), p. 96
2. INF 1/292, Home Intelligence Weekly Report 73 (16–23 March 1942), Appendix.
3. *Parliamentary Debates*, 363 (1940), col. 1307.
4. CAB 66/12, WP 402 (40) (8 October 1940).
5. CAB 66/14 (23 December 1940).
6. CAB 65/9, WM 267 (40) (7 October 1940).
7. CAB 66/12, WP 402 (40) (8 October 1940).
8. See, for instance, C. King, *With Malice Toward None* (ed. W. Armstrong) (London, Sidgwick & Jackson, 1970), pp. 94–99 and 103–7.

9. H. Cudlipp, *Walking on the Water* (London, Bodley Head, 1976), pp. 134–36; INF 1/282 Home Intelligence Weekly Report 78 (23–30 March 1942); *Parliamentary Debates*, 378 (1942), cols 2233–2308.

10. Simon, CAB 66/23, WP 124 (42) (17 March 1942); Bevin and Churchill cited in A. J. P. Taylor (ed.), *Off the Record: W. P. Crozier, Political Interviews 1933–43* (London, Hutchinson, 1973), pp. 311 and 325.

11. Eden cited in J. Harvey (ed.), *The War Diaries of Oliver Harvey 1941–5* (London, Collins, 1978), p. 94; Churchill cited in Lord Moran, *Winston Churchill* (London, Sphere, 1968); INF 1/292 Home Intelligence Weekly Report 72 (February 1942).

12. In fact the *Globe* was suspended only briefly.

13. CAB 65/25, WM 35 (42) (18 March 1942).

14. A. J. P. Taylor (ed.), *Off the Record: W. P. Crozier, Political Interviews 1933–43* (London, Hutchinson, 1973), p. 325.

15. Cecil King was medically unfit for the armed forces. This was the reason why he had not joined up in the first place.

16. INF 1/187, Letter to Censorship Bureau (10 September 1939).

17. INF 1/238, Memorandum from R. H. Parker (15 April 1942).

Chapter 7

Fable of market democracy

A leading historian of the British press, Stephen Koss, portrays the post-war period as the apotheosis of political journalism. 'By 1947,' writes Koss, 'the party attachments of papers – as they had been understood to operate over the preceding hundred years – were effectively abandoned.' The press became fully independent of political parties and hence government, thus completing the 'halting transition from official to popular control'.[1]

This supposedly resulted in a marked improvement in the quality of political reporting and analysis. According to Koss:

> Newspapers grew steadily more catholic and less partisan in their ordinary news coverage. When confronted by a general election, they usually expressed a party preference, but always with at least a gesture of pragmatism and often for a different party from the one they had previously endorsed.

This more open-minded style of journalism is attributed by Koss to the emergence of a new type of proprietor who was 'a businessman first and foremost', oriented towards what sold rather than what furthered a party interest or ideological viewpoint. The man who 'personified' this pragmatic, undoctrinaire approach, in Koss's judgement, is Rupert Murdoch, whose 'papers, both in Britain and elsewhere, lurched from one party persuasion to another for reasons that were seldom articulated and manifestly more commercial than ideological'.

This analysis is broadly echoed by many other accounts of the post-war press. Their common theme is that newspapers were emancipated not only from party tutelage but also from the personal dominion of press magnates. According to John Whale, for instance, 'the newspaper's staff is left to get on with the job' in the modern press because many of the new proprietors 'have global problems of trade and investment to occupy their minds'. Like Koss, he sees control of the contemporary press as residing increasingly with readers.

Like all persuasive mythologies, these portrayals connect to an element of truth. But their overall assessment is misleading because they inflate short-lived trends into permanent transformations, and ignore developments which run counter to their conclusions. The press after 1945 was not transformed by the advent of 'market democracy'.

Growth of press autonomy (1945–74)

During the immediate post-war period a substantial section of the press remained subject to the personal control of interventionist proprietors: the second Viscount Rothermere, Beaverbrook, Camrose, Kemsley and, after 1948, David Astor. The labour movement papers, the *Daily Herald* and *Reynolds News*, were also tethered to the editorial line laid down by their political masters.

However, this hierarchical pattern of control gave way to a greater delegation of editorial authority in the regional press and in a growing section of the national press. The person who typified this change was Lord Thomson, who acquired the Kemsley empire in 1959 and *The Times* in 1967. Within the framework of an agreed budget, his editors enjoyed a high degree of autonomy. Publicly he declared, 'I do not believe that a newspaper can be run properly unless its editorial columns are run freely and independently by a highly skilled and dedicated professional journalist.' His British editors have broadly corroborated this statement. Harold Evans, for instance, could recollect only one occasion in his fourteen years as editor of the *Sunday Times* when he received political guidance from Lord Thomson: the proprietor, he was told in 1974, would be unhappy if the *Sunday Times* supported the Labour Party in the forthcoming general election.

Fleet Street became less hierarchical in the 1960s and early 1970s. The *Daily Herald* was freed from following the Labour Party line; Sir Max Aitken proved to be less dictatorial than his father, Lord Beaverbrook; Astor's proprietor-editor régime at the *Observer* came to an end; and, perhaps most important of all, Cecil King was ousted in 1968 after authorizing a front-page article in the *Daily Mirror* calling for the removal of the Prime Minister and the establishment of a national government without discussing the matter with the paper's editor. King's lordly action was in the *seigneurial* tradition of his uncle, Lord Northcliffe: his dismissal by his fellow directors in response to what they called his 'increasing preoccupation with politics' seemed, at the time, to signify the end of an era.

These changes in the control of the press coincided with the rise of specialist correspondents. Their number increased and they acquired a greater degree of autonomy than general reporters. As Jeremy Tunstall's research in the late 1960s showed, specialist correspondents tended to hunt in packs and to regularly exchange information and ideas with each other. This fostered the development of a group consensus and encouraged journalists to resist pressure from their news desks.

The devolution of authority within newspaper organizations, at a time of broad political consensus, encouraged a more bipartisan approach to political reporting and commentary. This was reflected, for instance, in the growing number of newspapers which invited politicians to write articles opposing the editorial line of their leaders during general election campaigns. However, although the interventionist tradition of proprietorship waned during the 1960s, it did not disappear. This was highlighted by a private management inquiry commissioned by publishers, which concluded in 1966:

> When all allowances have been made for variations within the industry, its most striking feature, and possibly its greatest problem, is its dominance by a small number of highly individualistic proprietors with their own personal interests and philosophy of management.

This was clearly a reference to the proprietorial régimes at the *Telegraph*, *Express*, and *Mail* groups.

The extent to which political partisanship declined has also been overstated. Thus Stephen Koss's sweeping claim that national newspapers 'often' supported 'a different party from one they had previously endorsed' was not in fact true of this period. Every single national daily slavishly supported the same political party at every general election between 1945 and 1970, with the sole exceptions of the pre-Murdoch *Times* and the *Guardian*.

However, the national press came to reflect the post-1945 political consensus in favour of welfare protection, state economic intervention and social unity. Newspaper partisanship was tempered, and there was a period in the early 1960s when Conservative papers were strongly critical of the Conservative government. And as a consequence of the legacy of the Second World War, there was a closer political correspondence between press and public than there had been earlier (or was to be later). Thus, in the 1959 general election, the Conservatives' share of national daily circulation was 54 per cent, and of the national vote 49 per cent; Labour's press share was 38 per cent and its electoral share was 44 per cent.[2] This pattern broadly held in all elections after 1945 until the polarised election of February 1974, dominated by a national miners' strike. This registered the beginning of a seismic shift in the British press and British politics.

Rise of coalitional journalism (1974–92)

In February 1974, the Conservative government was brought down in effect by industrial action. This marked a key moment (though prefigured by earlier developments) in which the Conservative Party moved to the right and turned against the post-war settlement based on full employment policies, high welfare spending and corporatist conciliation between organized labour, management and the state. The later 1970s marked the beginning of a successful right-wing mobilization against trade union power, welfare 'pro-fligacy' and economic policies that had encouraged high inflation. It was followed in the 1980s by the establishment of a new political settlement, based on neo-liberal economic management, anti-union legislation, and the rejection of democratic corporatism – the way Britain had been run since 1940.

During 1974–92, newspapers became more politically partisan, and the balance of the national press moved to the right. This was partly a response to the shift in British politics, but also to the assertion of authority by a new generation of interventionist, right-wing proprietors. Rupert Murdoch became the dominant press proprietor during this period. His papers moved to the right primarily in response to his views rather than those of readers. Thus, the *Sun* left the Labour fold in 1974 and became a right-wing Con-servative paper in opposition to the views of the majority of its readers. Even during the 1987 Conservative landslide victory, only 40 per cent of *Sun* readers supported the Conservatives.[3] Similarly, *The Times* and *Sunday Times* evolved into Thatcherite papers during the early 1980s, a time when the right-wing tide receded in favour of political centrism.[4]

Only *Today*, acquired by Murdoch in July 1987, exhibited some inde-pendence, though within strict bounds. It developed a green tinge, returned to the Conservative fold in time for the 1992 general election, strayed briefly to the left and was then closed down.

Murdoch imposed an editorial reorientation of his papers in Britain through a personalized style of management reminiscent of the earlier press barons. 'I did not come all this way,' he declared at the *News of the World*, 'not to interfere.' Stafford Summerfield, its long-serving editor, found to his dismay that the new proprietor 'wanted to read proofs, write a leader if he felt like it, change the paper about and give instructions to his staff'. A series of clashes with Murdoch, partly over the issue of whether the editor should be accountable to the paper's board or to Murdoch personally, hastened Summerfield's departure.

A subsequent editor of the *News of the World*, Barry Askew, also records Murdoch's extensive editorial interventions when he was in London. 'He would come into the office,' Askew recalls, 'and literally rewrite leaders which were not supporting the hard Thatcherite line.' Askew, who was not a Thatcherite enthusiast, lasted for only nine months.

Murdoch reconstructed the *Sun* by working closely with a talented but compliant editor, Sir Larry Lamb, whom he had hand picked for the job. However, he adopted a more circumspect approach towards *The Times* and *Sunday Times*. During his bid for Times Newspapers in 1981, he was asked whether he would change their character. 'Oh no, no, I would not dream of changing them at all', he had replied. But to assuage sceptical critics, Articles of Association and independent directors were imposed at Times Newspapers with the intention of preserving their editorial independence.

Although Murdoch never issued a direct editorial instruction to Frank Giles, the editor of the *Sunday Times*, he made his views forcibly known.

'Murdoch, the paper spread out before him,' Giles recollects, 'would jab his fingers at some article or contribution and snarl, "What do you want to print rubbish like that for?" or pointing to the by-line of a correspondent, assert that "that man's a Commie"'. Further pressure was funnelled through Gerald Long, the new managing director appointed by Murdoch, prompting the editor to establish a dossier called the 'Long Insult File'. Undermined by a series of calculated humiliations (on one occasion, Murdoch entertained guests by firing an imaginary pistol at his editor's back), Frank Giles retired early. His replacement was a more reliably Conservative journalist, Andrew Neil, who moved the paper further to the right. According to Neil, 'Rupert expects his papers to stand broadly for what he believes: a combination of right-wing republicanism from America mixed with undiluted Thatcherism from Britain.'

The editor of *The Times*, Harold Evans, recalls similar pressure from his proprietor. Murdoch 'creates an aura', recollects Evans:

> The aura he created in 1981–2 was one of bleak hostility to Edward Heath and the Tory rebels, and contempt for the Social Democrats. He did this by persistent derision of them at our press meetings and on the telephone, by sending me articles marked worth reading which espoused right-wing views, by jabbing a finger at headlines which he thought could have been more supportive of Mrs. Thatcher – 'You're always getting at her' – and through the agency of his managing director, Long.

Long bombarded the editor with memos containing reprimands such as 'the Chancellor of the Exchequer says the recession has ended. Why are you having the effrontery in *The Times* to say that it is not?' Evans was also kept in a dependent position by not being given a fixed editorial budget. Consequently, he was compelled to seek permission for editorial decisions involving significant spending. As relationships soured, due to the centrist political orientation of the paper, and its slow growth of circulation against a background of heavy losses, Murdoch actively fomented opposition among a group of journalists personally hostile to the editor. In an atmosphere thick with intrigue, in which Evans' personal aide was secretly reporting to the opposition group, Evans resigned in 1983 rather than 'be subjected to a thousand humiliations, challenged on every paperclip'. He was followed by a succession of editors, all of whom were right-wing. However, the launch of the *Independent* in 1986 forced *The Times* to respond to new competition by being less predictably conservative and, later, by slashing its price.

Another active interventionist, Victor (later Lord) Matthews, was head of the Express Group between 1977 and 1985. 'By and large editors will have complete freedom,' he promised, 'as long as they agree with the policy I have laid down.' During his first flush of enthusiasm as proprietor, he forced his editors to endure lengthy discourses of homespun political philosophy, which then had to be recreated as editorials. Only the most outrageous *ex cathedra* judgements seem to have been resisted. 'I had to plead against the *Evening Standard*,' remembers Simon Jenkins, its former editor, 'being expected to call for a nuclear first strike on Moscow, to rid the world of communism, just like that.' Lord Matthews's staff were also a little taken aback by his novel sense of news values. 'I would find myself in a dilemma,' he publicly declared, 'about whether to report a British Watergate affair because of the national harm. I believe in batting for Britain.'

However, what perhaps most clearly reveals how little Matthews conformed to Koss's idealized view of the new generation of proprietors as market-led pragmatists was Matthews's troubled relationship with his new paper, the *Daily Star*, launched in 1978. Ironically this paper owed its existence to commercial considerations, since it was conceived primarily as a way of making better use of underemployed printing plant and staff. Matthews was persuaded initially that it had to be relatively radical since it was aimed at a 'downmarket', mostly Labour-voting audience. But when the *Daily Star*'s editor, Peter Grimsditch, argued that the paper should actually support the Labour Party in the 1979 general election, Matthews vetoed this on explicitly political grounds. Even after the election, he responded to the paper more as a partisan reader than as a market-oriented publisher. For example, on reading the proofs of a *Daily Star* leader critical of the Thatcher government's first budget, he angrily phoned the editor, 'There aren't any poor. You can take my word for it. There are no poor in this country.' The leader was duly modified to accommodate this insight.

In the end, Grimsditch was sacked and the paper became another Tory tabloid. It vigorously supported the Conservative Party in the 1983 election, even though only 21 per cent of its readers voted for Mrs Thatcher. Even when Lord Matthews was ousted by Lord Stevens in a corporate take-over in 1985, the *Star* continued to be a right-wing paper that reflected the Conservative views of its new proprietor rather than the predominantly centre-left views of its readership. As Lord Stevens explained, 'I would not be happy to be associated with a left-wing paper. I suppose the papers echo my political views ... I do interfere and say enough is enough.'

The third dominant personality to emerge in the national press was Robert Maxwell, a former right-wing Labour MP who acquired the Mirror Group in 1984. He brought to an end the relatively autonomous régime that had existed when the group was owned by Reed International during the 1970s and early 1980s. In the early days of his proprietorship he was in the office almost every night, phoning repeatedly his political journalists. 'I certainly have a major say,' he declared, 'in the political line of the paper [*Daily Mirror*].' Running newspapers, he added on another occasion, 'gives me the power to raise issues effectively. In simple terms, it's a megaphone.'

However, his control over the megaphone slackened when he became involved in ever more desperate attempts to save his heavily indebted media empire, including stealing from his employees' pension fund. Facing imminent ruin, and a jail sentence, he drowned in 1991 (probably in a deliberate act of suicide).

The other dominant publisher to emerge was the right-wing Canadian businessman Conrad Black, who acquired the Telegraph Group in 1987. He adopted initially a hands-off strategy after appointing senior executives who were, as he put it, 'in general sympathy ideologically and philosophically' with his outlook. However, in 1989 he established a base in England, and expressed concern about the *Daily Telegraph*'s 'flirtation with incorrect thinking about Ulster and about South Africa'. The editor, Max Hastings, who had been appointed as a new-broom editor and had presided over a major purge of journalistic staff, found himself the butt of increasing pressure. Eventually, he made way in 1996 for a more reliably right-wing editor, Charles Moore.

The revival of personal proprietorship was accompanied by an assertion of authoritarian editorship. Sir David English, editor of the *Daily Mail* (1971–92), was a domineering force who moved the paper sharply to the right. He was unusual in that he acted relatively independently of his tax-exile proprietor, the third Viscount Rothermere. Although Rothermere claimed to map 'the overall strategy my papers will take', he was probably less of a back-seat driver than he professed. More representative of the new style of assertive editor, albeit in an extreme form, was Kelvin MacKenzie, editor of the *Sun* (1981–94). He had a licence to bully and intimidate within the news room, providing he performed satisfactorily as his proprietor's *alter ego*, pushing up sales and giving vent to Murdoch's right-wing, anti-Establishment views. However, when the *Sun*'s circulation declined and its excesses became a political liability, MacKenzie was squeezed out.

The two notable exceptions to this general pattern of resurgent proprietors and assertive editors in the national press, during this period, was the liberal régime at the *Guardian*, controlled by the Scott Trust, and the turbulent years of the *Observer*, under Lonrho's control (1981–1993). Lonrho's head, Tiny Rowland, never succeeded in dominating the *Observer*, though this was not, as we shall see, for want of trying. These two papers were, in any case, small circulation centre-left papers that were out of kilter with the rest of the press.

The rise of radical Conservative proprietors and radical Conservative politics were linked. The strengthened right-wing press contributed to the right-wing shift that took place in the country after 1974, culminating in the election of Margaret Thatcher in 1979. A series of folk demons – most notably black muggers[5] and welfare scroungers[6] – were projected as being part of a deepening social *malaise*. These attacks tapped into already existing resentment against immigrants, the 'undeserving poor' and the 1960s generation. Trade unions were portrayed as selfish, irresponsible and over-powerful. This representation gained increased force from the way in which reports of industrial conflict repeatedly focused on their harmful consequences rather than on their causes, in this way implicitly pitting strikers against the public.[7] These attacks culminated, during the notorious 1978 'winter of discontent', in an assault not just on Labour government incompetence, but on 'beer and sandwiches at No 10', press shorthand for failed corporatist politics.

This sustained criticism contrasted with the overtly cheerleading relationship that most of the press developed with the Conservative government under Margaret Thatcher's premiership (1979–90). It provided enthusiastic support for the Falklands War, privatization of public utilities, anti-union legislation, neo-liberal economic management (especially after 1983), and Euro-scepticism. And it campaigned against the government's opponents, including the 'loony left', which was lampooned partly on the basis of factually inaccurate reports.[8] As a Thatcher government minister, Sir Ian Gilmour, commented with undisguised contempt, the press 'could scarcely be fawning if it had been state controlled'.[9]

But the adjective 'fawning' misrepresents the true nature of this relationship. A large section of the national press, during this period, *went into coalition with the government*. Both Conservative journalists and ministers shared the same conviction politics. They were partners in arms, colleagues in a shared project that repudiated what was perceived to be the shabby compromises and unprincipled politics of the past. They were intent on regenerating British society and reviving its ailing economy. Their relationship was not that of courtier and political ruler, but that of colleagues embarked on a common enterprise who felt warmth and respect for each other. Thus, Rupert Murdoch confided to the Conservative journalist-MP, Woodrow Wyatt, 'how much he admired what she (Margaret Thatcher) had done'. On being told this, the prime minister responded by saying how much she appreciated the 'wonderful support' of the *Sun* and *The Times*.[10]

However, this press–government coalition did not reflect a national consensus. On the contrary, the radical conservatism of the Thatcher administration deeply divided the country, with the majority rejecting key tenets of Thatcherism.[11] The Thatcherite political dominion owed more to a divided opposition and a first-past-the-post electoral system than to ideological hegemony. Nor did the Conservative press reflect the balance of opinion and political allegiance in the country. Thus, the Conservative share of national daily circulation in the three general elections (1979–87) that led to a Thatcher victory ranged between 71 and 78 per cent: yet, the Conservative share of the vote in these elections ranged between 42 and 44 per cent.[12] In other words, the Conservative Party's share of national daily circulation was over half more again than its share of votes.

Pragmatism and journalism (1992–2009)

The press–government coalition fell apart during the 1990s, in part because of a battle inside the Conservative Party. Margaret Thatcher's allies, in both

Parliament and the press, were alienated when she was ruthlessly deposed as prime minister in 1990 in an internal party *coup*. They soon came to view her successor, John Major, as equivocal and weak. He was reviled for signing in 1991 the Maastricht Treaty, surrendering further sovereignty to Europe. He lost authority when the government was forced out of the Exchange Rate Mechanism in 1992. His administration became mired in minor financial and sexual scandals, for which it was attacked mercilessly by the Conservative press.[13] To many right-wing journalists, his government seemed not a torch-bearer for Thatcherism, just another grubby, failed administration.

Meanwhile, the Labour opposition assumed a new identity as New Labour under a dynamic new leader, Tony Blair (elected in 1994). New Labour was strongly pro-market, Atlanticist, and openly dismissive of its former radical politics. The leading press magnate, Rupert Murdoch, was a global businessman without sentimental attachment to the tribal affiliations of the Westminster village. Forced to choose between a failing government that had betrayed the Thatcher legacy, and a market-friendly opposition politician, he was ready to do business.

There followed an elaborate mutual courtship. Tony Blair was invited to address the massed ranks of News Corporation executives in Hayman Island, Australia in July 1995. In an eloquent speech, he made clear his commitment to an open and free economy. The meaning of this was spelt out when New Labour shifted its position on monopoly controls. It had supported, in a Lords debate, the then Conservative government's intention of blocking large press groups from buying ITV or Channel 5. It then attacked this policy in the Commons in April 1996 on the grounds that it 'treat[s] newspaper groups unfairly in their access to broadcasting markets'.[14] New Labour in effect proposed itself as Murdoch's champion. Further political flirtation followed, culminating in Murdoch's support for Blair in the 1997 general election.

In March 1998, Tony Blair returned the favour by phoning on Murdoch's behalf his Italian counterpart Romano Prodi, asking him whether the Italian government would block Murdoch's proposed £4 billion bid for Berlusconi's Italian TV network. When information about the call leaked out, the Cabinet press office first denied it, then proclaimed that Blair was backing Britain.[15] However, Murdoch's bid for the football club Manchester United was referred in 1998 to the Monopolies and Mergers Commission, and subsequently rejected. There then developed an outwardly warm but wary relationship between Blair and Murdoch in which both sides sheathed their swords. Blair's government never exerted pressure on Murdoch's BSkyB to reduce its large import of cheap American programmes in accordance with the Television Without Frontiers Directive, despite nudges from the Independent Television Commission. New Labour also redeemed its 1996 pro-monopoly stand by making it possible for Murdoch, through the 2003 Communications Act, to buy Channel 5 (but not ITV). Murdoch's papers, in turn, occasionally snarled at but did not maul the Blair administration.

In effect, a tacit deal was forged between two power holders – one a market-friendly politician and the other a pragmatic ideologue – in a form that sidelined the public. This was consistent with Murdoch's record over the past thirty years. He has at every opportunity promoted right-wing views and causes, yet has always been willing – when his economic interests were significantly involved – to draw back and make compromises.[16]

The other architect of the press's realignment behind New Labour, though a much less significant one, was Richard Desmond. Attacked as a 'pornographer' whose vital assets included the adult Fantasy Channel and *Asian Babes*, he was the target of a 'stop Desmond' campaign when he gained control of the Express Group in 2000. A number of MPs pressed for the take-over to be referred to the Competition Commission on the grounds that another soft-porn publisher, David Sullivan, had previously been declared 'unfit' to acquire the *Bristol Evening News*. Desmond's instinct, in this situation, was to gravitate towards official power. Bearing a gift (a large donation to the Labour Party), he was received warmly at the New Labour court. The *Express*, though a Conservative paper in the 1997 election, rooted for New Labour in 2001.

The third major prop of press support for New Labour was the Mirror Group, the publisher of the only popular daily and Sunday papers which had consistently supported Labour since 1945. However, the press realignment towards New Labour was as unrepresentative of public affiliations as the press conversion to Thatcher had been in the 1980s. Labour's share of national daily circulation was 61 per cent in the 1997 general election, and 70 per cent in 2001 election, yet its share of the vote never rose above 43 per cent in these two elections. New Labour's support in the press thus greatly exceeded its support in the country.

However, the Murdoch and Desmond papers (the latter only briefly) changed their political loyalties without changing their politics. Their underlying conservatism endured almost undiminished: their papers supported neo-liberal economics, the Iraq War, law and order policies, opposition to European social market politics and, in the case of the Express Group, extreme animosity towards immigrants. In 1997, the *Sun* argued in effect that Tony Blair was worth supporting as the only credible conservative leader in the field. In 2005, it reiterated its support for New Labour, while also expressing general boredom with the election.[17] The political crusade of the 1980s had changed to pragmatic accommodation.

Some national newspapers remained within the Conservative Party fold: the Mail Group, and the Telegraph Group, whose proprietor, Conrad Black, was jailed for fraud for six years in 2007, and whose place was taken by wealthy businessmen the Barclay brothers.

Concentration of press ownership

The development of the British press after 1945 was not simply shaped by changes in press ownership and British politics. There were also underlying structural shifts in the economy of the British press, and in the culture of society, that also contributed to the evolution of post-1945 journalism.

Thus, the reason why the decision of just two men – Murdoch and Desmond – changed so dramatically the political profile of the press in the later 1990s was because so many large circulation newspapers were bundled together in a small number of groups. Much is made sometimes of the fact that the British press has ten national daily and ten national Sunday papers, and that the trend has been for national daily concentration to decline since the 1980s (see Table 7.1). But a much greater degree of joint daily and Sunday newspaper ownership developed after 1947.[18] And due to the dominance of the national press, press concentration is much higher in Britain than in most other European countries. In 2008, just three groups controlled two out of every three national papers sold in Britain.

National press concentration is paralleled by a high degree of local press concentration. Four newspaper groups controlled in 2007 almost 70 per cent of regional daily and local weekly circulation, representing a significant increase of consolidation.[19] Like national press groups, most of these have extensive other media interests.[20] This is part of a more general picture of extensive international cross-media concentration, exemplified by News Corporation, which controls newspapers around the world (such as the *New York Post*), a major publishing house (HarperCollins), a major film company (Twentieth Century Fox) and, above all, Fox TV in the USA, BSkyB in Europe and Star TV in Asia. Rupert Murdoch is, in Bagdikian's phrase, a 'lord of the global village'.

Compromising ties

This trend towards concentration was accompanied, during the period 1965–85, by the growing integration of the press into businesses such as engineering, transport, oil and banking. In some cases, corporations outside the press acquired major publications; in others, established press groups diversified.

This was partly a response to the worsening finances of the press. Newspaper publishers sought a source of cross-subsidy by expanding into more profitable industries. Newspaper losses also made ailing papers relatively cheap for non-publishing companies to buy (though not to support).

Table 7.1 Concentration of national newspaper circulation, 1947–2008

	Big Three % of national					
	1947	1961	1976	1989	2002	2008
Daily circulation	62	88	72	73	70	62
Sunday circulation	60	82	86	80	79	79

Note: The three leading publishing corporations have been defined in terms of their market share of *each* of the categories of publication listed in this table.

However, when conglomerate controllers bought up the rotten boroughs of the fourth estate, they were seeking more than just an immediate return on their investment. Their motives were mixed. Some were lured by the social prestige that newspaper ownership brought or the excitement induced by what Leonard Woolf described as the 'magnetic field of highly charged importance, influence ... and vocational delusions'. For other business leaders, newspaper ownership was little more than an investment in corporate public relations. It extended their range of business and political connections, increased their corporation's prestige and, through judicious editorial appointments, contributed to the maintenance of public opinion favourable to private enterprise. As the Chairman of Atlantic Richfield (which spent approximately $20 million subsidizing the *Observer* before selling it to Lonrho) explained to his shareholders in 1978:

> Despite the social upheaval of the last few years, Atlantic Richfield's primary task remains what it has always been – to conduct its business within accepted rules to generate profits, thereby protecting and enhancing the investment of its owners. But ... senior management recognise that the Company cannot expect to operate freely or advantageously without public approval.

The winning of 'public approval' tended to be linked to support for the Conservative Party during this period. A number of major press groups – Trafalgar House (which controlled for a time the Express Group), United Newspapers and Pearson – gave substantial donations to the Conservative Party in the 1970s and 1980s. Owning (and subsidizing) newspapers and making political donations to the pro-business party were part of the same project.

While journalists on right-wing papers tended to accept that their proprietors' support for business interests *in general* was legitimate, they were reluctant to puff the specific interests of companies in the same conglomerate group. However, there developed 'grey areas' where journalists stepped gingerly for fear of treading on corporate toes. As *The Times*, then owned by the conglomerate Thomson Organization, candidly told the third Royal Commission on the Press: 'Coverage of Thomson organization activities [including oil and travel] in Thomson newspapers tends, certainly, to be drily factual.'

This period of conglomerate control contained seedy, unheroic moments when compromises were made (and often resented). One of the beneficial consequences of the new print technology introduced in the mid-1980s was that it restored, for a time, the profitability of the press. This coincided with a general trend towards the de-conglomeration of industry, and led to the refocusing of the press around its core business, and related media and leisure activities.

But while conflicts of interest became less extensive, they did not go away. One form in which they resurfaced was in relation to cross-media promotion within the same organization. For example, when Murdoch's newspapers gave disproportionate coverage to the British launch of their sister company Sky Television in 1989, journalists on *The Times* made a formal protest to the papers' independent directors, who declined, much to their discredit, to investigate the protest beyond speaking to the editor.

Another source of pressure came in the area of international news, and related to the regulatory politics of global media expansion. Thus Rupert Murdoch was threatened by the Malaysian government in 1994 with reprisals against his business empire at a critical moment in the development of his Asian satellite TV business, following prominent reports in the *Sunday Times* that senior Malaysian officials and ministers had received backhanders in the building of the Pergau dam, funded with British aid. Murdoch remonstrated with the *Sunday Times* editor Andrew Neil: 'You're boring people. You are doing too much on Malaysia ... They're all corrupt in that part of the world.' This contributed to a souring in the relationship between the two men, culminating in Neil's transfer to the United States.

Yet right-wing newspapers never became, even in the era of conglomerate compromise, mere mouthpieces of big business. This is because they had to maintain credibility among readers, and also because they were influenced by the professional concerns of editorial staff.

Compliance and resistance

If the trend after the 1960s was for more centralized systems of editorial control to be established in the national press, this did not go unchallenged. Strongest resistance occurred in the broadsheet press, where journalists had become accustomed to a greater degree of autonomy than their tabloid counterparts, and where the new régimes represented therefore a bigger rupture with the past. Yet there was only one occasion when journalists actually succeeded in decisively defeating their proprietor.

When Tiny Rowland acquired the *Observer* in 1981, he intended to make substantial changes. The paper's liberal coverage of Africa, he warned, was abetting the advance of communism. In traditional proprietorial style, he appointed a new roving Africa correspondent without consulting the editor.

However, he had been forced, like Murdoch, to accept new Articles of Association and independent directors at the *Observer*, designed to prevent him from taking editorial control. The independent directors at the *Observer*, unlike those at Times Newspapers, had been chosen by staff, which made them more of an obstacle. And whereas Murdoch moved with consummate skill at Times Newspapers, first appointing caretaker editors and encircling them with people he could trust, Rowland blundered in with an ill-judged ultimatum that undermined his authority.

Donald Trelford, the *Observer*'s editor, wrote an article in April 1984 reporting that Zimbabwe's armed forces were torturing and killing their own citizens in the dissident Matabeleland province. This put Rowland in a difficult position, since his corporation, Lonrho, derived £15 million of its profit from investments in Zimbabwe. Rowland also had an uneasy relationship with the Zimbabwe Prime Minister Robert Mugabe, since he had backed his principal rival, Joshua Nkomo, in a recent election. Seeking to protect his commercial interests, Rowland told Trelford to withdraw the article.

Trelford refused and was backed in his stand by all his editorial staff and independent directors. In the highly publicized row that followed (in which Lonrho reportedly cancelled advertising in its own paper), Rowland had little real choice but to back off. Lonrho's image had already been damaged by the Conservative leader Edward Heath's well-publicized attack on the corporation as 'the unacceptable face of capitalism'. To have accepted Donald Telford's resignation, in these circumstances, would have been to court a public relations disaster.

Even so, this incident proved to be only the opening skirmish in a long-running battle. The *Observer* again came under pressure from its parent company, this time to attack the way in which the Al Fayed brothers had worsted Lonrho in a take-over battle for the House of Fraser group. 'In summary,' read one internal note, 'Mr Rowland [Lonrho's chief executive] would greatly appreciate any assistance in persuading Mrs Thatcher to publish the report of the inspectors into House of Fraser' that was strongly critical of the Al Fayeds. Between 1985 and 1989, the paper responded by publishing a series of articles criticizing the Fraser take-over, and calling for it to be quashed. This culminated in the publication of an unprecedented midweek issue, dedicated to attacking the 'Phoney Pharaoh' Mohamed Al Fayed, to coincide with Lonrho's AGM. *Observer* journalists protested to their independent directors who, after a formal inquiry, concluded that the paper's reputation had been 'tarnished'.

The same pattern of pressure and resistance was repeated on other occasions. David Leigh, head of the *Oberver*'s investigative team, refused to return in 1989 to a story about British Aerospace malpractice in selling Tornado aircraft, on the grounds that it had been planted by Lonrho executives and was being inflated for reasons of corporate rivalry. He eventually resigned over the issue, declaring that the *Observer* 'had become a sick paper'. His verdict was echoed by the paper's former deputy editor Anthony Howard, who publicly declared that 'without any overt pressure being applied, there has developed a tendency to anticipate Mr Rowland's wishes and to cater for his interests'.

Yet, corporate self-censorship had been actively opposed. In the event, Trelford survived as editor until 1993. He walked a difficult tightrope, balancing the demands of his proprietor with those of his suspicious and increasingly critical staff. An easier life beckoned when Trelford 'retired' to become a journalism professor.

The partial success of journalists' resistance on the *Observer* was in marked contrast to what happened on the *Sunday Times*. This is worth documenting because it draws attention to something that the academic literature tends to ignore: the pressures and sanctions that a determined new management can bring to bear in order to change the culture and ethos of a news organization.

The *Sunday Times* evolved into a neo-Thatcherite paper in the early 1980s partly in response to the increasing influence of new-right ideas in the early phase of the Thatcherite era. However, the principal cause of change was a management-imposed shift of editorial direction. Murdoch's appointment of Andrew Neil as editor in 1983 was part of a general shake-up in the editorial hierarchy of the *Sunday Times* in which section editors from the pre-Murdoch régime were gradually weeded out. This removed the buffer that had helped to insulate reporters and feature writers from the full impact of the change in the paper's ownership. Neil's régime inaugurated, according to Claire Tomalin, the paper's former literary editor, 'a reign of terror'. 'I was extremely aware of a great deal of misery and bullying,' she recalls. Her recollection of this period is echoed by other journalists whom we interviewed. For example, Peter Wilby, the paper's former education correspondent, recalls: 'There was a tone of fear ... a horrible, "totalitarian" atmosphere.'[21]

What Neil called typical 'wet' or 'lefty' stories were discouraged or downplayed. Thus Donald McIntyre, the paper's labour correspondent, had a running battle over his reporting of the miners' strike (1984 to 1985) in which he was regularly pressed by the editor to adopt a less critical attitude towards the National Coal Board and the government. Sometimes McIntyre felt that the editor's criticism was justified; sometimes he argued back; but at other times, he admitted, he censored himself 'to some extent'. The trouble with arguing back, McIntyre explained, is that it 'starts to become counter-productive and you get to the point where you either had to leave or you just become a sort of joke'. McIntyre chose to leave.

At times the pressure on journalists from the old régime was extremely abrasive. On one occasion, John Shirley, the paper's chief reporter (and right-wing Labour supporter), was denounced by Neil as a 'left-winger' and 'Trotskyist' in a voice so loud that the news room fell into a hushed silence. Shirley became so enraged by changes on the paper that he cancelled its delivery to his home. 'A lot of people were being bullied,' according to the *Sunday Times*'s former features editor, Don Berry. 'Life was deliberately made unpleasant for them in the hope that they would go.' Thus Joan Smith, who had complained about the way in which her report of the Greenham Common anti-nuclear protest had been altered, was told by the news editor, Anthony Bambridge, on 25 January 1984: 'The editor feels you have got in a rut on nuclear matters. He would like to see you broaden your range. He would like to see you in the paper more often.' Smith asked how often and was told every week, ideally. She then pointed out that she had had forty-six stories published in the past forty-four weeks. Bambridge replied, 'You are to be congratulated. I am having a terrible time. You are not the only one who is thinking of leaving.' Two months later, Smith left the *Sunday Times.*

But the principal way in which the paper was propelled editorially to the right was through a cumulative process of attrition. This is graphically described by Isabel Hilton, the Latin American specialist at the *Sunday Times* until July 1986:

> What would happen is that you would write a story and it would disappear. The copy would vanish around the building and people would write little things into it and take out other things. It would eventually appear in a very truncated form with the emphases changed. It had all been done at stages along the way. To try and make a fuss about this on a Saturday when everything was very busy was very difficult.

The accumulation of pressures led some journalists to internalize controls. 'The sense of intimidation,' according to Hilton,

> was so strong that people actually started censoring themselves because it is very unpleasant to get into this kind of argument all the time. It is not just a collection of incidents, it's a collection of incidents *and* the atmosphere, which in the end is so depressing. You stop functioning as a journalist. There are things you just don't bother to pursue because you know you just won't get them into the paper.

Hilton eventually left. Her example was followed by many others, although not all went for the same reasons. In early 1981, there were some 170 journalists on the *Sunday Times*. At least a hundred journalists left the paper between February 1981 and March 1986. This exodus included most of the best-known *Sunday Times* journalists from the pre-Murdoch era.

The changes in the *Sunday Times* during the period 1981–86 were part of a more generalized assertion of hierarchical control in the national press. However, the level of overt conflict at the *Sunday Times* was atypical. A number of factors generally minimized clashes. Proprietors usually influence the ethos of an organization in a cumulative way.[22] They chose the editors they wanted, and got rid of them if they 'failed'. Editors' freedom of action was curtailed by the house tradition of the paper, budgetary controls, management guidelines, and an implicit framework of understanding about how the paper should develop. Increasingly editors in the changed managerial environment of the 1980s also came to accept proprietorial intervention as legitimate. As Max Hastings, then editor of the *Daily Telegraph*, put it: 'I've never really believed in the notion of editorial independence as such. I would never imagine saying to Conrad [his proprietor], "you have no right to ask me to do this, I must observe my independence."' Additional considerations perhaps came into it. When Hastings was woken up late at night by his proprietor and was expected to converse fluently for an hour or more, his new wife whispered to him: 'Think of the money, think of the money.'[23]

A variety of other influences cushion conflict in a newspaper. Journalists tended to be selected in the first place partly on the grounds that they would 'fit' in. Conforming to hierarchical requirements brings rewards in terms of good assignments, high exposure, promotion and peer-group esteem. Resistance invited escalating sanctions. As Anthony Bevins, the late distinguished political journalist, wrote (with an element of overstatement):

> It is daft to suggest that individuals can buck the system, ignore the pre-set 'taste' of their newspapers, use their own news-sense in reporting the truth of any event, and survive. Dissident reporters who do not deliver the goods suffer professional death. They are ridden by news desks and backbench executives, they have their stories spiked on a systematic basis, they face the worst form of newspaper punishment – by-line deprivation ... It is much easier to pander to what the editors want.

Accommodation is facilitated by other factors. Newsgathering is done under pressure of time, and tends to be organized around powerful groups and institutions as key sources of news.[24] The political culture of British society, during the post-corporatist era, was strongly pro-market, at least until the 2008 crash. The casualisation of the press industry that took place from the 1980s onwards increased the economic insecurity of journalists, and probably made some of them more biddable. While there are no recent data, Jeremy Tunstall's pioneering survey of specialist correspondents in 1968 provides a possible indication of national newspaper journalists' political orientation. He found that only 2 per cent of those working for right-wing Labour or centrist papers said that they were 'well to the left' of these publications.[25]

Restoration of market controls

While proprietors are constrained by the need to persuade people to buy their papers, the consumer is not 'sovereign' in the way that neo-liberal theory claims. This is partly because the national press market developed in an imperfect form.

A key change in the functioning of the market occurred in 1956, when newsprint rationing was abolished. This led to a more unequal distribution of advertising between titles because advertisers were no longer constrained by space scarcity in their choice of paper. However, the advertising redistribution that took place was not influenced on a significant scale by political prejudice.

A small number of advertising agencies told the second Royal Commission on the Press (1962) that their clients sometimes vetoed left-wing publications. The ill-fated *Scottish Daily News*, founded as a radical co-operative in

1975, was told by an irate advertiser: 'I'm not going to keep a newspaper which, the first time I get a strike, will back the strikers.' A pre-launch feasibility study for another failed left newspaper, the *News on Sunday*, also concluded, on the basis of interviews with agency executives, that its politics would deter some advertisers.

However, political considerations played a smaller part in advertising selection in the post-1945 period than they had done before. Precise calculations of the cost of opportunities to see advertisements in rival publications, analysed in terms of the social characteristics and, later, buying behaviour of readers, became the main basis for drawing up press advertising schedules. Intuitive assessments of editorial influence, in which ideological judgements sometimes crept in, became less significant. This was reflected, for example, in the first two handbooks on advertising media planning published under the auspices of the Institute of Practitioners in Advertising. The first, issued in 1955, included a whole chapter on the 'character and atmosphere' of advertising media containing speculation about 'the intangible effects of accompanying editorial and advertising'. Its successor, published in 1971, was openly disparaging about this approach.[26]

The initial advertising redistribution that took place in the 1950s was determined largely by economic inequalities between readers. It led to a reallocation in favour of midscale and upscale papers. This operated against the left press because, generally speaking, its readers were less affluent than those of the right-wing press. Certain contingent factors exaggerated this distortion. The rapid growth of employment and financial advertising benefited primarily upscale papers, while downscale papers suffered more than others because their readers tended to be heavy viewers of commercial television.

The death of radical papers

The redistribution of advertising in the 1950s coincided with a fall in national circulations. These reached a peak in 1951, dropped and then rallied, only to fall sharply after 1957. This induced, in turn, a rapid escalation of expenditure as newspapers desperately tried to escape the general circulation decline by spending more on bigger papers no longer subject to strict newsprint controls. Detailed evidence shows that there was a marked deterioration in the financial position of the national press between 1957 and 1965 because its costs rose much faster than its income.

Popular social democratic papers thus found themselves in a double bind. They were exposed, like the rest of the press, to the general deterioration in the cost and revenue structure of the industry. They tended also to be particularly badly hit by the redistribution of advertising, following deregulation. This was especially true of the *Daily Herald*, which had three drawbacks in advertising terms: its readership was disproportionately working class, male and ageing. In the advertising space famine of 1945, its advertising per copy sold had been more than that of either the *Daily Express* or *Daily Mail*. By 1964 it was less than half of either paper.

The *Daily Herald* also lost readers partly as a consequence of its continuing commitment to the Labour Party during the Conservative ascendancy of the 1950s. But its loss of advertising far exceeded its loss of sales, and was a more important cause of its downfall. In 1955 the *Daily Herald* had an 11 per cent share of both national daily circulation and advertising revenue. By 1964 its share of circulation had declined modestly to 8 per cent but its share of advertising had slumped to 3.5 per cent.

Indeed, despite its loss of sales, the *Daily Herald* still retained a substantial following. It was not true, as Sir Dennis Hamilton (Chairman of Times Newspapers) suggested, that the *Daily Herald* 'was beset by the problem which has dogged nearly every newspaper vowed to a political idea: not enough people wanted to read it'. When it closed in 1964, it had a circulation of 1,265,000 – more than five times the circulation of *The Times*.

The *News Chronicle*, a long-established Liberal daily, succumbed in 1960 with a substantial circulation of 1,162,000. This was roughly on a par with the highly profitable *Daily Telegraph* buoyed up by upmarket advertising. Similarly the *Sunday Citizen* (formerly *Reynolds News*) folded in 1967. This was a quality paper in terms of the relatively extensive coverage it gave to public affairs, but by 1965 it obtained per copy sold one-tenth of the advertising revenue of the *Sunday Times*, because it did not appeal to an élite audience.

The closure of these three social democratic papers was part of an epidemic that also killed off the *Empire News*, *Sunday Dispatch*, *Sunday Graphic* and *Daily Sketch* between 1960 and 1972. All these papers succumbed to similar pressures to those that decimated the centre-left press. They all had a predominantly working-class readership and, in terms of mass marketing, relatively 'small' circulations. They thus fell between two stools: they had neither the quantity nor the social 'quality' of readership needed to attract sufficient advertising necessary for their survival in a deregulated economy.

Adjusting to the advertising system

One response of downscale papers to the economic realities of post-war publishing was to try to break out of the working-class market. The editorial implications of this are graphically illustrated by the troubled post-war history of the *Daily Herald*.

The *Daily Herald*'s management responded initially to the paper's growing shortfall in advertising not by modifying its editorial policy but by seeking new and more imaginative ways of selling the paper to the advertising industry. In particular, it sought to combat the negative image of the paper's readers as poor by initiating research which showed that they were heavy spenders on certain products such as canned meat, desserts, cereals and beer.

The diminishing success of this promotion encouraged the *Daily Herald*'s management to undertake in 1955 a fundamental review of the paper's editorial strategy and market position. Two clear options emerged from this review. One, inspired partly by market research into what people read in popular papers, was to devote less space to political and industrial coverage and more to human interest stories, photographs and strip cartoons. This was identified as the most promising way to rebuild a mass circulation and, in particular, to 'bring in women – vital to the advertising department'.[27]

The second option, and the one that was eventually adopted, was to attract more advertising by seeking to upgrade the paper's readership both socially and educationally. This strategy led to the appointment of John Beavan as editor in 1960 with the remit to lure former *News Chronicle* readers and, above all, to attract 'the intelligent grammar school boy'. The paper moved upmarket and included features about books, classical music and even ballet. It also loosened its ties with the Labour Party and the TUC, and moved politically to the right.

Yet despite these changes, the *Daily Herald*'s readership remained obstinately proletarian. Indeed, even in 1963–64, only 13 per cent of its readers were middle class. Yet its owners were conscious that the traditional, loyalist union subculture from which the *Daily Herald* sprang was in decline. The paper's management, influenced by the Gaitskellite revisionism of the early 1960s, concluded that the cloth-cap, traditional Labour Party identity of the paper was putting off potential readers and that the only way to blast the paper successfully into the middle market was to relaunch it under a new name, the *Sun*. As a prelude to this, the TUC was persuaded to sell its share of the paper in 1964 to the International Publishing Corporation (IPC), which had acquired Odhams's shares in the paper three years earlier.

The intention behind the relaunch was to construct a new coalition of readers composed of working-class, 'political radicals' (the old *Herald* readership) and young, upwardly mobile 'social radicals'. 'The new paper,' according to an internal memorandum, 'is to have the more representative make-up essential to advertisers.'[28] But the difficulties inherent in this strategy were dauntingly revealed in prelaunch research which showed the enormous gulf that separated the two wings of the coalition. 'Social radicals', defined largely in terms of their attitudes towards race, hanging and issues such as increasing access to (but not abolishing) public schools, turned out to be only marginally more inclined to vote Labour than Conservative or Liberal, and to be not greatly more likely to read the *Daily Herald* than the *Daily Telegraph*. Ranking high among the favourite reading of 'social radicals' were the society gossip columns of the *Daily Express* and *Daily Mail*, expressing social values fundamentally at odds with the class-conscious, often resentful attitudes of many *Herald* readers recorded by Odhams's previous surveys.

These findings suggest that it would have been more sensible for the *Daily Herald* to have been relaunched as a more popular, working-class daily. But this strategy was rejected by IPC because it would have meant spending money attacking another paper in the same group, namely the *Daily Mirror*. Instead, the launch proceeded along its preconceived lines, seemingly unaffected by the corporation's own research.

In the event, the editorial staff of the *Sun* never succeeded in finding an editorial formula which reconciled the two very dissimilar groups that they were seeking to attract. IPC's market research showed that the paper failed both to please old *Herald* readers and to attract young, affluent, social radicals.[29] The paper struggled on as an underfinanced, deradicalized hybrid until it was sold to Murdoch at a low price in 1969.

The *Sun* was then reoriented towards a mass working-class market. The recasting was done with consummate skill, making the *Sun* Britain's best-selling daily. It greatly increased its entertainment coverage, in particular human interest reporting of show business and TV stars, developed a more explicit style of soft porn, and shrank its coverage of public affairs. It evolved a complex editorial formula – mistakenly dismissed by some critics as simple-minded – which was both hedonistic and moralistic, iconoclastic and authoritarian, generally Conservative in its opinions and radical in its rhetoric. It also anticipated the Thatcherite era by expressing new-right arguments before Margaret Thatcher herself.

It was an ironic ending for a daily that had been the only consistent supporter of the Labour Party for over half a century. Revealed by market research to have had the most devoted readership of any popular daily as late as 1958,[30] it was first enfeebled and then converted into a paper which stood for everything that the old *Daily Herald* had opposed.

Consensual pull of the mass market

Other reformist papers adjusted to post-war market conditions by muting their radical commitment in a bid to maximize sales. This pattern of accommodation is illustrated by the post-war history of the *Daily Mirror*. It emerged triumphant from the radical wartime and immediate post-war period to become the top circulation daily paper in 1949. But during the 1950s, the *Mirror's* management became increasingly aware that the tide of radicalism which had helped to sweep the paper to the top was receding. The 1951 general election inaugurated a long period of Conservative ascendancy. Other indicators registered a change in the market environment. The *Daily Mirror's* growth of circulation slowed down in the early 1950s, and began to fall after 1955. It also failed to retain the substantial share of advertising it had won in the 1940s. The paper's management responded by steering the *Daily Mirror* more towards the centre of gravity in the mass market – the political centre. The class divisiveness of the paper's 'us and them' rhetoric of the 1940s softened in the 1950s and early 1960s into the more inclusive and acceptable rhetoric of 'the young at heart' against 'the old', the modern against the traditional, 'new ideas' instead of 'tired men'. The *Daily Mirror*'s commitment to the Labour Party remained but it changed in character. Increasingly it took the form of opposition to the Conservative Party rather than positive advocacy of a socialist alternative.

In the late 1950s, the paper also pursued, for a mixture of motives, young and upwardly mobile readers. They brought in additional advertising because they were particularly sought after by advertisers; they seemed to embody important, new social trends; and they were an accessible part of the market because their newspaper-reading habits were relatively unfixed. The effect of this redirection was to make the paper's readership more socially and politically heterogeneous. By 1964 one-third of the paper's readership opposed the Labour Party and its readership profile was considerably more upmarket than it had been in the 1940s. This was perceived by the *Mirror*'s management to impose a limitation on the paper's radicalism. As Cecil King, then Chairman of the Mirror Group, explained in 1967:

> Today newspaper circulations are vast assemblies of people of all social classes and all varieties of political view. A controller who tried to campaign for causes profoundly distasteful, even to large minorities of his readers, would ... put his business at risk.

However, Cecil King's market fears, and those of his senior colleagues, perhaps rationalized their own personal inclinations. King's youthful radicalism waned as he grew older. Hugh Cudlipp, his close colleague and successor as chairman of the Mirror Group, subsequently left the Labour Party to join the SDP. Their centrism was reflected in the choice of political advisers to the Mirror Group in the 1950s and 1960s – Alfred Robens, George Brown and Richard Marsh, all right-wing Labour politicians who subsequently defected to the Conservatives or Liberal–SDP Alliance (later Liberal Democrats).

The *Daily Mirror* succeeded in recouping the circulation it had lost in the late 1950s, and displayed flashes of its old radicalism during the 1960s, until it was challenged by the renascent *Sun*. Between 1969 and 1985, its sales fell into almost continuous decline and this free-fall was resumed again in the early 1990s. The paper's successive managements responded defensively by cutting back on the *Daily Mirror*'s campaigning journalism. The paper also experimented with different populist registers in an attempt to find a new voice that would appeal to a younger readership. Its inner uncertainty and waning radical commitment were symbolized by its changes of masthead. Under the Maxwell régime, its old campaigning masthead slogan 'Forward with the People' was resuscitated in a patriotic form, 'Forward with Britain'. This was replaced in turn with a slogan defining the paper's identity exclusively in market terms: 'Colour Newspaper of the Year'.

By the mid-1990s, the *Daily Mirror* had in some ways more in common with its rival the *Sun* than with its former incarnation in the 1940s as one of Britain's greatest radical papers. In the late 1990s, a brave attempt was made to recapture some of the *Mirror*'s former radicalism under the editorship of Piers Morgan (1995–2004). Its opposition to the 2003 Iraq War recaptured some of the panache that had made it successful in the past. But still the paper's slide in circulation continued remorselessly. And its rekindled radicalism was contained within a package that was overwhelmingly entertainment centred. This reflected another key change that took place in the press after 1945.

Depoliticization of the popular press

The commercial pressures reshaping the *Daily Herald* and the *Daily Mirror* affected popular papers more generally. These emerged from their cocooned existence in the 1940s and early 1950s into an intensely competitive environment where the mounting pile of dead titles was a constant reminder to publishers of the consequences of failing to adjust to change. The decline of circulation that began in the 1950s continued in a seemingly remorseless way, with a temporary recovery of popular newspaper sales only in the late 1970s and early 1980s. Underlying this decline was a reduction in the proportion of adults reading national papers from 1967 onwards. Editors of popular papers became acutely aware that they were swimming against the market tide.

Falling sales were accompanied by rising costs. National newspapers more than quadrupled their paging between 1945 and 1975 and almost doubled them again in the subsequent period up to 1996. Between 1946 and 1974, the annual costs of the average national and London daily increased fourteen-fold.[31] Soaring expenditure intensified the need to stay ahead in the circulation battle.

How this could be achieved was spelt out in extensive market research commissioned by increasingly anxious publishers. The most-read items were found to be human interest stories and certain entertainment features because their appeal transcended differences of age, class and gender. Sport was popular among men, as were women's features among women. However, public affairs coverage attracted generally low average readership scores because it appealed less to women than to men and less to the young than to the over-35s.

The managements of popular newspapers responded by giving more space to content with a common denominator appeal. They expanded human interest content, entertainment features, sports and women's articles (see Table 7.2).[32] This growth took place at the expense of public affairs coverage, which declined, as a percentage of editorial space, by at least half in all our sample popular papers between 1946 and 1976. Indeed, public affairs took up less space than sport in all these papers by 1976.

In effect the make-up of popular papers reverted to their pre-war character in response to similar market pressures. However, the downgrading of political coverage was carried to even more extreme lengths in three sample papers – *The People/Sunday People*, the *Sunday Pictorial/Mirror* and the *Daily Herald/Sun*. In the latter case, public affairs as a proportion of editorial space was down

Table 7.2 The editorial contents of a selected national daily and Sunday newspapers, 1936 to 1976[a]

Percentage of editorial space	Daily Express			Daily Herald/Sun			Daily Mail			Daily Mirror			Daily Telegraph			Sunday Express			People/Sunday People			Sunday Pictorial/Sunday Mirror			Observer		
	1936	1946	1976	1936	1946	1976	1936	1946	1976	1936	1946	1976	1936	1946	1976	1936	1946	1976	1936	1946	1976	1936	1946	1976	1936	1946	1976
Advertising (proportion of total space)	43	18	44	42	17	40	46	18	36	29	16	42	47	35	48	51	16	56	38	22	44	24	25	46	46	36	49
Editorial (proportion of total space)	57	82	56	58	83	60	54	82	64	71	84	58	53	64	52	49	84	44	62	78	56	76	75	54	54	64	51
Photographs[b]	13	7	13	9	5	16	15	7	14	21	8	18	8	2	9	14	4	13	11	4	21	26	25	20	3	3	12
Illustrations[b]	4	4	5	2	4	6	5	4	5	7	15	8	1	1	1	4	6	9	2	2	2	6	6	6	1	–	3
Public affairs news[c]	14	29	12	23	34	8	15	27	12	10	18	9	19	40	26	8	20	5	10	15	2	7	10	5	20	28	16
Public affairs features[c]	4	10	6	10	11	6	4	12	8	2	7	4	3	9	4	10	19	12	4	11	6	10	16	6	6	19	14
Finance	10	4	7	6	1	1	9	3	10	4	–	1	20	8	20	5	2	2	1	1	1	2	–	2	7	2	10
Sport	22	18	27	19	20	30	20	19	23	15	9	28	14	11	15	21	20	25	25	28	30	18	20	27	17	12	16
Human interest news	20	20	16	14	14	14	14	19	17	21	29	17	14	12	13	15	11	12	18	15	13	11	14	13	7	5	5
Human interest features	10	6	12	8	4	20	15	3	10	27	5	16	10	10	2	23	9	17	23	17	22	15	26	28	6	7	8
Consumer and women's features	7	2	4	5	3	2	8	2	5	6	4	2	3	1	5	4	2	10	3	3	5	8	5	5	4	2	11
Horoscopes, cartoon strips, quizzes and competitions	4	3	6	3	3	8	3	4	5	6	16	10	1	1	1	4	6	6	8	8	6	14	3	5	3	5	1
Arts and entertainments	6	4	7	6	4	7	5	5	9	4	1	8	6	3	10	3	4	6	3	2	6	7	3	6	25	20	15
Other features	5	5	4	6	4	7	7	6	3	7	10	5	9	7	3	8	7	4	7	2	10	9	3	4	5	4	5

Notes: [a] Sample 252 issues. [b] These are tabulated in terms of their content. [c] Defined as political, social, economic, industrial, scientific and medical affairs. All figures have been rounded off to their nearest whole number.

by almost two-thirds in 1976, compared with thirty years earlier. Evidence for the subsequent period is incomplete and contradictory.[33] What seems to have happened is that the depoliticization of the popular press deepened in the 1980s, but was at least partly reversed between 1987 and 1997.[34]

Gap between quality and popular newspapers

To a much greater degree than the popular press, broadsheet papers maintained a commitment to serious political coverage. Between 1936 and 1976, both the *Daily Telegraph* and the *Observer*, for example, actually increased their relative coverage of public affairs, while reducing or merely maintaining their human interest content (see Table 7.2). The very rapid growth in the size of broadsheets after 1985 contributed to a large *absolute* increase in entertainment content. However, as a percentage of the total, political stories only declined markedly in the early and mid-1980s, and rose again subsequently to a level that was higher in 1997 than in 1957.[35] A significant difference thus remained between a politicized élite press and a relatively depoliticized mass press.

This evolving divergence was not primarily the consequence of profound differences between what quality and popular paper readers liked. For example, the most-read stories in Sunday quality papers during the period between 1969 and 1971 were human interest stories about ordinary people, followed by human interest stories about celebrities – precisely the most-read stories in the *Sunday People* and *Sunday Mirror* during the same period.[36]

The polarization between the two sectors arose primarily from the divergent ways in which they were funded. The quality press generally derived over two-thirds of its revenue from advertising, secured through appealing to high-spending, niche audiences. The popular press, on the other hand, obtained over half of its revenue from sales and its value to advertisers was rooted in its circulation success. Thus one sector needed to 'select' its readers as a way of safeguarding its advertising income, while the other needed to build and retain a mass circulation.

These divergent economic pressures affected the way in which each sector related to the market. Popular papers catered for the lowest common denominator of mass demand, in the process ignoring the preferences of a significant minority of the readers who would have liked more public affairs coverage. By contrast, quality papers privileged the politicized minority among their readers as a way of avoiding the indiscriminate expansion of circulation. This often coincided with the concerns of senior journalists in the quality press.

Advertising thus encouraged prestige and popular papers to define their target audience differently. It also conferred a higher level of subsidy for prestige than popular papers. The reason why approximately 25 per cent of the market sustains half the number of national daily titles in 2009 (five) is because this is the most affluent part of the market, and generates a large advertising bounty.

The consequence of advertising funding is thus to ensure that the only papers that offer detailed coverage of public affairs are those that cater for affluent minorities. This gives these minorities extra firepower, and a disproportionate influence on public life.

Economic power is thus converted into ideological power. Yet this comes about not through blackmailing pressure exerted by advertisers on editorial content – the usual concern of radical critics – but through an impersonal process in which advertising influence is largely unsought. Economic inequalities in society give rise to unequal advertising outlays on the press. This influences, in turn, the structure and balance of content of the national press.

Curtailment of choice

The escalating costs of publishing in the first four decades after the Second World War imposed a further limitation on the ideological spectrum of the press. The rise in staffing, paging and promotional expenditure had the effect of stifling competition. Only established national newspaper enterprises, able to economize by making use of existing print capacity and services, were able to incur the enormous cost of launching a new national paper. Others were excluded or were deterred by the high cost involved. During the 1970s and early 1980s the trade union movement discussed the possibility of starting a new national daily, and even commissioned a detailed feasibility study through the TUC. Reluctantly it concluded in 1984 that it lacked the funds to go ahead with the project despite the fact that its privately commissioned consumer research indicated that there was a substantial market demand for a new left daily.

The only new voices to be heard in Fleet Street before the advent of new technology merely amplified the existing chorus. In the half century before 1986, just four new national papers were established: the *Sun*, *Daily Star*, *Sunday Telegraph* and *Mail on Sunday*. All these papers originated from leading press groups, and consolidated their oligopoly. Politically, they were all on the right and strengthened Conservative domination of the national press.

Mythologizing of new technology

Between 1986 and 1989 a technical revolution took place in the national press. Digital typesetting with direct input by journalists and advertising staff was introduced, and photocomposition fully replaced the manual casting of copy in hot metal type. Pages were designed and made up on computer terminals linked to plate making rather than being pasted up on a board. Powerful, new web-offset machines, requiring fewer production staff, were installed and colour printing was introduced. Facsimile transmission was adopted, enabling the physical separation of editorial and production processes and the simultaneous printing of newspapers at different sites. This reduced distribution costs and facilitated the more intensive use of printing presses.

These technical innovations were accompanied by a revolution in the social organization of production. Thousands of printers were made redundant between 1986 and 1988. The old system of production, in which shop-floor control was effectively subcontracted to trade unions, was streamlined into a low-cost, mass-production process controlled by management. After 1989, a number of national publishers also enforced individual contracts with journalists, and derecognized the National Union of Journalists.

The introduction of new technology was funded principally in two ways. Reuters, owned jointly by leading press groups, was floated in 1984 and produced a windfall sale of shares. Most national publishers also sold their historic properties in the centre of London and moved to cheaper sites. In 1989 the last national newspaper rolled off the last printing press in Fleet Street, marking the end of a historic tradition that went back almost to the beginning of British journalism.

A skilled public relations campaign prepared the way for this transformation. Press managements argued that computerized technology would transform the national press by reducing costs. New papers would be easy to set up, and minority journalism would flourish with the aid of low-cost technology. These arguments were echoed by distinguished journalists and politicians on the centre-left as well as the right in a general mobilization of public opinion against Fleet Street's printers. 'Murdoch may have done more for the freedom of the press than a dozen Royal Commissions,' enthused Bill Rodgers, Vice-President of the SDP, after the press tycoon shed his Fleet Street production workers. Only the intransigence of some in the print unions, argued Ian Aitken, political editor of the *Guardian*, prevented the emergence of 'entirely new newspapers representing all points of view'. His counterpart at the *Observer*, Robert Taylor, also wrote enthusiastically about how new technology would undermine 'the tyranny of the mass circulation press, with its mindless formula journalism appealing to the lowest common denominator'.

The man who initially embodied all these hopes for the future was Eddy Shah, a publisher of freesheets in the north-west and the victor of a famous confrontation with a print trade union, the National Graphical Association. He announced in 1985 to general acclaim that he was setting up a new national daily and Sunday paper in a green-field site, miles from Fleet Street, using the latest in print technology. He was widely hailed as the harbinger of a new era.

But it was in fact Rupert Murdoch who made the first, decisive move by building a new printing plant in Wapping, East London. Although he told the print unions that he intended merely to print a new local daily there, he secretly established a large, new plant, costing over £66 million, capable of printing all his national newspapers. An alternative production workforce was recruited with the help of the maverick electricians' union and trained to operate the new technology. An alternative distribution system was also established through an Australian transport company, Thomas Nationwide Transport, to prevent effective sympathy action by organized labour. As a final precaution, Murdoch reconstituted his Wapping plant as a separate company so that picketing by his Fleet Street employees outside Wapping would be technically illegal.

Murdoch then issued an ultimatum to the print unions requiring them to accept a legally binding no-strike agreement in which 'new technology may be adopted at any time with consequent reductions in manning levels' and in which anyone involved in industrial action during the term of the contract would be dismissed without appeal. The print unions, although agreeing belatedly to new technology and voluntary redundancy, refused to sign an agreement which effectively removed union protection. A strike was called and Murdoch's Fleet Street production workers mounted a forlorn, nightly vigil outside the coils of razor wire surrounding the Wapping plant. Their frustration flared into occasional violence during ritualized mass pickets, which resulted in some print workers being gaoled and their unions heavily fined. After more than a year, the strike was called off amid bitter recriminations.

Murdoch's success was followed by a wave of redundancies in Fleet Street as rival press groups introduced new technology. New papers were also launched in the period 1986–89, seemingly fulfilling optimistic predictions about the impact of new technology. But these predictions were based, as it turned out, on a myth: the widespread belief that overpaid and underworked print workers accounted for the major part of newspaper costs. In fact, production wages comprised only an estimated 21 per cent of Fleet Street costs before new technology was introduced.[37]

'Downsizing' the production force thus did not change fundamentally the economics of publishing. The launch and establishment of new national newspapers still required large resources. *Today* and *Sunday Today* were launched with an initial outlay of £22.5 million; the *Independent* with an establishment fund of £21 million; the *News on Sunday* with around £6 million; the *Sunday Correspondent* with £18 million; and the *London Daily News* with an outlay of well over £30 million in its first year.

Outlays remained high because new technology was relatively expensive and had only a limited impact in lowering non-wage costs. Newspapers still had to attain relatively high circulations in order to break even. The run-in period when new papers were building circulation, and trading at a loss, added to the effective establishment cost.

Just how little things had changed was revealed by Shah's supposedly mould-breaking launch of *Today* and *Sunday Today*. Shah's central problem – apart from lack of editorial ability – was shortage of money. A substantial part of his launch fund was spent on setting up a modern plant. This led him to economize on prelaunch preparations, which contributed to the production problems and indifferent editorial quality of the early issues of his papers. He then ran out of money after only ten weeks and found it impossible to secure further credit, largely because the equity proportion of his capital amounted to only £8.5 million. As a consequence the first national newspapers to be launched by an outsider in half a century were taken over by a leading press conglomerate, Lonrho. Along with other sub-sidiary backers, Lonrho injected a further £24 million into the Today Group in 1986–87, effectively doubling the establishment outlay. *Sunday Today* was closed down and *Today* was acquired by the leading monopolist Rupert Murdoch, who attempted to resuscitate it as a commercial proposition and failed.

One problem Shah shared with other would-be publishers was that he had to leap over the publishing equivalent of a high jump from a very short run-up. The length of the run-up was affected by how much money the publisher was able to spend on getting the paper right, and building a substantial reader-ship. The height of the jump depended on the advertising bounty that readers brought with them. A paper aimed at the working class, such as the *News on Sunday*, needed in 1987, using the latest technology, around 800,000 circulation to break even. A paper aimed at the affluent, such as the *Independent*, required approximately half this circulation in 1988.

The net impact of new technology was modest because it did not lower entry costs substantially or change the distorting role of advertising. Of the small shoal of minnows that swam for a time near the hulks of the estab-lished press, only two survived. Casualties included two left papers, *News on Sunday* (1987) and *Sunday Correspondent* (1989–90), the first of which was editorially dismal and both of which were undercapitalized. Shah again attempted with too little money to launch a new national paper, *The Post* (1988), which lasted for only thirty-three issues. The *London Daily News* (1987) was killed off with the help of a short-lived spoiling paper launched by the monopoly *London Evening Standard*. The only mainstream newspapers to stay the course were the *Independent* and *Independent on Sunday*. However, they only avoided closure by surrendering their independence. Initially, the *Independent* attracted talented journalists, breathed new life into a bi-partisan tradition of journalism, and made great headway in building circulation. It then depleted its limited resources by launching a Sunday paper during a recession, lost momentum, and was finally torpedoed by Murdoch and Black, who slashed the prices of rival papers. The *Independent* and *Independent on Sunday* limped into harbour, and were taken over ultimately by an international media group based in Ireland.

The only partial exception to this record of relative failure was the launch of *Sunday Sport* in 1986, and its expansion into a weekday title, *Sport*. These caricatured the excesses of tabloid journalism, with invented stories such as 'World War II Bomber Found on the Moon', and its predictable follow-up 'World War II Bomber Found on the Moon Vanished'. However, their diet of sport, crime and pornography, without public affairs coverage, make them specialist publications rather than national newspapers. They are also not very popular: their survival has been due to their paring down of costs, with skeletal staffs, no general news service, and a heavy reliance on cheap, bought-in material.

The expansionary period of the national press is now probably over. The major press groups forestalled the threat of further challenges by forcing up costs. They multiplied newspaper sections, held down prices and in the late 1980s poured money into promotion. No new national newspaper has been launched since 1989, apart from the specialist *Sunday Business* started in 1996, and the Sunday stable-mate of the *Star*, launched in 2002. The latter – the product of a powerful press group – probably typifies what, at best, we may expect in the future.

In short, the technical transformation of the press never produced a corresponding editorial revolution. It led to a cleaner, cheaper system of production; it gave rise to fatter newspapers with new sections; and it added two centrist titles to the already crowded top end of the market. But what it did not do was enrich popular journalism through the proliferation of viable minority newspapers, or by significantly extending the ideological range of the press. The Fleet Street 'revolution' was a rainbow that came and went, though not before dazzling impressionable journalists.

Internet and journalism[38]

The internet is likely to have a much greater influence on journalism than computer-aided print technology did. Some of the internet's effects on journalism are wholly positive. Crucially, it has lowered entry costs, enabling self-publishing bloggers to gain a significant audience. It has made it easier and quicker for journalists to gain information, and this has sometimes helped them to gain rapid access to grassroots voices (typified by the soldiers' website, ARRSE). New international e-zines have come into being, promoting dialogue between nations.

But some consequences have been negative. A recent study, based on over 120 interviews with journalists and mini-ethnographies of news rooms, found that the internet is encouraging scissors-and-paste, routine journalism.[39] It is contributing to greater work pressure, with some journalists being required to deliver on different 'platforms'. It is also giving rise to an increased blizzard of information, prompting some journalists to compensate by relying more on a limited repertoire of authoritative news sources, and monitoring ever more anxiously what other journalists are doing. This is giving rise to a surprising degree of uniformity between numerous national news websites, reflected in the same story lines, quotes and even pictures.

The internet is also undermining the business model for delivering news in the heavily advertising dependent sectors of the press – the quality national and regional/local press. Between 2005 and 2007, internet advertising doubled as a percentage of total media spending (from 8 per cent to 16 per cent). This was accompanied by a decline in the press share (especially pronounced in the regional press), which was accentuated by the 2008 recession. Budget cuts and redundancies in the press are gathering momentum. They are likely to result in a significant number of newspaper closures during the next five years; and the conversion of newspapers into website-only operations (with smaller staff).

But amid these positive and negative developments, there is also continuity. The principal news brands remain in control, dominating both online and offline journalism. The dominant gatekeeper role of the professional journalist has been supplemented but not undermined by citizen journalists. And the commercial organizations that professional journalists work for are mostly driven by the same imperatives of profit and power as before.

Power without responsibility

Intense competition in the 1970s and 1980s gave rise to a number of well-publicised newspaper excesses:[40] inventing an overnight love tryst between Prince Charles and Lady Diana Spencer on a lonely railway siding in the royal train (*Sunday Mirror*); fabricating a fictitious interview with Mrs Marica McKay, the widow of the Falklands VC hero (*Sun*); touching up a photograph of 'Lady Di' to give a hint of nipples in a low-cut dress (*Sun*); offering 'blood money' to relatives and friends of the 'Yorkshire Ripper', Peter Sutcliffe (*Daily Mail*, *Daily Express*, *Daily Star* and *News of the World*); pillorying a child as the 'Worst Brat in Britain' without mentioning that he was ill due to contracting meningitis (*Sun*); and, most notoriously of all, reporting as 'The Truth' misleading claims that football hooligans had urinated on police officers, attacked rescue workers and stolen from injured fans in the Hillsborough football stadium disaster (*Sun*).

The same competitive dynamic prevailed in the 2000s, and produced predictable results. One strategy for winning and keeping readers is to make them angry. As *Sunday Express* journalists were commanded in 2003 'We must make the readers cross … ' The office memo went on to itemise the things that make *Express* readers especially angry, from teenage pregnancies to the mismanaged railway system.[41]

This 'tabloid' approach led to ever more inventive ways of arousing indignation. Thus, in mid-2003, the British public read a succession of stories about 'asylum seekers' doing objectionable things: for example, killing swans (*Sun*, 4 July 2003), a few days later poaching fish ('Now They Are Eating Our Fish!', *Sun*, 7 July 2003), and eating donkeys (*Daily Star*, 31 August, 2003). The first of these articles was perhaps best judged to raise readers' blood pressure. Swans in Britain are a symbol of national heritage, protected by law since Norman times. To eat swans is to transgress a national taboo, at a time when anti-immigrant hostility was already increasing.

The *Sun* judged the issue to be so important that it cleared its front page. Under the banner headline 'SWAN BAKE', the article began with an emotive cue: 'Callous asylum seekers are barbecuing the Queen's swans ... East European poachers lure the protected Royal birds into baited traps, an official Metropolitan Police Report says.' The *Sun's* continuation story, inside the paper, recorded unambiguously: 'Police swooped on a gang of east Europeans and caught them red-handed about to cook a pair of swans ... '

It subsequently transpired that there was no Metropolitan Police Report, merely an internal, one-page memo 'advising officers about the law should they come across people interfering with swans'.[42] There were in fact no police arrests of any immigrant 'gang' laying swan traps. The *Sun*, concluded the official Press Complaints Commission (PCC), 'was unable to provide any evidence for the story'.[43]

If one way to engage readers' attention is to make them angry, another is to frighten them. In 1998, Andrew Wakefield and his associates published a paper in the *Lancet*, a leading medical journal, which suggested that there might be a connection between the Measles, Mumps and Rubella (MMR) triple vaccine and the onset of bowel disorder and autism. The study was based on a small – and selective – sample of twelve children, and it did not claim that a connection had been proven. But in a press conference launching the study, Andrew Wakefield advised that it might be sensible to avoid the triple vaccine until further research was done.

This press conference provided the launch pad for a tabloid campaign against the vaccine, sustained over a number of years, in which the *Daily Mail* and *Sun* took the lead. At the height of the MMR scare, in January 2001, the *Sun* published an article about the vaccine, on average, every other day for the entire month. This is typified by its report that 'anguished mother Mary Robinson' is 'convinced' that the MMR jab 'caused autism in four of her kids and behaviour problems in another'.[44] The article offered no medical support to back up Mary Robinson's conviction, but quoted her as saying that 'they [the authorities] withdraw a hairdryer if there is a problem – why aren't they withdrawing this drug' (by which she meant vaccine). Celebrities were also mobilized in the cause. 'TV star Carol Vorderman led calls for a safe measles jab last night', reported the *Sun*, adding that the Countdown star had 'talked to many people' with children who had been damaged by the vaccine.[45]

However, the problem with this and other unqualified diagnoses is that autism often first becomes apparent at around the age of 2, when children are given the triple vaccine. This is coincidental, and not causally connected. The overwhelming body of medical evidence – including major studies in the US, Japan and Finland, and regular annual reviews of available research – concluded that the vaccine did not cause autism, and was safe.

But leading popular papers gave the impression that to allow one's children to receive the triple vaccine was to play Russian roulette with their health. Its take-up fell sharply in the wake of alarming press coverage, leading both to increased individual exposure to infection, and reduced collective immunity.[46] As a consequence, cases of mumps soared, and the incidence of measles rose year on year after 2005. In 2008, measles cases in England and Wales increased by no less than 36 per cent.[47]

Measles is a potentially serious illness that can lead to pneumonia or brain damage (and claimed the life of a child in 2005). The prominence given by the popular press to maverick medical opinion, and the outbursts of anguished parents, made compelling reading. It also helped to revive an avoidable disease. These, and other scares, go some way to explaining why Britain has the least-trusted press in western Europe.[48]

Notes

1. S. Koss, *The Rise and Fall of the Political Press in Britain*, vol. 2 (London, Hamish Hamilton, 1984) p. 4.
2. D. Butler and G. Butler, *Twentieth Century British Political Facts 1900–2000* (Basingstoke, Macmillan, 8th edition, 2000), p. 537.
3. MORI, June 1987. This excludes those who were undecided or intended to abstain.
4. Butler and Butler, *ibid.*, 2000, pp. 274–75.
5. D. McQuail, *Analysis of Newspaper Content*, Royal Commission on the Press Research Series 4 (London, HMSO, 1977).
6. S. Hall, C. Critcher, T. Jefferson, J. Clarke, and B. Roberts (1978) *Policing the Crisis* (London, Macmillan, 1978).
7. P. Golding and S. Middleton, *Images of Welfare* (Oxford, Martin Robertson, 1982).
8. J. Curran, I. Gaber, and J. Petley, *Culture Wars* (Edinburgh, Edinburgh University Press, 2005).
9. I. Gilmour, *Dancing with Dogma* (London, Simon and Schuster, 1993), p. 223.
10. S. Curtis (ed.) *The Journals of Woodrow Wyatt* (Basingstoke, Macmillan, vol. 1, 1998), p. 125.
11. A classic essay making this argument is I. Crewe, 'Has the electorate become Thatcherite?' in R. Skidelsky (ed.) *Thatcherism* (London, Chatto and Windus, 1988). For a summary of more extensive evidence, see Curran, Gaber and Petley, *Culture Wars*.
12. See note 2.
13. R. Greenslade, *Press Gang* (Basingstoke, Macmillan, 2003).
14. Amendment to Broadcasting Bill moved by Dr John Cunningham, *Parliamentary Debates*, 275 (84), col. 551, 16 April 1996.
15. N. Chenoweth, *Virtual Murdoch* (London, Secker & Warburg, London), p. 201.
16. B. Page, *The Murdoch Archipelago* (London, Simon and Schuster, 2003).
17. M. Scammell and M. Harrop, 'The press: still for Labour, despite Blair', in D. Kavanagh and D. Butler (eds.) *The British General Election of 2005* (Basingstoke, Palgrave Macmillan, 2005).
18. By 1989, for example, the three dominant groups controlled 57 per cent of *total* daily and Sunday paper circulation in Britain compared with 42 per cent in 1947 (*Annual Report of the Press Council 1989* (London, Press Council, 1990), table 4; *Royal Commission on the Press 1947–9 Report* (London, HMSO, 1949), appendices 3 and 4. No comparable figures are available for 2008. But unlike 1947, the three groups dominating the national daily and Sunday press in 2008 were the same.
19. House of Lords Select Committee on Communications, *The Ownership of the News* (London, Stationery Office, 2008), vol. 1, p. 46.
20. *Ibid.*, 2008, tables 1 and 2, pp. 42–44 and 47–48.
21. My thanks to Brendan Wall for help in conducting interviews.

22. For recent evidence of how ownership and senior management influence the culture of news organizations, see House of Lords Select Committee on Communications, *The Ownership of the News*, vol. 2 (Evidence), (London, Stationery Office, 2008), pp. 338 *et passim*.

23. M. Hastings, *Editor* (Basingstoke, Macmillan, 2002), p. 235.

24. This is perhaps the key point of a highly illuminating book: N. Davies, *Flat Earth News* (London, Chatto and Windus, 2008).

25. J. Tunstall, *Journalists at Work* (London, Constable, 1971).

26. J. W. Hobson, *The Selection of Advertising Media* (London, Business Publications, 1955); J. R. Adams, *Media Planning* (London, Business Books, 1971). There was, however, a reaction against overdependence on quantitative approaches in media planning during the late 1970s.

27. 'Daily Herald reader interest surveys recommendations', p. 8 (London, Odhams Ltd records, 1955).

28. 'Attitudes to newspapers and newspaper reading' (London, International Publishing Corporation (IPC) records, 1964), p. 3.

29. 'Report of an investigation into the transition from the *Daily Herald* to the *Sun*' (London, IPC records, 1968).

30. 'Report of a survey to study attitudes to daily newspapers' (London, Odhams Ltd records, 1958).

31. Estimated from *Royal Commission on the Press 1947–9 Report* (London, HMSO, 1949), table 4, p. 82, and *Royal Commission on the Press Interim Report* (London, HMSO, 1976), table E5, p. 96.

32. A representative sample (twelve issues of dailies and six of Sundays per year) was selected in a way that gave appropriate weight to each quarter of the year, each week in the month and each day in the week. A code–recode comparison of a representative sample of 1491 items yielded 83 per cent agreement in their classification.

33. D. Rooney, 'Thirty years of competition in the British tabloid press: the *Mirror* and the *Sun* 1968–1998', and S. McLachlan and P. Golding, 'Tabloidization in the British press: a quantitative investigation into changes in British newspapers, 1952–1997', both in C. Sparks and J. Tulloch, *Tabloid Tales* (Lanham, Rowman & Littlefield, 2000).

34. S. McLachlan and P. Golding, *ibid.*, fig. 3.11, p. 86.

35. *Ibid.*, fig 3.12, p. 87.

36. *Sunday Times*, Marketing Research Studies, 1969–1971; Sunday Paper Readership Surveys, International Publishing Corporation Marketing and Research Department, 1969–71.

37. The latest available figure for the national newspaper press in the pre-new print technology period, as reported in the *Royal Commission on the Press Interim Report* (London, HMSO, 1970), table E.11, p. 101.

38. The internet is discussed elsewhere in this book, in particular Chapters 16–18, and 24.

39. N. Fenton (ed.) *New Media, Old News* (London, Sage, 2009).

40. H. Porter, *Lies, Damn Lies and Some Exclusives* (London, Chatto and Windus, 1984); P. Chippendale and C. Horrie, *Stick it up Your Punter* (London, Heinemann, 1990).

41. Cited N. Cohen, 'Going nowhere fast', *Observer*, 12 October, 2003.

42. N. Medic, 'Swan bake: making a meal of a myth', in R. Cookson and M. Jempson (eds) *The RAM Report* (Bristol, Mediawise, 2005).

43. N. Medic, 'Making a meal of a myth', in M. Jempson and R. Cookson (eds) *Satisfaction Guaranteed?* (Bristol, Mediawise, 2005), p. 29.

44. *Sun*, 26 January 2001.

45. *Sun*, 8 January 2001.

46. T. Boyce, *Health, Risk and News* (New York, Lang, 2007).

47. BBC News, 'Rise in measles "very worrying"', 6 February 2009. http://newsvote.bbc.co.uk/mpapps/pagetools/print/news.bbc.co.uk/1/hi/health/787254 Accessed on 21 February 2009.

48. Eurobarometer survey, 2002, cited in the *Guardian*, 24 April 2002.

Part II

Broadcasting history

Chapter 8

Reith and the denial of politics

There are two accounts of the origins of the BBC. The first is that the Corporation was the personal achievement of John Reith. The second is that its emergence was accidental. According to the first view, the BBC's monopoly of broadcasting was an inevitable consequence of the Corporation's cultural mission, while for the second, as R. H. Coase has written, 'The problem, to which the monopoly was seen as a solution by the Post Office, was one of Civil Service administration. The view that a monopoly in broadcasting was better for the listener was only to come later.'

These theories appear to conflict. According to one view, Reith made history fit his vision. According to the other, a great institution took a particular form because no one appreciated its future importance. Both, however, have a central flaw in common: they disregard political and social change in the world outside broadcasting.

Discovering an audience, a director, and the money

Broadcasting – the transmitting of programmes to be heard simultaneously by an indefinitely large number of people – is a social invention, not a technical one. The capacity to broadcast existed long before it was recognized. 'Wireless telegraphy' was developed during the First World War for military purposes. It was used as a substitute for the telephone, but one with the disadvantage that it was impossible to specify the audience which heard the message. An American engineer, David Sarnoff, first saw the possibilities of radio in 1916. 'I have in mind a plan of development which would make radio a "household utility" like the piano or electricity,' he wrote. 'The idea is to bring music into the house by wireless.'

Yet for some time after popular broadcasting had started in the 1920s, wireless was regarded as little more than an experimental toy. It took Northcliffe, a pioneer in the commercialization of leisure, to demonstrate the potential audience for the new invention. He arranged a promotion stunt for the *Daily Mail*. Dame Nellie Melba was to be broadcast singing from Chelmsford. This event, which began 'with a long silvery trill' and ended with *God Save the King*, attracted a much larger audience than had been expected. It made the wireless manufacturers aware for the first time of a potentially huge market for them to supply.

In 1922 there were nearly a hundred applications to the Post Office from manufacturers who wanted to set up broadcasting stations. This demand created the need for control. As Peter Eckersley, one of the company's first employees, wrote later, 'The BBC was formed as an expedient solution to a technical problem. It owes its existence to the scarcity of air waves.' The Postmaster General solved the problems of radio interference by persuading rival manufacturers to invest jointly in one small and initially speculative broadcasting station: The British Broadcasting Company. John Reith was made its Managing Director.

How would the BBC have developed if its first director had been a career civil servant, a banker, or a Bloomsbury intellectual? Many of the features of broadcasting which are taken for granted today would certainly be absent. Reith's domination of the Corporation in its early days was massive, totalitarian, and idiosyncratic, and for many decades the traditions of the BBC seemed to flow directly from his personality. The British Broadcasting Company was set up as a business. Reith turned it into a crusade. 'Scotch engineer, Calvinist by upbringing, harsh and ruthless in character', as A. J. P. Taylor has described him, Reith used 'the brute force of monopoly to stamp Christian morality on the British people'. While waiting to find out whether his application for the directorship had been successful Reith wrote in his memoirs, 'I kept my faith alive night and morning and encouraged myself with the text "Commit thy way unto the Lord, trust also Him and He shall bring it to pass".' Later he was to exhort his staff to dedicate themselves to 'humility in the service of higher pursuits. The desire for notoriety and recognition', he warned, 'sterilizes the seeds from which greatness might spring'.

This ability to impose his will on staff was helped by his size. Churchill nicknamed him 'Wuthering Heights' and senior staff would stand on the stairs to argue with him, 'so that I can see you eye to eye, Sir'. His administrative style, and indeed his private diary, were characterized by abuse. Memoranda sent to Reith would return peppered with 'rubbish', 'stupid', 'soft minded idiocy', 'he lies'. Frequently he saw his life in nautical terms: the Corporation was a ship and he was at the helm. He was pompous, humourless, arrogant and, like most megalomaniacs, paranoid and self-pitying. Yet the near absurdity of his vision enabled him to foresee the power of the new service.

Broadcasting was to be financed partly by a tariff on wireless sets, and partly by a licence fee. These sources soon proved inadequate for the rapidly expanding station. Listeners evaded the tariff by building their own sets with cheap foreign components. They then evaded the full licence fee by applying for experimental licences. The BBC complained, and the manufacturers were angry that the monopoly of wireless production was not proving as profitable as they had hoped. Hence in 1923 the Sykes Committee was set up by the Post Office to inquire into the Company's finances. This rejected advertising as a source of revenue because 'The time devoted to it ... would be very small and therefore exceedingly valuable.' Radio advertising would interfere with market competition by favouring large firms. Instead the report recommended that a simple licence fee should be raised to finance the service.

The Crawford Committee, two-and-a-half years later, unquestioningly accepted the necessity of a broadcasting monopoly, and recommended that the private company be replaced by a 'Public Commission operating in the National Interest'. The service was felt to have outgrown the petty limits of a business enterprise. 'Formed at a moment when broadcasting was still embryonic – regarded by many as a toy, a fantasy, even a joke', the report argued, 'the company by strenuous application to its duties aided by the loyalty of its staff has raised the service to a degree which reflects high credit on British efficiency and enterprise.'

In 1926 the British Broadcasting Company closed, and the new British Broadcasting Corporation opened. Reith was delighted that the unique status of his organization was recognized. 'The Royal Academy and the Bank of England function under Royal Charter', proclaimed the 1927 *Handbook*. 'So does the BBC. It is no Department of State.'

The BBC as a public corporation

The BBC came to be seen, in the words of William Robson, as a 'sociological invention of immense significance', and a 'breathtaking administrative innovation'. Hilda Matheson, the first head of the Talks Department, wrote in 1933 that the Corporation was 'wholly in keeping with the British constitution, and it is more and more common to find it quoted as a possible model for the management of other national services for which private control and direct state management are equally unsuitable'. What, then, was the novelty of the BBC's organization and to what extent was Reith responsible for it?

Reith did not invent the notion of a public corporation. Neither did the Corporation simply emerge accidentally. Reith exploited a theory because it was convenient to do so. The Post Office, which played a critical role in the BBC's development, was itself an early example of a nationally run business. William Beveridge had commented in 1905 that the GPO was the 'one socialist experiment ... that now works well'. Forestry, water and electricity were all important public corporations set up in the years before the BBC was even thought of. Lincoln Gorden, the economist, wrote that by the 1920s, 'Public boards had become all the rage, politicians of every creed when confronted with an industry or a social service which was giving trouble or failing to operate efficiently – create a board.'

The First World War had been critical in establishing the conditions for the acceptance of a 'Public Service Utility'. Despite bitter opposition, the centralized control of health, insurance, coal, and ultimately the rationing of food had been introduced. These were seen as exceptional wartime measures. By the 1920s, however, a generation of reformers who had been civil servants during the war were experienced in organizing the centralized distribution of resources. Indeed for a brief period after the war even the government accepted a more interventionist role. The BBC was formed in this period.

The development of the public corporation depended on the rejection of both market forces and politics in favour of efficiency and planned growth controlled by experts. Briggs has pointed out that the acceptance of the BBC and its monopoly was a consequence of the 'substantial and influential support' the Company received between 1924 and 1925. The monopoly remained in Reith's keeping because 'a large number of important people and a large section of the interested public felt that it was right that this should be so'. These influential people were those who were personally impressed by Reith: the Post Office officials; the director of the wireless manufacturers' association; even the Prime Minister, Baldwin.

However, the idea of the BBC also had more general support. There was a widespread dissatisfaction with the *ad hoc* nature of industrial competition. Even in the 1920s, during the first post-war slump, there was a sense that there must be alternative ways to manage the distribution of resources. Men like Beveridge, who had demonstrated the justice of centralized control in the arrangements for social security and in the rationing of food during the First World War, were opposed to the social consequences of industrial competition. In 1934 Beveridge was to argue:

> In a free market economy consumers can buy only that which is offered to them, and that which is offered is not necessarily that which is most advantageous. It is that which appears to give the best prospect of profit to the producer.

This kind of attitude, which Beveridge later developed and popularized in his broadcasts, was surprisingly widely held in the early 1920s. For example, Sir Stephen Tallents, who was to play a prominent role in the BBC as well as in the British documentary movement, had worked on rationing with Beveridge, and held very similar opinions. Reith's view that capitalist competition was not wrong but could be inefficient was therefore hardly original.

The BBC was to be used repeatedly as a prototype of the public corporation, especially by Herbert Morrison. Perhaps the feature which particularly attracted socialist writers was the BBC's distance from the world of capitalist industry. The Corporation made no profits. But in addition the goods it made, programmes, were in theory accessible to an infinite number of consumers. It was also a completely new enterprise with no capitalist inheritance to weigh it down. As Robson wrote, 'The BBC is an engine of the mind ... it represents socialized control not encumbered with compensation.'

It was this aspect of broadcasting which Reith grasped. He argued that it was in the very nature of the medium that it should be available for all, for it 'ran as a reversal of the natural law that the more one takes, the less there is left for others'. In broadcasting, he wrote, 'There is no limit to the amount which may be drawn off. It does not matter how many thousands there may be listening; there is always enough for others.'[1] In order to exploit broadcasting fully, Reith had argued, it must be governed by social and not financial priorities.

Thus considerations of profit would have restricted the service to the populous urban areas. Reith was determined that the BBC must serve the whole nation. However, Reith also saw that a national service was vital for the defence of the Corporation's monopoly. 'About a week ago', he wrote in 1923, 'we got wind of a projected attack.' This was to be 'based on the grounds that under the present system we had already reached the limits of our expansion. The deduction to be drawn was that the British people would never be supplied with adequate services unless the principle of competitive commercialism were admitted.' Reith rejected commerce because it would have diminished his empire and lowered its status. But he also believed it to be inefficient in the management of national resources. Many shared this view.

Even the government had come to see some kinds of goods as exceptional. In 1927 the film industry, suffering from foreign competition, was protected by import controls, because films were of 'outstanding national importance'. The BBC had been established because the government was anxious not to exercise unfair patronage by granting a monopoly to any one commercial company. But it had also been considerably affected by the report of a Post Office official, F. J. Brown, on a visit to the USA where 'an epidemic of broadcasting was raging'. Thousands of American companies had started broadcasting and President Hoover had demanded central control over the new technology, claiming that it was as if '10,000 telephone subscribers were crying through the air for their mates'. As a result of interference, Hoover declared, 'the ether will be filled with frantic chaos'.[2] The British government realized, on the basis of the American experience, that broadcasting was a new kind of resource whose management demanded a new form of administration.

The BBC was founded on a rejection of politics. From the start of broadcasting there had been anxieties that the service would become an agency of government propaganda. Sir Charles Trevelyan, a Labour representative on the Sykes Committee, asked the Company's lawyer whether 'for public reasons a government could intervene to prevent anything it regarded as undesirable being broadcast'. He was told that there might be control of the news, but that a government was unlikely to bother with concerts, lectures, speeches, or the weather.

While Reith believed that the BBC should be above politics, politicians at first believed the BBC to be beneath them. Direct public ownership was rejected because it was felt 'A Member might well shrink from the prospect of having to defend in Parliament the various items in a government concert'.

Reith despised politicians and disliked party politics. Although at various times he had political ambitions, he hated the 'toadying, the cringing pursuit of popularity' which he believed characterized politics. 'It is pathetic', he wrote, 'how apprehensive Labour leaders are of their followers and how little control they seem to have over them'. Reith often misjudged the significance of political events (he felt that the split and collapse of the Labour government in 1931 was unimportant, 'Silly, over money'). 'The whole horrid technique of politics should be abolished', he wrote in his diary. 'Government of a country is a matter of proper administration, in other words efficiency. It need not be different in nature from the government of a business – only in degree' (29 November 1936). Perhaps the most significant feature of Reith's distaste was the sense that politics led to vacillation and compromise when firm government was needed. Reith was not alone in this view. Indeed an interest developed during the late 1920s and early 1930s, from the extreme right to the fellow travelling left – and including the Keynesian centre – in the benefit of planning.

'The Next Five Years Group' and Political and Economic Planning (known then as PEP!) were groups involving members with different political allegiances but who were agreed on the need for more social planning. 'It may be', wrote one reformer in *The New Outlook*, 'that the Party structures will act for some time as an obstacle in the way of new developments'. Macmillan summed up this position:

> Most of us recognize that the old system of free unplanned Capitalism has passed away. Most of us agree that a leap forward to complete state planning is politically impossible. But ... our search is for some practical scheme of social organization ... which is neither.[3]

On the left, the XYZ club and the New Fabian Research Bureau soon became the natural home for planners and economists.

It has been argued by Scannell and Cardiff that the BBC legitimized its model of broadcasting not by the huge audience the service soon attracted but by reference to the élite of 'the great and the good who trooped into studios to educate and inform on every subject from unemployment to the Origin of the Species: Shaw, Wells, the Webbs, Beveridge, Keynes and Huxley – the roll call is endless'. Broadcasting, they argue, was dominated by a specific, reforming, fraction of the middle class. 'They saw themselves as superior to the aristocracy, for they were efficient and uncorrupt, and claiming to act for the general good, they presumed (naturally) to speak and act on behalf of the working classes'. Robert Skidelsky has argued that Keynes's economic theories provided the basis for a new liberal politics in the 1940s, which avoided class struggle and yet implied 'Keynes's most characteristic belief: that public affairs should and could be managed by an elite of clever and disinterested public servants' (*Encounter*, April 1979). The BBC provided a cultural institution which performed the same function. Indeed the economic and political structure of the BBC was also a product of the experience and beliefs of this reforming intelligentsia. Reith's view of what he intended the BBC to be, those pressures he perceived as threatening, and the alternatives he rejected, were typical of what has been seen as a 'middle opinion'. Indeed it might be claimed that the success of the BBC vindicated the view that a strong middle-class consensus lay beneath the dissent and turmoil of the 1930s.

However, this view should perhaps be modified. Marwick has admitted, in an article called 'Middle opinion in the thirties', that 'They did not in their own day achieve much, these advocates of political agreement, the "soft centre" as they were not unjustly called'. Indeed, the 'great and the good' were, as Hugh Dalton wrote in 1936, 'more or less eminent persons who are disinclined to join any existing political party, but who are prepared to collaborate with others in writing joint letters to the Press, and in such organizations as the Next Five Years Group'. They were a band of leaders – but they had no followers. As Pimlott has argued in *Labour and the Left in the 1930s*, their policies might have developed 'into the basis of a powerful campaign for a British New Deal as a frontal assault on mass unemployment'.[4] But in fact the supporters of middle opinion were politically isolated. Keynes and Beveridge had to wait until the Second World War to see their ideas implemented. Yet the BBC was not merely a dream or a plan for reform. It was a rapidly growing institution. By the middle of the 1930s it had become an established and central component of British culture.

Perhaps pressures other than those of the liberal intelligentsia were at work in the making of the BBC? Certainly, unlike Beveridge's plans for insurance, the BBC cost the government no money. The personal connections of the BBC producers were with Bloomsbury literati rather than with liberal reformers. Reith was more an evangelist than a liberal. 'Anything in the nature of a dictatorship is the subject of much resentment these days', he wrote in 1924. 'Well somebody has to give decisions'. While liberals planned, Reith bullied, wheedled, and built an empire. 'It is occasionally indicated to us that we are apparently setting out to give the public what we think they need and not what they want – but few know what they want, and very few what they need'.

Reith was authoritarian and successful. In the 1930s the new liberals were neither. Moreover, although they dominated broadcast talks, this category hardly dominated the BBC's output. Despite Reith's preoccupation with culture, contemporary critics most frequently accused the Corporation of philistinism. 'The company undoubtedly saw itself as a cultural force', wrote

R. S. Lambert, 'by which it meant something constituted to avoid the postures of vulgarity'. Perhaps the BBC was less dominated by the concerns of the liberal intelligentsia and more successful in the 1930s because it was paternalist. Perhaps, also, it gave the public what it wanted rather more than Reith was prepared to admit. For, as the BBC *Handbook* shows, by 1934 the BBC was broadcasting more light music, comedy, and vaudeville than any other European station. It was hardly the stuff of social revolution.

The BBC and political independence

How was the BBC's independence from partisan political pressure to be achieved? The directors of the private company were replaced by publicly appointed Governors in 1926. These were to be the trustees of the public interest. At first the Governors and Reith disagreed about how the responsibility should be divided between them.

Thus Philip Snowden's wife Ethel – described in Beatrice Webb's diaries as having 'caricatured social climbing' (19 March 1932) – arrived at the BBC expecting an office, a secretariat and a full-time job. Appointed a Governor as a 'convenient representative of both Labour and Women', she believed the Director General should play an administrative role, and that the Governors should make all policy decisions. Reith detested her, and commented that she thought that 'there ought to be a board meeting every day … an abominable exhibition by her. A truly terrible creature, ignorant, stupid and horrid'. He saw her as a threat to his own position. Indeed he was quite correct to do so. Hugh Dalton, the Labour politician, recorded in his diary (3 August 1930) that Ethel Snowden had asked G. D. H. Cole – another Governor – to help her get rid of Reith. 'Who would she suggest as his successor?' Cole had asked. 'I would gladly take it on myself', Ethel had replied.

Herbert Morrison wrote in his important work on nationalization, *Socialization and Transport*, 'It is a matter of argument whether the Director General of Broadcasting should, or should not, be a strong personality'. Reith's views were quite straightforward: he wanted to be in control, and he wanted the Governors to back up his decisions.

The Corporation was supposed to be independent and non-partisan: in practice it was not even indirectly accountable to parliament. In a Report on the Machinery of Government written in 1918, the Webbs had opposed the increased use of public corporations because when a board is set up without explicit status provided for ministerial responsibility to parliament – the situation is obviously unsatisfactory. Only ministerial responsibility provides safeguard for the citizen … and consumer.

However, these objections were not understood. The government had felt in 1925 that: 'The progress of science and the harmony of art would be hampered by too rigid rules and too constant supervision by the state'. So, between Reith, anxious to avoid having the content of broadcasting politically manipulated, and therefore determined to evade political control, and the government, anxious to avoid responsibility for trivia, the BBC was left with no effective accountability. This omission came to be treated as though it were a principle. Herbert Morrison later claimed to have invented it. Robson wrote in 1935 that it was

> in strict conformity with the English tradition ... derived as a practical expedient to perform a particular function, without any concern for general principles – or indeed any awareness that questions of principle were involved.

It is perhaps better seen as the elevation of an uneasy compromise into an ideal type.

The BBC and the General Strike

The BBC's practical interpretation of impartiality was soon tested during the General Strike in 1926. Reith knew that the survival of the Corporation (whose constitution had not yet been formally accepted) depended on its conduct during the crisis.

One effect of the strike was to create a national audience for broadcasting. At the end of 1926 Hilda Matheson was able to write, 'The public and wireless listeners are now nearly synonymous terms'. Beatrice Webb noted in her diary that 'The sensation of the General Strike centres around the headphones of the wireless set'. Although there were only 2 million licence holders these represented a far greater number of listeners, and 'communal listening' was a feature of the crisis as people gathered in halls and outside shops to hear the news.

The BBC seemed more important because of the absence of all other sources of information. An old-age pensioner in the 1950s told Julian Symons that he still had 'the little homemade crystal set which worked lovely with the iron bedstead for an aerial ... and which told me what was *really happening*'. Despite the inadequacy of its news, the Corporation emerged from the strike with a national audience and increased authority.

Another effect of the General Strike was that the BBC invented modern propaganda in its British form. During the First World War persuasive techniques had been crude. All Germans were characterized as vicious beasts intent on murdering children and raping nuns. Anthony Smith has argued that a rejection of the propagandists of the First World War, and the ensuing reaction against the black-out that they had perfected, were among the profoundest influences on the men who came to lay the foundations of broadcasting in the early 1920s.

The First World War view of propaganda was still accepted by many during the strike. Its main proponent was Churchill and its main instrument the *British Gazette.* This was a daily news-sheet that few took seriously, so evidently biased were its contents. Churchill wanted to commandeer the BBC, as the government had the right to do. Reith argued that if the BBC was taken over the strikers would merely close the service down. Apart from destroying 'the pioneer work of +3g years', by shattering public confidence in broadcasting, 'It was no time for dope, even if the people could have been doped'. He argued that to suppress information was likely to exacerbate the crisis. His most telling point was that by gaining the trust of both strikers and the government the BBC could positively facilitate a resolution of the crisis:

> In the end conciliations of some kind must supervene and ... the BBC could act as a link to draw together the contending parties by creating an atmosphere of good will towards its service on both sides.

Reith argued that the trust gained by 'authentic impartial news' could then be used. It was not necessarily an end in itself.

He stated, however, that 'Since the BBC was a national institution and since the Government in this crisis was acting for the people ... *the BBC was for the Government in the Crisis too.*'

Indeed it was Reith's own political judgement which controlled policy throughout the strike. Briggs has pointed out:

> He preferred mediation to showdown. If his views had coincided with those of the sponsors of the *British Gazette* he would have had fewer qualms about allowing the BBC to fall directly into the hands of the government. As it was, his personal conviction gave strength to his resistance on constitutional principles.

Reith, as another writer, Patrick Renshaw, has argued, 'would have supported the union against the owners. But he was certainly not prepared to support the TUC against the Government'. However, Reith's 'distinct' view seems very close to that of the most implacable opponent of the strike, Churchill. Martin Gilbert argues that Churchill was quite prepared to accept a conciliatory policy towards the resolution of the coal-miners' dispute with the owners; it was only the general and political strike he was opposed to.

Until 1926 the press had prohibited the BBC from collecting any news. The strike allowed the Company to develop a news service of its own. This reported statements by the strikers as well as the strike-breakers. One of the bulletins on 4 May started with the TUC statement, 'We have from Land's End to John O'Groats reports of support that have surpassed our expectations.'

During the strike no representative of organized labour was allowed to broadcast, and the Leader of the Opposition, Ramsay MacDonald, was also banned. These restrictions were imposed by the government. Reith thought them wrong, but said he could do nothing about them. Willie Graham, one of the strike leaders, wrote angrily to him:

> The Government emphatically deny that they interfere with the BBC in any way. On the other hand the company states that it was not a free agent. I am sure that you will agree that it is impossible to make any sense of these two statements.

Called by some workers the 'British Falsehood Corporation', the BBC learnt how to censor itself during the strike in order to forestall government intervention. Nevertheless the General Strike marks the end of propaganda based on lies and the start of a more subtle tradition of selection and presentation.

Throughout the strike the government had emphasized that the strikers were politically motivated and hence unconstitutional. The BBC emerged from the crisis with an ethic of political neutrality, which was expressed as much in the tone of its broadcasts as in any formal regulations. This was to have profound consequences for politics.

Governments and the BBC in the 1930s

The General Strike initiated a pattern that was to recur throughout the 1930s: the BBC was forced to pass off government intervention as its own decision. In 1935 it was proposed to include talks by a communist and a fascist – Harry Pollitt and Sir Oswald Mosley, respectively – in a series on the British constitution. The Foreign Office protested, arguing that Pollitt could not be allowed to broadcast, as he had recently made a speech supporting armed revolution. The BBC responded by referring the matter to the Governors, who declared that, 'More harm than good could be done if a policy were adopted of muzzling speeches'. A BBC official told the Foreign Office, 'We can't chuck Pollitt unless, under our charter, we are given instruction from government that he is not to broadcast'.

The Foreign Office remained adamant that Pollitt should not broadcast. They suggested, however, that the question could resolve itself into the undesirability of *Mosley* speaking.[5] The matter was finally brought to an end when the Postmaster General wrote to Reith pointing out that, as the Corporation licence was due for renewal, it would be wiser to comply with government demands. The BBC then asked for permission to say why the programmes had been banned.

The government reacted sharply. According to a Cabinet minute:

> It would be neither true nor desirable to state publicly that the talks would be an 'embarrassment to the Government' at the present time. But it would be true to say that 'they would not be in the national interest'.

Despite the feeling of Corporation officials like Tallents and Graves that the BBC's chances of survival were better if it were seen to be acting in strict accordance with the Charter, the series was dropped and no mention made of government pressure.

An even more remarkable example of the BBC's relationship with the government occurred in the period immediately before the outbreak of the Second World War. On 25 August 1939 the Labour leaders Hugh Dalton and Harold Laski, together with the General Secretary of the TUC, Walter Citrine, wanted to broadcast a direct personal message and warning to the German people. In an interview with them, the Director General of the BBC, Ogilvie (who had replaced Reith in 1938), refused to tell them whether their request would be granted. In the event, news that a 'statement' had been made was broadcast, but nothing whatsoever was mentioned about its contents.

Ogilvie, Dalton pointed out, clearly wanted to consult the Foreign Office but refused to admit this. The next day the Labour leaders complained to the Foreign Secretary, Halifax, of the way in which the BBC had treated them. By this time Ogilvie apparently claimed that he had told Dalton and Citrine that he was going to consult the Foreign Office.

Walter Citrine complained to Halifax that 'Our people are getting pretty fed up with being expected to shout with the government one day and being treated like a lot of children or nobodies the next'. He went on to say that Ogilvie (who had been a Conservative MP) 'might be good enough to help them [the Tories] collect material to rag Lloyd George with – but that doesn't satisfy me that he is fit to be Director General of the BBC'.[6] This incident demonstrates the continuous and insidious dependence of the Corporation on the government. It is not merely that the decision whether to broadcast the message was referred to the Foreign Office. In addition, Ogilvie was predicting Foreign Office policy, and indeed covering for it. Earlier, the BBC had been concerned to make government pressure on its decisions public. In 1939 it was protecting the Foreign Office, and passing off Foreign Office demands as its own policy.

Since 1927 the BBC had been strenuously courting government departments in an attempt to evade press restrictions on its reporting. 'We ought to be the arbiters of what Government news goes out', wrote a Corporation official, 'not a commercial company like Reuters'.[7] A close relationship with civil servants grew up and government pressure was often exercised informally and personally. 'Vansittart would like the BBC to get pro-France in our news and stop using words like insurgent', Reith wrote in his diary in 1937. The Corporation was most concerned that disputes with government should not be resolved by the emergence of any official regulations.

This cautious self-protection was shrewd, and may have been the only strategy available. However, it made the BBC vulnerable to bullying. At various times it was implied that the licence fee might not be allowed to rise, or even that the Corporation's licence to broadcast might be terminated. As a result, the most important constraint came to be the Corporation's anxiety to pre-empt the threats.

The BBC, society and programmes

During a decade of depression and industrial decline, the BBC grew, quadrupled its staff, raised salaries and acquired vast buildings. One writer, D. G. Bridson, recalled his shock at being asked to work for the BBC. 'In 1935 I mentally bracketed it with Parliament, the Monarch, the Church and the Holy Ghost', he wrote.

However, the Corporation also intended to become part of the Establishment. Its development into an authoritative institution was a complex process. This was expressed in the choice of outside broadcasters, and what they were allowed to say. It was also expressed in how the Corporation treated them, and its own staff. It was expressed in the distance between what it claimed to do and what it did.

In a decade of hunger marches and 'red united fighting fronts', the BBC regarded a succession of royal broadcasts as the triumph of outside broadcasting and actuality reporting. Broadcasting in the 1930s was dominated by state openings, royal anniversaries, visits, deaths and births, and by the Coronation. 'The floral decorations for His Majesty's broadcast', ran one press release, 'will be one bowl of hiskura (mauve) and a small vase of grape hyacinths'.

In 1923 Reith had exercised a servile cunning in his attempt to persuade the Dean of Westminster to allow the Duke of York's wedding to be broadcast. It would, he suggested, even have advantages 'from the devotional point of view'. Many who 'by sheer force of circumstance, or negligence had little to do with the Church' would hear the 'measured cadence of the sacred words'.[8] The experience, Reith implied, might change their hearts.

Reith's greatest *coup* was the annual Christmas message delivered by the Monarch. These events were usually preceded by an 'Empire programme', making contact with far-flung colonial stations. 'Goodbye Wilmington', ran one, 'and a Happy Christmas to you all ... behind us the mountains which encircle Vancouver are still lost in darkness ... though a faint radiance announces that dawn is on its way'.[9] George V's funeral resulted in an eighty-page BBC policy document, 'Procedures on the death of a sovereign'.

Reith and the Corporation did not merely present traditional pageantry to a wider audience. They established a new manner for royalty which was more appropriate to the twentieth century. Reith made suggestions for what royalty should say, and how they should say it. He recognized what kinds of occasion a royal presence would grace – and benefit from. One of the bitterest complaints of

Reith's old age was his omission from royal Garden Party invitation lists. He felt he had 'done much to serve the House'. Indeed the BBC was responsible, at least in part, for moulding a new domestic and populist image for the Monarchy.

The BBC was a little less sensitive to the needs of trade unionists. One of the clearest aspects of what came to be known as the 'William Ferrie incident', was the incomprehension of the Corporation's *bourgeois* but liberal-minded staff, when confronted with a worker.[10] Ferrie, a communist trade unionist, was invited to reply to a talk given by Sir Herbert Austin, who had spoken on the immense improvement of working-class conditions during the twentieth century. This was in 1932. Ferrie committed the Corporation equivalent of original sin by departing from his written script when he reached the microphone. He began to tell the public how the BBC had censored him, and horrified Corporation officials rushed to fade out the programme. Ferrie later wrote:

> I was particularly incensed at their demand that I should put across that the slogan 'Workers of the World Unite' is not a revolutionary slogan. I also refused to drop my h's and talk as they imagine a worker does.

His talk had quite clearly been altered to make it more politically accep-table. But the way in which it was done is even more revealing. The BBC censored him in ways that the officials would hardly have recognized as such. 'Your language', commented Mary Adams, 'was too literary and impersonal'. Ferrie, to her surprise, came 'in an agitated state', to see her at her Chelsea home. He arrived at the studio with three colleagues 'for support'. All of this seemed odd to middle-class BBC producers, even though Mary Adams was sympathetic to the union case. It seems in retrospect a perfectly regular way for a working-class trade unionist to deal with an institution that seemed bent on intimidating him.

The BBC was more intentionally autocratic in its treatment of its own staff. Reith would banish rebels from the centre of the empire to the peri-phery. 'You're a very dangerous man Harding', Bridson recalls Reith telling one, 'I think you'd better go up North where you can't do so much damage'. Indeed, by 1937 the only doubts about the Corporation's monopoly were centred on the rights of its staff. There were several symptomatic scandals during the 1930s. The first was the forced resignation of P. P. Eckersley, an engineer and programme innovator of enormous talent who had worked for the Corporation since 1926. Eckersley wrote his own epitaph, 'He had ideas: We stopped them'. He was obliged to resign because he was cited in a divorce case.

The second was over the pressure brought to bear on the editor of the *Listener*, R. S. Lambert, to discourage him from continuing with a libel action. Lambert was warned that he had no future career in the Corporation if he pursued the case. Later he argued that 'This opinion crystallized the dangerous doctrine that the individual owes more loyalty to his employer, than to his fellow employees'.

Reith's view was succinct. 'It's a mug's game', he wrote in a book called *Personality and Career*, 'to pull contrary to your boss'. In 1937 the Ullswater Report recommended, under pressure from Attlee, that a Staff Association should be set up, and for the first time the BBC's workers had organized representation.

The BBC saw itself as a humane and enlightened employer, which had always pursued strictly egalitarian and meritocratic appointment procedures. In 1934 an internal report commented complacently that there was 'a good proportion of women to men on the staff'. This was true, but most of the women were secretaries.

Hilda Matheson and Mary Somerville had set up the key Talks Department and the Education Service when the Company started. It was a woman's initiative which had started the Sound Archive. Women, however, were never announcers, rarely presenters, and the proportion of women in administrative and creative posts declined. Between 1926 and 1936 the Corporation's staff had increased fourfold, yet, as the BBC's annual reports show, the number of women in creative jobs had risen by little more than one-third, and in senior administrative positions by barely one-quarter.

Nevertheless, the atmosphere in the BBC, a new, exciting, glamorous place where it was better, as Peter Eckersley remarked, 'to have discreet affairs than to remarry', is summed up by Maurice Gorham:

> The BBC secretaries were beginning to bloom though they reached full flower later. By that time many of them were pin money girls. It was a great sight to see them going out at lunch, high heeled, sheer stockinged, beautifully made up, talking disdainfully in high clear voices.

By the 1930s the BBC had become an august institution. It was not a crude agent of the *status quo*, rather it advocated acceptable change, in some areas, in certain circumstances, sometimes.

The BBC and journalism

Indeed, by the end of the decade the sheer amount of news that broadcasting and the press were flooded with was so large that, had it wished to, a government could hardly have pre-censored it all. However, a new tradition in reporting imposed new criteria of selection on the news. Journalists stopped being passionate advocates, saw themselves rather as independent professionals, and their writing as a negotiated product of conflict between partisan views. This self-image and its practical consequences were most fully developed in the BBC. Reith was not opposed to conflict. On the contrary, he fought the press for the right to broadcast on contentious issues. But the BBC and the new 'professional journalist' retained a monopoly over deciding its limits.

The BBC and appeasement

The BBC's brokerage was subject to pressure. In the eyes of the BBC's programme-makers, politics was an activity which only happened between major political parties. Two kinds of political dispute never reached the air waves: divisions within parties and the expressive politics of the streets. Winston Churchill, repeatedly excluded from broadcasting because his views were seen as eccentric, wrote to Reith saying he wished he could buy broadcasting time. He preferred the American commercial system 'to the present British method of debarring public men from access to a public who wish to hear'. In 1933 Churchill and Austen Chamberlain complained that the BBC 'had introduced an entirely new principle of discrimination into British public life, namely the elimination from broadcasting of any Members of Parliament who were not nominated by the Party leaders or the Party Whip'. Such a crucial innovation, they protested, should be decided by parliament, not arbitrarily imposed by the BBC.[11]

The most important dispute the BBC ignored, and one which cut across party loyalties, was that of the government's policy of appeasing German territorial ambitions. Churchill claimed that the BBC conspired with the press to exclude all opponents of this policy from any access to the public. Gilbert and Gott have suggested that appeasers were effective for so long mainly because of their success in keeping the opponents of German rearmament out of public office. However, the control of public knowledge and opinion was also crucial. An early reference to Polish rearmament lost a producer his job in 1932. Speakers were banned because of their hostility to the fascist states. Later, the BBC was to apologize for its attitude during the 1930s by explaining that, while mistaken, it was merely following the trend of opinion of the times. Yet the BBC's silence is extraordinary, as it was itself making extensive plans for the Corporation's conduct and survival during a possible war.

Reith's diary first mentions preparations for war in 1933: plans for the physical protection of transmitters and broadcasting stations were in hand by 1935; Reith was involved in discussions over the organization of a Ministry of Information in the event of war by 1936; details of trains in which to send personnel from London were established by 1937. Thus the BBC was secretly preparing for a war which it did not officially expect, while the public were kept in ignorance of these cautious foresights.

The BBC at the end of the decade

Reith resigned in 1937, restless and dissatisfied. The BBC no longer stretched him, and he hoped for something better, which never came. Increasingly, as the prospect of high office receded, he regarded the Corporation which he had created with resentment. It had not, he came to feel, treated him well.

By the end of the 1930s the BBC seemed a natural and inevitable solution to the problem of administering a national broadcasting system. It had won the right to discuss controversial politics against the determined opposition of suspicious governments and a jealous press. But it developed unnecessary conventions, and had become too defensive. The real test of the Corporation's independence was to come during the Second World War.

Notes

1. J. W. C. Reith, *Broadcast Over Britain* (London, Hodder & Stoughton, 1924), p. 52.
2. F. J. Brown, 'Broadcasting in Britain', *London Quarterly Review*, 145, 3 (January 1926).
3. H. Macmillan, 'Looking forward', in the Next Five Years Group, *The New Outlook*, 1 (8 May 1937).
4. See B. Pimlott, *Labour and the Left in the 1930s* (Cambridge, Cambridge University Press, 1977).
5. 'The citizen and his government' (1935–36), *BBC Written Archives*.
6. The unpublished diary of Hugh Dalton (25–29 August 1939). For a further development of this affair, see J. Seaton and B. Pimlott, 'The struggle for balance: the BBC and the Labour Movement 1920–45', in J. Seaton and B. Pimlott (eds), *Politics and the Media in Britain* (Aldershot, Gower, 1987).
7. 'Relationship between the government and the BBC: the Foreign Office', *BBC Written Archives*.
8. Duke of York's wedding, *BBC Written Archives* (Royalty).
9. Christmas broadcasts, *BBC Written Archives* (Royalty).
10. The William Ferrie incident, *BBC Written Archives*.
11. The Churchill and Chamberlain complaint, *BBC Written Archives* (Churchill).

Chapter 9

Broadcasting and the blitz

The 'Dunkirk spirit' and the comradeship of the air-raid shelter during the blitz have long been part of our national self-image. How much was this myth and how much reality? Officials concerned with civilian morale in the Ministry of Information and the Home Office who had seen ordinary people as unintelligent and weak during the phoney war in 1939 came to see them as dependable, shrewd and courageous by 1940. What was the cause of this change?

It is clear that the BBC, almost certainly the most important instrument of domestic propaganda during the war, conducted a campaign intended to convince the public of its own endurance and solidarity. The BBC emerged from the war as both a symbol and an agent of the victory. More than at any other time, the BBC was part of, and seen to be part of, the history of the nation.

'The people will break'

When war was declared in 1939 most people expected a cataclysm. Pre-war pessimism about popular morale had largely been forgotten, yet it had been common to many groups who were otherwise opposed to each other.

During the 1930s another war was felt to be imminent. The main aim of many politicians was to avert the repetition of a disaster like that of the First World War. Even pacifists organizing peace pledges came to feel, like Vera Brittain, that they were trying 'Canute-like to reverse the inexorable'. Indeed, memories of the First World War dominated the British as they entered the Second.

The success of the fascist dictatorships had led to a growing distrust and fatalism about the political will of the 'masses'. J. A. Hobson argued in the left-wing *Political Quarterly*:

> No one could have predicted the possibility of the collapse of all codes of decent conduct, all standards of justice, truth, and honour, not only in international affairs but in the revealed nationalism of the brutalitarian

state, the facile acquiescence of whole peoples in the absolute domination of self-appointed masters, and the amazing credulity of the educated classes under the spells of the crudest propaganda.

(January 1938)

Many on the left believed that the organization of the resistance to fascism would lead to totalitarianism at home. 'If you go to war to save democracy', Kingsley Martin wrote in the *New Statesman* (1 September 1939), 'you will give up democracy in doing so, and find that you are fighting for the overseas investment of your own capitalist classes'. Even after the outbreak of war Sir Charles Trevelyan, a former Labour Minister of Education, wrote privately, 'I have a deep-seated feeling that none of the people want to fight, and that the war will collapse'. It was thus felt by some on the left either that the workers would refuse to fight a war against fascism abroad, because it would only lead to fascism at home, or that they would not fight anyway, because of the iniquitous lack of justice in Britain.

The marches and demonstrations of the 1930s had led the right to believe that British workers were too anarchistic and socialist to be trusted to fight. Those in authority were also anxious about the effects of class division on morale. As early as 1926 a pioneering social scientist, Lasswell, had written, 'Governments of Western Europe can never be perfectly certain that a class-conscious proletariat will rally to the clarion of war'.

Indeed the whole concept of 'public morale', which so preoccupied the government during the war, originated in the 1930s. It was a concept based on naïve psychological and sociological assumptions; in particular, that individuals' attitudes and behaviour were peculiarly susceptible to manipulation in the conditions of modern 'mass' society. 'Morale' was seen as single and malleable. The success of the fascist dictators had confirmed these views, and demonstrated that the urban masses acted in response to crowd psychology and not according to rational political calculation. One reason for this view of the masses, as Bruntz indicated, was the widespread belief that superior allied propaganda had helped to shorten the First World War. *The Times* in 1918 had argued that effective propaganda had hastened victory by a year, and consequently saved a million lives. Indeed, as Shils pointed out, the Nazis may have overestimated the effect of propaganda, because they concluded that 'If Germans failed to be tricked by propaganda this time, success was assured'. In addition, the decades between the two wars had seen the dramatic success of commercial propaganda in advertising. The people, then, were thought to be persuadable.

Parallel to this anxiety was the belief that the new technology of destruction, the bombing attack on cities, would lead to a collapse of civilian society. These fears were based on exaggerated projections of the number of deaths which could be expected for each ton of explosives dropped, and on the biased intuitions of military 'experts' about how civilian populations would respond to bombing. 'In simple terms', Titmuss wrote, 'the experts foretold a mass outbreak of hysterical neurosis among the civilian population'. Psycho-analysts argued that, under the strain of bombing, people would 'regress', and behave like frightened and unsatisfied children. A group of eminent psychologists reported to the government that 'The utter helplessness of the urban civilian today when confronted with the simplest task outside his ordinary work is likely to be a potent factor … in the war effort'. Experts confidently predicted that for every survivor injured by bombs at least three others would be driven mad.

It was therefore widely believed that the British worker would be devastated by an attack from the air. Perhaps this fear explains the curious official ambivalence about the approaching war during the late 1930s. Detailed preparations were made for war, yet rearmers were still banned from the microphone. An atmosphere of dignity, gloom and appeasement dominated broadcasting even after the declaration of war. Harmon Grisewood recalled that at the end of September 1939 the new Director General, Ogilvie, sug-gested that a lady cellist, playing a duet with a nightingale in a wood, should be broadcast to Germany. Ogilvie believed that the sound would induce peaceful and harmonious thoughts in the belligerent fascists.

The first months of war

When the war started normal programmes were replaced by news bulletins interspersed with serious and appropriate music. 'Almost everything is obscured at present', the *New Statesman* commented on 9 September. 'For the first days of the war the BBC monotonously repeated news which was in the morning papers and which it had itself repeated an hour earlier. While each edition of the papers repeated what had already been heard on the wireless'. The news black-out was as complete as the black-out of the streets. During the phoney war the BBC paid for nominal independence by doing exactly what the government wanted. Jack Payne noted that the music department was 'deep in memos', one of which listed the eighty banned German and Italian composers, including Monteverdi, who had died in 1643. Another BBC employee claimed that the only explanation for the failure of the Germans to devastate Bush House was that 'no BBC administrator had remembered to send Hitler the memo reminding him to have it done'.[1]

When more varied programmes started from new provincial centres in unlikely country houses, they were rather less well-organized versions of what had gone on before. Basil Deane, who ran the Entertainment National Service Association (ENSA), the organization responsible for the entertain-ment of the troops, wrote, 'Public anxiety was not lessened by the forced gaiety of variety artists whose personal jokes and excessive use of each other's Christian names – syndicated familiarity – savoured of self-advancement and was out of key with the national mood'. Many early propaganda broadcasts had a peevish, hectoring tone. A month after the outbreak of war a British Institute of Public Opinion poll showed that 35 per cent of the public were dissatisfied with the BBC and 10 per cent did not listen to it. In the winter of 1939 to 1940 Mass Observation reported that rumours were rife; the people apparently did not believe the newspapers, the Ministry of Information, or the BBC. They trusted only their friends.

The 'phoney war' forced the BBC to regionalize and extemporize. The most important change was the Corporation's dramatic growth in size. In 1939 the BBC had 4000 staff, by the beginning of 1940, 6000, and by November of that year nearly 11,000. Roger Eckersley, the staid brother of Peter Eckersley, wrote, 'I knew directly or indirectly most of the senior staff up to the outbreak of war. Now, I shared lifts with complete strangers'. It became increasingly difficult to control the hordes of new staff and this in itself led to a period of anarchy and change. The new employees were quite different from the regular Corporation men. George Orwell broadcast to the colonies and India, William Empson to China, Herbert Read organized poetry readings, Edward Blunden arranged talks, and Basil Wright and Humphrey Jennings made programmes on the principles of documentary. According to Orwell:

> The British Government started the present war with the more or less openly declared intention of keeping the literary intelligentsia out of it, yet after three years almost every writer, however undesirable his political history or opinions, had been sucked into the various ministries or the BBC ... No one acquainted with Government pamphlets, the Army Bureau of Current Affairs lectures, documentary films and broadcasts to occupied countries ... can believe that our rulers would sponsor this kind of thing if they could help it.

The notion of a Corporation converted from philistine reaction to progressive culture became part of the fable of the BBC at war. It was a particularly public example of a common tension that characterized much war work. Conservative administrative authorities were forced to work with creative intellectuals. Scientific 'boffins' invented curious bombs for the military; literary and artistic 'boffins' did intelligence work. The Ministry of Information was notorious for the strange collection of dilettantes, anthropologists and advertising copy writers which it employed. Duff Cooper, who directed the ministry, wrote that a monster had been created, 'so large, so voluminous, so amorphous, that no single man could cope with it'.[2] 'Frustrated' was the word he came to hate most: the plaintive cry of brilliant amateurs thwarted by bureaucracy. Yet the intellectuals were more prepared to take risks, as they had no careers to jeopardize. The *Radio Times* became filled with pictures of distinguished chemists putting bicycle power to strange purposes, and professors of literature 'thinking' about future programmes; the image of 'boffin' at least provided an accommodation and role for experts. For a brief period it was respectable, and even useful, to be serious. Nevertheless the BBC, wrote Orwell, felt 'halfway between a girls' school and a lunatic asylum'.

Programme changes

The first radio personality of the war was not a patriotic politician or a staunch common man, but Lord Haw Haw. By 1940 William Joyce dominated German propaganda to England. His voice was rich, apparently upper class, 'Cholmondely-Plantagenet out of Christ Church',[3] and caused much speculation. It was difficult to avoid Joyce's wavelength when tuning into British stations, as Rebecca West recalled. 'There was an arresting quality about his voice which made it a sacrifice not to go on listening'.

Everyone in Gosport knew that Haw Haw knew that their town hall clock was two minutes slow. In Oxford everyone knew when the Germans were going to bomb the Morris works; Lord Haw Haw had told them. The myth of the English aristocrat with inside knowledge of the German High Command – a kind of diabolical Peter Wimsey – was powerful. What Lord Haw Haw said was less important than what the British came to believe he had said.

It has been argued that Haw Haw was ineptly used by the Germans, who failed to keep him adequately informed about military developments. However, both the government and the BBC were seriously worried about the broadcasts. Robert Silvey of the Audience Research Department was commissioned to conduct a survey of Joyce listeners for the BBC. 'It produced highly reassuring results', he wrote in the BBC *Handbook*. 'It showed that the British welcomed the new guest to the fireside as a diverting entertainment in the first bleak wartime winter'. But the survey included some less comfortable findings: by the end of 1939 over 30 per cent of the population was listening to Joyce regularly. The BBC's Home Broadcasting Board had sneered that only 'adolescents, and middle-aged women' listened to him. Silvey's work revealed that every kind of person heard the programmes. The reassuring feature of the audience, little understood at the time, was that Haw Haw's listeners were particularly discriminating ones. Most read one or more newspapers; 34 per cent of the listeners were *Times* readers. Those most exposed to enemy propaganda were those least likely to be taken in by it. Yet Joyce's ability to hold an audience demonstrated either that the BBC was failing to entertain or that its news was distrusted.

The fall of France in 1940 demonstrated the potential power of enemy propaganda. It was widely believed that German broadcasts were responsible for the failure of the French civilians to resist the German invasion, and for the strength of the French 'fifth column' of collaborators. British officials felt that radio was crucial, yet the BBC was too solemn, aloof and boring. The problem was urgent.

1940 and cheerful patriotism

Dunkirk has been seen by most historians as a key turning point in the war. A massive defeat was turned into triumph, and the British, curiously relieved to be without allies, found a new determination to win the war. Calder sees Dunkirk as the point at which the 'old gang' of pre-war reactionaries was finally exposed. Found to be guilty, they were thrown aside. After Dunkirk, he argues, people were concerned with winning the war, and ensuring a 'New Deal' for the peace. Mass Observation noted a steady growth of left-wing opinion from this period.

What is remarkable is the absence of any evidence of popular pressure for a negotiated peace. Rationally, invasion seemed certain, and defeat, accompanied by appalling devastation, seemed likely. Yet where, during the 'phoney war' period, there had been a degree of indifference, now there was a closing of ranks. It was not that morale was high, nor that anybody believed Britain was likely to win the war: rather, the war was accepted. The public decided to try to survive it as best it could.

Broadcasting contributed to this shift in mood. It ceased to be merely exhortative. It became more sensitive to popular feeling and, in consequence, more successful in moulding or at least channelling public opinion.

Dunkirk meant that the war changed from being an affair of soldiers abroad to one of civilians at home. It was quickly followed by the Battle of Britain and then the blitz. The kind of war that people had expected had arrived. Yet, though devastating, the catastrophic effects widely predicted in the 1930s did not occur. Survivors went on with what Churchill called 'their job of living through the blitz'. Even Mass Observation, which documented the panic and virtual disintegration of civilian life in the worst-hit towns at some times during the winter, noted the remarkable capacity of the public to adapt to new conditions. In London, Tom Harrisson wrote, 'the unfailing regularity' of German attacks 'greatly raised the ability to adjust, and created the best organized centre in the country'.

The First World War was traumatic partly because the horror of a large-scale modern conflict had been far greater than anybody had ever imagined. The Second World War – especially on the civilian front – was bearable precisely because literature, memory and rhetoric had led everybody to expect a repetition. Yet civilians in cities, like men in trenches, were prisoners. In the First World War the troops called trenches on the Western front by familiar names, Piccadilly, Liverpool Street, Elephant and Castle, Penny Lane. In 1940 it was the real places in Britain which suffered. They could not escape. There were civilian front and relief lines. In the First World War men would be regularly moved back from the front to security behind the lines. In the Second World War (as Titmuss argued) the underprivileged survived the stress of attack partly because there was a variety of 'safety valves' they could use. The government never stopped the nightly 'trekking' out of the city centres, nor did it resist the take-over of tube stations as deep shelters. On any one night of the blitz seven out of ten Londoners slept in their beds. But in any single week during the blitz nearly everyone spent at least a night in the shelters or the equivalent. Civilians thus survived the stress partly because – like the soldiers in the First World War – they took some relief from the front.

The prevailing atmosphere in 1940 among the civilian ranks was, as in the 1914 army, one of 'us' against 'them'. The opposition was as much to the unbelievable bureaucracy of British administration as to the Nazis themselves. Strachey expressed this mood when he wrote:

> There is no public record of the labour of the interdepartmental committee, of the co-ordinating committee, the Board of Enquiry, or of the Treasury minute, or indeed of the final Cabinet minute which settled upon the word 'incident' as the designation of what takes place when a bomb falls on a street.

One way of dealing with the Second World War was to refer firmly to the First. Like many of his listeners, the broadcaster J. B. Priestley's own image of fighting was based on memories of 1914–18, and he particularly liked to draw parallels between trench life in the First World War and civilian mores in this one.

In his memoirs, Priestley referred to a folksong of the Great War:

> 'It's hanging on the old barbed wire
> I've seen 'em, I've seen 'em'.
> ... [E]ven the devilish enemy, that death-trap the wire, has somehow been accepted, recognized, acknowledged, almost with affection.

A similar point about public attitudes in the Second World War was made by John Strachey:

> No the people didn't call Germans Huns ... or dirty bastards. No one knows in what region of the unconscious the English people decided that their formidable enemy were best called Jerry. ... There is in it an acceptance of destiny; of a destiny to resist. There is a refusal to take the panoply of the German might at its own evaluation.

Both writers are pointing to an attitude of familiarity, though not of contempt, for the enemy. This had first developed among soldiers in the proximity of the trenches. In the First World War it had separated them both from those who lived in the security of high commands, and from everyone in the safety of home. In the Second, such irony was an appropriate attitude for civilians' nightly encounters with bombers.

To what extent did the BBC lead, follow, or play a part in the creation of a new rhetoric to handle the experience of being bombed nightly?

The war brought the blue joke and an anarchistic, almost surreal, assault on authority to the radio. Shows like ITMA (It's That Man Again) never challenged the basis of authority; rather, they consolidated it by making a joke of its misuse. In the 1930s radio comics had been warned that there were to be 'no gags on Scotsmen, Welshmen, clergymen, drink or medical matters'. ITMA thrived on innuendo, and on a skilful nudging at the previously taboo.

The programme was based on a formula. It had a repertoire of characters with stock phrases. Funf, 'the enemy agent with the feet of sauerkraut', made a joke of the spy panic of 1940. 'This is Funf speaking', he would intone, muffled by a glass. 'After you Claude – No, after you Cyril', RAF pilots would quip as they queued to begin the attack, using another ITMA catch-phrase. Each programme had eighteen-and-a-half minutes of talk into which an attempt was made to pack 'at least one hundred laughs'.[4]

A great strength of the show was its topicality. The writers visited factories and army camps to pick up current slang. The programme would be rewritten up to the hour before it was broadcast in order to include jokes on the latest news. ITMA summed up public frustration and gave it vent. In an early show transmitted from Bush House, itself next door to the Ministry of Works, Tommy Handley issued a memo. 'To all concerned in the Office of Twerps. Take notice that from today, September the twenty-fourth, I the Minister of Aggravation, have power to confiscate, complicate and commandeer'. In 1940 there was a period of remorseless exhortation of the public by the government. Frank Owen noted in the literary magazine *Horizon* that he was obliged to pass thirty-seven government posters on the way from his house to the Post Office. The Ministry of Food was particularly active in impressing on the public the virtues of the carrot. An ITMA sketch took note:

> *Door opens.* Voice: Do you know what you can do with a carrot?
> Tommy Handley: Yer.
> *Door closes.*

Frank Worsley, the producer, thought that the humour of ITMA was 'the closest radio had come to the everyday jokes that ordinary people have always made ... The characters were not trying to be funny in themselves, they were only funny in relation to the situation'.

One of the show's most popular characters was 'Mrs Mopp, the vamping vassal with the tousled tassel', a charlady who worked for a pompous civic dignitary. 'Can I do you now sir?' she would ask. Mrs Mopp was perhaps the most famous version of a familiar figure of the period. She glares at German bombers during an attack in an *Express* cartoon by Giles (20 November

1940). 'Never mind about it not being arf wot we're giving them – let's git 'ome', demands her husband. The same figure – phlegmatic and grumpily imperturbable – was dug out of ruins. She was a mythical figure, and real people were frequently credited with her well-known characteristics. 'Mrs Wells is an obstinate woman', John Strachey wrote about one lady who survived an air raid. 'You may drop big bombs on her, you may kill her dearly loved husband before her eyes, you may bury herself and her daughter under her home: but you do not alter her'. People who signed themselves 'Mrs Mopp' sent letters to the *Listener* and the *Radio Times*; she was discussed in the *New Statesman* and she asked the Brains Trust questions.

Mrs Mopp was an image of the working-class woman at war. Her characteristics were an indefatigable appetite for work, and stubbornness. She did not mean to be heroic, but simply to get on with things. Titmuss saw her in 'a certain Mrs B., a beetrootseller by trade', who brings order and comfort to a shelter in Islington but who returns daily to her stall.

When 'charladies' had first been mentioned in a broadcast in 1938 by John Hilton, the programme received hundreds of letters correcting his language. He should have called them 'charwomen' for, wrote the aggrieved listeners, they were hardly ladies.[5] By 1942 charladies were featuring regularly in BBC programmes – recognition of a kind of the importance and power of working-class women. 'Kitchen front' programmes were broadcast 'for the busy working woman – the charlady'. 'Mrs Mopp', said Priestley on the radio, 'could easily believe there weren't any women in Germany ... just tramping, bragging, swaggering males, silly little boys'. 'When I think of the country now', said another speaker on the Home Service at the height of the blitz (*Listener*, 9 September 1941), 'I see representing the country an embattled Mrs Mopp shaking her fist at the sky. "I'll do yer," she says, "I'll do yer"'.

The other woman the BBC gave the nation was 'the girl next door', Vera Lynn. She sang sweet but not sexy songs. The typical 'crooning' style implied an intimate relationship between the singer and her listener. This was hardly appropriate, and possibly embarrassing, to the communal listeners of the Forces Programme. Vera Lynn was the solution. A Vera Lynn song was a cross between a hymn and a pub song.

Yet nostalgia and sentiment were not thought by the BBC to be proper fare for fighting men. 'Why should we hear so much from Vera Lynn?' Deputy Director Graves wrote angrily. 'How can men fit themselves for battle with these debilitating tunes in their ears?' The BBC Board of Governors remarked testily, 'Sincerely Yours deplored – but popularity noted'.[6] Military authorities demanded something more martial, yet the show survived, simply because it had such a vast and enthusiastic audience. 'The girl next door' was loyal, sincere, faithful, ordinary and unsophisticated. She was 'the mainstay of most war fiction', Tom Harrisson noted in a review of war literature written in *Horizon* (December 1941) and was the heroine of a number of films.

'The people are changing'

According to contemporary commentators, the war made the public more serious minded. This view has been accepted by later historians. Perhaps it should be qualified. Robert Silvey certainly felt in 1946 that there was no evidence that public taste had 'deepened'. Val Gielgud, Director of Drama during the war, recalls that when a 1940 production of *Hamlet* was interrupted at the grave scene, the BBC was inundated with letters from people who wanted to know what happened next. Yet there was undoubtedly a shift in interest. The public appetite for news broadcasts became insatiable. Less predictably, the audiences for serious music increased sharply, and drama ratings doubled between 1939 and 1941. At the start of hostilities the BBC had assumed that the people would be 'too tired for much heavy stuff', and in too sombre a mood to appreciate variety. Both assumptions were revealing – and both proved wrong.

It was generally believed that the masses were becoming more informed, and the success of programmes like the Brains Trust was seen as evidence of this. 'One of the surprises of wartime radio', wrote Howard Thomas, the programme's producer, 'is that five men discussing philosophy, art and science, should have a regular audience of ten million listeners'. As many people listened to the Brains Trust as to the most popular variety shows. Such was the influence of current affairs and discussion broadcasting that the Brains Trust formula replaced orthodox debating in innumerable social clubs and societies. It was particularly popular with local Conservative Associations.

The Brains Trust panel consisted of three regular members and two visiting guests. The original trio were Julian Huxley, the scientist, the philosopher Joad, and Commander Campbell, a retired soldier. In retrospect Campbell seems like a character from Evelyn Waugh, or perhaps Captain W. E. Johns – an enjoyable, overdrawn caricature with a background of exotic experience: he claimed to be able to sleep with his eyes open, to have solved the mystery of the *Marie Celeste*, to have seen and smelt sea serpents, and to have 'married' a South Sea Island girl by eating some fish with her.

Brains Trust questions were wide ranging. 'Why should we learn algebra?' asked a class of Manchester schoolgirls. 'Why can you tickle other people but not yourself?' asked a bus conductor. 'What is hate?' enquired a schoolmistress. A group of RAF pilots who asked why flies could land on ceilings started a dispute which lasted months. To be mentioned on the Brains Trust was fame indeed. A week after *War and Peace* had been recommended by the panel it had gone out of print. This kind of impact was hard to ignore. In 1941 the Ministry of Food was exhorting women to make the new, economical, soya 'Joad in the Hole'.

The importance of the show was recognized by Whitehall in other ways. There was concern about the programme straying into delicate political areas, highlighted by the fact that Joad and Huxley were socialists. In 1942 questions on religion were banned because the churches complained that the programme had an agnostic bias. In 1943 the government banned the discussion of politics, and MPs were excluded from the panel. When Huxley attacked patent medicines and called for a National Health Service the Tories complained. After a period of increasing restriction the original panel were forbidden to appear together. From 1943 each was allowed to broadcast only one programme in three.

The Brains Trust was somewhere between a culture and an institution. Like other programmes, it provided a new currency of conversation. Women in shelters discussed Campbell's views on hypnosis. (He claimed it could be beneficial: 'I knew a man who put his wife to sleep with it at weekends'.) In 1940 the *Listener* reported that Gilbert Murray's jokes were swapped in bus queues. 'Veni, Vidi, Vichy', he had said. 'I came, I saw, I concurred'.

The success of the Brains Trust was the basis for many theories about public opinion during the war: left-wingers felt that a population interested in the panel's views on social justice would also be susceptible to socialism. Whether or not this was right, the programme presented to the listener an image of himself as engaged, participant and capable of confounding experts. Perhaps the real significance of the Brains Trust was that it represented a shift not just in public attitudes, but in the Corporation's willingness to cater for them. Despite restrictions and political interference, the Trust provided for and encouraged an immense public curiosity about the natural world, the world of affairs, and about questions of ethics, philosophy and psychology, and in so doing it began to foster a less aloof and distant image of the Corporation.

Yet the most dramatic image of the radio at war is of families clustered around their sets, listening with reverence to speeches by Churchill, the news, or J. B. Priestley's Sunday night talks. These commanded some of the largest audiences ever known. 'By 1941 over 50 per cent of the adult population listened to them', reported Silvey. It is therefore worth considering them closely.

Before the war the BBC had rarely allowed Churchill to broadcast. The Corporation even censored him after the war had begun. He was considered too anti-German. Churchill had come to hate the BBC. Yet his speeches as Prime Minister, always delivered first to parliament, were perhaps the most dramatic events of wartime broadcasting. He claimed that he merely gave words to what people felt: 'The people's will was resolute and remorseless, I only expressed it, I had the luck to be called upon to give the roar'. Churchill believed that military success, rather than propaganda, was the only way to win a war. 'If words could kill', he broadcast in 1939, 'we would all be dead already'. Despite his claim to the contrary, Churchill was of course an expert propagandist, and the government, whatever it said in public, remained desperately concerned with the public mood throughout the war.

If Churchill expressed confidence in the people, J. B. Priestley claimed to represent them. His first series of 'Postscripts' started after Dunkirk, at the peak listening time after the Sunday evening news. The series turned him into a household name. 'I found myself', he wrote, 'tied like a man to a gigantic balloon – to one of those bogus reputations that only the media know how to inflate'.

Churchill combined an appreciation of practical problems with a deep, almost metaphysical romanticism, based on an appeal to honour, national pride and a sense of history. Priestley was just as practical but looked to the future. He helped to give the war an aim beyond military victory by focusing attention on the world to be built in the aftermath. Priestley talked about a level of society with which Churchill had had little contact and of which he understood less. While Churchill talked of Henry V and quoted Macaulay, Priestley's examples were Falstaff and Sam Weller.

Priestley's success, however, had essentially the same foundation as that of Churchill. It was based on an appeal to traditional values; indeed, on an appeal to a traditional social order. Priestley's Postscripts make a virtue of getting on with the job in hand, even when there were no alternatives. Like Churchill, Priestley linked current events with the past. He reminded listeners after Dunkirk of Hardy's descriptions of the Napoleonic wars, and described it as another English epic. 'So typical of us, so absurd, yet so grand and gallant that you hardly know whether to laugh or cry'. Official propaganda, Priestley claimed, encouraged people to see the war as an interruption. It was, he said, rather 'a chapter in a tremendous history'.

Postscripts continually emphasized the rural nature of Britain. In the First World War officers read *The Field* and *Country Life* in the trenches, and war poets contrasted the seasons and images of nature with the war. Priestley, broadcasting to the most urbanized population in the world, referred in ten out of his seventeen talks to the country and nature. 'I don't think that there has ever been a lovelier English spring than this last one', he said at the start of the Battle of Britain, 'now melting into full summer'. Later, after the news that the British had been obliged to sink the French fleet, he started the broadcast by saying that he had seen two heartening things that week. 'The first was a duck and the second was a dig in the ribs'. The duck swimming with her ducklings, 'triumphant little parcels of light', was in a country pond; the dig in the ribs was given by Churchill to Bevin in parliament before the grim announcement. Priestley talked about factories and the blitz, British restaurants and London humour, but the village or the Welsh hills were more frequently the setting for his talks. Priestley provided his listeners with a way of handling their experiences. 'I don't like danger', he said in November 1940, when Londoners were facing their twenty-eighth consecutive night of bombing, 'but the fact that we are all at least within reach of danger seems to me a better, not a worse, feature of the war'. In the First World War men in the trenches, and the writers who recorded their lives, had survived its horrors by rejecting romantic heroism. In the Second, Priestley made the everyday and commonplace heroic.

Priestley demanded 'more flags and less red tape, hard work and high jinks'. He challenged the old order and called for more social justice. Like Ed Murrow later, he praised the courage of individuals and criticized their leaders for ineptitude. In his second series of Postscripts he proposed to talk about money, class and equality. 'I received', he wrote, 'two letters'. One was from the Ministry of Information, telling him 'that the BBC was responsible for the decision to take me off the air'. The other was from the BBC saying 'that a directive had come from the Ministry of Information to end my broadcasting'. They were both anxious to make it clear that 'the order to shut me up had come from elsewhere'. The Minister of Information, Brendan Bracken, had seen Priestley earlier and warned him to say more about Dickens and less about the government. As with the Brains Trust, there had been complaints in parliament about Priestley's socialism. Churchill felt it intolerable that the BBC should broadcast criticism of the government, and ordered Priestley to be gagged. Already, within the Corporation, the Controller of Talks had written to Ryan, the Controller of News:

> Priestley has definite social and political views which he puts over in his broadcasts ... The question which I want to raise is one of principle, whether any single person should be given the opportunity of acquiring such influence ... merely on the grounds of his merits as a broadcaster, which are, of course, very great.[7]

Priestley's removal was widely greeted as a sign of government censorship. The *New Statesman* printed a selection of the letters of protest, 'representative of the many others we have received'. Even the *Radio Times* printed letters of complaint for several weeks.

The removal of Priestley showed how limited was the official concern for reform. Priestley's programmes proposed different priorities from the war aims laid down by Churchill. To talk of new orders and redistribution was, in the view of the government, merely to distract the public from the urgent business of winning the war. Yet it was at precisely this point in the war that even the officials in the Ministry of Information were beginning to urge the government to plan post-war reconstruction. The public, they argued, needed the prospect of a better future to enable them to cope with the rigorous present. Priestley had merely started the shift in propaganda a little early. Later it was to be taken up with growing enthusiasm by the government itself.

Harold Nicolson dismissed the talks as 'sentimental banalities'. Priestley himself was puzzled by their success. Subsequently they have been seen as a major contribution to a change in public mood. Yet the most notable feature of Priestley's talks was that a concern for ordinary people and their future emerged and was expressed by very traditional images of rural England, village communities and nature. This was hardly the rhetoric of a revolutionary.

The news

The most important wartime programme was the news. Information about the conduct of the war was the main determinant of morale on the Home Front. Indeed the BBC's claim to accuracy and objectivity was, in itself, a propaganda weapon – a demonstration of the superiority of democracy over totalitarianism. This was particularly true because the BBC – much more than the press – was the 'voice of Britain'. Unlike newspapers, its messages reached a wide foreign audience in neutral and occupied countries. Broadcast news also seemed to be an authoritative reflection of official policy and opinion. There were allegations on the left that the real facts of the situation were kept from the people; these were particularly relevant during the period of the 'phoney war', when many on the left expected imminent defeat. The Service Ministries, on the other hand, viewed radio news with suspicion for a different reason: they saw it as a threat to morale.

News, like everything else for the duration, was determined by the necessity of winning the war. The Corporation's sense of priorities was often very close to that of the government. There was narrow-minded and bigoted censorship. But some of the omissions which the BBC was later blamed for were more a result of the contemporary understanding of what could be done in the war, than of deliberate suppression. Thus, for example, the BBC did not so much fail to inform the public about the holocaust – indeed what it knew, it told – rather, this news was not given a prominent position, and there was little consideration of what might be done to save the remaining Jews. This was largely because the BBC accepted the government's views that the allied victory was the only 'realistic' condition for effective action.[8]

However, such was the demand for news that when little of the real thing was available because of military inactivity, the public created its own. Rumours acquired a special influence. The Ministry of Information waged a relentless and unsuccessful campaign against them. Mass Observation divided them into three categories: impressive, informative and inhibited.[9] The first were a compensation for non-involvement in the war; the second were based on an attempt to improve the teller's prestige, and the third kind, the inquiry claimed, were based on fear. Mass Observation argued that rumours arose from a general distrust of published and broadcast sources, and so were a product of official censorship. But they may also have been a simple reflection of anxiety, a context in which to talk about the war. The BBC always argued that rumours could be stopped only by more comprehensive news.

Several departments contended for the right to control the BBC. Even more believed that they deserved it. The Ministry of Information was concerned to encourage morale at home; the Political Intelligence Department to scavenge information from abroad; the Foreign Office to maintain friendly relations with allies and neutral countries; while the Ministry of Economic Warfare was interested in the immediate effects on the enemy's industry and morale, even if this involved ignoring the interests of the neutrals.

At the start of the war an official wrote that the Ministry of Information 'recognized that for the purpose of war activities the BBC is to be regarded as a Government Department'. (He added: 'I wouldn't put it quite like this in any public statement'.[10]) This implies a rather different relationship between broadcasting and the government than that which the BBC claimed. Yet the control by the ministries was often irregular and contradictory. For a time even the BBC's Director Generalship was divided: one Director to say yes to the ministry (broadcasters joked) and the other to say no to the staff.[11]

The Ministry of Information, which had most direct control over broadcasts, had been the butt of much humour when it was formed: the inefficiency of its organization seemed to be surpassed only by the scale of its notional operation. It was believed to be staffed by brilliant but dotty amateurs. Nigel Riley (who resigned from the ministry) pointed out that in 1940, of 999 ministry employees only 47 were journalists. The ministry was supposed to build morale, yet until 1941 it based its judgements on little except hunches and intuition. Stories about the department's gentlemanly eccentricities were legion. One incident involved a ministry official dispatched to lecture in the provinces on the wickedness of gossip. Complaints came back that his speech had been almost entirely composed of long quotations in Latin. 'Oh', replied the department, 'Latin? It's usually Greek with him'.

Reith, who was appointed Minister of the department in 1940, was deeply depressed by its pointlessness and disorganization. Nevertheless, before Churchill dismissed him later in the same year he had begun to define the work of the ministry and to discipline its staff. Reith believed that it was essential to have news and propaganda controlled by the same authority. By the end of the war, Ian Maclaine has argued, the ministry was actively defending the press and broadcasting from the Service Ministries.

Broadcasting and the press

Which did people believe more, the newspapers or broadcasting? Intellectuals certainly did not trust the Corporation. They recalled its role during the General Strike. 'What could possibly take the place of newspapers?' wrote the editor of the *Picture Post* (18 December 1940). 'There surely cannot be any sane man or woman who would argue that the Ministry of Information, or its near relation the BBC, have so far offered a serious alternative to the newspapers in conveying information?' Yet there were also grounds for distrusting the press. Newspapers had deceived the public in the interest of the Establishment over the abdication crisis.

The war heightened a long-standing rivalry between press and radio. The *Listener* was voicing a widely held BBC view in 1941 when it claimed that while radio was concerned to report events as they occurred, news in the press was regarded as entertainment. A Home Service talk in March 1941 maintained that newspaper stories might have come 'from a report from a Mexican correspondent of a Portuguese journal quoted in a Roman paper'. The public had little idea of the tricks employed by the press in presenting events.

Mass Observation reported that radio was the most important medium of information in 1941, and that by the end of the war it had replaced the newspapers for some kinds of news, particularly immediate accounts of battles.[12] When more systematic surveys asked people to rank the media on which they based their opinions, radio came far below personal experience and several points below newspapers. Yet between January 1940 and the end of the war in Europe the authority of the press fell steadily, from third to sixth place in people's ranking. In contrast, the position of broadcasting remained constant throughout this period, between fifth and sixth place.[13] By the end of the war people had come to trust broadcasting more — at least in comparison with other sources of information.

Topicality and the BBC

The Second World War made topicality the dominant news value. German scoops had shocked the public and done much to discredit the Corporation at the start of the war. Topicality then became the key weapon in the BBC's defence against the expansionist censorship of the Service Ministries. The Ministry of Information recognized the importance of getting news on the air as quickly as possible. A memorandum ordered 'Action to strengthen confidence in BBC news. Confirmed items to be included in earliest available bulletins, even at the expense of friction with the Press'.[14]

From 1939 the BBC's news section grew rapidly, gathering material from an increasingly wide range of sources, including monitoring foreign broadcast sections. The BBC also developed the ultimately 'topical' news, the 'on the spot' or 'outside' broadcast. By late 1944 teams of broadcasters were regularly accompanying British units both in France and in the Far East. Commentators developed a way of reporting conditions at the front which related the soldiers' experience more closely to their families at home. 'If you've got a brother or a husband or a sweetheart in Normandy today', started one famous report from the war zone in 1944, 'there's a fair chance you might see your name riding along the dusty roads, your name on a truck, on a lorry, on a bulldozer, on a tank, somewhere in France'. The style of war reporting was also closely modelled on an earlier form of outside broadcasting: sports programmes. A reporter describing a bombing raid on Hamburg was angrily compared by a *Radio Times* correspondent (30 September

1944) to 'someone at a Welsh Rugby International – not a person watching death and destruction'.

The war led to a victory for those who believed in the superiority of the scientific assessment of public opinion. At the start of the war the government believed that this could be tested by consulting pressure groups and opinion leaders. By the end of the war the public was being polled, probed and tested by a multitude of official surveys. These new sources of information made it clear that, in everyday matters of which the public had experience, it was essential that news should be given quickly and accurately. If people had been bombed out of their homes and their towns devastated, it was imperative that the BBC should be able to say so. Knowledge of the extent of destruction was an important factor in coming to terms with it. At the start of the blitz Maurice Gorham had written, 'The news sounded all the more alarming for being so vague'. But by November 1940, although scrupulously censored for information which might be useful to the Germans, it had become more precise. In Britain, at least, 'topicality' became the dominant news value as a consequence of the war.

The 'manner' of the news

Before the war the BBC's announcers had been anonymous: this was felt to be more dignified. However, from the start of the war they were named, and this innovation excited considerable comment at the time. The change was introduced in order that, in the case of invasion, the public would not be taken in by orders issued by the enemy. After the war it was discovered that the Germans had carefully trained substitute announcers to sound like Alvar Lidell and Stuart Hibberd to be used during the proposed invasion of England. However, the BBC maintained some pre-war standards. The announcers, despite sleeping in a lavatory adjoining the studio, and living for days underground, continued to present the news in dress suits. When the BBC received a direct hit which made an audible thump in the middle of a bulletin, the announcer paused, a whispered 'Are you all right?' was heard, and then he continued, with Corporation-bred aplomb, to read the news without comment.

Before 1939 style had often seemed more important than comprehensibility in BBC news broadcasting; during the war ease of understanding became paramount. There was a new anxiety about syntax and vocabulary, and scripts were scrutinized for difficult words and constructions. The Corporation also became more sensitive about the voices of its news readers. Clement Attlee, Deputy Prime Minister as well as leader of the Labour Party, complained that the monopoly of upper-class voices was likely to offend workers. Indeed this anxiety was shared, and a Home Morale Emergency Committee in the Ministry of Information suggested that 'something might be done to diminish the present predominance of the cultured voice upon the wireless.

Every effort should be made to bring working-class people to the microphone.' The Corporation responded by employing Wilfred Pickles, whose voice combined the properties of being both working class and northern.

Broadcasting had developed a unique pitch of speech in the 1930s and 1940s, a high and hard voice. One news reader, Joseph Macleod, wrote that he had two voices. One was low, gruff and Scottish. The other, which he always used when broadcasting, was 'young, suave, rather pedantic and intolerant, a voice in a higher register'. The war also made the tone of voice a more sensitive matter than before. Macleod lost his job, ostensibly because his style of announcing was too 'tendentious'. He was accused of putting too much emphasis on certain words, and apparently sneering at the government. He was dismissed, according to Harold Nicolson, soon after Bracken had 'spoken openly about the left-wing fanaticism of certain members of the BBC, especially in the news room'. Clearly, the tone of an announcement could establish the public attitude towards the news. One news-reader wrote of the problems posed, for example, by announcing the suicide of the Commander of the *Graf Spee* after the ship had been lost. If the announcer sounded pleased the item 'would sound gloating. While if he sounded sympathetic it would sound fifth column'. The BBC's solution to this problem was that announcers should sound as 'official, neutral, and unaffected as possible'. The BBC announcer, it had been decided, should sound like a civil servant.

Another, more urgent, reason why announcers became so careful of their words and their timing was the problem of the sarcastic comments which German broadcasters had at first managed to slip in during pauses in bulletins. The only way to stop this was to read the news smoothly and unhesitatingly. By the last months of 1940 the only comment a German commentator managed to intrude was an exasperated, 'Oh that's not fair!'

The news, enemies, allies and neutrals

Another, more romantic image of the Corporation at war was of the BBC as provocateur, spy and supporter of resistance movements. The Corporation recruited many refugees to staff the foreign broadcasts, and these formed a new and exotic element within the Corporation's staid departments. 'The Hungarian Unit', read a dry memo of the period, 'a duel averted by Duckworth'. A recurring tension in all of these sections was between the demands of the centrally controlled news service and the interests of individual nations. The Danish section complained that they were not allowed to deal with events in Denmark itself in sufficient detail. According to Bennett, the correspondents who supplied the service with its information from neutral Sweden even organized a news strike in an attempt to change the BBC's policy.

Other countries complained that the broadcasts implicitly criticized the occupied countries. Listeners who took risks to hear the BBC felt that they should be complimented on their resilience, rather than condemned for their failure to do more. Indeed, like home broadcasting, the Foreign Service suffered from a tendency to exhort rather than inform or support in the first year of the war. Richard Crossman argued that too many of those employed in directing propaganda had come from the advertising world. 'Do you suffer from National Socialism?' was their line. 'Then buy British Democracy!'

Another tension was the extent to which the broadcasts should encourage (as one BBC administrator put it) 'listeners to *do* something rather than *feel* something'. It seemed presumptuous to instruct foreigners in sabotage when the British had little experience of it, and were themselves safe. More significantly, the dramatic success of the 'V' campaign, when in 1941 Dutch, French, Belgians and Scandinavians in occupied Europe were asked to use the letter 'V' as a rallying sign, revealed the dangers of such a strategy. In one Vichy town, Moulins, graffiti Vs for 'victoire' were so numerous that the Germans imposed fines and penalties on the whole town. In Prague 'multitudes of little Vs had appeared on all sides'. From Belgium it was reported that 'never had so much chalk been sold so quickly'. The campaign, initiated almost accidentally, was evidently a success. Its effects, however, were disastrous. It merely exposed those who were prepared to be active resisters to the Germans at a time when there was no possibility of any allied invasion. Men lost their lives in a campaign with no practical goal. In addition, the BBC was in effect making foreign policy. The campaign was stopped. Crossman later argued that it was a great mistake for those involved in psychological warfare to suggest that they have 'a mystical substitute for military action'. Broadcasting had to be as concerned with preventing resisters from acting unwisely as with prompting them to action when the right moment came.

It is not easy to assess the effect of the BBC's foreign broadcasts. Indeed it is difficult enough to decide what the overall impact of resistance was on the German war effort. Every clandestine listener, however, had already committed an act of resistance, and the BBC's service provided information – even if of a selective kind – to populations who were starved of news. The BBC's bulletins provided most of the material for the underground press in occupied Europe. M. R. D. Foot has concluded that the role of broadcasting was to 'keep the mechanism of the canal gates of freedom oiled and in decent order, till the water levels of fluctuating public opinion could move up and down again'.

This image of the heroic BBC was not, however, shared in the USA. 'To Americans, not very enthusiastic about British cooking, the warmed up remnants of the original meal were not very palatable. News bulletins – one half an hour long – often contained items from yesterday's American press', wrote an academic, Emmanuel Katz, in 1944. The constant stress on the collapse of social barriers in Britain only emphasized how tenacious they had been, and to what extent they still survived. However, American public opinion was never wholly pro-British, and the attitudes towards broadcasting were part of a wider feeling about the war.

In matters concerning the allies, the BBC's policy was dictated by government. When the Russians started to fight the Nazis, the cover of the *Listener* was devoted to a pageant in honour of Russia, while the *Radio Times* was packed with tributes to Russian workers. This was a period of extraordinary enthusiasm for Russia and all things Russian. As Elizabeth Bowen wrote of a character in her wartime novel, *The Heat of the Day*, 'The effect of her was, at first glance, that of a predominating number of London girls this summer when the idealization of Russia was at its height – that of a flying try at the Soviet comrade type'. However, the BBC was told not to include the 'Internationale' in the popular Sunday evening concert of allied national anthems. The Corporation abandoned the series rather than be embarrassed by the sound of the communist song.

Conclusion: 'my country true or false?'

In 1939 the Home News Service editor had said that in the event of war the BBC would 'tell the truth and nothing but the truth, even if the news was horrid'. By the end of the war the Corporation was arguing that the pursuit of truth had been victorious. 'Today', the 1946 *Handbook* proclaimed, 'we can point to the history of broadcasting in Europe and say that certain good principles in broadcasting have defeated the worst possible principles'. During the war the BBC seldom lied if it could avoid doing so. Indeed, as the war began with a series of devastating defeats for the allies it might have been difficult to disguise the situation. However, that the BBC could claim independence was at least partly because it suited the government that it should do so. For the government continually intervened in the conduct of the Corporation, and merely chose not to control it directly.

Veracity, however, was perhaps the only acceptable aim for a democratic news policy. More practically, telling the truth was probably the most effective propaganda with which to face a sustained war. 'You must hate propaganda to do it well', Richard Crossman wrote, 'and we British did hate it and therefore took more trouble to conceal what we were doing'.

The contemporary judgement of the BBC's performance was enthusiastic. 'In a world of poison the BBC became the great antiseptic', said Léon Blum, the French socialist leader. Recently the claims of broadcasters that they have independence have been challenged. 'Bias' and opinion are fundamental conditions of the production of news, not accidental pathologies. Hence the work of the BBC during the war has been viewed with greater scepticism. A belief in its independence is little more than a self-adulatory part of the British myth.

The BBC cannot simply be distinguished from its totalitarian opponents in terms of its intentions. In both Britain and Germany broadcasting was seen as a crucial instrument in the war effort. Indeed both countries even shared practical concerns: hopes should never be raised unless they could be met; controversy between enemy allies was, as Goebbels claimed, 'a small plant which thrives best when it is left to its natural growth'. He continued that 'News policy is a weapon of war. Its purpose is to wage war and not to give out information'. The BBC also viewed news as part of propaganda. However, the use of the 'news' weapon was determined by quite different constraints and pressures in a democratic society.

British home propaganda depended on an informed public. The BBC remained a civilian institution, whose employees saw themselves primarily as broadcasters. Once committed to a policy of informing the public, the war acted as an incentive within the Corporation for an improvement in the news services. Although the BBC broadcast optimistic official figures for enemy fighters shot down in the Battle of Britain, tended to treat raids on Germany as victories, cut, edited and censored news, its main purpose remained that of telling people what was happening.

If the Service Ministries and the government were concerned to limit the amount and kind of information broadcast, the main pressure within the Corporation was to tell the people as much as possible. This did not mean telling them everything, but the heritage of obligations imposed by the Corporation's public service monopoly meant that the public knew more than might have been expected.

In Britain, Asa Briggs has observed, the mystique of radio meant little. In Germany, the new medium had been credited with almost magical powers of suggestion. These views affected the way in which broadcasting was used in both countries. The dominating image of the BBC during the war (indeed the dominating image of the war in Britain) was one of relentless domesticity. 'Every time I listen to these programmes I cry', a factory worker told Mass Observation about a radio link-up between soldiers and their families. 'You hear the women giving the men their messages ... they can hardly get through sometimes'. Another describes her day. She gets back from work 'about nine o'clock, and they've got the wireless on. Dad's asleep in the chair – the kiddies are in bed'. Families were united around the radio; 52 per cent of respondents to one survey always listened to the news with their families, 76 per cent preferred to do so if possible. In Titmuss's classic account of the development of welfare policy during the war, he saw the security of the family as the crucial guarantor of good morale. By 1945 the radio had become an essential element of the image of the family in its home.

Before the war the BBC had regarded the regular expectation of particular kinds of programmes as 'lazy listening'. In contrast, during the war the BBC made considerable efforts to develop such habits. Regular programmes produced predictable audiences. The knowledge of these could be used in propaganda appeals and information campaigns. Indeed the predictability of the daily broadcasts was a kind of security in itself. 'At the moment, all similes for safety are slipping', wrote C. A. Hodson in 1941. 'How can one say as safe as houses?' But the BBC at least seemed dependable. Modern programme planning, a matter of inducing habit, was at least in part a consequence of the war.

By 1945 the Corporation had apparently become less aloof. Programmes like ITMA, Hi Gang, and Worker's Playtime introduced a more vigorous tradition of speech and humour to broadcasting, one that was closer to the music hall tradition than the well-mannered 'variety' of pre-war programmes. They were part of a feeling that the British war, unlike that of the prudish Germans, was taken seriously, but never solemnly. Even government propaganda came to appreciate the 'common man's sense of humour':

Those who have the will to win
Eat potatoes in their skin,
Knowing that the sight of peelings
Deeply hurts Lord Woolton's feelings

exhorted the Ministry of Food. Humour was part of the protective self-image with which the British faced air attacks and the possibility of invasion. It was an image that the BBC helped to create, and was determined to encourage. Harold Nicolson even broadcast talks on the subtle superiority of British humour to that of the status-conscious Germans (*Listener*, December 1942).

There was, of course, another war which did not get much broadcasting time. This was one of apathy, and dingy making-do rather than cheerful resilience. Life in shelters was not always a protracted East End party; it was squalid, with inadequate sanitary arrangements, little food and chaotic overcrowding. Novels of the period document the dreariness and austerity of life in Britain after several years of war, and newspapers campaigned against the petty-mindedness of official regulations and bureaucracy. The BBC did not campaign for the public on any of these issues.

However, the Corporation succeeded in producing a dignified but humorous image of what kind of people the British were. It was not that the BBC 'came closer to the people'. Rather it represented them as a liberal, compassionate, reforming administrator might have seen them. The BBC innovated within a repertoire of very traditional ideas. Subsequently it has been argued that there was a significant change in public mood during the war. The people became determined that there would be greater social justice after it. Certainly the war changed the BBC, and it changed public taste.

Yet the day after the war in Europe ended, the public changed again. The audience for the news dropped by half, and never returned to wartime levels.

Notes

1. D. G. Bridson, *Prospero and Ariel: The Rise and Fall of Radio* (London, Gollancz, 1971), p. 269.
2. D. Cooper, *Old Men Forget* (London, Hart-Davis, 1953), p. 79.

3. Harold Hobson, *Daily Express* (14 January 1940).

4. T. Kavanagh, *Tommy Handley* (London, Hodder & Stoughton, 1949), p. 73.

5. *Listener* correspondence, *BBC Written Archives* (John Hilton).

6. Board of Governors' Minutes (5 July 1941), *BBC Written Archives.*

7. Maconachie to Ryan (6 September 1940), *BBC Written Archives.*

8. See for further development of this example, J. Seaton, 'The BBC and the Holocaust', *European Journal of Communication*, vol. 2, 1, 1987.

9. Mass Observation (October 1940), File 473, 'What the people are talking about today'.

10. A. P. Waterfield to W. Palmer, *Ministry of Information Files*, INF 1/238.

11. A. S. Hibberd, *This is London* (London, Macdonald & Evans, 1950), p. 307.

12. Mass Observation, *The Press and Its Readers* (London, Art & Technics, 1949), p. 41.

13. 'The British Institute of Public Opinion Survey, the attitudes towards the press and broadcasting and other sources of information (1940–45)', in H. Cantril (ed.), *Public Opinion 1935–46* (New Jersey, Princeton University Press, 1951).

14. *Ministry of Information*, INF 1/250, Home Morale Emergency Committee, Item 13 (22 May 1940).

Chapter 10

Social revolution?

It is a commonplace of twentieth-century social history that world war has been the agent, or at least the catalyst, of major change. What has been less noticed is the extent to which wartime forms of organization – born of the unusual conditions and needs of the moment – have created structural fossils in important areas of policy, surviving immutably in peacetime, but with no particular relevance to the post-war world.

Broadcasting and education provide interesting examples of this process. Both were drastically reorganized at the end of the Second World War. In each case the most striking feature of the reforms was the imposition of a 'tripartite' division, based on a supposed hierarchy of talent. The changes represented a sharp move away from a view of society as an aggregate of individuals and towards an official concept of particular groups with separate needs.

Broadcasting

Reith's programme policy depended on an assumption of cultural homogeneity: not that everybody was the same, but that culture was single and undifferentiated. He had been determined to avoid the mediocrity which he believed would accompany freedom of choice. 'It is occasionally indicated to us that we are apparently setting out to give the public what we think they need and not what they want', he wrote in 1924. '[B]ut few know what they want, and very few what they need'. Advisory panels of 'experts' were established to lay down canons of taste in music, and to adjudicate correct pronunciation. Their purpose was to give authority to cultural values, not to represent listeners' interests.

Reith believed that the function of broadcasting was primarily educative: its purpose was to train 'character'. According to this view, your class of origin and what you learnt mattered less than how you lived and how you learnt. This principle was the basis for his programming policy. Men might be unequal, but they could all try equally. Hence the Corporation defended a policy of mixed programming, in which talks, light music, chamber music, quizzes, vaudeville and plays succeeded each other. The service was not planned to provide appropriate listening for different interests, or to allow people to avoid what was serious in favour of the trivial. Reith was determined that the audience should encounter everything that broadcasting could offer.

Mixed programming determined many aspects of the Corporation's policy between the wars. In 1934 a BBC administrator wrote that 'the most advantageous single extension or change in programme policy'[1] would be to stop broadcasting programmes at regular times and so break the audience's conservative listening habits. This was part of the Corporation's campaign against what was contemptuously known as the 'tap' listener 'who wants to have one or more very light programmes available at all hours between breakfast and bedtime'.[2] 'The BBC', the 1932 *Yearbook* claimed, 'definitely aims at having an interval of four or five minutes between programmes ... it is obviously irritating for a listener who, switching on his set to hear, say, the news, finds himself listening to the last minute of an opera or vaudeville turn'. Listening was a serious business.

The BBC's belief in cultural homogeneity was a useful weapon in the defence of its broadcasting monopoly, particularly against the commercial wireless exchanges. These retransmitted a selection of BBC and continental programmes to simple home 'speakers', improving reception and making it cheaper. The number of such stations had risen from 34 in 1929 to 343 by 1935. The BBC argued, in the 1931 *Handbook*, that the relay system contains within it forces which, uncontrolled, might be disruptive of the spirit and intention of the BBC charter. The persons in charge of wireless exchanges have power, by replacing selected items of the Corporation's programmes with transmission from abroad, to alter entirely the general drift of the BBC's programme policy.

The BBC was defending its own position, and what it assumed was a generally recognizable set of cultural values. Reith's objection to audience research was also based on the principle of cultural homogeneity. He did not want to know popular preference, because of the danger that programme organizers would pander to it.

The BBC had a distinctive model of the listener. 'Broadcasting is not mass projection, though it seems to be so, it is an individual intimate business', wrote Hilda Matheson, the first head of the Talks Department in the *Sociological Review* (no. 3, 1935). The personal relationship between listener and programme was elevated into a principle. The class and tastes of groups of listeners were irrelevant. Any variety in programmes was justified by the changing moods of the average listener and not by reference to the interests of different groups. In this way, 'entertainment' had its appropriate place: it was meant to provide periods of relaxation in the broadcasting diet of the Reithian 'average' listener.

The Reithian approach was paralleled during the 1920s and 1930s by similarly 'unitary' assumptions in state education. The content of state education between the wars was common to all schools: children merely received more or less of it. At the top of the ladder children had access to 'the whole world of learning', while at the bottom they had 'the hems of learning only'.[3] The curriculum was governed by notions of a 'general liberal education', a direct legacy of Matthew Arnold's philosophy of education.

Educational policy reflected the traditional psychology of the nineteenth century, argued the Spens Report on secondary education in 1938:

> with its emphasis on faculties and its belief in the doctrine of formal education and mental transfer which played an important part in perpetuating a curriculum common to all pupils.

It was assumed that most boys and girls were equipped with the same mental endowments, that most of them developed the same way, and at almost the same rate of progress. Although some scholarships were available to the academic secondary grammar schools, these were very scarce, and most pupils paid fees. University scholarships were even more rare. Yet all the children in grammar schools followed a pattern of education which was designed to secure university places which only 3 per cent of them actually attained. Even in non-academic secondary schools, the curriculum was merely a weaker version of the university-dominated teaching of the grammar schools.

State education, like state broadcasting, was (in theory) designed to enable the hard-working and able to develop those faculties which were regarded as common to all. In education there was also emphasis on the development of 'character', a nebulous and undefined moral concept, taken undiluted from the 'muscular Christian' ethos of leadership training which governed public schools. Until Cyril Burt's ideas on scientific intelligence testing were accepted during the 1940s and 1950s, the ideology of 'character' pervaded educational policy as well as broadcasting.

In many ways, of course, education and broadcasting are not comparable: for one thing, state education hardly grew at all during the 1930s, while broadcasting developed very quickly. For another, broadcasting was centrally controlled with a national monopoly, while education was administered locally, and alongside (rather than in competition with) a prestigious private sector. Nevertheless, broadcasting and schooling as communicators of accepted values have enough in common for the similarity to be striking. The similarities in the organizational changes, which occurred as a result of the impulse for reform created by the Second World War, are more remarkable still.

Reform, the war and education

The needs of war radically altered education and broadcasting. The Education Act, 1944, which introduced compulsory secondary education for all, has been seen by many as the finest achievement of a great reforming minister, R. A. Butler, who based it on what he described to his biographer, Ralph Harris, as a 'sensationally ingenious report'. More recent assessments have been less enthusiastic. According to Brian Simon,

> Through the late 1940s and 1950s when so much might have been accomplished, the development of secondary education for all was restricted and distorted by the dead hand of a doctrine brought to a point during the depressed 1930s – the doctrine that in effect secondary education is not for all.

The Education Act recommended that schools be reorganized 'firstly to provide opportunities for a special cast of mind to manifest itself ... indeed to develop specialized interests and aptitudes'.[4] The Act was not the result of radical political pressure, but of official initiatives within the Board of Education itself. In 1938 the Spens Report had suggested that 'It is becoming more and more evident that a simple liberal education for all is impractical'. It drew a distinction between those children 'who work with hands, work with tongue, or work with pen' and suggested that 'one child differs from another far more than is generally supposed'. The Norwood Report and the 1944 Act went further and argued that these differences were held in common by groups of children. They distinguished between three kinds, the child 'who is interested in learning for its own sake, who is interested in causes and who can grasp an argument ... [He] is sensitive ... he is interested in the relatedness of related things ... he will have some capacity to enjoy from an aesthetic point of view'. A child of this kind was to go to a grammar school, the distinct feature of which 'lies in the intellectual ideal which it upholds'. This category of school was to retain the values which had been intended for all schools before the war, and was to produce the new professional and managerial élite.

The second kind of child 'often has an uncanny insight into the intricacies of mechanisms, whereas the subtleties of language construction are too delicate for him. To justify itself to his mind, knowledge must be capable of immediate application'. These children would 'go into industry' and were to attend the new technical schools.

The third kind of child 'may have much ability but it will be in the realm of facts. He is interested in things as they are ... he must have immediate return for his effort'. These residual children were to attend the new secondary modern schools. These schools were to be separate but equal and were, according to the report (incredibly) to have 'parity of prestige'. The purpose of the modern schools was distinct because these children would need education for their leisure: 'This homely aspect of education is often the basis of future happiness, and is as vitally necessary as it can be interesting'. It was implicit in the Norwood Report and the Act that there were children who could think, children who could do, and the rest.

This division of schools and children was not consciously based on any scientific evidence, but was justified on the grounds that 'these rough groupings have in fact established themselves in general educational experience'. Immediately the Act was published Cyril Burt attacked its underlying psychological assumptions. He argued that his own work had long since demolished the myth of separate 'mental types', and that the proposed reforms had overlooked the fundamental discovery of his work on intelligence: that anyone who was above average in any one aspect of intellectual performance was likely to be above average in all of them. 'It is difficult to see', he wrote, 'how even administrative necessity can lead us to discern the indistinguishable and to find three types of mind when they do not exist'. However, Burt's attitude was surprising, for the process of selection and division was to be carried out with his own 'scientific' intelligence testing. More strikingly, the proportions of children which it was projected would attend each kind of school closely approximated to Burt's 'normal curve' of the distribution of intelligence within the population. Indeed, in an article devoted to 'The psychology of listeners', Burt wrote: 'Politically no doubt all men are born equal. Mentally however, as the results of surveys incontestably show, the range of individual differences is far wider than had ever been suspected'.[5]

The classification of children proposed by the Act depended on the war experience of Burt's followers in training and assigning members of the armed services to appropriate jobs. Psychologists used increasingly detailed tests developed from Burt's work, not only to guarantee that the various services had equal shares of intelligent personnel, but also to distinguish between 'skill' and 'character', and to identify a whole range of special mechanical, logical and clerical abilities. 'The value of vocational or educational classification', wrote Vernon and Barry about their work as psychologists during the war, 'lies not merely in the closer co-ordination of human capacity with job ... but also with their effects on morale'. Workers, they argued, were happier if they were not disturbed by association with those with abilities far beyond, or behind, their own. Thus during the war 'streaming' was developed and rationalized.

The effect of the war is also revealed in the provision of the new 'technical' schools. During the war there had been a shift in the subjects in which children were examined towards the sciences, in response to the increased need for technical skills. Lord Hankey wrote in 1941 that 'Technical colleges, although ill housed, ill equipped and understaffed had responded without hesitation to the needs of the services and industry and had magnificently reorganized themselves to train men and women for the war effort'. It was these experiences, a dramatic increase in the need for technical and scientific workers, and the reorganization of schools and training to produce them, which had led to the creation of the new 'technical schools' and the perception of the 'practically able' child.

In the Act it was expected that these new schools would take some of the children who would previously have gone to grammar schools, and direct them into more technical and industrial work. These schools simply failed to appear. This was partly because money was not available. Also, during the war the government had been able to direct the allocation of the entire workforce; in a post-war world this was far more difficult. Moreover, hopes that private industry would seek technically educated school-leavers for training did not materialize; employers continued to prefer young people with a 'general' academic education where they could get them.

R. A. Butler had written in 1942 that

> Education cannot by itself create the social structure of a country. I have
> to take the world as I find it and the world I find is one in which there
> is a very diversified range of types. Educational progress must be along
> the grain of human nature.[6]

Yet arguably the Act and its implementation was precisely an attempt at
massive social engineering. It was not, as Simon has argued, merely a rationalization of the *status quo*, but marked a major change in the official perception of the child. It also represented a new recognition of class, and the
fragmentation of culture. The old, liberal culture survived, but was confined
to the curricula of the 'professionals' in their grammar schools; while in
modern schools children for whom exams were inappropriate were to be
taught how to entertain themselves.

Reform, the war and the BBC

The war also revolutionized the BBC. During the war Reith's 'cultural unity'
was abandoned. After a visit to the troops in France, Ogilvie, Reith's successor as Director General, had come back convinced that the morale of the
forces would be improved by knowing that their families at home were listening to the same programmes with them, but also that the Corporation's
whole programming would have to change. Ian Hay, a BBC comptroller,
had written in 1939, 'We shall need a lot of entertainment before this business
is over'. It was recognized that the new forces service would have to be quite
different from a 'watered-down version of our peacetime programmes', for 'if
we give them serious music, long plays, or peacetime programme talks they
will not listen'.[7] The lure of the continental stations could not be ignored
during the war and programme changes would inevitably have more long-term
consequences. An official wrote ominously, 'We shall not be able to return to
our Sunday policy when the war ends'.

More light music, comedy, crooning and jazz were justified not only by
the immediacy of wartime demands, but also, crucially, by a new model of
the psychology of the listener. The first step argued that the service had to
be changed because troops were listening to it communally in the mess
or in camps. Then it was suggested that different programmes were appropriate to different occupations. Very quickly the audience research department was trying to establish which kinds of music had the best effect on
factory production.

Modern wars change the status of entertainment: leisure is seen as an
aspect of 'public morale'. This was particularly true in Britain after 1940.
Nevertheless, the Corporation was anxious not to be accused of producing
'programmes fit for morons', and the *Listener* printed many letters on this

subject. 'I think you will find this army more highbrow than you suppose', wrote one officer (15 February 1941).

What had first been seen as a temporary expedient became a permanent feature when the General Forces Programme was changed to the Light Programme in 1946. Grace Wyndham Goldie commented on the consequences of this innovation for the internal structure of the Corporation. 'It is not only that this is lighter, more gay, fresher in its approach; but for good or evil it is more closely related to the box office than any broadcasting in England has ever been before' (*Listener*, 26 December 1940). Competition was introduced between various parts of the Corporation. It meant the recognition of distinct groups whose tastes the BBC was obliged to identify rather than to change. This internal reform was of more fundamental importance than the competition later offered by commercial television. An editorial in the *Listener* claimed that 'the position is that the Forces Programme is carefully planned and not a casual proliferation of high jinks for low brows' (13 March 1941). Yet providing the public with what it wanted had become central to the Corporation's plans.

The introduction of a 'Light' Programme inevitably had implications for the Home Service. As early as 1940 the Home Service Board had decided that the 'barometer of listeners' preferences' should be a regular item on its agenda. However, the Home Service also broadcast the main news bulletins, and came to be seen as the part of the BBC which was most concerned with 'citizenship, family and home'.

The final and most revealing innovation was the introduction of the Third Programme. An internal memorandum in 1944 had suggested that the BBC should provide three competing services. Programme A 'should be of the highest possible cultural level, devoted to artistic endeavour, serious documentary, educational broadcasting, and the deeper investigation of the news, corresponding in outlook to a *Times* of the air'. Programme B, 'the real home programme of the people of the United Kingdom', would 'give talks which would inform the whole democracy rather than an already informed section, and be generally so designed that it will steadily, but imperceptibly, raise the standard of taste, entertainment, outlook and citizenship'.[8] Programme C was to divert, and needed little detailing.

The Third Programme was a survival of the Reithian ethic of 'mixed' programming. It emphasized that it should be judged by the whole programming of the service rather than individual items.

> The daily broadcasting schedules rush by the listener like the scenery past the windows of an express train ... The Third Programme from the beginning has arrived at a standard which has brought it into conflict with this ephemeral characteristic of broadcasting.[9]

Elsewhere, Harold Nicolson wrote, 'Every cultural pill is coated with sugar; and an item which it is felt might be unpalatable is tendered with a tone of apology, or with the horrid cheeriness of the scoutmaster, the padre, or the matron'. The Third regarded broadcasting as an art.

The 1950 White Paper on the future of broadcasting argued that 'listeners will now normally have a wider choice of contrasting programmes', while Nicolson, who had been involved in the creation of the Third, was at pains to point out that 'at no time, I am glad to say, did we entertain the doctrine that the listening public should be segregated between sheep or goats'. Sir William Haley, the Director General who had originally thought of the Third, put the classification clearly in a lecture given in 1948:

> Before the war the system was to confront [the listener] with pendulum-like leaps. The devotees of [Irving] Berlin were suddenly confronted with Bach ... Since the war we have been feeling our way along a more indirect approach. It rests on the conception of the community as a broadly based cultural pyramid, slowly aspiring upwards.

This concept resembled the hierarchy of ability.

Progress or rationalization?

By the end of the war British broadcasting and education had been radically reformed. Is it a coincidence that the two most important vehicles of national culture were reorganized almost simultaneously and in each case along very similar lines?

The reforms may have been made possible by the new weight given to public opinion by the war. However, in both areas of policy the form which the changes took depended on a new official way of looking at children on the one hand, and at listeners on the other. In this, distinctions were in effect being made between the tastes, abilities and interests of different social groupings.

Listeners and children are not obviously analogous. Yet what is striking is the similarity in the proportions of people assigned, quite independently, by education and broadcasting authorities to three categories. It is as though in the natural order of things there were three types of children and three types of listeners reflecting a three-way divide in society as a whole. It was expected that the population would divide as follows:[10]

Grammar schools 5%	Third Programme 6%
Technical schools 15%	Home Service 20%
Modern schools 80%	Light Programme 74%

In both cases the figures were based more on a hunch than on statistics, and in both cases they proved wholly unrealistic. In education the technical schools barely got off the ground and completely failed to produce the technical administrators that had been expected; instead the grammar school section expanded. The estimate of the Third Programme audience of serious listeners was wildly optimistic; it never attracted more than 1–2 per cent of listeners. Neither projection was officially justified in terms of social class; yet in both cases what seems to have occurred is the imposition on social policy of official assumptions based on military and administrative experience.

There has been much discussion about the social effects of the war. Calder and Marwick have pointed to a major upheaval; Addison has suggested the culmination of a long, slow revolution in attitudes; Pelling argued that there was not much fundamental change at all. What is clear is that there was a dramatic and permanent increase in the power and scope of government. Whitehall's view of society and human nature, essentially meritocratic and hierarchical, pervaded policies which in normal times would have been fought out in the political arena. The reforms in both broadcasting and education reflected an approach to organization which had more to do with a civil service conception of the world as itself writ large, than with the reality of the world as it existed. Thus, in Whitehall there were administrative, executive and clerical grades (and in the services there were officers, NCOs and privates). Officials found their own tripartite system natural and efficient. In creating new structures for the public they assumed a similar pattern of talent and need. In broadcasting, as in education, reforms contained a contradiction. On the one hand they were progressive in that they sought to cater for the whole society; but on the other they reinforced class divisions by giving new life to old hierarchical assumptions.

Notes

1. Filson Young to Dawney, BBC Internal Memorandum, 'Programme policy', *BBC Written Archives* (3 March 1934).
2. 'Programme revision committee', *BBC Written Archives* (June 1934).
3. Board of Education, *Inspectors' Report* (1932), p. 12, para 7 [Cmd 4068].
4. *The Nation's Schools: Their Plans and Purposes*, Ministry of Education Pamphlet 1 (London, HMSO, 1945).
5. Sir Cyril Burt, 'The psychology of listeners', *BBC Quarterly*, IV, 1 (April 1949), p. 7.
6. Lord Butler, *The Education Act of 1944 and After*, The First Noel Buxton Lecture, University of Essex (Harlow, Longman, 1965), p. 21.
7. Ryan to Nicolson, BBC Internal Memorandum, *BBC Written Archives* (17 January 1940).
8. 'Programme development', BBC Internal Memorandum, *BBC Written Archives* (14 February 1944).
9. BBC, *The Third Programme: Plans for October–December 1944*.
10. Sources for education figures, Ministry of Education circular 731 (1944), quoted in P. H. J. H. Gosden, *Education in the Second World War* (London, Methuen, 1976); and for broadcasting, *Listener* (February 1946), and BBC Internal Memorandum, 'Projection for the Third Programme', *BBC Written Archives* (14 May 1946).

Chapter 11

The BBC under threat

In 1946, when television broadcasting was resumed, the BBC's popularity at home and prestige abroad were even greater than before, largely because of the wartime experience. Yet barely a decade later, the BBC's monopoly of the air waves was destroyed. Television and, subsequently, radio were placed on a new competitive footing. More than anything else, this has shaped the aims, structure and output of all television programming since about 1984.

The change was not brought about by public pressure, but by a small group within the ruling Conservative Party. It was opposed by bishops, vice-chancellors, peers, trade unions, the Labour Party and most national newspapers. Reith compared the introduction of commercial broadcasting into Britain with that of dog racing, smallpox and bubonic plague.[1] The objections to commercial broadcasting were diverse, but most were anti-American, and opposed the encouragement of crude materialist desires. Criticisms of this kind were particularly vehement on the left. More recently, however, some socialist writers have taken a different view, arguing that commercial television was, in fact, a cultural liberator, taking the control of broadcasting out of the hands of a patronizing and paternalist establishment, and increasing the scope of genuinely popular influences.

Austerity, monopoly and the Beveridge Report

The BBC's prestige contributed to its undoing. The Corporation had assumed that it was invulnerable, and so had the 1945 Labour government, which consequently did not hurry to renew its licence. In 1947 Beveridge was asked to conduct an inquiry into the BBC's affairs. He might have been expected to sympathize with Reith's legacy of benevolent, high-minded despotism at the BBC, for Beveridge had once claimed that his ideal society would be run by neither parliament nor dictators, but by professional administrators – 'social doctors' – who would organize society 'to adapt the social and economic relations of clients so as to produce the maximum economic health'.[2] However, as a liberal, Beveridge was highly critical of the Corporation.

He distrusted the tone and character of the BBC, which, 'beginning with Londonization, going on to secretiveness and self-satisfaction, and ending up with a dangerous sense of mission became a sense of divine right'. He was constantly on the watch for 'the four scandals of monopoly: bureaucracy, complacency, favouritism and inefficiency'. Written in Beveridge's inimitable style, the report nevertheless finally recommended that the Corporation's licence be renewed, because the alternative, American-style commercial television, seemed far worse.

The recommendations of the Beveridge Report were ignored by the Conservatives after they beat the Labour Party in the 1951 general election. Instead, Selwyn Lloyd's dissenting minority report, which was in favour of commercial broadcasting, became the basis for the commercial lobby. Nevertheless, Beveridge's findings influenced the form of British commercial broadcasting. First, the report preferred spot adverts to sponsored programmes because they gave advertisers less control over programme content. 'A public broadcasting service', the report commented, 'might have its controlled and limited advertisement hour, as every newspaper had in its advertising columns, without sacrificing the independence of standards of broadcasting'. Second, the report advocated the regionalization of broadcasting and the decentralization of the BBC. These arguments affected the organization of the commercial system when it was introduced.

The commercial television lobby has been seen by some writers as a tiny group of back-bench MPs, 'who worked night and day on the project'. However, they were supported by the immense power of the great entertainment industries. Pye Radio, the largest West End theatre management, and J. Walter Thompson, the advertising agency, were all involved in the campaign. Although a member of the group declared in the House of Commons that 'Any suggestion that the Bill was fostered by commercial interests is a complete figment of the imagination of the Party opposite', the speaker at the time was a director of various electronics firms who expected to profit out of an increase in the market for televisions.[3] 'At what point', H. H. Wilson asked, 'were the members speaking as MPs representing their constituencies, and when were they speaking as directors, managers or employees of advertising agencies, market research organizations or radio and television manufacturers?'

However, the most important organizer of the lobby was a broadcaster, Norman Collins. He had been director of the Light Programme, and controller of BBC Television. When he was not appointed Chief Executive of Television, Collins resigned from the BBC. He told *The Times* that he had left

> because of a clash of principle ... whether the new medium of TV shall be allowed to develop at this, the most crucial stage of its existence, along its own lines and by its own methods, or whether it shall be merged into the colossus of sound broadcasting.

The commercial lobby fought a hard and frequently unscrupulous battle. It was successful because important members of the government, including the Prime Minister, Churchill, were not prepared to defend the BBC. Significantly, the campaign also had the active support of Lord Woolton. He had modernized the Conservative Party organization before the 1951 election and brought a new kind of candidate into parliament. This group represented industry and advertising rather than law or hereditary wealth.

Woolton wanted free enterprise to dominate the 'new age of post-war prosperity'. 'Our individual lives today', he complained in a broadcast, 'are hemmed in by no less than 25,000 controls'. He wanted to associate the party with the long-term material aspirations of the people, and believed that commercial television would help to do this.

The opposition to commercial television was organized by the National Television Council with Christopher Mayhew as its secretary. Support came from surprising quarters. 'The Establishment', wrote Henry Fairlie, 'came as near as it has ever done to organizing a conspiracy against the government of the day – a Conservative Government'.[4] This group objected to the cultural consequences of commercial television: it would 'vulgarize, bowdlerize, and coarsen', wrote one critic.

The argument became more fierce when it was learnt that in the USA the Coronation had been shown interspersed with NBC's television chimp, J. Fred Muggs, selling tea. A deodorant had been advertised just before the ritual anointment. Horrified MPs suggested that if a commercial system were started here, royal tours would be interrupted by commercial breaks extolling the makers of the Queen's chairs and carpets.

Nevertheless the Act introducing commercial television was passed in 1954 because most Tories believed that in some way it would promote industry, commerce and the free market. The new service was named, by some genius of euphemism, 'Independent Television'.

Commercial television and the new world

'A whole new world has come', proclaimed the first commercial television *Yearbook* in 1955. 'We've won, and now we can really get going', said Norman Collins. 'The importance of the introduction of commercial TV goes far beyond any question of the merits of commercial versus public service broadcasting', wrote Wilson, 'for it may also seem to symbolize a change within the Conservative Party, and give expression to an accumulation of influences which are securing the future of British society'. ITV brought about a revolution, it has been claimed, because it challenged the complacent pre-war conservatism of the BBC. The Corporation was staffed by narrow-minded, middle-class professional bureaucrats who had little sympathy for working-class interests. Norman Collins complained of the 'apathy, disinterest and often open hostility towards the new medium' that existed within the

BBC. Lord Simon of Wythenshawe, chairman of the BBC Governors, claimed that during the early 1950s only about one-fifth of the business the Director General presented to the board was concerned with television. Indeed in 1946 when Haley was shown a television demonstration he had remarked that he would not have one in his house.

The BBC, one producer wrote, regarded radio as 'the father figure, established and responsible', while television was seen as a 'spendthrift tiresome adolescent'.[5] The BBC bureaucrats, secure in the imperial comforts of Broadcasting House, deluged television producers in the unheated wastes of north London with memos. These detailed the proper procedures for the purchase of books and why it was outrageous to suggest that book covers should be cut up, even to be shown on the screen. The tensions were exacerbated by the influx into television of cameramen, technicians and directors who were used to the high living which characterized the precarious film world. 'Disorder has been repeatedly reported from the television studios ... new employees do not seem to have become one with the Corporation', read one ominous memo of the period. 'Perhaps', another memo replied, 'a brief course on the history of the Corporation might be of assistance?'[6]

Indeed, during the 1950s the Corporation appointments policy was apparently designed to keep the new service in order, rather than accelerate its development. Gerald Beadle was an amicable BBC administrator, quietly approaching retirement in the Western Region, when the call came. 'About 1953', he remarked, 'every BBC directorship in London was filled by younger men than me ... but then in 1956 something quite unexpected happened ... at the age of fifty-seven I was appointed Director of TV'. Beadle was to hold this post during the critical early years of commercial television.

Beadle was a typical example of the BBC administrator of this period. The Corporation man, as Burns has argued, did not work for the BBC, he worked *in* it – as a secular church of professional excellence. One writer noted that a Corporation producer 'breathes the BBC ritual welcome to eminent persons as they arrive' (to have their personalities 'brought out', rather than be put on the spot), 'How good of you to come!' (*Encounter*, October 1960). The Corporation saw itself as a particularly dedicated branch of the civil service, and this image affected its approach to television.

However, the BBC's performance during the 1950s needs scrutiny. Despite the overwhelming bureaucracy, a remarkable generation of television producers and directors started work during this period. They were to dominate the entire output of British television, on both channels, for the next twenty years. Even the Corporation's lack of interest in television had benefits. Because it was seen as relatively unimportant it was left alone. Goldie claims this allowed programme makers far greater initiative.

The most serious charge against the BBC was that it starved the new service of funds. In 1950 the BBC's television budget was only one-half of that allocated to the Home Service. However, in the period of experimental broadcasts during the 1930s, television had been able to develop only because the BBC had been willing to subsidize it out of wireless revenues. (In the USA, where it depended on advertising funds, the service was forced to close because the pictures and reception were inadequate to attract a commercially useful audience.) The BBC also pursued a policy of national coverage and, by 1956, 98 per cent of the country was able to receive television. This was achieved only by a massive redistribution of resources away from the rich south-east, where there were many television owners, to the more remote regions. A national service was an investment which could not at first have been made by the commercial companies.

Competition new and old

It has been argued that commercial competition changed the BBC. Competition forced the Corporation to consider public wants more seriously. 'The BBC will have to abandon the ivory towers for the beaches! People prefer fun', wrote one critic (*Daily Mail*, 15 February 1957). Peter Black comments that a kind of myth developed, based on an image of 'the energetic thrusting showbiz visionaries elbowing aside the complacent bureaucrats of the BBC, by presenting a series of audacious novelties that blew the stale air of monopoly out of television and sent the invigorating breezes of free enterprise whistling through it'.[7] Others have argued that subsequently broadcasting has been dominated by the need to maximize the audience.

Yet competition came to the BBC long before Independent Television was thought of. The decisive break with Reithian paternalism occurred during the war, when the General Forces Network was established. Similarly, the BBC had always been obliged to prove that the size of its audience legitimized its receipt of the licence fee. Indeed the BBC had been subject to competition from foreign commercial stations since the 1930s. It was the challenge of Luxembourg which had broken the dismal Reithian Sunday on the radio. However unctuously it was defended, the BBC had abandoned the concept of planned programming considerably before the introduction of Independent Television, while programme makers have always been most sensitive to the competition offered by colleagues. Anthony Smith has argued in *British Broadcasting* that 'Producers within the BBC were more often conscious of an internal competition within the different sections of the BBC'. This, he claimed, led in the 1960s to 'an enormous flowering of talent and inventiveness'. Such internal pressure had the greatest effect on standards and innovation within both authorities.

In addition, the threat posed by commercial competition was more limited than its advocates have suggested. At first the two authorities fought a bitter ratings war. They soon discovered that the public would watch anything in preference to a party political programme. (The parties reacted swiftly and

ensured that these broadcasts were shown simultaneously on both channels.)
When ITV offered the audience the Hallé Orchestra, the BBC's share of the
audience rose. When the BBC offered the people *La Bohème*, the numbers
watching fell to 2 per cent. However, both soon discovered the comforts of
competition and the security provided by the dependability of the enemy's
programming. It was found that documentaries and current events programmes achieved their maximum audience only if they were shown at the
same time. As Burns commented, 'Competition now seems to be accepted as
a fact of life for both the BBC and ITV, and is defended by both. There is
one obvious reason for this; it makes life easier for them'. A rigidly conventional
use of time and categories of programmes was reinforced by competition.

Commerce and the audience

It is often assumed that ITV changed television because it won the battle for
the audience. This is not the case. Indeed commercial television had little
effect on the growth of the television audience, nor did it decimate the
numbers watching BBC.

Between 1955 and 1956 the commercial companies struggled to acquire
an audience. Howard Thomas wrote that by January 1956, 'The situation
was very grim. The costs of running commercial television were enormous
for the audience was simply not large enough to attract advertising revenue'.

However, the situation improved. In a well-publicized campaign in 1957
Sir Kenneth Clark was claiming a 79:21 preference for the commercial channel.
In December of the same year, out of 539 programmes listed by TAM in the
top ten ratings, 536 were from ITV and only 3 produced by the BBC. 'Once
they had a choice', Black wrote, 'the working-class audience left the BBC at a
pace that suggested ill will was more deeply entrenched than good'. The first
ATV Showbook put the point more jubilantly: 'We've got the audience', it
proclaimed. Norman Collins said that the BBC would soon 'grind to a halt'.

Certainly the BBC panicked. *Ariel*, the staff magazine, became full of
warlike metaphors about 'beating back the enemy' and getting into 'fighting
formation'. As large numbers of staff left the Corporation for the higher salaries
and more makeshift offices of the commercial companies, Sir Ian Jacob wrote,
'I doubt whether any organization in peacetime has been subject to comparable
strain' (*Ariel*, 3, 1956).

Corporation officials became obsessed with maintaining a 30 per cent share
of the audience. Television was typically being interpreted in terms of the
audience distribution of radio. Furthermore, its audience was being seen in
terms of an obsolete distribution of the population between classes. According
to this view, the commercial companies would concentrate on entertainment
(like the Light Programme, which drew 68 per cent of the audience), leaving
more serious programming to the BBC (like the combined Home and Third
services, which drew 32 per cent of the audience).

The apparent collapse of the audience posed a dilemma. The BBC might be destroyed because its share of the audience would no longer justify the collection of a licence fee from all viewers. Or the BBC might be destroyed because it would be forced to emulate the commercial programmes.

However, the argument about which service had won the largest audience was confused, in the first place because the two authorities counted their audience in different ways. 'For us', wrote Robert Silvey, the head of the BBC's audience research, 'it meant people, and for ITV it meant TV sets. Our method was based on questioning samples of the population about their previous day's viewing; ITV's on metered records of when TV sets in a sample of homes had been switched on'. Although both methods showed trends in viewing behaviour, they could not be directly compared.

Indeed the commercial companies had not 'won' a 70 per cent share of the total viewing audience as Clark had implied. Rather, this was the proportion of those viewers who had purchased a new television set which could receive both channels. At first this was a tiny fraction of the total audience. Even as late as 1960 the ITA estimated in its annual report that fewer than 60 per cent of licence holders had two-channel sets. Given their considerable financial investment, it was hardly surprising that viewers with new sets at first preferred the novelty of commercial television. Nevertheless, throughout the period the BBC's total audience was over twice that of ITV.

Indeed the introduction of commercial television had no independent effect on the overall growth of the television audience.

As Table 11.1 shows, this was fast but steady. The pattern of gradual growth was interrupted only once, when two years before the start of ITV the Coronation produced a dramatic rise in numbers of viewers. The BBC did not 'lose' an audience, nor did commercial choice increase the speed of audience growth.

Table 11.1 Growth of Television Audience

Year	No. of new TV licence holders
1946–7	14,560
1947–8	57,000
1948–9	112,000
1949–50	344,000
1950–1	420,000
1951–2	685,319
1952–3	639,192
1953–4	1,110,439
1954–5	1,254,879
1955–6	1,235,827
1956–7	1,226,663
1957–8	1,123,747
1958–9	1,165,419

Source: BBC Handbooks (1946–59)

Public service: private enterprise

Commercial television in Britain was hardly revolutionary. Indeed it was carefully modelled on the BBC. The traditions of public service were inherited by the new authority.

The ITA was responsible for regulating the commercial stations and made no programmes. Like the BBC, ITV was licensed only for a limited period, a system which ensured that the whole of British broadcasting came under periodic review. Like the BBC, it had a publicly appointed controlling board. 'The BBC triumphed', Peter Black wrote, 'because all of those chosen as members of the IBA might equally well have been BBC Governors'.

The new service was more limited than the BBC. It was banned from broadcasting its own opinions, and the injunction that it should observe 'impartiality in the treatment of all controversial issues' has been interpreted narrowly to imply a balance of views within each programme. As Smith points out, the prohibitions 'listed in the 1954 Act are broadly consistent with the general editorial policy of the BBC, but they have been used over the years to oblige independent TV not to do certain types of programme'. Hence ITV has been given less political independence than the BBC.

Thus Independent Television was made in the image of the BBC. Introduced after a controversy which *The Economist* called 'a soufflé of high principles and politics' (15 June 1954), which disguised a simple profit motive, commercial television was nevertheless formed as a public service.

Commerce, finance and television

Indeed television was so expensive it had always seemed likely that it would have to be financed commercially. 'Had there been no war in 1939', Briggs remarks, 'it is conceivable that commercial TV would have come to Britain fifteen years before it did'. Even in the limited experimental stage, television was an exorbitantly expensive medium. In 1937 a BBC *Handbook* had estimated that an hour of television cost twelve times as much to produce as the most expensive programme on the radio. Even Reith, in his evidence to the Selsdon Committee in 1934, claimed that he had 'no objection in principle to the sponsor system and we do in fact do something which is near to that and might do it in the future'. Sir William Haley wrote in 1945, 'Television will cost more than the Corporation's usual sources of funds can easily provide'. Beveridge had rejected sponsorship, but was not hostile in principle to some commercial involvement in television.

The BBC itself had been pressing for some kind of commercial financing of television since the 1930s, partly because it was felt that business interests could have little serious effect on what was seen as a trivial means of entertainment. Within the BBC, television was regarded as an extension of the Light Programme. As such it might be expensive, but it could hardly be important. 'In terms of the ethos which had been cultivated within the BBC during the fifties', wrote Burns, 'Light Entertainment remained an unfortunate necessity, its marginal character inescapably perpetuated in the adjective tagged to it'. Commerce, television and programme policy had been closely linked since the 1930s.

New programmes and the new style

Perhaps the most important innovation which ITV introduced was the change of mood which it brought to broadcasting. The atmosphere of the new companies, owned and run by showmen like Val Parnell and the Grade brothers, was quite different from the stifling solemnity of the BBC bureaucracy. 'It was more like Klondyke than Maida Vale', wrote Howard Thomas. When Thomas went to see Lew Grade at ATV about new programme ideas he would be met by a cloud of cigar smoke, and Grade would throw open a drawer bulging with receipts and bills. The haggling would then begin. Describing Parnell and Grade negotiating a new contract for ATV Thomas wrote, 'They sat like boxers pausing between the rounds of a heavyweight championship'.

Once ITV had begun broadcasting, it no longer had to fight the moral scruples of the establishment and its first priority was to capture an audience. 'Variety', claimed the first *ATV Showbook*, 'although accumulating the largest number of viewers, has been taken to task by critics of commercial television who have asked for "more cultural programmes and less airy frolics"'. The article continued, 'Many will agree with ATV chief executive Val Parnell when he says there is a lot of culture to be gained from watching a great clown performing'. However, it was not the big top or the *Commedia Dell'Arte* which drew the ATV audience, but rather the giveaway shows, Double your Money, Take your Pick, and Beat the Clock. The Labour MP Tom Driberg compared the audience's howl of laughter at one of these shows to that of the circus crowd in ancient Rome (*New Statesman*, 25 December 1959).

Independent Television did not, however, 'soundly beat the BBC at its own game', as a *Daily Mail* critic claimed in 1956. BBC drama, serials and documentaries were consistently preferred to those of ITV. Consequently, in 1956 news, documentaries, classical music, current events and drama on ITV were cut by one-third. 'A craven definition of "serious"', Black claims, 'killed off promising programmes whose only offence was that though entertainment, they were a novelty'.

ITV's most important contribution to television was to develop a format for the news. The BBC bulletin had been read by an unseen newscaster accompanied by still photographs. Cardiff and Scannell argue that this failure left a gaping hole in the very centre of television programme output. The function of a daily news service is not simply the continuous up-to-the-minute monitoring, processing and defining of immediate national and international news events. It also serves to define the currency and topicality of events and issues for current affairs programmes.[8]

Independent Television News attracted an immense audience. It used journalists as news readers, allowed them to write their own scripts, and showed them on the screen.

Robin Day, one of ITN's first newscasters, commented in his memoirs that 'The man on the screen had a further task, to win the professional confidence of his colleagues'. ITN developed television journalism in new directions, despite the limitations imposed upon it by the Television Act. The obligation to exercise balance proved particularly difficult. 'Any problems?' Day once asked the news director. 'Yes', Cox replied bitterly, 'a call from a chap called Pontius Pilate who says his case has not been properly put'. The success of the ITN approach in turn provoked the BBC into improving its own news services.

However, ITV also inherited many traditions from the BBC. One disgruntled critic claimed, 'The BBC has precedents for everything, for handling a monarch's abdication, a State Opening of Parliament or a boy scouts' jamboree'.[9] The opening years of television seem little more than an extension of the wireless, where history was relentlessly marked by a succession of royal events (with outside coverage).

More significantly, the BBC solved many of the political and social dilemmas that confronted television. The BBC showed the first televised election, and established the rules governing politicians' access to television, while the practical consequences of 'neutrality' and 'balance' in a visual medium were developed by a new generation of BBC producers and presenters. Goldie employed several young Labour ex-MPs defeated in the 1951 general election to make current events programmes. Later she claimed her choice was vindicated because Mayhew, Taverne and Wyatt moved from the left to the middle and right of the political spectrum. These shifts in attitude might also demonstrate the power of the ethic of consensus which came to dominate television journalism. The commercial companies simply took over the conventions developed within the BBC. Both, wrote Stuart Hood, 'interpreted impartiality as the acceptance of that segment of opinion which constitutes parliamentary consensus. Opinion that falls outside that consensus has difficulty in finding expression'. Hood suggests that the median of acceptable opinion may shift, but the consensus, once arrived at, is always shared by both companies.

The BBC had also set precedents for the solution of technical dilemmas in television journalism before ITV started. New rhetorics of documentary and current affairs coverage were established. At first most cameramen had been trained in the cinema, and had little experience of journalism. 'In those early days', one producer wrote, 'I often discarded glamorous pictures of cherry orchards, or flocks of bleating lambs, or children dancing in playgrounds because, though improbably useful in a travelogue, they did nothing to a study of, say, the relationship of Yugoslavia to the USSR'.[10] She concluded that, as pictures would always override words, a style had to be found which ensured that they would reinforce rather than distract from the meaning of a piece. It was also recognized that the use of film raised problems of authenticity. Viewers could easily be led to believe that a film taken in the past actually portrayed events happening in the present. One solution was to use someone who had helped to make the film as the programme presenter. Reviewing the BBC magazine series Foreign Correspondent in the *Listener* (May 1959), Goldie had written that they

> were using film but we were not trying to make films. We wanted the programmes to be dominated by the personality of the commentator ... We were all feeling our way but when the series finished we felt that we had hit on a new form that had come to stay in television. The key to the new form is the use of film to illustrate a personal experience.

This form was quite opposed to the style of the British documentary movement, in which the film purported to represent an authoritative reality, rather than any personal view.

These innovations and cautious explorations of the specific properties and opportunities of televised politics and current affairs were made well before ITV started. They solved dilemmas that were common to any television service. ITV did not challenge or alter the rules established by the BBC; it merely helped to develop them further.

End of a monopoly: vulgar new world

The introduction of Independent Television did not mark such a decisive break with the BBC. Rather, the brash new companies owed more to the Corporation than has usually been recognized. The BBC had already begun to change in fundamental ways before ITV was started. The commercial station provided a stimulus for the maturing of a national television service. Sir Hugh Greene claimed that dramatic changes were to come later in the 1960s, and these were as much to do with a shift in the political climate as with any administrative innovations.

This is not to deny that the BBC had a radically different manner and organization from Independent Television. Like the British Raj, the BBC combined privilege and moral purpose. It was a world in which 'unsoundness' was a major crime. Independent Television provided an alternative source of employment for dissidents and had no deadweight of custom or dignity. Personnel moved continually and freely between the two authorities by the 1960s.

However, commercial television was also modelled on and limited by the BBC. Originally intended as a political counterweight to what was seen as the BBC's 'red' bias, ITV was as vulnerable to political pressure. The BBC depended on public support for the legitimacy of its licence fee, as ITV depended on it for advertising revenue.

It has often been claimed that ITV was a vulgar debaucher of cultural standards. In the pursuit of profit it merely pandered to the lowest common denominator of public taste. More recently a far more subtle case has been advanced which is not so crudely anti-commercial. This claims that ITV was, rather, an energizing, populist force which gave expression to working-class culture.

Notes

1. J. C. W. Reith, *House of Lords* (22 May 1952), H. L.176: 1293–1451.
2. Quoted in J. Harris, *William Beveridge* (Oxford, Clarendon, 1977), p. 311.
3. Captain L. P. S. Orr MP, *House of Commons Debates* (22 June 1951), 529:327.
4. H. Fairlie, 'The BBC', in H. Swynnerton Thomas (ed.), *The Establishment: A Symposium* (London, New English Library, 1962).
5. G. Wyndham Goldie, *Facing the Nation: Television and Politics 1936–1976* (London, Bodley Head, 1977), p. 45.
6. 'Television staff policy', *BBC Written Archives* (1955).
7. P. Black, *The Mirror in the Corner* (London, Hutchinson, 1972), p. 115.
8. P. Scannell, 'The social eye of television', *Media, Culture and Society*, 1, 1 (1979).
9. H. Fairlie, 'TV: idiot box', *Encounter* (August 1959).
10. G. Wyndham Goldie, 'TV report', *Listener* (23 October 1968).

Chapter 12

Class, taste and profit

Post-war affluence was measured in consumer durables. Cars, refrigerators and washing machines made it easier to do what had always been done. Television changed people's social life and habits. Commercial television was believed to alter their aspirations and values as well.

In the late 1950s and early 1960s television was central to a debate about supposed changes in the British class structure. The growth of a mass television audience and the setting up of a commercial service were seen as agents of a revolution that was eroding class distinction and increasing social mobility. Television has more often been seen as a destructive than as a creative force. In the 1950s many regarded it as a threat to traditional ways of life, and hence to the basis of traditional political loyalties.

In 1962 the Pilkington Report summed up this debate. The Director General, Sir Hugh Greene, later called the report 'the most important piece of work on the purposes of broadcasting which has appeared in this or any other country'.[1] Pilkington attempted to establish the criteria for producing – and judging – good broadcasting. In fact the report was very much a product of its time, and was constrained by current sociological fashions.

The myth of the disappearing working class

During the 1950s it was argued that affluence was destroying the working class. The general elections of 1955 and 1959 seemed to support the view that there were no longer two nations: fewer and fewer people were prepared even to support the Labour Party. Two complementary explanations were put forward. According to the first, as the working class had become richer it was actually disappearing through assimilation into the middle class. According to the second, a working class had continued to exist but prosperity had undermined an awareness of its own interests: capitalism was successfully eradicating the consciousness (though not the reality) of class.

The first view was particularly popular among right-wing Labour politicians (who used it to justify an attempt to remove socialism from the party's constitution). 'The steady upgrading of the working class', wrote Anthony Crosland in his book *The Future of Socialism*, 'both occupationally and still more in terms of political and social aspirations, renders Labour's one-class image increasingly inappropriate'. It was also widely held by social scientists, who invented the inelegant term 'embourgeoisement' to describe the alleged process. As Butler and Rose wrote after the 1959 general election, 'It is more than ever possible to speak of the Conservatives as the country's usual majority party ... the Labour Party has to face the fact that its support is being eroded by the impact of age and social change'.

Between 1951 and 1958 real wages rose by 20 per cent. The proportion of manual workers who owned their own homes rose from 32 per cent to 39 per cent in the four years before 1962.[2] Between 1951 and 1964 the number of television sets rose from 1 million to 13 million. Indeed, as televisions were clearly not useful, the widespread ownership of sets merely appeared to confirm what Crosland called the 'pubs, pools and prostitutes' view of the working class, which was seen to 'waste all its higher income on alcohol, tobacco, gambling and fun ... if not actually women'.[3]

During the same period working-class habits also changed. People went on more holidays, went to the cinema less frequently, began drinking more at home and less at pubs. As these goods and habits had previously been the prerogative of higher social classes, it was assumed that their use also entailed middle- and upper-class views and beliefs.

The second explanation of the decay of the working class depended on the centrality of culture. The rituals which were a source of strength to working-class life were disappearing, partly (so it was argued) because of the homogenizing influence of television. Paradoxically, working-class culture was celebrated just as it seemed to be about to vanish. Indeed its condition was detailed by a generation of academics whose origins were working-class, but all of whom had been upwardly mobile.

'To live in the working class', wrote Richard Hoggart, 'is to belong to an all-pervading culture, one in some ways as formalized and stylized as any that is attributed to the upper classes'.[4] Jackson and Marsden in their book on working-class life argued that two-and-a-half centuries of urban life 'have established distinct working-class styles of living with very real values of their own. Values which are perhaps essential to society and which do not flourish that strongly in other reaches of society'.[5] In a chapter headed 'An acceptance of the working-class life', they remarked that obliterating these values and way of life 'can be so quick in a technological society ... the mass media, the central planning office, the bulldozers are all characteristic instruments of change'. In a related series of studies Wilmott and Young compared the warm closeness of a Bethnal Green working-class community with the more isolated life of a new suburb. In the East End the emphasis was on the informal collective life and the extended family, the pubs and the open-air market. 'There is a sort of bantering warmth in public', they claimed, which in the new suburb, Woodford, was reserved for the family home. There seemed to be more uniformity in gardens, attitudes and behaviour in Woodford than in the East End. 'Maybe uniformity is one of the prices we have to pay for sociability in a more mobile society', they concluded.[6]

Television was important because it was seen as replacing old communal forms of leisure with isolated and standardized entertainment. 'In many parts of life', Hoggart argued, 'mass production has brought good: culturally the mass produced makes it harder for the good to be recognized'. Indeed for writers like Hoggart, culture was the most important aspect of a society's achievement.

Hoggart applied F. R. Leavis's concern with the moral quality of élite literary culture to a broader problem of working-class life. For Leavis, Annan wrote, 'The analysis of the text is only important in so far as it reveals the profundity or morality of the writer's moral consciousness'.[7] Leavis was concerned to evaluate the purpose of literature. 'Where there is not in the literary critical sense a significant contemporary culture', he wrote, *the mind* is not fully alive'.[8] Hoggart was concerned to judge modern working-class culture. He concluded that 'Most mass entertainments are in the end what D. H. Lawrence described as "anti-life". They are full of corrupt brightness and improper appeals and moral evasions'. Progress had been reduced to material improvement: 'It only offered an infinite perspective of increasingly good times. Technicolour TV, all smelling, all touching, all tasting TV'.

Thus the Pilkington Report was the product of two contemporary concerns: that the working class was being absorbed into the middle class, and that working-class culture was decaying because of the industrialization of leisure. Raymond Williams wrote that 'From 1956 to 1962 there was an intense development of ideas in the field of culture and communication, and by the time of the Pilkington Report this had reached the level of open and conventional politics'.[9] The committee had been asked to review the development of television. In fact they did much more, producing a report which judged the nation's culture. Television, the report argued, was 'one of the major long-term factors that would shape the moral and mental attitudes, and the values of our society'.

Yet the working class did not disappear, and neither did working-class culture. There is little evidence that people lose a sense of their social identity simply because they become comparatively better off. Indeed the really remarkable feature of the period was not affluence – the rise in living standards looks far less impressive when it is compared with the growth in other European countries – but full employment. For the first time there was work for everyone, and it gave working-class culture, taste and life a confidence which it had rarely had before.

The Pilkington Report depended on a sentimentalization of an earlier 'golden age', just as Hoggart and Wilmott and Young had before it. Indeed it demonstrates a puritanical distaste for the effects of improved material conditions. Although its concern with the influence of television on social and cultural behaviour is important, the standards by which it judged the mass media were based on false premises about the nature of working-class life.

The power of the media

The Pilkington Report also depended on a crude view of the power of the media to influence individual behaviour. Advertising, and in particular its newest and most dramatic form, the television commercial, was regarded as immensely persuasive. The effect of advertising was dramatized by the contrast with the war, when advertising had not only been limited, but also pursued rather novel goals. A cartoon by Fougasse in 1942 wryly made the point: it compared the huge pre-war billboard extolling the public to 'Eat more and more Meatio' with the tiny wartime poster which read, 'Save Meatio, don't use more than you need!'[10] In this context the post-austerity explosion of advertising amazed the public, and academics and politicians became very sensitive to its effects.

Television advertising in particular was regarded as sinister. It was often equated with 'brain-washing' techniques which had been exposed during the Korean War. 'It may well be', wrote Daniel Bell in the *Listener* (December 1956), 'that our fears are excessive, that the pliability of the consumer, like that of the "indoctrinated" communist youth, is an exaggerated fact'. The fashion for 'motivation research' seemed to suggest that advertisements relied on an appeal to people's irrational and subconscious feelings in order to sell goods. The model of the consumer as a rational hedonist was replaced by another in which many goods were purchased not for their intrinsic worth or usefulness, but in an attempt to assuage anxieties. Marketing, dependent on the 'eight hidden needs' (most of which could be reduced to one – sex), was claimed to have dramatic effects. 'The ability of advertisers to contact millions of us simultaneously through television has given them the power to do good or evil on a scale never before possible', one persuader put it.[11] Leavis wrote that 'a new brand of applied psychology ... and a highly specialized profession' had been developed. 'Years of carefully recorded and tabulated experiment [led advertisers] to develop their appeal in the confidence that the average member of the public will respond like an automaton'.[12] Television advertising, which reached people in the defenceless privacy of their own homes, seemed to assume that consumers were unable to introspect sufficiently to understand their own motives.

The working class were felt to be the group most vulnerable to the ambitions of advertisers. 'There is one kind of person who seems particularly responsive to advertising: the man or woman who is moving up from one class to another', Mark Abrams argued in a broadcast in 1956. 'These people – and there are an incredible number in Britain – have to shed their old buying habits and acquire new ones. The class-destroying function of modern advertising is cumulative', he suggested:

> The initial effect is to encourage people to want to buy consumer goods
> formerly enjoyed by their social betters. As they achieve this and become
> more socially mobile, advertising and television provide them with
> knowledge that enables them to fill their new role.[13]

Indeed the first television commercials seemed to confirm this view of the
direct impact of the media on behaviour. Shops almost immediately sold out
of the advertised goods, and jubilant market researchers discovered that the
public recalled the commercials long after they had first been shown. But
this was only a temporary effect.

Indeed, later research has shown how complex the relationship between media
message and audience behaviour is. The public is not a passive, empty box merely
waiting to be filled with the injunctions of advertisers. How people react to what
they see is determined by their class, age and the beliefs they already hold. Nor is
the public subconscious so easily manipulated as many assumed. As one contemporary market researcher pointed out, surveys which concluded that housewives did not like macaroni which cooked to a wet sticky mass because wet sticky
masses aroused sexual guilt in them were not treated with the scepticism they
deserved.[14] Some critics reacted cautiously to the power of advertisements: 'I
cannot think so poorly of British Fathers', wrote Tom Driberg in the *New Statesman* (20 December 1958), 'as to accept the diagnosis proclaimed by one ITV
advertiser last week, "Every daddy *deserves* a Brylcreem home dispenser for
Christmas"'. However, most critics believed it to be overwhelming. Advertising
executives were credited with a power they would have been delighted to exercise,
but which was far in excess of their rather unpredictable performance.

This overestimation of the manipulative power of the media influenced
the Pilkington Report. It led to a crude view of the public – particularly the
working-class audience – as passive, gullible and misled.

Real and false wants

The Pilkington Report dismissed expressed public preferences as unreal and the
product of commercial manipulation. A Labour Party report on advertising written in 1962 developed some of these arguments. Advertising, it claimed, could
not be defended by the assertion that it merely reflected the times. For, in order
to make advertisements, individuals were obliged to make decisions. Insofar as
advertisers determined what was shown they were responsible for their choices.
Some people, the report argued, had claimed that advertising 'reinforces attitudes
of materialism, only too prevalent in society'. In the committee's opinion,

> This charge is probably the opposite of the truth: for it seems more
> likely that what advertising does is to interfere with the appreciation of
> material goods to the extent that it substitutes for a genuine assessment
> or perception of their qualities, vague sentiments and fantasies.

The choices that were expressed under these conditions were consequently not 'real'.

The Pilkington Report's assessment of commercial television depended on a similar view of the exploitation of working-class false consciousness for profit. The argument was based on two premises. First, that the public's expressed choice was not a real one because it had not been offered the entire range of possible options from which to choose. It made its choice of television programmes from a culture already limited by the imperatives of profit. Second, the public was in itself limited: the choices it made were deformed by the inadequacies of its education, wealth and leisure. The working class has, of course, been particularly damaged in these ways.

The report's attitude towards cultural choice was particularly clear in its discussion of entertainment. ITV defended itself by arguing that its programmes were popular. Pilkington replied that

> to give the public what it wants is a misleading phrase ... it has the appearance of an appeal to democratic principle, but the appearance is deceptive. It is in fact patronizing and arrogant, in that it claims to know what the public is but defines it as no more than the mass audience, and it claims to know what it wants, but limits its choice to the average of experience.

The commercial companies suggested that there was no need to consider entertainment as it was so unimportant. However, for Pilkington, the individual programme was analogous to the text for the literary critic. As such, it was as essential to judge 'trivial entertainment' as more serious programmes. Pilkington found most entertainment programmes unsatisfactory.

However, as Crosland pointed out, it was patronizing and perhaps unwise to dismiss expressed public wants as irrelevant. He argued that the range of newspapers and television programmes was 'still considerable, certainly wide enough to offer genuine comparison'. Indeed most people, for most of the time, chose the escapist, the diverting, or the trivial. Policy should not ignore these needs, but should also seek to encourage minority interests.

The Pilkington Committee's fears that the public was passive led it to consider audience preferences as little more than the expression of commercial manipulation. Consequently the report became insensitive to public taste. Indeed it endorsed the BBC's popular music policy when this was clearly out of touch with what people wanted to hear, as the success of the pirate stations soon demonstrated.

Entertainment, politics and advertising

The Pilkington Committee was romantically committed to a concept of folk culture. Its emphasis on the importance of the 'authenticity' of cultural products meant that many other considerations were ignored. For instance, television entertainment programmes often implicitly supported particular political values. Yet the report's emphasis on the cultural purposes of programmes has meant that long-term political consequences have rarely been discussed. In addition, the report depended on a series of misleading images about the nature of working-class life and culture which affected its tone and distorted its recommendations. Often Pilkington seemed perilously close to despising what was popular and entertaining, and approving only that which was rigorous and demanding.

This was unfortunate, because the report's identification of programmes as the central focus for any assessment of broadcasting is crucial. Moreover, its recognition of the structural effects of advertising on the quality of programmes is original and shrewd, and still pertinent a generation later. In addition, attempts by Pilkington to mitigate the impact of advertising by giving the third channel to the BBC, and by strengthening the power of the ITA over the companies, were important factors in improving the commercial service. In particular, the report, which had been wonderfully orchestrated by Sir Hugh Greene, also gave the BBC the *élan* and confidence which were the basis for its most exciting expansion in the 1960s.[15] For the first time, the Corporation attempted to make broadcasting something like a quality popular newspaper. This is perhaps the most challenging model for a national broadcasting service.

Notes

1. Sir Hugh Greene, 'The future of broadcasting in Britain', Granada Guildhall Lecture (1972), p. 24.
2. M. Pinto Duschinsky, 'Bread and circuses: the Conservatives in office 1951–64', in V. Bogdanor and R. Skidelsky (eds), *The Age of Affluence* (Harmondsworth, Penguin, 1970), p. 55.
3. C. A. R. Crosland, 'The mass media', *Encounter* (November 1962).
4. R. Hoggart, *The Uses of Literacy* (London, Chatto & Windus, 1957), p. 16.
5. B. Jackson and D. Marsden, *Education and the Working Class* (London, Routledge & Kegan Paul, 1962), p. 223.
6. P. Wilmott and M. D. Young, *Family and Class in a London Suburb* (London, Routledge & Kegan Paul, 1960), p. 129.
7. N. Annan, 'Love among the moralists', *Encounter* (February 1960), p. 37.
8. F. R. Leavis, *The Common Pursuit* (London, Chatto & Windus, 1952), p. 192.
9. R. Williams, *Communications*, revised edn (London, Chatto & Windus, 1966), p. 10.
10. Fougasse (pseud. C. K. Bird), *The Changing Face of Britain* (London, Methuen, 1950), p. 15.
11. V. Packard, *The Hidden Persuaders* (Harlow, Longman, 1957), p. 259.
12. F. R. Leavis and D. Thompson, *Culture and Environment* (London, Chatto & Windus, 1953), p. 48.
13. M. Abrams, 'Advertising', *Listener* (15 December 1956), p. 1089.
14. M. Abrams, 'Motivation research', *Advertising Quarterly* (November 1959), p. 311.
15. See M. Tracey, *A Variety of Lives: The Biography of Sir Hugh Greene* (London, Bodley Head, 1983).

Chapter 13

How the audience is made

Commercial television produces audiences, not programmes. Advertisers, in purchasing a few seconds of television time, are actually buying viewers by the thousand. The price they pay is determined by the number of people who can be expected to be watching when their advert is shown. Hence, advertisers regard programmes merely as the means by which audiences are delivered to them. The sequence of programmes in any evening, week or season reflects the quest of commercial customers to get the largest or most appropriate public they can. 'The spot is the packaging', wrote a market researcher in *Advertising Quarterly*, 'the product inside the package is an audience'. These are the realities which help to determine what kinds of programmes are made, when they are shown and who sees them.

Commercial television was introduced in the 1950s because it was claimed that it would bring competition into broadcasting, and make the service more responsive to popular demands. The Independent Television channel was supposed to break the narrow élitism of the BBC's cultural policy. Indeed, once it had been given a regional structure, it was also supposed to promote provincial culture and oppose the BBC's metropolitan bias. Finally, commercial television, its advocates claimed, would be less vulnerable to political pressure. Unlike the BBC, its finances would be independent of official control.

Few of these hopes were fully realized. The allocation of the franchise areas in which commercial companies were given the right to broadcast was designed to produce a system in which four (later five) of the largest and wealthiest regions made most of the programmes for the national network. The smaller companies made most of their programmes for local consumption; only a few of their products were to be shown nationally.

The first commitment of the commercial companies was to make a profit. Hence they were concerned to minimize the financial risks involved in making programmes. The smaller regions, whose audiences were not so attractive to advertisers, could not afford to invest in expensive programmes unless they were guaranteed a national showing. Similarly, the large networking companies needed to be able to show their programmes in every region in order to cover their costs. Consequently decisions about which programmes were to be networked became centralized.

This centralization was formally established when the Independent Television Companies Association (ITCA) was set up in 1971. This decided which programmes were to be shown on the national network, and how much the smaller companies had to pay towards the costs of the major programme producers. The smaller companies, however, complained that the ITCA was dominated by the five major programme networking companies.

The Independent Broadcasting Authority

Yet British 'commercial' television was not merely a product of market forces. If financial pressures were the only influence, the programme makers' aim would always be simply to reach the largest possible audience for the smallest amount of money.

In practice this would have meant a diet of American soap opera, variety shows, filmed series, quizzes and chat shows, based on proven formulae, endlessly repeated. 'Minority' programming would cater only for groups defined primarily in terms of their consumption patterns. Current affairs would have been confined to news bulletins, and advertising spots would have been longer, more frequent and more intrusive. In addition, even more programmes would have been bought from abroad – particularly the USA – and fewer programmes made in Britain or directed at a British audience. Commercial broadcasting did not develop all of these features in Britain, because of the framework of public regulations within which it was obliged to operate. Nevertheless, these pressures remain the dominant features of a commercial service.

The Independent Broadcasting Authority (IBA) exerted a major influence on commercial television. The powers of the authority were widened following the report of the Pilkington Committee (1962), but the most public job of the IBA was to license television franchises, and to reallocate these periodically. The authority was also required to ensure 'balanced programming', 'due impartiality' in the treatment of controversial issues, and a high quality in programme production as a whole. To enforce its recommendations the IBA could determine the broadcasting schedule, prohibit the transmission of particular programmes, or even revoke the franchises of offending companies. In addition, the IBA monitored and controlled the amount, timing, quality and content of advertisements shown on commercial television.

When commercial television started in Britain in 1956, there was little idea of what form it would take. 'All we had in the beginning', recalled Sir Robert Fraser, the first Director General of the ITA, 'was an Act of Parliament, an untested authority, a little prefab in a mews by Marble Arch, and a bit of money we had to pay back'.[1] Nevertheless, the new controlling authority quickly developed a commitment to public service. Thus, in the first months of broadcasting, as Sir Kenneth Clark recalled, the IBA threatened to make current affairs programmes itself to counter a proposal to abandon such programmes by the commercial companies. The determination of the authority to maintain minority programming in peak viewing time was similarly demonstrated when it came to reallocate franchises. In 1967 some of the original commercial franchises were not renewed. As a result, programme scheduling on ITV had an important though secondary goal, that of securing the reallocation of franchises. 'Advertisers understand that current affairs and news programming is a condition of the survival of the commercial television companies', wrote one advertising executive. 'It is no good complaining about them'.[2]

The IBA also intervened in the construction of the programme schedules, requiring that one-third of all material broadcast by commercial TV companies should be 'serious non-fiction, sensibly distributed over the week as a whole in appropriate times'.[3] Without this intervention, a service which many people relied on as their primary source of news might have carried very little current affairs coverage.

The IBA's intervention also helped to maintain a wider range of cultural output than would otherwise have been the case. In 1956 'serious programming' accounted for 19 per cent of the companies' schedules. This rose to 26 per cent in 1959, and 36 per cent in 1965, a proportion which was maintained. However, official figures were inflated by the growing number of programmes which were classed as serious documentaries, but which were on entertainment topics (such as Alan Whicker's series). In addition, there were an increasing number of consumer-oriented programmes (on cars, holidays and gardening, for example), some of which scarcely qualified for their official classification as 'serious and informative'. Nevertheless, programming on commercial television undoubtedly included more serious material because of the IBA's influence, and many of these programmes gained large audiences. The most striking example was ITN's News at Ten, which was enormously innovative in its presentation of news and which regularly featured in the IBA's yearly 'Top Twenty' popularity ratings.

The Authority was also important in maintaining the standards of entertainment on commercial television. It limited the number of cheap American imports and the frequency with which programmes were repeated. The IBA also assisted the smaller regional companies by charging the more profitable regions a higher rent for the use of the television transmitter which it owned, and thus made them subsidize the rental of the poorer companies. In addition, through its position on the committee which decided which programmes were shown on the central network, it ensured that some of the regional programmes were shown nationally.

Regions and audiences

The Television Act, 1954, had not specified how commercial television was to be organized. It had laid down no principles to guide the allocation of contracts. When commercial companies began to submit proposals to the ITA they suggested many different ways of dividing commercial broadcasting between competitors. Thus, some contractors offered to provide particular kinds of programmes, all the light entertainment, or all the music; others proposed to make the programmes for particular times of day, 6–9 pm or 3–7 pm. However, Sir Robert Fraser decided that the system should be based on regional companies. In this way, he intended to prohibit the growth of a centralized monopoly based on London, and to 'give real creative power to the regions'.

Yet the principle of the federal structure seemed threatened from the very start. During the first two years commercial television was so expensive to run, reached such a small audience, and was so unprofitable that there was little interest in the smaller regions. It was during this disastrous period that Roy Thomson acquired Scottish Television at a very low cost. It was only when this company overcame its initial difficulties that the other regional services began to develop. Thomson, famous for having said that owning a commercial station was like having a licence to print money, soon made Scottish Television profitable. 'I like monopolies', he said, 'when I operate them'.[4]

Regional commercial broadcasting has survived, but in a form that makes sense in economic rather than cultural terms. Thus, Tyneside and Teesside have little in common apart from geographical proximity. Yet they were given a combined television station because only the joint purchasing power of their audience was sufficient to make up a marketing unit. A more serious case was that of Harlech Television, supposedly a Welsh station, but actually required, for commercial reasons, to cater for a large English audience as well. It has been argued that some regional television stations, for example Border Television, may have strengthened, or even created, a sense of local identity. However, most of the regions have no real justification except in marketing terms. Apart from London, television regions have not even approximately coincided with local authority areas. This has at least inhibited the discussions of local political issues.

The regionalism of commercial television appears less firmly rooted in popular needs than in the convenience of the market.

Indeed the most important response by the commercial companies to regional differences within Britain was to identify and sell distinctive characteristics in marketing terms. 'Granada has the skilled workers: surveys prove it!' read an advertisement in a 1959 trade magazine. 'Westward where women cook', read another in *Campaign* in 1962. In 1979 Southern Television was pointing out that its A, B and C1 housewives cook, and have time to be *femmes fatales* afterwards (*Campaign*, 5 July 1979). The differences between the habits and tastes of the various regional audiences became an essential feature of sales campaigns. In 1962 one writer claimed that 'The television regions made scientific selling more possible than ever before'.[5] New products could be launched in regions where they were most likely to be successful, and advertising campaigns could be tested by pilot surveys in a particular region. In the same way, regional television meant that additional advertising pressure could be applied in any area where sales were slumping. The most important effect of the regional structure of commercial television was to change the marketing map of Britain.

Franchises and owners

The cost of developing commercial television was at first so great that franchises had to be given to syndicates which had the resources to undertake the necessary capital investment. This brought an important change in the kind of people who controlled broadcasting. Hitherto in the BBC responsibility had been vested in professional administrators whose social origins, training and attitudes reflected the 'public service' philosophy of the Corporation. Independent television introduced a new type of executive, business-oriented and entrepreneurial, geared to the commercial criteria of the sponsors. Thus, while the BBC was directed by Sir William Haley, who had started his career as a journalist on the *Manchester Guardian*, and who became editor of *The Times*, Associated Television's first director was Lew Grade, a show business and theatre impresario.

By the time that the franchises were reallocated in 1967, commercial television had become highly profitable, and consequently the justification for allowing it to be controlled by speculative capital no longer held good. Indeed such vast profits had been made from a publicly owned asset, the air waves, that the prospect of their reallocation created a flood of applications. There was an atmosphere reminiscent of Klondyke gold fever. Many of Britain's major corporations financed 'prospecting' companies composed of theatre managers and entertainment moguls, spiced with a few peers or eminent members of the BBC. Although changes were made in the new franchises, instead of widening control, the redistribution, in practice, merely consolidated the power of the great media empires.

This pattern continued until the 1980s; the government encouraged the oligopolistic tendencies of the broadcasting industry itself – in the name, of course, of freedom. If one contradiction of this period was that free market rhetoric was accompanied by interventionist practice, another was that talk about a media marketplace was accompanied by its virtual eradication. Technological change, with its requirement of long-term investment and large-scale capitalization, produced a bureaucratic jungle of profit-taking conglomerates which now own huge shares in all the media which the public consumes.

By 1990 the small number of corporate owners were not competitive in a sense that could be conceivably expected to produce an improved product: but their financial rivalry undoubtedly imposed pressure to produce a cheaper one. That meant an almost inevitable lowering of standards: it is cheaper to buy in agency news than to send a reporter to the scene, it is cheaper to buy in internationalized soap opera than to make your own drama, and so on.

The victims of media concentration are variety, creativity and quality, while the future proliferation of broadcasting channels in the hands of a shrinking band of operators is certain to make matters worse.

Ownership and control of television

However, the control of commercial television companies could not simply be equated with ownership. Those who actually produced commercial television programmes enjoyed a significant degree of autonomy. But, most important of all, the pressure of market forces imposed powerful constraints on what could and could not be broadcast. These operated irrespective of the formal ownership of commercial television. In a study of the way in which programming is determined in the USA, Wolf argued that ownership does not explain the differences in programming between stations. 'It may be', he suggested,

> that those who saw such influences labored under a false analogy between the small town newspaper editor who may have shaped every word in his paper, and the television corporate executive, who according to the analogy controlled what was shown on the air.[6]

Indeed he concluded that in the USA the more diversely owned companies were less likely to take the networked programmes, particularly the news, current affairs and documentaries, and more likely to replace them with old movies, old quiz shows, or old operas. They did this simply because of the pressure to attract the largest possible audience.

The economic and social organization of broadcasting is very different in Britain from that which Wolf describes in the USA. There, the more diversely owned companies were the smaller and less successful ones, which were more vulnerable to market pressures. Nevertheless, the inevitable pursuit of profit within a commercial system must have some similar consequences for the programming decisions which can be made in any country. Market forces operate as a continual limiting pressure on any commercial broadcasting system. Yet it is also clear that more socially diverse patterns of ownership could be an important factor in creating the conditions for more adventurous and varied programming.

The audience that advertisers want

The most important pressure on television scheduling and programme making is that of advertising expenditure. If television companies sell audiences, what kinds of audiences do advertisers want, and how are they packaged to attract sales? Indeed, how does the real purpose of producing audiences for advertisers affect the apparent purpose of producing programmes for audience consumption?

The American system of programme sponsorship, in which advertisers pay for individual programmes, was rejected when commercial television started in Britain, on the grounds that it gave advertisers direct power over programme content. Instead only 'spot advertising' was permitted. Advertisers could buy time slots only between or within programmes. At first, advertisements were limited to an average of six minutes per hour. Later, when it was seen that this led to an accumulation of advertisements in peak viewing times, which had above-average amounts of advertising, it was decided to limit advertisements to no more than seven minutes in any one hour.

The decision to adopt restricted spot advertising had been hailed as a victory for public service broadcasting. 'The prohibition of sponsorship was an inspiration of the Television Act', declared Fraser, 'since it established the supremacy of the editorial principle'.[7] Spot advertisements were compared with newspaper advertising. They were seen as guaranteeing the independence of programme making from the influence of advertisers: no rational person, it was argued, supposes that what newspapers publish in their editorial columns is determined by advertisers. Spot advertising would protect the editorial integrity of commercial television. 'Advertising will be an asset worn as a bright feather in the cap of free TV', Sir Robert Fraser wrote, 'not as a soiled choker around the throat'.

Sponsorship of all programmes except news and current events was finally permitted in 1988. However, on the ITV channels there continued to be a fierce battle about who could sponsor what – and considerable anxiety about potential commercial abuses of the authority of some programmes. Such niceties, of course, were not part of the satellite broadcasting régime. Here there were few restrictions on sponsorship and far more advertising was allowed. Indeed, one of the oddities of the intense political campaigns of the period was the BBC's failure to point out, in its own defence, that while the British public enjoys some adverts, repeated research has shown how irritating they find too many. Historically, the British public has enjoyed and endured less advertising per hour of viewing than any American or European viewer. It may be appalled when the full commercial diet of adverts reaches it.

However, during the 1980s powerful interests complained to a sympathetic government that the ITV companies and the IBA were using their monopoly too effectively. Between 1981 and 1989 the advertising revenue of commercial television doubled in real terms, fierce competition for air time raised the price of advertising and increased the discretionary power of companies. Thus, there was great commercial pressure to create alternative sources of air time: cable, satellite and a competing commercial terrestrial Channel 5 were proposed, in order to bring down advertising costs. Advertisers believed they had a strong interest in breaking the economic basis of the existing ITV companies' cultural power.

Hostile critics argued that the IBA had become too closely identified with the ITV companies. A new body, the Independent Television Commission (ITC), was set up to preside over the 'deregulated' commercial system, but with far more limited powers than its predecessor. Thus, franchises for ITV (which after 1993 became known as Channel 3) were to be auctioned. Auction winners will then hold franchises for ten years. The ITC will have little authority to demand changes in programme performance. Thus while the Commission is obliged to ensure that public sensibilities about images of sex or violence are not offended, it has limited authority with which to perform the more critical task of ensuring that good programmes continue to be made and shown by companies desperately trying to recoup the huge capital expense of their franchise bid.

The IBA's powers, however imperfectly exercised, stemmed from its economic sanctions within the ITV system. Since its inception, the ITC has developed imperialist ambitions. Clearly it would like to use its controls to bring traditional public service criteria to bear on the enlarged commercial sector. Indeed, the ITC is probably responsible for a profound metaphorical change in ministers' language. In 1986 guarantees of programme quality were to be a 'factor' in allowing applicants to enter the auction for Channel 3 franchises; by 1987 they were being discussed as a 'hurdle'; they rose during 1988 to a 'fence'; and by 1990 they were confidently described as 'a barrier to the inferior'. But metaphors alone will not control commercial pressures to maximize profits, and it remains to be seen how far the ITC can realize its ambitions.

Yet many of the pressures exercised by advertisers on the content of programmes have remained remarkably consistent since the start of commercial broadcasting. The extent to which they affect programmes and schedules depends on the ways in which they are balanced and regulated.

Thus it is clear that even spot advertising does not preclude advertisers from calculating how the editorial content of programmes affects the impact of their advertising message. 'After all', as an advertiser wrote as early as the 1950s, 'an advert is seen as part of a programme' (*Campaign*, 14 March 1956). Advertisers have prior knowledge of programme schedules, which are published each quarter in advance of their transmission. They thus know the general character, if not the precise content, of the programmes with which their advertisements will be shown. There have been cases in which advertisers have avoided certain programmes on the grounds that their content is unlikely to dispose viewers to respond favourably to their advertisements. This is most common when the content of the programme clashes directly with the appeal of the advertisement (for example, airlines have withdrawn advertisements from appearing in documentaries about air disasters). However, it has also occurred when a programme is thought to have associations that detract from the broad image of the product.

In contrast, some programmes may be preferred because they provide an editorial environment conducive to a favourable response to particular advertisements, or because their prestige is thought likely to enhance that of the product or service advertised within them. Thus, advertisements for newspapers appear near the news, and those for beer are often placed close to programmes on sport. The very fact that such intuitive judgements associated with programme content can influence how advertising time is bought must affect the decisions made by the companies about scheduling.

This pressure is, however, marginal. The main consideration of advertisers is not the programme environment of their advertisements, but the size and composition of the audience that the programmes will attract. Advertisers buy television time in two ways. Sometimes they buy a 'guaranteed audience', that is, a fixed number of viewers. This may be made up of many small sections of the audience and spread over a whole range of programmes with low ratings. Alternatively, it may be composed of a few large audiences during peak viewing times. In either case, what is bought is viewers. However, advertisers may also purchase particular advertising slots. The television companies may oblige advertisers to buy a 'package' of slots, composed of some of the peak viewing times the advertisers want, but combining other, less attractive slots. Nevertheless, advertisers are more in control of the kinds of audiences their campaigns will reach if they buy specific slots.

Commercial television rapidly became the leading advertising medium for mass consumer products and so was under pressure to put on programmes with an appeal to a mass audience. However, many patrons of commercial television have sought to reach particular constituents within the mass market, in particular women (who are the key decision makers in many consumer purchases) and young people. Since commercial television derives its revenue from advertisers and not from viewers, the commercial system is thus led towards catering for these groups. Thus the success of commercial breakfast television depends almost entirely on its capacity to attract an audience rich in consuming housewives.

Market research can provide a detailed breakdown of the audience profile for particular programmes. A massive investment is made in monitoring how many and what categories of people watch each programme. This research assists the television companies to produce programmes that will deliver the required audiences, and provides them with an accurate measurement of the audiences which they have sold.

Research also helps advertisers predict from advance programme schedules what audiences they can expect to buy. This research takes the form of continuous monitoring of a representative sample of viewers, providing detailed figures for programme viewing analysed in terms of the size and class of audience. It is supplemented by additional surveys that analyse other, more specialized characteristics of viewers. This research has established that certain types of programmes – soap operas, situation comedies, the main news bulletin and variety programmes – have a generalized appeal that transcends differences in social class, age and sex. It also reveals that other types of programmes – most notably political documentary programmes and serious drama – are not watched as much by women and young people. The results have shown a remarkable stability of viewing preferences since the intro-duction of commercial television. There has been little change in the pattern of mass viewing, apart from a small shift away from variety and sport.

The way in which commercial television time is sold generates pressure for quantity of audience, rather than quality of audience appreciation. It has even been suggested that some advertisers prefer television programmes not to be too involving, for fear of detracting from the impact of their adver-tisements. This has been called the 'Let's-give-the-public-the-shows-they-*least*-like-so-they'll-watch-the-ads' theory.[8] The widespread use of video-recording machines has made research into the effects of advertising even more complex. Little is yet known about the extent to which the public uses this technology to avoid adverts. But it is assumed that 'spooling on' is a common habit.

The IBA attempted to offset the pressure for quantity of audience by cir-culating the companies with a weekly Audience Appreciation Index, which monitors the quality of audience response to individual programmes. This index has consistently shown that information programmes are more highly appreciated than those concerned with entertainment. There seems to be an inverse relationship between audience size and audience enjoyment.

However, it is doubtful whether this intervention had much influence on the time-buying decisions of advertisers, as no connection has yet been established between the audience's enjoyment or involvement in pro-grammes, and their responsiveness to advertisements shown at the same time. The implications of audience appreciation research have only lately begun to be developed. It has been argued that, within the two categories of information and entertainment programmes, those with large audiences tend to have higher appreciation scores than those with small audiences. Indeed some market researchers have come up with the less-than-remarkable finding that the more demanding a programme is, the better it has to be before people will watch it.[9]

The pressure on commercial television to maximize audiences naturally leads to a preference for 'entertainment' as opposed to 'serious' programmes. Within the broad category of entertainment there is a preference for pro-grammes which have previously demonstrated their appeal to women and young people. Hence there is a bias against showing sport at some times of the day, as it mainly appeals to men. Commercial pressures have also led programme makers to emphasize the personal and human interest aspects of documentary stories. Thus, structural social problems are treated in the form of individual case studies. This kind of programme reaches a wider audience, particularly among women, than other documentary styles. The prominence given to certain types of programmes on commercial television is a direct consequence of the pressures generated by advertising for the production of certain types of audiences.

Advertising also generates a strong pressure for the television companies to produce predictable and regular audiences, as well as to maximize them. While the ratings for any particular programme may be hard to predict, because they depend so much on factors outside the control of any commercial company (in particular what the BBC is showing), viewing patterns over a year, as well as the categories and sequences of programmes, have been easy to predict.

Advertisers rely on programme schedules to produce the audiences which they pay for. This has encouraged attempts to use the sequence of programmes in order to manipulate the size of an audience over an evening. Consequently, programmes with a broad audience appeal are shown early in the evening, in an attempt to capture viewing families for a particular channel for the rest of the night's programmes. Scheduling attempts to expand and consolidate the mass audience throughout the evening. It is this pressure which leads to the screening of 'minority' information programmes outside peak viewing times, and to the 'twinning' of BBC and ITV schedules for current affairs programmes. By doing this the companies may minimize choice, but they also minimize the loss of audience from programmes that get low ratings. In addition, current events programmes are thus seen by a far larger general audience than would otherwise be the case.

The proliferation of broadcasting channels which was so enthusiastically advocated by advertisers will, however, make many of these calculations increasingly insecure. Already the use of videos makes the assessment of impact of adverts more difficult. Accelerating fragmentation of the great national audiences previously enjoyed by the duopoly may provide, as some have argued, many new specialized concentrations of consumers, or it may provide nothing more than smaller, more unpredictable audiences. Indeed, the most enthusiastic advocates of 'deregulation', the advertisers, have begun to be anxious about the future effectiveness of advertising on TV at all.

Whatever happens, there is evidence that these commercial attempts to manipulate the audience are only partly successful. Goodhardt has argued that most families watch television sporadically. The 'inheritance factor' (or the likelihood of watching the programme that comes next) seems effective for only one programme, not the whole evening's viewing. Nor would it seem that people become loyal to a channel because they are addicts of particular series. Out of forty serials screened in the spring of one year only 54 per cent of people who saw one episode of any serial also saw the next. Most of the people watching the second half of the story were different from those who had seen its beginning.[10]

Nevertheless, the commercial companies necessarily continue to try to maximize their audiences. The pursuit of the largest possible audience is not in itself harmful. But if it is narrowly interpreted, it may lead to schedules that are cautious, conservative and that very rarely break established patterns.

The needs of all advertisers using commercial television are not the same. Some have sought more specialized groups within the mass audience, and the financial significance of this kind of advertising is growing. This is indicated by the growth of corporate advertising, in which giant companies are merely concerned to project an image of their activities rather than any specific product. In addition, there has been an increase in consumer durables and motor advertising. These categories have risen as a proportion of total television advertising expenditure from 7 per cent in 1968 to 30 per cent in 1988.[11] This has been accompanied by a fall in food, drink and household advertising directed at the mass market. Furthermore, there has been a growing tendency even among mass market-oriented advertisers towards directing their campaigns at particular segments of the market.

The impact of this shift, however, has been muted by the difficulties involved in translating the aims of marketing strategies into buying television time. There have been fashions in market research which determine how the audience is offered to the advertiser. In the 1950s and 1960s motivational research was dominant. 'Beecham's buyers are a little more likely to strive, and are a little more neurotic', stressed an Associated Rediffusion survey in 1962. 'Compared, that is with Aspro, Anadin and Disprin buyers, however, they are noticeably more extrovert'. Increasingly, though, there was a trend towards pilot studies of particular products and towards attempts to segment target markets with a fine precision.

However, despite attempts (by Leo Burnett and the British Bureau of Market Research in particular) to develop 'psychographic' profiles of television viewers, such methods remain impressionistic. No satisfactory method has been developed that enables advertising men or women to select time slots in a way that allows them to reach the types of personalities believed to be particularly susceptible to their advertising campaigns. Consequently, commercial television companies have not been obliged to cater for particular groups (at least those defined by psychological categories) to any great extent.

Advertisers have been most interested in reaching 'light viewers', who are like the 'floating' voters in election studies. The success of a campaign may depend on the proportion of light viewers, who might not otherwise know about the product, that it can reach. For a time, light viewers were regarded as being particularly selective in their televisionwatching habits. This was partly because a large proportion of light viewers were middle class, and were believed to be discriminating.

However, this view has now been challenged. Goodhardt has suggested that light viewers tend not to watch particular types of programmes, nor do they prefer low-rating minority programmes. They tend to be as unselective as heavy viewers, but merely watch less television. Hence, support of minority programmes does not seem to be a means of reaching the light viewer. On the contrary, it appears that advertising on high-rating programmes represents the most efficient way of reaching light viewers. Another study suggests, furthermore, that the pursuit of light viewers is in itself misguided. What matters is not how many advertisements of a particular product are seen, but how many in relation to the number of advertisements of a competing product.[12] The light viewer sees less than the heavy viewer of *all* the competing products on television. It may, therefore, be better to reach him or her through other advertising media.

A further problem for the advertiser is that neither minority programmes nor particular genres of programmes can be relied on to deliver specialized audiences. Goodhardt's analysis of the housewife audience for twenty different categories of programme showed that only Westerns are positively sought out by any viewers. Westerns were the only kind of programme with a slightly higher level of 'duplication viewing' – that is, the likelihood of a viewer seeing more than one programme within this category – than could be explained by channel loyalty or overall rating figures. Most people, Goodhardt's work suggests, see further programmes of any particular genre only because they prefer one channel, or because the programme has a high rating, not because they are specifically interested in its content. 'People who watched one arts programme', according to Goodhardt, 'had no more tendency to see another arts programme than to see, say, a Western or a religious programme, or a sports programme with a comparable weighting'.

This characterization of television audiences as indiscriminate and promiscuous in their viewing habits has been challenged. Sue Stoessel argued that the results of Goodhardt's research were misleading because they aggregated behaviour over several weeks. This obscured major changes in viewing behaviour from week to week. It is only by examining these detailed changes in viewing behaviour, she suggested, that preferences for individual programmes could be revealed. An analysis of changes in viewing figures over successive weeks reveals the effects of positive choice and preference, as does an analysis that distinguishes between audience behaviour in the different regions. In London, she argued, light viewers are more heavily concentrated among the audiences of some specific programme types. There are significant groups of viewers, at least in the London area, who do choose to watch programmes because of their content.[13]

This debate is likely to continue. The apparent failure of different categories of programmes to divide audiences into conveniently specialized groups has important implications. It may reduce the potential for commercial television to create new patterns of programmes. A low-rating current affairs programme has little to offer advertisers if it delivers not a discriminating élite (like a 'quality' national newspaper), but large numbers of heavy viewers so hypnotized that they cannot even summon the energy to switch off the ballet or Third World poverty programme offered at the margins of peak viewing times.

Indeed, the audiences for specialized programmes do not necessarily share other characteristics which would make them marketable packages for sale to advertisers. A shared interest in Westerns does not imply, for instance, a propensity to trade in a new car each year or a tendency to be a young couple setting up home for the first time. On the other hand, if Stoessel is correct, there is a market for élite and quality advertising in television, but it may not be most efficiently reached through this medium.

Indeed insofar as advertising has promoted minority programming hitherto, it has tended to be in a form that produces groups of viewers which are marketable. Travel programmes, and those about cars and cooking, have all developed partly because they cater for audiences with a shared interest in buying certain sorts of products. The advertising for cable and satellite television depends on the development of this commodity-based 'narrowcasting'. The greater choice of channels will, it is suggested, offer advertisers more refined groups of audience interest. However, those with fewer material interests in common have been, and will continue to be, less favoured.[14]

Public regulation and the public interest

In its time the IBA played an important role in mitigating the adverse effects of advertising on broadcasting. Nevertheless, at times the Authority was passive. For example, it was reluctant to ensure that companies adhered to the programme policies on which they won franchises. It was difficult for the Authority to be more active in its surveillance, partly because its statutory obligations were imprecise in many areas. However, political realities limited its power more fundamentally. The commercial television lobby is highly organized and politically effective. It employs public relations officers and cultivates an able group of MPs. In addition, many newspapers are sympathetic to the commercial television lobby. Its interests are also protected by an extensive network of contacts based on the interlocking directorships linking commercial television companies to other banking and industrial organizations. In contrast, the IBA was less effectively organized as a political lobby, and its powers of supervision – which were inevitably the product of political negotiation – were consequently constrained. Finally, the IBA would be 'punished' for its interventions into schedules or programme decisions. Thus, having been required to present more balanced programming over Christmas, the companies could retaliate by showing programmes which got only very low ratings.

However, the aims of the IBA were furthered by the presence of the BBC as a 'public service' institution, committed to broad social and political objectives rather than to the maximization of profit. There was in Britain a great convergence between public and commercial broadcasting in which the two systems influenced each other.

In addition, for much of its history, commercial television was in a strong bargaining position in relation to advertisers. ITV was able in the past to resist some advertising pressure precisely because it was in a seller's market.

Companies sold advertising time in ways which reduced the pressures to maximize audiences. The high profits and monopolistic position of commercial television created an environment in which the IBA could be more effective.

Swinging sixties and sober seventies

In the 1960s and 1970s television came of age. Since 1970 there has been a remarkable revolution not in the technology but in the content of broadcasting. In this period, television rapidly developed its own forms – in the treatment of politics, interviews, documentaries and plays – which were quite different from the earlier styles of radio or film. During the 1960s television humour began to take the form of satirizing itself – an indication of how widely the conventions of the new medium had been publicly absorbed.

This was partly a product of a more generally liberal mood, which made a wider range of possibilities available for broadcasters. After the Pilkington review of 1962, the BBC became a more adventurous organization. At the same time, the independent television companies became more secure and more profitable. By the 1960s, moreover, television had taken over from the cinema a mass working-class audience.

In many ways the vast size of the television audience has posed problems for the medium. There is a continual pressure to screen programmes that will attract the largest audiences and cause offence to the smallest numbers of viewers. Yet the attempt to reach a big audience while meeting 'public service' criteria has been a creative tension.

Some commentators, like Stuart Hood, Michael Tracey, Anthony Smith and even Sir Hugh Greene, have seen the period since the early 1970s as one of increasing caution in television. Not only did the reporting of the troubles in Northern Ireland provide many problems for the broadcasting institutions, but also the BBC and ITV became more vulnerable to government threats over a broad range of issues.

Channel 4, minorities and money

Yet it was a reinterpretation of the public service principle which produced Channel 4. The ideas behind the creation of this new channel were a product of the tensions identified during television's most creative and expansionist years. But it was also influenced by the political problems of the period. However, by the time the station opened there had been a change not only in the general economic climate but also, more damagingly, in the conditions of competition for television audiences.

Channel 4 'publishes' programmes made by independent production companies. It does not make any programmes of its own, although it does commission them. Originally it was financed by the existing commercial companies who supplied much of its material. As it did not sell its own advertising time it was somewhat removed from the direct pressures experienced by the rest of the commercial sector. The 1990 Broadcasting Act changed this: the channel was now to be made more vulnerable to advertisers' interests. However, it is still obliged to screen programmes for the various 'minority' interests that are not well served elsewhere in the television system.

The minority-based rationale of Channel 4 had a number of origins. Perhaps the most important was the experience of even the most distinguished and 'marketable' producers and directors, that it was impossible to work, in Britain, outside the BBC or ITV companies.[15] Those who wanted to make programmes that did not conveniently fit into the patterns of viewing developed by the duopoly, or those who simply wanted a greater control over their own material, found it difficult to raise the necessary finance or find buyers for what they made. It was argued that there evidently were audiences within the mass of viewers with more distinctive tastes and needs, but the existing channels allowed these consumers little opportunity to demonstrate their preferences. A new pattern of differently organized production companies, liberated from the limitations of the ITV or BBC systems, would be able to find and develop these more specialized audiences. Therefore any innovation in the television service ought to make it possible for 'independent' producers to explore the interests of these minorities.

It was also strongly argued that television had failed to reflect Britain's contemporary cultural diversity. Reformers emphasized the needs of the various Black and Asian communities, as well as those of minorities like the young and the old, for programmes which dealt with their concerns and ways of life. Any new service, it was suggested, should produce material for these social and ethnic minorities.

Finally, some market researchers believed that the blunt instrument of television advertising could, by the 1980s, be refined. A new channel could offer programme incentives that attracted discriminating 'minorities' of selective television viewers and could sell them the things they had particular interests in. For the first time, television would be able to deliver higher concentrations of the more affluent consumers that advertisers wanted.

The logic of Channel 4 looked appealingly neat. It would offer greater freedom of choice, and serve minorities neglected elsewhere. Unfortunately, the minorities that producers, social reformers and advertisers were interested in were somewhat different.

Channel 4 represents an important (and perhaps the last) reinterpretation of the public service role of broadcasting. In this version, the freedom of creative individuals to risk making the programmes they want to make is seen as the guarantor of public good. It was a Labour government which decided to back the new channel (although a Conservative one presided over its birth). Labour support was based on a feeling that the political consensus

developed by the existing broadcasting services was too restrictive. Consequently the channel was given the opportunity to create new conventions for
dealing with controversial and political issues. It is not obliged to balance
views within a programme, but only over the whole schedule and over time.
It can, therefore, broadcast more clearly partisan material.

However, the channel's capacity to innovate depends on the politics of
money. The only ultimate defence Channel 4 has for its style and programmes is their ability to attract advertising revenue. By the 1980s the
Conservative government was using the success of Channel 4 to attack public
service broadcasting, by demanding that greater numbers of programmes
should be produced by 'independent' companies. Yet Channel 4's innovations
had been completely dependent on the development of public service ideals.

In the late 1980s both the BBC and ITV companies were obliged to take
an increasing proportion of their programmes from the 'independent' sector;
by 1993 this was expected to account for 25 per cent of their output. This has led
to the emergence of some culturally important and commercially successful
companies – and of innovative programmes. 'The Media Show', the astutely
topical series on Stalin, and many others were made by production companies
outside the duopoly. However, whether such companies are actually independent,
except in the formal sense, is dubious. A survey by the London Business School
showed that they were all financially precarious, with low profit margins.[16]
People set up independent television companies because they want to make programmes – not because they want to make money. The study also showed how
completely dependent these companies were on the patronage of the established
channels. The new satellite companies were, as yet, hardly interested in their
quality products.

The limitations of commercial broadcasting are largely the result of the
economic pressures to which it is exposed. That British commercial television
has been in some ways superior to others is due to the public service traditions and institutions that have so far determined its development. Nevertheless, the implications of a comment by Sidney Bernstein, the television
industrialist, should always be borne in mind. 'Commercial television is a
very unusual business', he said, ' ... you don't necessarily make more money
if you provide a better product'.

Yet the market and the audience for television programmes is altering
dramatically under the impact of a whole series of technological changes.
Whether the advantage of increased variety will be enough to offset the
dilution of resources remains to be seen. Indeed this period may yet be
regarded, in television terms, as a lost golden age.

Notes

1. Sir Robert Fraser, *ITA Notes* (October 1970).
2. P. Todd, 'Scarcity of TV time!', *Campaign* (26 January 1979).

3. *IBA Annual Report* (1978).
4. R. Thomson, *Contrast: Television Quarterly* (Winter 1961), p. 107.
5. Associated Rediffusion, 'Cold and flu remedies', *Market Profiles*, 6 (1962).
6. F. Wolf, *Television Programming for News and Current Affairs* (New York, Praeger, 1972).
7. Sir Robert Fraser, *ITA Notes* (January 1970).
8. C. E. Setlow, 'TV Rating, there just might be a better way', *New York Times* (31 December 1978).
9. T. P. Barwise, A. S. C. Ehrenberg and G. J. Goodhardt, 'Audience appreciation and audience size', *Journal of the Market Research Society*, 21, 4 (October 1979), p. 269.
10. G. J. Goodhardt, A. S. C. Ehrenberg and M. A. Collins, *The Television Audience: Patterns of Viewing* (Farnborough, Saxon House, 1975).
11. Tables of advertising expenditure in *Admap*, No. 2, 1988.
12. A. Roberts and S. Prentice, 'Reaching light TV viewers', *Admap* (March 1979).
13. S. Stoessel, reply to Roberts and Price, 'The real weight of light viewers', *Admap* (June 1979), p. 277.
14. M. Johnson, 'Narrow-casting – problems and opportunities', *Admap* (June 1983).
15. See S. Lambert, *Channel 4* (London, British Film Institute, 1982).
16. *Independent Television Production: Finance and Dependency*, London Business School Report (December 1989).

Chapter 14

The first new media

Video, cable and satellite technologies, and their attendant communication novelties – ways of transmitting entertainment, words, pictures, data, voices and other services in huge variety, over vast distances, at ferocious speeds – have been discussed in such extravagant terms, and introduced with such little debate, that their wider social and economic implications have often been ignored. We are in danger of seeing emerging patterns as necessary, or, even more dangerously, as technologically determined, and accepting the consequences fatalistically.

Seventy-year-old audience habits have changed. The impact of these developments will go far beyond what people do with their leisure. There is also the likelihood of direct impact on political behaviour and institutions. Every previous innovation in communications, from the emergence of the mass circulation press through the development of radio and television, has profoundly altered not only how politics is understood in societies, but the nature of political negotiation itself. Such an immense set of changes as are now occurring will inevitably revolutionize political expectations, behaviour and institutions. We, as yet, can only speculate about the likely effects: but they will clearly influence the future of democracy. Yet we have seen thirty years of speculation driving policy. Audience behaviour has proved more stable.

Experts have been divided between the neophiliacs and the cultural pessimists. Neophiliacs write of the disappearance of class (by which they mean that traditional types of work will be replaced), the disappearance of workplaces (as the work-bench is supplanted by the home computer terminal) and the eventual relocation of the production process to the developing world as the management of information (about production and consumption) becomes the key commodity in the technologically advanced economies.

Such predictions seem premature. Neophiliac arguments bring to mind an earlier debate about the arrival of the 'post-industrial' society. Comments by Anthony Smith and John Howkins belong to the same tradition as Daniel Bell and Alain Touraine,[1] who argued that the expansion of the service sector, increasing expenditure on the production of knowledge, and ever larger investment in research, together with changes in the technologies of production and leisure, were creating a new social order. *Plus ça change:* as Krishan Kumar has argued, similar developments become apparent early in the history of industrialization, and do not represent any qualitative change.[2] Many of the neophiliac predictions of future patterns are based on naïve extrapolation from current trends, and ignore the idiosyncrasies of historical development.

The pessimists, on the other hand, see changes in mass commercial culture as a subversion of 'standards'. In the discussion of broadcasting technologies, the new 'cultural' pessimists, such as Nick Garnham and Richard Collins, joined hands with the 'industrial' pessimists, like Henry Braverman,[3] who shared concern over the impact of computer and information technology on employment. Thus, broadcasting becomes the fulcrum of a wider social and economic upheaval. The pessimists see little evidence for the emergence of new cultural patterns and much evidence for the irreparable damage to old ones.

In practice this 'revolution' represents the continued industrialization of the service sector. New technology performs old tasks more efficiently: in particular, the sorting, correlating and ordering of information in bureaucracies. Many of the current problems in broadcasting policy concern the next stage: the domestication of the computer.

Indeed, from both sides of the British political spectrum great, and perhaps unrealistic, hopes of industrial revival have been pinned on the exploitation of new communications technologies. On the one hand, those on the left have argued that the provision of a national cable network is similar to the laying down of the other great service infrastructures of industrial society: water, rail and road. It has been persuasively suggested that markets for goods and products increasingly exist not in physical space, but between those who are in contact via the networks of cable communication. Goods and services can be produced anywhere and to any specification with the complex exchange of data provided by cable facilities. It has thus been argued that the state should invest in a massive programme of cable provision in order to provoke a dramatic new regional and national economic revival. Advocates of this strategy point to the success of French governments' attempts to modernize communications. Using the notion of 'informatics', the French argued that access to, and understanding of, the most modern means of communication is part of being a contemporary citizen. Consequently, French policy makers have suggested that the state must educate the people and provide the means for the fullest possible public participation in this technology. The French government has also based its policy on the belief that the industrial possibilities of cable systems can only be developed if the technology is in the widest possible use. Thus, in France there has been a typically *'dirigiste'* development of cable and telephone services by the state, according to a clearly laid-down plan, with little room for liberal 'free market' principles.

However, those on the right have also been concerned to develop cable and computer services. Indeed, much broadcasting policy in the 1980s and 1990s was, as we shall see, directed at encouraging private, individual investment in cable and when this failed, it hoped to substitute satellite service. There has been no commitment in Britain to an extension of citizenship rights or knowledge. Indeed, the direction of broadcasting policy, which it might be argued should always be considered along with education, has been to exaggerate the divisions between groups of people. British broadcasting policy was previously based on the concept that it had to make the same rights available to all audiences, citizens, voters. This is no longer the case. Increasingly policy is based on one right only: the 'right' to pay for extra services. Thus, Conservative policy makers, while also emphasizing the importance of cable communication, have been prepared to reduce the access to information and services of most citizens in the belief that development could most efficiently be led by those who can pay for it.

There is also a key economic problem (a reflection of distinct patterns within the British economy) which influences policy decision within this area. The Conservative government during the 1980s, although it wished to encourage the private acquisition of cable television (so that the public would at least become a potential market for the other goods and services cable might offer), was also concerned, rather belatedly, with the provision of advanced communications to the financial and banking sector. So dominating was this interest in the British economy, that fulfilling its urgent needs for greatly expanded new information services became an overriding but unstated priority within government policy. Many of the decisions in this area were thus, covertly, determined by the perceived interests – or by the pressure exerted – by this sector of the economy.

The effects of the development of increasingly interdependent technologies of telephone, data and broadcasting services have all, in England, been used to diminish the democratic access to these services. Thus, traditionally, heavy (business) telephone users subsidized lighter (domestic) subscribers' long-distance calls, which tended to be shorter and less frequent. As the costs of communication became an ever more important item in commercial budgets, the pressure to reduce costs and to influence policy increased. Broadcasting policy, too, has been determined more by concerns to protect, for instance, the domestic electronics industry, than by an interest in the political and cultural obligations of broadcasting.

The problems posed by this kind of development are common to all countries. Few countries, however, have such strong broadcasting traditions as Britain, or have had such determined neophiliacs at the helm. When the Conservative government came to power in 1979 an official ideology of non-interference in the market was buttressed by a vigorously neophiliac view of information technology. A key Cabinet Information Technology Advisory Panel (ITAP), including experts in electronics and industrialists but nobody with any broadcasting experience, concluded that industrial revival was to be stimulated by 'cabling up' the nation. The necessary conditions for this economic miracle (a large proportion of homes linked to high-quality cable networks), it was argued, would best be created by providing an alluring range of television channels for the eager public. That these would inevitably offer a consistent diet of old films, sport, American soap opera and light entertainment was regarded as incidental.

In 1982 the committee urged the adoption not of North American models, but of the most sophisticated cabling system that would permit households to receive and use several hundred different channels. Thus the nation would be lured into the new infrastructure by stealth: having paid for cabling in order to receive more entertainment, television users would find themselves linked conveniently to a variety of multipurpose networks with opportunities for computerized shopping, working and learning. 'It is as if', one commentator suggested, 'the Roman Senate had sanctioned, without debate, the proposition that improvements to the supply system of the Roman legions should first be introduced by speeding up the chariots in the hippodrome'.[4]

So solid was the expectation of a virtually insatiable appetite for television, that official calculations were based on the assumption that the technological leap forward could be accomplished without support from public funds. Britain was the only country in Europe which expected the entire capital cost of laying a cable system to be paid for by the sellers and consumers of the recycled programmes and films. In West Germany, France and Japan, state investment in a comprehensive cable system became a major, and expanding, element in the annual budgets.

Apart from the problem of initial finance, there are other grounds for wondering whether neophiliac hopes are not premature. Thus, in the USA – where the success of cable had been seen as providing a model for Britain – the cable revolution seems to be failing, or at least stabilizing. In the last half of the 1980s more cable stations closed in the USA than opened.

Indeed, popular programmes aimed at mass audiences, supposedly the basis of cable expansion, have failed to find adequate markets. So far, where cable has succeeded commercially, there has been a price. In 1995 the most profitable American cable network offered its viewers a 'choice' of twenty movies repeated on a monthly basis.[5] The pressure of real or supposed mass taste has been inexorable: even in Manhattan, with its sophisticated viewers, CBS was forced to end the brief experiment of providing one quality station. Multi-channel television has since then taken off. In America pornography has been defined an issue of freedom of speech – and consequently given the protection of the Constitution in New York. One quarter of cable stations now offer pornography.

Indeed, in Britain there is an additional factor, more powerful than in the USA: video. The proportion of video-owning homes is already twice as great in Britain as in the USA and, despite the recession, video ownership continues to grow faster in Britain than in any other European countries. By 1995 most families possessed a video: a development not taken into account by official calculations earlier. Satellite TV at first took time to develop audiences: indeed it took the remaking of British football by Sky to really make the breakthrough into a mass medium. Oddly, by the twenty-first century the groups of interactors formerly known as audiences had become even more used to getting, and to playing with, free content. In some ways the BBC licence fee, for example, which is still very vulnerable in new ways, looked more exposed in the 1980s than it does now: free at the point of consumption is the modern internet way.

Unconstrained by the public service obligations, the first satellite station, Sky Television, owned by Rupert Murdoch, provided four channels pitched relentlessly at the supposedly popular tabloid market: a children's channel which offered nothing but cartoons, a film channel (for which, in addition to a dish, you have to buy a decoder), and two other channels showing replicas of exhausted formula programmes, mostly presented by familiar formula faces. This service so far has hardly added to the 'choice' the sovereign consumer could indulge in. Indeed, by buying up sports events it clearly diminishes public choice. So far, cable and satellite services have yet to be really successful here. In addition to these satellite services, Channel 5 was launched with radically simplified programme formats in 1997. These changes mean that the behaviour of the television audience as well as television production values and finance are bound to alter. Nevertheless, there is evidence that, in the battle for public viewing hours, these new 'viewing' opportunities face a more formidable task than had been expected. Certainly, in Britain there had been no cable 'revolution' by the start of the 1990s,[6] nor was a post-industrial society much in evidence.

The end of public service broadcasting?

Certainly satellite, cable and video in combination will accelerate the decline in audiences for existing networks: more viewing opportunities will mean fewer viewing hours. One change is a move away from 'family viewing'. Evidence from satellite television showed that, rather than arguing about what to watch together, family members were separating to watch different programmes. Thus, apparently, while fathers watch sport (in the sitting room), mothers are now relegated to viewing soap operas in the kitchen, while teenagers consume pop video channels in their bedrooms.[7] The take-up of satellite and video demonstrates that the public is willing to spend a higher proportion of its disposable income on entertainment, but this fragmentation of the audience has barely been explored by advertisers and its wider social implications have, as yet, hardly been considered. As ratings fall, financing programme content becomes more difficult. The range of quality programmes and perhaps even the possibility of innovative broadcasting may still be a victim. The public service ideal depends for its realization on funding. In the new, hyper-competitive climate, even advertisers, who had been so clamorous in their demands for more advertising time, were becoming anxious about the likely *over-supply* of time. As the White Paper on the Development of Cable Systems and Services pointed out, one hour of homegrown documentary could cost £20,000. By contrast, an hour of American soap opera could be bought for as little as £2000. One possibility, therefore, is a trend similar to that in the cinema of the 1940s and 1950s: fewer programmes made in Britain, and an ever-expanding proportion of imports.

Here, Thatcherite market liberalism had particularly disastrous effects. With the abolition of quotas for foreign programmes, there was little to restrain cable and satellite stations from importing much and commissioning little. With no rules to enforce a balanced diet of programming, the new stations naturally turned, like their American counterparts, to the lowest common denominator of pop, chat, soap and sport. Perhaps the wider range of viewing which satellite, cable and video provide will lead to an imaginative exercise by viewers of 'freedom of choice'. Existing evidence, however, suggests the opposite: audiences will not have the freedom to consume anything other than an even greater concentration of pop, chat, soap and sport than now.

If this analysis is correct, a shift of power within the networks is likely to follow. Where broadcasting is protected through subsidy, monopoly, or legislative requirements, producers can be given their head; where commercial pressures necessitate a heavy reliance on imported package deals and low-budget formula programming, producers will be reduced, in effect, to corporation men: executives carrying out company policy. With less money available, making fewer 'original' programmes, initiative will be at a low premium. In particular, there may be less incentive to make programmes about British subjects, political, social, or cultural, purely for domestic consumption. Indeed, it is ironic that much of the privately commissioned research for the satellite stations has shown just how wise the consumer is, and how badly served by neo-liberal belief in market forces. The public have found the existing satellite services repetitive, limited and based on-all-too familiar styles and formats. They also recognize that the BBC, ITV and Channel 4 offer a greater variety of programmes, and of course they still continue to watch far more of these than the satellite stations, albeit increasingly to their own schedules on video. Even in homes with high satellite or cable use, terrestrial television programmes are still key.

Some people do, of course, have specialist interests which satellite channels may serve. Nevertheless, so far the public remain more discriminating as a body of viewers than as newspaper readers. Yet, they seem oblivious to the likely disappearance of the services they value most. Under the current régime, market forces, not consumer interests, will come to determine programme making.

There is a further danger, or at least an area of uncertainty. Until recently the economics of television was determined by an invariable: people bought television sets to watch programmes put out by the networks. The relationship between programme maker and viewer, through the medium of a single-purpose instrument, and the role of public policy in regulating programme content, were based on this simple truth. The old relationship is rapidly weakening and soon will hold no more. Watching 'live' programmes ('live' in the sense of received from the ether) is already only one of the purposes of a television set. When it becomes increasingly common to use television not only for video, but also to make hotel reservations, monitor electricity consumption and place bets, 'live' viewing may become a comparatively minor factor in the calculations of those who buy, sell and produce television sets, with inevitable consequences for those who make programmes as well. At the same time, computers now offer broadcasting. The internet offers many services – the mix is altering. At the same time, the obligations of public policy become more difficult to define when the 'content' of television is no longer so evidently a single 'cultural' product.

Politics and new technology

There will also be consequences for politicians and political parties. Broadcasting, and especially television, has been a vehicle of political integration, establishing what Denis McQuail has called the 'common coin of values, ideas, information and cultural expression'. Arguably, television has set the political agenda: ordering public priorities and arousing public concern for good or ill.

Key to this process has been the national audience. The power of television has been based to a considerable degree on lack of choice: almost any nationally networked programme is certain to count its viewers in millions. Cable, video and satellite have increased the range of 'choice' without necessarily increasing variety or quality of subject matter (perhaps, as has been argued, reducing it). It was argued in the 1990s that a larger number of highly competitive commercial stations would fragment: the national audience would vanish. In fact, broadcasting still assembles national audiences around great events, and 'terrestrial' or national broadcasting has held on to much larger audiences than predicted. Indeed, we still need to avoid premature judgement. Such changes might have beneficial results or bad ones. Given the centrality of broadcasting to modern politics, however, it is virtually certain to alter the nature of the political game. Already some effects of increased 'choice' on political culture can be seen. Given the centrality of broadcasting to modern politics, however, it is virtually certain to alter the nature of the political game. Already some effects of increased 'choice' on political culture can be seen. The proliferation of news outlets has nevertheless lessened the impact of each. Moreover, as the press has sought to cover as many opinion bases as possible (through a wide variety of opinion columns) the political identity of the press has become, in some ways at least, more complicated. In the long run, this diminished authority will undoubtedly influence both the role and the standard of these newspapers. A similar process is taking place with television: the fragmentation of the national audience means that the significance of any one programme or channel has been greatly reduced. However, although in the 1980s audiences for a major news programme routinely reached 11 million viewers, and now ratings are usually nearer 3 million, nevertheless, over time, through 'watch again', downloads and so on, the accumulated audience is far greater. Moreover, no other medium has anything like the convening power of televison. All of these factors alter political influence: they do not get rid of it. It is important not to be confused here. It is not being suggested that the media will have less effect: just that their effects will be different.

These effects, however, remain speculative. Will national coverage be reduced in importance relative to local issues? Such a development might be positive. It might provide citizens with greater awareness of what affects them directly, and give more scope to local campaigns and pressure groups. On the other hand, the example of the existing local press gives little ground for optimism. Lack of initiative, cost, and the fear of writs have discouraged the vast majority of newspapers, including the big-circulation regional dailies, from acting as anything more than publishing houses for politicians' handouts.

If, therefore, a diversity of local television stations produces an increase in local political reporting, the benefits remain uncertain. What does seem likely is that the present 'privileged' status of news and documentary, which has been a prominent feature of public service television, will be eroded even further. Political coverage at least held its own as inter-channel competition increased: between 1956 and 1976 the time devoted to politics quadrupled on average. Channel 4 increased the variety and range of political programmes. But this trend began to be reversed in the late 1980s. During the 1992 general election, campaign coverage on the two major channels (BBC1 and ITV) was restricted to little more than a series of interviews with leading personalities: examination of campaign issues was relegated to BBC2 and Channel 4. Cable stations with small budgets and instant commercial targets are scarcely likely to widen the range or deepen the level of discussion. Indeed, for all its failings, television coverage of politics in Britain has been serious and sustained. As Scannell has argued, broadcast politics has widened access to political processes. Indeed, it may be argued that political programmes with the depth of reporting of the quality press (though with its definition of the limits of political discussion) are served out, for largely historical reasons to do with the public service origins of the BBC, to a *Sun*- and *Star*-buying public. Much recent research in the UK and the USA has shown the decline in time given to news, a fall in public interest in it – and especially, a marked decline in the provision of foreign news.[8] It seems likely that the commercial pressures of cable and video may ensure that, instead of deriving political information from television, large numbers of people will, in effect, be deprived of any reliable political information at all.

Even if there is no reduction in the time allotted to current affairs and documentary programmes, cuts in budgeting are bound to have a deleterious effect on quality and, in particular, originality. National and international reporting all too easily becomes a collaborative exposure of the viewpoint of the spokesman for a particular interest, provided that the interest in question has Establishment approval. The reason is cost as much as bias: investigative journalism, digging beneath the surface and asking uncomfortable questions, involves more time, resources and financial risk. Here competitive pressures are likely to be the enemy of imagination, professionalism, and above all, that which is controversial and radical.

Censorship

Some political effects of the new technology are speculative. Others are already frighteningly apparent. One development in the second category is the closing of doors which many had regarded as permanently unlocked: the reimposition of censorship in a new form, made the more dangerous because it is occurring in response to a public mood that owes much to fear of the new technology itself.

While dismantling 'public service' standards in broadcasting, and claiming to liberalize and free the system, the Thatcher government in fact presided over the introduction of an accumulation of supervisory quangos to control videos, satellite, cable and terrestrial broadcasting. All are concerned primarily with the exclusion of 'offensive' imagery. The movement started with the video recording bill. This introduced a system of bureaucratic pre-censorship of a kind unprecedented since Oliver Cromwell's 'licences of the press'. Ostensibly it was concerned with pornographic and violent home videos dubbed by the press as 'video nasties'. In practice the implications have been wider. The legislation set aside the earlier 'interpretative' view of screen images, held by the British Board of Film Censors (BBFC). This view was concerned with evaluating the meaning and intention of scenes, and emphasized that it was in context that any given act had to be judged. This view was replaced, in effect, with an index of prohibited acts. All videos have to be submitted to the board, and may be liable for censorship if they contain any material which deals with 'human sexual activity', 'images of human sexual organs' (potentially even if the films are made as part of training programmes for medical staff), or 'mutilation, torture, or other acts of gross violence' (like scenes of war and sporting events). Defence on the grounds of artistic or literary merit has been increasingly set aside.

Film censorship has a long, and in some respects a hilarious, history. The BBFC, however, had come to see its role as one of 'leading public taste as much as curbing it'. More recently, its board of nominees, for the first time directly appointed by the Home Office, has tended to apply specific standards of permissible and non-permissible sexual or violent acts. This style of regulation has come increasingly to determine considerations in all the other regulatory bodies. Thus, there has been a decisive shift in public policy towards the media: away from the encouragement of the good and towards the deletion of what government-appointed committees regard with distaste.

Perhaps the availability of unpleasant material to the public, especially young people, will be reduced by all these supervisory bodies. However, the history of censorship in general reveals little evidence of a beneficial effect on public morality or mental health. But whatever the possible benefits, the dangers of illiberalism are manifest: thus, for example, coverage of wars, deliberately and rightly intended to shock, may well be restricted.

Conclusion

Should we, therefore, side firmly with the cultural pessimists against the neophiliacs? The answer is that much depends on the behaviour of broadcasters and programme makers and, more particularly, governments, in the face of technological advance. Both neophiliacs and cultural pessimists emphasize the *power* of new technologies. Machines and inventions are not inherently powerful, nor is the use to which they are put inevitable. While the new technology brings with it many dangers, as well as many opportunities, its impact will depend crucially on how it is managed. We have now been through two episodes of technological brinkmanship, in which serious discussion has been stifled. All too often policy has been driven more by fantasy than realism. It has led to over-hyped and then over-extended telecommunications and IT industries.

Notes

1. See, for example, A. Smith 'The fading of an industrial age', in J. Curran, H. Smith and P. Wingate (eds) *Impacts and Influences* (London, Routledge, 1987).
2. K. Kumar, *Prophecy and Progress* (Harmondsworth, Penguin, 1978).
3. See, for example, R. Collins, N. Garnham and G. Locksley, *The Economics of Television* (London, Croom Helm, 1987).
4. *Parliamentary Information Review*, No. 2, Cable and Services (June 1988).
5. New York Cable Stations, 'Cable Digest: the Future of Film Channels', No. 3, (November 1995).
6. In societies where the state was prepared to take a more '*dirigiste*' role, like France and West Germany, the revolution was more advanced. See, for instance, G. Nowell Smith, *The European Experience* (London, British Film Institute, 1989); or Nick Costello, 'Telecommunication and cable in France, America and the UK', *European Commission Special Paper*, No. 3 (Jan. 1990).
7. MORI/NOP survey, *Satellite Television and Family Viewing* (January 1990).
8. See Steven Barnett, 'A small iceberg travelling south', report for the ITC, on broadcast news, 2001.

Chapter 15

Broadcasting roller-coaster

For most of the BBC's existence, the principle of 'public service' embodied in the 1926 Charter had not been the special preserve of the Corporation. Indeed, the idea that some organizations should operate for the public good and at the public expense was shared by all political parties, as well as the leaders of private industry and commerce, and ordinary voters. In the 1980s, however, the idea was strongly challenged for the first time. For broadcasters who had taken 'public service' for granted, life suddenly became uncomfortable.

One problem was the issue of political independence. Institutions like the BBC, whose *raison d'être* included the principle of impartiality, are never at ease with very ideological governments. Their distress becomes acute when there is only one party in office for a protracted period. In the case of public service broadcasting, it needs the threat of potential opposition power as a sabre to rattle warningly at governments. Yet, as the Conservative Party won one election after another from 1979 onwards, British politics became increasingly one-party rule. Indeed, the emergence of a coherent, highly ideological project for the transformation of British politics and society after 1982 put the BBC even more under threat.

The new Thatcherite project was highly individualistic: it argued that public interest could only be secured by maximizing the capacity of individuals to choose; and that government should seek to abandon controls, not exercise them. 'Deregulating', however, often had an ironic effect: a policy supposed to get government off people's backs often turned out, in practice, to be highly centralizing. Frequently, fiercely *dirigiste* measures of deregulation became instruments for delegitimizing, eradicating and diminishing any institution or organization that had alternative views. In addition, the project could be a politicizing one. The fashionable neo-liberal creed often ignored cultural constraints: like scientific socialism in a different era, it was over-rational.

'The New Right', as John Gray points out, 'failed to perceive the dependence of individualistic civil society on a dwindling but real patrimony of common ideas, beliefs and values'. In other words, the possibility of extreme individualism depended on the cultural, educational structures that formed active, independently minded individuals. Public service broadcasting had been founded precisely to shore up and improve the common store of ideas, values and knowledge. Thus, the story of public service broadcasting in the 1980s and 1990s had a far wider resonance than the question of whether people watch one chat show or another. It is a story of whether a plurality of voices can survive – and at what cost – in monolithic times.

Of course, the BBC and all responsible broadcasters always are, always have been, and always will be, worried about how to deal with politicians. The problem is that recently, handling politicians has become more important than making programmes, thinking of new programmes, relating creatively to audiences, or expressing what is going on within the nation. On the other hand, only if broadcasters abandon trying to provide a comprehensive and objective schedule, and opt instead for entertainment, will the pressures cease.

In turn, all politicians seek to influence, cajole, bully, manipulate and prejudice, if they can, how broadcasters deal with their affairs. Broadcasting is far too important to them for seemly good manners. Indeed, consideration of how the media will react is playing a larger part in political calculation than before. Policy, not just its presentation, is increasingly tuned to media reaction – despite, or perhaps because of, the declining capacity of media news organizations to interpret and process sophisticated news. In a sense, nobbling the media, however you do it, is just politics.

However, what marked out the 1980s was that political pressure assumed a new form. For the very first time since British broadcasting started in 1926, the issue became not merely what the BBC did, but whether it would survive at all. Indeed, to some members of the Conservative government, the BBC as an institution, and public service as an ideal, began to be seen as key obstacles to its attempt to revolutionize how Britain was run, and its ways of thinking. Public service was seen as the inefficient self-serving camouflage of groups who wanted to protect their own interests from the correcting force of competition. Mrs Thatcher put the case inimitably in her memoirs: 'Broadcasting was one of those areas – the professions, such as teaching, medicine and the law were others – in which special pleading by powerful interest groups was disguised as high minded commitment to some common good'.[1]

Regarding the BBC as an irritatingly arrogant, cosily protected establishment dinosaur, Thatcherites marked it down for eradication in the radical right cultural revolution. At first, Mrs Thatcher merely sought to harness two quite contradictory pressures to cure the BBC of the tendencies she objected to. The first consisted of the self-appointed moral regulators, such as Mrs Whitehouse's Viewers' and Listeners' Association, with vociferous support in the middlebrow press, who argued that television was to blame for a decline in morals in the country. Public service broadcasters, the Prime Minister put it, rephrasing the words of Adam Smith, 'were claiming the rights of poetry, but providing us with a push pin'. The second consisted of the commercial interests of her most influential supporters in the press, particularly those of Rupert Murdoch (whose name and organization, significantly, received no mention in her memoirs). Murdoch was interested in the profits that could be made if British television was 'deregulated'. This would make it easier for his present or future chances to succeed. As his deal with Tony Blair and the Labour Party showed in the run-up to the 1997 election, Murdoch liked to extract maximum commercial interest from his newspapers' political power. Mrs Thatcher, however, argued that increasing competition would lead to an improvement, 'raising' standards of taste and decency. This was an odd position, because everywhere else unregulated competition had tabloidized, coarsened and vulgarized broadcasting. Indeed, the Premiere showed a touching faith in Murdoch's capacity to raise standards – his previous contribution to halting moral decline having been the relaunch of the *Sun*.

Mrs Thatcher never saw much television, except when she was on it. However, her husband, who watched a lot, was widely reported to have given her daily resumés of its iniquities. But broadcasting happens to be almost the only industry which politicians ever see much of at work, as they slip in and out of studios. During Mrs Thatcher's premiership, College Green, a windswept triangle of grass with good shots of the Houses of Parliament behind it, virtually became part of the British, as yet unwritten constitution. College Green, and Millbank next to it, where the television stations broadcast much of their political reporting, increasingly took over from Parliament itself as the most critical area of public life, especially at times of crisis, the place where politicians hunt for attention, and journalists hunt for someone with an angle. Mrs Thatcher's observation of the television industry at work, 'too many men, too much waste!' fuelled her conviction that television embodied the hydra-headed enemy of British laxity: archaic union practices that preserved unnecessary jobs, and smug management. In contrast, print journalism caused the Conservative government few problems in the 1980s. In her first term of office, the Prime Minister gave knighthoods to the editors of the *Sun*, *Sunday Express* and *Daily Mail*. In return, these and other newspapers softened their criticism of the government and concentrated their attacks on its enemies – a novel interpretation of the duties of the fourth estate. One minister asked Mrs Thatcher about her favourable press, and she replied guilelessly, 'That's because I've been so kind to them'.[2] She did not think broadcasters treated her fairly, nor did she set out to be nice to them.

However, there were many other aspects of broadcasting that increased tension between broadcasters and politicians during the 1980s. The Prime Minister was angered by the sceptical ways in which some broadcasters dealt with her, and she believed they were promoting an out-of-date view of the contemporary world. Bernard Ingham, her abrasive No. 10 Press Secretary, called them (the broadcasters) – the Dimblebys and Elsteins – the unelected princelings of broadcasting. Less personally, but more provocatively, in practice, public service broadcasting was not merely any one organization – it was the product of a regulated market. In the regulated market the worst economic pressures to produce the cheapest programmes for the most viewers can be counterbalanced by the requirements to be impartial, to inform, to entertain and to educate, to match the audience share of the competition, and to secure licences to broadcast. Yet the guiding idea of the 1980s, and one that has survived Mrs Thatcher's departure, was that any market regulation impeded the proper outcome of market choice. The more sophisticated interpretation of choice, according to which regulation provides a wider variety of programmes for a wider variety of audiences, was anathema to governments for whom deregulation, privatization and the efficacy of market choice were the main instruments of reform and which had become, by the 1990s, ends in themselves. Thus the very basis of public service broadcasting made it peculiarly vulnerable to government attention.

However, it was inevitably politics that most inflamed the relationship. Sweeping government denunciations of the BBC's left-wing bias, and of alleged misreporting, and allegations against journalists, became routine. Individual presenters, television executives, journalists, particular items, and whole strands of coverage were targeted. The cumulative effects of such intimidation were profound. 'If the television of the western world uses its freedom continually to show all that is worst in our society', said Mrs Thatcher after the reporting of the riots of 1981, 'how can the uncommitted judge?'[3] As Hugo Young, in his biography of Mrs Thatcher, *One of Us*, argued: 'The less formal, but no less purposeful attacks, led by Mrs. Thatcher herself, on the BBC and other television broadcasters who threatened to loosen ministers' control over the agenda of the nation were ferocious'.

The Prime Minister's determination to reform broadcasting was given an added twist by the political challenges her government faced. First, she regard much of the BBC's reporting of the Falklands War (particularly the use, on news broadcasts, of the term 'the British troops', rather than 'our troops') as almost treasonable. She was incensed by a 1983 election phone-in which included tough questions by members of the public – as she wrote 'put up, not properly edited out' – about the conduct of the war, especially the sinking of the *Belgrano* (an Argentinian cruiser, sunk, controversially, within the exclusion zone around the Falklands while it was apparently attempting to leave the area). Above all there was the reporting of Northern Ireland.

Brian Wenham, an influential BBC programme maker and bureaucrat, contemplating the evidence about one programme, *Real Lives*, which caused an early prime-ministerial explosion, later observed that 'It was usually Ireland, it was usually the BBC, it was usually a row bigger, with more heads rolling, than you'd ever think possible'.[4] Eddie Mirzeoff, a senior BBC producer, talked about the pervasive self-censorship to which the rows led: 'the cost was always in programmes we did not make, ideas we dare not have'.

Certainly, the government's reaction to the BBC's handling of Northern Ireland was a major factor in the growing sense of panic within the BBC during the 1980s. It was, in part, a battle about unspecified constitutional rights. The BBC claimed, on the basis of its obligation to be impartial and to inform, the right to include Sinn Fein, the Protestant extremists and sometimes the IRA, as voices that needed to be heard, while the government claimed the political right to exclude from the BBC voices which they thought had to change in order to win a right to a voice. The government always interpreted exposure as endorsement. 'Publicity', said Mrs Thatcher famously, 'is the oxygen of terrorism'.

Mrs Thatcher often gave the impression that broadcasters existed to support her, correct, views. If they gave air time to other points of view they were, in effect, opposing her. As she had been elected and they had not, her views were legitimate, those of others were not. Impartiality – even over as intractable and complex an issue as Northern Ireland – was seen as a mischievous disguise for disloyalty. Time and again, broadcasters offended her over their handling of the issue: indeed, they were bound to. Mrs Thatcher's feelings on this issue need exploring, for they ran high. That they did so was understandable. Shortly after she was elected, the MP Airey Neave, a close friend and confidant since Mrs Thatcher had been an aspiring, unmarried young lawyer in the 1940s, was blown up by the Irish National Liberation Army (INLA), a splinter faction of the IRA. The BBC screened an interview with an INLA representative, who triumphantly boasted of the achievement. Many found the interview offensive, but revealing. Mrs Thatcher, mistakenly, saw it as support for INLA views. Later, in 1984, she and her husband survived an IRA bomb in the hotel in Brighton where she was staying for the Conservative Party conference. Perhaps not surprisingly, an intolerance of argument over Northern Ireland ossified into a narrow-minded zeal. Many observed that the bombing had profoundly changed her.

Thereafter, almost any television reporting in this area seemed to add to her fury. A number of incidents were interpreted as further evidence of subversion. There was the initial refusal of the BBC to hand over its film of the terrible mob lynching of two plain-clothes policemen; there were interviews with members of the IRA; there were attempts to include IRA and Protestant community political representatives in studio discussions; there were conflicts over a series of programmes – Real Lives, A Question of Ulster, Death on the Rock – which increased tension between broadcasters and politicians. After the Prime Minister had seen, and been enraged by, Real Lives, a programme which showed the 'everyday' lives and families of a Protestant and a Sinn Fein extremist, the Broadcasting Ban was imposed. This meant that when members of terrorist groups appeared on television, their voices could not be heard and actors had to read their words. This ban did nothing to reduce public interest in paramilitary personalities. It did, however, constitute a humiliation to the public service broadcasters, as it was little more than a visible badge of government power. It also meant that television executives did not make programmes about Northern Ireland if they could help it. However, the long-running Ulster saga did not go away, and its existence meant that government hostility to public service broadcasting continued to be underpinned by the Prime Minister's fierce passion about the issue.

In addition to this, the war on the 'complacent' public service tradition was ardently supported by a range of newspapers. The *News of the World* called the BBC 'The Boring Bonkers Corporation', the *Mail* said it was '(utterly) Biased (morally) Bankrupt and (politically) Corrupt'. The lead, however, in BBC bashing was provided by the *Sun*, *The Times* and the *Sunday Times*, shock troops of Thatcherism in its Maoist phase. The *Sun* described the BBC on one day as being 'Boring Old Auntie', and on the very next day accused it of 'Sleaze and Sluttery'. Broadcasting was attacked for loose morals, extravagance, fifth columnism and offending against public taste. *The Times*, for the first time since the abdication crisis, ran editorials on three consecutive days to the same theme: the inadequacy of the BBC. However, as newspapers, unlike MPs, are not required to declare an interest, none of these scions of Murdoch's News International felt called upon to mention that their proprietor happened to have growing ambitions for his satellite television stations. In every sphere, from the domestic British to the international market, the BBC and its World Service, and more generally the constraints of public service programming, with its emphasis on programme diversity and impartiality, stood in the way of News International. And indeed, anyone who stood in the way of the party most likely to deliver policies friendly to News International was also an enemy. As William Shawcross shows in his biography, Rupert Murdoch has little or no interest in news or programming, and while he routinely 'asset strips' news rooms, he has seldom invested in media content. His interest in politics tended to reflect the needs of his businesses: beyond that he was apolitical. Thus the News International campaigns against the existing broadcasting arrangements increased in parallel with the Corporation's interest in satellite. The *Sun*'s shrill demand that 'Aunty Must Go' was a pragmatic piece of commercial lobbying.

As if this fetid brew of political and economic hostility were not enough to seal the fate of the BBC, technological and social developments in satellite and cable broadcasting would have meant that any administration would have had to consider how to handle changes to what had been a relatively stable competition which had developed between ITV and the BBC over thirty years. Whatever happened, the 'duopoly' of public service broadcasters would have been bound to face considerable competitive challenge for audiences by the end of the decade. The adjustment, the possibilities, the role of 'public service' advantages in these changes were not inevitable. Different policies would have different outcomes, but a period of rapid and potentially difficult change was unavoidable.

Moreover, the era of public service broadcasting also seemed to have passed throughout the world. In many countries it appeared that 'public service' channels, of varying strengths and success, were being obliged to take on advertising, faced rapidly declining audience shares, and suffered a loss of authority. Even in sympathetic political climates, like those of Scandinavia and the old Commonwealth, public service broadcasters found it difficult to maintain distinctive broadcasting values. The sense of a regulated diet of programmes, even the sense of a scheduled progression of programmes and predictable audiences, looked as if it might fray or even disappear once the public had a larger choice of channels to choose from, and more things to do with their television sets.

All over the world in the 1980s, public service channels were being deregulated, and as a result saw their audiences collapse. Some even began to suggest that in any case the heyday of television had passed. The very peculiar capacity of the medium to assemble, address and touch the emotions of huge national audiences simultaneously seemed to be disappearing. Television had become one component of a huge entertainment industry that now included music, films, videos and the rapidly expanding computer market. Commentators began to suggest that television had lost its dominating cultural role. However, most people continued to watch television regularly. It was perhaps more accurate to say it was the power of the television corporations, the programmes and schedules which were changing.

Thus the alliance of political and commercial interests, arraigned against public service broadcasting in the mid-1980s, looked overwhelming. The radical ideas of right-wing think-tanks such as the Institute of Economic Affairs and the Adam Smith Institute, criticized for their extremism and impracticability in the early part of the decade, seemed positively mainstream and cautious later. In particular, they advocated the break-up of the BBC, the superiority of advertising revenue over licensing revenue, and the benefit of consumer 'choice' through increased channel availability. They argued that regulation was unnecessary, and praised the role of auctions in allocating commercial broadcasting licences. It was not just that the political climate had changed; everything that had previously been a source of protection for public service broadcasting suddenly made it vulnerable. The BBC was, as the decade progressed, under sustained commercial and political threat as never before.

Government attacks

How did the government go about 'dealing with the problem of the BBC' – the issue that Mrs Thatcher was so determined to address? The first line of attack was political. Part of the 'consensus' that Mrs Thatcher's administration set out to change was the idea that appointments to public bodies, such as the BBC's Board of Governors, should be more or less bipartisan. Prime ministers and home secretaries had, of course, liked to exercise choice in these appointments in the past. Thus, Harold Wilson had appointed the ITV Chairman, Charles Hill, as BBC Chairman in 1971 to bring the Corporation to heel. However, even Hill could not be regarded as a party political placement; he had been a Conservative, not a Labour minister.

The Conservative government believed that such delicacy on such a point was unnecessary, and indeed inefficient. If the BBC was to be encouraged to be friendly towards the government's project, you needed to be sure of the loyalty of those who ran it. Hence, during the 1980s, appointments to the BBC's Board of Governors became increasingly politicized. Qualified but unsympathetic candidates were not appointed, while ill-qualified ones were – a process of committee management which indeed applied to many other public bodies as well. Hugo Young, in his biography of Mrs Thatcher, quotes a colleague: 'Margaret usually asked "Is he one of us?" before approving an appointment'. It was the appointment of sympathetic chairmen of the Governors that gave the government its real power over the BBC. The first Chairman appointed by the new administration was Stuart Young, who happened to be the brother of a Conservative government minister. However, he showed signs of going native on the BBC. His successor, Marmaduke Hussey, was made of sterner stuff. Hussey, an ebullient Second World War veteran, had no background in broadcasting, had come straight from being the Chairman of Times Newspapers, where his confrontation with the unions had helped to change Fleet Street but had also led to the paper's being closed for a year. One of his qualifications may have been that he had worked for Murdoch and, in a sense, was unlikely therefore to cause Murdoch problems. A charming, forceful man, he saw his chairmanship as a full-time job to 'sort out the BBC'. Over the next decade, he oversaw all the major changes in the Corporation, brutally dismissed one director general, shabbily pushed aside the next, and appointed the third, John Birt, without even advertising the job or considering other candidates. Coming from newspapers, he treated the BBC, one critic remarked, 'rather as if he had owned it'. He was treated with a fearful deference by the Corporation until the end of his reign.

Hussey's influence was supposedly balanced by that of his deputy, Lord Joel Barnet, a former Labour Treasury minister who also chose to work at the BBC on a full-time basis. Barnet, however, accepted much of the Hussey diagnosis, and once even acknowledged that he did not, in practice, represent any difference in view from Hussey. Meanwhile, the Board of Governors, one critic commented, came to represent 'an unfortunate combination of low calibre and high prejudice'.

Of course, the 'packing' of boards, and in turn the administration of increasingly large tracts of contemporary life by committees and quangos rather than by elected government, had been an article of faith of the Conservative reforms. One argument was that there should be a move from 'representative' boards of directors, chosen because, however loosely, they stood for specific interests (in the BBC this might mean the regions, or writers, or women or educators) to so-called 'corporate boards', where individuals were selected on their merits. Well managed, this could be a useful development. In practice, however, it was taken to mean that members should be chosen for their adherence to an agenda. Indeed, against a background of mounting unease about the impact of some of these ideas on the quality of services, in 1994 the Nolan Committee on Standards in Public Life was asked to address the problem of whether the perceived bias in public appointments was a media-induced mirage – or a real issue. Nolan concluded that there was clear evidence of a political bias in those who had been appointed: '[I]ndividuals who are Conservative Party supporters, or whose companies donate to the Conservative Party, are more likely to be found on appointed boards, than those who support Labour or the Liberal Democrats'.[5] The report also recommended that when 'individuals had political interests they ought always to be declared'. The Committee recommended that an independent commissioner should oversee all such appointments. Nolan's 'public service' ethic incorporated the values of selflessness, integrity, objectivity, accountability, openness, honesty and leadership. In the case of the BBC there was evidence of direct interference in appointments to the Board of Governors and, perhaps more importantly than Nolan's virtuous criteria, individuals were nearly always selected for their compliance, and never for their independence.

With the Chairmanship in a safe pair of hands, and a politically packed Board of Governors, the government had a Trojan horse to take its policies right to the centre of the Corporation. There was a dramatic shift of power inside the BBC, with the Chairmen and the Board of Governors extending their power and interfering over an increasingly wide area. The Board of Governors is, constitutionally, the BBC, and as such has an immense authority within the Corporation: to have a Board that was hostile to everything the Corporation had done was deeply demoralizing. The first casualty was the independent-minded representative of an Olympian BBC tradition and elegant draughtsman of memoranda, the Director General, Alisdair Milne. In his memoirs Milne laid down his battle credits: a succession of brilliant, innovative programmes, whose object had been first, in *Tonight*, a hugely successful news magazine, to get on a level of conversation with viewers, and famously, in *TW3*, the pioneering satire show, 'to address, late on a Saturday night, people who are more aware of being persons and more aware of being citizens than at any other time of the week'. He had defined the job of Director General as being to engineer a harmonious relationship with the Chairman and, above all, 'to provide a climate of confidence in which programme makers can do their best work'.[6] Milne was certainly not able to achieve harmony with Hussey, nor was he able to control a sense of mounting hysteria in the BBC. Personality always plays a part in appointments and dismissals, and Milne and Hussey did not get on, partly for the good reason that Hussey regarded Milne as part of 'the problem' he had been sent in to sort out. Milne was peremptorily sacked. The first he knew of his departure was when, in a lunch break between meetings, Patricia Hodgson, the BBC's Secretary ('carved from deep frozen Oil of Ulay', according to one wit) used his Christian name – not the usual DG – in asking him to see Hussey, who disposed of him and told him to leave the building, in which he had worked for over thirty years, by tea-time. Milne was succeeded as Director General by Michael Checkland – an accountant who had never made a programme but who had nevertheless worked for the BBC for many years, and who was known for his prudent capacity to save money, and more interestingly, to save it to spend wisely on important projects. Checkland was finally replaced by John Birt, first as Deputy Director General, and then as his replacement. Mrs Thatcher's memoirs icily assert that 'the appointment of Duke Hussey, and later of John Birt, as Director General represented an improvement in every respect'. At last she apparently had her men in place.

During the late 1980s and 1990s it was widely believed that the Governors of the BBC were working behind the scenes to make programme makers not so much yield to government pressure as make it unnecessary. In many ways this was part of the new managerialism: managers and boards were not merely required to take hard decisions, but there was a macho pride to be taken in making these decisions as unpleasant as possible. In part, of course, this was merely an attempt to browbeat groups of people with values, or indeed the social capital of respect, into compliance. It was part of a far wider plan to limit the authority of professionals. However, it was also, in itself, an expression of the new orthodoxy: to manage properly, it had to hurt.

The second line of Conservative attack on the BBC was, of course, the licence fee. When there are periods of 'natural' revenue expansion, as when television ownership was increasing, or there was a switch to colour licences, when the BBC's funds increase because of a change in demand for its services, the Corporation has greater independence. There was no such natural increase in the 1980s, and television production costs were rising faster than general inflation. Thus, simply by not raising the licence fee, the government could impose savage cuts on the Corporation. Most prime ministers have probably warned the BBC's director generals that the licence fee would be cut. Most have not, in the end, meant it. During the 1980s and 1990s, the fee was eroded by a government that was intent on changing the nature of the BBC. Having abandoned its original ambition simply to abolish the Corporation, the government determined to exert its power, not only by interfering with the licence fee, but also by changing expectations, and radically altering the ecology of broadcasting institutions within which the BBC works. The aim was to change the kind of institution that the BBC aspired to be. Death by beheading was to be replaced by death by salami cuts. There had been no doubt, among politicians on both sides and in pressure groups, that the object of the 1990 Broadcasting Act had been intended to be the destruction of the BBC. The Peacock Report had not, much to Mrs Thatcher's chagrin, put advertisements on the BBC screens. By the late 1980s, as the next recession hit, the last thing any commercial station, or indeed even any advertiser, wanted was more broadcast advertising time; by the great recession of 2009–10 commercial televison was in considerable difficulty as advertising revenue leaked away to other media. Ironically, the loss of public service restraints had probably made it less, not more, attractive to audiences as well. Nevertheless, having been thwarted once, 'this time the feeling was', commented one politician, 'we'll get them'. The likelihood that the Corporation would disappear seemed high.

Survival or sea change?

Yet the BBC, despite the most determined onslaught it has ever faced, survived. The BBC was understandably reluctant to point out that it had won. It would not have been tactful. Yet, as Anthony Smith, one architect of Channel 4, remarked afterwards: 'It was a miracle. All the fire was deflected from the BBC on to ITV – the opposition got it'. And when the Broadcasting Act was finally passed it was indeed commercial television – the partner in a public service duopoly – that undoubtedly took the brunt of assault. Lord Thompson – a previous Chairman of the IBA – ruefully pointed out: 'When the BBC needed help, we gave it. But they kept their head down when we were under attack'. The campaign had been started by Brian Wenham's masterly organization of the BBC's evidence to the Peacock Committee. It developed through Extending Choice (that characteristic product of managerialism, the BBC's mission statement), through Producer Choice (the introduction of internal markets) and a continued process of management reorganization. The BBC ducked and weaved in every way it could, using reform both as an expedient political face saver, and sometimes as a real agent of necessary change. Thus, despite the strong pro-government bias on the Board of Governors (who seemed to dislike much of what the Corporation did, and who beguilingly claimed to be 'often too busy actually to watch television'), despite the animus of a very directed Prime Minister, and despite the pressure on revenue, the BBC survived. In this light, Hussey, Birt and all the rest are not villains but, on the contrary, heroes, doing what had to be done, or doing what had to be seen to be done, and radically propelling the BBC along the road to a real future.

But what BBC, for what purposes, and at what cost, survived? Most popular accounts of the reforms emphasize their costs and consequences. In two powerfully argued and sharply contrasting books, Chris Horrie and S. Clarke's *Fear and Loathing at the BBC*, and Steve Barnett and Andrew Curry's *The Battle for the BBC*,[7] it is suggested that at the very least the process of reform in the BBC was awkward, ruthless, inefficient, unhappy and self-destructive – and that, in the end, the Corporation only survived by voluntarily and lavishly doing to itself almost everything a hostile government wanted. Indeed, the debate is similar to one that recently raged among art historians, discussing the fate of much great medieval painting and sculpture during the Reformation, when previously sacred images were seen as idolatrous and attacked. It has been suggested that many great works were saved from the image breakers by being *slightly* defaced. A nose or an eye was sacrificed, say some, to save the whole. Others argue that, on the contrary, the sense and purpose of the whole was lost by the defacement and that afterwards the images simply decayed and fell apart. Is that what has happened at the BBC?

Another version of this account is that the quite horrible means by which the BBC secured change, the ruthless exclusion of alternative voices in the process, the application of management and production targets, the process by which, far from becoming less bureaucratic it has become (like many other institutions), it was asserted, far more top heavy, were all instituted not to make better programmes, but to deal with politics. Dissent, argument, creativity, such an account suggests, are the source of vigorous and creative programmes. Most people who have left the BBC now have little good to say for it. But then, on the other hand, their accounts may be biased.

Managers and the media

There is, first of all, no doubt that the organization needed an overhaul. A British Steel manager invited to talk to the BBC in the early 1980s said that he came away convinced that something had to change. The Corporation was over-bureaucratic, too large, too cumbersome. It did not, he added, feel like a modern, slim, confident organization.[8] Management was the big 1980s idea, and institutions, businesses and services throughout the nation were adjured to 'manage' themselves better.

However, the BBC had, in the past, been rather good at 'management'; indeed, when the Corporation was first set up, 'public service management' had itself been a huge innovation and was much praised and copied as a valuable new way of running an enterprise. Indeed, Ian MacIntyre in his biography points out that the first Director General, Reith, came to the BBC precisely as a manager, one with the highly relevant experience acquired on active service in the First World War, where his job had been to improve the quality of the hugely increased productivity of mass-produced American armaments factories. The BBC had grown fast, and gone on growing, because it was always an organization that took management seriously. On the other hand, 'management' within the Corporation was originally carefully separated from 'programmes'. 'Good Management', wrote Reith, 'is what is necessary to provide the conditions in which good programmes – far more important – can be made'.

During the early post-Second World War period, the BBC's response, both to staff shortages and to production problems, had been increasingly to assimilate wider aspects of the production process into the organization. The BBC had grown. Of course, the trend had been present since the BBC began, when, in order to have sound engineers or to build adequate transmitters, the Corporation had found that it had to train them itself: its problems were too specialized for the general level of technical training provided by the market.

However, with the emergence of television, the process accelerated. The BBC instigated make-up and make-up training, set-building, lighting, costume design, studio design, studio space and more and more engineering within the Corporation as it found it needed them. In so doing, the BBC both established production standards and became the main provider of training for the entire broadcasting industry. Although it could be argued that this had been an important infrastructure for broadcasting in Britain and that the industry was a vital one, nevertheless, as money got tighter, it became harder for the BBC to continue to be such a generous patron. The sense of an over-staffed, over-protected, over-bureaucratic corporation made the BBC vulnerable to calls for reform. But something had to change, it had become increasingly difficult to innovate – resources and money were used efficiently – but inflexibly.

However, one of the difficulties in analysing the impact of 1980s managerialism on the purpose and function of institutions like the BBC is that quite separate problems and solutions were deliberately confused in the project 'to manage better'. The first aim was to make sure that resources were used efficiently: this was often genuinely urgent. However, the second aim was to reduce dissent within organizations, while the third was to demonstrate that organizations were willing to be 'managed' better. In a rite of passage, it became a ritual of the Thatcherite cultural revolution that organizations like the BBC should admit their guilt, and perform acts of contrition and expiation before finally emerging, to use the fashionable managerial jargon, 're-tooled'. It was not merely that the BBC required direction and change, but that it was necessary that these should be seen to be difficult and that the end result should be a 'new' BBC.

The real problem, of course, is how you measure improvement in management in an organization like the BBC. As John Harvey Jones, the former Chairman of ICI and a prominent management 'guru' of the 1980s, pointed out, organizations have to change continually, and better management should mean greater scope for entrepreneurial innovation. But who are the 'entrepreneurs' in a broadcasting empire – the managers or the programme makers? Moreover, the BBC, like any large and old organization, has been perpetually reorganized ever since it was founded. In the early 1970s it had already undergone four major organizational changes in forty years. In the beginning, 'administration' had been firmly separated from programme making and output, and indeed the separation had become 'an article of faith', remaining as a convenient fiction as late as the 1970s. When Tom Burns talked to the top levels of the BBC hierarchy in the late 1960s for his book, several complained that 'Managers were seen by everyone else as lepers'. Managers and administration were still far less important than pro-grammes. It was still the roll-call of good, innovative, successful programmes that really ambitious broadcasting careers were made from. Burns reported one respondent as saying, 'Everybody in the Corporation, I suspect, sneak-ingly wants to get nearer and nearer to programmes, and I think, too, that one is always frightened as an administrator of stopping something'.[9] For the ambitious and driven, the pull, the gravitas in broadcasting was through making programmes, and remained so until the late 1980s. Yet the reality was changing. By then, the people who made programmes were far less important than the people who did the accounting for programmes.

Running a modern broadcasting organization almost inevitably develops a tension between industrialization and craft production. A great deal of tele-vision is in effect mass produced, falling into a narrow range of categories – sit-coms, game shows, chat shows, soap operas and so on. There are also other, more idiosyncratic kinds of programme. However, there is always pressure to reduce costs and standardize production. As we have seen, this became more acute during the 1980s. Nevertheless, within these constraints the challenge is to produce novel, intriguing, stimulating, fun, serious, enlightening programmes. Such creative products will always in part be a product of a culture, ways of thinking, a rewards system – what actually gets you on, and ultimately the kinds of personality that survive best in a system. Thus the question of creativity is never simply one of resources – although television is costly, in terms of both money and organizational needs. Nevertheless, the difference between good and indifferent programmes is one of giving permission and receiving encouragement.

However, one mounting pressure as the 1980s moved on was a sense not so much of permanent revolution as of permanent hysteria within the BBC. One young current affairs journalist, just down from Oxford, described it as 'a very volatile panicky place', where crises were always breaking out. Birt and Hussey calmed everything down.[10]

The BBC entered the process of being reformed with a naturally articulate and vociferous staff. The journalist recalled meetings in the BBC canteen at Lime Grove, an old labyrinthine building where news and current events were pro-duced, ripe with corners for conspiracies, 'where producers screamed and man-agement cowered'. Indeed, John Birt's initiation into the Lime Grove experience, confronting angry producers assembled to hear his plans, is said to have rocked him by its unrestrained hostility. He returned from the meeting determined to change the culture, no doubt to change the people and, while he was about it, to pull down the building – and to call in the management consultants.

Managers and management

The BBC called in four different firms of management consultants to oversee its reform during the late 1980s and 1990s. Such advice is not cheap. Such people do not make programmes. What do management consultants do? Ideally, they enable an organization to do what it does better, or they may help it to change what it does. This may be all very desirable and, as we have seen, the BBC may have needed something like it. However, management consultants tend, on the whole, to accentuate the role of managers. In a widget industry, managers, not workers, may be the people who create new opportunities for the firm. This is only partly true in broadcasting, where the people who make things make the opportunities. There was a radical shift in power within the BBC: what had been a producers' programme-led hierarchy became a management-led power structure.

Titles and salaries illustrate this trend. Thus, when an outstanding head of radio drama resigned, his job was replaced by that of a drama business unit manager. The change in title reflected a change in priorities, and a shift in the kinds of talents apparently required. Another indicator was that the salaries paid to the exhausting front-line current events and news personnel, who in a real sense are the BBC's 'face to the world', between 1980 and 1995 fell from having been equal to those of comparable managers to being less than one-third. Inevitably, management-led organizations recruit people who want to be managers.

The consultants, apart from harassing liberal-minded producers into line for the government, were also widely believed to be there less 'to make the organization run more efficiently', and more to increase the Director General's control over unruly troops. Certainly, one of the things management consultants can do is describe in apparently uncontestable, neutral and pseudo-technocratic terms, the apparently inevitable necessity of doing what those who call on them want. Yet, in order to meet the government's onslaught, greater discipline was necessary.

Management became increasingly fashionable and important during the 1980s. Many believed that better management was an instrument which could reform ailing British institutions and habits. Those in apparently radical think-tanks – such as Demos – endorsed the desirability of wholesale changes to the organization of institutions, and a steady stream of political pamphlets discussed efficiency, and how to measure outcomes. Indeed, for those organizations that were wealthy enough to measure what their impact was, it was a useful tool. 'Modernization' became synonymous with change brought in from outside an organization. The emphasis in whole rafts of social thinking moved from what kind of services were desirable to how they were to be delivered. Under this there was also – as is usual – a political change in emphasis. The 'new managerialism' substituted a legitimate concern for the efficiency of the process of production for an older and perhaps also legitimate question about distribution.

One of the problems in assessing the effect of these ideas was that there was an element of genuine utopianism in some of the thinking. Thus Charles Handy, a humane and liberal management guru, produced a series of ideas for the reform of organizations which he saw as both desirable for management and liberating for individuals. Later he was to ruefully acknowledge that their outcome – in practice – was often disastrous.

Some new principles of management were enthusiastically applied to enterprises everywhere. The first was the 'death of organization'. Handy had written that 'the telephone makes it possible for people to work together without being in the same place'.[11] He went on to consider the impact of communication changes and said that organizations, institutions, offices, careers, were all fast becoming irrelevant. It was not merely that commerce would become leaner – a new, radical division of labour should be developed. You could be liberated from the inflexible institution because its work would change more rapidly. Businesses should become increasingly 'federal', buying in and commissioning specialized work as they needed it: 'Life in more and more organizations is going to resemble a consultancy firm', he claimed. Handy's optimistic utopian vision of a new social order, with individuals freed from jobs and companies, and in charge of their own work destiny as never before, included a claim that in future hierarchies would be old hat, organizations would be 'flat'; workers, he claimed, would 'have a right to do their own things in their own way as long as it is in the common interest, that people need to be well informed, well intentioned and well educated in order to interpret their common interest'.

Handy's ideas suited the BBC well. The Corporation faced savage financial cuts, and the consequences of the 1990 Broadcasting Act – that it eventually commission 25 per cent of its programmes from outside the Corporation in the independent producers' sector. A plan for forcing through some drastic reorganization was needed and the new managerialism appeared to be one way forward. Such reform was also, no doubt, seductive, because, despite Handy's vision, delayering, federalist, re-tooled organization also happened to provide the upper of the hierarchies that survived with hugely increased powers.

Why did the BBC bother with all the management hoo-ha, and not just cut bits off? The benign interpretation is that management wanted to make sure it got rid of the right – that is, the worst – bits. The more sceptical view is that it wanted to legitimate what it did. The least attractive view is that, although there were endless meetings, guidelines, mission statements and flow charts, it had no clear vision of what a streamlined 'better' BBC would be like – except that it should be more docile and smaller; but perhaps it was trying to find out.

The process began slowly but gathered speed. Indeed, when Mrs Thatcher was replaced by decent Mr Major, the BBC juggernaut of reform went right on rolling. Part of the incentive for reform came from the need to cut production costs and to use plant and people more efficiently. This led to the 'TV Resource Study', which started from the assumption that regional BBC plant was under used and should be 'reorganized', i.e. that some of it should be shut down and that expensive London plant ought to be better used or disposed of. More to the point, perhaps, the management consultants suggested that 'plant', television studios and the resources and people should be utilized on a twenty-four hour-a-day, seven-day-a-week schedule. This plan, jauntily entitled 'The Twenty Four Hour Rolling News Day', claimed to be about a 'new concept in news readiness'. In fact, one critic claimed that its primary target was the rewriting of staff contracts. In the past, long hours had meant overtime payment; in the future they meant just that, long hours.

The structural supports now seen as 'irrelevant' or surplus were lopped wholesale. However, the problem was whether the way in which cuts were made was rational or even cost-effective. Expensive new Manchester studios were 'disposed' of before they even opened. Elstree Studios, tatty but fertile in programmes, were deemed to have the wrong image, and sold. But the 'TV Resource Study' was the place where the real motor of BBC reforms was invented. At first it was called the 'internal market', but a public relations alarm bell rang, and a special brainstorming session was set up to think of something better. It came up with 'Producers' Choice'.

This title, instantly recognizable as another example of 'Newspeak', sounded positive, programme centred, something you'd like to have. It did not sound like lots of meetings, lots of invoices and the 'wholesale transformation of perfectly good programme makers into second rate accountants', which is how one producer described it.[12]

'Producers' Choice' was intended, like the other artificial internal markets of the 1990s, to make costs transparent. In the past, not only had there been a good deal of cross-subsidization within budgets, but also many of the resources used in making programmes – studios, training and so on – had been paid for centrally. The new, stern philosophy in public affairs argued that this led to waste and extravagance because the true costs of using any resource were disguised. 'Producers' Choice' was supposed to make the real costs of making programmes apparent. However, it was also intended as a mechanism that would discreetly dispose of parts of the organization. So producers, having been allocated budgets, had to buy in the services they needed as cheaply as they could. That the real purpose of the exercise was to shut departments was made clear by the simple diktat that, while producers were encouraged to look outside the BBC for services, production departments were prohibited from trying to sell their services beyond the Corporation.

The trouble with artificially constructed internal markets – in all institutions – is that while they may drive down the costs of the central activity of the institution (replacing hips, teaching students, making programmes), they also require much of their resources to be spent on accounting and on monitoring financial systems. They redistribute resources away from the central activity. Producers (like teachers, nurses, doctors and so on) spent more of their time than was congenial, possibly a great deal more than was efficient, filling in forms and sending out invoices. Power usually flows from where the money is used – and so there was a further shift in power within the organization. In the early 1990s the staff magazine and the national press were full of BBC job advertisements: 'financial assistants', 'accountants', 'financial controllers' were much in demand. Many of the management consultants brought in from outside jumped ship and became BBC managers instead, not programme makers. Nevertheless, the reforms did deliver far greater resources back to programme makers in the end.

The second part of the agenda was to make the BBC more orderly. Was this a necessity in order to bring the Corporation into line with Conservative ideology so that it might survive, or did it, as some have claimed, bring about a collapse of traditional BBC values? John Harvey-Jones, the great industrialist, in his gospel of management *Making It Happen*, comments:

> 'our forebears have given our companies a tradition of open speaking and respect for differences of opinion which is, in my view, the most precious single inheritance we have. There is no way in which a vision of the future can be developed among a group of people unless they have a very high degree of toleration, and indeed enthusiasm for argument.[13]

Toleration was not a word that many felt characterized discussions in the BBC in the 1990s.

A guiding tenet of the new managerialism was that long-term careers within organizations are bad: not so much for people, but for organizations. Anyone who actually stays with an organization must be a dullard. People were supposed to hop from job to job. Indeed, there is now almost a cult of the 'outsider'. In the late 1960s, when Tom Burns was writing his book, most people within the BBC could think of their own long-term interests and those of the Corporation together. Although competition with ITV, and then Channel 4, gave individuals real freedom and flexibility, nevertheless they could focus ambition, groom experience, have expectations, and calculate.

During the 1990s, the BBC became a rich source of baroque fables about the impact of 'managerialism' on an articulate and competitive group of people and, moreover, a group well able to mobilize publicity on their own behalf. The conflict between the managers and staff often represented a battle about words. Language and the problems of its use had always taken a concrete form in broadcasting. Indeed, the early history of the medium was of the slow, cautious licensing of spoken ad-libbed speech, as opposed to scripted language. The use of scripts had been both a means of social and political control, ensuring that dangerous, untoward, or offensive things did not get said, and also a way of refining and attending to the impact of speech. Only very gradually were people's own voices and words permitted on air, legitimizing new points of view in public debate. Today, there is more unscripted broadcasting than ever. Nevertheless, the meaning and impact of language remains a vital and delicate part of broadcasting culture.

Words matter to journalists, and are what their work depends upon. As BBC journalists are not yet at the tabloid end of the market, they use words to describe, identify and discriminate.

Yet, one of the consequences of the new managerialism is the use of words for obfuscation rather than clarification. The use of words to disguise intention rather than to reveal it. It seemed to many that everything had to be translated into a new vocabulary: long-winded, tedious, pompous, technocratic. Journalists loathed the corrosion of words. A disgruntled wit called the new language 'Birtspeak'. It was easy to assume it had a purpose.

The management revolution at the BBC, as everywhere else, meant interminable meetings. It also created many examples of that newly fashionable ritual, the management 'away day'. This was accompanied by enforced *'joie d'esprit'* involving strange settings (once in a marquee, disconcertingly like a big top) which disguised the reality that real jobs, futures, the nature of the BBC, were all on the line. What gave rise to bitter jokes was the perverse distance between the ostensible intent and the manner of these events – the supposed 'open' discussion, 'exchange of views', jolly team-spirit building, and what was seen to be their real purpose, the identification and exclusion of opponents. Indeed, what journalists felt they reacted to was the undermining of language as a means of describing. Nevertheless, attention reality was refocused. If the first part of the project had been to save the Corporation from the government, the second was to re-engineer the BBC from within.

History and managers

Another aspect of 1980s managerialism was a contempt for history, and a cavalier rewriting of it. Of course, this may, in part, be necessary. The world changes: concern for how things were done may be an impediment to how they must now be done. On the other hand, institutions only really function at their best if people working in them want to do more rather than less than is necessary. Tradition and history – values even – and a pride in what has been done well can be invaluable stimulants to ambition. Institutions also have to remember their history so that they do not repeat their mistakes. The past can be a resource for the future, not just a hindrance to it.

Yet, within the BBC, 'looking back' was seen as being a characteristic of the 'old guard', the people who had run the Corporation in the inefficient past. To say why things had been done as they had, or to query the logic of innovation (for example, of spending a lot of time and money attempting to create a 'price' for studio time, when there was in no real sense a market for it) was to 'mark you down as a doomed, old-speak person', recalled one veteran. 'The past was a very dangerous place to mention', maintained another.[14]

But perhaps all the hostility to change was just part of a recurring romanticism about the past? Or perhaps the myth of a golden history is necessary to organizations like the BBC, where, unlike many industries, people ought not to be consensus minded. Being difficult (up to a point) may indeed be a very important part of good journalism.

Indeed, an organization like the BBC that has endured, and developed, always at the very edge of rapidly evolving technology, has a peculiar relationship with its own past. It is made all the more strange by the way in which it can *use* its past. Old programmes are continually reshown, readapted. The 'past' of the BBC is more visible than that of most firms, and the BBC's involvement in its audience's past is also complex. People remember events and themselves through what they saw or heard broadcast. Elaborating conservative tradition has been one way of handling dramatic technological change. Indeed, the fatigued sense that there has recently been too much change, which seems to characterize people working for the BBC, is a product not only of change – which the Corporation has always had to do – but of having to produce rationales as well as action.

The BBC shared this sense of 'too much change' with several other institutions. Indeed, those working in the Health Service, for example, just like those in the BBC, naturally have to deal with constant change because treatment is altering all the time. On the other hand, the core activity of other institutions, like education, that also complain of 'too much change' remains remarkably constant over time. But perhaps what all these services share is that they provide goods which cannot easily and perhaps ought not to be assessed by profitability. 'Good' broadcasting and 'good' education are not easy to measure – though we may feel quite secure about identifying them when we see them.

Nevertheless, the past's superiority is a recurring theme in the BBC's self-perception. When the Corporation moved out of its original, cramped offices on Savoy Hill in 1926, one broadcaster asserted that the old offices 'had been quite the most pleasant club in London'; before, he went on, 'all was intimacy and harmony. After, all was bureaucracy and conflict'. During the Second World War, one broadcasting official recalled 'the old, intimate, close days of pre-war broadcasting'; after it, others repined 'the urgent, close sense of purpose the war produced in the BBC'. Grace Wyndham Goldie, a doyenne of a whole generation of broadcasters and a stern innovator in political broadcasting, nevertheless said that 'the smaller BBC of the early 1950s meant that ideas flowed more freely'. Tom Burns pointed out that by the mid-1970s everyone he talked to in the BBC complained that it had recently become 'too big', yet in fact the Corporation had grown far less quickly than in the previous decade. By the 1990s, BBC employees were still saying that it was far too big, even though it had recently got much smaller. But, above all, they said that, in the past, working for the BBC had felt like a vocation; people were sometimes infuriated by it, but also proud of it as an idea and as a standard. Argument, they also claimed, had been allowed, encouraged and was not stoppable.

In the early 1990s, some distinguished voices expressed deep anxiety about the kind of place the Corporation was becoming. They were all the more impressive because none of them was under any threat: they mattered too much. Indeed, in different ways, they summed up, in the programmes they had made, the independence of their views, the accumulated concessions and stands they had taken and, in a creative authority, why public service broadcasting had been an important and exciting part of public and private life. David Attenborough, a great programme maker, and in his time a very distinguished BBC administrator, and Mark Tully, a legend in India, on which he had reported for years, argued that the BBC had become a hostile, demoralized, over-managed and secretive place. The dramatist Dennis Potter, in a scathing attack on Rupert Murdoch and the BBC at the Edinburgh Television Festival (1987), lamented the retreat of all television from innovative programme making.

Of course, the BBC culture is wordy, sarcastic, urbane, discontented, sometimes fashionable – and perhaps, properly, always likely to be disgruntled. Sniping, gossiping and griping are part of the atmosphere. Yet, in this period, the BBC, like many other managerialized institutions, became a feverish place, with the political pressure from outside transmuted into intense internal pressure. Perhaps again because, ultimately, the BBC makes ideas, trades in images, the impact of managers and their 'correct' and 'incorrect' ideas is felt more personally. 'I don't mind being told what to do by some chap in a suit who's never edited a programme', complained one BBC producer, 'but I'm buggered if I'm going to be told what to think'.[15]

Leaders

Part of the new managerialism of the 1980s was an importing of a kind of posturing ruthlessness. Everywhere, passengers, patients and those out on parole were renamed 'clients' in the public services. If Hussey was sent into the BBC by the Conservative government to bring it into line, John Birt was widely seen as his agent in the new tough mode.

Birt had been a very successful and innovative programme maker in the smaller but hugely fertile LWT. Trained as a scientist, one observer claimed that he thought in structures, and then tried to make the organization fit the ideas. He was, commented another, 'a facts and figures man'. Asked to speak about quality drama, he wanted evidence about numbers of plays shown, hours broadcast, percentages of viewers. Those who worked with him also commented that he was 'a rules man – his plan was always to decide on a "rule" and keep to it'. Privately energetic and charming, in public meetings, although always well prepared, he could, in the early days, be wooden, an odd mixture of shyness and bombast. He became more relaxed and confident as his tenure moved on. Yet arguably, the two previous, indisputably great Directors General – John Reith, and Hugh Greene in the 1960s – had both also often been accused of being overbearing and dictatorial. Greene was also a mischievous person. Both men combined aggressive style with a widely recognized – if not always approved of – image of what the BBC should do. Birt began his career at the BBC in the most difficult times the Corporation had ever experienced, but he did have a vision. He was subjected to a furious, unrestrained barrage of press opposition. At first, some sensed that he didn't particularly like the BBC. Roger Bolton, a former BBC producer and respected programme maker, wrote in the *Guardian*: 'The BBC has a deep and abiding hold on those who have worked for the Corporation'; he went on, 'The overwhelming impression given by those who now run the BBC is that they have no affection for it and for its past achievements, and no respect for its programme makers'. But then, some saw Bolton as a critic, in turn, with an axe to grind. Birt was, he would argue, focused on the future.

Simmering internal resentment, combined with a hawkish press, meant that Birt's every action was under media scrutiny. It didn't help that the twelfth Director General of the BBC got his job almost by fiat, and that able, respected competitors, like John Tusa, who had recently successfully reformed the prestigious World Service (and carried an enthusiastic staff with him), were told by Hussey that there was no point in applying. How he was appointed was not Birt's fault, but it made him look like the product of the kowtowing politics of the 1980s. What became known as 'Armani-Gate' also did damage. The title came from the Director General's preference for stylish designer suits. However, it shocked BBC employees (many of whom were now on short-term contracts and had recently been sternly warned by the rectitudinous Corporation that they must pay their taxes properly) when they discovered that the Director General himself apparently did not actually work for the Corporation. Instead, he was paid his salary through a holding company which permitted him to make a small – and indeed in the rest of broadcasting, routine – tax advantage. At the time it was as if a great British institution had been so undermined by the Conservative onslaught that those who were supposed to hold its future dearest were not committed to it.

Birt was saved as influential and objective commentators rallied to support him. Particularly important was a letter sent by senior journalists to the *Independent*, publicly backing him. 'Old axes are grinding', Polly Toynbee, Peter Jay and others wrote, and 'old scores are being settled in the attack on the Director General'. He was certainly helped by distinguished and, on the whole, left-wing members of the general committee. It was a delicate moment; Michael Checkland, the previous Director General, reduced a meeting to roars of appreciative laughter when he began a speech by quoting his BBC employee number. The problem was not whether Birt was or was not venal, but what people thought it meant for the BBC. Indeed, the incident may have been a turning point in showing that the public still cared quite passionately about the Corporation.

As the 1990s progressed the BBC calmed down. Perhaps this was because all the opposing voices had been shunted off, retired, or were too busy. Perhaps it was because political pressure from government and opposition had changed from volatile hysteria to a steady pressure of objections, attempts to arrange favourable news running order, lunches and telephone calls. Or perhaps it was because the BBC had been reformed and was more in control of its own agenda of change than in the volatile 1980s.

There was also a shift of power within the Corporation; Birt was even prepared to humiliate Hussey – soon to retire anyway. The Chairman, married to a lady-in-waiting to the Queen, was given no prior warning and was hugely embarrassed that the BBC had conducted a secret, and constitutionally damaging, deal with the Princess of Wales for a revenge interview to put her case against Prince Charles. It was seen by the BBC as a scoop – and it netted the Corporation a huge world audience. Whether it was proper, or properly conducted, or not, seemed to matter little. Certainly Hussey was ruthlessly sidelined as his influence waned.

By the 1990s, the BBC was undoubtedly more disciplined. Most important of all, it was producing some outstanding programmes. However, above all, under John Birt the BBC had, against all the odds, survived.

Who saved the BBC?

How was Mrs Thatcher thwarted? Part of the answer was just politics. There was an important element in her Cabinet who were determined to protect the BBC. Of these William Whitelaw was undoubtedly the most influential: no one could have been closer to her, making his determined opposition all the more effective. Whitelaw pointed out that when the Conservatives were in opposition in 1965 the BBC's Director General had been very determined to protect Conservative opposition interests against the then Labour government. It was a debt that was amply repaid. Whitelaw saw it as important evidence of the benefits of independent, impartial public service broadcasting.

'In a difficult field', he was to write, 'we should be most careful not to endanger what we have achieved'. Early on in government Whitelaw oversaw the implementation of a Labour plan, and introduced Channel 4. He remained a resourceful Cabinet player. Whitelaw had said, 'It's committee work and behind the door work, and respect that gets you what you want' and, almost in direct contradiction to his leader, concluded that 'I am always disturbed by talk of achieving higher standards in programmes at the same time as proposals are introduced leading to deregulation, and financial competition because I do not believe that they are basically compatible'.[16] Whitelaw knew what he didn't want, and traded his indispensability to the Prime Minister for it. After the early, lunatic faith that the Prime Minister held, that a technological transformation of Britain could be carried out on the backs of people's appetites for old movies, and after Rupert Murdoch had got everything he could wish for in terms of favourable policies for his new satellite station, Mrs Thatcher's attention also turned elsewhere.

The second factor was that, despite growing competition, people still liked watching BBC programmes. Popularity – and a sense that programmes

reflect and shape viewers' and listeners' interests, that there are some programmes at the edge of public opinion and pleasure – proves the most solid
defence for broadcasters. Yet, in the beginning, programmes seemed so very
removed from the heart of the new régime – and the fertile argument, and
sense of ideas flowing that encourage creativity, seemed so alien to the new,
neatly managed structure – that there was a fear that the Corporation had
been saved, but that quality broadcasting had not. There were continuous
and growing anxieties about radio, which worsened with the departure of
one of Birt's most respected appointees, Liz Forgan, from the post of Head of
Radio. She had left because the next stage in rationalization was to be the
creation of 'bi-medial departments', serving both radio and television. It was
feared that the specialized culture of, for example, children's television, or
the alternative news agenda of the World Service, would be lost. However, at
least by the mid-1990s, the argument was again about programmes.

One effect of the Broadcasting Act had been to create new opportunities
for all the people who could not bear the old broadcasting sector any more –
in the independent sector. Indeed, for at least one generation public service
broadcasting values (that you made programmes because they were important
and interesting and necessary) survived in the best of the independent companies. So the BBC exported values – and could import back programmes
made by its own kind of broadcaster.

The third factor was that the reforms cut costs at the BBC. However, huge
sums were wasted on the way. Early on, the producer's choice system was
discovered to be paying some costs twice, and money was 'lost' in the system
(malcontents grumbled that at least under the old scheme transferred funds
were spent on programmes, not 'lost'). Money was also mishandled in setting
up BBC Enterprises. This was a typical 1990s venture. The idea was that it
earned the BBC 'extra' revenue by exploiting BBC programmes. It cost more
than it ever brought in. Nevertheless, however ramshackle the process, a
leaner, more cost-conscious BBC did emerge.

Perhaps Birt was more in debt to all the dissidents than he realized. So vociferous was the campaign, as successive waves of reorganization cut swathes through
what journalists saw as central BBC ways of doing things, it certainly seemed that
the process was very painful. Loud complaints may, ironically, have served to
placate the government that the BBC was being reformed as it would wish.

Birt, and his team, managed to steer the Corporation through the greatest-
ever challenge to its existence. By the mid-1990s the BBC felt as if it was,
slightly grimly, on a course it understood. It is a story which may show how
flexible British establishment institutions can be. The BBC remained a
national and international institution; it had not, in the end, been fatally
politically compromised. It made good programmes. The public also actually
cared about it. It was Birt's particular capacity, in a way, to look forward,
and the Corporation began to prepare for how it might give a 'public service'
interpretation to the opportunities of digital television.

Public service can perhaps only be measured by what it is institutions agonize over. If you are only there to make a profit, everything is far simpler. Questions like *what do children need?*, *how ought the public to be informed about the election?*, *what new dramatists should be developed?*, *how do we reflect the debate about contemporary society?* and many others are simply not relevant in a commercial system. But they continue to be relevant in the BBC.[17]

Broadcasting in the twenty-first century

Indeed, by the beginning of the new millennium, the unthinkable had happened. The BBC emerged from two decades of political and technological (if not creative) turmoil as the strongest player on the British broadcasting scene and with an enhanced international presence.

At the start of the 1990s it had seemed possible that the Corporation was doomed to a twilight life of decreasing revenue, declining and fragmented audiences and enfeebled performance. At best it might expect a reduced role making programmes for élite minorities or worthy causes that commercial broadcasters would not touch because of their narrow appeal. The BBC, whose whole history has been one of combining popular and quality programming, would fade into insignificant mediocrity.

That this was its likely fate was all the clearer when what was happening elsewhere was taken into account. Other public service broadcasters all over the world had become pale shadows of their former selves. They had lost finance and clout. Even great national broadcasters like NBC in America had been eviscerated by a combination of deregulation, and a collapse in the will to protect information as a public good. Canadian public service broadcasting had lost monopoly rights, finance, and swiftly lost audience share: it was reduced to appealing for charitable funds from viewers to continue to make programmes. Australian public service broadcasting suffered a similar fate. A previously robust element of a broader commercial programme-making culture, public service barely survived either as an institution or as a set of values. Similarly RAE in Italy was reduced to a small, apologetic organization. Almost everywhere the story was the same. These precipitous declines were not inevitable but the predictable outcomes of broadcasting policy. On a more positive note, novel news services like CNN swiftly gained authority and reach in their reporting – yet CNN was more widely watched in the rest of the world than it was in America. All over the world, traditional public service broadcasters were in trouble – how could they survive here?

Meanwhile, throughout the 1990s, it was argued that 'broadcasting', or terrestrial broadcasting at least, was doomed by inexorable technological change (actually this was always talked about as if it were good; technology would promote progress). Experts confidently predicted that people would stop watching old-fashioned steam television, and that if they did watch it they would customize their programme choice from the huge range of new channels available. In any case, they would not be watching television or listening to the radio, because they would be too busy buying products and services off the net – or 'interacting' with it. The theorists of interactivity were very clear that this was absolutely novel, engrossing – and very superior to old, passive spectatorship. They dismissed any idea that when you look at a picture and are delighted by it, or read a novel and find yourself transported into the mind and understanding of characters within it, watch a drama and feel involved in the outcome of the story, or contemplate news with apprehension, you are altered by the experience. 'Interactivity' was, it was claimed, revolutionary.

Indeed, the main concern throughout the 1990s was the means of delivery of new services and not their content. Indeed, content delivery was changing; by 2002 nearly 40 per cent of British homes had access to cable or satellite television. Meanwhile sports, especially football, had been transformed as money was pumped into them in order, at least in part, to develop exclusive access to attract viewers to the new services. Of course, there were profound changes in audiences' behaviour. People spent time in the new sociabilities of the net, they spent time on video games and watched videos. Indeed, many movies began to look increasingly like video games, and were often made as much for the home video market as for public display. Evidence from the Independent Television Commission showed that multi-channel households watched a variety of offers, and browsed through entertainment opportunities more freely. There was some evidence that the multi-channel homes (that might soon be in the majority) did not watch television collectively, and watched television slightly less, overall, than previous generations. Younger people in a period of great affluence went to the cinema more.

Yet people went on watching television in far greater numbers and for far more of the time than had been predicted at the start of the new technological revolution. Moreover, the majority of them continued to watch terrestrial channels (however they received them) more than any other channels. Channel 5 – originally given very light regulation because it was not expected to last more than a few years – grew into a serious competitor for ITV. (The light-touch regulation made it attractive to buyers who saw it as a way to tabloidize the television market.) Channel 4 went from strength to strength in the 1990s. ITV, saddled with huge auction bids to pay off, lacking the regional tension that had once made it so creative, and having made many mistakes on its way to the new digital channels, began to have more acute problems. When the long boom of the 1990s stuttered to a halt, all the commercial broadcasters faced severe adjustments as advertising revenues collapsed. But these problems were trivial in comparison to a stark and unexpected reality: people still liked watching television for the same kinds of reasons that they had liked watching it in the past. Most startling of all, the BBC survived, flourished and became (for the moment at least) the dominant player. It was a remarkable outcome.

Partly it was the product of a frequently ignored problem – that of content. Despite the huge attractions of sports channels, which soon bought up all sorts of events and privatized them (and outpriced the terrestrial stations), and children's channels that offered a reliable diet of cartoons, steam television still made new programmes that people wanted to see – and imported the best of foreign production. In the case of the BBC the outcome was largely a vindication of the Birt–Hussey reforms. Together with an astute, well-prepared move into digital, the BBC offered new services that led people into a new era of broadcasting and information. BBC World, from a shaky and unconvincing start, improved and began to grow into an authoritative new international presence. The BBC website received more hits than any other in the UK: the BBC was again a persuasive representative of the nation all over the world. Ultimately, broadcasting services confounded the pessimists because they were still able to touch audience tastes, pleasures and hopes.

Yet broadcasters were also able to exploit a political and regulatory régime which – in the end – supported them. The public takes its leisure for granted, yet even fans enjoying their passion depend on structures of broadcasting that are politically determined. This is as true of wholly commercial systems of broadcasting as of those with a public service component. These political realities cannot alter the terms of international broadcasting trade – but they can modify their impact if there is the will to do so.

Nevertheless, the ideals of public service broadcasting were under powerful new strains. News, especially, suffered from many challenges. Rolling 'live' news is more vulnerable to unsubstantiated rumour than the old, slower kind. 'Representing' the nation is more complex, for you must find, for example, the 'representative' Muslim voices (not just the excitingly news-worthy extremist ones) – and broadcasters have to be acutely aware across a whole landscape of political interest. Audiences, through the long, comfortable boom years perhaps felt little to threaten them, and were less interested in threats to other people's safety, in the new, complicated international disorder of the post-Cold War world. As the press reacted to the dominance of broadcasting and became more campaigning and opinionated (and less concerned with news as such, which the broadcasters could do better), this in turn reflected back on broadcasters – who, despite their dominance, still seem to find it hard to establish independent news agendas. In America broadcast news has become more like the press: more partisan, less impartial. It is rather disturbing to watch – but many argue that it is the way forward for news. In addition, much political coverage seems to operate in a simple – and misleading – moral universe of rights and wrongs. As successful political negotiation always deals with making painful concession about strongly felt interests, the very basis of democratic politics is all too often traduced. In particular, the idea of politics as a discussion about genuinely difficult-to-resolve issues is being lost.

Legislation, technological change and evolving audience habits could swiftly alter the broadcasting landscape again. There is no divine right to broadcast. Yet, despite the threats and the problems – and the alternatives – we still seem to like it. Perhaps, grudgingly and almost unconsciously, we value broadcasting as part of a national conversation: it still remains a mirror we hold up to our increasingly diverse selves.

The BBC: an imperfect beauty

The problem with all of the media industries is that they are politically and socially very important indeed and economically of the middling rank. The asymmetry is more threatening now that they are all so international. If they are doing their work properly they act like a kind of antibiotic in public life – keeping the system clean. But this is in the public interest – not necessarily of any concern to the businesses that run them. The media are also like the canary that used to be kept in a cage in the mines – sensitive to foulness, they and their condition offer an early-warning system of political dangers. 'Broadcasting' driven by public service values has been an especial feature of the British media ecology. But it is in some ways under the most serious threat since the challenges of the 1980s. Increasingly. it is clear that many of the valuable producers of media content all over the world depend on some kind of 'gift'. Al-Jazeera was launched with one, the BBC has the licence fee. But they also have to be forged by intense competition. In the digital world, when – for example – research shows that the consumption of news programmes drops by almost 40 per cent, keeping the public attention is about as difficult as it gets.

For the first sixty years of its existence the threat to the BBC was political. Now it faces even more formidable foes: huge, rapacious, rich, multinational information/entertainment empires that see it as an inconvenient competitor which they would simply like out of the way. These are able to wield greater power because governments are more economically 'liberal', less willing and less able to protect public services. Behind closed government doors, and in the corridors of the regulators, in international regulatory venues, beyond the public eye, these commercial interests argue – often successfully – for their own interests. Indeed, while it is possible to have a clear battle with a political party, commercial interests are far harder for the Corporation (and those who seek to support public service values) to fight against: the public often does not like the pressure a government exercises on a broadcaster, but hardly thinks of the media conglomerates.

In America, there are public service ideals in the media – but no institutions to put them into practice. 'Public' values reside more in the press in the states – yet the newspaper industry is in severe collapse. President Reagan's abolition of the 'fairness doctrine' in 1988 (which had required political balance of broadcasters) led directly to this emaciation of public discussion in broadcasting. It has led to an American public ignorance that has squandered the authority of its 'soft' power, with consequences for the whole world. In Britain and Europe we have the institutions (although we barely value them or their practitioners), but will we permit them to innovate sufficiently to survive, if they can?

The BBC is an institution: it has been a broadcaster, it generates all kinds of content, it is many other practical things (the inventor, for example, of well-informed and expert help lines). But, most importantly, it is a set of values embodied in considered and evolving practices which it can use to re-engineer public life in the interests of the public. In this way content and public service content (which is not just a rump of glum, improving material, but the whole range of 'information, education and entertainment') is a habit of mind that has done much to change and mould – largely for the better British life. David Hendy's funny, witty, wise and gloriously imaginative account of Radio 4, *Life on Air*[18] answers the question of why the audience for a unique radio station found it 'stitched into the very fabric of their being', but in a larger way the BBC is part of the British unwritten constitution.

The BBC was not and never has been a 'state' broadcaster (although its relationship to the state is more complex than it looks at first sight). The 'licence fee' (a regressive poll tax, or a hypothecated tax of the kind most people resent) on the right to receive radio signals, gave it an income separate from a state grant. It was a brilliant invention because the BBC has never been like a department of state, precisely because of its separate finances. Like many British constitutional arrangements, this independence is a fuzzy, indistinct notion. Governments set the level of the licence fee. However, whatever its imperfections, the licence fee has been a real constitutional prop. The BBC had its own income. Indeed, as technological innovation and audiences grew there have been times when the income has grown quite separately from government control. Of course, now we have an institution – the BBC – the means of financing of which, new technology may make impossible.

In addition to an income, there were other constitutional niceties that protected the BBC from undue political pressure, up to a point. That politicians have sought to bring pressure onto the BBC is not the issue: how the BBC, and indeed politicians, have handled the pressure is what has mattered. The BBC is independent from any particular government – and indeed has particularly onerous responsibilities – because it outlives them all. But the BBC is an institution which, in some sense, has to pursue the same objectives as the state, and it has undoubtedly been one of the mechanisms that has kept politics decent. In turn, of course, it has been bullied, harassed, charmed, wheedled, chivvied, threatened and argued with by all governments. While there is little or no public discussion as to whether the press is reasonable or how it spends money, there is a heated debate, over all of these matters, about the BBC, and this in itself is a public good (even if the overwhelming hostility of the press increasingly represents the interests of commercial competitors).

However, the BBC time and time again has also negotiated with the British state – on the basis that there were some things it understood better than the political classes. This is most apparent in news and foreign broadcasting, when the Corporation has often felt that it has an especial expertise in understanding the 'hearts and minds' of audiences. Time and again the World Service has gone out and brought its understanding of the temper and views of foreign audiences to bear on government attempts to influence those audiences – not, it has to be said, always successfully. Nevertheless, the BBC has behaved as an expert and influential co-worker. On many domestic issues as well, from how to tackle teenage pregnancy (in soap operas or dramas), to how to approach great, state public crises, terrorist attacks, and Princess Diana's funeral, the BBC has brought a special expertise to the task. The BBC has not been a client of the state but an independent dealer with it.

This is one reason why we argue our mores and principles out in public over it. The *Daily Mail* (which has a higher proportion of BBC consumers in its readership than any other newspaper) quite often rails against it. But then the BBC is a place where the colliding morality of young and old fight it out. It often gets things wrong – sometimes casually, sometimes it makes the wrong choices carefully, but at least we can interrogate those decisions in public.

Ever since John Birt and his team made the counter-intuitive but visionary choice to put BBC content out on all platforms, the Corporation has been a leading market maker in technological innovation. The British public has taken to down-loading, I-playing, 'watching again' with enthusiasm. Conventional watching and scheduling are evaporating – but once the BBC has made a market, other commercial players want a slice of it. Although some have argued that the licence fee is peculiarly vulnerable in a multi-channel digital world, nevertheless the notion of content free at the point of consumption (which is what the licence fee provides) is actually very contemporary. In any case, the licence fee was never rational, it just worked, and has been preserved by political will. If the BBC goes, then that will have been a political, not a commercial decision. One attempt to answer the 'accountability' problem that some argued was the Corporation's weakness was to replace the BBC Governors – a mysteriously British institution – in 2007 with the BBC Trust. This body was set up to articulate more clearly the interest of the public. Actually, it has worked rather more flexibly and intelligently than many critics thought that it would, yet it too finds it difficult to speak 'for' the BBC. So the BBC combines a large, powerful, at times overwhelming voice with an incapacity to speak for itself. This may become more of a problem.

The BBC has become a world exporter of 'impartiality' and, more importantly, 'objectivity'. This is a very simple principle, important in news but with a wide, cultural reach: the ambition is to describe the world as it is, not through pre-set ideological blinkers of any kind. In news, you do it through attending to all sides, in culture you do it by creatively permitting a variety of truths to be expressed with all the fluency that can be mustered. In the old days, you were being impartial if you 'balanced' a 'left'-wing point of view with a 'right'-wing one, and the BBC could (and did) often argue that if both 'sides' complained, it was doing its job. If the nation is uncomfortable, then that makes things more demanding for the Corporation. As one BBC Chairman put it, 'A Nation on the rack puts the BBC on the rack'. Now, on almost any issue, there are many more varied opinions, and Britain is a more diverse society – with powerful, globally linked communities.

A recent BBC report attempting to grapple with multi-ethnic, multi-world connected audiences argued that now there was a 'wagon wheel' of contemporary, contending views. 'Impartiality', however, is testing work and not about being in the 'centre'. Thus, for example, one BBC news executive added a useful idea – that of 'hard impartiality', a robust determination to report what is happening, not what audiences or authorities are comfortable with. Thus, there should be no impediment to exploring and displaying the most alien of views, including those of our 'enemies' (or, one might say, especially our enemies) in any conflict. Thus, a report by David Loyn on the Taliban's changing tactics, from inside the group, by an 'embedded' reporter, which showed the Taliban as a group with political intelligence and indeed developing policy, was a perfect example of proper journalism in this tradition: despite some cries of treason, it told citizens what they needed to know, in the classic public service tradition. Yet 'impartiality' is often treated as if it were a thing, or a goal. It is neither: it is merely a tool, a sceptical injunction to avoid *a priori* assumptions. It also means that audiences trust a source which they know is not lecturing them for its own purposes, in which they can see their own views, but in which they are also exposed to other views and may come to appreciate them.

'Objectivity' is more important, as it demands judgement, not a weak 'balancing' of views. A proper journalist in a hard place has to come to a judgement of what is going on there. But, in turn, judgement does not mean campaigning. These are vital arguments and delicate decisions to make in a very opinionated but not very informed world. So we can demand that the BBC is impartial but that it uses this on the way to better judgements.

Freedom of speech is a lovely, buxom, bountiful idea about holding the court of opinion open: and this is also an issue for the BBC. Thus, another duty of public service news and other kinds of content is to provide a forum for the wide variety of views that exist. It is especially important in contemporary societies. You are bound into a society where your views and position are given a hearing. However, while public service ought to report and respect the sincerity of views, neither the strength of the belief, nor the authenticity of the believers, nor the fashionableness of the ideas are sufficient grounds for a capitulation of judgement. An objective report is likely to have been tempered by and adjusted to the widest possible range of views, yet reporting is not excused, by the process of consulting a variety of views, from the obligation to account for the world as accurately as it can. Creationists ardently believe what they claim to be the origins of the world, there are a lot of them about, they have all sorts of consequences in schools, we all need to know what they are saying and why. They certainly have a right to say what they want to. But the BBC does not fulfil its obligations if it is 'impartial' between the well-founded scientific evidence of evolutionists and the sincere beliefs of creationists. Nor is the formulation that it often seems to use, 'creationists believe' and 'scientists believe', acceptable. Scientists do not 'believe' their findings – their relationship to them depends on several thousand years of rational enquiry. Of course, sometimes scientists hold misunderstandings – but these are correctable by their own processes. Thus, the BBC must apply objectivity. But it must also hold the forum open to views that many find unpalatable.

In a rather direct way, the BBC is the inheritor of a great British pragmatic philosophical tradition – that of the utilitarian John Stuart Mill. Mill's elegant thought is simple, the argument is organic and it improves and grows. Arguments do not arrive at the table as fully formed, as they can be formed by interaction with other arguments. Arguments are not 'commodities' to be 'bought', nor are they armies that 'win' because they are the strongest. Rather, they are creative instruments of exploring and developing improved solutions. The BBC's respect for its audience and place in the analysis and interrogation of the world requires it to have and implement just such a view of ideas and solutions: that the cauldron of argument is the place to grow discussion.

The BBC is an engine of the mind. It has become a national treasure and world resource because it has been given the creative freedom and political responsibility to attract audiences, tell the truth and be playful. Even if it sometimes fails to adhere perfectly to its principles, at the very least we can argue that it should try harder. That it is 'ours', it belongs to us all, not its shareholders, is also part of its glory. Indeed, not only has it lasted longer than many media organizations, more significantly, it has constantly changed, yet in doing so has reimagined enduring social and political values and made them sparklingly relevant to shifting history. In doing so it has become a world by-word for reliability. Moreover, it has, over time, got it more right (and worried about getting it right) than most other organizations – and the public understand this. Indeed, the BBC is possibly more famous than Britain, more accepted all over the world, and as vulnerable as it has ever been.

Thus, in shanty suburbs of Addis Ababa and out in Ethiopia's rural villages, where there is a café there is a television which people pay small sums to watch. Standing in the smoky haze of freshly roasting coffee, one journalist recently saw the locals watching the war in Afghanistan on the BBC. In the middle of a refugee camp in the horror of war in Southern Sudan, an anthropologist friend saw a television powered by a generator, Ethiopians enthusiastically engaged in watching an Arsenal game on the BBC. Meanwhile, in America this summer, in Williamsburg in Brooklyn, New York, while sitting in the café with my cappuccino, I realized that two adjacent lap-tops, (each accessorised by an achingly fashionable youth), were checking the news on the BBC website. This is simply because the BBC has become one of the world's great objectivity traders. Such assets are very precious, very few in number, and are endangered in any number of ways.

How has the BBC survived? The Corporation has been repeatedly saved by three allies. First and most important, paradoxically, have been governments. They have often had rows and threatened the BBC, but nevertheless, in the last instance, governments of all political complexions have recognized something in the BBC which operated in the interests of public life. Politicians and politics are more beleaguered now than ever before. For nearly twenty years, governments all over the western world have been outsourcing political decisions: finding themselves unpopular, they have sought to divest themselves of power. However, it is probably to politicians that we must look still for engineering the solutions to the survival of values.

Second, public service broadcasting has been protected by a network of impartial institutions: impartiality is highly valued yet under tremendous threat. The British civil service has, time after time, gone out and adjusted the machinery appropriately to do its best to protect a service that it has understood is based on compatible principles. The regulatory bodies that we now have in place, both nationally and internationally do not always interpret their job properly. In America, the regulator is part of the problem. It has collaborated with the impoverishment of public discussion. Regulators today often have marvellously clean and tidy economic objectives; they have aims and principles, targets and standards by the cartload – yet running a creative institution is about independence to get on with the difficult job of inventiveness. Are the regulators working? They have taken over the nasty political work and turned it into the clean laundry of economic models. But, given the technological and social challenges, are they adequate?

Then there is the public. Being popular and valued has been the best political strategy for survival. However, this is more difficult to achieve, and when it is achieved, as we have often seen, the opposition ignores it. Technology is like a whirlwind, remaking public life and public expression (as well as overturning economic models for information and cultural creativity at a break-neck speed) in magnificent new ways. The BBC will survive – or not – if it continues to weave itself into our everyday lives and our aspirations – and if, we the public, value it.

Notes

1. Margaret Thatcher, *The Downing Street Years* (London, HarperCollins, 1995), p. 210.
2. Hugo Young, *One of Us* (London, Cape, 1992), p. 510.

3. Mrs Thatcher, speech to the Parliamentary Press Gallery, 11 July 1981.
4. Institute of Contemporary British History, 'Witness Seminar', *Real Lives* (February 1995).
5. *The Nolan Report on Standards in Public Life*, Cmnd 2850, 1995, 1, para. 70.
6. Alisdair Milne, *Director General: The Memoirs of a British Broadcaster* (London, Hodder & Stoughton, 1988), p. 74.
7. Steve Barnett and Andrew Curry, *The Battle for the BBC: A British Broadcasting Conspiracy* (London, The Aurum Press, 1994); Chris Horrie and S. Clarke, *Fuzzy Monsters: Fear and Loathing at the BBC* (London, Heinemann, 1994).
8. Interview with Chris Beauman.
9. Tom Burns, *The BBC: Public Institution and Private World* (Basingstoke, Macmillan, 1977), p. 43.
10. Author interview.
11. C. Handy, 'Balancing corporate power: a new Federalist paper', *Harvard Business Review*, 1992, p. 572.
12. Author interview.
13. J. Harvey-Jones, *Making it Happen* (London, HarperCollins, 1991).
14. Author interview.
15. Quoted in Barnett and Curry, *The Battle for the BBC*, p. 219.
16. William Whitelaw, *The Whitelaw Memoirs* (London, The Aurum Press, 1989), p. 285.
17. This chapter is based on a number of confidential interviews with policy makers, broadcasters and politicians.
18. David Hendy, *Life on Air* (Oxford, Oxford University Press, 2007).

Part III

Rise of new media

Chapter 16

New media in Britain

Introduction

The rhythm of change in the media does not resemble the regularity of the seasons. Thus the period 1900 to 1940 was a time of rapid transformation, when the hegemony of print, music-hall and piano was undermined by the rise of film, radio and gramophone (to say nothing of television, which first broadcast in Britain in 1936). By contrast, the following forty-year period was an era of relative stability, marked by a reshuffling of the media pack. Between 1940 and 1980, television became the principal mass medium, other media were demoted, and the transistor radio, Walkman and video recorder became popular media accessories. However, after 1980, the pace of change again quickened. The desktop computer became a mass medium; the internet and web came into their own; television channels – satellite, cable and digital terrestrial – mushroomed; production techniques changed across the media; and computer and video games won a mass following. Still greater innovations, we are told, are waiting in the wings.

This acceleration of change was fuelled by new communications technology. The invention of microprocessors brought into being powerful, compact computers, and facilitated the creation of the internet. Satellites orbiting in space and relaying information between terminals on earth, and fibre-optic cable systems transmitting coded impulses of light down hair-like strands of glass, transformed the carriage of communications. Above all, the digitization of communications (the conversion of words, numbers, sounds and images into electronic binary digits) initiated a chain reaction of innovation that still continues today. Digitization reduced production costs dramatically in many media industries. It offered enormous advantages in terms of compressing, storing, editing, copying and distributing communications. It enabled more digital television channels to be transmitted on the same spectrum. It also allowed new forms of interconnectivity to take place. For instance, it is now technically possible to email friends through an advanced television set, watch a video on a mobile phone, or view television on a computer. It is this potential for *convergence* – the coming together of different media technologies – that is giving rise to forecasts of imminent transformation.

New media, we are told, are remaking the world. According to the New Labour government, in 2000: 'The explosion of information has fuelled a democratic revolution of knowledge and active citizenship. If information is power, power can now be within the grasp of everyone.'[1] Its cheerleading White Paper *A New Future for Communications* descanted eloquently on the way in which new communications technology is expanding choice, extending media diversity (including the creation of over 250 new television channels in twenty years), and increasing pluralism of media ownership. Future developments, it concluded, will move us towards 'full and sustainable competition' in the broadcasting industry. The government's positive reading of technology-driven media expansion provided the main rationale for its decision to accelerate deregulation through its 2003 Communications Act.

However, New Labour's justification for change has a suspiciously familiar ring. Both the Thatcher and Major governments had invoked similar arguments when they had pressed ahead with media deregulation. Yet, the pace and impact of media change do not seem to match the forecasts that were made at the time.

It is worth looking more carefully at what was predicted and what actually happened. The wisdom of hindsight is a useful corrective to uncritical acceptance of seemingly authoritative opinion, especially when this is summoned to justify important changes of public policy.

Cable television

In 1982, few people were better placed to discern the future of the media in Britain than Kenneth Baker, the newly appointed Information Technology Minister. A rising star destined to become a long-serving member of Conservative cabinets, he had been briefed by civil servants and leading industry experts. His considered judgement, delivered in a Commons speech, was that the advent of cable television 'will have more far-reaching effects on our society than the Industrial Revolution 200 years ago'.[2]

His assessment was part of a euphoric moment of anticipation. Leading industrial experts had predicted that cable TV would be a great engine of economic growth.[3] The *Times Educational Supplement* compared the advent of cable TV to the coming of public libraries,[4] while the *Economist* concluded that the decision to green-light cable TV was 'the most important industrial decision' of the Thatcher administration.[5]

This optimism was based on the conviction that cable television was going to be unlike anything that had been seen before. 'Off-air cable television sets' would deliver new services such as banking, shopping, meter reading, domestic security systems and even visits from the doctor. Cable TV would provide narrowcasting: numerous channels for minorities, including the elderly, deaf and those seeking adult education. Above all, it would be immensely popular, generating an entertainment-driven information revolution. Its most compelling feature would be 'film-on-request', a service that would enable viewers to select the film they wanted to see from an electronic film library.

Successive governments leant over backwards to ensure that cable television was a triumph. Interim cable TV franchises were awarded in 1983, before the cable TV regulator had been even established, in order to take advantage of the commercial momentum building up among investors. While an initial tax break was not sustained indefinitely, cable TV was exempted from the high-cost, public service requirements imposed on its competitors. In 1987, cable television operators were given permission to compete in the telephone market. In 1990, the prohibition on non-European ownership of cable television was lifted. Restrictions on the growth of a cable TV oligopoly were also rescinded. By 1999, all but six of the country's 136 operational franchises were owned by just two companies, NTL and Telewest.[6] These were allowed to merge in 2005 to form a giant cable TV monopoly that was renamed Virgin Media in 2008.

However, we now know that what was foretold did not happen. The advent of cable TV did not change Britain more than had the Industrial Revolution. Indeed, even Kenneth Baker's (now Lord Baker) more precise and low-key pronouncements were way off the mark. He had predicted in 1982 that 'by the end of the decade [1980s], multi-channel cable television will be commonplace countrywide', and that cable TV 'will be used for armchair shopping, banking, calling emergency and many other services'.[7] In fact, far from becoming 'commonplace', cable TV was adopted in just 1 per cent of homes by the end of the 1980s,[8] and by only 13 per cent in 2008.[9] Many of cable TV's much-vaunted new services, such as home banking, calling emergency services and domestic security systems, either never materialized or were short lived.

Cable TV was also a let-down in television terms. The availability of films, on its delayed film-on-request scheme, was limited. The legion of worthy channels (i.e. adult education) that had been promised was not much in evidence. In fact, most of the programmes shown on cable TV were recycled; and a good many of them had been made originally for large audiences.

But if the output of cable TV was a disappointment, this was nothing compared to the prolonged agony of its long-drawn-out failure. Cable TV had great difficulty in attracting both investors and customers in the 1980s. It obtained a new lease of life during the 1990s, when there was massive inward investment, mostly from the US. All over Britain, roads were dug up to install fibre-optic cable, and hopes in the industry rose. Yet, even during the high point of expansion, 1993–99, the underlying participation rate – that is, the proportion of households passed by cable which subscribed to cable TV – remained almost static.[10] NTL and Telewest duly ran into financial difficulty, and were forced to cancel their ambitious investment plans in 2000–1. This left 50 per cent of Britain's homes without access to cable in 2007.[11]

Lastly, the private, unregulated development of cable TV in Britain did not become an engine of growth, because its off-air services largely failed. Instead, cable TV led to massive losses, and almost bankrupted the giant corporation NTL

Satellite television

Satellite television began in Britain as a feed to cable television in 1984, but only really came into its own with the launch of a direct broadcasting service to homes in 1989. Murdoch's Sky TV gained 'first mover' advantage by launching fourteen months ahead of its rival, British Satellite Broadcasting. There was then an extended period of bloodletting, marked by heavy discounting and promotion, that resulted in the two companies making a combined estimated loss of £1.4 billion.[12] Murdoch emerged as the victor, in effective control of the merged company, BSkyB. Despite being based in Britain, and becoming in effect the British satellite monopoly broadcaster, BSkyB was exempted from burdensome public service obligations, initially on the dubious grounds that it was a 'non-domestic' broadcaster.

This enabled BSkyB to dodge an obligation to originate programmes – a key dispensation that has been central to its parasitic existence. Unlike HBO in the US, or Canal Plus in France, BSkyB makes no drama of distinction. It is in the business of rights management rather than of broadcasting. Most of its programmes are imported, primarily from the USA.

This makes BSkyB no different from cable TV. But it had two key advantages over cable TV: it had lower costs, and eventually made a profit. This enabled BSkyB to buy better TV rights than cable TV, over a longer period. It overtook its rival, accounting for an estimated 18 per cent of homes by 2002.[13] This increased, after a rapid growth spurt, to 34 per cent of 'main TV sets' in 2008.[14] But BSkyB's staple of films, cartoons, music channels and live sport (and that of cable TV) still accounts, as we shall see, for a significantly smaller share of viewing time than public service broadcasting.

What the record of BSkyB reveals is that a combination of being a virtual satellite monopoly and being exempt from cost-bearing regulation can yield, in the hands of good management, a very large profit. But its history also reveals a bigger drama. BSkyB was a pioneer of interactive digital TV, launching Sky Digital in 1997. This realized a dream that had been eagerly awaited for years.

Interactive digital television

From 1994 through to the early 2000s, there was a steady flow of articles in the national press about the wonders of interactive TV. Essentially the same forecasts that had been made for cable TV in the early 1980s were reprised for interactive digital TV, only sometimes with different jargon. 'Two-way television' was now called 'iTV'; 'film-on-request' was renamed 'video-on-demand'. This last was to be even better than anything promised before. According to the *Independent*, 'video-on-demand, once fully operational, will allow us to call up almost any film in the world, to watch any TV programmes, and to compile "dream schedules" – our own perfect evening's viewing'.[15] Once again, new services, including banking, shopping and visits from the doctor, were trumpeted. And once again, it was foretold that the society would be significantly changed by new technology. '"Interactive TV"', according to the *Sunday Times*, 'is poised to revolutionise the way information, education, media, commerce and entertainment are channelled into the 21st century home'.[16]

But, in one important respect, this good-news message was pitched in a higher rhetorical register, with much greater emphasis on user empowerment than before. Readers of the broadsheet press learnt that viewers of iTV would be able to 'vote on key issues';[17] 'be able to choose the storyline for a drama and [specify] whether they want a sad or happy ending';[18] instruct their TV sets to scan and select from hundreds of channels of information overnight to report whatever news they were interested in;[19] have 'elaborate conversations' through their TV sets with travel companies about the kind of holidays they wanted;[20] try out new clothes on a virtual cat walk;[21] and saunter down a shopping mall, walk into virtual shops, and buy whatever they liked, without ever moving from their sofas.[22] In short, interactive digital TV meant the kiss of death for the couch potato, and would lead to a 'fundamental shift in power from the TV director to the consumer in the home'.[23]

In fact, the iTV that was developed in the late 1990s and early 2000s bore very little relation to this hype. Shopping on TV meant choosing between a limited range of heavily promoted products; video-on-demand offered a restricted number of often not very good films; home visits by the doctor amounted in the end to NHS Direct, in effect the accessing of a glorified medical dictionary; NatWest pioneered an interactive TV banking service in 1995, only to close it down in 2003;[24] there was a restricted choice of camera angles for some football games on certain subscription channels; and iTV provided an alternative way of placing bets.

Yet, despite the fanfare of press publicity, viewers were mostly unimpressed. A mere 20 per cent, in a 2003 Ofcom survey, indicated a willingness in principle to pay for interactive television services.[25] Indeed, these accounted for only 36 per cent of British television's *non*-broadcast revenue in 2006,[26] and most of this was attributable to premium-rate phone calls.[27]

The most important form of commercial TV interaction was probably mass voting in the *Big Brother* series. However, the principal way that votes were registered was through the nineteenth-century technology of the telephone. This became the only mode of interaction after the option of red-button voting was discontinued in 2004, and that of SMS voting in 2006.[28] This outcome was not what the transformation of 'dumb' television sets into 'intelligent machines' had been intended to achieve.

Indeed, according to a number of market research studies, only a minority with red-button facilities actually used them.[29] The number of interactive users even decreased between 2003 and 2006.[30] Yet, still the true gospel was proclaimed from press pulpits. For example, the distinguished journalist Emily Bell proclaimed in 2001 that 'iTV is threatening to be the hot platform of tomorrow'.[31] Seven years later, and now promoted to be the *Guardian*'s Director of Digital Content, she was still writing enthusiastically about the power of 'red button interactivism'.[32]

Going digital

In November 1998, the two giants of ITV joined forces to launch OnDigital, Britain's first digital terrestrial television channels. Part of their pitch had been that digital television would provide better clarity of sound and image. Yet, to general surprise, the picture and sound quality of these new digital channels was sometimes greatly inferior to that of conventional television. Indeed, in some parts of the country the sound simply disappeared. This technical failure was due to packing too many channels into the available frequencies, causing transmission power to be curtailed in order to prevent interference with existing analogue signals. With the incompetence that characterized the entire history of OnDigital, the new venture was launched before the new technology had been mastered.

OnDigital's conception was also flawed. It went head-to-head against BSkyB, a company with more money, more subscribers (built up over years), more channels and a smarter management. BSkyB did the obvious thing. It hit OnDigital as hard as it could before the new pretender found its feet. First, BSkyB's installation charges were cut, and then its set-top boxes were given away free. OnDigital's launch funds drained away, as it was forced to match this promotion. Only inspirational programming, at this stage, could have saved it. OnDigital's inspiration was League football, attracting fewer viewers (and smaller match crowds) than BSkyB's Premiership football. Observers watched with horrified fascination as ITV's finest presided over OnDigital's slow-motion death. Attempted mouth-to-mouth resuscitation, in the form of a belated relaunch as ITV Digital, failed. The company collapsed in 2002, with an estimated £1.2bn loss.[33]

The victor in this contest did not have it all its own way. BSkyB joined BT and others to launch the Open Channel on Sky Digital in 1989. It was a state-of-the-art digital shopping channel which, it was hoped, would revolutionize shopping. Open Channel received a fanfare of publicity, not least in newspapers owned by Murdoch (also controller of BSkyB). *The Times*, for example, reported that Open Channel was valued at £1.4 billion before it had even started trading, in anticipation of the profits that it would generate.[34] In the event, the Open Channel was an ignominious failure and closed in 2001.

At this stage, national conversion to digital television was running into difficulties. The key breakthrough occurred when the BBC, with junior partners BSkyB and the transmitter company Crown Castle, launched a 'Freeview' service of digital channels in 2002. Once a £99 set-top adapter had been installed, these digital channels were available without subscription. Others (including ITV and Channel 4) subsequently joined the scheme after it had proved to be a popular success. Thus, what drove the digitizing project forward was not interactivity but 'free' content. The new license fee settlement had funded the BBC to develop new digital channels and develop the 'freeview' package. This time round, technical problems were minimized by opting for fewer channels in return for stronger transmission power.

Freeview contributed to a sharp reduction in the number of analogue TV users, as did the increasing success of satellite TV. Even so, the government had been forced to delay its planned conversion from analogue to digital broadcasting, which had originally been scheduled for 2006–10. Even in 2008, 13 per cent of homes were without digital TV, a proportion that was significantly higher in some regions, like Northern Ireland.[35] The latest date for the completed switchover is now 2012.

Dotcom bubble

During the 1990s, articles about the marvels of interactive television had been accompanied by another story, mostly confined to the business pages of the press. This reported that the internet was about to transform buying and selling, and was already making fortunes for techno-savvy entrepreneurs. Thus, the *Independent on Sunday* recorded, under the headline 'Web Whiz-Kids Count Their Cool Millions', that 'the precocious and proliferating breed of "dot com" millionaires are fabulously rich and ludicrously young. Their fortunes reduce national Lottery jackpots to peanuts … '.[36] The implication was that readers could also share in this market jackpot. The *Sunday Times* reported that 'the mania for investing, to hitch a ride on the road to wealth, is reflected in the cover of the current *Forbes* magazine, which proclaims that: "Everyone Ought to Be Rich"'.[37] The *Sunday Mirror*'s advice was characteristically more direct: 'Your Wealth: Get on the Net to Get Ahead'.[38] Wildly overoptimistic forecasts, widely reported in the press, fuelled the dotcom bubble. For example, the *Independent* reported Silicon Valley venture capitalist Joel Schoendorf as saying in 1999: 'I wouldn't be surprised if we saw a 5 per cent increase in investment next year, and every year for the next five to ten years'.[39]

In fact, the dotcom boom came to an end less than twelve months after this pronouncement. Yet, very few British publications – with the notable exceptions of the *Financial Times* and the *Economist* – clearly foresaw the bust before it happened (resembling in this respect the American press, which was no less gullible).[40] For the most part, British newspapers were content to chronicle the accumulation of wealth during the dotcom boom without properly investigating whether it was based on a secure foundation. There was little informed discussion about the extent of cost reductions secured through net retailing (which varied widely between different market sectors), or analysis of which consumer groups were most accessible to net retailing. Indeed, there was very little awareness of just how low home internet penetration was in Britain in 1999.

In the event, a large number of dotcom companies went bankrupt during 2000–2 without ever making a profit. Pension funds were seriously depleted, and Britain only narrowly missed following the US into recession.

True dawn

Yet, the irony was that the mass adoption of the internet only occurred towards the end of the dotcom bubble, and persisted *long after* it had burst. The take-off moment was the summer of 1999. Between early 1999 and 2002, the proportion of UK households with internet access soared from 13 per cent to 46 per cent.[41] By 2008, this had increased to 65 per cent.[42] Thus, in just under a decade, those with ready internet access had grown from a small minority to two-thirds of the nation – a shift comparable in scale and significance to the growth of television ownership during the 1950s. Underpinning this quiet revolution was the rapid diffusion of household computers (in just over half of homes in 2002, and in 70 per cent by 2007).[43]

The expansion of the internet took primarily a high-quality form. By 2008, 56 per cent of homes had a broadband connection, compared to 9 per cent with a dial-up connection.[44] But, however accessed, popular adoption of the internet was the key development of the early twenty-first century. The internet offers a wider gateway to the world of information and entertainment than do satellite and cable television. Unlike new television, the internet enables retrieval from a vast storehouse of information, as well as real-time interactions with others. It also provides a means of self-expression and collective organization in the way that interactive television does not. The net is global in its reach, extending horizons potentially beyond the Anglo-American world of British cable and satellite television. It offers a variety of different pleasures; sharing videos on YouTube, downloading music from Last.fm, or maintaining contact with friends on Facebook. The ability to navigate on the web has also become a work skill that is desired for an increasing number of office jobs.

Yet the considerable advantages conferred by net access are distributed unevenly in Britain. In 2008, a third of British households did not have internet access, and a quarter of British adults have never used the internet.[45] The strongest factors influencing entry to the online world were education, class and age. In 2008, 93 per cent of those with a BA degree or higher had home access to the internet, compared with 56 per cent of those with no formal qualification (such as GCSE).[46] Those in the highest income category were more than twice as likely to use the internet (91 per cent) than those in the lowest income category (39 per cent), in 2007.[47] Household net access was highest in the affluent south of England, and significantly lower in the north of England (and also northern Ireland), in 2008.[48] Among those over 65, 70 per cent had never tried the internet: yet among the 16–24 year olds, there were no internet abstainers.[49] Non-users were higher among women (30 per cent) than men (20 per cent).[50] The main explanations given for not having home internet access, apart from lack of interest, were cost and absence of skills.[51]

Continuity and change

Digitization paves the way for technological convergence because it converts words, sounds and pictures into a *common* code of 0s and 1s. This will lead, it has been predicted ever since the mid 1990s,[52] to the imminent creation of a 'killer application' that will combine all media in a single, irresistible product.

However, this notional 'killer application' will need to utilize broadband digital networks. At the moment, these are not fully developed. The building of 'broadband Britain' will require a massive investment. It will be accomplished through a pragmatic combination of different technologies: fibre-optic cable, standard telecommunications upgraded by digital subscriber line (DSL), and wireless technologies. Until this modernization is completed, the conditions do not exist for an all-conquering, multimedia apparatus which will supplant all rivals, despite the advent of digitization.

Indeed, what we are now experiencing is not so much media convergence as media proliferation: the provision of not only television and radio, in analogue and digital forms, delivered through different carriers, but also the computer, internet, mobile phone, DVD player, video game, camcorder, view data, electronic book and other applications. Convergence is occurring at the level of cross-media ownership. *Quasi*-convergence, facilitated by digitization, is also taking place through the sequencing of the same product on different platforms (for example, the screening of the same digitized films in the cinema, on television and as DVD). However, convergence at the level of consumption has been much less rapid than was anticipated. In 2008, only 11 per cent of mobile phone users used their phones to browse the internet, and only 6 per cent used them to read emails during the preceding three months.[53] Indeed, the proportion accessing the internet through their mobile phones, whether via GPRS or UMTS, in 2008 was virtually the same as in the preceding year, suggesting that the advanced mobile phone 'bubble' has burst.[54] Perhaps a more significant portent of change is that 23 per cent of recent net users said in 2008 that they had downloaded a movie or video.[55] If the computer becomes a regular and widely used source of film and TV programme downloads in the way that it has for music, this will lead to a fundamental change in the media system.

But the majority currently watch most television programmes on a TV set, due its convenience and ease of access. Television is still the most popular medium in terms of the time it absorbs each day – more than fifty years after its launch. It also continues to be the dominant news medium. In 2006, 65 per cent of the British population said that television was their main source of news, compared with 6 per cent who designated the internet.[56] The proportion nominating television in 2006 was the same as in 2002, while those citing the internet had increased by just four percentage points in the intervening period.[57] While the rise of the internet represents an enormously important development, and digitization will lead to still greater change in the future, there is also an underlying continuity in the organization and use of the media.

The dominant media brands – organizations like the BBC and News Corporation (publisher of the *Sun* and *Times*, broadcaster of BSkyB, controller of the social network website Facebook, among other media) – are still dominant. These dominant brands control not only the most-consumed news media offline but, along with leading search engines, also the most visited news websites in Britain.[58] These news organizations are shaped by the same news values and network of sources as before, little changed by new technology.[59] And in terms of mass consumption, these dominant news organizations are still in control. In 2008, 21 per cent of recent internet users read a blog – a highly significant figure, because it registers an exciting new development.[60] But another way of looking at this finding is to note that four in five adults had *not* read a blog in 2008. The role of the professional journalist and the constrained institutional settings in which they work have not been undermined by 'citizen journalists'.

Proliferating channels

However, one major change that has taken place is a very large increase in the number of television channels. The growth in their number (over 550 accessible in Britain), the rise of multi-TV households, the diffusion of time-shift video technology (with its capacity to facilitate specialized programme consumption) and the spread of minority media have fuelled fears that social cohesion and democratic dialogue are being weakened. The fragmentation of the media system, it is argued, is eroding communication between social groups in a shared public space. It is allegedly subdividing the public sphere into 'sphericules'; encouraging individuals and sectional groups to assert their values and interests without regard to others; and more generally, undermining a shared sense of common purpose.[61]

In a British context, this argument overstates the extent of change in the TV system. Leading television channels in Britain are still relatively popular. Their ascendancy is of course much less now than it was in the early 1960s, when there were only two television channels to watch. Their dominance is also slowly fading (see Table 16.1). Even so, the four leading television channels in Britain (BBC1, BBC2, ITV and Channel 4) accounted in 2008 for 56 per cent of all television viewing. Their pre-eminence is even greater during prime time: in 2006, they accounted for 69 per cent of viewing. The national community still comes together on a regular basis, laughs together, shares a sense of regret or outrage, and is drawn into a debate about common social processes, through mass television channels during peak viewing hours. These constitute the primary public sphere of contemporary Britain.

Limits of globalization

The growth of new media has given rise to another elegiac sociological thesis. This points out that both satellite television and the internet transcend national boundaries. More generally, television is becoming integrated into the global economy and is increasingly, it is claimed, showing the same programmes around the world. In this view, the rise of transnational media and globalization are weakening identification with the nation. They are also said to be eroding engagement in national politics, since this derives ultimately from a sense of national belonging.[62]

While this thesis sounds plausible, it again makes the mistake of assuming that the core media system has undergone a fundamental change. In a British context, this is not correct. Although cable and satellite television

Table 16.1 TV channels' share of viewing time

	BBC1	BBC2	ITV1	Ch4	Ch5	All others
	% all viewing time					
2008	22	8	18	8	5	39
2006	23	9	20	10	6	32
2001	27	11	22	10	6	24
	% prime time (18:00–22.30)					
2006	24	9	27	9	6	25
2001	28	9	35	8	5	14

Sources: BARB (2008); European Audiovisual Observatory Yearbook 2007, vol 1 (2006); European Audiovisual Observatory Yearbook 2002, vol 2 (2001). All figures are rounded off to the nearest whole figure.

transmit a large number of foreign (mostly American) programmes, they account for less viewing time than do terrestrial channels. While these last buy more foreign programmes than before, their full integration into the global economy has been prevented by protectionist regulation. The licence fee is a protectionist device that funnels large funds into national TV production through funding the BBC which, on its main channels, originates the majority of its programmes in the UK. As late as 1998, ITV was required by regulation to generate 60 per cent of its programmes from Europe (in effect, mostly the UK), while Channels 4 and 5 had to fulfil a 55 per cent quota.[63] This was lightened in 2003, though terrestrial channels are still expected to originate the majority of their programmes (with exemptions) from within the EU.

More generally, British terrestrial television promotes national identification by giving prominence to symbols of the nation, providing a shared social experience for the nation and a news service strongly shaped by national news values (even down to its definition of the 'weather'). It also encourages involvement in national politics by keeping a spotlight continuously trained on Westminster, and by giving extensive coverage to general election campaigns.

Indeed, the argument that British television is weakening *national* identity and political engagement needs to be turned on its head. The problem is, rather, the other way round.

British television news is nation centred enough: only 29 per cent of the main news broadcasts on BBC and ITV were devoted to foreign affairs in 2007. Perhaps more important, their selection of foreign news was strongly influenced by traditional national allegiances. No less than 71 per cent of the time devoted to foreign TV news was concentrated on Britain's geopolitical sphere outside Europe – the US, Iraq, Afghanistan and the Commonwealth countries. Europe (excluding the UK) accounted for just 7 per cent, while whole areas of the world (including China and Japan) routinely received minimal coverage.[64] This imbalance is not offset by transnational news channels like CNN, since these have tiny audiences in Britain.[65]

A case can thus be made that British television journalism remains excessively insular and traditionalist in a way that discourages engagement in European and global politics. British television reporting has yet to respond adequately to the decline of the British state and the transfer of some of its sovereignty to global markets and agencies, and to the European Union.

Diversity gains and losses

One consequence of the increase in the number of television channels was that there was a massive expansion of broadcast output. In December 1980, 300 hours of television programmes a week were available in Britain, yet by 2000 this had grown to over 40,000 hours a week.[66] This includes an enormous range of programmes – from art house movies to classic

Hollywood, stand-up comedy to Bollywood, MTV music to continuous cartoons – that was either rationed or unavailable before.

However, calculations about increased diversity need to take account of diversity losses as well as gains. While the add-on service of cable and satellite television introduced greater variety, this tended to be at the expense of the variety of the core television system. This can be illustrated, in a simple way, by television sport. The creation of new satellite sports channels greatly increased the volume and diversity of sports coverage, but it also led to the withdrawal of live coverage of key sporting events that was once available free on public service television. In effect, some people obtained a better sports service while the majority received a worse one.

In this case, the losses and gains involved were relatively transparent. A more general assessment is more difficult to make. However, the indications are that the emergence of new television channels weakened the core system by destabilizing the ecology on which it was based. Channel expansion also justified the deregulation of broadcasting, which made a deteriorating situation worse.

ITV emerged as the weak link in the public service system during the late 1980s and early 1990s. During its first thirty years, between 1955 and 1985, it had been a distinguished broadcaster. It had found no difficulty in supporting high-cost, low-audience programmes, because it had been highly profitable as a consequence of its monopoly of television advertising. It had also been subject to an effective regulatory authority, especially after 1964. However, these two prerequisites of public service virtue – easy money and tough regulation – were subsequently eroded. ITV was exposed to advertising competition by the rise of cable and satellite TV in the late 1980s and early 1990s, the conversion of Channel 4 to the status of an independent advertising rival in 1993, and the launch of Channel 5 in 1997. In addition, the commercial television regulatory authority lost key powers as a consequence of the 1990 Broadcasting Act. This new legislation also replaced the traditional way of allocating ITV franchises, based on a programme and talent 'beauty contest', with an auction to the highest bidder (with some quality safeguards). As a consequence, ITV became subject to a less public service-oriented management. This was typified by Paul Jackson, Carlton's Director of Programmes, who proclaimed in 1992:

> If *World in Action* [ITV's flagship investigative journalism programme] were in 1993 to uncover three more serious miscarriages of justice while delivering an audience of three, four or five million, I would cut it. It isn't part of the ITV system to get people out of prison.[67]

During the same period, the BBC's sense of *élan* was weakened by a new style of leadership, which seemed out of sympathy with its public service tradition.[68] When John Birt took over as Director General in 1992, he instituted for himself a tax arrangement that symbolized his market-oriented approach. Instead of being employed by the corporation he headed, Birt chose to be paid as a freelancer employed by his private company. He proceeded to convert the corporation into an internal market, constituted initially in 1993 by no less than 480 separate, self-sufficient accounting units. Intended to curb profligacy, it encouraged caution and tended to stifle creativity. It was followed by enervating 'efficiency gains', culminating in year-on-year budget cuts in 1996–2001.

The effect of all these changes was to lower the overall standard of broadcast journalism. Their impact was most noticeable in ITV, where there was a cumulative shift towards tabloidization. Between 1987/8 and 1997/8, foreign coverage dropped from 15 per cent to a mere 7 per cent of ITV's current affairs programme content. This was part of a more general shift in which analysis of economic and political affairs gave ground to 'softer' crime and consumer features.[69] ITV also moved its main 10 o'clock news bulletin to a later slot in order to clear the evening for uninterrupted prime-time entertainment, until pressure forced the network to partially relent. Its new rival, Channel 5, joined this general drift away from public purpose. In the memorable phrase of its former programme director Dawn Airey, Channel 5 gave priority to 'films, fucking and football'.[70]

The quality of television drama also declined. Individual plays had been central to the golden era of television drama during the 1960s and 1970s. They provided the licensed space where new ideas and talent could be tried out and demanding scripts could be presented. However, between 1978 and 1998 individual plays declined as a proportion of terrestrial television drama, from 23 to 10 per cent. Their place was taken by an increasing emphasis on soaps and series, because these provided a safer and more predictable form of television, designed to deliver consistent ratings. This cumulative realignment was part of a more general pattern in which terrestrial television turned increasingly to tried and tested formulae, renewable series, recognized stars and upbeat storylines.[71]

However, the partial decline of public service broadcasting was caused only partly by cable and satellite TV, and the changes in policy that their rise justified. Furthermore, this decline was not monolithic. If some things got worse, others got better. New programme formats and styles broadened social access to television during the 1980s and 1990s. These ranged from brilliant, innovative reports in BBC2's prestigious *Newsnight*, which sought to break free from its reliance on a political élite, to daytime talk shows which gave working-class women a greater voice.[72] During the Birt era (1992–2000), a greater attempt was made to employ more British Asian and Afro-Caribbean programme makers, and to address the distinctive concerns of ethnic minority audiences. The continuing popularity of British public service television programmes – and the continuing public support for the maintenance of the public service broadcasting system in Britain – attested to its underlying strength.

Some past damage has since been undone, and new improvements initiated. The BBC's internal market was swept away in 2000, in a wave of reform that gave increased power to programme makers. The BBC's 2002 digital television initiative introduced successful new channels that enabled the corporation to connect more effectively to different age groups and minorities within the viewing public. There have been positive as well as negative developments, advances as well as reverses. Yet, it is difficult to avoid the impression that the extension of private choice in the form of pay-TV has been at the expense of public, collectively funded provision.

Retrospect

Time and again, the broadsheet press overstated the impact of new media. Cable TV, it was widely predicted, would be an engine of economic growth. Interactive digital TV would place the viewer firmly in control. The internet would transform the retail business almost overnight. All these predictions proved to be wrong. Cable TV was a consumer flop throughout the 1980s; interactive television generated not-very-inspiring services that many did not use; and the dotcom bubble burst, with losses so great that it almost induced a recession in Britain.

Why were broadsheet journalists – not a notably trusting group – so ready to believe the hype of self-serving sources: the cable and interactive television developers and dotcom entrepreneurs? The main explanation is that this hype was often part of the informed consensus of the time – endorsed by senior politicians, industrial and academic experts, and a flow of information coming from the US. New media hype also accorded with news values that stressed novelty, and satisfied the need to fill the expanding space devoted to consumer and lifestyle concerns. It also drew upon meta-narratives deeply embedded in the culture of society – a view of technology as the midwife of progress, and an instinctual belief that technology determines outcomes. In brief, journalists responded to the sources they talked to, the institutional demands of their work, and the cultural air they breathed.[73]

But even if many journalists overstated the pace and impact of technological change, the media landscape in the early twenty-first century was very different from what it had been in the early 1980s. The single most important development was the rise of the internet, comparable in importance to the advent of television. For this reason, the next two chapters are devoted to exploring further the internet's history and significance.

The other key change was the increase in the number of television channels. This manifestly increased the diversity of British television. Some critics complained that it also undermined social cohesion and a sense of national identity. But they exaggerated the extent of change: leading channels still reached a large audience. There is also a strong case that British television should become more open to European and global influences, rather than the opposite.

The growth of pay-TV probably led to a depletion of terrestrial broadcasting. Certainly, the hype that surrounded cable and interactive digital TV contributed to the growing deregulation of commercial broadcasting. That ensured that British television was not as good as it might otherwise have been, if better advantage had been taken of new technology.[74]

Notes

1. *A New Future for Communications* (London, Stationery Office, 2000), p. 8.
2. Kenneth Baker, *Parliamentary Debates*, Satellite and Cable Broadcasting, 20 April 1982 (London: Hansard, 6th series, vol. 22, 1982), p. 230.
3. Information Technology Advisory Panel, *Cable Systems* (London: Cabinet Office, HMSO, 1982).
4. *Times Educational Supplement*, 28 October 1983.
5. *Economist*, 6 March 1982.
6. C. Leys, *Market-Driven Politics* (London, Verso, 2001), p. 127.
7. P. Goodwin, *Television Under the Tories* (London, British Film Institute, 1998), p. 68.
8. D. Goldberg, T. Prosser and S. Verhulst, *Regulating the Media* (Oxford, Clarendon Press, 1998), p. 10.
9. *Communications Market Report* (London, Ofcom, 2008), p. 21, www.ofcom.org.uk/research/cm/cmr08/cmr08_1.pdf. Accessed 12 February 2009.
10. S. Lax, 'The Internet and democracy', in D. Gauntlet (ed.), *Web Studies* (London, Arnold, 2000), p. 166.
11. *Competition Issues Related to Core Premium Content* 30 September 2008 (London: Ofcom, 2008) p. 11. www.ofcom.org.uk/consult/condocs/second_paytv/annex8.pdf. Accessed 14 February 2009.
12. N. Chenoweth, *Virtual Murdoch* (London, Secker & Warburg, 2001), p. 98.
13. *Social Trends* 32 (London, Stationery Office, 2002), table 13.2, p. 211.
14. *Communications Report 14* (London, Ofcom, 2008), figure 3.64.
15. *Independent*, 12 January 1996.
16. *Sunday Times*, 4 October 1998.
17. *Guardian*, 21 June 1994.
18. *Independent*, 9 September 1996.
19. *Sunday Times*, 30 April 1995.
20. *Independent*, 24 October 1994.
21. *The Times*, 27 November 1994.
22. *Independent*, 6 October 1994.
23. *Sunday Times*, 30 April 1995.
24. Information derived from *Daily Telegraph*, 6 September 1995, and NatWest Customer Services.
25. Ofcom (2004).
26. Ofcom (2007).
27. Information obtained from interview with Ofcom executive, 2008.
28. Information provided by Nikki O'Shea, Factual Entertainment, Channel 4.
29. *New Media Age*, 27 April 2006.
30. *Precision Marketing*, 9 March 2007; cf. *New Media Age*, 6 April 2006.
31. *Guardian*, 7 May 2001.
32. *Guardian*, 24 November 2008. In fact, it is not the red button but the computer mouse that will provide the most signficant form of interactivism, as in the BBC's successful iPlayer (programme replay) application.
33. T. Lennon, 'Digital TV: a phoenix risen from the ashes', *Free Press*, 129, 2002, p. 2.

34. *The Times*, 15 April 1999.
35. *Communications Market Report 14* (London: Ofcom, 2008), figure 3.64.
36. *Independent on Sunday*, 25 July 1999.
37. *Sunday Times*, 26 December 1999.
38. *Sunday Mirror*, 17 October 1999.
39. *Independent*, 14 July 1999.
40. J. Cassidy, *Dot.Con* (London, Penguin Books, 2003).
41. *Family Expenditure Survey* (1998–2002), www.statistics.gov.uk.
42. Office for National Statistics, www.statistics.gov.uk/cci/nugget.asp?id=8. Accessed 14 February 2009.
43. *Family Expenditure Survey 2002*, Office for National Statistics, www.statistics.gov.uk/cci/nugget.asp?id=868. Accessed 14 February 2008.
44. *Internet Access 2008*, Office for National Statistics (2008), www.statistics.gov.uk/pdfdir/iahi0808.pdf. Accessed 14 February 2009.
45. *Ibid.*, 2008, pp. 2 and 4.
46. *Ibid.*, 2008, pp. 4.
47. *Family Spending 2007*, Office of National Statistics, www.statistics.gov.uk/downloads/theme_social/Family_Spending_2006/FamilySpending2007_web.pdf. Accessed 14 February 2009.
48. See note 44, p. 2.
49. *Ibid.*, p. 4.
50. *Ibid.*, p. 4.
51. *Ibid.*, p. 3.
52. N. Negroponte, *Being Digital* (London, Coronet, 1996).
53. See note 44, p. 7.
54. *Ibid.*, p. 8.
55. *Ibid.*, p. 8.
56. *New News, Future News* (London, Ofcom, 2007), figure 3.1, p. 17.
57. Ipsos survey, 2002, cited in *ibid.*, p. 17.
58. *New News, Future News* (London, Ofcom, 2007), figure 3.11, p. 34.
59. N. Fenton (ed.), *New Media, Old News* (London, Sage, 2009).
60. See note 44, p. 8.
61. For example, T. Gitlin, 'Public sphere or sphericules?', in T. Liebes and J. Curran (eds), *Media, Ritual and Identity* (London, Routledge, 1998).
62. E. Katz, 'And deliver us from segmentation', *Annals of the American Academy of Political and Social Science*, 546, 1996.
63. Information derived from the Independent Television Commission in 1999.
64. J. Curran, S. Iyengar, A.L. Brind, A. Salovaara-Moring, 'Media system, public knowledge and democracy: A comparative study', *European Journal of Communication*, 24 (1), 2009, pp. 5–26.
65. *European Audiovisual Observatory Yearbook 2007* (Strasbourg, Council of Europe, 2007).
66. *A New Future for Communications* (London, Stationery Office, 2000), p. 7.
67. Cited in S. Barnett and A. Curry, *The Battle for the BBC* (London, Aurum Press, 1994), p. 249. *World in Action* was duly discontinued.
68. See Chapter 15.
69. S. Barnett and E. Seymour, '*A Shrinking Iceberg Travelling South*' (London, Campaign for Quality Television, 1999), p. 16.
70. Cited in C. Leys, *Market-Driven Politics* (London, Verso, 2001), p. 127.
71. See note 68.
72. J. Curran, 'Television journalism: theory and practice: the case of *Newsnight*', in P. Holland, *Television Handbook* (London, Routledge, 2nd edn, 2000).
73. J. Curran, 'Technology foretold', in N. Fenton (ed.), *New Media, Old News* (London, Sage, 2009).
74. See Chapter 24 for a discussion of how the media can be reformed.

Chapter 17

History of the internet

Introduction

In the nineteenth century, people were awed by the emancipatory power of the newspaper and periodical that it became the convention to refer to the press with an upper case 'P'. When this awe gave way to familiarity, the press was demoted to a lower case 'p', and commentary about the press became more sensible.

We are still in the awestruck stage as far as the internet is concerned. Convention requires that the internet be designated with an upper case 'I', and the world wide web with upper case 'Ws' (though we have resisted this here). The wonderment this convention expresses goes some way towards explaining why so much current discussion of the net is so inadequate.

There are two leading schools of thought. One sees the internet as a technology of freedom that is empowering humankind, making accessible the world's knowledge, building 'emancipated subjectivities', promoting a new, progressive global politics, and laying the foundation of the 'new economy'.[1] The other sees the internet as an over-hyped technology whose potential value has been undermined by 'digital capitalism' and social inequality.[2]

We will explore these two rival perspectives by means of a circuitous route that takes us through the history of the internet (this chapter) and its sociology (Chapter 18). When combined together, this body of research points to a clear verdict: neither perspective is correct.

Historical overview

The internet has gone through four main phases. In its first phase, during the 1970s, it was used by scientists as a way of sharing expensive computer resources, exchanging research data and corresponding through email. It was the research tool of a techno-élite.

During the early and mid-1980s, the internet (broadly defined) entered its subcultural and proto-commercial phase. Its use widened as a consequence of the proliferation of computer networks, and became more varied. Usenet groups (specialist discussion groups) were formed; 'virtual communities', forged through the net, took shape; and some early internauts played identity games. Knowledge of a new argot, often derived from science fiction, became part of the grass-roots net subculture, introducing new acronyms such as MOO (a chat room represented as a physical place) and MUD (multi-user dungeon or, more soberly, multi-user domain). This was the period when a number of *digerati* enthusiasts proclaimed to the uninitiated that the internet was a life-changing, world-redeeming invention. However, the rise of grassroots networks in the early 1980s coincided with the emergence of commercial online services, and a sustained growth of business networks – and these were to prove a more significant development in the long run.

The third phase, from the later 1980s to the mid-1990s, was a period of transition when the deployment of the net as a research tool and subcultural playground gave way increasingly to commercial use. In 1991, prohibitions on the commercial use of the core internet were lifted. In 1993, commercial software was introduced which made the web (created in 1990) more accessible. In 1995, the American core internet backbone was privatized. This transitional period closed with the sleeping giant of Microsoft awakening to the success of the web, and assessing how best to profit from its growing popularity.

The fourth phase, from the mid-1990s to the present, marked the commercialization of cyberspace. Net companies, selling directly to the public, mushroomed. Net advertising became widespread, and new ways were devised to monitor users for commercial purposes. General portals sought to simplify the internet experience for the public in profitable ways. Commercial content became more prominent, and civic discourse less so.

However, this commercial takeover was incomplete. The net's culture and uses, shaped by its early pre-market development, did not disappear. The new commercial régime encountered strong resistance both from within the computer world and from the public at large. The net was pulled by opposed forces in different directions.

As a consequence, the net contains contradictory features, and can develop potentially in different ways. To make sense of the present, and glimpse into the future, it is necessary to examine the past more closely.

Underlying science

One way of viewing the history of the net and the web is to see it as the culmination of scientific innovation. It is an important perspective that tends to be neglected by non-scientists.[3]

One strand of innovation that led to the internet was the development of the computer. In the 1940s the first operational electronic digital computers were built – the British 'Collossus' in 1943 and the more advanced

American ENIAC in 1946. These and subsequent 'first generation' computers were massive machines, costing vast sums, attended by a white-coated priesthood and dependent on thousands of notoriously unreliable valves. Three key developments subsequently transformed the computer, enabling it to become smaller and more powerful. In 1947 transistors were invented, and gradually replaced computer valves. In 1958 integrated circuits were introduced in the form of silicon chips incorporating thousands of miniaturized transistors. In the early 1960s, this led to the introduction in research and business organizations of so-called 'minicomputers' – though these were enormous by today's standards. This led to the final decisive breakthrough: the microprocessor invented by Ted Hoff in 1969. This is the integrated circuit that incorporates the functions of the central processing unit of a computer, its 'heart'. Its invention led to the development of microprocessor-based personal computers, the first of which were manufactured in 1975 in the form of a do-it-yourself kit for hobbyists. The late 1970s marked the beginning of the personal computer boom that has continued to this day.

A second strand of innovation, the development of computer networking, was also a cumulative process. During the 1950s, a computer language evolved that drew on the pioneer work of a number of scientists, most notably Konrad Zuse. This still left unresolved how computers, using different systems, could communicate with each other. The first step was the building of an intermediary computer (IMP) in the late 1960s that functioned as a processing link between the computer 'host' and the network. This was followed in the early 1970s by the development of conventions (*protocols*) governing the dialogue between machines. This began with formulating shared codes for transporting communications (Transmission Control Protocol, shortened to TCP), and for addressing computers (Internet Protocol, shortened to IP). These eventually were adopted both in the United States and globally, though only after much difficulty. The other, linked breakthrough was the development of packet-switching during the 1960s and 1970s. This was an ingenious system whereby messages were disaggregated into units (*packets*) before dispatch; sent through different routes, depending on the flow of communications traffic; and reassembled on arrival. Each packet was wrapped in a kind of digital envelope containing transport and content specifications.

Protocols governing computer interaction and packet-switching technology made possible the development of the internet. This began in 1969 as a computer network (ARPANET) established by the US Defence Department, with nodes in four American universities. It grew rapidly in the 1970s and 1980s to become the backbone of a larger system that encompassed a number of networks. Its rise was paralleled by the development of a second major network, started in 1982 by the US National Science Foundation. This second network became linked to the first; built links with national networks around the world in the late 1980s; and took over ARPANET's backbone role in 1990. In the United States a cumulative process of convergence also took place in which a variety of outsider networks – business, commercial and grass-roots services – developed closer links to the American public system during the period between 1983 and 1995. The modern internet, in the sense of a publicly accessible, worldwide network of computer networks, came of age in the late 1980s and took off in the 1990s.

An ancillary development that facilitated the building of this global network was the improvement of modern communications infrastructure. Initially, computer networking was conducted through telephone wires, but later it came to use routinely both satellite and advanced cable. Satellite communication dates from the launch of Telstar in 1962, but developed fully only from the 1970s onward. The first, local *broadband* cable systems were laid in the early 1980s, while transcontinental systems were extended across the Atlantic and Pacific Oceans in the late 1980s. Between 1996 and 1999 there was a tenfold increase in transatlantic cable capacity, underlining the point that the sea still matters, as well as the sky, in coping with the growing volume of communications traffic.[4]

The third strand of innovation took the form of advances in computer software. The revered pioneer of software design is Vannevar Bush. He argued in the 1930s and 1940s that computers should be viewed not as giant calculating machines but as a technology that can assist human beings to store, retrieve and analyse creatively all kinds of information. Some claim to discern in his 1945 outline of a hypothetical 'memex' machine the essential elements of what became scroll bars, home pages, computer displays and scanning. However, it was not until 1963 that Douglas Engelbart and his team developed in a concrete form recognizably modern software, including graphics-based interfaces and the now ubiquitous 'mouse', the pointing device used to roam the computer screen. This was followed by the emergence of *hypertext* software, first developed in a simple form by Ted Nelson in 1965 and greatly refined subsequently. The key benefit of hypertext is that it enables computer users to move from one part of a text to another, linked text by clicking on an icon or symbol. In this way, it offers flexible and lateral intellectual pathways.

In 1990 Tim Berners-Lee and his associates at CERN, Geneva invented the world wide web. This took the form of a software program that enabled people to access, link and create communications in a single global 'web' of information. This was achieved through the development of new conventions governing the interaction between machines. One convention specified the location of the information (URI, later revised usually to URL); a second specified the form of information transaction (HTTP); and the third a uniform way of structuring documents (HTML). Before their general adoption, people experienced enormous difficulties in finding information on the net, and also in releasing information that others could find. Various protocols that had evolved for exchanging information were not compatible, and there was no generally accepted way of linking information in different documents.

While the web proved to be a momentous development, it built upon advances that had preceded it. The web was superimposed on the internet, and incorporated its protocols. Without the prior existence of global computer internetworking and the development of communications infrastructure underpinning it, the web would not have been possible. The popularization of personal computers was also a precondition of the web. It provided the dispersed computer power that enabled users to put their own content on the web, as well as the technical means to run web software. Finally, Berners-Lee's invention incorporated past software innovations, not least hypertext links that were a key feature of his project. Indeed, the world wide web may be viewed, in one sense, as part of a continuum of software development: subsequent innovations made the web easier to navigate, and introduced an audio and video dimension.

The web thus marked the coming together of three different strands of innovation. *It joined personal computing to networking through connective software.* This gave rise to a technological development with the potential to change the world. The internet and the web provide a global medium of communication in a context where the world's media system is overwhelmingly national and local. It allows individuals and groups to send as well as receive communications, in contrast to the one-way communication flows of conventional media. It is highly versatile, lending itself to different uses. Above all, the internet began as the least controlled part of the media system, subject to neither state nor market domination.

Birth pangs of the web

A central theme of the 'history of ideas' approach to scientific discovery is that most important inventions have a clear intellectual bloodline. They are usually the product not of a flash of insight coming from nowhere, but of an incremental progression of thought and practice. The invention of packet-switching, central to the birth of the internet, provides a case in point. It was conceptualized by Paul Baran in 1964; developed and implemented by Donald Davies and Lawrence Roberts in the later 1960s; revised significantly by Vinton Cerf and Robert Kahn in 1974; and refined thereafter. The 'auteur' theory of the creative process, to be found in some versions of film theory, gets short shrift in the academic history of science.

While this fastidious approach is broadly correct, it tends to downplay the excitement of discovery, at least as it is experienced in the low-key register of academic life. Yet the birth pangs of the web were not entirely free of drama. Its inventor, Tim Berners-Lee, was low down in the food chain of academic grants when he began work on the web. He was a scientist, without a Ph.D., on a temporary fellowship in the European physics laboratory, CERN. His repeated requests for additional resources all met with polite refusals. Indeed, he began to fear that his web project – justified on the less-than-straight-forward grounds that it would facilitate information sharing between scientists *within* the laboratory, rather than around the world – might be cancelled. When he first unveiled his visionary work it met with a lukewarm response from his CERN colleagues, with the exception of Robert Cailliau.

The future of the web thus seemed to depend upon winning external recognition. Berners-Lee was convinced that the way to achieve this was to present his project at a key conference, due to be held in 1991 in San Antonio, USA, where all the people who mattered in the computer science world would be present. He and his colleague Robert Cailliau submitted to the conference what was arguably one of the most important scientific papers of the last quarter of a century, only for it to be rejected on the pedantic grounds that it failed to situate its arguments adequately within the relevant literature. However, they were given permission to present the web in the second-division form of a demonstration.

The two young scientists flew to San Antonio, only to discover that the hotel where the conference was due to be held had no direct internet access. They persuaded the hotel to extend a phone line to the demonstration room, and charmed staff in the neighbouring university (identified by a local taxi driver) into allowing use of its dial-in service to their home computer. They had then to hunt down, at the last moment, a soldering iron in their hotel in order to bypass an American plug that did not fit their Swiss modem. The demonstration was a triumph. 'At the same conference two years later', Tim Berners-Lee recalls with a trace of smugness, 'every project on display would have something to do with the Web'.[5]

Political economy of invention

If scientific advance often takes the form of a logical or associative progression of thought, it is also crucially shaped by the wider context of society. A number of societal factors affect *when* and also *where* scientific progress takes place. One of these – patronage – was especially important in the case of the development of the internet.

The internet is an offspring of the Pentagon. When the USSR launched the first space satellite in 1957, the US Department of Defense responded by establishing the Advanced Research Projects Agency (ARPA), with the aim of mobilizing American universities and research laboratories more fully behind the country's Cold War effort. Among the new agency's many projects was a scheme to promote interactive computing through the creation of ARPANET, the world's first advanced computer network. Although the network was conceived originally as a way of sharing expensive computer time, it subsequently acquired a more important rationale. Computer networking would facilitate, it was argued, the development of a sophisticated military command and control system. It would also provide a means of sustaining communications channels in the event of a nuclear attack from the Soviet Union.

When ARPANET was identified as part of America's last line of defence against the 'evil empire', it became a spending priority. The development of packet-switching technology and the creation of a rapidly expanding computer network – both central to the birth of the internet – received major funding from the US Department of Defense.

Military spending also indirectly assisted the internet by fostering external conditions favourable to its development. The army funded the first American computer in 1946. So great was the armed forces' subsequent support of 'the nascent computer industry' that it became, in the words of a leading analyst, 'virtually a military subsidiary'.[6] This financial backing helped to establish the USA as the world's leading computer manufacturer and producer of computer software. The American state also sponsored the American space programme, whose by-product – satellite communications – facilitated the functioning of the global internet.

In effect, the American state underwrote a major part of the research and development process that gave birth to the modern internet. This was not something that the private sector would have readily undertaken, because it was not apparent, in the early days, that computer networking between academics, linked to the defence programme, had any commercial future. Indeed, the commercial giant AT&T was actually invited in 1972 to take over ARPANET, the forerunner of the internet, and declined, on the grounds that it lacked profit potential. It was the American state that picked up the bills in a context of limited commercial interest. Yet, after underwriting the cost of technology development, and the creation of a significant user base, the American state then proceeded to shepherd the internet to market. During the 1980s, the government provided financial support for the design of new computers to be modified in order to facilitate commercial internetworking.[7] The lifting of the prohibition on commercial use of the public internet in 1991 was followed by privatization of the public backbone of the internet in 1995. In effect, the internet became a state-sponsored commercial system.

The actual developmental role of the American state in funding, managing and then commercially floating the internet did not accord with the minimalist, 'night-watchman' conception of government in American neoliberal ideology. Its interventionism corresponded more closely, in fact, to the social market vision of the state as 'capitalist entrepreneur' that was once strongly advocated by European social democrats.[8] One reason why American political reality deviated from political rhetoric was the significant influence exerted by business on American telecommunications policy. However, the very much more important reason was that the American state allocated enormous resources to establishing military and technological superiority over the Soviet Union during the height of the Cold War. The internet was a Dr Strangelove project.

Similar levels of public investment were not available elsewhere, even in countries where the conditions for early internet development were promising. Britain built the first modern computer in the 1940s; developed a significant computer industry in the 1950s; and was the first country to develop packet-switching, in prototype, in 1968. But this auspicious start did not gain extensive state financial support, especially in relation to computer projects that offered only a long-term return.[9] It was not until 1981 that the Post Office launched a full-scale packet-switching service – using, after this long delay, expensively licensed American hardware.

Cultures of invention

The internet was the product not only of human ingenuity and state patronage, but also of the values of the people who first developed it. Data-processing systems do not have a fixed form determined by some inner technological logic but are influenced by the concerns and goals of their inventors, and of the contexts in which they operate. For example, IBM developed a highly centralized communication system for business organizations, in which the main computer had a master–slave position to terminals, and the relationship of users to the production and consumption of the data system depended on their position within the corporation. The IBM system both reflected and reproduced, Patrice Flichy argues, the hierarchical culture of the firm.[10]

By contrast, the internet came out of a very different world, though its supposed Edenic character has become the subject of much mythologizing. According to conventional accounts, the early internet reflected the freedom-loving values of the American scientists who designed it, and of the grass-roots activists who took it up. This love of freedom was then secured by the freedom of the marketplace, ensuring that the internet became a great engine of human enlightenment.

There is just enough truth in this account to ensure its longevity. However, it greatly simplifies by editing out or downplaying features of the net's development which do not accord with its story-line. It also grossly distorts by failing to acknowledge the central conflict that developed between the freedom of the net and the assertion of market control. What actually happened is different from the legend.

Jane Abbate's pioneering history shows that the American military was not a benign, self-effacing 'sugar-daddy' of the net whose role was confined to paying the bills. On the contrary, she concludes, 'networking techniques were shaped in many ways by military priorities and concerns'.[11] One over-whelming military priority was 'survivability'; in other words, a communication system that would be invulnerable to devastating attack. This led the military to sponsor a decentralized system without a vulnerable command centre that could be destroyed by the enemy. It also led to the development of network technology that would enable the system to function if parts of it were destroyed – a key attraction of packet-switching that dispensed with dedicated, open lines between sender and receiver. Another military priority was to secure a diverse networking system, since this was best suited to different, specialized military tasks. This gave rise to the net's modular structure in which different networks could be added on easily, once minimum requirements were met. It also resulted in the addition of satellite and wireless for internetworking, since these were well adapted to communications with jeeps, ships and aeroplanes.

However, if the military strongly influenced design objectives, academic computer scientists actually conceived and implemented the net's design. Indeed, academics working for ARPA had a significant degree of autonomy, helped by the fact that military objectives largely coincided with scientific ones. Thus the military concern for survivability dovetailed with the desire of the different university departments, which constituted the early internet, to retain their freedom and independence. Similarly, military endorsement of network diversity accorded with the academic goal of making the internet a better research tool by incorporating more networks. When there was a serious clash between paymasters and scientists over the issue of security, it was resolved amicably through the division of the internet into military and civilian networks in 1983.

Partly as a consequence of this harmonious relationship (sustained, seemingly, even during the Vietnam War), scientists were in a position to impose their values on the general development of the net. The ideology of science is committed strongly to the open disclosure of information and, in principle, to intellectual co-operation in order to further the shared goal of scientific advance. This was manifested in the co-operative way in which internet protocols were developed. It was also reflected in the open release of these protocols, since the internet's builders were seeking to promote good science, not to make money through proprietary exclusion. The culture of science also fosters interaction and discussion, and this influenced the way in which the early internet came to be used. Emailing soon eclipsed remote computing as the early internet's principal function.

However, the culture of academic life is, in largely unconscious ways, exclusionary. Academic work is seldom addressed to people outside the relevant knowledge community, which is why so much of it is buried in obscure publications and self-referential vocabulary. This exclusionary tradition was also a feature of the early internet. Considerable computer expertise was needed for people to go online, and academic computer scientists showed little interest in changing this.

The third cultural influence shaping the early internet was the American counter-culture of the 1980s. This was constituted primarily by three overlapping (and not always harmonious) subcultures: a hippy subculture centred on individual self-realization through the development of self-knowledge and freedom from repressive convention; a communitarian subculture seeking to rebuild a sense of togetherness by changing social attitudes, and experimenting with new forms of social organization; and a radical subculture committed to emancipation from patriarchal capitalism or, in a more populist mode, to giving 'power to the people'. While this counter-culture was very much in decline by the Reaganite 1980s, it directed considerable energy towards redefining the online world – perhaps from disappointment about how things had turned out offline.

The counter-cultural movement redefined the meaning and purpose of the internet. Even in the early days of ARPANET, computer use was not confined solely to work, since some of its users had emailed each other about science fiction. Commercial online services in the early 1980s also offered chat rooms and the opportunity to shop online. But the counter-culture helped to develop new uses for the net. This was the product of a long-running collaboration between computer scientists (who were told, for the first time, that they were 'cool') and the graduates of flower power (looking for a way of hanging on to their dreams). This creative relationship was facilitated by techie journalists and cultural entrepreneurs. Computers were reimagined and adapted as tools of personal liberation, organizers of virtual communities and weapons of political struggle.[12]

It was often local area networks, run usually as co-operatives heavily dependent on volunteer labour, which proved to be the most inventive. For example,the WELL (Whole Earth Lectronic Link), set up in the San Francisco area in 1985,[13] was the brainchild of Stewart Brand, then a radical rock concert impresario, and Larry Brilliant, a left-wing doctor and Third World campaigner. Brilliant enrolled numerous fellow former members of Hog Farm, a large, self-sufficient agricultural commune in Tennessee. They created an electronic commune that grew into 300 computer-mediated 'conferences' which brought together social and political activists, as well as enthusiasts of all kinds. One of its largest subgroups was composed of followers of the radical rock group the Grateful Dead. Deadheads (as they were disrespectfully called) spent hours online discussing the Grateful Dead's enigmatic lyrics and exchanging music recorded at live gigs – something the group supported as part of its public stand in favour of the 'pirating' of its music.

There also developed geographically dispersed grassroots networks, usually set up by students in university campuses. These included Usenet (1979), BITNET (1981), FidoNet (1983) and PeaceNet (1985). The most important of these were Usenet news groups built around the UNIX system. They were set up initially to discuss issues to do with UNIX software and troubleshooting. They proliferated to cover a wide range of issues, growing from three sites in 1979 to 11,000 by 1988. During these early years, Usenet created a significant space for the expression of minority views, and exploited the global potential of the internet by building extensive international links.

The counter-culture also contributed to the emergence of radical computer capitalism. Thus Steve Jobs and Steve Wozniak, who launched Apple in 1980, came out of the alternative movement. Jobs had travelled to India in a quest for personal enlightenment, while Wozniak was heavily involved in the radical rock scene. In 1982, Wozniak personally funded the organization of a rock festival dedicated to the Information Age. At the festival, which attracted more people than Woodstock, there was a giant videoscreen on which was projected a simple message:

> There is an explosion of information dispersal in the technology and we think this information has to be shared. All great thinkers about democracy said that the key to democracy is access to information. And now we have a chance to get information into people's hands like never before.[14]

In addition, the counter-culture influenced American university computer science departments during the 1970s and 1980s. This reinforced the stress on freedom, open disclosure and interaction as formative influences on the technical evolution of the net. It also created a milieu that sustained a determined defence of the pre-market internet when it came under attack (about which more below).

The fourth cultural influence shaping cyberspace was a tradition of public service. If the internet was incubated primarily in the United States, the world wide web was a European invention and came out of a legacy which bequeathed mass public service television and radio, parks in the hearts of cities, public libraries and art galleries, and a subsidized art-house film industry throughout much of Europe. The web's principal architect, Tim Berners-Lee, was inspired by two public service precepts: the need to create *free* public access to shared cultural resources (in this case, the storehouse of knowledge contained in the world's computer system), and the need to bring people into communion with each other (in this instance, through the connective potential of the computer). Underpinning Berners-Lee's approach was a strong public service orientation opposed to the exaltation of market values above all else. A frequently asked question, he says, in the United States (though less so in Europe) is: Does he regret not making money out of the world wide web?

> What is maddening is the terrible notion [implied in this question] that a person's value depends on how important and financially successful they are, and that this is measured in terms of money ... Core in my upbringing was a value system that put monetary gain well in its place.[15]

Berners-Lee's decision not to promote the web through a private company was prompted mainly by a concern that it could trigger competition, and lead to the subdivision of the web into private domains. This would have subverted his conception of 'a universal medium for sharing information'. Instead, in 1991 he persuaded CERN to release the world wide web code as a free gift to the community. He subsequently became the head of a public service agency regulating the web (World Wide Web Consortium (W3C)), since this enabled him to 'think about what was best for the world, as opposed to what would be best for one commercial internet'.[16]

The fifth cultural influence shaping the net was the values of the market. At first, these seemed benign and progressive. Their initial effect was to counter the exclusionary norms of academic life by democratizing the web. In 1993, a commercial web browser (Netscape) was launched that used colour images, and made the web more accessible. Indeed, it played a key role in popularizing use of the web. It was followed by the creation of commercial websites that were fun to visit.

In the mid-1990s, all aspects of the internet seemed enormously positive. Even if the internet was a product of a superpower war-machine, its military legacy was terminated in 1990 when ARPANET handed over control of the public internet backbone to the National Science Foundation. A combination of academic, counter-cultural and public service values had created an open public space which was decentralized and seemingly uncontrolled. It had established a tradition of co-operation in which software codes were freely disclosed, and it had greatly extended the uses made of the net, not least through the creation of the world wide web. The growing influence of commerce seemed merely to be extending the benefits of this new medium to more people, without detracting from its fundamental nature.

Commercialization of the internet

The largely uncritical reception given to the increasing commercialization of the net during the mid-1990s accorded with the ethos of the period. This was a time when deregulated capitalism was trumpeted as the only way to organize an efficient economy, and when capitalism's victory over communism was hailed as the 'end of history'. The mood music of the time was reinforced by the outpourings of net experts. The MIT guru Nicholas Negroponte set the tone in a celebrated book, published in 1995, which portrayed the internet as the centrepiece of a democratizing digital revolution. 'The information industry', he declared, 'will become more of a boutique business ... the customers will be people and their computers agents'. The public, he predicted, will *pull* what it wants from the internet and digital media, rather than accept what is *pushed* at it by media giants. Fundamental change was already upon us. Media consumption, he claimed, is becoming 'customized' according to individual taste, and 'the monolithic empires of mass media are dissolving into an army of cottage industries', making obsolete 'industrial-age cross-ownership laws'.[17] Similarly Mark Poster, another revered net expert, also concluded in 1995 that we are entering the 'second media age', in which monopoly is being replaced by choice, the distinction between senders and receivers is coming to an end, and the ruled are being transformed into rulers.[18] In these, and most other commentaries, the market was not viewed as a limitation on the emancipatory power of the net.

The coalition that had created the pre-market internet fractured during the mid-1990s. Some academic computer scientists set up internet companies and became millionaires. Others quietly acquiesced to software licensing restrictions. University administrators looked for ways to make money out of their computer science departments. A new generation of computer industry managers emerged whose informality and populism seemed to set them apart from the stuffy corporate culture of their predecessors. In this changed environment, capitalism seemed hip: the way to make money, express individuality and prevent the state from taking control. The language used to discuss new media changed. The metaphor of the 'information superhighway', with its 1950s' association of statist modernism, gave way to the romantic image of 'cyberspace', derived from science fiction.[19] Everything seemed wondrous, transformative, positive.

However, the accelerating force of commercialization began to change the internet in ways that had not been anticipated. The open disclosure of information in pursuit of scientific advance that had shaped the net began to be superseded by the imposition of intellectual property rights in pursuit of profit. Software codes were no longer disclosed openly on an automatic basis, but were often restricted by licensing arrangements. Still more potentially undermining of the traditions of the early net was the transparent desire of some leading net companies to charge website fees. They intended to make free visits only a temporary measure, in order to foster a 'habit' that users would be willing to pay for once they were hooked. This threatened to change the internet out of all recognition, transforming an open electronic commons into fees-only, private enclosures.

The belief that 'peripheral voices' would move centre-stage in the digital era – central to a naïve mid-1990s' view of the internet – became increasingly implausible. This was partly because some search engines evolved into general portals which 'mainstreamed' the internet experience.[20] Their central objective was to retain users for as long as possible in order to sell their 'eyeballs' to advertisers and, also subsequently, to sell information about their net behaviour. This led general portals to construct 'hub and spoke' websites, in which users were encouraged to follow defined pathways and return to the home base before venturing out again. These pathways led to 'channels' which structured the internet experience. For example, in 2002, Yahoo! UK offered a basic choice between shopping, information, fun, business, personal and connect channels, while many of its rivals offered variations of the same.

Within content 'channels', prominence was given to what was popular (since the aim was to retain users) and also to what was sponsored. Thus, in 2002, AOL UK had a tie-in with Blockbusters for entertainment; MSN UK with Encarta for 'learning'; and Freeserve with Barclays Bank for business information. In short, the rise of general portals encouraged a middle-of-the-road, convergent use of the internet, strongly dependent on established sources. This way of organizing the internet experience was increasingly eclipsed by the less intervensionist model of Google. However, its way of ordering listings tends to funnel people towards the more popular sites, and to result in less-prominent sites being overlooked. Most people do not go beyond Google's top entries on any specific topic.[21]

A small number of companies, most notably Microsoft and America Online (AOL), gained pole position in the early commercial development of the net. The net's growing popularity then prompted leading media corporations – Time Warner, Vivendi, Disney, Bertelsmann, News Corporation, among others – to launch sophisticated websites or to form joint ventures with major telecommunications or software companies in order to establish a significant online presence. These media superpowers had enormous assets: back catalogues of content, large reserves of cash and expertise, close links with the advertising industry, brand visibility and cross-promotional resources. Although their start-ups sometimes floundered, enough succeeded for them to dominate cyberspace in a remarkably short period of time. In 1998, over three-quarters of the thirty-one most visited news and entertainment websites in the US were affiliated with large media firms.[22] In 1999, the websites of broadcast TV networks and MSNBC were the most visited sites in the US by 'news users'.[23] In 2006, the most visited news sites in Britain (apart from search engines) were all controlled by leading press and broadcasting organizations.[24] Creating and maintaining a multi-media, audience-pulling website became an expensive business, offering few openings to those with limited resources (although, as we shall see, they were not left unchallenged).

A side effect of commercialization was to promote net advertising. The advertising industry introduced first of all the banner advertisement (a horizontal strip, reminiscent of early press display advertisements). This was followed by advertisements of different shapes such as 'button', 'skyscraper' and pop-up 'interstitials', and by new types of advertisements that contain audio-visual or dynamic elements (more like television commercials). Online selling to the public also became a more prominent feature, especially after the adoption in 1997 of a standard protocol for credit card transactions.

In this new commercial world, professional conventions – such as maintaining a 'fire-wall' between editorial and advertising – were weakened. In particular, the emergence of stand-alone, promotion websites converted advertisers into controllers of editorial content, rather than buyers of space, designated as advertising, in environments controlled by professional media staff – the offline norm. Typifying this new net phenomenon was the Pepsi website, which in 2002 offered a Britney Spears mini-site, games, music, and an opportunity to learn about the 'Joy of Pepsi'. This 'ad-free ad' approach can lead to abuse. Naomi Klein cites as an example of lowered standards a website called Parent Soup, paid for by Fisher-Price, Starbucks, Procter & Gamble and Polaroid. It calls itself a 'parents' community', and imitates a user-driven newsgroup. However, when parents go to Parent Soup, they receive 'branded wisdom' such as a good way to improve your child's self-esteem is to take Polaroids of her.[25]

New layer of control

A central feature of the early net, its absence of central control, was weakened as a consequence of commercialization. Net entrepreneurs developed 'cookies' – markers deposited by websites on computer hard drives – in order to log and transmit information about user behaviour. They also introduced authentication procedures for identifying users and the status of communications (for example, by developing a digital watermark registering whether a communication has been paid for). A whole new technology of commercial surveillance came into being during the 1990s.

This surveillance was deployed very extensively. In the United States, an estimated 92 per cent of commercial websites aggregate, sort and use for commercial purposes data about people's use of the net, wherever they are.[26] Many people make themselves vulnerable to this monitoring by waiving their rights to privacy in order to gain website access. Overriding 'human rights' protection of privacy is minimal in the United States, though there is more protection in Europe. In addition, people's use of the net is often monitored at work. According to a study released in 2000, 73 per cent of US firms routinely check on their workforce's use of the net.[27]

The internet has thus ceased to be an anonymous place and instead has become a glasshouse (although many people appear not to be aware of this when they go online in the privacy of their homes). Moreover, while surveillance technology was developed for purely commercial purposes (to sell data about users, protect financial transactions and prevent piracy) it began to be used in other ways. In the late 1990s, government agencies used surveillance technology to identify net users, share information about them and prosecute them (as in the case of international paedophile rings). While there is nothing wrong in governments intervening to protect the vulnerable, such as abused children, it underlines the point that the internet is no longer 'uncontrolled'. Indeed, authoritarian governments have become adept at using the vulnerable point in the internet system – internet service providers – in order to snoop and suppress.[28]

Corporate pressure was also brought to bear in the United States (and elsewhere) for the net to become subject to stronger property protection. In

1976, the United States passed a Copyright Act which extended copyright to software. This was buttressed in 1998 by the Digital Millennium Act, which greatly strengthened legal provision against 'circumvention'. Its effect was to overprotect intellectual property rights in cyberspace at the expense of 'fair use'.[29] The likelihood is that increased pressure will be exerted in the future to strengthen still further intellectual property rights, in both national and international jurisdictions, since the music majors are currently losing their battle against music piracy.

Opposition

In short, the internet changed profoundly as a consequence of the establishment of a market system, the successful incursion of media majors into cyberspace and the imposition of a new layer of technological control. However, these trends did not go unopposed.

When the progressive coalition which shaped the early internet fell apart, one group stood firm. This was an informal community of hackers who set about opposing 'proprietary software' – programs whose use was restricted by private patent or copyright. They may be likened to the nineteenth-century Chartists on several counts, even if their central objectives were different. Hackers played a significant part, as did the Chartists, in keeping open channels of free expression;[30] they were inspired, like many Chartists, by an ethic of co-operation; and, like numerous Chartists, some sought to defend a nostalgically remembered past against the new market order. But, above all – and this is perhaps the key point – they participated in the *same*, continuing battle for media freedom.

The cyberchartist revolt began in 1984 when Richard Stallman, a radical programmer at MIT, set up the Free Software Foundation. He had been outraged when a colleague had refused to pass on a printer code on the grounds that it was now restricted by licence. This seemed to Stallman something new and alien, an enforced form of selfishness that violated the norm of co-operation on which his professional life had been based. His outrage turned to anger when AT&T announced its intention to license the widely used and previously unrestricted UNIX operating system. In his view, this amounted to the corporate capture, with the full authority of the law, of a program that had been communally produced.

Richard Stallman, a bearded, romantic figure with the appearance of an Apostle, gave up his secure job and set about building almost single-handedly a free alternative to the UNIX operating system. It was called GNU (standing for 'GNU is not UNIX'). Between 1984 and 1988, Stallman designed an editor and compiler, which were hailed by the cyberchartist community as masterpieces of skill and ingenuity. Subsequently, his hands became damaged from overwork, and he slowed down. The GNU project was still some way from completion. However, a then unknown Finnish student, Linus Torvalds, who had heard Stallman give a charismatic talk in Helsinki, filled the gap. With the help of his friends, Torvalds developed in 1990 the missing kernel of the GNU system. The hacker community collectively improved the resulting GNU/Linux system, making it one of the most reliable in the world. Such was its sustained success that IBM decided in 1998 to hitch its wagon to the hacker star. It officially backed the Linux system, agreeing to invest money in its further development without seeking to exercise any form of proprietary control.

IBM also embraced the Apache server, on the same terms. This derived from a program released free by a publicly funded agency, the National Center for Supercomputing Applications (NCSA) at the University of Illinois. Initially full of bugs, it was transformed by the hacker community through cumulative improvements ('patches'), and renamed Apache. It became a widely used free server – its success again accounting for its open source adoption by IBM.

What partly underpinned the effectiveness of this concerted protest was that it enlisted the protection of the state (something that libertarian hackers tend to ignore). The Free Software Foundation set up by Stallman released its projects under a General Public License (GPL). This contained a 'copyleft' clause (the wordplay is typical hacker humour) requiring any subsequent improvement in free software to be made available to the community under the GPL. Contract and copyright law was thus deployed to prevent companies from modifying free software and then claiming the resulting version as their property. It was also used to ensure that future refinements in free software were 'gifted' back to the community. A similar legal formula was adopted by the less radical, 'open' (as distinct from 'free') source movement, though in a more permissive form.

The cyberchartist revolt kept alive the tradition of the open disclosure of information. It perpetuated the co-operative norms of the scientific community in which people make improvements or develop new applications (such as the world wide web) on the basis of open access to information, and then return the favour by making the basis of their discoveries freely available. In this way, cyberchartists perpetuated the moral economy of academic science, with its belief in co-operation, freedom and open debate in pursuit of scientific advance. They also undermined attempts to impose a market régime on the net by making available free or open source alternatives.

Who were these remarkable people, and what inspired them to challenge corporate power in cyberspace? They were a relatively homogeneous group, consisting mainly of highly trained computer workers employed by universities, research laboratories and the computer industry, as well as university students and knowledgeable computer enthusiasts. Their first chronicler, Steven Levy, argues that they tended to subscribe to a shared set of beliefs.[31] These can be summarized as five precepts: information should be free; respect should be earned through constructive achievement, not position or credential; never trust authority; computers have the power to improve the world; for this reason, they should be put to work for the benefit of humanity. While cyberchartists' motives were philanthropic, it is also clear that many enormously enjoyed hacking. They gained satisfaction from the thrill of creativity in building or improving new programs. They were gratified by the recognition they received from their peers. Many also derived a sense of purpose from working for the good of society, and living by a set of values superior to those of conformist corporate culture. The hacker tradition combined pleasure with service to others, and drew upon a hybrid culture that married individualism to collectivism. This conjunction is expressed succinctly in a stanza quoted admiringly by Richard Stallman:

> If I am not for myself, who will be for me?
> If I am only for myself, what am I?
> If not now, when?[32]

As the cyberchartist revolt developed, splits emerged on generational lines. Older cyberchartists, like Stallman, were intent upon preserving the values of the pre-market internet, while younger ones, like Torvalds, tended to be less anti-market. The computer industry boom also winnowed the ranks of cyberchartists, separating the dedicated from the dilettantes. As Eric Raymond, another chronicler of the hackers' revolt, comments:

> commercial demand for programmers has been so intense for so long that anyone who can be seriously distracted by money is already gone. Our community has been self-selected for other things – accomplishment, pride, artistic passion, and each other.[33]

Yet, in media legend, hackers are destructive and threatening: they spread viruses, break into computer systems in ways that imperil lives, and engage in online theft. This demonization obscures a crucial distinction between 'hackers' and 'crackers', 'white' and 'black' hats, those who work for the good of society and those who are antisocial, which is widely understood within the computer activist community. To lump the two together is to seek to delegitimate cyberchartists in much the same way that an attempt was made to stigmatize the Chartists in the 1840s.

User resistance

The cyberchartist revolt was effective partly because it was accompanied by user resistance. The pre-market internet had accustomed people to expect software and content to be free. Net companies found it difficult to re-educate them into paying.

This is illustrated by early attempts to commercialize the web. In 1993, the publicly funded agency NCSA released its pioneer browser Mosaic, free on the net. Within six months, a million or more copies were downloaded. Members of the Mosaic team then set up a private company and offered an improved, commercial version, Netscape, on a three-month, free-trial basis. However, demands for payment after the free trial were widely ignored. Netscape's management then had to decide whether to insist on payment or change tack. It opted to make its service free because it feared – probably rightly – that continued attempts to charge would cause people to migrate to a free alternative. Netscape turned instead to advertising and consultancy as its main source of revenue.[34]

Companies which tried to charge website fees also ran into trouble. A large number failed.[35] The only type of web content for which a significant number of people seemed willing to pay was either pornography or financial information. This also had the effect of propelling pioneering net companies towards advertising as their main source of revenue.

The virtues of net advertising were widely trumpeted. The net reached a mainly young and affluent audience. Its technology enabled advertising to be targeted towards specialist groups, with almost surgical precision. Above all, the net offered a unique selling point: consumers could click on an advertisement, be taken direct to the advertiser's site, obtain more information and buy the product or service in question.

The only problem was that there appeared to be built-in resistance to net advertising because it was viewed from the start as intrusive. An early warning signal came in 1994 when the US law firm Canter and Siegel posted an advertisement for its immigration law advice service to thousands of news groups. The following day, it was so inundated with abusive replies ('flames') that its internet service provider crashed repeatedly.[36] In 1995 a survey found that two-thirds of Americans did not want any net advertising.[37] People became adept at avoiding ads by clicking the delete button. New ways of engaging user interest ran into problems: audio-visual ads were expensive and took time to download. In the UK, crude banner ads still accounted for 52 per cent of net advertising expenditure in 2001. Worse still, the extent of net user resistance to advertising became embarrassingly transparent. In 2001, the numbers of users 'clicking through' to advertising sites were generally less than 1 per cent.[38] For all of these reasons, net advertising grew at a much slower pace than had been anticipated. In 2002, it still amounted to only 1 per cent of the UK's total media advertising expenditure.[39] However, it grew rapidly thereafter, to 16 per cent of total media expenditure by 2007.[40]

Direct selling on the net also proved to be much more difficult than anticipated. It tended to be confined to a limited range of products, such as music, live events, books and holidays. Many people, it transpired, liked to shop in person and were doubtful about the security of online credit card purchases. The dawning realization that net retailing was going to take a long time to establish successfully, and would require a heavy investment with a deferred and speculative return, was the main cause of the dotcom crash of 2000–1.

The entire internet economy was weakened by the crash. It was not only small net companies that ran into trouble. Even market leaders such as Yahoo! were forced to issue profit warnings, and major conglomerates such as AOL Time Warner and Vivendi had to restructure, partly as a consequence of failed net investments. Venture capital which had poured money into the internet economy lost confidence and withdrew support.

Yet, the irony is that internet retailing did expand during the 2000s. By 2008, 55 per cent of the British population said that they had bought something online in the past. Most of these (81 per cent) had done so in the last three months. The most popular items bought online were to do with travel, accommodation and holidays. But while the number of online buyers increased steadily, it is less clear that the volume of individual online consumption has also grown in the way one would expect if people were becoming increasingly reliant on online retailers. Certainly, between 2006 and 2008 the proportions buying differing volumes of online goods remained almost constant.[41]

In short, commercialization did not fully take hold, partly because the economy of the internet proved fragile. Online advertising grew slowly in Britain until 2003; online shopping developed even more slowly; dotcom enterprises lost money; and above all, most users could not be persuaded to pay for web-based content.

In short, commercialization did not fully take hold because the economy of the internet proved to be precarious. Underlying this fragility was the unwillingness of the public to buy heavily online, respond to net advertising and pay website fees. A revolt within the computer world, and unobtrusive resistance from the public, stalled – at least for a time – the market takeover of the net.

Contested space

The history of the internet is thus a chronicle of contradiction. In its mainly pre-market phase, the internet was powerfully influenced by the values of academic science, American counter-culture and European public service. It began as a research tool. It blossomed into a subcultural playground and medium of grassroots concerns, and it developed the world wide web as a public space open to all.

However, this early formation was overlaid by a new commercial régime. Major media organizations established well-resourced websites. Search engines, seeking to harvest advertising, signposted visitors to popular destinations. The growth of online entertainment tended to marginalize political discourse. Net entrepreneurs sought to populate the web with virtual shops and to make users pay for information. Computer companies turned software into profitable commodities. New surveillance technology was developed to monitor user behaviour and to extend digital rights management.

Yet the old order refused to surrender without a struggle. Dissenting computer workers resisted the new régime of enforced intellectual property rights by making available free or open source software. Users, conditioned by the pre-market norms of the net, declined to be re-educated into becoming paying consumers. Instead, they diverted from sites seeking to charge a fee to sites that were free.

As a result, the internet came to exhibit incongruent features. It is still a decentralized system in which information is transmitted via independent, variable pathways through dispersed computer power. But on top of this is imposed a new technology of commercial surveillance which enables commercial operators – and governments – to monitor what people do online. In a similarly contradictory way, the internet is managed by public service trusts, a legacy from its pre-market past, but most of the net's major players are now private companies. Yet, if the drive to commercialize the web intensified in the 2000s, the DIY culture of the web also found new expression.

This was exemplified by the founding of Wikipedia, a web-based, free-content encyclopedia, in 2001. It was written by a growing legion of volunteers, numbering some 75,000 active contributors in 2008. It encompassed an enormous range of subjects, covered in 10 million articles in more than 260 languages. It became a global phenomenon, attracting 684 million visitors in 2008.[42] And it achieved a remarkable (though variable) level of quality, supported by the self-correcting mechanism of revision, a shared norm of adhering to factual accuracy, unobtrusive safeguards and an academic tail of hypertextual links.

The rise of Wikipedia was accompanied by the meteoric growth of other websites based on user-generated content. Facebook was set up by Harvard students in 2004, took off as a young élite social networking site, and then grew exponentially when it became open to all in 2006. It provides a way in which users can publish, in effect, to their friends, while excluding unwanted attention. YouTube was created as a video-sharing website in 2005 and became a rapid success around the world. It offered a way in which users could circulate what they enjoyed, grade collectively what was available, and in the process provide an opportunity for marginalized artists and creative talents to connect to a wider public.

The emergence of Web 2.0, a part of the web based on user-generated content, represented a strengthening of the non-commercial traditions of the web. Some corporations sought to incorporate this grassroots activity, and transmute it into profit, by buying up high-traffic sites that would generate advertising revenue. Thus, Google bought YouTube in 2006, while Murdoch acquired the popular social networking site Facebook, also in 2006. Meanwhile, major film and TV companies sought to use YouTube and similar sites as extensions of their publicity departments. Their attempts were less than successful, because users were the gatekeepers determining prominence on these sites, and proved less susceptible to influence than time-pressured, PR-fed journalists reporting the entertainment industries.

In effect, the spirit of co-operation that had re-imagined the computer and discovered new uses for it in the 1980s, that had defended the internet through the open source movement, that had created the world wide web in 1990–91, was renewed through the development of social networking sites in the 2000s. Cyberspace is now much more commercialized than it was ten years ago; yet, it is still not a controlled market system.

The balance struck between the old and the new is inherently unstable, and may well change quite rapidly; but, as of now, the two leading understandings of the net both seem simplistic. The net is not an autonomous space where the 'push' culture associated with powerful media corporations has been vanquished in favour of the 'pull' culture of the sovereign user; yet, equally, the internet is not a featureless mall of digital capitalism. It remains a contested space, exposed to the opposed influences of pre-market and market forces.

So far, we have offered a history of the internet which foregrounds its technology and American origins, and contrasts a period of professional and grassroots influence with the subsequent attempt to impose a new order of market control. This largely leaves out wider questions about the consequences of the net, and its relationship to the structures of global society. These issues are best addressed by sociologists, to whose work we now turn.

Notes

1. Leading exponents of this position are N. Negroponte, *Being Digital* (London, Hodder & Stoughton, 1996 [1995]); and M. Poster, 'Cyberdemocracy: internet and the public sphere', in D. Porter (ed.), *Internet Culture* (New York, Routledge, 1997), and, in a more circumspect form, H. Rheingold, *The Virtual Community* (Cambridge, MA, MIT Press, 2000, rev. edn).
2. D. Schiller, *Digital Capitalism* (Cambridge, MA, MIT Press, 2000), a bold and innovative attack on internet orthodoxy. See also a more guarded exposition of a similar position in R. McChesney, *Rich Media, Poor Democracy* (Urbana, University of Illinois Press, 1999).
3. The best introductory accounts of the underlying science involved in the development of the internet are J. Naughton, *A Brief History of the Future* (London, Phoenix, 2000) and J. Gillies and R. Cailliau, *How the Web Was Born* (Oxford, Oxford University Press, 2000).
4. A. Briggs and P. Burke, *A Social History of the Media* (Cambridge, Polity Press, 2002) p. 291.
5. T. Berners-Lee, *Weaving the Web* (London, Orion, 2000), p. 56.
6. B. Winston, *Media Technology and Society* (London, Routledge, 1998), p. 218.
7. M. Cassells, *The Internet Galaxy* (Oxford, Oxford University Press, 2001).
8. S. Holland (ed.), *The State as Entrepreneur* (London, Weidenfeld & Nicolson, 1972). This position now has more support in Scandinavia and mainland Europe than it does in Britain.

9. J. Abbate, *Inventing the Internet* (Cambridge, MA, MIT Press, 2000); J. Gillies and R. Cailliau, *How the Web Was Born* (Oxford, Oxford University Press, 2000).

10. P. Flichy, 'New media history', in L. Lievrouw and S. Livingstone (eds), *The Handbook of New Media* (London, Sage, 2002).

11. J. Abbate, *Inventing the Internet* (Cambridge, MA, MIT Press, 2000), p. 144. Although this is the best relevant history, it mistakenly portrays the commercialization of the net as extending the freedom and diversity traditions of the early internet.

12. F. Turner, *From Counterculture to Cyberculture* (Chicago, University of Chicago Press, 2006).

13. H. Rheingold, *The Virtual Community* (Cambridge, MA, MIT Press, 2000, rev. edn).

14. P. Flichy, 'The construction of new digital media', *New Media and Society*, 1 (1), 1999, p. 37.

15. T. Berners-Lee, *Weaving the Web* (London, Orion, 2000), p. 116.

16. *Ibid.*, p. 91.

17. N. Negroponte, *Being Digital* (London, Hodder & Stoughton, 1996 [1995]), pp. 57–58 and 85.

18. M. Poster, *The Second Media Age* (Cambridge, Polity Press, 1995).

19. T. Streeter, 'Romanticism in business culture: the Internet, the 1990s and the origins of irrational exuberance', in A. Calabrese and C. Sparks (eds), *Toward a Political Economy of Culture* (Boulder, CO, Rowman & Littlefield, 2003).

20. V. Miller, 'Search engines, portals and global capitalism', in D. Gauntlett (ed.), *Web Studies* (London, Arnold, 2000).

21. M. Hindman, *The Myth of Digital Democracy* (Princeton, Princeton University Press, 2009).

22. R. McChesney, *Rich Media, Poor Democracy* (Urbana, University of Illinois Press, 1999), p. 163.

23. C. Sparks, 'From dead trees to live wires: the Internet's challenge to the traditional newspaper', in J. Curran and M. Gurevitch (eds), *Mass Media and Society* (London, Arnold, 2000, 3rd edn), p. 283, figure 13.8.

24. *New News, Future News* (London, Ofcom, 2007), p. 34.

25. N. Klein, *No Logo* (London, Flamingo, 2001), pp. 42–43.

26. L. Lessig, *Code and Other Laws of Cyberspace* (New York, Basic Books, 1999), p. 153.

27. M. Castells, *The Internet Galaxy* (Oxford, Oxford University Press, 2001), p. 74.

28. M. Price, *Media and Sovereignty* (Cambridge, MIT Press, 2002); L. Stein and N. Sinha, 'New global media and communication policy: the role of the state in the twenty-first century', in L. Lievrouw and S. Livingstone (eds), *The Handbook of New Media* (London, Sage, 2001).

29. L. Lessig, *The Future of Ideas* (New York, Random House, 2001).

30. See Chapter 2.

31. S. Levy, *Hackers* (London, Penguin, 1994).

32. Cited S. Williams, *Free as in Freedom* (Sebastopol, CA, O'Reilly, 2002), p. 102.

33. *Ibid.*, p. 167.

34. T. Berners-Lee, *Weaving the Web* (London, Orion, 2000), pp. 107–8.

35. D. Schiller, *Digital Capitalism* (Cambridge, MA, MIT Press, 2000); C. Sparks, 'From dead trees to live wires: the Internet's challenge to the traditional newspaper', in J. Curran and M. Gurevitch (eds), *Mass Media and Society* (London, Arnold, 2000, 3rd edn).

36. G. Goggin, 'Pay per browse? The Web's commercial future', in D. Gauntlett (ed.), *Web Studies* (London, Arnold, 2000), p. 106.

37. R. McChesney, *Rich Media, Poor Democracy* (Urbana, University of Illinois Press, 1999), p. 132.

38. L. Cheshire, 'What influence has advertising had upon the development of the Internet?' (Unpublished BA dissertation, Goldsmiths College, University of London, 2002).

39. *Advertising Statistics Yearbook 2002* (London, Advertising Association, 2002).

40. D. Freedman, 'The political economy of the "new" news environment', in N. Fenton (ed.), *New Media, Old News* (London, Sage, 2009), table 2.1.

41. *Internet Access 2008* (London, Office of National Statistics, 2008), p. 10.

42. All these figures are self-reported in '*Wikipedia: About*'. http://en.wikipedia.org/wiki.wikpedia: About. Accessed 20 February 2009.

Chapter 18

Sociology of the internet

Introduction

There is a very large literature, dubbed 'internetphilia' by Korinna Patelis,[1] which argues that the internet will solve many of our social ills: the decline of community, political apathy, national prejudice, social discrimination, public disempowerment, and much else besides. This tradition argues that the virtual world is free, egalitarian, interactive, self-expressive and global. It is superior to the physical world which it will redeem.

The counter-argument to this is that the impact of the net is determined not by its technology but by the structures and processes of society. In this view, the real world shapes the online world more than the other way round.

This is a central debate in net sociology. It also provides a good starting point for assessing the role and influence of the net.

Global understanding

It is often argued that the internet is shrinking the universe and promoting international understanding.[2] This view focuses on the potential of internet technology to enable free and equal exchange between people around the globe. What it ignores is the way in which this global interchange is distorted by unequal relations between rich and poor.[3]

At the end of the twentieth century, 20 per cent of the world's population disposed of 86 per cent of its wealth. This affluent fifth is in general the best educated, most technologically advanced section of the globe: it also has the highest density of computers per head, and accounts for most of the world's full-time online workers. These advantages structure the opportunity to communicate in cyberspace. Thus, in 2000 London generated more internet websites than the whole of Africa.[4] More generally, the United States, western Europe and affluent parts of Asia produce much of the content of the web, while whole areas of the world contribute very little.

The capacity to win attention is even more unequal than the opportunity to communicate in cyberspace. Media conglomerates have well-visited websites because they have large resources and high visibility. These advantages help to create privileged centres of online communication. In 2000, the USA produced almost two-thirds of the top thousand most-visited websites. Still more remarkable, it accounted for 83 per cent of the total pageviews of internet users.[5]

This dominance is facilitated by language. Less than 10 per cent of the world speak English as their first language. But English is becoming intelligible to a growing number of people, and has begun to assume the function once occupied by Latin in medieval Europe as the shared language of a transnational élite. In the late 1990s, an estimated 85 per cent of the web was written in English.[6]

There are thus strong pressures that act like a magnetic force of attraction pulling people towards the USA and northern centres of the world wide web. The converse is also true. Communications not written in English and not positioned at the top of search engines' hierarchies obtain scant attention. For example, anything written in Marathi is likely to be ignored in the global dialogue of the web, even though the population of Mahrashtra and adjacent Marathi-speaking areas, in India, exceeds that of Britain.

If the opportunity to win attention on the web is distributed unevenly, so too is the opportunity to visit. In 2000, a mere 0.16 per cent of the Indian population were internet users, compared with 41 per cent in the United States. This disparity was replicated around the world, and gave rise to a global community of internet users which bore little relationship to the distribution of the world's population. North America and western Europe accounted for 66 per cent of internet users in 2000, while the whole of Latin America and Africa accounted for only 5 per cent.[7]

This distortion was modified by the rapid diffusion of internet use in Korea (now one of the most online-active countries in the world) and Japan, and in urban India and China. But this adjustment reflected not only Japan's great wealth, but also the economic growth of south Asia. Net access remains geographically unequal, with Africa, and to a lesser degree Latin America, enormously unrepresented.

In short, the imbalance of power and resources in the offline world structure the online world. The minority who use the net are recruited primarily from the affluent; they consume content generated mainly by the rich centres of the world; and they communicate usually in languages that most of the world do not understand. It is a self-deluding fantasy to imagine that the dialogue of the internet is bringing all parts of the world closer together in mutual understanding.

Freedom from place

Another frequently invoked claim is that the internet is transforming our relationship to the physical world.[8] This is based primarily on inferences derived from the nature of internet technology. Because the net is global, its use is thought to be weakening identification with place ('deterritorialization'), and in particular with the nation. And since the net enables the formation of virtual communities of like-minded people, unconnected to where they live or work, it is also said to be loosening ties to specific contexts ('disembedding'). Physical and virtual geographies are allegedly de-merging in a form that is weakening national prejudice and eroding the link between social interaction and locality.

These arguments seem plausible. However, they appear rather less commanding when they are assessed in the light of actual evidence about internet use. Empirical research shows time and again that the virtual world is best viewed as an extension of the structures and processes of the real world, rather than as a technologically determined space that is reconfiguring society.

To illustrate this, we will turn to Daniel Miller and Don Slater's illuminating ethnography of the net in Trinidad. The net, they argue, is absorbed into the everyday life and social practices of its users. For this reason, it promotes, rather than detracts from, a sense of place. A number of Trinidadian websites parade symbols of national identity or express pride in national achievements. Chat rooms celebrate a strong sense of being 'Trini' by enacting through 'ole talk' and 'liming' what are widely perceived to be national traits – the ability to communicate, to be witty about everyday things, to be warm and expressive. Encounters with people of other nations in virtual space heighten rather than diminish a sense of national belonging. Many Trinidadians view themselves as 'virtual' envoys, seek to convey a favourable impression of their country, and are sometimes taken aback by how little other people seem to know about their culture and traditions. Indeed, Miller and Slater conclude (with perhaps an element of debunking overstatement) that '"being Trini" and "representing Trinidad" were not always the central or most conscious aspect of internet activities, but we rarely found an internet experience in which they did not feature'.[9] The net also facilitates an idealization of Trinidad among Trinidadians living in Britain, and provides a concrete way of staying in touch with relatives in Trinidad.

It may be that this case study is untypical. There is, argue Miller and Slater, a widespread desire among Trinidadians to identify with a stable, national community, partly as a consequence of the dislocations caused by slavery, migration and colonial subordination. In some other countries with a less traumatic past, where the tug of national identity is weaker, the net may promote a different relationship to place.

Yet, at the heart of Miller and Slater's account is a core theme that does seem to provide a secure basis for generalization. The virtual world emerges in their analysis not as a featureless space determined by its technology, but as a field of interaction shaped by local contexts. People relate to the net in terms of attitudes, cultural references, and concerns derived from diverse, *real-world* locations, and this strongly influences in turn what they get out of the net. This insight accords with all that we know about media consumption in general, accumulated through two generations of audience research.[10]

This stress on the socially situated basis of net consumption also accords with other studies. The net is generally used as an extension of everyday relationships: it provides a way of staying in touch with friends and relatives, much like the phone, and – in the past – the mailed letter.[11] Whether it also supports an identification with place depends upon the particular orientations and social contexts of net users. Thus, Larry Gross reveals the growing importance of the net in providing a source of identity and moral support for isolated, gay teenagers, without links to local gay subcultures, and for gay men in countries where gay sex is illegal.[12] In this case, the net seemingly provides an escape from an oppressive local context to a placeless, global gay village.

By contrast, Madhavi Mallapragada argues that the net helps to sustain an imperilled Indian identity among diasporic Indians living in the United States. The net offers them a channel of communication with friends and relations in India. It disseminates symbols of Indian identity and culture, and provides a forum of discussion on identity themes (such as how to persuade Indian-American teenagers to identify with their Indian heritage). The net also offers a socially acceptable way of searching for eligible Indian life partners.[13] In this case, then, the net fosters identification with a national homeland.

These two case studies point in opposite directions. Yet they have one thing in common: they both show that the meanings derived from the net are shaped by users' concerns and terms of reference. Their overarching implication is thus that different user inputs and contexts give rise to different symbolic uses of the net.

Given the current stock of knowledge about the net, it is not possible to say whether the net promotes 'freedom' from a sense of place; but what we do know is that this is certainly not true in relation to some users. Confident generalizations about how the net is promoting deterritorialization and disembedding, inferred from its technology, are simplistic and misleading.

Social emancipation

This insistence on the need to contextualize the use of the net in its social setting in order to assess the net's wider influence on society runs counter to another widely canvassed view. This sees the virtual world as a vanguard social space in which a more tolerant, egalitarian and emancipated universe is being forged. This virtual realm of the imagination is promoting social emancipation in the real world.

The progressive nature of the online world is derived, allegedly, from its 'postmodern technology'.[14] This enables anonymous interaction, in which people are able to escape from the visible markers which proclaim their gender, age and ethnicity, and position them in ascribed social roles. People can assume online whatever identity they want, and also talk about themselves with unaccustomed frankness, in this way exploring fundamental questions about who they are and whom they want to be. Role-playing (as in pretending to be a member of the opposite sex) can also be liberating, it is argued, because it enables people to experience at first hand socially conditioned responses and to acquire new insight about others.

'Virtual disembodiment' – being taken out of one's physical self in the virtual world – is thus said in cybercultural studies to assist the building of emancipated subjectivities and the gaining of enlightenment. This claim is invested with added significance as a consequence of theoretical developments in poststructuralist theory. These stress that there is no fixed and essential self, defined by biology, nature or reason, but rather identities that are always 'performances' enacted in relation to others. Seen in this light, the virtual world is a place for working out: the equivalent of a health club where bodies can be remoulded through relentless exercise. The internet is also, in some accounts, a prefigurative space in which the patterns of the future – in particular fluid, mobile identities freed from the constraints of tradition – can be cultivated.[15]

However, there are good grounds for thinking that the significance of online role-playing has been exaggerated. While identity games received much attention during the early, experimental phase of the internet in the 1980s, their popularity declined. When net use became more widespread, it also became more mundane. A major American survey found in 2000 that 91 per cent of users regularly use email, compared with 28 per cent who participate regularly in chat rooms or online discussions.[16] Online role-playing, it seems, was increasingly favoured by the young, and in particular by teenagers.

Some analysts overstate the empowerment of online fantasy games by examining what happens in these games in a form that is abstracted from the social context of the real world. Consider, for example, Mizuko Ito's acclaimed account of the 'virtually embodied' in which she describes how Melissa assumes the identity of Tenar on entering Multi User Dungeons (MUDs). Tenar is apparently 'a powerful and well-liked figure' who has had virtual sex with, and married, a number of other MUDders. This, we are told, is very strengthening because Melissa is able to import aspects of her dynamic Tenar personality into her everyday world, and her fantasy life 'animates her real life'.[17] Since we are told almost nothing about Melissa's real life, we are forced to take this claim on trust. However, there is one aspect of Melissa's online identity that provokes scepticism. Melissa describes her body online as it used to be when she was a svelte 18-year-old. What, one wonders, are the social pressures and personal anxieties that cause Melissa to present herself as younger and, by implication, sexier than the person she has become? Does Melissa's wish fulfilment really make her stronger, or does it increase her sense of loss and reluctance to come to terms with increasing age? It is an entirely characteristic weakness of this celebratory account – and others like it – that such questions are not even addressed.

This 'cyberculture' tradition of research has another recurring flaw. Its underlying notion of empowerment is based on 'self-constitutive strategies of being' – put simply, on individuals taking control through redefining who they are. The virtual world is celebrated because it assists imaginative forms of redefinition and re-enactment. However, this approach tends to discount the compelling ways in which social roles and identities are imposed through early socialization and peer-group pressure, and tends to ignore the structures of power that underpin these forms of social regulation. By focusing attention on the transformative properties of cyberspace, it tends also to downplay the importance of organization and political action needed to effect far-reaching change in the real world. It has taken the women's movement over a century to effect the legislative reforms, institutional changes and cultural shifts needed to achieve what is still an uncompleted social revolution.[18]

Political emancipation

If the internet does not deliver effortless social emancipation through online fun, perhaps it is advancing a progressive politics. After all, it is argued with undeniable eloquence that internet technology converts the desk into a printing press, broadcasting station and place of assembly.[19] This enables 'many-to-many communication' which allegedly is transforming politics. In this view the net is rejuvenating civil society, generating political activism and launching exciting experiments of popular participation in government. Established centres of power, and monopolies of communication, are being bypassed ('disintermediated'); counter-public spheres are being created through net-mediated conferences and chat rooms; and a process of progressive mobilization is under way that will empower the people.

Again, this infectious optimism follows a now familiar pattern. It extrapolates from the technological potential of the net the view that a powerful engine of change is at work, and then fastens on to a few hopeful straws of evidence to confirm the advent of a brave new world. What this approach fails repeatedly to grasp is that the virtual world is not 'determined' by its technology, and 'programmed' to promote progressive change. Rather, the online world is shaped powerfully by the dynamics of the offline world. This can limit the power of the net to effect change, or it can accentuate its impact. It is not the technology of the net, but the interaction between technology and context, that is the key to understanding the nature of the net's impact.

Thus, in most advanced liberal democracies, political activism is a minority pursuit and many people's interest in politics, in ordinary circumstances, is limited. For example, tracking surveys in the USA show that, between 1980 and 2000, fewer than one in ten Americans attended a political meeting, gave to political funds or helped a political organization.[20] Indeed, the indications are that, for a variety of reasons, the level of political engagement in long-established democracies is falling. In Britain, membership of political parties is in long-term decline, a trend experienced in a number of other European countries.[21] Voting turnout in the 2005 general election (61 per cent) was lower than in any election between 1922 and 1997, when it never dropped below 70 per cent.[22]

This low, and probably declining, level of political involvement in the real world influences the content of the virtual world. This was borne out by an analysis of net content undertaken by Kevin Hill and John Hughes.[23] They found only 6 per cent of web pages in 1997, and only 12 per cent of Usenet news group messages between 1995 and 1996, to be 'political'. The net is no different from most other media in that it marginalizes politics.

Hill and Hughes also found no evidence that the internet was helping to connect the disaffected or disengaged to the world of politics. On the contrary, political users of the net were more inclined to vote than the average, and tended to seek out not dissident information but the websites of the leading media organizations. They wanted more, not different, political information. Hill and Hughes also found no support for the view that the net offered support for progressive causes: on the contrary, the right seem better organized on the net than the left during the latter 1990s.

However, notwithstanding this sceptical account, the net did affect American politics. It enabled outsider candidates (most notably Howard Dean in 2004) to mount serious challenges for presidential party nominations. This culminated in the success of a relative outsider, Barak Obama, in winning the Democratic nomination aided by the internet, which helped him to raise large campaign funds from citizens as well as corporate sources, and to mobilize a broad-based activist coalition. These assets contributed to his eventual victory in the 2008 presidential election, although it was the 2008 economic crash, and the flatlining of so many Americans' incomes during a period of almost thirty years' economic growth, among other factors, that created the conditions in which the internet (and other forms of campaigning) were an effective political tool for the left. The same tool can be – and will be – deployed by the American right to secure electoral success in different circumstances.

In other words, the impact of the internet is contingent upon the wider context of society. However, this does not mean necessarily that the external environment functions as a 'drag', limiting the net's effects. The reverse can also be the case: the context can accentuate the impact of the net. This point is illustrated by our next example, comparing the role of the internet in two countries.

The People's Action Party (PAP) has ruled Singapore since 1965, and has exercised control partly through a restrictive National Security Act, manipulative defamation law, and the annual registration of civil society organizations.

But it has also ruled by consent as a consequence of rising economic prosperity and the prevailing national ideology that stresses Asian values, public morality and the need for ethnic harmony. One-party dominance has resulted in the local internet being co-opted in support of the régime through largely non-coercive means.[24] Even a critical website which is directed at the local population from outside the city-state's jurisdiction, and which is therefore free from state intimidation, is relatively restrained in what it says.[25] The internet has been tamed in Singapore by the dominant culture of a one-party state.

By contrast the National Front (Barisan Nasional), the dominant political coalition in Malaysia, is more fractured and divided than PAP. It has also been beset by allegations of crony capitalism, and rides uneasily the tiger of Islamic fundamentalism. The much greater degree of political division and opposition within Malaysia, by comparison with Singapore, was accentuated when Anwar Ibrahim, the deputy prime minister, was imprisoned in 1997 for unsubstantiated charges of corruption and homosexuality. Growing dissent found expression in online newspapers and magazines critical of the régime, which gained a substantial audience in the late 1990s and 2000s, when many people distrusted the mainstream press and television.[26] Critical online journalism both reflected and amplified political differences in Malaysia, culminating in the 2008 elections, when the National Front did worse than it had done for decades, and lost its two-thirds parliamentary majority. In brief, the difference of national context resulted in the internet strengthening opposition in Malaysia, but in being co-opted in Singapore.

E-government

However, it is often claimed that the interactive technology of the net enables people to engage in public decision making in new, more direct and meaningful ways. This may become true in the future, although the evidence so far is not very encouraging.

The best-known public participation project in Europe is Amsterdam's Digital City (called DDS in the Netherlands). It began in 1994 as a ten-week experiment to improve communication between the council and local people. Proving to be unexpectedly popular, it was then reconstituted the following year under a publicly funded Foundation as a virtual city structured around the metaphor of the square. Different squares were given over to particular topics (such as film, art or politics) and, in each of these, cybercafés were established as meeting places. The net was then still a relative novelty and the experiment brought together diverse groups in the city – hackers linked to the university, artists and musicians, radical activists drawn from the squatters' movement, among others. At its height, the project involved thousands of people; facilitated popular access to computers and online services; and organized votes on a range of issues. It became celebrated in radical circles (as did a similar experiment in Bologna, Italy). However, the level of public involvement fell away after the initial excitement wore off. Acute conflicts undermined the project from within, and adequate, long-term public funding proved not to be forthcoming.

Other more modest but, in the long term, probably more significant experiments have been attempted. One approach involves using the net to extend existing procedures of consultation, typified by the work of Citizens Online Democracy (UKCOD), founded in Britain in 1995. For example, in 1997 it co-ordinated and published submissions to the Cabinet Office in response to publication of the Freedom of Information White Paper. What made this first online scrutiny of proposed government legislation noteworthy was that 30 per cent of submissions came from individuals – very much higher than the norm.[27] The net offers, seemingly, a channel in which the unorganized can more easily become involved in democratic consultation.

However, in general, five recurrent problems have bedevilled online participation in government.[28] The first is that citizens' inputs can be divorced from policy outputs: they are mere simulations of open government, unconnected to the real structures of policy making. The second linked problem is that some online innovations are really public service promotions: they are about improving consumption of services rather than about participation in policy making. The third problem is linked to the first two: some people are reluctant to take part in online participation experiments because they think that they will not be taken seriously. The fourth problem has to do with the status of online participation: instant judgements based on pressing a button are open to the republican objection that democracy needs to be accompanied by debate and deliberation. The fifth difficulty is still more fundamental, and at present undermines all attempts to use the net as an agency of direct democracy. Quite simply, cyberdemocracy is not representative. In most countries, there are large disparities of internet access between rich and poor, young and old, graduates and early school leavers. This was the case, for example, in Britain in 2007–8.[29]

E-commerce

The internet is said to be transforming the way business is done. According to Philip Evans and Thomas Wurster, the internet is redefining the relationship between businesses and three groups of people – customers, suppliers and employees – by changing the mode of communication between them. 'In a deconstructing world', they conclude, the foundations of traditional business strategy are 'blown to bits'.[30] The internet is also said to be the driving force in the creation of a mysterious new entity – the 'new economy'.

What substance do these claims have? Certain industries, sometimes lumped together under the heading of the 'information and knowledge economy' – electronics, computing, telecommunications, media and information content producers – are among the fastest-growing sectors of advanced economies. They have generated new streams of wealth without changing the goals and dynamics of the market system. They have also displaced unskilled work with skilled work, creating increased rewards for the highly educated and already affluent, but shrinking opportunities for lower socio-economic groups. However, the internet is a relatively late and small-scale entrant to the information economy. While it has given birth to prosperous internet service providers, it has failed so far to sustain a substantial profitable net content-producing industry (apart from computer games).

Nor has the advent of online selling to the public brought into being an important 'new economy' retail sector. Net marketing expert Crispin Jameson points to seven factors limiting its growth.[31] The internet, he points out, does not eliminate the need in many sectors to invest heavily in stock, promotion, delivery and service: for example, Amazon made a massive outlay in creating the world's largest bookshop before becoming a successful online bookseller. Some people are nervous about credit card security online, especially in relation to small, unknown companies. In addition, some consumers enjoy (often unconsciously) the experience of shopping; want to see the product before buying it; expect the immediate gratification of possession; lack ready access to a personal computer; and are sometimes intimidated by the technical requirements of buying online. However, the internet has made significant inroads in some sectors, such as travel and accommodation, and seems set to enjoy an incremental growth without usurping the high street store.

Online shopping is eclipsed by online business-to-business sales. The latter represents, it is claimed, an area of innovation which has changed the dynamics of business.[32] Computer mediation has diminished administration and transport costs in a way that has probably helped the small company. It has enabled a greater number of buyers and sellers to connect to each other. It has extended the geographical reach of their interactions (with European, American and Asian companies regularly competing against each other in open tenders for major contracts). It has also enabled some companies to bypass 'old economy' intermediaries to sell directly to business customers.

However, even this thesis is not quite as straightforward as it seems. Some of the changes wrought by the internet were first set in motion by the electronic data interchange (EDI) systems initiated in the 1960s. Indeed, one reason why new information technology has so strongly influenced business-to-business commerce is precisely because it is the culmination of long-term change that preceded the internet and extranet.

The internet, or rather computer networking linked to the net, has also facilitated the development of globally interdependent financial markets operating in real time. These markets have greatly increased capital flows across national boundaries, added to the instability of the global economy and exerted a powerful cumulative pressure on national governments to converge around market-friendly policies. This said, modern communications technology is only one facilitating factor in the rise and growing political influence of financial markets (and is much less important than the dismantlement of the Bretton Woods system of economic regulation, for mainly political reasons).[33] Once again, the argument that the net has effected a major transformation is not as strong as it at first appears.

The claim that the net is changing the economic order now centres on the argument that the modern firm is 'adapting to the internet as its organisational form'.[34] This takes the form of a decentralized network enterprise, guided by a flat hierarchy, making extensive use of casual labour, able to respond quickly and flexibly to market feedback, with the capacity to deploy customized production strategies in response to specialized demand. This 'new economy' model, it is claimed, takes full advantage of new communications technology to secure productivity gains, to innovate and to adapt to the requirements of the global economy. It is the way of the future.

The only problem with this argument is that it relies very heavily on a small number of examples of success (usually featuring Dell and Cisco Systems), some of which have proved to be transient. Giant corporations, able to reap economies of scale and scope, dominate most sectors from bio-chemicals and car manufacture to oil and food retailing. It may be that the 'network enterprise' (formerly called the 'cluster model') will prove triumphant in some markets, particularly those that are fragmented or subject to rapid change. But the case has yet to be made convincingly that it is the business template of the new global order.

In the relevant literature, there is one significant absence. The internet offers an interactive, many-to-many channel of communication ideally suited to promoting deliberative forms of employee participation. But this aspect of the internet's potential is rarely discussed, because it does not fit the profit agenda of the e-commerce debate. The main reason why the internet has contributed so little to work-based democracy is that this has been actively discouraged by managements, many of whom now monitor their employees' emails.

Wonders of the net

The limitations of the view that the virtual world is determined by its technology have been highlighted for two reasons. This view has a prominent place in the internet literature, and warrants critical scrutiny in its own right. It also offers misleading solutions to problems for which the real remedy lies elsewhere. For this reason its emptiness needs to be exposed.

Yet, if the technological determinist argument is recast as a question – Does internet technology make any difference? – it prompts an immediately affirmative response. Internet technology opens up new possibilities and hopes, and new forms of fulfilment. It makes available a treasure trove of information, well over a thousand million unique pages of internet content, most of which is freely accessible.[35] It offers new forms of pleasure, not least the 'file sharing' of music and films. It provides a convenient way of staying connected, through email and social networking sites, with an extended network of people. However, of its many functions, we will focus in conclusion on just three which could make a significant difference to the future organization and direction of political life.

First, the internet makes it easier to transmit alternative views to a wider audience. Its email, conferencing and chat room functions facilitate expression of minority views. Software – now freely available – makes it *relatively* easy to establish and develop a website. The cost of 'publishing' online is lower than it is offline because costs are partly laid off on readers, who pay for reproduction and distribution through their personal computer and connection charges.

However, the evolving online distribution system is a serious obstacle to gaining attention on the web. Search engines are the key mechanism for determining which sites are visited. Only a quarter of websites are listed by directory-based search engines such as Yahoo![36] In the case of spider-based search engines (which use software to content-analyse websites), only 16 per cent of sites are included on individual engines, and only 42 per cent in total on all the major engines. Yet inclusion is only the first hurdle. The next is to be listed in the top ten or twenty in a search engine's rankings, since most people do not persevere beyond this point. This is where most websites drop from sight. While their originators can buy prominence through payment to search engines, this becomes expensive for more than a very short burst of promotion.

In effect, alternative voices tend not to be heard in the main square of the electronic public sphere, but they still get heard in some online back streets. This is because market censorship remains less developed and effective in the online world than it is in the offline world.

The other source of censorship is the state. Although the internet is no longer 'uncontrolled', its decentralized global structure makes it more difficult for authoritarian governments to censor than is the case with offline media. Although governments can usually screen out unwanted websites by exerting pressure on internet service providers, this can be circumvented by using unbanned proxy websites, accomplished through entering a URL address which the proxy websites fetch and display.

Second, the net provides a very effective tool of collective organization. The net played a significant part, for example, in the planning and mobilization of the anti-globalization protests from 1999 onwards. However, it was only one of a number of means of agitprop communication, including leaflets, posters, mail-outs, mobile phones, mainstream media publicity, graffiti and, increasingly crucial, cheap air travel.[37]

Third, the global, interactive nature of the internet makes it an important democratic tool at a strategic moment. The power of the nation-state is waning, with its authority, especially in the economic sphere, shifting towards international agencies, global financial markets and transnational businesses. These growing centres of power are not held adequately to account because participatory democratic politics is still organized mainly around nation-states. This problem is exacerbated by the fact that news media around the world (save for a tiny number of broadcasting channels) are overwhelmingly national and local. Their news values tend to be inward looking; their scrutiny of global agencies consequently inadequate; and they foster primarily nation-centred political debate.[38]

A democratic void is thus opening up as a consequence of a general failure adequately to supervise global power-holders, and the failure of nation-based news media to maintain adequate oversight of their activities. However, the rise of the net offers an opportunity for organized groups to communicate their concerns, and engage in reciprocal debate, in an international context. A new generation of web-based international magazines of political and cultural debate (typified by openDemocracy and Chinadialogue) is now beginning to emerge that will contribute to this process. Some national websites, such as that of the *New York Times*, will probably become more international in orientation, in response to the increasingly globalized nature of their online audiences.

A key limitation on the internet as a democratizing force remains its enormously unrepresentative social base.[39] However, this is likely to be partly corrected over time. The development of the global television market brought into being major exporting production centres, from Hong Kong to Brazil, catering for different socio-linguistic markets, which weakened American dominance.[40] As the internet has developed, a similar process is occurring, with computer hosts growing rapidly outside the USA–European bloc and communicating in languages other than English. The continued diffusion of computers will reduce social disparities of net access within affluent countries. This said, the composition of the internet community is likely to remain skewed in favour of privilege for a very long time to come.

Conclusion

The wide-eyed, internetphiliac approach is deeply flawed. The net has changed out of all recognition from its pioneering days, when the vision of the net as the redeemer of social ills was first promulgated. The civic discourse and subcultural experiment that so impressed early net commentators has given way to an increased emphasis on entertainment, business and electronic mail. The second defect of this approach is more fundamental. It failed to grasp that inequalities in the real world distort cyberspace and limit its potential for improving society.

Yet the position squarely opposed to this tradition is also open to criticism. It mistakenly argues that the whirlwind force of digital capitalism has overtaken the internet and converted it into another consumer media service. In actual fact, a formidable combination of computer workers, recalcitrant consumers and Web 2.0 activists has staged a highly effective rearguard action preventing the commercial takeover of the web. The web is still a contested space, its future unresolved.

There is also an awareness of the distinctive attributes of the net, at the centre of the internetphiliac approach. The global reach of net technology, the way it facilitates self-expression and interaction, the avenue it opens up to the world's knowledge and entertainment, all make the net and the web life-enhancing inventions. The net also offers an opportunity for groups to connect and organize beyond national frontiers, and coalesce in a global context. In a world where national sovereignty is eroding in favour of global agencies, the net has emerged at a strategic moment as a key tool of global communication in defence of popular influence.

Indeed, further thought needs to be given to how to develop, through new public policies, the potential of the internet. The forces of commerce will overwhelm the web in the long term, unless there is a countervailing force. In the twentieth century the democratic state intervened to prevent the commercial takeover of radio and television, and developed a form of organization and public funding that empowered the public in Britain and elsewhere. The challenge now is to consider how this rich tradition can be re-imagined in relation to the internet; how it can be extended from the national to an international arena; and how it can be funded.[41]

Notes

1. K. Patelis, 'The political economy of the Internet', in J. Curran (ed.), *Media Organisations in Society* (London, Arnold, 2000).
2. H. Rheingold, *The Virtual Community* (Cambridge, MA, MIT Press, rev. edn, 2000).
3. This is now part of a standard (but valid) left critique of the internet, to be found, for example, in C. Sparks, 'The internet and the global public sphere', in W. Lance Bennett and R. Entman (eds), *Mediated Politics* (New York, Cambridge University Press, 2001), G. Murdock and P. Golding, 'Digital possibilities, market realities: the contradictions of communications convergence', in L. Panitch and C. Leys (eds), *A World of Contradictions: Socialist Register 2002* (London, Merlin Press, 2001), and numerous other analyses, all quoting significantly different figures (though mostly from the same ultimate source).
4. M. Castells, *The Internet Galaxy* (Oxford, Oxford University Press, 2001), p. 264.
5. *Ibid.*, p. 219.
6. C. Kramarae, 'The language and the nature of the Internet: the meaning of global', *New Media and Society*, 1 (1), 1999, p. 49.
7. Castells, *The Internet Galaxy*, p. 260.
8. J. Stratton, 'Cyberspace and the globalisation of culture', in D. Porter (ed.), *Internet Culture* (New York, Routledge, 1997).
9. D. Miller and D. Slater, *The Internet: An Ethnographic Approach* (Oxford, Berg, 2000), p. 86.
10. J. Tulloch, *Watching Television Audiences* (London, Arnold, 2000) and J. Curran, *Media and Power* (London, Routledge, 2002), among others, provide accounts of the development of this research.

11. For an insight into how frequent letter writing, and an efficient mail service, sustained interconnected middle-class networks in the mid-nineteenth century (in much the same way that email functions in contemporary Britain), see J. Uglow, *Elizabeth Gaskell* (London, Faber and Faber, 1994).

12. L. Gross, 'The gay global village in cyberspace', in N. Couldry and J. Curran (eds), *Contesting Media Power* (Boulder, CO, Rowman & Littlefield, 2003).

13. M. Mallapragada, 'The Indian diaspora in the USA and around the world', in D. Gauntlett (ed.), *Web Studies* (London, Arnold, 2000).

14. M. Poster, 'Cyberdemocracy: Internet and the public sphere', in D. Porter (ed.), *Internet Culture* (New York, Routledge, 1997). The best collection of essays, in this tradition, is D. Bell and B. Kennedy (eds), *The Cybercultures Reader* (London, Routledge, 2000).

15. For a useful critical review, see D. Slater, 'Social relationships and identity online and offline', in L. Lievrouw and S. Livingstone (eds), *The Handbook of New Media* (London, Sage, 2002).

16. N. Baym, 'Interpersonal life online', in L. Lievrouw and S. Livingstone (eds), *The Handbook of New Media* (London, Sage, 2002), p. 62.

17. M. Ito, 'Virtually embodied: the reality of fantasy in a multi-user dungeon', in D. Porter (ed.), *Internet Culture* (New York, Routledge, 1997).

18. S. K. Kent, *Gender and Power in Britain, 1640–1990* (London, Routledge, 1999).

19. H. Rheingold, *The Virtual Community* (Cambridge, MA, MIT Press, rev. edn, 2000).

20. National Election Studies (University of Michigan, Center for Political Studies), 'The NES guide to public opinion and electoral behaviour', www.umich.edu/nes/nesguide/nesguide. htm (2002).

21. D. Butler and G. Butler, *Twentieth Century British Political Facts* (Basingstoke, Macmillan, 8th edn, 2000), pp. 141–42, 158–59.

22. D. Kavanagh and D. Butler, *The British General Election of 2005* (Basingstoke, Palgrave, 2005), p. 236.

23. K. Hill and J. Hughes, *Cyberpolitics* (Lanham, MD, Rowman & Littlefield, 1998).

24. G. Rodan, *Transparency and Authoritarian Rule in Southeast Asia* (London, CurzonRoutledge, 2004).

25. Y. Ibrahim (2006) 'The role of regulations and social norms in mediating online political discourse', PhD dissertation, University of London (LSE).

26. C. George, 'The Internet's political impact and the penetration/participation paradox in Malaysia and Singapore', *Media, Culture and Society*, 27 (6), 2005, 903–20; Rodan, *Transparency and Authoritarian Rule*.

27. S. Coleman, 'New media and democratic politics', *New Media and Society*, 1 (1), 1999.

28. J. Slevin, *The Internet and Society* (Cambridge, Polity Press, 2000); A. Willhelm, *Democracy and the Digital Age* (New York, Routledge, 2000); S. Coleman, 'The new media and democratic politics', *New Media and Society*, 1 (1), 1999; C. Bellamy and J. Taylor, *Governing in the Information Age* (Milton Keynes, Open University Press, 1998).

29. See Chapter 16

30. P. Evans and T. Wurster, *Blown to Bits* (Boston, MA, Harvard Business School Press, 2000), p. 228.

31. Interview with Crispin Jameson, senior executive Brand Union.

32. P. Lovelock and J. Ure, 'The new economy: internet, telecommunications and electronic commerce?', in L. Lievrouw and S. Livingstone (eds), *The Handbook of New Media* (London, Sage, 2002).

33. D. Held, A. McGrew, D. Goldblatt and J. Perraton, *Global Transformations* (Cambridge, Polity Press, 1999).

34. M. Castells, *The Internet Galaxy* (Oxford, Oxford University Press, 2001), p. 66.

35. R. Mansell, 'New media and the power of networks' (London, London School of Economics and Political Science, Inaugural Professorial Lecture, 2001), p. 17.

36. L. Introna and H. Nissnbaum, 'Shaping the web: why the politics of search engines matters', *The Information Society*, 16, 2000.
37. S. Lax, 'The Internet and democracy', in D. Gauntlet (ed.), *Web Studies* (London, Arnold, 2000).
38. These arguments are developed further in J. Curran, *Media and Power* (London, Routledge, 2002).
39. J. Curran and T. Witschge, 'Liberal dreams and the internet', in N. Fenton (ed.), *New Media, Old News* (London, Sage, 2009).
40. J. Sinclair, E. Jacka and S. Cunningham (eds), *New Patterns in Global Television* (Oxford, Oxford University Press, 1996).
41. See Chapter 24.

Part IV

Theories of the media

Chapter 19

Metabolising Britishness[1]

Is there such a thing as 'Britishness'? More than ever, being 'British' is voluntary, not necessary. What is it? Where can we find it? What part do the media play not merely in representing it but in forging changing national realities? What, indeed, about 'Englishness'? If the nature of the union between the different nations that compromise Britain is a problem – then the meaning of the 'English' nation is even more perplexing. Even raising the subject seems, in one kind of way, indelicate. Is it somehow offensive to even mention the idea of the nation in which we belong but towards which we have complicated allegiances – or which we may feel barely a part of? Surely we are all global citizens, all have multiple identities, which we shuffle and balance? It is quite acceptable, it seems, to assert and celebrate religious and cultural differences, or 'being Scottish' – or any number of the national minorities that so gloriously complicate our communities. In any case, we often like to think of ourselves as rather doughty, beleaguered members of minorities bravely asserting our identity against the nasty (and large) nations, or nasty (and large) majorities. As we are frequently shockingly ignorant of the alternative lives of other people we live in close proximity with, many injustices still occur. But actually, it is quite hard to assert, for example, English working-class identity, without being suspect. Of course, 'nationalism' can be a very dangerous force and typically, in harsh economic times, it is an appallingly destructive one. But does that mean we should abandon any sense of a unique national identity? What part do the media play in relating us to a common predicament?

The media, however inadequately, tell us both much of what we know of others we live with, and even more of what we believe. Images are perhaps one thing; it is when insensitivity turns into acts which alter how people can lead their lives that we need to consider more carefully. Despite many forces dissolving the capacity of nation-states to determine their own future and the nature of the economic and political interconnectedness of international fate, nevertheless we still live in nation-states. We still go to school in them, we get treated by their healthcare systems (or not), are policed within them, walk on national roads and drink national water. But do we live within them in our imaginations?

Perhaps we have, here, a special problem. No one quite knows what it is to be British. 'Britishness', British history, customs and habits seem especially questioned. Indeed, everywhere there is an anxious inspection of national tea leaves for what they might portend (except, of course, we British don't drink as much tea as we used to – perhaps even our auguries have become unreliable?). What is 'Britishness'? This is not the first tentatively anxious enquiry into the mystery. It tends to come up when people are uncertain about it – for if you are clear about what it is and that you feel it, there is no question to be asked. Despite the revolutions in how we live, are there continuing sensibilities and processes that provide a recognizable architecture to what we want to be?

The problem is not that Britain has changed, but rather, whether we need it any more. The national project has, it is argued, been unsettled by colliding forces which play out in confusingly opposite directions. The media have a direct and symbiotic relation to the mystery of the British constitution. Unlike America, or France or indeed Russia, we have no written constitution, no set of legal documents that specify what we are and the nature of the contract we have all made in order to agree to live together. Of course, written constitutions do not guarantee the good life in themselves (the Russians have had a magnificently liberal constitution for nearly a hundred years, but the written rules have had no impact on how Russians have lived during any of that time). The British tradition is unwritten, based on experience and case law and a great, fragile machine of institutions that operate (at their best) according to a flexible interpretation of the duties and rights of individuals and the collective good. The media, in different ways, are central to this – for better and for worse. So in one way the media in Britain, as well as holding local, regional and national political actions to account (or failing to), play an especially important – although informal – part in our collective condition.

Nevertheless, slightly subversively, one might observe that 'Britishness', and certainly the British constitution, have always been a muddle: we just have a new, emerging muddle which has given some power (but by no means all or the most sensible bits) to a new, fairer settlement, recognizing Scottish and Welsh relative autonomy, wanting to include rather than exclude groups and religions and ways of life. Messiness sometimes works rather well. However, the great contemporary priority is tidiness and written-down-ness. The holy grail of 'transparency' has been understood to mean that codifying everything that moves is seen as a solution to abuses of power, when a code is often merely a map of formal relations – when the most deadly of transgressions might still flourish in what people actually do. Many propose that we should write down more of the rules into a more formal constitutional settlement, and in some areas this is just what has happened over the last decade. Although the worry is that the muddle no longer has any coherence, simply tidying up 'Britishness' will not make it real.

There are a number of things nibbling and gnawing at our sense of our selves. Firstly, there is the most fundamental disappearance of the sense of the physical frontiers of the nation. The British now have almost no grasp of the fact that they are still 'an island nation' (let alone Shakespeare's 'sceptred isle'), as people come and go by air not sea, communicate by internet not mail, when the lives of other lands (India or Turkey) are all so easily accessible through the media, where TV land (even if grasped over the internet) or 'Facebook land' occupy a large space in people's sense of themselves. The vivid apprehension of our coastal edges and what they have meant (and still mean) has almost disappeared, and while we are still more geographically aware than most Americans, and can identify Europe and the continents, we do not have a strong national image of our parameters. Even within these regional limits (perhaps in contrast to the social mixtures of the myriad of national groups from elsewhere that now compromise British society) there is a sense of dissolution.

The most obvious way that 'Britishness' is under strain is the rise and rise of nationalisms within the union. Scotland, and to a lesser extent Wales, bustle with novel institutions and 'feel' no Britishness – on the contrary, they often define themselves in opposition to it. Scotland apparently wants to be shot of 'us'. The political scientist and commentator Anthony King has written a mordant and shrewd assessment of the state of the British constitution. He argues that the devolutionary engine we have landed ourselves with has an in-built friction that will inevitably lead to separation as the 'nations' demand more of the centre and set themselves in opposition to it. Then what about England? (Which, as a child a very long time ago, I just assumed *was* Britain; the titles seemed interchangeable – as they did to many writers in the late twentieth century.) King's conclusions are marred by a sharp and magnificent glumness, but, despite some acute observations (a reformed House of Lords, the author fears, could wind up comprising 'a miscellaneous assemblage of party hacks, political careerists, clapped-out retired or defeated MPs, has-beens, never-were's and never-could-possibly-be's'[2]), it is perhaps too deterministic. As recent political and economic crises unfold a new sense of the need for the larger union may again emerge. But more profoundly his analysis is limited by a blindness to the shifting nature of power in every aspect of contemporary lives.

In particular, he misses the huge, society-wide shifts in power that are the cultural consequences of media technological change. Power has moved from producers to some aspects of consumer choice. Across all of the media industries there is a real revolution going on, from the music industry to the mutating publishing trade, to news, and from surveillance to consuming, in every aspect of private lives and societies there is a technologically driven Wild West frontier remaking old relationships of authority. This is not the utopia we were promised; there are many aspects that damage common and collective goods. But it is irreversible and has tremendous unfolding consequences. Constitutional change must mirror a new compact that other forces are making with British citizens. The shape of power is changing, and what a nation is must change with it.

There are many separatist enthusiasts around in the political and intellectual classes. It is nevertheless perhaps worth noting that at least some of the advocates for the 'break up'-of-Britain scenario tend to ignore Northern Ireland, which is far more settled in Ireland and in the EU and in the union than it has been for thirty years of bloody, grinding conflict, not least because, as Roy Foster shows in a *tour de force* of evidence and argument in *The Luck of the Irish*, the Irish state has changed out of all recognition – although in fits and starts. He sardonically points out with a certain glee that none of this has happened in any of the ways in which the instigators of the conflict hoped or predicted. Because Ireland has become secular, feminized, venal, successful, vulgar, and the very last thing it wants or is interested in is Northern Ireland.[3] But perhaps Northern Ireland – for so long the most agitated of the nations – has become an inconvenient and complicating reality that many of the protagonists of dissolution prefer to ignore.

While the political geography of the nation is fretfully bothersome (were Scotland to declare independence the political geography of voting would consign England to a one-party state for the foreseeable future), the issue of national identity has been dislocated by many other forces as well. Many other aspects of 'geography', and indeed social and political landscapes, have disappeared. As Robert Colls points out in his troubled interrogation of national spirit, a 'local' and 'regional' map of Britain recognizable since 1840, at which policies were directed and in which people lived, has been replaced since the Thatcher government of the 1980s by a range of uncoordinated, unlocated 'schemes' and agencies driven by a multiplicity of public/private bodies. What they have instead of region or local as a driving force is 'efficiency', and these 'agencies' have measured their achievements in (sometimes invented) 'markets' – not by how they elicit and represent different local interests. Colls observes, 'as forces not entirely of the centre, nor in the centre, yet structured by the centre they came to replace the discourse of "geographical region" or "away from the centre"'. With this new way of talking the periphery ceased to be just geographical. 'At a time when the centre lost the confidence in its power to order things and the metropolis felt less responsible for the rest of the country, the old national shape began to dissolve. This truly odd condition prevails'.[4] Indeed, the whole landscape of Britain has disappeared since the 1970s, as factories became (in a way best captured by the dystopian novels of J. G. Ballard) 'gated communities' and 'lofts', while Methodist chapels – which were the engines of moral and political reform of the industrial revolution and after – have become paint shops. Cities and towns and the British countryside have all mutated, died away and sparked to life under many different pressures. Some cities have been rekindled by government policies which have promoted new kinds of commercial development. Yet, glamorous new areas in Manchester, London, Liverpool, coexist beside enduringly poor areas. However, public spaces in cities have been revitalized in the past decade – money has gone into parks and decent play areas for children as an expression of a common value. But Colls points to a perturbing lack both of locality and of nation in our ideas of ourselves.

There are aspects of 'Britishness' that are above locality, although no doubt also shaped by it. There is certainly uniquely 'British' media ecology. It is altering fast under the pressures that are causing media industries everywhere to adapt or to disappear. Nevertheless it remains a very particular process. It has balanced a partisan press – which, like the press everywhere, is in sharp economic decline, but which is hanging on better here than in many other places – with a broadcasting landscape that is still 'impartial' and non-partisan. It has seen, most catastrophically, an absolute decline in local and regional news vehicles. How can Wales understand itself with only one local newspaper? How can councils operate without the scrutiny that the local media used to bring? We are losing the capacity to think locally.

Yet the business patterns of the British media are distinctive, and so too is the tone. The popular press is far less polite than the American press, and, although often appallingly irresponsible, not corrupted to the extent of the Italian press; religion plays less a part than it does in Holland, and radical news less a part than it does in France – and so on. But the determining difference is the existence of impartial news. The top of the British press has become more intelligent and more comprehensive: the opposite has occurred at the bottom. While individual opinions and views flood the net, those that get megaphoned by broadcasting are still largely managed in the pursuit of representative and balanced views. You may want to swamp the broadcasters with your opposition to a view or a programme, but they will still, in the public interest, interrogate your position, evaluate it and contextualize it. 'Impartiality', objectivity and the fierce contest about the limits of free speech are still features of the complicated media scene here. This has important repercussions for our understanding of international events

Then there is the class system. It has been very unfashionable to discuss class recently, yet differences still persist. Moreover, class and shifting class images are clearly represented in changing media systems and the changing fortunes of different media, as well as the more obvious symptom of content. The poor (what Orwell called 'the common man', and what we have learnt to call 'the socially excluded' – what, one wonders will another government call them?), the unhappy, how we talk to our children (or increasingly and horrifying fail to), the elderly, the changed role of women and the extraordinary challenges for young men, these are everywhere and common. How to think of the best nurture for young lives when children and parents have legal rights but there is no way of discussing in court the only thing a child can thrive in – a home with, however it is constituted, a family – is a shared issue. When we talk and think of the nation, surely we also mean such broad sociological realities that together give us the flavour of the life within it. We also mean literature, plays, art, architecture, design, films, dance, music, humour: we mean sensibilities and environments. These broader realities are shaped in collaboration with the media.

The next big challenges to 'Britishness' are the Siamese-twinned issues of the multi-faith, multi-ethnic, multi-ness and the conjoined question of limits to the elasticity of 'Britishness'. 'Multiculturalism' has been a short-hand way of talking about the first set of issues, and the very title shows how important the media have been to this. Finding representative voices, reaching out to communities, learning sensibilities, has been one side of the task. Discriminations have been fought with differing degrees of success. Just as the British way of dealing with these realities has been very different from, for example, the German way, so our media response has also been different. There are national differences in how to confront a shared experience of more varied societies.

Yet there is another side to the problem – which was hardly mentionable until recently. Is there a lowest common denominator of consensus about what defines belonging, which cannot be breached? Have we worried too much about diminishing hostility to new pieces in the national jigsaw and not worried enough about whether there is a shared reality? On the one hand, there is the problem identified so well by Geoff Dench in his work on the East End, that thirty years of well-meaning 'triage' in cash-strapped public services, housing, health and education have, in rationally allocating recourses to the neediest incomers from abroad, accidentally actively dis-advantaged a section of the British working class, with disastrous political consequences.[5] On the other hand, there is the problem of including and celebrating many differences.

Finally, to be a nation, there has to be a sense of exceptionalism, of a unique inheritance and worldview. Often such a concept of destiny has been forged through conflict with an outside force. Raphael Samuel argued 'national sentiment as a historical force can hardly be studied without refer-ence to the demonisation of enemies both within and without'.[6] Yet the last national story that we could tell ourselves that had a legitimate and satis-factory 'us and them' in it – the story of the Second World War – fades and loses purchase. For several generations a sense of British 'exceptionalism' had been based on a myth, but also a powerful reality, and that is now increasingly frail. Nevertheless, this 'us versus them' view of national identity is a fairly conventional view, and there can be a more generous interpretation of pleasure in a heritage.

The life of nations depends on how the past is lined up with the present. This seems the great failure and a great opportunity of the moment we are struggling through. One of the things we need to revitalize is an unembarrassed national history once more. 'A nation', claimed Edmund Burke in 1782, 'is not only an idea of local extent, but it is an idea of continuity, which extends in time as well as numbers and in space'. Terry, a character in *Whatever Happened to the Likely Lads* on the BBC, commented in 1973, 'Not one of our memories is left intact'. Most people simply don't know what matters about our history any more. Moreover, in a nation which has always used history to explore itself (just as the French have philosophers, and the Americans have political economists and Hollywood, we have history) there is a loss of historical memory and ways of remembering. Indeed, this is more than ever important, as in much of the wider academy, at least, there has been an almost complete abandonment of 'Britishness' as a source of understanding or study. Some universities, turned into businesses, have ducked the challenging task of rethinking a fit-for–purpose way of scrutinizing the Britishness of disciplines. Thus, despite being equipped with cohorts of able historians, many of whom still aspire to write stylish, clear English, we have been dreadful at re-inspecting our history collectively. A coy discomfort at aspects of the story has led us to bury it. We have recently failed to tell children any coherent (let alone interesting) national story. While they are taught about Hitler and the Tudors, older students learn little of the nineteenth-century struggle for the franchise; and while it is true that all 10-year-olds learn about an empire in school, it is not ours, of course, it is the Spanish empire and the Incas that they toil over. Who lives where and how on the streets of Britain is shaped by our history. So surely, by now we could confront the awfulness *and* the admirableness of our own imperial past?

Meanwhile 'globalization', despite being a more peculiar process, with more complex impacts than almost any of the 'theorists' who easily proclaim it have recognized, does mean that we share some cultures internationally – and perhaps lose our own. Yet, conversely, one of the most disturbing aspects the 'globalization' of the media is that it has led to cross-continental cultural ghettos and silos of narrow interests in which people only encounter the like-minded. 'Nation shall speak unto nation' – the BBC's founding mission is far easier than it used to be, but it is far harder to get people to pay attention to anything other than the familiar and comfortable. Moreover, there is a wider sense of tectonic plates moving: Brazil, China and India are storming into the world arena. Where do we fit into this new, emerging map, and does anyone care?

There is another problem: this is not about what we may or may not have lost, but about the dominant way of thinking about 'Britishness'. It has become common to see a sense of the nation as a plastic and fluid construct. Linda Colley's stimulating and influential book *Britons: Forging the Nation 1707–1837*, in itself an attempt by someone who, as she explained, was not clear that she would go on living and working in Britain, was a pioneering example of this. In an authoritative and original account, she demonstrates that a British identity was 'forged' in the eighteenth century out of popular anti-Catholicism and the real threats of French aggression, but also the comfort of watching successes in wars abroad with little direct experience of the reality at home, and out of a reworked monarchy. The British state pre-dated the 'idea' of Britain. However, she also argues that there was a material basis to a sense of nationhood: 'For all classes and both sexes, patriotism was more often than not a rational response and a creative one as well'.[7] She is clear that the contemporary media played a large role in this nation-con-structing enterprise. Elsewhere the notion of the constructed nature of nationality gained ground. Benedict Anderson's definition of nations as 'imagined communities' was influential, as were, in a way, a wonderful set of essays edited by Eric Hobsbawm and Terence Ranger, *The Invention of Tradition*,[8] which considered, with a glorious wit, the ways in which ideas of nationality were invented and accepted (I learnt that those kilts I had worn were the late survival of a Highland fantasy). But while Colley was austerely aware that the enterprise of founding a national collective project was pre-carious and vital, for many of the other writers, as all national sentiment was really little more than a ruling-class trick, there was the sense of the ridicu-lousness of much national invention, and its ephemeral duplicity. We have ended up with a comforting, moralized version of fluidity in which 'the nation' is seen as endlessly plastic. Indeed, many who have written about the media have persuasively written about the media's capacity to alter and mould: but never asked questions about limits.

These ideas of national remaking were picked up eagerly – and bowdlerized. In a world where advertising can mould desires with such ease, why not remake – or 'rebrand' as it came to be called – the nation? Anthony Giddens, who famously thinks history is irrelevant, as it happened in the past, with his 'Third Way' was, in effect, one such immensely powerful, 'rebrander', while Mark Leonard's branding Britain is another version of the same idea. We are in another bout of 'designer' Britishness now. Thus, what started out in the past as an empirical interrogation of collective processes in the hands of accomplished historians has turned into something quite different. It turned into a proposal to 'redesign' Britishness. New, more sellable ways to describe us were advanced with breathy excitement, for it was suggested if you could describe us differently, perhaps, hey-presto, we would be different. It was an essentially propagandistic and certainly ideological view of Britishness, self-consciously shaped for selling us to ourselves and abroad.

The idea was especially attractive because it proposed a way of harnessing the power of the media into a reinvention of our purposes. The media do indeed seep into and chemically alter much of our collective lives, and the mix of outlets that we have ended up with says all sorts of things about the national psyche. The British popular press, gaudy, sentimental, ruthless and dispiriting, is increasingly brutal with ordinary lives as well as with the more powerful (think Sally Clarke, the women who was wrongly convicted of murdering two babies, on the basis of misleading expert evidence for which the expert has lost his job, and a local and national press campaign, for which no one lost their job – or ever apologized). The press tells us little about the wide world we find ourselves in, and in increasing cash-strapped times is marked by a narrow provincialism. Nevertheless, it is occasionally savagely truth telling, more often hysterical and ruthless – as only a wounded beast can be. Meanwhile, the utopia of better-informed, more intelligent and more deeply contextualized information is provided by a whole range of media – for the stratum of the educated and wealthy. In this way the prospect of 'using' the media to rebrand us looks like a way of managing the media to mould us for more useful ends – nevertheless, you cannot 'remake' British-ness as an advertising campaign. It will not work, because – dears – that is not what the 'British' are prepared to put up with. Actually, in such stubborn, prosaic refusals may still lie a national sentiment we can conjure with.

Indeed, 'Britishness' can only be a co-production. The public has to collaborate – but will only do so in something that is useful and meaningful to it. 'Britishness' cannot be done to us – it has also to bubble up. This is especially the case in times of crisis – which has often been forgotten by the happy-clappy evangelists of re-engineering national identity. 'Britishness' has to be grounded in the soil of contemporary life, even if that is unsettling. Unfortunately, modern political and academic language is saturated with the easy encomiums of the seminar room, in which people 'negotiate' meanings and 'discourses' are 'contested'. But these words disguise the reality of sharply felt losses and brutish triumphs. It is the real needs and desires of the public, not mythologized or convenient ones, that is the place to start a proper dusting down of Britishness. Being British is more voluntary than it has ever seemed before, but it has to start from realities.

So is there anything 'British' left? Where can we look for our exceptionalism? Actually, there is more of it around than people think: they look for it in the wrong places. But it is not a set of 'things' or 'essences'. George Orwell, whose writing critically (and at times romantically) inquired into the British condition so influentially in the twentieth century once characterized British life as 'Heavy breakfasts and gloomy Sundays'. Although Orwell's essays still resonate with brilliant insights and indeed offer a model of scrutiny and wit, there is no point in trying to pin down 'Britishness' to any such list: Orwell's modesties have been swept away in a blizzard of shopping. The Conservative Prime Minister John Major's attempt to specify Britishness as 'maiden aunts on bicycles and warm beer' certainly never hit the mark, even in the late twentieth century. Early New Labour's 'Cool Britannia' has been spat out. Yet there are qualities which, on closer scrutiny, endure, although some of them we may find deeply unattractive: that surely is part of the British point.

The 'media' play a special role in representing (and at times whipping up) national characteristics. But what is unusual in Britain is that British 'exceptionalism' has been defined and reinforced by a unique media institution which has played a role in metabolizing the nation's sense of itself, but which has also represented 'Britishness' abroad: the BBC. The Corporation may, or may not, survive the next decade of rocky problems, with technology, rapacious international businesses – perhaps even more threatening than domestic political vandalism – and a certain capacity for auto-destructiveness posing a set of interrelated looming threats. Nevertheless, inspecting how it has done Britishness is illuminating. The Corporation has an obligation to the nation because it is for the nation – so it has endlessly to try to sort out what the nation is. Mainly, the BBC metabolizes the nation by worrying about it. It adds reflective anxiety and creative imagination to the problems it confronts. This is clearly a quality in news and journalism: but it is as much an issue in drama and documentary and in the very administrative principles of the thing. In particular, it is the 'newsiness' of the programming in general – the way in which news provides moral and political climate for other kinds of creativity – and in turn the embedded nature of news in the wider programme-making milieu, that can make for a fertile and sensitive Petri-dish culture. Of course, the BBC cannot and does not survive alone, but that, perhaps, is the point. It is enmeshed in ways of doing things and values elsewhere in other British institutions. So examining what it does tells us something about it, but it may also tell us something more general about the puzzle of us and our present uncertainties.

The Corporation metabolizes Britain (when it gets it right) by airing its virtues; by bestowing recognition on groups, issues, achievements, and failures; by including the mad aunts and errant teenagers in the family group; by show-casing and polishing up the crown jewels of culture; by washing as much of the dirty linen as it can find right out there in the street and by taking the mickey out of the whole attempt.

The Corporation has been able to do this because it is part of the British 'unwritten' and informal constitution and, as such, it has related to the British public as citizens, but in a quite different way from any other official body. It consumes an alternative set of data about the British people on the move socially, technologically and aesthetically from any department of state: for it lives in the minds and hearts and imaginations of people at play. People have always had to choose to spend their time with the BBC, and even though the competition for attention has become far more intense, the Corporation has always had to win and woo. So it has never been able to ignore what the people want for long (although it has at some times been out of step with the national mood, and at others it has been able to express and lead it). Yet, at the same time it is enjoined to engage with the public not only as consumers but as members of an evolving society. So the BBC's sense of the nation is at an angle to any government's.

The BBC metabolizes the nation materially by distributing recourses according to a political and citizenship map of Britain, not an economic or market one. The media have, over time, been given many privileges: even very broadly defined as the content-producing organizations they still are. They acquired these benefits because, ultimately, they have to serve the public good. The argument for this remains simple: in democracies, electorates need to be recognized and informed; now there is plenty of information available, but navigating it or having attention focused on the things that matter is far more difficult. Distributing resources has meant access to radio, television and now digital technologies, and reshaping the production and ideas map of the country. If the BBC *is* national, then it has somehow to be part of the wider nation. This is so 'taken for granted' that it is almost invisible in the British mind, yet it has been a powerful engine of integration. A shrewd media regulator, Ofcom, which is empowered to try to make sure that the commercial and public roles of the digital and broadcasting industries are properly conducted, observed that the whole of the independence tussle was being played out in Scotland 'through the prism of broadcasting'. Yet there is a devilish paradox in the drama unfolding north of the border: market forces alone would not support an independent production market of any size in Scotland, yet the Corporation is being asked to invest in one. Those campaigning for this are not interested in a better service for any audience, but in developing an economic capacity at home: and yet the decision to invest such resources can only come (and is coming rather generously) from the 'British' BBC: the logic of economic and political decisions is quite different.

Then there is the 'representing the nation' to itself. This is, in part, an issue of representing the bits of the nation to themselves, partly an issue of representing the bits of the nation to the whole and partly a matter of correcting the overall picture by the nuancing that regional perspectives and realities bring. It has done each task variably well over time, at sometimes falling into clichés, but at others creatively harvesting local differences and local contributions to enrich the national brew. Some of this is to do with news, putting the nations and regions on the collective mind-map, as keeping them alert to their own condition is one part of the task. It requires political will.

But metabolizing the nation has to be continually reinvented. Take Northern Ireland: the BBC in the 1960s and the early 1970s was part of the problem that was about to erupt. It was staffed solely by members of the Protestant community, failed to 'see' the minority community and was unreflectively 'Unionist'. But slowly it became more responsive, its staff became more representative, the voices it gave access to became more varied, and then, as the troubles gathered venom, it evolved into an admirably pioneering institution. This was a matter both of getting the balance of staff, news stories, plays, documentaries and children's programmes appropriately right to the local audiences and of telling that story into the rest of Britain. Yet at first, when the sensitivity to the variety of Northern Irish voices had improved, another error emerged: an understandable attempt to emphasize the positive distorted the story yet again. The BBC had to learn that it did not exist in order to 'build the peace' or 'build the community'. Later still, visiting journalists from London, hungry for a scoop and some drama but who did not appreciate the local consequences of stories, had to be managed: they were too unresponsive to local meanings. Another corrective lesson: the BBC did not exist to tell exciting stories that were over-dramatized; 'stars' hunting for scoops did damage to the reality on the ground, and that reality was too important to be oversold back on the mainland. Yet, and this is also true, the visiting, observing journalist was also an important part of carrying meanings from community to community. 'Outsiders' brought something to the mix in the province and to the understanding on the mainland. Over time, the BBC learnt how to do it – and on the way produced a world-class news outfit in the region.

Pat Loughrey, the first Catholic to be appointed to a senior position there, and now Head of the Regions and Nations for the BBC, argued that the single most important programme that started the move in Northern Ireland was a phone-in called *Talk Back*, a loud, opinionated, shouting shop at first. There was political pressure to close it down, as it was thought to incite inter-communal violence, but the BBC held steady. After 'about five years of both communities screeching poisonously at each other, they got it out of their system, realised there was a space in which they could be heard, and then they started to listen to each other'.[9] This is one key way the BBC does Britishness: by listening to and allowing an arena for the variety of voices that reflect real communities. But in Northern Ireland the struggle to get it right was part of the bigger solution: there are no easy, quick fixes to attempting to be truthful.[10]

Indeed, one of the things the regions need to do is to correct the metropolitan bias of almost everything in Britain, but the process is more complicated than it appears at first inspection. The BBC has to be part of and let the regions speak their minds on issues and pleasures to themselves. One way is to make programmes about them – another way is to make programmes in them. But devolving to the regions only does its transformative, enlarging work if then the regional insights are brought back to amend and correct the whole picture. This is the trick we have to learn more generally, and it is more complicated than it looks to get this right. In this way, as one ex-BBC mandarin pointed out, putting production capacity out to the regions was not enough: the regional production needs to be able to engage and catch the attention of the centre and the centre needs it to do so. Thus, for example, the whole issue of Europe looked different from the shires and the provinces. In the close Westminster village there is traditionally a good deal of hostility to the whole EU policy, and the BBC political and cultural élites are largely, unavoidably, part of that central mind set – yet reporters working where the EU has brought benefits, out in the valleys of Wales and the Yorkshire Dales, corrected the dominant Westminster-centric view.[11] Indeed, what is true of the regions is true of the world. Going and seeing, bringing back views and understanding, is the single most critical way in which the whole BBC news-gathering and processing machine contributes to our comprehension of our place in all of the worlds that we all live in as a part of.

These dilemmas are merely reproduced when dealing with the increasingly diverse communities that live within Britain. An old BBC problem, that of what constitutes a representative voice, which stands legitimately for a point of view, becomes especially acute when times are dangerous. The Corporation's determination to represent the Northern Irish 'street' of opinion brought it into conflict with successive governments and took time to get passably right. Yet the inclusion of voices – which does legitimize them – also exposes them to scrutiny. Inclusion is insufficient: every voice must be properly challenged, yet inclusion in the national arena of nation remains one of the most important ways of defining Britishness. Regions, classes, faiths, communities all need recognizing.

Yet what vision of Britishness does the BBC work with? It is perhaps easier to see the kinds of interpretations that have to be balanced in something less contentious than religion, or politics. Take classical music in the BBC as an example of the dilemmas that have to be resolved in practice. The BBC is one of the largest patrons of music in Europe and the world. But working out (and 'balancing') different aspects of Britishness has all sorts of conflicts within it. To render 'British' musical life the best service, what must you do? Well obviously, you must support orchestras in the centre and in the regions – and keep live music performance and performers vitally alive. But that is not enough. You should also play the repertoire of 'British' music, from the great mediaeval choral tradition of Tallis and Bird, through Handel and Purcell, to Elgar, Delius and Walton. However, you ought also to be rediscovering new bits of the repertoire, which at some times the BBC has done almost single handedly – not just the British repertoire of course, but music in general. However, 'British' music should not just be a heritage trinket, and so, of course, you must commission new work from new composers, John Tavener, Harrison Birtwhistle and the baby avant-garders, even perhaps at times if no one much listens to it, though finding new ways of presenting music is part of the trick. Meanwhile 'British' music must not get out of touch with the world, so you must also get the best foreign performers and conductors to play here, and continually relaunch great music at the audiences. However, then there is the obligation to nurture young British performers and musical life in the schools. 'Young Musician of the Year' was invented brilliantly to do just this, when a BBC producer noted with dismay that there were few young British performers appearing in the international competitions. It worked: and can somebody please un-dumb it down right away? Today's one-size-fits-all populism, with ignorant 'celebrity' presenters asking accomplished young people asinine questions and an interference with the judging system so that the most 'news friendly' performer wins – not the most skilled – gets in the way of the real capacities and interests it is capable of encouraging and displaying. The principle of 'recognition' is one that governments have no purchase on – yet is a powerful, necessary cultural tool.

However, occasionally the whole balancing act of allocating money and attention hits the rocks of invention: thus the BBC has always cared obsessively about the quality of sound it has put out, but in the 1970s a new musical kid on the block was the 'early music' movement, with performances on original instruments. Unfortunately, as few had built or played sackbuts for several hundred years, they tended to sound – well – odd. But it was a British movement, and so, after some resistance, the indomitable BBC Producer (a wonderful breed) grasped it – with lots of expensive rehearsal time. But when all of that is sorted into an acceptable division of resources and energy there is another big problem: how do you balance your obligation to interest as many people as possible, and to the music and its development? The answer is all of the above, but in addition replayed in the shifting sands of contemporary musical history and taste. Balancing what is best for 'Britishness' is no easy task. It is a complex business of money and imagination.

The problems and perplexities of getting right the 'British' in classical music were just a model for the more commercially pressured issue of somehow getting popular music 'right'. Or of how to commission drama or comedy that was representative, innovative, and spoke to problems yet entertained. Moreover, it never stops all of the lessons having to be re-explored as the parameters and sensitivities alter.

Yet there is another paradox of Britishness: it is often best done when it is not attempted at all. Thus, the BBC World Service wonderfully represents the British interest best, precisely insofar as is not pursuing a 'British' agenda or indeed British 'interests'. It does it by doing impartiality, balance, and when it arrives at them, through hard-won, necessarily imperfect, properly objective judgements. In many ways it (and the 'mother ship of values', the larger BBC) relates to the world on our behalf by setting standards. The receiving audiences will use the World Service because it is useful and accurate for their lives, not because it represents a 'British' voice. Indeed, the perception that it is inflected by our interests damages it. This commitment to trying very hard to describe reality, as opposed to influencing it, has been the basis of the World Service's authority. Perhaps what is true abroad (or indeed increasingly at home, because of the way in which such services now include diaspora audiences scattered throughout Britain), is also true of how we need to see 'Britishness', not as a set of things or values; it is not that 'the beer is bitterer the coins are heavier and the grass is greener, the faces knobblier and mild',[12] but rather a set of processes which engage us in our contemporary reality.

David Hendy's sparkling, thoughtful account of Radio Four, *Life on Air*, makes a similar point. It is the 'how' public service broadcasting processes thoughtful playfulness that matters more than the passing scenery of programmes which reflect not only continuities but also changing tastes and agendas. In representing the nation, the 'immense variation in tone', from the warm homeliness of the shipping forecasts to the cerebral investigations of *In Our Time*, has been part of the 'diversification which was embedded as a fundamental goal' in the station's purposes. Radio Four embodied in 'one service a variety of ways with which the nation could view itself. It provides a national kaleidoscope'.[13] The author Lynn Truss put well the odd sense of community it can engender, 'The idea that other listeners, in other kitchens, in other baths, in other traffic jams, are yelling at the same thing is a comforting notion'. Thus, the World Service and Radio Four both show the way to some qualities, of fair representativeness, that are not things or even values, but habits of mind, processes, that are far more pervasive than any of the end-of-Britain doom mongers appreciate. Perhaps the thing is not to 'do' Britishness at all.

One of the last great successful inspections of Britishness was as a consequence of the Second World War, when a series of writers defined national characteristics in ways which critics have spent many years dismissing. Some aspects of these are more relevant to a very much changed Britain than appears at first sight. Not the modesty, or the class structure, let alone the cups of tea or the boiled cabbage. In 1957 Nickolas Pevsner, the great architectural historian, gave a series of BBC Reith lectures on the 'Englishness of English Art' (by which, being a German, like many of the most anglophile of post-war thinkers, he endearingly claimed he meant, 'just the most commonly acceptable name for that which is the essence of Britishness'). The lectures became a smash hit, selling out by their millions. For Pevsner, whose dry yet utterly comprehensive catalogue of vernacular architecture sought to distil the qualities of national life built in local bricks and mortar, the defining quality of British culture was an emphasis on narrative and preaching. It was, he claimed, epitomized by Hogarth with his great, popular morality tales – criticizing in Gin Lane and The Rake's Progress the corruption of British society. But, Pevsner notes that the most effective British artistic sermon 'is the recounting of what a sharp eye sees around it'. The hallmark of the British spirit, he claimed was 'Keen observing and quick recording together with an intense interest in the details of the everyday world and a preference for personal experience'.[14] But he also claimed to see (in our great cathedrals, along with extreme length and height) qualities of 'detachment as against passionate single mindedness', although he also argued that the nation's 'rationalism and matter of fact-ness' was matched by an enduring penchant for the 'romantic, weird and the irrational'. Meanwhile George Mikes (a Hungarian this time) observed on a Home Service programme that 'the British will not tell you a lie, but would not dream of telling you the truth'. He also added, that in Britain, 'If you go for a walk with a friend don't say a word. If you go with a dog never stop talking to him ... '[15]

Of course this elaboration of empiricism, open mindedness and critical scrutiny was part of an image of Britain widely shared then. Karl Popper's 'Open Society' was an immensely influential underpinning to all of this exploration. Popper's inspiring work provided a stern injunction to keep the arteries of criticism open. It demanded vigilance against the comforts of complacency. Like John Stuart Mill before him, but after the terrible lessons of totalitarian oppression, Popper reminded people that they might find challenging argument very uncomfortable – but that it was always a good thing. The 'Open Society' argument still rages and is what we British still perhaps have as a substitute for the American preoccupation with freedom of speech. In many ways the BBC, at its best, also puts some of these habits of mind into practice: sceptical, evidence driven, committed to the possibility of understanding others and, in as far as it tries to, continually pushing the boundaries of what we might be.

For perhaps there is no easy answer to 'Britishness' – and the recognition is in itself part of the answer. You *could* invent civic ceremonies. Governments keep proposing them. Yet we have quite good ones around the place: the Queen's Jubilee (for example) was not supposed to be going to be popular, but the people, as far as could be discerned, rather enjoyed it. You *could* do something with flags, but I, for one, will certainly not be swearing allegiance to any fluttering bit of civic religion. You *could* make the contract between us and the state more explicit. You certainly ought to do something about interpreting our history again: without polite omissions. You must represent the voices and instincts that exist within the national arena. You absolutely must permit, encourage and develop creative, imaginative energy. Museums, and children reading great books for fun (not dull, pointless reading schemes), artists, theatres and dancers all have much to add to our sense of what matters. But do not try to tidy the 'Britishness' up – after all, one enduring quality is our national hypocrisy. Once one understands that Robespierre energized the murderous Terror in the French Revolution in the eighteenth century by whipping up hatred for hypocrites and demanded that a new 'openness of heart' rule, one begins to see the necessary utility of a quality often associated with the British. Indeed, the contemporary British press seems sometimes to do little else than accuse other people (especially politicians, celebrities, people in public life) of two-faced hypocrisy. It is all of course a wonderfully hypocritical concoction; the British divorce, have affairs, break up marriages, live with each other more than ever before – they just enjoy disapproving of any passing public figure who behaves like they do.

Insofar as the BBC has found ways to be part of a national discussion about our condition, redistributed resources, tried to balance – however inadequately – competing claims, puzzled and questioned whether it is doing the right thing, learnt by trial and error, and above all, attempted to avoid ideological capture for all of the 'purposes' people would like to impose on it, then it has, indeed, most usefully 'metabolized' Britishness. Insofar as the British media more generally remain a place where real vices and virtues are called to our attention, then they do their public work. But do they?

George Orwell, that quintessentially most British of writers, is also the least parochial. His great fables, *1984* and *Animal Farm*, are as relevant to life in oppressive régimes as they ever were – and alert us in more sedate and lucky places to threats all the time. What he wrote in the middle of the last century still resonates and makes readers everywhere more inquiring of their predicament. Perhaps he also provides a way to see the contemporary quandary of our national identity. Writing in the 1930s, he claimed that Britain was 'the most class ridden society under the sun. It is a land of snobbery and privilege, ruled largely by the old and silly'. It was like a family, but one 'with the wrong members in control – and cupboards stuffed with skeletons'. He was pitiless about its double standards, snobbery, pomposity, xenophobia, inability at languages, and the terrible social divisiveness that separated the comfortable from the needy. As Ben Pimlott argued about Orwell, 'Being "British" we have to be reminded, perhaps does not mean that the list is full of things we approve of. Orwell sniffs orthodoxy at a hundred yards and having sniffed it, seeks to upset its adherents'.[16] Yet Orwell also 'refused to scorn qualities of common sense, empiricism and toleration'. Elsewhere, Orwell distinguished between patriotism as 'devotion to a particular place and a particular way of life, which one believes is the best in the world but has no wish to force on other people', and nationalism (which he said could be applied to ideologies like communism and fascism as well as nations), 'which is inseparable from the desire for power. The abiding purpose of every nationalist is to secure more power and more prestige, not for himself but for the nation or other unit in which he has chosen to sink his own individuality'. Orwell was, in short, a critical patriot, and everything he wrote was an extended polemic on the side of seeing the truth – however ugly – in ourselves. It was an embarrassing, awkward intimacy with ourselves that Orwell proposed, but it was above all a state of mind, a way of looking at the world that was fleshed out in his invitation to be critical, find shamefully distasteful – and yet appreciate that which was individual.

Perhaps the only way forward in our current national quandary – and yet one (and that is the delight) that is part of a long history that is distinctly British – is a stroppy-minded, slightly resigned toleration and defence of where we are as a nation. And it is in this slightly bleak describing, recognizing, relishing and laughing at our accurate condition (even if that is a somewhat dissolving condition) that really lies doing 'Britishness' better – because this is the place from which we can hope for better. Orwell wrote of Britain: 'There is something in it that is continuous, it stretches into the future and the past, there is something in it that persists, as in a living creature. It has a flavour of its own'.[17] We may or may not need to go on 'being British', but we do all need to go on being critical, open-minded realists – if we can, and if the media keep us informed, and bring us uncomfortably to face those things about ourselves that we don't want to know. 'Freedom', observed Orwell 'is the right to say what other people do not want to hear'.

Chapter 20

Global understanding

Gosh, with so much information around, organized in quite new ways and available so easily, surely we are all more knowledgeable than before? A connected world ought to be a more intelligent world. There are thrilling engines of enquiry developing, almost limitless information available, people to relate to, why do we need anything like the news? When worldwide publics can share events as they unfold, send immediate pictures from the hearts of disasters, can more or less communicate with anyone anywhere, who needs story finders, assessors and sellers any more?

In the brave new world of boutique views, grazing media-snackers, bespoke news consumption, when you take your information Indian, American or football style, with auto-didact news producers and content swappers, 'citizen journalists' sending images as events roll, happy connected chatters, posters and eager opionators all jostling for attention over the net, could it possibly be suggested that there is actually a new problem with ensuring 'news' diversity both nationally and internationally? Don't we have more of the stuff than ever before? Villagers in Africa can text aid agencies to say that the aid has not arrived in their village, and that local officials are corrupt. Pictures from conflicts (well, some conflicts) ricochet about the net, as incendiary as the bullets they show. Anyone can post their view on anything. At least in some societies (like ours) the very detail of political decisions, the documents that drive and make political policy, can be made available for all the public to scrutinize within hours of decisions. The blogosphere bustles with attitude. Like termites, colonies of information workers create huge edifices of knowledge. Isn't all of that teeming life diversity?

But the criteria of judgement remain the same – even in the new world. For the first condition of a decent society is some kind of common discussion, in public, of the realities of that society. It is a discovery that goes back to the sceptical empiricism of the enlightenment, but it is not 'western', or 'élite', it is just what makes the difference between civilized justice and many graduated degrees of oppression. It is a universal truth and it is what makes 'the media' potentially a public good. The media do this by bringing independent witness to scrutinize events. Many connecting and interactive new conversational forms may do it. Although comedy, drama, the rules and mores of reality shows, radio chat programmes, programmes about animals, children's programmes, interactive games – anything really – play their own creative and vastly important role in elaborating and challenging power – and do some of the vital work of amusing and informing audiences as well as the imperative of delivering their attention and interest – nevertheless they and the news all matter if the apprehending of reality is at the centre of the project. This is not to advocate 'realism' as a style – on the contrary; but satire and absurdity also have to speak to reality if they are to really hit home truths. Art adds its own creative interpretation to new understandings. But, if we are shown verities we recognize (and of course it is a messy, awkward business capturing the zeitgeist and yet moving it on), such realism engages us in a mobile dialogue about who we are, what is happening and what we wish to be.

The democratization of the means to communicate globally is a machine transforming knowledge and power. Yet reality is surprisingly hard to recognize. Moreover, it is perplexing enough to understand the conditions of communities we live in close proximity to; appreciating the more distant lives of others is still more challenging. In the past this was a matter of physical distance (which is still more important and complex than people understand –what do you know of the other lives lived in the road you live in?). Now it is as much – perhaps – about psychological and imaginative distance. But the distance is also a material one.

It is quite simply the most exciting period of cultural change for generations. Thus, magnificent opportunities of the new communications order are transforming relationships between traditional power hoarders and some publics. Across all the so-called media industries, all of which are converging but which we recognize, from music, to publishing, to 'broadcasting' (the production of certain kinds of content delivered on any platform), to the news industry, the first great revolution for two hundred years, combining new technology, an upturning of creative relationships and unfolding new economic models, is remaking our imagination and understanding. Yet, precisely because of there is so much choice it is easy to ignore anything that we do not agree with or find uncomfortable. We can choose only to consult news and knowledge that fits our view of the world. We can find evidence that supports any prejudice or preference we fancy. We can build a comfortable silo for ourselves. We can also just ignore everything: who needs news about far-away places? The most recent research about the impact of the web on cultural goods (and perhaps, by extension, on cultural products – like news) is that the combination of web and media makes the largest, most popular, most discussed 'celebrity' goods hugely successful, but that smaller, less recognized goods and events disappear. You need a louder, bigger voice to attract attention in the noisy party of the digital world. It is harder to attract attention for things we need to know. It is harder for smaller, less fashionable voices to get heard.[1]

Informed myopia

Indeed, even the most educated publics may follow conventional thinking as unquestioningly as ever. Technological sophistication does not necessarily lead to challenging thought *per se*. For example, the economic crisis of 2008– 9 was often described as a 'credit crunch', because huge economic turbulence was caused by a sudden collapse in the availability of money to lend and this in turn was based, at least in part, on a collapse in confidence. Yet it could also legitimately have been called a 'cognitive crunch'. It was caused by a failure of comprehension. People did not understand the financial instruments that were being used to spread risks, they did not understand the models of finance, they did not understand the consequences of what was in many ways a classic speculative 'bubble' – but one whose impact was swift and global in a quite novel way. It turned out that even those ostensibly wielding the financial tools did not understand them. A priestly caste of experts wielding a formidable set of jargons delivered us all considerable economic benefits: so it was more comfortable for us all to believe that someone else understood the mystery, even if we did not. We delegated understanding. Hard questions requiring simple answers put at earlier stages might have transformed behaviour. It was a lack of comprehension and the assertion that it was all too technically sophisticated for people to comprehend that was one cause of an economic catastrophe. Public understanding is thus not an optional luxury – without it, terrible things happen.

It is also the case that the relationship between the digital world and the 'old' media world is still more interdependent and complex than many assume. The digital world is not 'substituting' for the older media world, but they coexist and amplify messages across each other in different ways. 'Celebrity' events become famous by multiplying their fame across all platforms – old and new.

Yet, despite more interaction we have not arrived at anything like common measures of the scale. For example, wars and conflicts, human suffering of many varieties, caused by natural and man-made disasters, continue to have quite different impacts on the different publics. There is no common register in which they are assessed and attended to. One aspect of this is political. Different public audiences with different political positions interpret conflicts (and are moved often to rage, not compassion) according to their own persuasions.[2] In this way images of suffering still have huge consequences. They agitate and whip up feelings, they are important evidences of injustice, they mobilize action which is sometimes redemptive, sometimes angrily punitive. Yet the relationship between the digital-swapping world of online communication and the news agenda of the apparently more traditional agenda is very close – large movements of engagement and feeling are nearly always amplified through a new co-relationship. Agendas still get set in remarkably traditional ways.

There is another issue – those conflicts, disasters, unfolding catastrophes, issues that get a distorting kind of attention. The world may be inter-connected, but much of what happens is noticed by no one beyond the site of the events. Indeed, it is even more specific and odd: it is pictures of suf-fering that matter. Without images, events do not have a wide purchase on attention. Thus, take the example of famine. These are usually long-running, slowly gathering emergencies. They take time to develop, there is plenty of evidence that they will occur, they can be reliably predicted, and they are most usually privatized – they happen slowly to people, where they live and only in the very last, absolutely disastrous phases do populations move or end up in relief camps. Indeed, and this is difficult to accept, all famines are essentially political phenomena; they are not caused by absolute failures of food supply but by a political failure to give people access to food. However, such emerging disasters are hard to capture pictorially and governments and relief agencies have spent the last thirty years trying to produce more rational ways of dealing with them. The charities (who get their money in Britain from the public), however, need to catch public attention with dramatic imagery. Thus there is a bizarre concentration on campaigns around visible suffering.

There are also the catastrophes that for various reasons – governmental control, distance, complexity of story, stereotyping – but most usually quite simply because of lack of traditional coverage, simply get no attention. One example would be the cholera outbreak in Zimbabwe in 2009. We had radio reports but, because of the Zimbabwean government's exclusion of journal-ists, and especially its exclusion of the BBC, which, despite an ingenious attempt to get around the censorship, could get few pictures out of the ravaged country, no one really understood the extent of the social breakdown that such an epidemic represented. Another, different example would be the long-running and horrifically brutal war in Goma, a war with far higher casualties than any other contemporary conflict – but which has had little or no media attention. 'News' still sets our mental map of concern, and if there is no reporting, then we do not notice.[3]

Of course many governments in many places and many cross-national groups are not at all interested in any public understanding at all. Govern-ments have been able to control the description of reality and to restrict the views of dissident voices despite new technological opportunities. Take many of the countries of 'new' Europe. Despite twenty years of development since the collapse of communism and its controls of the media, we need a name for the odd and strangely threatening moment these societies are in. The media are controlled – but in a different way. A report by the Soros Open Society Foundation[4] demonstrates that something novel, yet disconcertingly familiar, was already remaking these societies' capacity to understand themselves long before the economic crisis. Moreover, this engine has been moving fast in the wrong direction: if things were bad in the early 2000s three years later, by

2008, they were definitely worse. When the Cold War ended, democracy was supposed to bloom, a movement towards independent thought and better government to spread through political systems. The chemistry of decency was to go about altering political parties, and these would improve public services, and the economies becoming rule governed would profit and grow in everyone's interests – and all of it to be tested and made better by the power of scrutiny that free media bring to political situations. But it has not happened. A new political malaise – with no precise name – nationalism, nepotism, corruption, clientalism are all part of it, stalks the post-postcold war. The disease is the repoliticization of broadcasting (and no doubt everything else). It is not an ideologically coherent movement – but it is about the capture of recourses by élites. It is the era of kleptocracy.

This forensic and chilling report by the Open Society Foundation showed how political control of the crudest and most vulgar kind has taken repossession of television, from the Urals to Umbria. Freedom of thought, impartiality of information, wise exploration of the public condition (whether discussed in news, comedy, soap operas or relevant drama), the notion of broadcasting as informing citizens has retreated, not advanced in these countries. Politicians capture regulators, broadcasting is commercialized and bastardized, news is puppetry, drama has all but disappeared. This is a common story all over the former Eastern Europe, but beyond that as well: Italy at the heart of 'old' Europe has a media system in corrupt political control.

Does it matter; does 'television', the main object of the report matter any more? Don't young people do other things, isn't the internet replacing it, can't people get information from elsewhere? Yet, as the researchers for the Soros report comment, 'reports of the death of television are greatly exaggerated' – it remains the most important window on the world for most people in those societies. Of course the new technologies pose all broadcasters immense and intriguing problems: ones that the political influence largely appearing as commercial exploitation leaves most of these ailing European beasts badly positioned to deal with. Populations still depend on broadcasting for their knowledge and entertainment: they are, however, using it differently. Nor has the 'need' for the engagement that broadcasting can foster (as well as the enjoyment and knowledge) disappeared because of the opportunities of the new technology. The report identifies the more general drivers to the present condition, audiences fragment, ownership consolidates and technology converges. Who, then, represents the public interest or the need for citizens to be informed? Not the weak regulators, certainly not the owners, and barely the broadcasters. The process is not a passive one but an aggressive one. 'Professionals are being replaced by loyal mediocrities', comments the Polish section of the report, managements change in tune to political power, and the rich cultural capacity of the Polish film industry, for example, to create telling fictions is pushed to the very margins of programmes. In Albania, 'Information is neither impartial nor fair. There is almost no media outlet without vested economic or political interests'. In Italy, with Berlusconi back in power, a dark farce plays itself out.

Yet the report in itself was a hopeful thing. You can trust what it shows and you can understand what it tells us. In this way reliable knowledge about advertising revenue, the political manoeuvres, the attempts by some broadcasters to serve their publics better, the impact of the EU trying to wrest propriety back into some systems, the report in itself helps to move the situation from dire to remediable. It ought to make the scrutiny and compliance of the media a higher priority in the EU. Political will and action depends on knowledge.

In another continent the story is different – but related. Reporting of African affairs in Africa has, many experts believe, got worse over the last twenty years. Intimidation, politics and the lack of an independent market for the news are problems. While aid agencies have supported local media they have been inexperienced and uneasy with thinking about business models which might give local media in Africa the absolutely vital economic independence they need in order to flourish. It is not a good thing that the 'good' guys in the media world are dependent on aid. Nevertheless, the mobile telephone is a powerful tool in the hands of the communicating citizen. Many of the media organizations and journalists have been heroic – they know witness makes the difference. Meanwhile, the coverage of developing nations back into our world has also declined. We in Britain, for example, feel far less engaged with the story of India than we did even twenty-five years ago. Although this, too, is complex, because it is, of course, very easy for British citizens from the subcontinent to tune into news and information directly themselves – but we do not all share this knowledge any more. Or to be more accurate, although wealthy, information-rich people now can get much more detailed and comprehensive reporting if they pay and look for it, general understanding has been diminished.

However, everywhere the situation is made more complex and far more hopeful by the opportunities of the digital platforms, which provide new spaces for discussion to creep in. In the Middle East a wild west of talk shows, phone-in discussions, music competitions and cooking marathons has produced a vivid, swirling world of opinion. This is combined with new news capacity. Although some believe that the early radical impartiality of Al-Jazeera, the news channel, has been captured and tamed, nevertheless there is more and better news available. The media flood across borders. The story is never simple – Egypt imprisons journalists, controls expression and yet the well-off can watch the equivalent of *News Night*, a challenging questioning of events on a satellite station. In Saudi Arabia, on the one hand fatwas are issued against opponents, and yet a liberal website has recently been reopened. The American scholar Mark Lynch argues that people are learning to argue, exchange views, question governments, challenge opinion in an exciting new way all over the region.[5]

Yet against this hopeful background there is one stark and growing impediment to knowledge: the acute increase in the threats to journalists and reporting organizations. Telling the truth is no easier than it ever was (even though we are all very sophisticated about what 'the truth' might be). In communist Russia, towards the end of the régime, if the state did not like what you said, you might find it hard to publish what you wanted – but, for the second decade since the end of the communist rule, journalists have been targeted, assaulted and killed, not necessarily directly by the state but by mysteriously opaque interests. It is dangerous to challenge official interpretations of events in many places. This is part of a wider pattern. During the whole of the Second World War, seventy-eight journalists were killed. In 2008 Human Rights Watch listed the names of the 184 journalists killed in that year alone. In the past, independent reporters witnessing conflict had a curious protection: they were the means for both sides in any engagement to get their story out. Yet, as the importance and worldwide nature of propaganda (the significance of mobilizing international diaspora has become a vital part in the ambitions of many groups) has grown, those in conflicts have other ways of getting their own version of events out to supporters. Repeatedly, media organizations have been targeted. Al-Jazeera, the BBC, the news agencies Reuters, Associated News, Agence France-Presse have had buildings quite deliberately targeted during conflicts all over the world. Even more threateningly, individual journalists and the local reporters who are often the life-blood of foreign reporting have been threatened, kidnapped attacked and killed – as journalists. Meanwhile journalists in many political systems are threatened, and indeed killed, because they challenge authority. Although this is a romantic version of journalism – under whose mantle many journalistic abuses attempt to hide – nevertheless it is also an important aspect of the power and value of the media. So, in addition to the commercial threats to news making there is a steep rise in the hazards journalists face. Public understanding comes at a cost.

Amoral

What is the commodity that the media carry that makes everything better, without which decency cannot break out, which is under such threat and which people everywhere hunger for (and perhaps find less palatable when they get it)? It is something like objectivity and the stroppy-minded capacity to confront reality. It is not on one side or the other, or at least tries to tell, insofar as it can discern it, what is happening. Journalists are not there to save the world, they are there to report on it. Indeed, news is amoral in the simple sense that it at its best struggles to perceive what is actually happening – it is not there to change the world. Paradoxically, this lack of moral compass is what makes the news useful as a moral guide. Moral news tells us what has happened – that is all it does, and that is everything it does. News does reality, not nice.

Now we need to distinguish more clearly what is actually valuable in the thing we have previously called 'news'. The bits that matter are not necessarily the bits we are familiar with. We believe we live in a world in which 'news' has been made redundant by a super-fecundity of information. However, although the information world seethes with many kinds of plenty, this is not necessarily more original and reliable knowledge. Indeed, the muddle about what news now is has produced a fog of soggy thinking – which, of course, suits some interests very nicely. There is a fatal confusion between news selling (of which there is a great deal more) and news gathering, assessing and making – (of which there is a good deal less). Ofcom, the British regulator, in its 2007 *New News, Future News* report, full of state-of-the-art economic analysis of the costs of 'news', committed this fundamental category error – and failed to consider news *gathering* costs. Sellers commoditize the news for audiences, but few invest in finding out anything that they and we do not already know. Previously, in the old mass world 'news' was just what 'newspapers' and 'news broadcasts' did. It was the heady mixture of (sometimes) novel information and eye-catching sensation – all of the processes were aggregated and were easily recognizable in the end product. But now, to mistake the variety of vehicles that sell news for the news unearthing they depend on is to mistake the wood for the trees. The broadcast news cliché of the female 'blonde in blue' plus 'elder chap in grey' combo – or the even worse smarmy chap in sun tan version – that is a truly global phenomena is a way of selling news, it is not the bit that matters, there is an almost infinite supply of it. We need to take the production of news apart to see what is of consequence to the public interest.

It is the hunter-gatherers of the news ecology who inform our collective lives. Too much news capacity is confined to the back rooms where information is processed and not enough is spent on people on the street. It is often argued that now all we need is news processors directing news, like human traffic lights. But unless you know what you are directing, understand the stories and the background to the stories that have not yet broken, the news directors will be useless. Already news is like a ticking clock, with too much attention focused on the second hand moving around – when the shape of time the shape of meaning into which an event can be framed is more important and requires a greater, deeper knowledge of what stories mean. Thus, in addition to hunter-gatherers proper news also requires editorial intelligence. It is the integrity of news decision making back on the ranch that also makes news valuable. That editorial sophistication nearly always comes from editors who have been and seen and understand stories directly and personally. They must not (in our interest) just respond to what we are presumed to be interested in, but have to have wider, deeper values. Moreover, news generates creative thought far more than is often recognized – and feeds on culture, in turn. It is the pulling of discussion based on trustworthy judgements (and the resonating of public issues out into comedy and drama and back again) that matters. The diversity that is of public interest is in a variety of news sources and the choice selection of stories.

We may also need rumour squashers just as much as we ever did. One of the things news can do is the opposite of 'whipping up' – it is the proper allaying of fears. The speed of communication has altered everything. The relatives of injured or dead soldiers are now woken, if necessary, in the middle of the night to receive the terrible news – it can no longer be left till the morning, as families might stumble across the news on twenty-four-hour broadcasting. Prime ministers and presidents are expected to react to political events immediately: the time for consideration and assessment has vanished. Indeed, the speed of the news-agenda churn is having profound impacts across a whole terrain of economic and political life. Not following the herd is more than ever vital in breaking stories.

There is another common confusion: innovative audience consumption patterns are also mistaken for 'news' variety. Of course audiences, with their creative exploration of technical opportunities, are remaking all the media industries, from music and art to book publishing and the news. New cultural forms are blossoming. Yet audiences' hunger for experience and the anxious inspection of consumers' new habits has led to another fallacy. People nibble on news from steam television and radio, on the net, on their phones, iPlayers, on bits of paper; at whatever times, for whatever purposes, they pluck news cherries for their own interests and hand them round to their friends. Nevertheless, more and different consumption patterns do not mean there is more newly originated news out there. One change is that audiences are able to *avoid* what they are not 'interested' in more effectively than ever before. But the news that we have to be concerned about is still the new knowledge, alerting you to your environment and having a collective discussion in public about things that, it turns out, matter.

Another weary old-speak confusion that gets in the way of clear thinking about now: wrong definitions of the freedom of speech problem. In pre-lapsian time (like a decade ago) the problem was to secure space for a variety of views in the opinion bazaar. The problem was keeping the arteries of opinion open, because there was a shortage of opinion-expressing opportunity. The argument for public service broadcasting, for example, was that it required an enforced variety of opinion to compensate for its powerful position. Yet this negative anxiety evolved into a positive injunction to use impartiality as an instrument that produces better-informed accounts of events and their causes. The idea became a determination to evade ideological, commercial, political and special-interest capture: this value is as relevant as ever.

However, now you can find any opinion you fancy, find somewhere to express any view you want. You can catch Fox News, with its dedicated partisanship, visit evangelical websites, while phone-ins, message boards and chat rooms throb with people all eager to show and tell what they think. Much of the current affairs blogosphere is stridently masculine, and a worrying new gender divide is emerging – leaving half of the human race bored by political discussion. The old argument that there was nowhere to express *opinions* is surely far less relevant than before. You can find somewhere to parade a view. Nevertheless unfashionable views, ones that challenge orthodoxies of any kind (depending on where you are), still find it far more challenging to attract attention and space. More intriguingly, how we can differentiate between reasonable-*looking* propaganda, and information that is reliable, accurate, trustworthy is challenging.

'Trust' is itself different now. A fear haunts many modern governments of the democratic kind that the public no longer give public institutions enough 'trust'. Fear of a 'trust' shortage has preoccupied many areas of life, from medical to political, from the game show competitions to official statistics. John Lloyd has argued with elegance and force that the media in liberal democracies have played a malign role in unreasonably denying democratic politics any space to articulate political action – they have deliberately dissolved the trust in the political process.[6] It is an important argument. However, the contemporary map of trust is altering. There is not some Maginot Line of trust, an unmoving wall that has to be defended: the public trusts differently from how it trusted in the past.[7] It is more individualistic, expects a greater intimacy and directness of communication. it is argumentative and, while at some times sceptical, it is also often enchanted with irrational beliefs. Such 'personalization' may indeed make public attitudes more vulnerable to hysterical media campaigns (whether of the *Daily Mail* jihadist or the real kind). However, on balance, it remains very important that the public trust the trustworthy.

Nevertheless, perhaps the problem now is not so much what publics believe, but what they know. People have so many opportunities to have opinions that this is not any longer the scarcity we have to worry about. Now it is evidence that matters. This is why impartiality and objectivity are as salient as they ever were. It is also about the opinion agenda. Nearly seventy years of empirical research has shown that the media do not determine what you think, but do set the agenda of what you think about. People have many ways of forming views, false ideas can be as influential as facts if lots of people believe them and they are not corrected by sceptical reality checkers. Properly funded news polices veracity and stretches public horizons: it also represents and amplifies public concerns. Yet, it is the fertile facts that map reality and form the basis for views that we need to be concerned to preserve.

The other 'opinion' problem is how we are to be brought into relationship with uncongenial views: the 'others' that we may try to avoid. All that opinion expressing is also confused with a variety of opinions: more does not mean wider. More may be a mob. Niche–partisan news selling means that the range of acceptable expression within communities is often a spiralling, narrow one. Both nationally and internationally, great swathes of opinion talk and listen only to other like-minded publics. News can speak across these boundaries if it tells reliable and recognizable accounts of events. People attend when they hear their own reality accounted for justly. It is part of the task of enlarging our collective imagination and attaching our fickle attention to uncomfortable things that we don't understand, that we would often prefer to ignore but which will affect our lives. Proper news is a rationality explorer: it shows you unflinchingly why people, in their circumstances, have the attitudes they have. So the diversity that matters is the diversity of the unexpected and plain reporting.

Moreover the 'new information' bit of the 'news' is not growing. All over the western world we have lost scrutiny capacity. Startlingly, in a world where everyone says everything is 'global', news values have become more parochial under the intense heat of competition. While simultaneously we are losing genuinely local understanding at an alarming rate, the consequences of the economic collapse of 2008–9 mean that Wales, for example, will have almost no local reporting left. It will have political structures of its own, councils, a national assembly – but no vehicle for discussing what they are doing – except public service broadcasting. The online story of news is one of concentration, not diversity. Thus, more genuinely novel sources of reliable news on the net are difficult to identify because search engines are inadequate. But even so, one recent study showed that the '4,500 news sources updated continuously'[8] from all around the world, about which one search engine boasted, were overwhelmingly lifted and pasted from just four places: three news agencies Agence France-Presse, Associated Press, Reuters and the BBC. The news sellers and opinion strutters were adding their interpretations to a limited set of sources. Another study looked at the decline of 'local' reporting in cities across the world.[9] Yet those who put new things on the collective radar provide an early warning system without which we know that democratic institutions simply fall into weary corruption.

This is why a big, well-resourced news organization like, for example, the BBC's, may be likely to produce more diversity than a small one. Many people are experimenting with ways of assessing news sites so that the public can know which places to turn to for reliable and trustworthy news. But some organizations have a record of appraisal and discovery and a history of reliability: and our own BBC is in this way a potential world resource as well as a national one. Calming news which is accurate needs to be present on the web, and the public have to be able to find their way to it when they need it. News gathering and assessing must be reinvented. Nevertheless, it is the feet on the ground with the Taliban, with the outcast political parties in India or in the back streets of Birmingham that matter. There is no alternative to people witnessing events: reporting is a kind of testimony, and we need more quizzical interrogation of the world. 'Citizen' journalism is a magnificent democratic tool, but it needs situating by people who understand how the world on the ground smells. Variety still depends on independent-minded journalists just pursuing stories that are of consequence.

Global institutions: global public

However, being interconnected also means that we need information processors and attention graspers big enough to understand and confront global phenomena. We still need big news organizations – or at least a better way of co-ordinating and testing information so that public understanding has the range to match the institutions we live within. Modern government is large. Global forces impact on individual lives. Huge, international info-tainment businesses often regard news as an expedient political instrument or a branding instrument. Their first concern is not with the quality of information that democratic citizens need. Why should it be? Meanwhile, all of these commercial players seek to translate their interests into politically favourable situations, lobbying is powerful, expensive and rarely sponsored by citizens. The BBC, for example, can bring variety to public discussion because it is large enough and belongs to the public. Moreover, somehow we need to support robust organizations, because the resources devoted to fixing favourable news stories are far larger than those devoted to resisting them.

Some argue that 'partisan' news is the way forward. Yet scandals are exposed by commitment to accuracy, not advocacy. It is not that advocates are not useful – but they also need testing. Recently, in Afghanistan the only footage that was available of the biggest military engagement the British army had been involved in since the Falklands, the taking of Musi Quala, was taken by military film units. It was propaganda. Only the BBC was able to explain what had actually happened: it took a reporter who had been there often to understand the significance of what was occurring. The army still seems to fail to understand that independent journalism is the only reliable way of guaranteeing trust. Meanwhile, aid agencies are paying film makers to make the documentaries, but who will scrutinize the agencies themselves – now nearly all large, multinational enterprises and remarkably unaccountable? Partisanship is one aspect – but limiting.

Diversity is in the public interest – but modern societies suffer from collective attention deficit disorders. How can people concentrate, when it matters, on things that matter? In the fidgety, non-linear world of the disaggregated attender, how do you mobilize people to notice things? One answer has been sensation, a febrile brew of self-righteous indignation, stirring, shock, salaciousness and attack journalism. Another is to punch a message across all platforms. One of the things democracy needs, that the news can do, is shout and make a fuss about things citizens ought to know. We still need ways of amplify the message across all of the carefully coloured outlets responsive to different audiences. The public interest has to work harder to be noticed, and we need agile but resourceful media to do that.

There is another reason for supporting or creating new vehicles like the big news organizations in the spinal column of our cultural content providers: because news becomes the nervous system of a variety of engagements. News is often considered as a public-service good in its own right (which it is), but there is little discussion of how news seeps into the tissues of an organization or institutions. The traffic is creatively two way: comedy, games, drama and children's programmes metabolize news into stories that foster different kinds of discussions of the issues of the day. News alerts programmes to reality, they nurture creative engagement with our predicament. There are a variety of objectivity traders in the world market for knowledge; there are news agencies who are impartial because they sell news to all comers; many news organizations, especially in places that are difficult to work in, fight tenaciously to tell accurate stories. But we need some big, well-resourced and perhaps innovatively organized news producers to test and contextualize stories internationally. But objectivity is hard to do, expensive to produce and more challenging to bring off successfully to the satisfaction of complexly polarized audiences in the contemporary world. Yet the economic model that supports such organizations is under severe economic pressure. On the one hand, we need original models that trade in and test the news that everyone now can produce. It has to be tested because it may, just like old-style news, be accurate but partial. Or it may be a rumour. Or it may be deliberately misleading. The news providers are beginning to get better at handling this material. But it is not enough. We still need news hunters and assessments based on local understanding. We still need the capacity to translate stories from one culture and set of political assumptions into another.

Then there is the really urgent need – a national and an international democratic deficit – to hold international NGOs to account and to argue about it. After all, charities which are now international big businesses, for example, act in our name, with our money, and what they do influences everyone's future. The world is developing world institutions, they cannot thrive without an international public to address and mould them. Meanwhile, since the 1980s NGOs have boomed. They have become part of a new kind of fifth estate, but they are not all the same. Many critics argue that they are unaccountable; some critics are increasingly cynical about the value of what is called 'aid'. We need to distinguish between those NGOs that are self-interested oligarchies, the ones who, pursuing benign ends, have bad effects, and the ones whose purposes and impacts are valuable, and we really do need to subject them to the kind of scrutiny that tests them. Americans need to know what is done in their name in places they can barely find on a map.

Finally, we need global media with a broad international reach because we have other, invisible and powerful global institutions, and without media scrutiny they will fall into corruption. We, somehow, need a questioning and testing and capacity to argue with institutions that matches their range and size. Some of them are global businesses, who operate a good deal more agilely than the media to cover them, some are supra-governmental. Many operate below the radar of any public – let alone the interconnected world audiences to whom they need to be held accountable.

Actually, we at home (wherever that is) need more reporting of distant foreign places for practical issues of self-interested survival – not because it would be nice of us. The first problem is what we understand about our own situation. After all, some of the places we barely bother about have some of the highest economic growth rates and the youngest, most energetic populations and the most difficult economic and political circumstances. Africa, for example. Yet, even the most narrow minded must have noticed that what happens in Britain, down-town Manhattan or Mumbai is hardly a domestic matter any more. Of course there is trade, but there are also bombs. Comprehending what happens in Luton, Walthamstow or Brixton already depends on some kind of understanding of what is happening in Pakistan. The failure to understand foreign places, from their ground up, not out of our preconceived, comfortable stereotypes or sheer blindness, has already had dire consequences in Iraq and Afghanistan, as well as in London and Madrid. But this is two way. We need to come to terms with unpalatable views. But so does everybody. We need to understand the voices that we do not like and do not agree with even more than those we admire or support. They need to understand us as well. In particular, we have to be concerned about the stories we *will* need to know about – that at the moment seem distant or trivial. Future stories are as important as or even more so than present ones.

Experienced understanding of this kind depends on knowledge and local wisdom. In order to understand the world, not simply interpret it through ideological or info-tainment spectacles, people need to have a historical context within which to place events. Which way things are blowing is only accurately answerable by reference to experience – without it we all too often get the trend of an event (the only thing that matters about it really) quite wrong. Where are the sources of such nuanced, local, deep, long-historical, experienced knowledge of the world in Britain (and indeed in the world)? They are in some government departments, they are in commercial organizations, and they exist in communities. But many of these are woefully incapable of also engaging the public – which they have to learn how to do. Lost local understanding is mirrored by lost international understanding. Indeed, comprehension and explanation requires immersion and local intelligence. It may require friendship. It certainly requires respect and local voices. We need to lay the seeds of our future intelligent knowledge of places now, and we need reporters out, reporting – not editing. Such reporting is expensive, and while much journalism has improved in sympathy and quality – especially the focusing on the voices and views of those who are the subjects of stories, who now increasingly give their own account in their own words – it is also fragile. Just as we all need to know more, we are in danger of making ourselves more stupid. Of course, the cost of ignorance and a loss of knowledge is often catastrophic.

In the twenty-first century the front line of every bloody conflict – as well as every commercial endeavour – is in human minds. Fortunes are made and battles won far away from battlefields – in the ideas people have. News making is a knowledge industry: part of the advanced economy of under-standing that is remaking the world. Stupid societies make bad decisions. Those that cannot have a common discussion on the realities (both the jolly and the unnerving) of their predicament become tyrannies – either aggres-sively nasty or myopically stumbling places, replete with trivial comforts but unaware of simmering problems. Getting the thinking around news making right, so that it goes on discovering and alerting us to the unexpected (as well as comforting us with the deliciously shocking familiar), and inventing new ways to tickle the public fancy is important. But the variety that matters is in the hard slog of telling us little stories that we will come to see as import-ant – it is news gathering and news agendas that we have to think about. Keeping information honest is not a luxury: it is a matter of self-interest.

Notes

1 See Ed R. Sambrooke, *Global Voice* (London, Premium Publishing, 2007).

2 See Jean Seaton, *Carnage and the Media* (London, Penguin, 2005), chs 1, 7 and 11 for an extended discussion of these issues.

3 See Suzanne Franks, 'Media, Aid and Disaster', Ph.D. dissertation, University of West-minster, 2007, and in 'Trust and Aid', *Political Quarterly*, 78 (3), 2007.

4 Open Society Foundation, *Television Across Europe: Regulation, Policy and Independence* (EU Open Society Institute, 2008).

5 Mark Lynch, *Voices of the New Arab Public* (London, Columbia University Press, 2007). Naomi Sakr's excellent *Arab Television Today* (London, I.B. Tauris, 2007) also argues for the exciting developments in some media spaces in these societies.

6 John Lloyd, *What the Media are doing to our Politics* (London, Constable and Robinson, 2007).

7 See Jean Seaton, 'Trustworthiness: ancient and modern', *Political Quarterly*, 79 (3), 2008, 300–14.

8 Chris Patterson, *News Agency Dominance in International News on the Net*, Research Paper, University of Leeds, 2005, p. 47.

9 Thomas Johnson, 'Young People and City News', Shorenstein Centre, 2007, www.ksg.harvard.edu/presspol/index.htm.

Chapter 21

The liberal theory of press freedom

According to classical liberal theory, the freedom to publish in the free market ensures that the press reflects a wide range of opinions and interests in society. If a viewpoint is missing in the press, this is only because it lacks a sufficient following to sustain it in the marketplace. As the heroine puts it in Tom Stoppard's play *Night and Day*, 'The *Flat Earth News* is free to sell a million copies. What it lacks is the ability to find a million people with ... a conviction that the earth is flat. Freedom is neutral'.

The free market, it is also argued, makes the press a representative institution. 'The broad shape and nature of the press', proclaims John Whale, 'is ultimately determined by no one but its readers'. This is because newspapers and magazines must respond to the concerns of their readers if they are to stay in business.

Some liberal theorists view the market as an analogue of the electoral process. They claim that newspapers submit themselves to public judgement every time they go on sale, whereas politicians stand for election at infrequent intervals. Consequently newspapers are closer to the people than are their elected representatives.

The market-based press is independent because it owes allegiance only to the public. The press is the people's watchdog, scrutinizing the actions of government and holding the country's rulers to account. Its reporting of the news keeps readers abreast of important events and developments, and enables them to exercise informed judgements at election time. By providing a forum of public debate, the press also facilitates the formation of public opinion. This opinion is then relayed by the press – the people's tribune – to those in power.

There is thus a clear sequence of argument, which begins with the claim that the free market renders the press diverse, representative and independent. The press's autonomy enables it to fearlessly scrutinize government, brief the electorate, stage a national debate and relay public opinion to authority. To this are sometimes added ancillary functions such as expressing the shared values of the public, assisting society to adapt to change and exposing wrongdoing.

This classical liberal theory of the press has been repeated so often that it has acquired a seemingly unshakeable authority. But its chain of argument contains a number of weak links. This will become apparent when we compare the reports of the three major inquiries into the British press and consider what ensued during the official silence that followed.

Freedom to publish

'Free enterprise', declared the first Royal Commission on the Press (1949), 'is a prerequisite of a free press'. Underlying this belief was a relatively untroubled conviction that the unrestricted freedom to publish produces a diverse and representative press. The Commission expected to find that 'the press as a whole gives an opportunity for all important points of view to be effectively presented in terms of the varying standards of taste, political opinion, and education among the principal groups of the population'. Wartime regulation was blamed for preventing new publications from springing up to meet changes in public demand. Anticipating deregulation, the Commission rejected proposals for assisting the launch of new papers as unnecessary. The natural creativity of the market, it assumed, would again make the press representative.

This assessment was queried by the next Press Commission (1962), and openly disputed by its successor (1977). The latter's blunt conclusion was that 'anyone is free to start a daily national newspaper, but few can afford even to contemplate the prospect'. It also noted that the national press was overwhelmingly right wing and manifestly unrepresentative. Indeed, 'in February 1974 ... the share of newspaper (national daily) circulation held by papers supporting the Conservative Party was 71% greater than Conservative votes as a percentage of the votes cast'.

High entry costs were found to curtail the freedom to publish in other sectors of the press. Even establishing a new local evening paper in a town with no direct competition would cost in 1977, according to the Commission, between £2 million and £3 million. The cost of launching a new magazine in the main consumer sectors was also found to be high. As for new paid-for weeklies, there are 'not many places left with the right conditions to provide a permanent market'.

The assumption that 'anyone' is free to start a new paper has been an illusion ever since the industrialization of the press. That it is an illusion was exposed in unsparing detail by the last Commission. In effect, it dislodged a key foundation stone of liberal theory.

Since then, the advent of the internet has enhanced the freedom to publish by lowering entry costs. But the list of the ten most-visited news sites is dominated by large news organizations like BBC News, the *Guardian*, *The Times*, *Sun* and *Telegraph*.[1] It is always possible to set up small websites, the equivalent of small corner shops. But this is not the same thing as publishing well-resourced news websites – the equivalent of supermarkets – which large numbers of people visit.

Diversity and chain ownership

The 1949 Commission argued that proprietors should be free to conduct their publications as they wished. This was justified partly on the grounds that proprietors had the right to safeguard their financial investments in a high-risk industry. The Commission also believed that publishers' freedom from restraint underpinned the diversity of the press.

This hands-off approach assumed that chain ownership would not develop into a major problem. 'There is no reason to expect', declared the Commission, 'that the aggressive expansion of chain undertakings [in the daily and Sunday press] which characterized the early period will be resumed. Neither in the local nor in the periodical press nor in the news agencies do we expect a significant trend towards further concentration of ownership'.

The 1962 Commission was obliged to revise this assessment. It found that the share of circulation controlled by the major chains had 'substantially increased' in all parts of the press. The leading three proprietors' share of the national daily press had soared to 89 per cent. There were, it added, 'spectacular movements towards concentration of ownership' in the periodical press. Only among local weeklies was concentration 'negligible'.

This latter conclusion had to be discarded. Acceleration of chain ownership since 1962 had been greatest, concluded the 1977 Commission, in the local weekly press. Unlike before, new acquisitions had also resulted in the same three proprietors dominating both the national daily and the Sunday markets. In addition, the Commission highlighted a phenomenon which had previously received little attention – the emergence of subregional monopolies in which all or nearly all 'competing' local morning, evening and weekly papers were owned by the same group.

These changes in press ownership led to a shift in perspective. Whereas the first two Commissions had taken for granted the right of proprietors to determine editorial policy, the third Commission talked of the need to 'protect editors and journalists from owners'. The exercise of proprietorial power no longer appeared to be legitimate as a basis for securing press diversity, at a time when only three men controlled over half of total daily and Sunday newspaper sales in Britain.

In the thirty years after 1977, there was a major expansion of local press concentration, but a small reduction in the dominant three groups' share of national press circulation. Overall, the level of press concentration remained especially high in Britain, much higher than in most European countries (due to the dominance of the British national press).

Loss of independence

Other changes contributed to growing misgivings. The first Commission had advanced as a subsidiary justification for proprietorship the claim that it safeguarded the independent integrity of the press. 'It is undoubtedly a great merit of the British press', declared the Commission, 'that it is completely independent of outside financial interests and that its policy is the policy of those who own and control it'. The Commission thus invoked the classical liberal view of the press as an independent fourth estate, uncompromised by vested interest.

However, most of the British press was bought up by, or diversified into, interests outside publishing during the 1960s and 1970s. By 1977, all but one of the leading publishing groups in both the national and regional press were part of larger conglomerates with holdings in fields as diverse as oil, transport, mining, construction, engineering, finance or the leisure industries. 'Rather than saying that the press has other business interests', concluded the last Commission, 'it would be truer to argue that the press has become a subsidiary of other industries'.

This clearly undermined the case for proprietorial control as a guarantee of the press's independence, to which the first Commission had paid such fulsome tribute. It also cast in a new light the Commission's contention, cited above, that proprietors had the right to exercise control over their investments in the high-risk press industry. If investigative journalists discover wrongdoing by a parent or sister company, should their employers have the legitimate right to suppress what they found? More generally, can the freedom of the press be equated with the freedom of conglomerates, owning much of the press, to promote their business interests? These questions clearly troubled the 1977 Commission, and partly explain why it was much less enthusiastic about 'the rights' of proprietors than were its predecessors.[2]

Since the Commission's report, most large press groups have refocused their activities on communications, though many still retain some non-media interests. However, this shift has compromised in a new way rather than restored the press's independence. Most major press groups have interests in other media (such as books, TV, film, magazines, radio or the internet), not merely in Britain but abroad. They are not subsidiaries of big business: they *are* big business. They are also active lobbyists of government, seeking to change public policy in their favour[3] – something that is not consistent with the disinterested actions of an autonomous fourth estate.

Competition, choice and new technology

The first Commission attached great importance to the role of competition in making the press responsive to the public. Due to competitive pressures, argued the Commission, 'whatever a paper's purpose and however it is owned, it cannot escape the necessity of offering the public what some at least of the public will buy'.

Although the Commission was troubled by the large number of newspaper closures during the inter-war period, it viewed this as a temporary lapse caused mainly by publishers' extravagance and lack of adaptability. 'In the provincial press as a whole', it concluded, 'there is nothing approaching monopoly and we can see no strong tendency towards monopoly'.

The 1962 Commission introduced a Keynesian analysis which suggested that a trend towards contraction and monopoly was a built-in feature of the newspaper market. 'The natural tendency', concluded the 1962 Commission, 'of the economic factors affecting [newspaper] production and sale is to diminish the number of papers ... '. Successful papers are usually able to outspend their rivals because they have both greater sale and advertising revenues, and also lower unit costs, due to their higher economies of scale. In the long term, this tends to result in weaker rivals going to the wall. The 1977 Commission broadly concurred with this analysis, adding two things. Economies of consolidation were enabling strong press groups to buy out rivals in the local press, at above the market rate.[4] The large financial resources and accumulated expertise of leading press groups also equipped them to launch new publications more successfully than small independents.[5]

The 1977 Commission found some solace in the emergence of freesheets. However, the rise of local freesheets during the 1980s reduced the number of paid-for weeklies. It eroded local press autonomy by generating papers totally reliant on advertising. Freesheets also became organized increasingly into chains, many of them the same chains that dominated the local press. By 1988 the five largest publishers of freesheets were responsible between them for 338 free newspapers, and a further 243 paid-for papers.

The 1977 Commission also placed much hope in new technology. During the 1980s, new, computer-aided print technology did in fact lower entry costs, and enable the launch of new papers in the national press (though rarely in the local daily press). However, most of these new publications failed. Costs rose again when leading national papers greatly expanded their size, forcing their less well-endowed rivals to follow suit. Once again, entry into the national press became prohibitively expensive. The last new national daily to be launched was Eddy Shah's short-lived *Post* in 1988. With the exception of the *Star*'s Sunday edition (launched in 2002), the last new national Sunday was the ephemeral *Sunday Correspondent* (1989–90). Computer technology did not ride to the rescue for long.

In the period 1948–2002, there was a reduction in the total number of paid-for newspapers in the UK from 1441 to 646. The biggest decrease was in paid-for weekly papers, and in local morning dailies, though there was a marginal increase in the number of national papers during this period (see Table 21.1). The result was a long-term weakening of competition, and spread of monopoly in the local press. Between 1921 and 2002, the number of urban centres with a choice of paid-for *local* morning papers fell from twenty-seven to none, and of paid-for *local* evening papers from fifteen to two.[6]

The rise of the internet seemingly offers a technological remedy to this contraction, since it extends choice. However, the benefit of this has been

Table 21.1 The number of newspaper titles, 1921 to 2002

	1921	1937	1948	1961	1976	1988	2002	% reduction 1921–2002
National press								
National daily	14	11	11	10	9	12	12	14.3
National Sunday	14	10	10	8	7	9	11	21.4
Regional/local press								
Morning	41	27	27	22	20	18	19	53.6
Morning freesheets	–	–	–	–	–	–	6	–
Evening	93	83	80	77	79	74	74	20.4
Sunday	7	7	6	5	6	8	11	(57)
Sunday freesheets	–	–	–	–	–	–	10	–
Weekly and bi-weekly	1485	1303	1307	1219	1072	801	509	65.7
Freesheets	–	–	–	–	185[a]	896[b]	640	–
Total[c]	1654	1441	1441	1341	1193	922	646	61.6

Sources: Royal Commission on the Press 1947–9 Report, Appendix 2, Tables 2–3; *Royal Commission on the Press 1961–2 Report*, Appendix 3, Tables 3 and 5; *Royal Commission on the Press 1974–7 Final Report*, Annex 3, Table 4, *Press Council Annual Report 1988*, Table 1 and Table A.
Notes: [a] This relates to 1975. [b] In addition, there was one local daily and one Sunday freesheet. [c] Excluding freesheets.

diminished by two things. Newspapers have poured money into developing news sites, thereby pre-empting the rise of rivals. And, as mentioned earlier in this book, the press is now reeling from the loss of advertising. Advertising expenditure on the internet overtook that in the national press in 2006, and in the regional press in 2007.[7] Press advertising is not relocating in the main to newspaper websites, but to other parts of the web. The business model for delivering news – based on a large advertising subsidy – is beginning to break down. The result will be editorial budget cuts and cumulative newspaper closures, for many years to come, that will bite into the national as well as regional press.

In short, the *deus ex machina* of classical liberal theory – free market competition that is supposed to render the press diverse and representative – has fallen into disrepair in the regional press, and is threatened in the national press.

Reappraisal

The standard themes of liberal theory are open to more far-reaching objections than that provided by the Press Commissions. The press is not representative, because it is owned and controlled by the powerful.[8] Newspapers do not 'represent' their readers' views in a literal sense, because readers buy papers partly to be entertained: thus, survey research shows that only a minority of the *Sun*'s readers actually voted the same way as their paper in the four general elections of the Conservative ascendancy (1979–92). And a narrow focus on the alleged representative role of the press ignores the far more significant source of representation provided by civil society.

But the Press Commissions represent, nevertheless, staging posts in a journey of disenchantment with traditional liberal theory. In particular, what had seemed plausible to the first Commission seemed increasingly implausible to its two successors. They drew attention to four underlying problems. High entry costs render the press less accountable; the growth of chain ownership limits press diversity; wider business entanglements weaken the press's claims to disinterest; and the recurrence of market failure undermines those processes which are said, in liberal theory, to make the press the servant of the people.

These long-term problems are not specific to Britain, but are manifested all over the world. One response to them has been to promote the ideals of social responsibility and objective journalism among journalists as a way of ensuring that the press serves the public. It is a strategy that has been pursued vigorously in the United States, partly as a way of mitigating the consequences of increasing press concentration and monopoly in the decentralized American press. It has also become, in practice, a way of relegitimating the market system. However, in a British context it has radical implications, since it upholds professional autonomy and impartiality in a way that challenges the partisan, hierarchical character of the national tabloid press.

The alternative route is the social market strategy pursued particularly in northern Europe. This has taken various forms: general press subsidies, selective grants to minority papers, aid for the launch of new publications, and press-specific anti-monopoly measures.[9] This approach seeks to sustain diversity and competition through public intervention, and is also a way of relegitimating the market system. However, even this option has radical implications in Britain, because it means deviating from the traditional British press policy of having no policy.

In the event, the last two Royal Commissions dithered between these two strategies without fully backing either. Their indecision was the root cause of their ineffectiveness.

Social market flirtation

Perhaps the closest the Press Commissions came to following a social market strategy was to advocate special anti-monopoly measures for the press. This was tentatively initiated by the 1949 Commission, which proposed that the Monopolies Commission should monitor changes in press ownership with increased vigilance. This proposal had no discernible effect.

In 1961 its successor recommended the setting up of a Press Amalgamations Court. A variant of this proposal was adopted in 1965. It required all large press groups to obtain the permission of the Secretary of State before they were allowed to purchase a newspaper. The 1977 Commission demonstrated that this approach had failed: all fifty press acquisitions between 1965 and 1977, falling within the terms of anti-monopoly controls, had been allowed. The Commission argued that anti-monopoly legislation needed to be strengthened in five ways. Its advice was ignored.

Since its report, nothing has happened to suggest that feeble anti-monopoly legislation has had any significant influence on the press. Out of 172 transfers of newspaper ownership to major press groups between 1980 and 2000, only three applications (all involving minor papers) were refused, and a further five were approved subject to conditions.[10] All major acquisitions – including Murdoch's purchase of *The Times* and *Sunday Times* in 1981[11] and the Guardian Group's acquisition of the *Observer* in 1993 – were allowed.

The last two Commissions placed enormous faith in the power of legislation to restrain the growth of press concentration. They rejected proposals for divesting the major press groups – originating from the centre as well as from the left of the political spectrum.[12] They also opposed the introduction of selective press subsidy systems, now operating in a number of Britain's neighbouring countries. In effect, they put most of their weight behind one particular strategy. It failed.

Restriction on joint media ownership

The Press Commissions had slightly more success in seeking to keep the press and broadcasting industries separate, in the interests of maintaining media pluralism. However, this success came late and proved to be short lived.

Against the prescient advice of the first Press Commission, newspaper owners were allowed to be investors in commercial television when it was launched in 1955. The second Press Commission was critical of this involvement, but was prevented from making an explicit recommendation by its terms of reference. Contrary to the spirit of its report, press groups continued to retain shareholdings in commercial television. Indeed, they were even given a prescriptive right to participate in setting up local commercial radio stations in their circulation areas when independent radio was introduced in 1972.

This prescriptive right was ended by the 1981 Broadcasting Act, on the recommendation of the 1977 Press Commission. The IBA also adopted a policy of reducing substantial press interests in commercial television and radio in response to the urging of both the 1977 Press Commission and the 1977 Annan Committee on Broadcasting. This was codified in the 1990 Broadcasting Act, which prevented any press group from having a controlling stake in a television franchise.

However, the tide turned during the deregulatory 1990s. The 1996 Broadcasting Act partly reversed previous policy by allowing most news-paper groups (with less than a 20 per cent share of the national market) to expand into terrestrial television, and by relaxing the rules about cross-own-ership of local press and local radio. The New Labour administration indi-cated its willingness to go further down this path in 2001, after protracted public soundings dominated by self-interested media lobbying. The Com-munications Act (2003) opens the door to Murdoch's acquisition of Channel 5, if it becomes available for sale.

This was preceded by the adoption of more liberal rules governing the development of satellite and cable television (and later digital multiplexes), allowing extensive cross-ownership to develop. The key turning point was 1990, when Rupert Murdoch, controller of the largest press group in Britain, was allowed to dominate British satellite television by retaining control of the merged satellite broadcaster BSkyB.

Self-regulation

If the Press Commissions' flirtation with social market policies was a relative failure, the tentative steps they took to promote the professionalization of the press were scarcely more successful. The most concrete reform to emerge from their efforts was the establishment of a self-regulatory agency. This was conceived by the 1949 Commission as a well-funded and widely respected public body concerned not only with investigating complaints against the press but also with such matters as the recruitment and education of jour-nalists and the promotion of substantial research into the press. The 'General Council of the Press', envisaged by the Commission, would be similar to the General Medical Council. It would embody and promote a professional culture among journalists.

The Press Council was reluctantly set up by the industry in 1953, in an enfeebled form, following the threat of statutory regulation. The Press Council's shortcomings were roundly condemned by the 1962 Commission, which urged government legislation if there was no improvement. This produced some reforms – notably, the appointment of an independent chairman and the annual publication of press concentration statistics. However, these reforms failed to impress the third Commission. 'We hope', concluded its scathing report, 'that in future the Press Council will be more vigilant in demonstrating the independence and impartiality to which it lays claim'.

The 1977 Commission made twelve recommendations for a complete overhaul of the Press Council's organization and procedures. Nine of these (including most of the important ones) were rejected. However, the fresh threat of legislation, with all-party support, led to another round of reluctant reforms in 1989 to 1990. This included, after twenty-seven years of foot dragging, the formulation of a code of conduct for journalists. However, these reforms were judged to be too little and too late by the Calcutt Committee, which recommended that the Press Council be disbanded and replaced by a more effective agency.

The Press Complaints Commission (PCC) was established in 1991. When it was investigated by Sir David Calcutt in 1993, it was also found to be failing the public:

> The Press Complaints Commission is not ... an effective regulator of the press. It has not been set up in a way, and is not operating a code of conduct, which enables it to command not only press but also public confidence ... It is not the truly independent body that it should be.

This indictment led eventually to the appointment of a new chairman, Lord Wakeham, in 1995. Once again, the cycle of public scrutiny and condemnation, followed by contrition and the promise of reform, was resumed. Once again, minor improvements were made. The PCC became a more user-friendly, efficient, publicity-conscious organization. The backing of key figures in the industry ensured that it carried more clout than the 1980s Press Council had done. Wakeham proved to be adept at courting the powerful, until he resigned his PCC chairmanship in 2002 in order to spend more time with his lawyers, as a consequence of his alleged entanglement (as a non-executive director) in the Enron fraud case.

However, despite some improvements, two fundamental problems besetting press self-regulation were not resolved. The PCC was not fully independent of the industry which funded it. It was also not very effective. It had no power to command evidence, award fines or order the payment of compensation. It also lacked moral authority, because it did not enjoy the whole-hearted consent of the press industry, and was only accepted as a 'lesser evil' to statutory regulation. Its main function was to assist informal conciliation between outraged members of the public and the press. The PCC made much of the fact that its adjudications were published in the offending paper, and that this was a powerful deterrent against abuse. What it omitted to point out was that in its first ten years (1991–2001), the PCC upheld only 1.5 per cent of the complaints it received.[13]

The deficiencies of the PCC have now been brought into sharp relief by the establishment of the Irish Press Council in 2008. This last, unlike the PCC, has a vigorous and effective Press Ombudsman; reaches conclusions on the 'balance of the evidence' rather than being reluctant to judge; and accepts third party complaints, subject to certain conditions. The difference between the two bodies was highlighted when they assessed the same racially offensive article (published in both countries in July 2008).[14] The complaint was upheld in Ireland, and rejected in Britain.

However, the principal shortcoming of British press self-regulation is not its lack of independence nor even its dismal record in judging complaints, but its dearth of ambition. It does not publish substantial research; it does not stage formative debates about press ethics; it does not honour great journalism; and it makes no significant input into journalism education. Indeed, it does not embody in any meaningful way a professionalizing project. Unwanted by the press, it has settled for being a customer complaints service.

The first Press Commission had pinned its hopes not only on the creation of a Press Council but also on education as a way of fostering a public interest culture among journalists. It wanted the content of journalism education to be broadened, and its organization streamlined nationally – objectives ardently sought also by the third Commission. In the event, journalism training continued to impart a narrow range of skills and knowledge, and to foster an unquestioning attitude. Its organization, always piecemeal, became more fragmented in the 1990s. The National Council for the Training of Journalists (NCTJ) qualification never became, as the third Commission hoped, a respected yardstick of professional competence. It is possessed by only a minority of journalists.[15]

While narrow vocational training was overtaken by the student-led expansion of media studies in British universities during the 1980s and 1990s, this was neither anticipated nor desired by the first and third Commissions, which echoed the industry's hostility towards undergraduate media degrees. This hostility turned into angry denunciation when the press experienced the novelty of being subject to watchdog scrutiny. 'This paper regards a degree in media studies as a disqualification for the career of journalism', thundered one respected daily (*Independent*, 31 October 1996), a view echoed by other papers. A major investment was thus made in media education without British universities acquiring an accepted role in supporting and interpreting the ideals of professional journalism, in the way that it did in the United States and elsewhere.

The Commissions' professionalizing project failed also because it was overwhelmed by stronger forces than it was able to command. Powerful commercial pressures were unleashed in the national press after 1956, when newsprint rationing was lifted, and again in the 1980s with the introduction of new technology. In the national press, this led for a time to a decline in standards of accuracy, notorious cases of chequebook journalism, more prurient intrusions into private grief not justified by the public interest, the parading of imaginary folk devils, and outbreaks of sadistic bullying of sad people. In the regional press, a tendency towards lazy, public relations-led journalism was reinforced by editorial cost-cutting, falling sales and the consolidation of the freesheets.

However, it was tabloid excess which most outraged public opinion. By 1993, only 10 per cent of the public believed that journalists could generally be trusted to tell the truth. This was a drop of almost half by comparison with ten years earlier, and placed journalists at the bottom of fifteen groups in terms of public credibility, below even politicians.[16] In 2002, a reformulated question elicited another damning response: 75 per cent in the UK said that they 'tended not to trust' the printed press – a much higher proportion than in any other country in the European Union.[17] There could scarcely have been a more telling indictment of the Press Commissions' professionalizing strategy for reforming the press.

Uneasy ambivalence

Press Commissions have also advocated other reforms – that newspapers should display prominently the name of their owner, that they should declare an interest when reporting on topics in which their parent or associated companies are financially involved, and that the press should abide by a Charter of good practice drawn up by the last Commission, which would be policed by a reformed Press Council and, if it proved necessary, by statute. All these proposals were ignored.

However, the last of these is worth examining briefly because it highlights the uneasiness, borne of misgivings about the liberal inheritance, that informed the work of the last Commission. At first glance, its Charter reflected a completely traditionalist position. It had been inspired by the publishers' campaign against the union 'closed shop', and contained detailed prohibitions against union influence. The Charter was prefaced by acceptance of the newspaper publishers' argument that 'in reality editorial and managerial decisions were inseparable'. The publisher's pregorative was also justified by an idealized image of the free market as a guarantor of 'the right of a man to express what he believes'.

However, another part of the Commission's report had questioned whether the market really functioned in the freedom-enhancing way in which it was supposed to. The Commission was in fact more ambivalent than it appeared to be at first sight. Press freedom, it suggested, should not only be equated with publishers' freedom from restraint; it also had something to do with the freedom of people who edit and work in newspapers. This approach was reflected in the clauses of its proposed Charter which upheld the freedom of conscience of individual journalists, and the right of the editor to accept any contribution 'notwithstanding the views of his proprietor'. However, the Commission then found itself in deep waters because the strengthening of staff rights is advocated by some as a way of securing the independence of the press. Internal democracy, it declared hastily, is 'a complex and disputed subject' about which it was unable to 'express a view'.

This dalliance with reformism ensured that the proposed Charter was quietly buried at the behest of publishers. The same kind of reformist ambivalence is to be found elsewhere in the Commission's report. Newspapers, it declared, should behave 'with proper restraint'; the press should recruit, like broadcasting, more graduates; young journalists should attend improving courses and 'learn about society'. Indeed, the Commission seemed intent, at times, on transplanting the public service rationale of broadcasting to the press, but its moves in this direction were hesitant and contradictory. It wanted a public service orientation, but not the framework of public regulation underpinning it. It favoured a more balanced, responsible approach, but saw merit in the free market tradition of outspoken comment. Unable to define precisely what it meant by professionalism, the Commission was not very successful at promoting it. But its flirtation with the idea of public service was nevertheless revealing: it was an attempt to co-opt a different theoretical tradition in a bid to bolster the increasingly threadbare classical theory of press freedom.

Weak reformism

The three Commissions were sharply critical of the press, yet failed to come up with solutions to the problems they identified.[18] The sum total of their efforts was failed anti-monopoly legislation and ineffectual self-regulation. No major reform of the press was attempted after their appointment.

Publishers were the main cause of this cumulative failure. They opposed at every turn any statutory reform of the press. Apart from the *Guardian* management's brief apostasy in the 1960s when it lobbied privately for a press subsidy system, publishers on both left and right made common cause in resisting any public intervention in the press. Their opposition was fired by a righteous libertarianism which equated their freedom from restraint with public liberty. This became the central idea shaping the regulatory environment of the press.

This was partly because the press was an important disseminator of ideas about itself. Publishers draped the mantle of freedom around their shoulders, and created doubt and uncertainty about the desirability of reform. However, the main reason why reformism failed was that the press intimidated the political class. The political cost of 'doing something' about the short-comings of the press was judged to be too high. For example, Clement Atlee, the astute prime minister of the first majority Labour governments (1945–51), was opposed to appointing the first Royal Commission on the Press on the grounds that this would upset the press.[19] The Callaghan Labour government (1976–79) quietly buried the third Commission's proposals for tougher press monopoly legislation because it did not want to add to its political problems.

Politicians' loss of nerve was cumulative, and now seems unlikely to be reversed, at least in the short term. In 1931, Stanley Baldwin, leader of the Conservative Party, spearheaded a campaign against the 'power without responsibility' of the press barons. It was inspired by revulsion against the abuses of the press, outrage at the pretensions of a newly independent power, and above all a desire to save his career and strike back at his principal critics.[20] However, this campaign was followed shortly afterwards by the forging of an uneasy rapprochement between the Conservative Party and the predominantly right-wing press, which persisted for much of the subsequent period.

The case of the Labour Party was more complex.[21] It was traditionally critical of the 'millionaire press' but its antagonism mellowed a little in the 1930s when it became a publisher of a mass circulation daily. However, the labour movement ceased to be a major stakeholder in the press system when its newspapers closed down in the 1960s. Its alienation turned into mounting hostility when the trade union movement became the target of sustained press attack during the 1970s. The first sign of a political shift occurred in 1974, with the publication of the Labour Party Study Group report *People and the Media*, most of whose proposals became official policy. Reworked versions of these, committing the party to curbing press concentration and promoting press pluralism, were incorporated into its 1983 and 1987 general election manifestoes. However, by the 1990s, the Labour leadership became increasingly mute on the subject of press reform. Greater priority was given to winning press support, symbolized by Tony Blair's 1995 trip to Hayman Island, Australia, to speak to News Corporation executives about the need for an 'open and competitive market'. This was followed by a sustained courting of right-wing newspapers after New Labour was elected in 1997 and twice re-elected. Legislative reform of the press dropped off the agenda because it threatened New Labour's fragile bonding with right-wing press tycoons.

The voices calling for change were thus marginalized. The Campaign for Press and Broadcasting Freedom (CPBF), established in 1979, continued to be an eloquent exponent of reform. However, its principal initial sponsors, the press unions, were crushed. The CPBF's thoughtful representations went largely unheeded by government, regardless of which party was in power. Its arguments tended not to get a hearing in the press it wanted to reform.

Public dissatisfaction with the press, registered periodically in opinion polls, continued to be high. However, this dissatisfaction was channelled by backbench MPs in the direction of limited proposals – in particular, private members' bills for privacy protection or right of reply – partly in response to their own concerns about shielding their private lives from critical scrutiny. There was thus no powerful force subjecting the press to sustained criticism, and building support for major reform.[22]

However, the politics of radio and television proved to be different from that of the press. If reformers failed in the press, they had more success in broadcasting. This produced, as we shall see, a fundamental inconsistency at the heart of media policy.

Notes

1. *New News, Future News* (London, Office of Communications, 2007), figure 3.11, p. 34.
2. Colin Seymour-Ure (an academic adviser to the Commission) argued that the transfer of control of the press from political parties to unaccountable business conglomerates weakened the legitimacy of the press (see his 'National daily papers and the party system' in *Studies*

on the Press, Royal Commission on the Press Working Paper 3, London, HMSO, 1977). His paper was symptomatic of the misgivings that were expressed at the time.

3. See, for example, Bruce Page, *The Murdoch Archipelago* (London, Simon and Schuster, 2003).

4. N. Hartley, P. Gudgeon and R. Crafts, *Concentration of Ownership in the Provincial Press*, Royal Commission on the Press 1974–77, Research Series 5 (London, HMSO, 1977)

5. *Periodicals and the Alternative Press*, Royal Commission on the Press, Research Series 6 (London, HMSO, 1977).

6. *Royal Commission on the Press 1947–9 Report*, Appendix 2, table 1 (London, HMSO, 1949); Newspaper Society database (as of January 2002).

7. Des Freedman, 'The political economy of the "new" news environment', in Natalie Fenton (ed.), *New Media, Old News* (London, Sage, 2009).

8. This is a central theme of Part I of this book.

9. P. Murschetz, 'State support for the daily press in Europe: a critical appraisal', *European Journal of Communication*, 13 (3), 1998; E. Skogerbo, 'The press subsidy system in Norway', *European Journal of Communication*, 12 (1), 1997; P. Humphreys, *Mass Media and Media Policy in Western Europe* (Manchester, Manchester University Press, 1996).

10. Department for Culture, Media and Sport (DCMS), *Consultation on Media Ownership Rules* (London, DCMS, 2001), p. 25.

11. The government failed to refer Murdoch's purchase of Times Newspapers to the Monopolies Commission on the grounds that the newspaper group was in such financial difficulty that its immediate future was in doubt. This was not the case.

12. Proposals for divestment came from, among others, Sir Geoffrey Crowther (Royal Commission on the Press, Oral Evidence, Vol. 1, p. 5, London, HMSO, 1962), and Professor Jeremy Tunstall (Royal Commission on the Press 1974–77, unpublished evidence), both from the centre left of the political spectrum.

13. C. Frost, 'The Press Complaints Commission: a study of ten years of adjudications on press complaints', *Journalism Studies*, 5 (1), 2004, pp. 101–14.

14. 'Africa is giving nothing to anyone – apart from AIDS', *Independent*, 10 July 2008.

15. A. Delano and J. Henningham, *The News Breed: British Journalists in the 1990s* (London, London Institute, 1996).

16. R. Worcester, 'Demographics and values: what the British public reads and what it thinks about its newspapers', in H. Stephenson and M. Bromley (eds), *Sex, Lies and Democracy* (London, Longman, 1998).

17. Eurobarometer Survey, 2002, cited in the *Guardian*, 24 April 2002.

18. The 1977 Commission contained a minority report, signed by two members, proposing a National Printing Corporation and a Launch Fund to assist the establishment of new publications. These recommendations were ignored.

19. Its appointment was secured through a private member's Bill, and pressure from the National Union of Journalists.

20. For a brief description of the context of this campaign, see Chapter 5.

21. Sean Tunney, *Labour and the Press* (Brighton, Sussex University Press, 2007).

22. For different interpretations of the politics of press regulation, see J. Curran, 'Press reformism 1918–98: a study of failure', in H. Tumber (ed.), *Media Power, Professionals and Policies* (London, Routlege, 2000), and the more optimistic T. O'Malley and C. Soley, *Regulating the Press* (London, Pluto, 2000).

Chapter 22

Broadcasting and the theory of public service

British broadcasting was started as a public service, and this proved as creative commercially as it was innovative culturally. Indeed, until recently every stage of its development, from the emergence of the BBC, through the introduction of commercial television, to the founding of Channel 4, depended on a set of linked and radical expansions. First, at each stage a novel source of finance was discovered. In turn the growth of broadcasting was financed by the licence fee, advertising revenue, and then a tax on the profits of the commercial companies (but one devoted to making pro- grammes). These sources of finance did not compete with each other, and were key to the possibility of political independence. Each stage produced new audiences for broadcasting – the BBC creating an image of its audience as 'participants' in the great affairs of the nation, commercial television popularizing the medium, and Channel 4 decisively registering and enhan- cing the interests of minority audiences. Finally, of course, at each stage new kinds of programmes and styles of addressing audiences were evolving. Until the 1980s, broadcasting in Britain was not fettered, but liberated for cultural and political expansion by the requirements of public service.

The principle of public service – which has always been fought over and continually reinterpreted – was not the paternalistic and abstract rule which critics have suggested. Nor has it been damaging to entrepreneurial initia- tive. Indeed, public service regulation has secured the survival of a successful broadcasting industry, one which has become more significant economically and which has become an important exporter of programmes while con- tinuing to discuss and mould national issues. It has, of course, also never been perfect. Broadcasters have often failed to perceive the public interest and, even more frequently, have been too acquiescent to political pressure. Broadcasting has often been used by dominant political actors. Nevertheless, it has provided a flexible means of managing and developing an important utility which has been commercially successful and also served the public.

In the 1980s 'public service' became unfashionable. Yet those who derided it often had a financial interest in weakening it or, alternatively, disliked the political autonomy of broadcasting. However, public service is not a static or dated ideal, it is one we need to redefine and develop. What were the origins of the principle and how did it come to be undermined?

Broadcasting in Britain – monopoly or duopoly – always depended on an assumption of commitment to an undivided public good. This lay beneath all official thinking on radio and television until the 1970s. In 1977 the Annan Report abandoned this assumption, and replaced it with a new principle of liberal pluralism. The ideal ceased to be the broad consensus – the middle ground upon which all men of good sense could agree. Rather, it became, for Annan and those who supported and inspired him, a free marketplace in which balance could be achieved through the competition of multiplicity of independent voices. The result has been confusion and crisis, from which no new received doctrine has yet emerged.

So, by 1982, the Hunt Report on the introduction of cable television could begin to modify the principles of balance and quality even further. These were relegated to a part of the national service in the BBC and ITV. Although both the Hunt Report and the subsequent White Paper advocated some safeguards to protect the British system from the damaging effects of foreign satellite transmissions, and to guarantee the rights of the networks to televise events of national interest, the basis of public service broadcasting was abandoned. Thus cable television, free from constraining ideals, was left to produce programmes that 'were sufficiently attractive for the public to buy'.[1] The 1990 Broadcasting Act suggested that contenders for broadcasting franchises should produce 'sufficient amounts of quality programmes', but not only was this undefined, it only occupied two paragraphs in the Act. By contrast, conditions governing the financial arrangements for the auction of franchises took up fifteen pages.

However, the most obvious long-term symptom of the change in the status of the concept has been a shift in terminology. The concept of public service is elaborated in all broadcasting reports before that of the Annan Committee. As early as 1923 the Sykes Report argued that broadcasting was 'of great national importance as a medium for the performance of a valuable public service'.[2] The next report – that of the Crawford Committee in 1926 – suggested that in view of the scale, significance and potentialities of broadcasting, the duties and status of the Corporation which it had just created 'should correspond with those of a public service, and the directorate should be appointed with the sole object of promoting the utmost utility and development of the enterprise'.[3]

Later reports developed the consequences of this view. 'The influence of broadcasting upon the mind and speech of the nation', commented the Ullswater Report, made it an 'urgent necessity in the national interest that the broadcasting service should at all times be conducted in the best possible manner and to the best possible advantage of the people'.[4] In 1950 the Beveridge Report on broadcasting characterized the ideal of public service more actively. 'Like the work of the universities', Beveridge suggested, 'the work of broadcasting should be regarded as a public service for a social purpose'.[5] The Pilkington Report, which considered both the BBC and the commercial service in 1962, added to this definition: 'The concept of broadcasting has always been of a service, comprehensive in character, with the duty of a public corporation of bringing to public awareness the whole range of ... activity and expression developed in society'.[6] Indeed the organization of commercial television was as much a product of the ideal of public service broadcasting as the BBC's had been originally. Thus successive reports developed the idea of broadcasting as a public service – catering for all sections of the community, reaching all parts of the country regardless of cost, seeking to educate, inform and improve, and prepared to lead public opinion rather than follow it.

The Annan Report in many respects broke with this tradition for the first time. This change was noticeable, both in the evidence which was presented to the committee, and in the conclusion of the report. Even the reformers, whether of the left or right, disregarded the public service principle entirely. The BBC referred to it in only the most apologetic tone. The Annan Committee itself took a pluralist view: broadcasting should cater for the full range of groups and interests in society, rather than seek to offer moral leadership. 'For the individual life is a gamble, he is entitled to stake everything, if he desires, on one interpretation of life', it argued. 'But broadcasting organizations have to back the field, and put their money on all the leading horses which line up at the starting gate'.[7] In one elegant metaphor, much of the basis of public service broadcasting had been dismissed, despite the fact that Channel 4 was, in many ways, in practice an extension of it.

Indeed the Annan Report's reinterpretation of public service unintentionally left British broadcasters defenceless against the threats posed by recent technological developments. By so transforming public service it left no grounds on which to manage or control the impact of the inevitable introduction of cable, video or satellite broadcasting. Since 1977, reports and White Papers on the future of these very technologies have not even attempted to assess the impact of unregulated competition for audiences, revenues and programmes on the television system as a whole. Thus it was possible for the Hunt Report to suggest that viewers' willingness to pay for cable television simply constituted a new source of revenue. It was claimed that this would not divert resources from existing channels. (However, it was not apparently thought necessary to support this assertion by either evidence or argument.)

By contrast, there was a radical development in the 1986 Peacock Report, which reinterpreted the role of the market in broadcasting.[8] While advocating what Samuel Brittan, a leading monetarist journalist and theorist and member of the Peacock Committee, called 'the goal that British Broadcasting should move towards a sophisticated market system based on consumer sovereignty', the report perceived public service commitments as actually protecting consumer sovereignty. Brittan commented that 'The existence of a

tax-financed BBC and the IBA regulation of commercial television were justified by Peacock as a second best, but very successful, attempt to replicate artificially the programme structure of a true broadcasting market'. More than that,
the committee took up the elaboration of the public service ideal developed
in Channel 4 provision, and suggested that a mature broadcasting service
would operate like the publishing industry. 'Pre-publication censorship, whether of printed material, plays, films, broadcasting or other creative activities
or expressions of opinion, has no place in a free society', the report argued,
and recommended that the government 'embark forthwith on a phased programme for ending it'. Brittan went on to point out not only that the report
widened the scope of its enquiries far beyond its original brief of considering
the introduction of advertising into the BBC (which it rejected), by assessing
the future of broadcasting and how that could be best managed in the context of technological developments, but also that the report demonstrated the
fundamental social significance of broadcasting. As Brittan commented:

> Peacock exposed many of the contradictions in the Thatcherite espousal
> of market forces. In principle, Mrs Thatcher and her supporters are in
> favour of de-regulation, competition, and choice. But they are distrustful ...
> of plans to allow people to listen to and watch what they like, subject
> only to the law of the land. They espouse the market system but dislike
> the libertarian value judgements involved in its operation: value judgements
> which underlie the Peacock Report.[9]

The Peacock Report put public service back on the agenda just at the
point when the broadcasting organizations seemed to have abandoned it.

In fact, this abandonment by the broadcasting organizations is a problem,
for the authority of British broadcasting has always depended on the pursuit
of public service. Indeed, by relinquishing any claim to this, the broadcasting institutions have put into jeopardy a whole set of complex relationships between themselves, the state, their audiences and their programme
policy. What caused this crisis? What are its consequences?

The state and broadcasting

One cause of the collapse of the principle of public service broadcasting has
been the deterioration in the relationship between the state and broadcasting
institutions. In the Sykes Report, Charles Trevelyan argued that 'We consider such a potential power over public opinion and the life of the nation
ought to remain with the state'. Because broadcasting was so important it
was seen as 'essential that permission to transmit, and the matter to be
transmitted should be subject to public authority'.

Air waves were a scarce resource which did not obey national boundaries.
Consequently the state was obliged to control the right to broadcast in all

societies. In the early British broadcasting reports, however, there is a consensus that state regulation is the best guarantee of broadcasting independence and accountability. As the Crawford Report put it, only the state could license the BBC to be 'a public corporation acting as trustee for the national interest'.

In the 1920s the problem of the relationship of government with broadcasting was dealt with by making new rules and creating new machinery. It was taken for granted that the control over the administration of an organization could be kept quite separate from whatever the organization did. Hence it was possible for broadcasting to be politically accountable, and yet remain independent of any political influence. The Sykes Report noted that any detailed control of the work of the Corporation would make a government 'constantly open to suspicion that it was using an opportunity to its own advantage'. It was therefore decided that the minister responsible for the service would be able to answer questions in the House on matters of principle and finance, but he should not be held responsible for the programmes themselves. Later the problem seemed to disappear. Complaints about government intervention were rare, and the issue of excessive interference no longer seemed to exist.

In 1936 the Ullswater Report commented, 'We have no reason to suppose that, in practice, divergent views of public interest have been held by the Corporation and government departments'. Pilkington argued in 1962 that 'The practical resolution of the problem was made easier because the first priority of the department concerned with exercising the government's responsibility (the GPO) is with technical matters'. No conflict had arisen between broadcasters and governments over the definition of public interest.

However, by the 1970s this pragmatic argument was felt to be inadequate. Imperceptibly the problem had become one of defending broadcasters against the state. The relationship was increasingly characterized as one of vigilant and stealthy hostility. A cold war had been declared between them.

This was partly a consequence of the changing nature of politics in Britain. In a world of increasingly sophisticated news reporting this posed problems for both the BBC and the IBA. 'Politics' and political balance could be treated simply in two- or three-party terms in the 1950s. By the 1970s this was no longer the case. The emergence of centre parties made the work of 'striking a balance' far more difficult for broadcasters. In addition, many fields which had previously been regarded as non-controversial and administrative had moved into the political arena. But also because of a proliferation of parties, interests and pressure groups, because of a widening gap between the major parties and, most of all, because of the rise of issues – of which Northern Ireland was the most critical – for which the gentlemanly and constitutionalist assumptions of the early rule makers could not cater. The problem of providing 'balance' in dealing with treasonable activities in Ulster – when, whether and under what conditions to interview terrorists or members of illegal organizations, how to discuss the issue at all – forced the broadcasting directorates to make new rules and, in effect, to add to the corpus of Britain's unwritten constitution.

The questions which the public asked about broadcasting, the Annan Report claimed, were becoming 'more critical, more hostile and more political'. At the same time, there was a new public mood, 'at once inflationary in the expectation of what political power could achieve, and deflationary towards those in power who failed to give effect to these expectations'.

The interests of governments had come, by the late 1970s, to be seen as inimical to those of broadcasting. The distinction between the broadcasting bureaucracies and what they produced had been challenged. Previously the quality and balance of a company's programmes were believed to be guaranteed by the good order of the administration. This view was now replaced by one of increasingly detailed suspicion. More than that, broadcasters' institutionalized caution about the power of governments had developed into a rejection of all kinds of intervention by the state.

This has had profound consequences for the legitimacy of the public service broadcasting organizations. The Annan Report argued that the authorities have a dual role: on the one hand they exist to ensure that broadcasters operate in the public interest and are responsive to public opinion, particularly as expressed in parliament. On the other hand, they exist 'also to defend broadcasters from undue pressure from whatever quarter'. But these are not complementary obligations; rather they are contradictory. The authorities are supposed both to reflect political pressure and to resist it. It used to be possible for the authorities to perform these two functions when the interests of the state and the broadcasting organization were seen as similar, if not identical. However, once their interests are opposed, the two aspects of the authorities' role are increasingly difficult to reconcile.

Accountability and broadcasting

This situation would matter less if other mechanisms designed to relate broadcasting institutions to society seemed less perfunctory. Since 1926 they have all suffered from attrition.

Reith rapidly turned the BBC Governors, supposedly 'the trustees of the national interest', into creatures of the Director General. In both commercial television and the BBC, the Boards of Governors depend for their information upon the organizations they were designed to supervise, and they have no independent secretariat or research function. The Governors have remained relatively powerless, and do not see their job as one of representing external interests or views. Similarly, the role of the advisory committees was ingeniously reinterpreted. Reith ensured that these acted as specialists (whether in music, speech or religion) who merely offered their advice over particular policy issues to the Corporation, rather than experts in broadcasting as such.

Indeed the only independent source of power left within these supposedly governing bodies is that of the Chairman of the Board. This power derives from the Chairman's close personal association with the Director General – or the administrative head of the independent service. Yet this intimacy leads to what Heller has called 'the tendency of broadcasting authorities to identify their interests, and by implication the national interest very closely with the survival of the organization they supervise'.[10]

However, in the 1980s a series of political crises in which the role of broadcasting was crucial – the Falklands War, continuing trouble in Ireland, disputes about the interpretation of foreign events, and profound disagreements about the management of the economy – all exposed the potential vulnerability of the governing body and the Chairman to political influence. Indeed, the Conservative government sought to dominate the governors more directly than any previous administration, by swamping the board with its own supporters. In the 1980s, the problem was not so much the identification of the Chairman with the institution, but rather the identification of the Chairman with the government in power.

Yet the broadcasting organizations had given up so much of the ground themselves. By the 1980s the IBA was to claim that accountability was only a minority interest. The Annan Report had endorsed a system which was little more than a pious rhetoric. 'On balance', the report concluded, ' ... while some improvements could be made, the relations between government and parliament and the broadcasting authorities do not require much adjustment: the chain of accountability is adequate'. Annan apparently believed that accountability was a purely abstract idea – one which includes no reference to the public. But the paragraph nevertheless ends, 'We do not consider, however, that the relations between the broadcasters and the public are satisfactory'. If, as Annan suggested, broadcasting is to abandon the independence of public service, and be based, rather, on a principle of representative pluralism, then the inadequacy of the Governors, and advisory committees, becomes even more serious. By the 1990s accountability had almost been dispensed with as a value. It had, up to a point, been replaced by that of market success.

Independent professionals or men with an interest?

The independence of broadcasting from the state has recently been seen as the most important condition of the service's accountability. This independence has in turn been reduced to the freedom of programme makers. Yet, as Beveridge once commented, 'To whom is a broadcaster responsible? If it is only to his own conscience the decision might better be described as irresponsible.'

This emphasis on broadcasters' rights is a consequence of focusing the assessment of broadcasting on individual programmes. Pilkington was the last report to elaborate the tradition of public service, and it also argued that 'A service of broadcasting should be judged, not by the stated aims of the broadcasters, but by its achievements'. The Annan Report endorsed this approach.

Nevertheless, broadcasting and broadcasting institutions cannot be understood merely as a collection of separate programme 'texts'. As a report by one of the televison unions commented, judging broadcasting organizations by their product 'was like being asked to evaluate the Milk Marketing Board by drinking milk – relevant, but not adequate'.[11]

Broadcasting is a process which cannot be entirely understood from its products. Few would claim that the whole nature of the industrial enterprise can be understood from the shop floor of one factory. Neither can all the pressures which condition broadcasting institutions be revealed by an examination of what Tracey has called 'the world of determination of a television programme'[12] – however important that study might be. The emphasis on programmes as the most important criterion for judging broadcasting reinforces the arbitrary role of professionals at the expense of more general considerations of public service.

The Annan Report claimed that 'Good broadcasting would reflect the competing demands of a society which was increasingly multi-racial and pluralist'. In turn, this variety could be secured only by giving the 'talented broadcasters' greater freedom of expression.

However, broadcasters are not necessarily influenced by a wide variety of interests. Much research has shown how little producers and directors consider their audience. The only information about viewers which seriously affects producers is knowledge of the size of the audience. This is not because audience research is incapable of providing more complex detail, but because to know more would put producers under even greater stress. 'For a sociologist', commented Burns, 'it was rather like watching the whole practice of medicine being reduced to the use of a thermometer'.[13] Producers value the opinion of their colleagues most, but they see very little even of them.

The public interest cannot simply rely on the quality of broadcasters, because to do so is to ignore the pressures which determine broadcasting choices. 'When one stresses the role of individuals manning the system', Garnham argues, 'one is tempted to await a Messiah who will come over – and help transform the system'.[14]

However, the relationship of broadcasters to their organization has also altered. Burns argued that there had been a considerable change in attitude since the 1960s. Then staff expressed a devotion to public service 'and a belief in the BBC's normative role in the cultural, moral and political life of the country'. By the 1970s this had been replaced by a commitment to professional values. Indeed, as Kumar points out, the emergence of professionalism as the dominating ideology is the product of a particular moment in the evolution of broadcasting organizations. Even the notion of 'lively broadcasting' which determines the professionals' judgements 'expresses a particular stance towards the audience, a judgement of what the audience can and cannot take, which reflects a particular conception of the purposes of broadcasting'.[15]

Indeed the new 'scientific management' of broadcasting organizations has greater power than earlier administrations, whose main concern had been to protect and assist programme makers who had far higher status within the organization. 'Because of the need to allocate time and resources economically', Burns argued, 'working relations became impersonally functional'. The steady march of rational managerialism had led to a withering of institutional ardour.

Indeed, professionalism is now being superseded in many broadcasting organizations by crude financial managerialism. The pursuit of profit rather than excellence is more likely to dominate decisions in the next decade. Government reforms, culminating in the 1989 Broadcasting Bill,[16] and the auctioning of Channels 3 and 5 to the 'highest bidders' (who in order to bid had to pass a programme quality 'threshold', but who were awarded franchises solely on their ability to raise the largest amounts of capital)[17] will inevitably reduce the power of programme makers. These pressures are already evident: in the past broadcasting administrators had often been programme makers first; in a survey of appointments to top posts in television the majority of posts were given to 'accountants, bankers, and financial managers'.[18] Consequently not only were the talented programme makers upon whom Annan, for instance, rested the future of broadcasting less committed to public service than before, but also they had become less important within broadcasting organizations.

Independence and the theory of broadcasting

The significance of broadcasting independence is also disputed. One side suggests that the independence is functional and must be extended to guarantee accountable broadcasting. The other argues that this same independence poses a serious threat to political institutions, whose control over broadcasting should be strengthened. Working from the same assumptions about the role of the media, Anthony Smith and Colin Seymour-Ure arrived at diametrically opposed diagnoses and solutions.

According to classic liberal theory, the independence of a journalist depended on his ability to follow the uninhibited dictates of his conscience. According to Smith, this is an illusory ideal. In discussing the 1968 crisis in French broadcasting he argues that, 'The ORTF strikers had stumbled across the central dilemmas of broadcasting and were demanding in the name of freedom ... a right which no broadcaster has ever really achieved – the right to be an individual member of a Fourth Estate'. In its place Smith put forward a far more sophisticated and powerful version of the theory, in which the independence of broadcasters is not an individual right – but rather a functional necessity.

Broadcasters are not free, but are 'brokers and megaphones, impresarios and mediators', he suggested. The 'independence' of broadcasting institutions from political control was one solution to a dilemma all broadcasting systems had to solve: namely the necessity not only of regulating the right to broadcast but also of ensuring that broadcasting served the interests of all sections of society. For, Smith suggested, 'The institutions of broadcasting inaugurated a special problem of unlegitimized and unselective power'. Broadcasters are obliged to negotiate political conflict and not take sides in it – precisely because of the immense and dangerous nature of their power. In stable systems, countervailing interests would always be able to enforce damaging sanctions if broadcasters became partisan.

This model implies that all political interests in society can, in practice, be reconciled. It is a logical extension of broadcasting institutions' own view of their role as arbiters that they come to see conflict and opposition as the products of failures in communication. Nevertheless, if there are real differences in interest, incompatible policies, and irreconcilable principles, then the role of the broker becomes untenable.

However, the functional independence of broadcasting institutions has many of the same policy consequences as the older liberal individualism. For, Smith argued, the way to meet recent criticisms is to give broadcasters more independence. The more perfectly broadcasters can do anything they want, the more adequate the service will be. As he is reported as commenting to the Annan Committee:

> If I am free to say anything I want to say except the one thing I want to say then I am not free ... In broadcasting ... a single prohibition imposed on a national broadcasting authority or within it tends to corrode the whole output.

Colin Seymour-Ure views the 'independence' of broadcasters rather differently. The independence of the press – no longer the client of political parties – and 'now part of vast corporations who may have very direct interests in the outcomes of policy decisions' is vulnerable because it is compromised by ownership. Broadcasters, moreover, having abandoned the protection of 'public service' ideology are also susceptible to accusations of bias. Seymour-Ure argues that:

> Some Labour politicians used to take comfort in the fact that although the press might be disproportionately conservative, at least broadcasting was balanced. This is no longer true. No doubt broadcasters are not wilfully biased. But the simple fact of deciding their own programme content may in the extreme case lead to a projection of party politicians and leaders that might run entirely counter to the parties' own views.

He suggests that the current interpretation of broadcasting independence has seriously damaged the political system.

The ideal of broadcasting independence – unlimited by any obligation to public service – has become increasingly inadequate. It has contributed to a growing anti-government ethos. It is hostile to many forms of political partisanship. It may inhibit political change and development. It may be that, as Seymour-Ure comments, the period of mass-based party organization is ending, for one effect of television in many countries seems to be 'the erosion of intervening structures between representatives and electors'. Nevertheless, any increase in the autonomy of broadcasting institutions may have more serious political consequences than had been expected. Rather, it is the democratic processes which need support: not because broadcasters are malign but because of the inexorable pressure of broadcasting independence on the handling of politics. And the devotion of increasing amounts of political energy to managing the media – rather than managing politics.

Choice versus public service?

Double think, according to George Orwell, is the 'power of holding two contradictory beliefs in one's mind simultaneously and accepting both of them'. Through successive régimes, *double think* has nevertheless precisely defined the attitude of politicians towards broadcasting. On the one hand there are people (government ministers, for instance) who tend to believe that the worse excesses of broadcasting, as of the trade unions, should be curbed. There are others (shadow ministers, for instance) who look to broadcasting as a means to correct political bias.

Never, however, have the contradictions been so glaring as in the recent past. The politics of the 1980s and 1990s were orchestrated in a language of freedom, choice, non-intervention, withdrawal of the state: yet they were deformed with successive governmental limitations on the public right to be informed. Where individuals have sought to challenge state manipulation of the news, the government showed neither mercy nor moderation in making an example of offenders. Indeed, the effective range of discussion and investigation is probably narrower here than in most modern democracies – including France, Sweden, West Germany and possibly even the USA. It may not be long before the former Eastern bloc leaves us behind in the matter of broadcasting freedom. Who can imagine the Home Office giving a foreign camera crew *carte blanche* to film what they liked in the Maze Prison – in the way that the Soviet authorities recently provided open access to a western team in one of the USSR's remaining political gaols?

In addition to this, during the 1980s the Conservative government blatantly used television for government propaganda – with a massive increase in public sector advertising. Between 1980 and 1989, commercial television revenues doubled in real terms, and the proportion of advertising revenue generated by the public sector over that period quadrupled, indeed by 1989 it had become the largest single buyer of television advertising. The privatizations of public utilities were the single largest source of television advertising finance between 1990 and 1995.[19] If the ostensible purpose of the advertising was the sale of shares in the shortly-to-be-privatized public sector industries, it also furthered the ideology of privatization.

Throughout the period, public service broadcasting was compared unfavourably with 'the real choice offered to consumers by a more effective market'.[20] Successive reports, government green papers and Bills proposed to 'set free broadcasters from the narrow constraints of control' and it was repeatedly argued that satellite, cable and a deregulated broadcasting system would offer the public a greater choice of programmes more sensitively tailored to their wants by the competitive pressures of the market. In part, of course, government policy was attempting to adapt to a new situation in which cable and satellite would deliver such a multitude of channels and services that the previous régime of regulation would become practically impossible. But more than this, policy was driven by a profound hostility to the principles of public service broadcasting.

Yet the ideology of 'choice' was absurd. Commercial broadcasting is based not on the sale of programmes to audiences, but on the sale of audiences to advertisers. Thus the introduction of more competitors will reduce advertising revenues both by spreading them between a greater number of channels and by splitting potential audiences into even smaller groups. As the main incentive will remain the attraction of the largest possible audience, the competing channels, less constrained by regulation to produce a variety of programmes, will tend to show more of the same or similar programmes.

Indeed, if one contradiction of Thatcherism was that free market rhetoric was accompanied by interventionist practice, another was that talk of the marketplace was accompanied by its virtual eradication. Technological change – with its requirement for long-term investment and large-scale capitalization – has produced a bureaucratic jungle of profit-taking conglomerates which own shares in all the media which the public consumes. The small number of corporate owners is not competitive in a sense that could conceivably be expected to produce an improved product; but their financial rivalry will undoubtedly impose pressure to produce a cheaper one. That means an almost inevitable lowering of standards, since it is cheaper to buy in internationalized soap opera than to make your own drama, and so on. The result is likely to be a lesser variety of the kind of programmes that many of us watch some of the time, and some of us watch most of the time, but which do not attract top audience ratings. We are all, on occasions, members of minorities. Thus the victims of media concentration are variety, creativity and quality, while the proliferation of broadcasting channels in the hands of a small band of operators, 'liberated' by government policy from the obligations of public service variety, is likely to make matters worse.

'Choice', without positive direction, is a myth, for all too often the market will deliver more – but only more of the same.

Conclusion

Broadcasters have come to see the state as their enemy. Yet broadcasting institutions ultimately depend on the state for their legitimation. This authority cannot be replaced by a pluralist ideal of reflecting social and cultural variety. Indeed the adoption of this principle has left broadcasters peculiarly vulnerable to the more general attack on public service broadcasting.

Moreover, arguments with quite different aims from those of the broadcasters, but apparently related, are being used to undermine broadcasting responsibility and independence. Thus neither the emphasis on the authority of the viewers' right to choose from a greater variety of programmes, nor the elaboration of some aspects of the local and regional role of the media, let alone the distinction between a 'service' the public will pay for and a public service, are intended to strengthen the creative autonomy of broadcasters. On the contrary, they are arguments which enhance the power of commercial interests in determining the patterns of broadcasting provision.

Thus, without a commitment to public service, broadcasters are increasingly vulnerable to detailed political interference in the content of programmes. Broadcasting in Britain has in the past had a considerable degree of autonomy from other institutions: it has not in any simple sense been biased. This autonomy is now threatened, partly because the consensus about what constitutes the 'middle ground' of agreed opinion has broken down, partly because the reliance on the skill of professional broadcasters which has replaced it is unjustified, and partly because of the erosion of public service broadcasting. Broadcasting needs to find a new relationship to the state – and a new form of commitment to public service, and indeed a new definition of public service that will work in the conditions of increased competition.

Notes

1. *Report of the Enquiry into Cable Expansion and Broadcasting Policy* (Hunt Report, 1982) [Cmnd 8697].
2. *Broadcasting Committee: Report* (Sykes Report, 1923) [Cmnd 1951], X, 13, para. 21.
3. *Report of the Broadcasting Committee* (Crawford Report, 1926) [Cmnd 2599], VIII, 327, para. 49.
4. *Report of the Broadcasting Committee* (Ullswater Report, 1936) [Cmnd 5091], VII, 617, para. 7.
5. *Report of the Broadcasting Committee* (Beveridge Report, 1951) [Cmnd 8116], IX, 1, para. 217.
6. *Report of the Committee on Broadcasting* (Pilkington Report, 1962) [Cmnd 1755], IV, 259, para. 23.
7. *Report of the Committee on the Future of Broadcasting* (Annan Report, 1977) [Cmnd 6753], XVI, para. 311.

8. *Report of the Committee on Financing the BBC* (Peacock Report, 1986) [Cmnd 9824], II, para. 636.
9. S. Brittan, 'The fight for freedom in broadcasting', *Political Quarterly*, 58 (1) (March 1987).
10. C. Heller, *Broadcasters and Accountability*, BFI Television Monograph 3 (London, British Film Institute, 1978), p. 39.
11. ACCT report, quoted in C. Heller, *Broadcasters and Accountability*, BFI Television Monograph 3 (London, British Film Institute, 1978), p. 50.
12. M. Tracey, *The Production of Political Television* (London, Routledge & Kegan Paul, 1978), p. 13.
13. T. Burns, *The BBC: Public Institution and Private World* (London, Macmillan, 1977), p. 137.
14. N. Garnham, *Structures of Television*, BFI Television Monograph 1 (London, British Film Institute, 1973), p. 21.
15. K. Kumar, 'Holding the middle ground: The BBC, the public and the professional broadcaster', in J. Curran, M. Gurevitch, and J. Woollacott (eds), *Mass Communication and Society* (London, Edward Arnold/Open University, 1977), p. 232.
16. Broadcasting Bill, Bill No. 9, December 1989 (London, HMSO, 300906).
17. See Martin Cave, 'The conduct of auctions for broadcasting franchises', *Fiscal Studies*, 10 (1), February 1989, pp. 17–31.
18. 'New managers, new talents', *Vision* (December 1989), pp. 15–31.
19. 'Television advertising by sector', *Campaign* (July 1989); 'Public utilities flotation advertising spend 1990–95', Hargreaves & Whitticker, Spencer Report, *Adcam*, 1996.
20. S. Velachesky, 'Broadcasting choice', *Hobbart Papers on Liberal Economics* (June 1989), p. 7.

Part V

Politics of the media

Chapter 23

Contradictions in media policy

Introduction

To inform, to discuss, to mirror, to bind, to campaign, to challenge, to entertain and to judge – these are the important functions of the media in any free country. The purpose of public policy should be to enable the media to perform them more effectively. Yet historically, very different traditions of promoting these ideals, or indeed pursuing no ideals at all, have developed in relation to different media. Traditionally, press policy has taken the form of having no policy, and the functioning of newspapers has been left largely to market forces. By contrast, television and radio have been required to pursue objectives set by parliament, and have been subject to regulation.

However, during the Conservative ascendancy of the 1980s and early 1990s, there appeared to be a revolution in official thinking about the media. It was argued that broadcasting should be shaped more by the market, and less by public bureaucracy. The state was portrayed as a threat to media freedom, and regulation was attacked as an obstacle to satisfying the consumer. These themes were invoked, for example, by supporters of the deregulatory Broadcasting Acts of 1990 and 1996. The clear implication was that the gap between press and broadcasting policy should diminish, and the market should be allowed to reign.

A new version of policy consistency was pursued under New Labour, in power for over a decade after 1997. The formerly separate worlds of broadcasting, telephones, computers and print were coming together, it was proclaimed, as a consequence of technological convergence, and this necessitated the development of a common approach for all communications. 'Sectoral policies' for separate media, of a kind pursued by previous administrations, needed to be replaced by a single, coherent vision for the communications industry as a whole.

A new, unifying theme was also advanced by New Labour. 'Communications industries', declared a 2001 government consultation document, 'constitute a large and growing part of our national income'. Their continued growth will promote investment, employment, innovation, choice, diversity and lower consumer prices. However, Britain's communications industry is also faced with intensified competition in a more globally integrated market. Consequently, a key objective of communication policy must be, in the words of the government's 1998 Green Paper, 'not only to defend the domestic position, but also to attract a share of global revenues and jobs to the UK'.

A new ministry was also created to brush away the cobwebs of the past, and impose a new sense of direction and purpose. In 1992, the John Major government established the Department of National Heritage (the nearest synonym to 'Culture' that conservative sensibilities would then permit). It was renamed the Department of Culture, Media and Sport (DCMS) by the incoming New Labour government in 1997, and was rededicated to the task of developing an 'integrated' communications policy.

Yet, over ten years later, New Labour had still failed to fulfil its promise of 'coherent regulation in a converging environment'. Like the New Right Conservative administrations that preceded it, New Labour merely added another layer of piecemeal reform. Indeed it added to, rather than detracted from, the confusion at the heart of British media policy.

Efficiency

This confusion has survived repeated attempts to inject order and clarity. Indeed, superficially, official reports on media industries over the past sixty years appear to have much in common. One recurrent theme has been the emphasis on greater efficiency. Thus, in 1949 the Gater Report on the British Film Industry called for more effective financial planning, while the second (1962) Press Commission urged that better machinery for negotiation should be established, a point also stressed by the Prices and Incomes Board Report on the press in 1967. In the same way the Annan Report (1977) concluded that 'clear lines of decision making, fewer chieftains, better communications' were needed, and the Peacock Report on the BBC (1986) argued that 'the assessment of efficiency is one of our Committee's chief aims'. Such comments, few of which have ever had any significant effect, have become part of the ritual of investigation.

Most official reports have also taken an optimistic view of the independence of journalists and programme makers, and their capacity for autonomous reform. Thus two Royal Commissions on the press stressed in identical words that 'on the quality of the individual journalist depends not only the status of the whole profession of journalism but the possibility of bridging the gap between what society needs from the press and what the press is at present giving it'. Similarly, the Annan Report argued that 'the strength of British broadcasting lies in the creativity of people who make programmes'.

Hence successive reports have suggested better recruitment policies, improved training and education, greater integrity and responsibility among communicators, and new opportunities for independent producers. Annan

(1977) proposed an Open Broadcasting Authority which would show minority programmes made by 'small independent production groups', a term which is reminiscent of the 'small independent producer' which film policy has been trying unsuccessfully to help since the Moyne Report in 1936, and which Peacock (1986) championed for mainstream television. In the same way, three Royal Commissions put their faith in individual entrepreneurs as the best way of sustaining a varied press. Even the Calcutt Report (1990) on privacy suggested that newspaper ethics depended 'on the calibre of the individual conscience' – an engagingly innocent view of the solution to tabloid exploitation.

This emphasis on individuals as the mainspring of improvement has resulted in economic and institutional constraints being neglected. Repeated attempts to boost film production have foundered because they have not been combined with reform of film distribution and exhibition. Public funding of films swelled the profits of large production companies when there was a buoyant film industry, and led to some films being made that were never shown in commercial cinemas, when the film industry went into decline. Similarly, the Annan Committee proposed an Open Broadcasting Authority (Channel 4, as it became known) to introduce more adventurous minority programmes, yet failed to suggest how its finance could be arranged to protect it from the economic pressures which inhibited experimental programming on the other channels. In the event, an ingenious cross-subsidy scheme was introduced, initially in a form which insulated Channel 4 from conformist market pressure, but this owed nothing to Annan's vague advice on funding. In much the same way, the Peacock Committee hoped that by forcing the BBC and ITV to take a fixed quota of programmes from production companies, a new legion of fearless, independent programme-makers would spring up to create more diverse, popular programmes. What the Committee did not anticipate was that the independent production quota (first introduced in 1986 and extended in 1990) would expand a vulnerable, casualized, low-paid sector of the television workforce that lacked either the power or the autonomous resources to fulfil what was expected of it. Yet the Peacock Committee (chaired by a noted neo-liberal economist) was in fact more alert to economic structures than most such committees. Although appointed by a government hostile to the BBC, it nevertheless protected the BBC, because for the first time its main object was to consider the financial structures that underlay cultural considerations. If the BBC was funded by advertising, Peacock warned, the result would be reduced choice and worse programmes.

However, this inattention to economic constraints occasionally had positive outcomes, though more by accident than by design. When the Annan Committee recommended a minority television channel, it did not anticipate that this would provide a shot in the arm of the ailing film industry. By giving individual, one-off British art movies a secure, predictable audience on television, Channel 4 initially improved film makers' capacity to raise film finance. By offering an additional distribution system, Channel 4 also gave new opportunities for people to see the work of a network of creative and important film makers. However, this failed to solve the financial crisis of British film making. In France, where the film industry was relatively more successful, state-generated funding was more readily and consistently available – a crucial factor in artistic and commercial success.

Government and lame ducks

Government intervention has sometimes been justified as an exceptional measure that will make subsequent interference unnecessary and restore a stable and competitive market. This has been particularly true of British film policy, which has been shaped by a combination of crisis-driven expediency and unfulfilled optimism. Thus, in 1927, a Board of Trade inquiry into the film industry advocated special measures to deal with 'unfair, devious and improper trading' by American competitors. This report resulted in the Cinematograph Act, 1927, which obliged distributors and exhibitors to purchase and show quotas of British films. But this was intended to be only a short-term measure, to promote 'free and equitable trade'. In 1949 the National Film Finance Corporation was set up to provide loans for film production. It was seen as a response to a temporary inability of British film producers to obtain private investment capital. The Eady Levy, introduced during the same period, was designed to promote national film production through a tax on box-office takings, which was supposed to fall most heavily on successful foreign imports. Similarly, the last Royal Commission on the press recommended that newspapers should be offered cheap loans in order to pay for the introduction of new printing technology during a period of financial crisis. Its advice was sensibly ignored.

Most of these measures, though advocated as temporary expedients, became settled features of public policy. The 'temporary' import quota introduced in 1927 was strengthened in 1938, supplemented during the 1940s, and abandoned only in 1983. The National Film Finance Corporation, set up as a self-financing agency, was forced to write off many loans and so became a continuing source of state finance for the film industry. It was closed in 1986, subsequently replaced by the anorexic British Screen Finance (with some public money), and then revived, with infusions of lottery funds, as the Film Council in 2000. The Eady Levy survived until 1984 even though it reinforced American domination of the British film industry by subsidizing American-backed films which were only nominally British. The rationale for the levy had changed, and it came to be seen as a way of maintaining employment rather than supporting national culture. All these one-off interventions proved more long-lasting or served different purposes than were originally intended. They might all have been more successful if they had been designed to address long-term problems rather than short-term crises.

Thus, official media reports display over the years many of the same shortcomings and engage in the same ritual responses, while glossing over problems which their recommendations failed to solve. Yet the essential conservatism of official policy is less important than its contradictions. Good policy is not necessarily consistent policy, but one of the most curious features of government relations with the media has been the way in which reports on the press, broadcasting and film industries have often conflicted sharply with one another.

Divergent policy goals

Thus, broadcasting regulation has long sought to preserve a space for national collective expression. As late as the 1970s, no more than 14 per cent of television programmes on BBC or ITV were allowed to be foreign (excluding Commonwealth countries). 'Foreign' was changed to mean non-EEC countries in the 1981 Broadcasting Act, but strict rationing of foreign programmes continued. The foreign allowance was raised to 35 per cent of commercial, terrestrial TV programmes in 1993, and to slightly higher quotas for Channels 4 and 5 in 1998. This protectionist policy was backed up by limitations on foreign ownership of broadcasting. Until 2003, non-EU corporations were not allowed to acquire ITV and Channel 5, though the restriction on majority holding of cable TV companies was lifted in 1990, and that on new multiplex, digital enterprises was waived in 1996.

However, what was thought desirable in television and radio was not deemed important in the press. There has never been any restriction on foreign ownership of British newspapers. Official inquiries into the press, unlike those into broadcasting, have never seen this as an issue. In film policy, by contrast, cultural autonomy has been believed to be important but it has been eclipsed as an objective by the need to sustain a film industry under-written by American money. This was acknowledged tacitly by the 1968 review of film legislation when it argued that the National Film Finance Corporation should be maintained not to defend British cultural production, but because 'it constitutes a real attraction for foreign investment'.

The competing claims of the economy, 'culture' and the political system are negotiated in media policy, and resolved in divergent ways in different industries. In film policy, priority has come to be given to maintaining jobs; in television, more attention has been given to cultural concerns. This has resulted in films being conceived and regulated in quite different ways, depending upon whether they are watched in the cinema, on video or on 'live' television.

In the case of television, resources have been redistributed in order to promote quality and diversity. The obligation imposed by the Independent

Television Commission (ITC), and later Ofcom, on ITV companies to provide a mixed schedule ensures that some of the revenue generated by programmes (including films) reaching large audiences is invested in more demanding or more minority-oriented programmes watched by smaller audiences. Yet the same principle was never applied to the allocation of film funds through the Eady Levy. This tax on cinema takings was paid to production companies in proportion to the box-office revenue for their films. It constituted a bounty distributed according to market demand. 'The levy', concluded the 1968 Board of Trade review, 'should not be used to breed indifference to economic reality'. Underlying this argument was a concern that cultural or qualitative concerns should not encroach upon market efficiency and the survival of British film making. By contrast, there has never been a policy in relation to videos and DVDs, apart from a prohibition against objectionable sex and violence.

State as threat

One reason for these underlying tensions and contradictions is that media policy has been shaped by different philosophies. A common feature of much official thinking about the working of the media has been a liberal suspicion of the state. However, this suspicion assumed such evangelical proportions in the case of successive Royal Commissions on the press that it led them into an implicit confrontation with other media inquiries.

Thus, the last Royal Commission on the Press (1977) advanced a sweeping definition of what was acceptable:

> We are strongly against any scheme which would make the press, or any section of it, dependent on government through reliance on continuing subsidies from public funds. We are also opposed absolutely to the establishment of any body which could, or might have to, discriminate among publications in such a way as to amount to censorship in the sense of preferring to support some publications and not others.

Selective subsidies targeted towards weak publications were rejected on the grounds that this could lead to pro-government favouritism. Yet non-selective subsidies were repudiated because they failed to offer special help to the vulnerable. The first approach was found wanting because it might lead to political partiality, the second because it was ineffectual. This catch-22 formula in effect ruled out most forms of market intervention.

Yet the political dangers that successive public inquiries into the press detected in allocating public resources seemed less of a problem in other sectors of the media. 'No public body', thundered the third Press Commission, 'should ever be put in a position of discriminating like a censor between one applicant and another'. This is exactly what the Independent

Broadcasting Authority, among other public agencies, did when this advice was given. It is what the Independent Television Commission and Radio Authority did subsequently – and what Ofcom, the Film Council and Arts Council (whose grants include small publications) do now. The processes of public selection that press inquiries, steeped in a tradition of anti-statism, found so alarming have long been common practice.

The Press Commissions' objection to all policies that can lead potentially to state dependence is no less maverick. If this precept were introduced into the broadcasting sector, it would lead to the immediate privatization of the BBC and Channel 4, the deregulation of all channels, and the free trading of their shares on the open market. Yet not even the most right-wing broadcasting inquiry – chaired by Sir Alan Peacock – was willing to go this far.

Press Commissions' negative view of the state contrasts with their positive view of the market. This is seen as the sheet-anchor of press independence, a view that coloured their opinion of market processes in general. Having rejected public subsidies that induce economic dependence or involve a process of choice, they perceived no difficulty in another kind of subsidy – advertising – that induces economic dependence, involves a process of choice and indeed tends to favour Conservative papers because of their affluent readerships. In the Commissions' view, public subsidies are fraught with dangers; private ones are not. Similarly, successive Press Commissions failed to make an explicit connection between the high costs of market entry and the predominantly right-wing character of the national press. To have done so would have meant questioning their idealized view of the market as neutral, in contrast to the partiality they perceived to be lurking in the actions of state-linked agencies.

Benign state

By contrast, public reports on broadcasting generally view the state in a more positive light. Conservative paternalism and an Arnoldian concern with moral and cultural values originally contributed to this view. A liberal corporatist tradition also played a part, equating central planning with the rational and scientific use of resources, as did a radical commitment to redistribution through the state. Broadcasting was also viewed as being so powerful an influence that it needed to be harnessed to the general good.

All nine major reports on British broadcasting argued that a publicly appointed agency could act in the public interest, if it was established by the state for this purpose. As the Crawford Committee (1926) put it, 'The actual commission should be persons of judgement and independence, free of commitments, and … they will inspire confidence by having no other interests to promote than those of public service'.

Broadcasting has been repeatedly presented in reports as serving the public interest as a consequence of being subject to regulations framed for the public good and controlled by people committed to the best interests of the entire community. The BBC was financed from licence revenue and was therefore, in the words of the Pilkington Report (1962), under 'no obligation, express or implied, to pursue any objective other than that of public service'. Public regulation was seen as both necessary and desirable even after the introduction of commercial television.

This conception of state-sponsored public service has depended on a number of principles. First, that broadcasting services should be made available to everyone in the UK, and not merely developed in areas where it was easy or cheap to do so, or restricted to those who could pay for them. Second, that public service broadcasting should produce a wide variety of high-quality programmes because it is not controlled by the forces that make for low standards and uniformity. Finally, that public regulation should ensure broadcasters' accountability through the relationship of the broadcasting authority with parliament.

Whereas press inquiries are in general pro-market, the opposite is generally the case with broadcasting inquiries. Indeed, public service is deemed necessary in order to make up for the deficiencies of free enterprise. The Crawford Committee (1926) argued that 'no company or body constituted on trade lines for profit ... can be regarded as adequate ... in view of the broader considerations which now begin to emerge'. The Ullswater Committee (1936) regarded commercial advertising as incompatible with 'the intellectual and ethical integrity which the broadcasting system in this country has attained'. Much of this opposition was based on the belief that what the Beveridge Committee (1951) called 'competition for numbers' results in standardized programming. This view was justified by references to the deplorable condition of commercial broadcasting in the USA. 'Experience in other countries', concluded the Pilkington Report in 1962, 'is that this kind of competition, so far from promoting the purposes of broadcasting, or extending the range of programmes, or helping to realise the potential of the medium, serves rather to restrict them'.

The necessity of extensive public regulation was never questioned in official reports on television or radio until the Thatcher era. There were signs of unease before that, most notably a concern about the relationship between government (and in particular, party politicians) and broadcasting. But this gave rise to reform, not repudiation, of the public service system. There was also a gradual weakening of the sense of cultural purpose associated with Lord Reith. As the Annan Report commented, 'the ideals of middle-class culture, so felicitously expressed by Matthew Arnold a century ago ... found it ever more difficult to accommodate ... the variety of expression of what is good'. The Annan Committee found it harder to define what 'good' broadcasting was than did Pilkington. Nevertheless, Annan did make qualitative judgements, finding the BBC's output, on balance, superior to that of ITV. Annan was opposed to the unrestricted commercial control of broadcasting, and saw the fact that ITV made 'some programmes which both stimulate and entertain, and are not concocted in order to drug their audience into an uncritical stupor' as a product of public regulation. Even the Peacock Committee, which in certain important respects broke with the broadcasting consensus, nevertheless clung to a conception of public service broadcasting as 'a commitment to produce a wide range of high quality programmes to maximise consumer appreciation'. Collective provision and public regulation was producing, in its judgement, a 'mixed diet' of programmes 'at a low cost' that 'has broadened the horizon of a great number of viewers'. While it favoured long-term deregulation, it still made the case for a residual public service system which would secure 'programmes of merit which would not survive in a market where audience ratings was the sole criterion'. These were, it added, not just minority programmes but included ones that attract 'medium sized audiences of which virtually all the population at some stage form a part'.

Broadcasting and press reports do not each constitute a single unity. The second Press Commission was more critical of the market than other Press Commissions, while the Peacock Committee was more anti-statist than the broadcasting inquiries that had preceded it. But in general broadcasting policy has been framed within a pro-state, anti-market framework, while press policy has been formulated within a framework that is anti-state and pro-market. This has produced recurrent inconsistencies that cannot be explained away in terms of technological differences between the two media. For example, the idea that government should give money to a publishing corporation, even one with a publicly appointed managing authority, would have been anathema to all Press Commissions, which could not countenance even selective subsidies. Yet this is what the Annan Committee proposed when it suggested that a government grant could be given to start an Open Broadcasting Authority, and what the Peacock Committee recommended when it suggested that its proposed Public Service Broadcasting Council could be financed by the taxpayer.

Divergent histories

Differences of perspective are rooted partly in different histories. The press began as an agency of news and political comment. It was also organized as a free market system from 1695 onwards. Traditionally, it has been viewed within a taken-for-granted market framework, and evaluated primarily in terms of its functioning within the democratic system. A neo-liberal, 'politics of information' approach has coloured the work of all major public inquiries into the press.

By contrast, during the 1920s radio was not allowed to compete fully with the news service of the press, and was organized as a public service monopoly. It was evaluated primarily in terms of its contribution to culture, education and entertainment, defined by formative Victorian debates. This legacy had an enduring influence on how broadcasting was viewed by subsequent public inquiries.

From the outset, it was also accepted that broadcasting had to be regulated by the state because spectrum frequency was a scarce public resource which needed to be managed in the public interest. This was always an ideological argument, masquerading as a technical one, since it presupposed that public interest management of spectrum scarcity was best entrusted to the state rather than to the marketplace. But it powerfully influenced the approach of all public investigations into broadcasting, even that of the Peacock Committee which sought to challenge and renegotiate this statist legacy.

Consequently, press and broadcasting reports have tended to approach their work in different ways. While Royal Commissions on the press have focused generally on the quality of news and political comment, and formulated their conclusions within a free market system of thought, broadcasting inquiries have concerned themselves generally with the full range of programmes, and promoted reform from a public service viewpoint. This has regularly produced divergent or incommensurate conclusions. Thus, in 1960 the Pilkington Committee recommended a ban on television advertisements 'appealing to human weakness'; yet two years later the second Royal Commission on the press did not even consider the content of newspaper and magazine advertising, let alone recommend its reform. Similarly, the Annan Committee recommended that the joint ownership of commercial broadcasting companies and record or music publishing companies should be banned, on the grounds that there was bound to be a conflict of interest between them. The third Royal Commission on the press, also reporting in 1977, did not propose (or even discuss) a similar measure in relation to the music press and record production.

These discrepancies merely illustrate the different intellectual frameworks in which press and broadcasting policy are conceived. However, these frameworks no longer make sense. Popular newspapers devote less than a quarter of their editorial content to reporting and commenting on public affairs. Indeed, television has usurped the role of the press as the principal source of news. The distinction between media of 'information' and those of 'culture and entertainment' has completely broken down. The spectrum-scarcity justification for public service broadcasting has also been undermined by the development of cable, satellite and digital television. Hence the different policy approaches which have been developed to deal with broadcasting and the press are completely inadequate.

Pressure groups and policy

Another source of inconsistency in media policy derives from the fact that it is shaped by public inquiries confined to one media industry. These have not been given common terms of reference, and they have not been set to work within an integrated framework of communications policy.

The inevitable consequence has been that public inquiries have responded to the divergent pressure groups and economic interests at work in different media industries. Broadcasting inquiries have been powerfully influenced by the BBC, and for this reason have tended to uphold the principles of public service. Press inquiries have been shaped by publishers – who have invested large resources to influence them – and have tended to champion their *laissez-faire* approach.

This sectoral narrowness has also tended to nurture self-interested inconsistency. To take but one example, the 1977 Press Commission favoured limited press holdings in profitable television and radio franchises because, following press lobbying, it came around to the view that these were a valuable, potential source of cross-subsidy for vulnerable newspapers. Similarly the Prime Minister's Working Party on the Film Industry (1977), influenced closely by the views of the industry, proposed that television should finance film making. On the other hand, the Annan Committee (1977) was exposed to broadcasters who were hostile to the idea that broadcasting should subsidize less profitable media. It consequently opposed the view that 'like an aged parent, the film industry has a right to look to television to support it in its old age'. It rejected the proposal (already endorsed by the Working Party on the Film Industry) for money for film investment to come out of the television levy. It was also much more hostile than the 1977 Press Commission to cross-ownership between press and broadcasting.

A second consequence of the uncoordinated way in which communications policy has evolved is that reforms, proposed and implemented for one industry, have had unforeseen consequences for other media. For example, the decision to establish commercial television in 1955–56, in the wake of Selwyn Lloyd's minority report, contributed almost certainly to the epidemic of newspaper and magazine closures that the second Press Commission was then appointed to investigate in 1961.

This source of inconsistency has yet to be rectified. New Labour (like the Major government that preceded it) has produced policy proposals covering more than one medium, and invited comment. But it has yet to initiate a full-blown public inquiry into the communications industry which critically scrutinizes divergent media policy and proposes a coherent alternative.

Continuing confusion

Of course, a degree of variation in approach to different media could reasonably be justified in terms of their contrasting characteristics. In practice, policy differences are rooted in the histories of different media, and the polarized politics of communication that these have produced. Policy divergence is not the product of rational differentiation between media, nor is it presented in these terms.

However, during the 1980s and 1990s, the rise of the New Right held out the promise of greater policy consistency, at least on its impoverished terms. It sought to reorganize broadcasting on the free market lines of the press. However, while it made policy inroads, and while market values were strengthened within the broadcasting system, its project failed ultimately through lack of political and public support. The BBC and Channel 4 were not privatized. Although a 'light touch' regulator of commercial TV (ITC) was established in 1990, it had a much heavier hand than its press counterpart, the Press Council/Complaints Commission. The ITC licensed the right to 'publish' on domestic airwaves; it excluded television companies which failed to submit adequate public service programme plans; and it was able to impose fines – a power that it used. Unlike the supine Press Complaints Commission, the ITC exerted a significant and positive influence on the industry it regulated.

Indeed, the New Right phase of media reform introduced new contradictions. The ostensible purpose behind rolling back public bureaucracy was to enlarge freedom. However, the Conservative government did not approve of the uses to which this freedom was put. In 1984, it introduced legislation to outlaw video 'nasties'. In 1988, it established the Broadcasting Standards Council (BSC) to monitor levels of sex and violence on television. In 1990, it required broadcasting bodies to reflect BSC codes in relation to sex and violence. During the later 1980s, the Conservative government also lobbied unsuccessfully other European governments to take a tough stand against television sex in the Television without Frontiers Directive (1989). Although committed ostensibly to increasing freedom of expression, the Thatcher government also introduced in 1988 a ban on broadcasting the voices of supporters of terrorist organizations (including democratically elected Sinn Fein politicians). This conflict between the pursuit of market freedom and the increase of state censorship reflected an underlying tension, at the heart of modern conservatism, between market liberalism and social authoritarianism.

However, New Labour proved to be no more successful than its predecessors in rationalizing media policy. One reason for this was that the Department of Trade and Industry (recast in 2007 as Business, Enterprise and Regulatory Reform) in effect continued to be a second 'media ministry', and promoted a market brief, while the Department of Culture, Media and Sport was more oriented towards public service policies. A second reason was that New Labour's promotion of global media competitiveness as a central objective tended to clash with its aims of promoting media quality, diversity and access. A third reason is that its reappraisal focused on telecommunications, broadcasting and print, but sidelined film (even though film is now funded and distributed partly by television, and the two media are inextricably linked). Nothing that Ofcom has done during its watch has significantly diminished these inconsistencies (though this is partly a consequence of the legislative framework within which it works).

Incommensurate media policies that have arisen out of different cultural traditions and the impact of different industrial lobbies could be represented as a triumph of organic pluralism, or at least rationalized in some way. But this has yet to happen. In New Labour's green, white and consultation papers on communications, public service broadcasting is defended, without any equivalent attempt being made to justify an entirely different approach to the press. The latter is just assumed to be right, without any argument or reason being given. In this way, the contradiction at the heart of media policy persists – unacknowledged, unexplained and unjustified – as it has done for over eighty years. All that New Labour's rhetoric about the need for an integrated communications policy has achieved is to expose how incoherent it remains.

Chapter 24

Media reform: democratic choices

Introduction

The media absorb over thirty hours a week in the average person's life. They are central to the democratic life of Britain. They are a vehicle through which different social groups connect to each other, and join in the shared conversations of society. They are also major sources of pleasure and cultural fulfilment. How the media are organized and regulated matters.

Yet public policy about the media is often presented as an arcane subject to do with regulators, 'governance' and 'externalities'. It seems to belong to a rarefied world where only experts are qualified to speak, and where complex issues are susceptible solely to technocratic solutions.

But in essence the debate about how best to organize and manage Britain's media is exceedingly simple. It also involves choices that affect everyone. It is not something that can be left safely to specialists, powerful lobbies and politicians who – unexposed to public pressure – will tend to curry favour with media magnates.

What follows is a summary of public discussion about media policy. It reports not only the principal policy alternatives that are available, but also the thinking behind these. The aim is to provide a map that marks clearly the main points of entry into the democratic politics of the media. It also seeks to highlight the way in which media politics is no longer purely national – the exclusive concern of national government and national electorates – but is acquiring a significant European and international regulatory dimension.

Free market

Free market ideas have been the main driving force shaping media policy since the early 1980s. They have encouraged the adoption of deregulatory policies under successive Conservative administrations during the 1980s and 1990s, and under New Labour since 1997.

The starting point of the free market approach is that consumers are the best judges of what is in their interests. Media policy should seek therefore to create the conditions of greatest possible competition, thus enabling consumers to exercise sovereign control. This produces media that people want, a wide range of choice, and media independence from government. There is no conflict between the needs of society and the functioning of the market system. On the contrary, 'all provision for the consumer on a competitive basis in a non-distorted [media] market', according to the *Financial Times* journalist Samuel Brittan, 'is a public service'.[1]

The market not only empowers the consumer and fosters freedom but also makes for efficiency. It follows from this that there is very little need to reform the press, since it is organized along free market lines. The opposite is true of public service broadcasting, which is indicted on four main counts. It is controlled by an unrepresentative élite who foist their cultural values on the public. It is vulnerable to government pressure because it is dependent on state-sponsored privileges. It is run by bureaucracies prone to waste and profligacy. And, according to some critics, the BBC and Channel 4 are unaccountable havens for radicals. This is in marked contrast to the competitive environment of the press, where the consumer is in control and where, consequently, unpopular radical views get short shrift.

The case for deregulation, argue neo-liberals, has been further reinforced by technological change. It was once maintained plausibly that broadcasting channels had to be managed in the public interest because the scarcity of airwave frequencies produced a natural oligopoly. But cable, satellite and digital technologies have multiplied the number of television channels, and these have been supplemented by DVDs, the web and – in the pipeline – a new generation of convergent, digital media. The technical justification for public service broadcasting, based on the need to manage spectrum scarcity, has been undermined.

The world is also changing, it is argued, in a way that makes media competitiveness a key objective of communications policy. The media are part of the expanding information sector, and generate both jobs and exports. But British media are now exposed to increased competition as a consequence of the growing integration of the world's audiovisual markets. Leading British media companies should be free to accumulate increased economies of scope through mergers and acquisitions if they are to compete successfully against heavyweights in the international market. 'Some concentration of [media] ownership', suggests New Labour's Green Paper on *Regulating Communications*, 'has been regarded as inevitable, and possibly desirable, since it confers advantage in terms of global competitiveness'.[2]

These different arguments contributed to a cumulative policy of broadcasting deregulation. The 1990 Broadcasting Act inaugurated the sale of ITV franchises. It also established a 'light touch' regulator (Independent Television Commission), and weakened public obligations on commercial broadcasters. This was followed by the 1996 Broadcasting Act, which relaxed restrictions on ITV and commercial radio concentration.

The 2003 Communications Act is the most recent staging post in market-friendly reform. It sanctioned a further increase of commercial radio and television concentration. It allowed British terrestrial television channels to be bought by an owner outside the EU. And it established a new regulator, the Office of Communications (Ofcom), with a brief to 'roll back regulation promptly when regulation becomes unnecessary'.[3] In the official view, the growth of media outlets, supported by the digital revolution, lessens the need for regulation.

Yet the pace of deregulation has still not been fast enough for committed neo-liberals. The Adam Smith Institute believes that the BBC should be broken up into 'an association of independent and separately financed stations' funded partly by advertising. It argues that the market should prevail, since 'the only fair criterion of judging a programme is by how many people like it'.[4] Similarly, Rupert Murdoch holds that increased cross-media ownership should be actively encouraged, since it increases investment and is therefore 'a force for diversity'.[5] Some conservative commentators have also called for the lifting of the legal requirement on broadcasters to be impartial on controversial issues. This limits free speech, they argue, in support of an ideal of objectivity that is unobtainable and illusory (echoing, ironically, a standard left claim during the 1970s).

Pressure for deregulation comes not only from the right in Britain, but also from neo-liberals entrenched within some parts of the European Commission. Broadcasting was exclusively a national policy area until 1989, when the European Union's Television Without Frontiers Directive was introduced. Revised on successive occasions, it was recast as the Audiovisual Media Services Directive (2007), covering both conventional television and new online services.[6] Its underlying objective has been to remove barriers to cross-border competition between television organizations in Europe. To this end, it established a country of origin principle: satellite television companies can be regulated only in the country where programmes are 'uplinked' rather than in the countries where their programmes are received. This led some radical critics in the 1990s to predict that European law would lead to a competitive 'race to the bottom'. National governments in Europe would vie with each other to scale down television regulation in order to attract inward TV investment, while television companies would engage in 'regulatory arbitrage' – securing deregulation though threatening to relocate to a low-regulation country.

In the event, this did not happen on an extensive basis. Only two European countries – Britain and Luxembourg – extensively deregulated their satellite television companies. They became the headquarters of a number of satellite television companies broadcasting to other countries. Some deregulation was enforced by the European Court of Justice on reluctant governments (as in Sweden and the Netherlands) which sought to regulate incoming satellite TV content.[7] However, most national governments refused to outbid each other in terms of deregulation but clung, in some form, to public service broadcasting régimes. The economic incentive of inward investment was thus trumped by 'politics', based on a wider understanding of what best served the public interest of their countries.[8]

But if neo-liberals failed to secure TV deregulation though the European state, it was not through want of trying. The European Commission's Competition Directorate proposed in 1998 that public service broadcasters should be prevented from making programmes of a kind made by commercial broadcasters[9] – a proposal that was fiercely resisted and got nowhere. In the 2000s, a variety of interested parties sought to prevent national public broadcasters from developing online services, on the grounds that this represented unfair competition. So far, their objections lodged with European competition authorities have all failed.

Neo-liberals have also sought to advance their aims through international trade negotiation, conducted under the auspices of the World Trade Organisation (WTO).[10] The United States government sought to impose global free market media policies during the Uruguay round of negotiations, only for this to be strongly opposed by European and other countries in the early 1990s. A fresh attempt was made to outlaw subsidies for media production (including the television licence fee) and eliminate programme quotas during the stalled Doha round of trade negotiations, not yet completed. This time round, the neo-liberal agenda was more strongly in the ascendant (at least until the 2008 crash). There was acceptance in principle that there should be free trade in services (formalized in the General Agreement on Trade in Services (GATS)). The issue was how far this Agreement should be extended to media services, and in what form. In the event, the EU vigorously resisted any change imperilling public service broadcasting and selective film subsidies (its negotiating position having been strengthened by a prior political campaign in Europe). The neo-liberal strategy of multilateral negotiation – that had secured the international deregulation of telecommunications (completed in Europe in 1998) – thus seems to have run out of steam. It is likely now that the US government will place greater emphasis on making bilateral agreements with individual countries, where it is able to exert greater leverage in favour of a neo-liberal media settlement.

Market radicals can also be reformers. The principal way in which they address market shortcomings is to cultivate a tradition of media professionalism. Through careful recruitment, strong leadership, the honouring of great journalism by professional associations and the development of appropriate journalism training and education, reforming neo-liberals hope to instil a public interest culture among journalists. In this way, they seek to enhance the quality of journalism without undermining its independence through state intervention. This approach can lead to the adoption of self-regulation – for example the Press Complaints Commission, which has no formal powers and is funded by the press industry – as a way of discouraging abuse, mollifying angry customers and offering an alternative to state intervention. The furthest down this road that reformist neo-liberals are usually willing to travel is co-regulation: that is, a combination of limited government regulation (for example, over media mergers) and self-regulation – what some lawyers call 'soft governance'.

Social market

Neo-liberals have thus occupied the high ground, launched numerous initiatives, and operated on national, European and global fronts. They have had more influence on media policy in Britain than in much of Europe. Yet, even in Britain, neo-liberals have been less successful in relation to the media than in some other sectors of the economy (such as energy and financial services – until the 2008 crash). This is partly because neo-liberal lobbying for media reform has been weakened repeatedly by their unreliable allies, 'social market' liberals.

Social market liberals are the wild card in the media politics pack because they are to be found among the left as well as the right. Within the right, they have caused havoc by making the case for controls, while within the left they have caused consternation by advocating market solutions. Their thinking, and also their maverick influence, is best illustrated, first, by two policy documents produced during the Conservative era of the 1980s and early 1990s.

The key social market text of the 1980s is the Peacock Report (1986). The Peacock Committee was set up to investigate whether the BBC should take advertising. It widened its brief to consider the development of the entire broadcasting system. Dominated by clever neo-liberals, the committee recommended – as expected – that 'British broadcasting should move towards a sophisticated market system based on consumer sovereignty'.[11] It also advocated a transitional strategy of cumulative deregulation that significantly influenced the 1990 Broadcasting Act.

Yet, instead of pressing for rapid liberalization, the Peacock Committee surprised everybody by making a right-wing case for public service broadcasting as a necessary, short-term response to market failure. There was insufficient advertising, it argued, to fund good programmes on both the BBC and ITV. A ratings war between the two would reduce programme diversity. Subscription television was too underdeveloped to sustain adequate minority provision. The best way to secure the benefits of a free market, it argued, in a situation where the market was underdeveloped, was public service policy. This is because 'collective provision or regulation of programmes does provide [now] a better simulation of a market designed to reflect consumer preferences than a policy of *laissez-faire*' because it generates a greater choice of programmes for the consumer.

The significance of this report, published during the height of Thatcherism, was that it took the wind out of the growing political campaign to fast-track deregulation. The report made in effect a short-term market case for the BBC and regulation of commercial broadcasting. However, many of its longer-term proposals, which the committee wanted to be implemented in the next fifteen years, were ignored. Thus, new television sets were not required to be manufactured in a form suitable for pay-TV systems; the BBC's licence fee was not abolished; a new fall-back agency that would channel grants towards 'programmes of a more demanding kind' was not put in place in order to make acceptable a lurch towards deregulation. In the event, the Peacock Report was drawn upon selectively in order to defend rather than to destroy public service broadcasting.

The key social market document of the 1990s was the Conservative government's White Paper on *Media Ownership* (1995). The government's policy review had been prompted by a powerful media lobby pressing for a major liberalization of anti-monopoly controls, in the context of the rise of cable and satellite television. There was also growing internal pressure within the Conservative Party in favour of a media-friendly initiative, as a way of mending fences with estranged media allies. This pressure was increased by the shifting position of the New Labour opposition, which outflanked the Conservative government from the right by championing the right of press tycoons to move into commercial broadcasting. In these circumstances, it required social market nerves of steel to hold the line. The occasion produced a remarkable White Paper (issued by National Heritage Minister Stephen Dorrell) which proclaimed:

> A free and diverse media are an indispensable part of the democratic process. They provide the multiplicity of voices and opinions that informs the public, influences opinion and engenders political debate. They promote the culture of dissent which any democracy must have. In so doing, they contribute to the cultural fabric of the nation and help define our sense of identity and purpose. If one voice becomes too powerful, this process is placed in jeopardy and democracy is damaged. Special media ownership rules ... are needed therefore to provide safeguards necessary to maintain diversity and plurality.[12]

While the fostering of a successful and competitive media industry was an 'important objective' of public policy, 'the main objective must ... be to secure a plurality of sources of information and opinion, and a plurality of editorial control over them'. The needs of democracy must come first.

General competition legislation, the White Paper argued, is not an adequate basis for regulating the media; it is framed primarily with economic objectives in mind, and permits levels of media concentration that are too high, given the media's strategic role in the democratic process. While the expansion in the number of media outlets makes possible some liberalization of controls on a cumulative basis, significant limits still need to be placed on the expansion of large media corporations. In the event, the White Paper's proposed limits were relaxed in response to strong industrial lobbying when a more receptive Heritage Minister, Virginia Bottomley, framed the 1996 Broadcasting Act. They were eased a great deal more in 2003, under New Labour. Even so, the 1995 White Paper remains a significant expression of social market thought.

It is now sometimes argued that we should move from structural to behavioural regulation of media corporations.[13] In plain language, this means that a much greater degree of media concentration is acceptable, providing steps are taken to prevent the abuse of market power. The focus should be less on setting limits on media amalgamation, and more on preventing possible damaging consequences. Thus it is entirely acceptable for a major corporation to monopolize a 'gateway technology', such as set-top boxes or electronic programme guides, providing regulatory steps are taken to ensure that competitors have access to this technology at fair prices. However, this 'behavioural' approach still does not address the central argument of the 1995 White Paper – namely, that anti-monopoly media regulation is needed not only to maintain fair competition but also to prevent the distortion of democracy.

The most recent social market texts of importance are written by two Keynesian economists, Andrew Graham and Gavyn Davies (who later became Chairman of the BBC). They attempt to justify the existence of public service broadcasting in terms of market theory. Their first argument is that television has 'public good' characteristics: its programmes can be consumed – unlike a Mars bar – by an infinite number of people without additional cost. Public service broadcasting is a way of enabling this public good advantage to be retained by the public.

Second, extensive intervention is needed, they argue, to cope with a built-in tendency for a small number of companies to dominate the broadcasting market. 'Thus, while one source of monopoly, spectrum scarcity, has gone, it has been replaced by another – the natural monopoly of economies of scale and of scope'.[14] Economic advantages of size foster oligopoly, and limit real choice. Regulation alone is not a sufficient response to this problem because regulators tend to be influenced unduly by the industries they oversee. Publicly owned organizations such as the BBC are also needed because they produce 'merit goods' that set standards, and influence both the wider broadcasting industry and public demand.

These arguments clearly influenced New Labour's White Paper on communications policy (2000).[15] However, the White Paper's overt thrust was that there should be, over time, a movement away from onerous regulation of broadcasting in favour of self-regulation and the setting of general objectives. But this explicitly pro-market message was incorporated within an intellectual framework that expressed a continuing commitment to public control of broadcasting. Programme quality, impartial briefing of the electorate, content diversity, a pluralism of voices were all desirable goals, but not things that the market at present can be relied upon to deliver. The entire document – and indeed New Labour's entire broadcasting policy – can be viewed as an attempt to square a circle: a fervent belief in the market, combined with a highly developed sense of its limitations. This is a standard social market position that justifies – and indeed elevates – the regulator as champion of the public interest.

Outside Britain, perhaps the best-known social market experiment is the Swedish press subsidy system that keeps alive (with increasing difficulty) 'political papers' that would otherwise die in free market conditions. The justification for this scheme is that these minority papers extend the diversity of the press and enhance the working of democracy. Their economic viability is imperilled because they lack the economies of scale of their bigger-circulation rivals. So, a compensatory grant is given to non-market leading newspapers. The size of the grant is determined in relation to circulation and the volume of newsprint, without reference to editorial content, and is administered by a public body with all-party representation, in order to prevent political partiality. In addition, subsidies are provided as incentives to competing newspapers to lower costs by sharing distribution or other functions. Various alternative subsidy schemes designed to support press diversity operate in other countries, such as Norway, Finland and the Netherlands.[16]

The Swedish example is unusually ambitious because it seeks to restructure the terms of competition of an entire industry in order to sustain minority voices. The more conventional approach is to intervene on a more limited basis in order to further one of three objectives: encourage new media ventures, facilitate distribution or avert closure.

Thus, the production of new films is assisted by seed money provided by the UK's Film Council. A more ambitious seeding exercise is the legal requirement (first established on an extensive basis by the 1990 Broadcasting Act) on major broadcasters to commission 25 per cent of their programming from independent production companies.

Barriers to press distribution are overcome by legislation in France, Germany and Greece that asserts the legal right of lawful newspapers to be stocked and displayed by newsagents, subject to a handling charge. In a similar vein, independent films (including an endangered species, Norwegian films) can gain access to cinemas in Norway because most cinemas are municipally owned. Public ownership ensures that a variety of films – not just an exclusive diet of commercial American films – are screened.

Closures of a wide range of cultural institutions and organizations – theatres, art galleries, varied music, dance and creative arts organizations, independent publishers and others – have been averted partly through ongoing grants from the Arts Council, with an increasing emphasis on supporting regional activity.

In brief, the social market approach believes in principle in the free market but can find it wanting in practice. This gives rise to public interventions, usually intended to sustain media diversity, pluralism of ownership or 'quality' of output.

Protectionism

Social market liberalism can shade into protectionism. This last takes the form of production quotas, import duties, restrictions on foreign media ownership and subsidies designed to support domestic media production and control.

The European Union is protectionist. It argues that American film and television programme makers have an enormous competitive advantage over their counterparts in Europe. While the European film and television industry is fragmented into national industries catering for different national publics, the American audiovisual industry is highly concentrated and serves a vast domestic market. This enables the American majors to achieve large economies of scale, and both outspend and undercut their European rivals. Thus, American television companies can sell the rights of a TV drama for as little as one-tenth of the cost of making its equivalent in Europe. This is because American TV companies normally recoup their costs and make a profit from their domestic market: the sale of foreign rights, which entail little additional cost, yields a high rate of return, enabling heavy discounting. The cheapness of some American programme rights (often bundled together in packages) creates a very strong incentive for European television companies to import US content, even if audience research indicates a strong preference in most European countries for home-grown TV products.[17] Likewise, American film makers can exploit the advantage conferred by the size of their home market to generate high-cost blockbusters; they also dominate the international film distribution system, and have close ties to national cinema chains. Against these steep odds, programme and film makers in Europe need, according to the European Commission, a helping hand.

The second reason why the European Union is protectionist is that it is seeking to develop the cultural infrastructure of a new state (something which official publications tend to be reticent about). The European Commission wants to promote Europe-wide media companies, co-productions and reciprocal cultural trade between European partners, as a way of promoting a 'we feeling' among European nations. Shared cultural experiences, and a strengthened sense of European identity, will encourage increased levels of political participation. People will be more inclined to vote in European elections and to connect to European politics if they feel themselves to be 'Europeans'; and this will facilitate, in turn, a greater degree of European political integration based on the increased pooling of national sovereignty.

The European Commission's main protectionist weapon is the Audiovisual Media Services Directive. Like its predecessor (first introduced in 1989), this lays down that, where possible, half or more of TV programming transmitted in Europe (with some exemptions) should be generated from within the EU. However, the quota's optional nature results in variable national enforcement. In 2004, the overall compliance rate within the EU was 63 per cent. This average concealed big differences. In protectionist France compliance was 96 per cent, whereas in neo-liberal Britain it was 45 per cent (because the quota has never been enforced on British satellite and cable TV).

The Directive is also intended, as mentioned earlier, to promote cross-border media competition within Europe. In this way, it is hoped, European media champions, with bulging economic muscles, will emerge to take on the might of the six Hollywood majors. This aspiration even led the Commission to flirt for a time with the idea of encouraging media concentration. This arose, paradoxically, from a European Parliament proposal, in 1990 and 1992, for Europe-wide legislation that would strengthen anti-monopoly controls. Media lobbyists sought to subvert this initiative by proposing a permissive form of legislation that would supersede strict national monopoly controls. They won the broad support of the European Commission, which argued that increased media concentration in Europe might be desirable because it would make for greater international competitiveness.[18] However, the idea of having a Europe-wide media monopoly policy foundered in the mid-1990s because it was fiercely opposed by some member states.

The Commission also seeks to support the European audiovisual industry through a subsidy scheme. This was initiated in 1990, and is now in its fourth incarnation. The Media Programme currently makes a financial contribution towards training, production, distribution and promotion costs in the audiovisual industries. Its budget is relatively modest in relation to the magnitude of the task it is tackling.

The Commission's protectionist policies have been unsuccessful. New media ventures attempting to build a pan-European public – such as Europa, a pan-European satellite TV channel launched by five national public service broadcasting organizations with a great fanfare in 1985, only to fold one year later[19] – have failed to secure significant audiences because Europe is linguistically and culturally divided. There is still no pan-European media sphere supporting identification with Europe and involvement in European politics. During the lifetime of the EU's audiovisual subsidy scheme, Hollywood's share of the European film market relentlessly increased.[20] There is also a large European television programme trade deficit with America.

European protectionism coexists with national cultural protectionism. Britain, despite its public neo-liberal stance, is part of this tradition. During the 1980s, programme imports from outside the EU were limited to a draconian 14 per cent of commercial TV transmission time (with some exemptions). Public service commercial TV channels then became subject to a requirement to 'originate' (in other words, make or commission) set proportions of programmes that varied in relation to different channels. These proportions were specified in 1993 by the Independent Television Commission, and revised in 1998. However, much the most important form of protectionism is the television licence fee, a public subsidy that gives strong financial support to national TV production (organized through the BBC).

Neo-liberal critics argue that all forms of protectionism injure the 'hidden hand' of the free market, and subvert the dynamic that should give rise to a diverse, free and responsive media system. Some cultural studies libertarians join in this attack, arguing that protectionism feeds the cancer of nationalism, limits media diversity and serves the interests of élites who use protectionism to support their ascendancy.[21]

There are two standard responses to these charges. The first is that limited forms of protectionism are intended to extend, not shrink, media diversity, since they seek to offset overwhelming forms of economic power that limit competition and choice. Second, the élitist charge is answered by the argument that constructive protectionism seeks to maintain rather than undermine the accountability of power. The nation is still where democracy is primarily organized. Effective national media are needed to provide an intermediary link between elected government and citizens, and afford a communication space where national concerns, issues and solutions can be debated. And since democracy is evolving to include a continental dimension in the form of the European Union, the media system should also evolve in a form that holds European government and power holders to account.

But if public service broadcasting is a recurrent target of neo-liberals and libertarians, it is also the most influential media experiment to have been attempted in Europe. As a form of media organization that has been imported around the world, from South Africa to South Korea, it warrants special attention.

Public service approach

While neo-liberals focus on satisfying the wants of the individual consumer, the public service approach is concerned with serving the needs of society. In essence, this comes down to three things: serving democracy, generating content that has cultural value and promoting social inclusion.

The locus of public service loyalty used to be exclusively the BBC. But as the public service system has developed over time, so it has come to mean not only the BBC but also regulated commercial broadcasting and Channel 4 (a public trust). It comprises that part of the broadcasting system which has a legal obligation to serve the welfare of society.

While the general justification for public service broadcasting has been referred to in different places in this book, it may be helpful to summarize here its main themes.

First, public service broadcasting is committed to reporting the news impartially and to giving due prominence to coverage of public affairs. It thus ensures that people are briefed properly as citizens, and contributes to the healthy functioning of the democratic system. In contrast, market-driven media tend to marginalize news in favour of entertainment, offer 'info-tainment' instead of informative analysis, and can follow partisan agendas (like Fox News in the US). Compare, argue public service advocates, the quality of the BBC's or ITN's popular news service with that of the market-based tabloids.

Second, public service broadcasting maintains high programme standards and contributes to the cultural resources of society, rather than merely offering what is profitable. It seeks to democratize culture by making widely available the best works of literature, drama, art and music. It aims to renew the culture of society by supporting innovation and experiment. It is also committed to catering for the diversity of the public and the enthusiasms of minorities, as well as of the majority.

Third, public service broadcasting is preferable because it is best at binding together and integrating an increasingly privatized society. It ensures that everyone has access to a shared, unifying experience, because it does not discriminate against outlying areas or low income groups on the grounds of cost or profitability. Its approach is inclusive, seeking to draw together society in its diversity and to frame public discussion in terms of what serves the general good. In addition, because it invests in making programmes rather than relying, like BSkyB, on imports, public service broadcasting maintains a cultural space through which society can express itself and define its collective identity.

Public service broadcasting is well funded in Britain because it has strong public support. Comparative figures for 2004 show that *per capita* funding for public broadcasting in 2004 was higher in Britain than in most other countries, including even Sweden, France and Japan. This has enabled the BBC to deploy large sums in developing a popular online website, a web-based replay facility (iPlayer), five new digital TV channels directed at different groups, a Freeview package of digital channels (with others), and a world TV and radio service. British governments may publicly champion free trade and deregulation, but they also quietly authorize the generous endowment of a nationalized corporation, the BBC. And it is not the thrusting entrepreneurs of the deregulated TV sector but the BBC that remains Britain's 'media champion'. The BBC is the principal reason why the UK is the second biggest exporter of television programmes in the world.

A protective shield has been forged around public service broadcasting, designed to repel neo-liberal attack. In 1997, the European Union's fair trade rules were amended through the adoption of the Amsterdam Protocol, which endorses the public funding of broadcasting for public service objectives. In 2007, the Convention on Cultural Diversity was ratified under the auspices of UNESCO. This international treaty authorizes each signatory to 'adopt measures aimed at protecting and promoting the diversity of cultural expressions within its territory', including the use of subsidies, regulation, quotas and publicly owned broadcasting.[22] In effect, it establishes cultural diversity as a legitimate objective of international negotiation, to be balanced against that of free trade. This potentially sets UNESCO on a collision course with the WTO, and is intended to block the imposition of a free market régime around the world.

But if public service broadcasting weathered the era of neo-liberalism, it also declined in quality (despite advances in some areas).[23] In particular, commercial public service television became more market driven as a consequence of being partly deregulated. This had a knock-on effect, compelling the BBC and Channel 4 to become more like their main commercial rival in order to maintain their audience share.

Commercial public service broadcasting also declined for economic reasons. Television costs rose, while audiences and revenue were subdivided between more television channels and a new rival, the internet. By 2012, the cost of the public service obligations of ITV1, according to Ofcom, will outweigh the benefit of its licence to broadcast.[24] Without financial support, ITV1 may wish to surrender its licence. Alternatively it will ration, even more than before, 'uneconomic' programmes – meaning that there will be still less serious current affairs, local news, challenging UK drama, UK-scripted comedy, non-imported children's drama and factual programmes. Likewise, Channel 4 is heading towards a large financial deficit, and will also find it difficult to finance its public service remit.

A way thus needs to be found to restore the financial viability of public service broadcasting outside the BBC. Proposed solutions entail three elements: first, the identification of a source of subsidy, such as top-slicing the licence fee, a levy on the rental of spare spectrum released by the planned 2012 switchover to digital TV, a levy on digital TV profits, or the generation of a cross-subsidy through a Channel 4 link-up to profit-making BBC World-wide Television; second, the bestowal of an ongoing public subsidy in return for the delivery of public service content; and, third, a regulatory requirement on TV that it deliver public service content.

This proposed refinancing represents a way of reviving the earlier broadcasting settlement. ITV was not merely required by law to transmit public service content: it was also enabled to do so because its licence to broadcast – in the era of oligopoly – constituted an indirect subsidy, since it was assured advertising receipts greater than its franchise dues. Initially, Channel 4 also received a cross-subsidy from ITV in return for handing over its advertising time to the commercial broadcaster.

The other part of the proposed reform is the re-regulation of British broadcasting. The standard public service obligations – accuracy and impartiality, diversity, quality and origination – should be imposed, to a varying degree, on all British broadcasting organizations. It could be extended in full to BSkyB – Britain's *de facto* monopoly satellite broadcaster, which has become highly profitable by developing a parasitic business model based on the management of TV rights rather than the making of programmes.

If broadcasting should be shielded from excessive commercial pressure, it needs also to be protected from government. All those appointed to chair the BBC during the Conservative ascendancy were government supporters. Indeed, Marmaduke Hussey, a long-standing chairman of the BBC (1986–96) was a brother-in-law of a Cabinet minister; Stuart Young, his predecessor (1983–86), was a brother of a Cabinet minister. The first chairman of the BBC appointed by New Labour, Gavyn Davies, was also a New Labour insider (although he proved to be strongly independent).

The appointments system has become corrupted and needs to be reformed. The best way to achieve this is to remove effective control of broadcasting appointments (including to the board of Ofcom as well as the BBC Trust) from government, and to establish an independent appointments committee. A further way of shoring up the independence of the BBC is to replace its royal charter – subject to periodic renewal, usually accompanied by pre-renewal government intimidation – with its formal establishment through an Act of Parliament. After nearly ninety years of distinguished service, the BBC should no longer be considered a probationer on a temporary contract.

What has sustained broadcast independence over the years is the determination of broadcasters not to be controlled, and the public backing they have generally received when governments have sought to clip their wings. This was manifested in the run-up to the 2003 Iraq War, when the BBC defied government pressure and insisted on critically scrutinizing the case for invading Iraq. This was in marked contrast to the uncritical pre-war reporting of the US media, which proved to be much more compliant, despite their lack of formal structural ties to government. This said, British television's greater independence on this occasion was assisted by the much greater cross-party and popular opposition to invading Iraq that existed in Britain compared with the US. Steps still need to be taken to insulate British broadcasters from political pressure.

The third theme of public service reform should be to learn from abroad. Traditionally, the British public service approach has delegated considerable decision-making power to programme makers at the level of producer. This is because the British model is more independent of the market than the US broadcasting system and more independent of civil society than the representative-ridden structures of mainstream European broadcasting. There is much to be said for this British approach, since it makes for programme quality.

However, this distinctive British approach also has weaknesses, which its more complacent champions overlook. British television is very insular – much more so than television in most other northern European countries. British television also tends to underrepresent the diversity of British society as a consequence of being excessively metropolitan and linked too closely to Britain's political élite.

Yet, there are reformist tendencies within the broadcasting community seeking to change this. Their hand could be strengthened by redefining the public purpose of broadcasting to include representative pluralism. Broadcasting organizations should be charged with a duty to give adequate expression to the different viewpoints and concerns of the public. Broadcasters' existing obligation to inform could also contain an explicit reference to the need to give due prominence to events and developments outside Britain.

Radical visions

Over the years, a number of radical visions have been advanced for the root-and-branch reform of the media system. While these have no chance of being implemented in the prevailing political climate, they are worth alluding to in order to keep in play alternative ways of thinking about the organization of the media. Socialist and liberal versions of this visionary tradition are best represented by, respectively, Raymond Williams and John Keane.[25]

The late Raymond Williams argued that collective control over the means of mass communication was needed to further a 'cultural revolution', based on a universal right to transmit and receive information. This would enable people to grow in the power to direct their own lives, extend collective understanding through the exchange of experience and develop 'the capacity for personal and independent response and choice'.

Broadcasting, according to Williams, has been stunted by authoritarian, commercial and paternalistic forms of organization. The untried alternative is a 'democratic' one. The BBC and commercial broadcasting should be replaced by public trusts which would own production and transmission facilities on behalf of society and lease these, on long-term contracts, to independent companies which would control programme making. These companies would be run by broadcasters in a democratic way: administrators would be required to work within the framework of 'elected policy'.

Similarly, newspapers should be acquired by newspaper trusts and leased to their editors and journalists. Newsprint companies should be in separate public ownership, and provide supplies at a 'fair and open price'. Within this system, working journalists should determine editorial policy.

The underlying principle behind this proposed reorganization is that 'the active contributors [should] have control over their own means of expression'. When the means of expression are so costly that they are beyond their financial resources to own, society should step in to enable media professionals to exercise control over their own work. This form of public intervention is enabling, since it secures the freedom of journalists and creative staff and protects them 'alike from the bureaucrat and the speculator'.

By contrast, John Keane approaches the task of restructuring the media from the perspective of a radical liberal who, in his own words, 'acknowledges the facts of complexity, diversity and difference, and – in plain English – harbours doubts about whether any one person, group, committee, party or organization can be trusted to make superior choices on matters of concern to citizens'. What is needed, in his view, is a pluralistic media system which involves different people in different ways in overseeing the exercise of power in society. Only some media, he suggests, should be subject to what he calls 'the time-consuming and unwieldy procedures of direct democracy', the strategy favoured by Williams.

Yet, despite their differences of approach, both Williams and Keane tread rather similar paths. They both mount a critique of market- and state-linked media. They both seek to create media that are independent – what Keane calls, in a Germanic formulation, 'non-market-non-state media institutions'. In both cases, this results in the search for self-effacing forms of public intervention that are positively enabling. In Keane's case, this means 'a wide range of different regulated markets for different audiences and services'. These could include, among other things, time-share and common carrier arrangements with private media corporations; the funding of local independent cinemas, recording studios, and lease-back broadcasting facilities; subsidized political newspapers; co-operatively run publishers and distributors; and a reformed BBC.

However, the 'third route' rhetoric of both Williams and Keane raises almost as many questions as it answers. One unresolved issue is how state influence is to be reined back in the way that they both want. The intricate cat's cradle of subsidies, allocations, interventions, regulations and market suspensions outlined by Keane would lead, in fact, to a very extensive exercise of authority over the media by agencies that are part of the state. The same is true, to a lesser extent, of Williams's scheme. He assumes, mistakenly, that leasing the technical means of communication on long-term contracts to communicator-controlled consortia will enable 'public trusts' to take a back seat. In fact these trusts or some other public agency would have initially to fund these consortia, and then decide whether to support them if they ran into financial trouble. By default, public authorities would exercise some of the power deployed formerly by what Williams calls (revealingly) 'functionless financial groups' within the market system. This is not to imply that public agency involvement necessarily leads to state subordination, something that the history of British television from the mid-1950s refutes. But Williams and Keane both deploy an anti-statist rhetoric that sits uneasily with what they actually propose. They also pay too little detailed attention to devising ways of preventing the abuse of state power, by conveniently excising this danger through the use of emollient words such as 'enabling' and 'facilitating'.

The second key issue is who should be entrusted with control over the media. Raymond Williams argued that control should lie with professional communicators, since 'any restriction of the freedom of individual contribution' is a restriction on the freedom of society. But why should professional communicators, who are unrepresentative of society and often surprisingly uninformed about their audiences even within market systems, be established as a communications élite with exclusive rights of control over the media? Indeed, why should they be elevated above others in the same organization, rather in the manner of the Master and Fellows of Oxbridge colleges (a mandarin élite to which Williams himself belonged)? Different people within the radical tradition give different answers to these questions. Some syndicalists favour workers' control in different spheres, with media staff controlling the editorial process, and other workers controlling production, distribution and sales. In the late Tom Baistow's view, editors or their equivalent should function as trustees of the public interest, and their autonomy should be legally protected from private employers and trade unions alike. Others, still, argue for consumer, party, social group, professional or local community representation in the organization of the media. For example, the Militant Tendency, a Trotskyist organization, proposes that broadcasting and newspaper organizations should be allocated to political parties in accordance with the votes cast in the previous general election, while magazines should be handed over to scientific, technical and professional organizations – a scheme that leaves little scope for the voice of the consumer and excludes organizations that the Militant Tendency regards as 'undemocratic'. By contrast, John Keane argues beguilingly that different media should be controlled by different people in different ways.

The dominant view is that media workers' power should be balanced in some way by the rights of the public. This still leaves open how much influence media workers should have, and in what form. The basic options, in ascending order of significance, are: staff entitlement to information; the right to be consulted about major decisions; participation in senior appointments; representation on decision-making committees (editorial committees, boards of management, supervisory boards and so on); regular staff elections to senior management posts; and full workers' control.

These blue-sky debates seem completely removed from the reality of pragmatic, market-oriented media politics steered by governments with an overdeveloped sensitivity to what powerful media organizations want; yet wider debate can open up new avenues of thought and action. In the 1970s, a growing volume of criticism was directed against the comfortable (small 'c') conservative duopoly of the BBC and ITV. This gave rise to a discussion, involving people from different backgrounds and political affiliations, about how public service broadcasting could be reinvented. This produced an informed consensus in favour of creating a new form of organization: a 'publishing house' which would commission rather than make programmes, be innovative, serve minorities and extend the ideological spectrum of television (though this last idea was largely missing from the 'official' literature). This novel conception won the backing of the Annan Committee, the support of the outgoing Labour (Callaghan) government, and of the first Thatcher administration, with the result that Channel 4 was born in 1982. The public service broadcasting tradition became richer as a consequence.

Developing the internet

Perhaps we should now be focusing on how the internet can best be developed as a medium of communication for the twenty-first century. The internet has special attributes: it is cheap, interactive, global and offers access to a vast storehouse of information. It is an especially effective tool for the organization of social and political networks and the collective exchange and expression of information and experience.

Human ingenuity has led to the utilization of internet technology for the public good in a variety of ways, from the remarkable rise of Wikipedia and the Google project for the creation of a virtual global library through to the growth of social network sites like Facebook and YouTube. However, the continued development of the net in this protean way is threatened potentially from two different directions. The first threat comes from illiberal governments which seek to censor the internet. Their principal strategy has been to intimidate internet service providers into blocking or filtering access to websites they disapprove of (such as YouTube in Iran). The other threat comes from the cumulative commercialization of the net, manifested in attempts to multiply fee-entry websites, develop a system of digital rights management embedded in technology, contemplate a possible tiered internet service (with premium payments for rapid email), and the degradation of the internet through the uncontrolled distribution of spam.

These twin threats have encountered strong opposition from the campaign for 'net neutrality' (a neutral broadband network free of restrictions on content, sites or platforms). In addition, state online censorship has been evaded primarily through the creation of proxy websites and virtual private networks, though this requires some degree of technical knowledge on the part of the user. Commercialization of the web has also been opposed by the Open Source movement, with its influential base among computer scientists, and by millions of anonymous users accustomed to free access to the web.

But in addition to repelling threatening developments, we should think also about how best to shape the future of the internet in positive ways. The democratic state played an enabling role, at least in the view of public service broadcast supporters, in funding and developing television and radio in the twentieth century. What might equivalent initiatives look like in relation to the internet in this century?

Perhaps the first preliminary step is to ensure that public service broadcasting organizations have the freedom and resources to develop major, unrestricted websites – something that is opposed on the grounds that it will crowd out commercial initiatives and distort the development of cyberspace as a free market. This battle has been largely won in Europe.

The second step is to develop new forms of online service. Some public service broadcasters (PSBs) have developed websites that are primarily a news platform and playback facility, cleaving very closely to the model that they are familiar with. But PSB websites also offer opportunities for creating user-generated content and interactions; programmes in different formats; wide-ranging access to the broadcaster's archives; new ways of connecting like-minded people within civil society; experimenting with dramatic genres and journalistic formats; and generating a search engine with different criteria of prioritization than ratings-driven Google.

The third step is to seek to build a pan-European public space, supported by the online providers of all public service broadcasting organizations in the European Union. These organizations have enormous journalistic, creative and institutional resources. They should be invited to step up to the plate, and create an amalgamated online service that people in Europe (and else-where) will want to visit in large numbers and that entertains, informs and educates. Given the linguistic and cultural divisions of Europe, this will be an enormously difficult thing to accomplish. That is the challenge to which some of the most talented makers of drama, factual entertainment, docu-mentaries and current affairs programmes in Europe should rise. It is a chal-lenge worth engaging with because Europe will only work successfully as a political community if it is also, at some level, a social and cultural community as well.

The fourth step should take the form of thinking how best social market policies might be implemented to assist global dialogue. The single most important news medium in most countries is still television. Yet, television is organized primarily as a national news medium: indeed, much-vaunted international satellite TV news channels like CNN attract audiences so small in some countries as to be almost unmeasurable.[26] National television focuses on national news (about 80 per cent in the US and 70 per cent in Scandinavia). What little international news there is tends to black out large parts of the world, focus primarily on regions where the domestic country has a connection, and to interpret this news within a nationally inflected framework.[27]

Yet, the global nature of the internet represents an opportunity to offset the national introversion of conventional television journalism, and build a dialogue between nations. Indeed, global web-based journalism can potentially play a pivotal role in contributing to the development of an international civil society and public sphere holding to account global structures of economic and political power. But this will require financial outlays. A study of the pioneer international e-zine openDemocracy found that it spent £4.35 million in the period 2001–8, even though it drew heavily on people who wrote for nothing, used a network of volunteers to help 'publish' its website and spent very little on promotion.[28] Doing international virtual journalism – com-missioning, editing and translating articles, facilitating interaction and hyperlinks, publishing content online, winning public attention – all costs money. However, despite the distinctive quality of openDemocracy's con-tent, and the significant international audience it built (averaging over 400,000 monthly visits in 2005), the international e-zine still failed to generate significant revenue through advertising and other means. The shortfall was made good – in the short term – by charitable trusts (like the Ford Foundation). But if web-based global magazines are to become a force in the future, they will need continuing financial support from a public agency.

There are four leading contenders as sponsors of web-based initiatives. The first is a global agency like UNESCO; the second, the EU; the third, nation-states; and the fourth (for certain projects) local government. In each case, careful measures should be taken to prevent the funding agency from exercising editorial control – a familiar but surmountable problem to which the reformist media tradition, in its many manifestations, offers creative solutions.

Basis of legal debate

So far, we have focused mainly on policy discussion concerned with media organization. Overlaying this discussion is another, related debate concerned with media law. Libertarians in this legal debate stress the importance of freedom of expression, and the public's right to know the basis on which all decisions affecting the common good are made. Interventionists tend to emphasize other concerns, such as the right to a fair trial, national security, a good reputation and privacy. The main dispute between these two groups is about where the balance should be struck between these competing rights. Their different conclusions are also informed by divergent perceptions of the public. Interventionists tend to emphasize the susceptibility of vulnerable members of society to media influence, while libertarians tend to stress the critical independence of the public.

There is also another axis of contention. Some interventionists argue that the media should be prevented from violating the norms and moral values of society. This goes beyond the standard case for limited censorship, based on preventing serious harm from being done to others, and potentially constitutes a rationale for a broad measure of control directed against anything that is deemed offensive. Libertarians respond to this challenge in different ways. Some reject the argument outright: liberty, argued George Orwell, means letting people say things you do not want to hear. Others demur by saying that a communication has to be offensive to *reasonable* people. Others, still, negotiate by making a distinction between media that are ubiquitous and those that are less intrusive, and between media that reach a general audience and those that are seen only by adults. In general, they suggest, it is better to restrict access to a communication than to suppress it entirely.

Legal paternalism

During the 1980s and early 1990s, the tide generally flowed in favour of greater legal control of the media. The Video Recordings Act (1984) introduced a far-reaching system of censorship directed at 'video nasties'. The

Broadcasting Standards Council was established in 1988 (and subsumed into Ofcom in 2003) to provide a focus of public concern about sex, violence and standards of taste and decency in broadcasting. It was strengthened by being given the power to compel transmission of its indictments in 1990.

Broadcasters were required by the 1990 Broadcasting Act not to transmit programmes offensive to public feeling. However, an attempt by the British government to secure comparable regulation of broadcasting in Europe met with only limited success, due to the resistance of some of Britain's partners. The most significant moral injunction in the 1989 Television Without Frontiers Directive (incorporated into the Audiovisual Services Directive in 2007) is that directed against 'programmes which might seriously impair the ... development of minors'.

Conservative administrations also exerted strong pressure, both through private channels and through public flak, for broadcasters to censor themselves, most notably in relation to Northern Ireland. When this encountered some resistance, a gagging prohibition was imposed in 1988 on direct transmissions of speech from Sinn Fein and other 'terrorist' organizations. This was lifted in 1994, following the announcement of a ceasefire in Northern Ireland.

This growth of prohibition and moral regulation did not go far enough, in the view of some. Obscenity and indecency laws should be strengthened in order to outlaw widely available pornographic images of women and gratuitous media displays of violence. The rationale for this is not necessarily that violence shown on television leads in a stimulus–response fashion to imitative acts. The more sophisticated argument is that routine exposure to violence on television strengthens already existing dispositions towards violence, both in particular individuals and in the culture of society; and that pornography reinforces misogynous attitudes, and consequently encourages harmful actions against women. But if some of these arguments appear plausible, they are also difficult to verify empirically. There is still, in Cumberbatch and Howitt's phrase, 'a measure of uncertainty' about the consequences of media pornography and violence.[29]

The second argument for taking tougher action against pornogaphy is that it is offensive; it is experienced as oppressive; it demeans, with its constant suggestion of women's sexual availability; and it encourages scorn and contempt. The counter-arguments are that safeguards already exist against the most offensive forms of pornography; suppressing freedom of speech is objectionable; and over-zealous puritanism is also oppressive.

Calls for stronger controls against sexism are paralleled by demands for greater protection against racism. Legislation against incitement to racial hatred was introduced in 1965 in the wake of Labour's loss of the safe seat, Smethwick, with the help of the slogan 'If you want a nigger for a neighbour, vote Labour'. However, prosecutions are usually only successful if it can be shown that racist statements are likely to lead to actual violence or a breakdown of public order. A more narrowly defined offence of promoting 'religious hatred' (seemingly regarded as less offensive than racism) is contained in the Public Order Act (1986), making prosecution still more difficult. In 2006 the 'encouragement of terrorism' became a crime (though it has to be shown that publication is not only reckless but intended to encourage acts of terrorism).

An area where curbs are most often pressed is privacy. Until recently, the right to privacy was legally protected only indirectly through copyright, property and confidentiality law. The second Calcutt inquiry (1992) recommended the establishment of a statutory press complaints tribunal with the power to impose prior restraint (i.e. pre-publication censorship) against unwarranted press intrusions into privacy – a proposal rejected by both the Major government and the then Labour opposition. However, in 1998 the European Convention of Human Rights was passed into British law as the Human Rights Act. It contains a clause that 'everyone has the right to respect for his private and family life, his home and his correspondence',[30] balanced by the right to freedom of expression. This countervailing right was accentuated in an amendment to the Human Rights Act (framed in response to press pressure) which directs the courts to pay special attention to freedom of expression. A privacy right against media intrusion is now emerging in a weak form, through cumulative judicial judgement.

Legal libertarianism

Those who press for more censorship are answered by those who argue for less. Heading the libertarian agenda is a proposal that freedom of expression should be given special protection by being embodied in a written constitution. Free speech, it is argued, is under increasing attack and needs to be entrenched as a constitutional right. This would mean, for example, that the BBC could turn to the law courts for protection if it felt that its freedom was being curtailed improperly by government. Opponents argue that this reform would be alien to the legal and political tradition of this country. Its effect would be to force judges to make 'political' decisions, a task to which they are unsuited.

During the later 1990s and 2000s, the tide flowed in the direction of cautious legal libertarianism, although there were also counter-currents. A major objective of the libertarian movement – a Freedom of Information Act – was passed in 2000, and became fully operational in 2005. It establishes the right to any official information unless the government or public authority can show that disclosure would cause real harm to essential interests such as defence, security, law enforcement or privacy. The continuing concern of campaigners is that exclusions should not be unduly restrictive in practice. They are also pressing for more disclosure in the private sector, if the information is of public interest.

A second target was defamation law, an area where there has been a significant shift. The Albert Reynolds vs *Sunday Times* case (in which the former Irish prime minister sued the paper over a critical article published in 1994) established a legal precedent for qualified press privilege. This became a major issue of legal contention, culminating in a key judgement of the Law Lords in 2006 that a newspaper can print untrue and defamatory information if it can show that it was in the public interest to do so and that it was the product of responsible journalism. The key issue of legal wrangling will now be what constitutes 'responsible' defamation.

A third campaign – reform of 'whistleblower' law – resulted in a pyrrhic victory in 1989 when the 1911 Official Secrets Act was repealed. A discredited law, passed during a national panic about 'Hun spies', was superseded by more tightly defined, enforceable prohibitions contained in the 1989 Official Secrets Act. These rendered Sarah Tisdall (a junior civil servant jailed in 1984 for passing information to the *Guardian* about the imminent arrival of the first cruise missile in Britain) liable to successful prosecution even though her real crime, according to her champions, had been to politically embarrass the government rather than to endanger national security. Libertarian critics argue that the relevant section of 1989 Official Secrets Act should be replaced with a narrower measure applying only where disclosure would cause serious damage to defence, security, international relations, law enforcement or safety, and, crucially, that it should contain a full public interest defence for breaches of official secrets. The counter-argument to this is that public servants should be deterred from breaching their position of trust, and the weakening of official confidentiality will hamper the war against terrorism.

In the general battle over media law, legal libertarians have the best tunes. They have developed an eloquent rhetoric in which media liberty is equated with the freedom of society. On one side, we are told, there is the cause of freedom and the people; on the other, state repression supported by secrecy and censorship. But what is generally concealed in this rhetorical presentation is that media freedom is usually defined in practice as the free-speech rights of media property owners and those they appoint. What is being argued for, in reality, is an enlargement of their rights at the expense of the rights of others, on the grounds that this is in the general interest.

This case is often powerful because the cause of freedom is compelling. But the limitations of this case are also highlighted when the issue at stake is *whose* free speech should be upheld. In the late 1970s and early 1980s, Fleet Street workers took industrial action on several occasions to secure the right of reply for targets of press attacks. From 1981 onward, a number of MPs proposed private members' bills, with cross-party support, that would give to victims of press distortion or factual misrepresentation a legal right of reply, broadly in line with right-of-reply laws that exist in a number of northern European countries. Both of these initiatives sought to enlarge rather than restrict freedom of communication through the press. In both cases, they were strongly resisted as an attack on the free-speech rights of press controllers to determine what goes into their newspapers. This underlined the sometimes exclusive nature of the freedom which uncritical libertarians present as universal.

A quizzical response also seems appropriate in the wake of repudiated attempts to strengthen the rights of media staff. These defined implicitly the freedom *of* the media as including freedom *within* the media. Thus, one proposal was for a freedom of conscience clause to be written into journalists' contracts of employment so that they would have legal protection to resist doing dishonourable things. This was rejected by the Newspaper Publishers Association (representing press owners). The freedom of the press remains the freedom of the people who own and control it, however it is presented.

Map of media politics

Policy discussion about media organization is dominated by the debate between advocates of the free market and public service. One side calls for the media to be free of regulation other than the law of the land. The other side sings the praises of the British broadcasting system and declares it to be the best in the world. Between these two polarities of market radicalism and public service complacency are a number of intermediate positions that we have explored. They tend to be allied, however, with either a market or a public service tradition.

There is also another discussion concerned specifically with media law. Here, the main split is between interventionists who want society to be protected from irresponsible media, and libertarians who emphasize the need to uphold freedom of expression. This second division cuts across the first. This produces four clearly identifiable groups occupying different quadrants. They can best be presented in ideal-typical form.

The authoritarian right generally want the media to enjoy market freedom but to be subject to strong legal controls. They are responding to what they see as a tension between the ideal of market freedom and evidence that market competition can lead to an increasing volume of media violence and pornography, encourage individualistic values that weaken the moral order and give rise to political licence that undermines legitimate authority. They seek to resolve this tension by simultaneously embracing market freedom while policing its 'ill effects' through a framework of censorious law.

Those on the libertarian-inclined left reverse this logic. They favour limited legal censorship, but active economic intervention. They, too, are responding to what they perceive to be a dilemma: the need to overcome market censorship (requiring state action) and a desire to limit state involvement in the media. Their solution is to set overall objectives for state-owned or regulated broadcasters and to subsidize minority media, while limiting the scope of legal proscription.

The libertarian right – represented by some in the Conservative Party – follow a different route. They are committed to minimizing the role of the state in all aspects of the media. They tend to subscribe to the classic republican view that the role of the state should be confined to that of 'night watchman'. They are thus consistent in arguing against 'bureaucratic' regulation of the media, economic intervention and heavy-handed legal censorship. They just want the market to prevail, and the state to take a back seat.

In the final quadrant, the authoritarian left – once well represented in radical municipal politics – favour a strong state presence in all aspects of life. They support public ownership and regulation of broadcasting; redistributive arts subsidies; a strong legal stand against pornography and racial hatred; and expect the state to actively foster greater equality of respect and economic rewards. They are 'joined-up' interventionists.

In short, the simple dichotomy of left and right no longer describes adequately the politics of the media. To add to this complexity, the sphere of media politics now operates at three levels: the nation-state (still the most important), the European Union, and the global politics of international trade regulation. Adding still further to this complexity is the advent of digitization. This will render a régime of state regulation in broadcasting and of self-regulation in the press increasingly contentious, since both media are converging towards each other.[31]

We are thus going through a period of transition in which media politics is being reconfigured, media regulation is being subdivided between jurisdictions and communications technology is changing fast. Perhaps it is possible to hope that out of this flux will emerge a new communications order: media that have power *with* responsibility to the public.

Notes

1. Samuel Brittan, 'The case for the consumer market', in C. Veljanovski (ed.), *Freedom in Broadcasting* (London, Institute of Economic Affairs, 1989), p. 35.
2. *Regulating Communications* (London, Stationery Office, 1998), p. 16.
3. *A New Future for Communications* (London, Stationery Office, 2000), p. 95.
4. Adam Smith Institute, *Omega Report: Communications Policy* (London, Adam Smith Institute, 1984); Adam Smith Institute, *Funding the BBC* (London, Adam Smith Institute, 1985).
5. Rupert Murdoch, *Freedom in Broadcasting* (London, News International, 1989), p. 9.
6. This Directive also legalized for the first time product placement promotion (that is, advertising and branded messages embedded in television programmes that are not identified and disclosed to the viewer). This controversial innovation has a national opt-out, and is subject to specified limitations.
7. Alison J. Harcourt, 'Institution-driven competition: the regulation of cross-border broadcasting in the EU', *Journal of Public Policy*, 27 (3), 2007, pp. 293–317.
8. Peter Humphreys, 'The EU, communications liberalization and the future of public service broadcasting', in Katharine Sarikakis (ed.), *Media and Cultural Policy in the European Union* (Amsterdam: Rodopi, 2007).
9. Colin Leys, *Market-Driven Politics* (London, Verso, 2001), p. 148.

10. Manuel Puppis, 'National media regulation in the era of free trade: the role of global media governance', *European Journal of Communication*, 23 (4), 2008, pp. 405–24.

11. *Report of the Committee on Financing the BBC* (London, HMSO, 1986).

12. *Media Ownership* (London, HMSO, 1995), p. 3.

13. For a useful exposition of behavioural regulation arguments, see David Goldberg, Tony Prosser and Stefaan Verhulst, *Regulating the Changing Media* (Oxford, Clarendon Press, 1998).

14. Andrew Graham and Gavyn Davies, *Broadcasting, Society and Policy in the Multimedia Age* (Luton, University of Luton Press, 1997), p. 1.

15. *A New Future for Communications* (London, Stationery Office, 2000), p. 50.

16. P. Murschetz, 'State support for the daily press in Europe: a critical appraisal', *European Journal of Communication*, 13 (3), 1998; E. Skogerbo, 'The press subsidy system in Norway', *European Journal of Communication*, 12 (1), 1997.

17. Jan Wieten, Graham Murdock and Peter Dahlgren (eds), *Television Across Europe* (London, Sage, 2000).

18. *Pluralism and Media Concentration in the Internal Market: Commission Green Paper* (Brussels, Commission of the European Communities Green Paper, 1992); *Follow-Up to the Consultative Process Relating to the Green Paper on 'Pluralism and Media Concentration in the Internal Market'* (Brussels, Commission of the European Communities, 1994); cf. *Strategy Options to Strengthen the European Programme Industry in the Context of the Audiovisual Policy of the European Union* (Brussels, European Commission Green Paper, 1994).

19. Richard Collins, *Satellite Television in Western Europe* (London, Libbey, 1992).

20. Toby Miller, Nitin Govil, John McMurria, Richard Maxwell and Ting Wang, *Global Hollywood 2* (London, British Film Institute, 2004).

21. David Morley, *Home Territories* (London, Routledge, 2000).

22. Cited in Des Freedman, *The Politics of Media Policy* (Cambridge, Polity, 2008), p. 205.

23. See Chapter 16 in this volume.

24. *Second Public Service Broadcasting Review*, Phase 1 and 2 (London, Office of Communications, 2008).

25. Raymond Williams, *Communications* (London, Chatto & Windus, rev. edn, 1966); John Keane, *Media and Democracy* (Cambridge, Polity Press, 1991). For an alternative version of this tradition, not summarized here, see James Curran, *Media and Power* (London, Routledge, 2002), Chapter 8.

26. K. Hafez, *The Myth of Media Globalization* (Cambridge, Polity, 2007).

27. J. Curran, S. Iyengar, A. Lund and I. Salovaara-Moring, 'Media reporting, public knowledge and democracy: a comparative study', *European Journal of Communication*, 24 (1), 2009, pp. 5–25; Hafez, *The Myth of Media Globalization*.

28. J. Curran and T. Witschge, 'Liberal dreams and the internet', in N. Fenton (ed.), *New Media, Old News* (London, Sage, 2009).

29. Guy Cumberbatch and Denis Howitt, *A Measure of Uncertainty* (London, Libbey, 1989); cf. Brian McNair, *Mediated Sex* (London, Arnold, 1996).

30. Cited in Eric Barendt and Lesley Hitchens, *Media Law: Cases and Materials* (Harlow, Longman, 2000), p. 248.

31. Jacob Rowbottom, 'Media freedom and political debate in the digital era', *Modern Law Review*, 69 (4), 2006, pp. 489–513.

Bibliography

Public reports and papers

Broadcasting

Broadcasting Committee: Report (Sykes Report, 1923) [Cmd 1951].
Report of the Broadcasting Committee (Crawford Report, 1926) [Cmd 2599].
Report of the Television Committee (Selsdon Report, 1935) [Cmd 3703].
Report of the Broadcasting Committee (Ullswater Report, 1936) [Cmd 5091].
Report of the Television Committee (Hankey Report, 1944) (Privy Council Office).
Broadcasting Policy (1946) [Cmd 6852].
Report of the Broadcasting Committee (Beveridge Report, 1951) [Cmd 8116].
Report of the Broadcasting Committee 1949 (1951/2) [Cmd 8117].
Broadcasting, Memorandum on the Report of the Broadcasting Committee (1951) [Cmd 8291].
Broadcasting, Memorandum on the Report of the Broadcasting Committee, 1949 (1952) [Cmd 8550].
The Television Act 1954, 2 & 3 Eliz. II, c. 55.
Report of the Committee on Broadcasting (Pilkington Report, 1962) [Cmnd 1753].
The Television Act 1964, 12 & 13 Eliz. II, c. 21.
The University of the Air (1966) [Cmnd 2992].
An Alternative Service of Radio Broadcasting (1971) [Cmnd 4636].
Sound Broadcasting Act 1972, 19 & 20 Eliz. II, c. 31.
Session 1971–2 Independent Broadcasting Authority, Sub-Committee B, House of Commons Paper 465 (1972).
Observations on the Second Report of the Select Committee of the Nationalized Industries (1973) [Cmnd 5244].
Report of the Committee on the Future of Broadcasting (Annan Report, 1977) [Cmnd 6753].
Broadcasting without Frontiers, EEC paper, No. 9 (1984).
Report of the Committee on Financing the BBC (Peacock Report, 1986) [Cmnd 9824].
Subscription Television: A Study for the Home Office (London, HMSO, 1987).
Broadcasting in the '90s: Competition, Choice and Quality (1987) [Cm 517].
The Future of Broadcasting, Home Affairs Committee (1988).
Broadcasting Bill, House of Commons (1989).
The Future of Broadcasting, House of Commons Home Affairs Committee 1987–88 (London, HMSO, 1988).
Broadcasting Act 1990 (London, HMSO, 1990).
The Future of the BBC (Department of National Heritage, London, HMSO, 1992) [Cm 2098].
Broadcasting Act 1996 (London, HMSO, 1996).

Independent Television Commission Annual Report (London, ITC, 2001).

European Audiovisual Observatory Yearbook 2002 (Strasbourg, Council of Europe, 2002), Vol. 2.

Television Audience Share Figures (London, Independent Television Commission, 2002).

Second Public Service Broadcasting Review, Phase 1 and 2 (London, Office of Communications, 2008).

The press

Annual Report of the Press Council (London, Press Council, 1985).

Competition Commission, *Johnson Press plc and Trinity Mirror plc: A Report into the Proposed Merger* (London, Stationery Office, 2002) [Cm 5495].

Department for Culture, Media and Sport (DCMS), *Consultation on Media Ownership Rules* (London, DCMS, 2001).

Monopolies Commission (1965–66), *The Times Newspaper and Sunday Times* (London, HMSO, 1966).

Monopolies Commission (1967–68), *Thomson Newspapers and Crusha and Son Ltd*, House of Commons Paper 66 (London, HMSO, 1968).

Monopolies Commission (1969–70), *George Outram and Company Ltd and Hamilton Advertiser Ltd and Baird and Hamilton Ltd*, House of Commons Paper 76 (London, HMSO, 1970).

Monopolies Commission (1971–72), *The Berrows Organisation Ltd and the County Express Group*, House of Commons Paper 224 (London, HMSO, 1972).

Monopolies Commission (1972–73), *Westminster Press Ltd and Kentish Times Ltd, Gravesend and Dartford Reporter Ltd and F. J. Parsons Ltd, Subsidiaries of Morgan-Grampian Ltd*, House of Commons Paper 460 (London, HMSO, 1973).

Monopolies Commission (1973–74), *Courier Printing and Publishing Company Ltd and Associated Newspapers Group Ltd*, House of Commons Paper 108 (London, HMSO, 1974).

Monopolies Commission (1974–75), *G. and A. N. Scott Ltd and the Guardian and Manchester Evening News Ltd*, House of Commons Paper 349 (London, HMSO, 1975).

Monopolies and Mergers Commission, *Wholesaling of Newspapers and Periodicals* (London, HMSO, 1978).

Monopolies and Mergers Commission, *The Observer and George Outram* (London, HMSO, 1981).

Monopolies and Mergers Commission, *The Supply of National Newspapers* (London, HMSO, 1993).

Monopolies and Mergers Commission, *Daily Mail and General Trust Plc. and T. Bailey Forman Limited* (London, HMSO, 1994).

Monopolies and Mergers Commission, *Northcliffe Newspapers and Aberdeen Journals Ltd* (London, HMSO, 1996).

National Board for Prices and Incomes, *Wages, Costs and Prices in the Printing Industry* (1965) [Cmnd 2750].

National Board for Prices and Incomes, *Costs and Revenue of National Daily Newspapers* (1967) [Cmnd 3435].

National Board for Prices and Incomes, *Journalists' Pay* (1969) [Cmnd 4077].

National Board for Prices and Incomes, *Costs and Revenue of National Newspapers* (1970) [Cmnd 4277].

Privacy and Media Intrusion (National Heritage Committee, House of Commons, 1992–93, HMSO, 1993).

Privacy and Media Intrusion: The Government's Response (London, HMSO, 1995).

Report of the Committee on Contempt of Court (1975) [Cmnd 5794].

Report of the Committee on Data Protection (Lindop Committee, 1978) [Cmnd 7341].

Report of the Committee on Defamation (Faulks Committee, 1975) [Cmnd 5571].

Report of the Committee on the Official Secrets Act (1972) [Cmnd 7140].

Report of the Committee on Privacy and Related Matters (Calcutt Committee, 1990) [Cm 1102].

Report of a Court of Inquiry into the Problems Caused by the Introduction of Web-offset Machines (1967) [Cmnd 3184].

Review of Press Self-Regulation (1993) [Cm 2135].

Royal Commission on the Press 1947–9 Report (1949) [Cmnd 7700].

Royal Commission on the Press 1961–2 Report (1962) [Cmnd 1811].

Royal Commission on the Press Interim Report (1976) [Cmnd 6553].

Royal Commission on the Press 1974–7 Final Report (1977) [Cmnd 6810].

Royal Commission on the Press Final Report Appendices (1977) [Cmnd 6810–11–6].

Select Committee of the House of Commons on Newspaper Stamps, *Parliamentary Papers*, xvii (1851).

Film

Cinematograph Films Act (1927) [Cmnd 2053].

Report of the Committee appointed by the Board of Trade (Moyne Report, 1936) [Cmnd 2053].

Report on Tendencies to Monopoly in the Cinematograph Film Industry (Palache Report, 1944) [Cmnd 4059].

Report of the Working Party on Film Production Costs (Gater Report, 1949) [Cmnd 7837].

Report of the Committee on the Distribution and Exhibition of Cinematograph Films (Plant Report, 1949) [Cmnd 7837].

Cinematograph Films Council, Distribution and Exhibition of Cinematograph Films (London, HMSO, Board of Trade, 1950).

Cinematograph Films Bill 1960, 8 & 9 Eliz. II.

The Films Act, House of Commons Paper 206 (1960).

Board of Trade Review of Films Legislation (1968) [Cmnd 3584].

The Prime Minister's Working Party on the Future of the Film Industry (Wilson Report, 1976) [Cmnd 6372].

Report of the Committee on Film Finance (1985) [Cmnd 7610].

Monopolies and Mergers Commission, *Report on the Supply of Films for Exhibition* (London, HMSO, 1994).

The British Film Industry (National Heritage Select Committee, House of Commons, 1995) (London, HMSO, 1995).

Media and information

A New Future for Communications (London, Stationery Office, 2000) [Cm 5010].

Commission of the European Communities (1994) *The EU and the Globalisation of Technology* (Forecasting in Science and Technology Report) (EUR 15150, Brussels).

Commission of the European Communities (1996) *Culture, Homes and the use of Information Technology* (EC EUR 174011, Brussels).

Consumers' Use of the Internet, Oftel Residential Survey, May (Office of Telecommunications, London, 2002).

Europe and the Global Information Society (Bangemann Report) (Brussels, European Council, 1994).

Follow-up to the Consultative Process Relating to the Green Paper on 'Pluralism and Media Concentration in the Internal Market' (Brussels, Commission of the European Communities, 1994).

Globalization of the Mass Media (Washington, United States Department of Commerce, 1993).

Liberalising Trade in Services: A New Consultation on the World Trade Organisation GATS Negotiations (London, Department of Trade and Industry, 2002).

Media Ownership: The Government's Proposals (Department of National Heritage, London, HMSO, 1995).

New News, Future News (London, Office of Communications, 2007).

Pluralism and Media Concentration in the Internal Market (Brussels, Commission of the European Communities Green Paper, 1992).

Regulating Communications: Approaching Convergence in the Information Age (London, Stationery Office, 1998) [Cm 4022].

Report by the Think-Tank on the Audiovisual Policy in the European Union (Vasconcelos Report) (Luxembourg, Commission of the European Communities, 1994).

Strategy Options to Strengthen the European Programme Industry in the Context of the Audiovisual Policy of the European Union (Brussels, European Commission Green Paper, 1994).

Miscellaneous public reports referred to in the book

Parliamentary Debates (1918–60; 1940–43) (London, Hansard).

Machinery of Government Report (1918) [Cmnd 9230].

Board of Education, *Inspectors' Report* (1932) [Cmnd 4068].

Board of Education Consultative Committee on Secondary Education (Spens Report, 1938), 10/119.

Report of the Department Committee on Curriculum and Examinations in Secondary Schools (Norwood Report, 1943).

The Nation's Schools: Their Plans and Purposes, Ministry of Education Pamphlet 1 (London, HMSO, 1945).

Royal Commission on Local Government (1969) (Redcliffe Maud Report), Research Paper 9, *Community Attitudes Survey* [Cmnd 3409].

Civil Service Department, *Computers in Central Government: The Year Ahead* (London, HMSO, 1971).

Report of the Committee on Privacy (1972) [Cmnd 5012].

Royal Commission on the Distribution of Income and Wealth, Report 4 (1976) [Cmnd 6626].

Report of the Committee on Standards in Public Life (1996) (Nolan Report) [Cmnd 1028].

Family Expenditure Survey (1998–2001) *Office of National Statistics*, www.statistics.gov.uk.

Expenditure and Food Survey (2001).

Office of National Statistics, www.statistics.gov.uk *Social Trends 32* (London, Stationery Office, 2002).

National Statistics Omnibus Survey, April 2002, www.statistics.gov.uk

The press

General historical perspectives

R.D. Altick, *The English Common Reader* (Chicago, Ill., University of Chicago Press, 1957; London, Phoenix, 1963).

A. Andrews, *The History of British Journalism*, 2 vols (London, Richard Bentley, 1859).

G. Boyce, 'The fourth estate: the reappraisal of a concept', in G. Boyce, J. Curran and P. Wingate (eds), *Newspaper History* (London, Constable, 1978).

P. Brendon, *The Life and Death of the Press Barons* (London, Secker & Warburg, 1982).

C. J. Bundock, *The National Union of Journalists: A Jubilee History, 1907–1957* (London, Oxford University Press, 1957).

J. Chalaby, *The Invention of Journalism* (London, Macmillan, 1998).

D. Chaney, *Processes of Mass Communication* (London, Macmillan, 1972).

M. Conboy, *The Press and Popular Culture* (London, Sage, 2002).

G. A. Cranfield, *The Press and Society* (Harlow, Longman, 1978).

J. Curran, 'Capitalism and control of the press 1800–1975', in J. Curran, M. Gurevitch and J. Woollacott (eds), *Mass Communication and Society* (London, Edward Arnold/Open University, 1977).

——'The press as an agency of social control: an historical perspective', in G. Boyce, J. Curran and P. Wingate (eds), *Newspaper History* (London, Constable, 1978).

——'Communications, power and social order', in T. Bennett, J. Curran, M. Gurevitch and J. Woollacott (eds), *Culture, Media and Society* (London, Methuen, 1981).

K. Drotner, *English Children and their Magazines, 1751–1945* (New Haven, Yale University Press, 1989).

M. Engel, *Tickle the Public* (London, Gollancz, 1996).

H. R. Fox Bourne, *English Newspapers* (London, Chatto & Windus, 1887; London, Russell & Russell, 1966).

J. Grant, *The Newspaper Press*, 3 vols (London, Tinsley Brothers, 1871–72).

D. Griffiths (ed.), *The Encyclopedia of the British Press, 1422–1992* (London, Macmillan, 1992).

M. Harris and A. Lee (eds), *The Press in English Society from the Seventeenth to Nineteenth Centuries* (London and Toronto, Associated University Presses, 1986).

R. Harrison, G. Woolven and R. Duncan, *The Warwick Guide to British Labour Periodicals 1790–1970* (Brighton, Harvester Press, 1977).

S. Harrison, *Poor Men's Guardians: A Record of the Struggles for a Democratic Newspaper Press 1763–1973* (London, Lawrence & Wishart, 1974).

P. Hennessy, *Whitehall* (London, HarperCollins, 1989).

——*Never Again* (London, HarperCollins, 1992).

H. Herd, *The March of Journalism* (London, Allen & Unwin, 1952).

F. Knight Hunt, *The Fourth Estate* (London, David Bogue, 1850).

P. Knightley, *The First Casualty: The War Correspondent as Hero, Propagandist and Myth Maker from the Crimea to Vietnam* (London, Deutsch, 1975).

S. Koss, *The Rise and Fall of the Political Press in Britain*, vols 1–2 (London, Hamish Hamilton, 1981 and 1984).

A. Marshall, *Changing the Word: The Printing Industry in Transition* (London, Comedia, 1983).

M. Milne, *Newspapers of Northumberland and Durham* (Newcastle, Frank Graham, 1972).

S. Morison, *The English Newspaper* (Cambridge, Cambridge University Press, 1932).

A. E. Musson, *The Typographical Association: Origins and History up to 1949* (London, Oxford University Press, 1954).

C. Pebody, *English Journalism* (London, Cassell, Petter & Galpin, 1882).

D. Read, *The Power of News: The History of Reuters* (Oxford, Oxford University Press, 1992).

G. Scott, *Reporters Anonymous: The Story of the Press Association* (London, Hutchinson, 1968).

F. S. Siebert, T. Peterson and W. Schramm, *Four Theories of the Press* (Urbana, Ill., University of Illinois Press, 1956; New York, Books for Libraries Press, 1973).

A. Smith, *The Newspaper: An International History* (London, Thames & Hudson, 1979).

——'Technology and control: the interactive dimensions of journalism', in J. Curran, M. Gurevitch and J. Woollacott (eds), *Mass Communication and Society* (London, Edward Arnold/Open University Press, 1977).

G. Storey, *Reuter's Century 1851–1951* (London, Parrish, 1951).

K. von Stutterheim, *The Press in England* (London, Allen & Unwin, 1934).

H. A. Taylor, *The British Press* (London, Arthur Barker, 1961).

J. Tunstall, 'Editorial sovereignty in the British press: its past and present', in *Studies on the Press*, Royal Commission on the Press 1974–77, Working Paper 3 (London, HMSO, 1977).

M. Tusan, *Women Making News* (Urbana, University of Illinois Press, 2005).

A. P. Wadsworth, 'Newspaper circulations 1800–1954', *Transactions of the Manchester Statistical Society*, iv (1955).

C. White, *Women's Magazines, 1693–1968* (London, Michael Joseph, 1970).

F. Williams, *Dangerous Estate* (Harlow, Longman Green, 1959; London, Arrow, 1959).

R. Williams, *The Long Revolution* (London, Chatto & Windus, 1961).

——'The press and popular culture: an historical perspective', in G. Boyce, J. Curran and P. Wingate (eds), *Newspaper History* (London, Constable, 1978).

C. Wilson, *First with the News: The History of W. H. Smith 1792–1972* (London, Cape, 1985).

Newspaper histories

Anon, *The History of the Times*, vols 1–5 (1935–58).

D. Ayerst, *The Guardian: Biography of a Newspaper* (London, Collins, 1971).

Lord Burnham, *Peterborough Court: Story of the Daily Telegraph* (London, Cassell, 1955).

P. Chippendale and C. Horrie, *Disaster! The Rise and Fall of the News on Sunday* (London, Sphere, 1988).

——*Stick it Up Your Punter! The Rise and Fall of the Sun* (London, Heinemann, 1990).

A. Christiansen, *Headlines All My Life* (London, Heinemann, 1961).

P. Cockburn, *The Years of the Week* (Harmondsworth, Penguin, 1971).

H. Cudlipp, *Publish and be Damned* (London, Andrew Dakers, 1953).

M. Edelman, *The Mirror – A Political History* (London, Hamish Hamilton, 1966).

W. Fienburgh, *25 Momentous Years: A 25th Anniversary in the History of the Daily Herald* (London, Odhams Press, 1955).

G. Fraser and K. Peters, *The Northern Lights* (London, Hamish Hamilton, 1978).

M. A. Gibb and F. Beckwith, *The Yorkshire Post: Two Centuries* (Leeds, Yorkshire Conservative Newspaper Co, 1954).

S. Glover, *Paper Dreams* (Harmondsworth, Penguin, 1994).

B. Hagerty, *Read all About it!* (Lydney, First Stone, 2003).

P. M. Handover, *History of the London Gazette, 1665–1965* (London, HMSO, 1965).

D. Hart-Davis, *The House the Berrys Built* (London, Coronet, 1991).

A. Hetherington, *Guardian Years* (London, Chatto & Windus, 1981).

D. Hill, *Tribune 40* (London, Quartet, 1977).

W. Hindle, *The Morning Post, 1772–1937* (London, Routledge & Kegan Paul, 1937).

H. Hobson, P. Knightley and L. Russell, *The Pearl of Days: An Intimate Memoir of the Sunday Times, 1822–1972* (London, Hamish Hamilton, 1972).

D. Kynaston, *The Financial Times* (London, Viking, 1988).

L. Lamb, *Sunrise* (London, Macmillan, 1989).

R. J. Lucas, *Lord Glenesk and the Morning Post* (London, Alston Rivers, 1910).

I. McDonald, *History of the Times 1939–66*, Vol. 5 (London, Times Books, 1984).

R. McKay and B. Barr, *The Story of the Scottish Daily News* (Edinburgh, Canongate, 1976).

H. Richards, *The Bloody Circus: The Daily Herald and the Left* (London, Pluto, 1997).

J. W. Robertson Scott, *The Story of the Pall Mall Gazette* (London, Oxford University Press, 1950).

H. R. G. Whates, *The Birmingham Post, 1857–1957* (Birmingham Post and Mail, 1957).

O. Woods and J. Bishop, *The Story of The Times* (London, Michael Joseph, 1983).

Nineteenth-century press history

W. E. Adams, *Memoirs of a Social Atom*, 2 vols (London, Hutchinson, 1903).

Anon, *Guide to Advertisers* (London, 1851).

A. Aspinall, 'Statistical accounts of London newspapers 1800–836', *English Historical Review*, lxv (1950).

——*Politics and the Press, 1780–1850* (London, Home & Van Thal, 1949; Brighton, Harvester Press, 1973).

I. Asquith, 'Advertising and the press in the late eighteenth and early nineteenth centuries: James Perry and the *Morning Chronicle*, 1790–1821', *Historical Journal*, xvii (1975).

P. Bailey, *Leisure and Class in Victorian England* (London, Routledge & Kegan Paul, 1978).

V. Berridge, 'Popular Sunday papers and mid-Victorian society', in G. Boyce, J. Curran and P. Wingate (eds), *Newspaper History* (London, Constable, 1978).

T. Boyle, *Black Swine in the Sewers of Hampstead* (London, Hodder & Stoughton, 1989).

L. Brake, A. Jones and L. Madden (eds), *Investigating Victorian Journalism* (London, Macmillan, 1990).

L. Brown, *Victorian News and Newspapers* (Oxford, Clarendon, 1985).

T. Catling, *My Life's Pilgrimage* (London, John Murray, 1911).

P. Catterall, C. Seymour-Ure and A. Smith (eds), *Northcliffe's Legacy* (Basingstoke, Macmillan, 2000).

I. R. Christie, 'British newspapers in the late Georgian age', in *Myth and Reality in Late 18th Century British Politics* (London, Macmillan, 1970).

C. D. Collet, *History of the Taxes on Knowledge* (London, T. Fisher Unwin, 1899).

S. Coltham, 'The *Bee-Hive* newspaper: its origins and early struggle', in A. Briggs and J. Saville (eds), *Essays in Labour History* (London, Macmillan, 1960).

——'The British working-class press in 1867', *Bulletin for the Society for the Study of Labour History* (Autumn 1967).

F. Dilnot, *Adventures of a Newspaper Man* (London, Smith, Elder, 1913).

J. A. Epstein, 'Feargus O'Connor and the Northern Star', *International Review of Social History*, xxi (1976).

T. H. S. Escott, *Masters of English Journalism* (London, T. Fisher Unwin, 1911).

K. Flint, *The Woman Reader 1836–1914* (Oxford, Clarendon Press, 1993).

J. Foster, *Class Struggle and the Industrial Revolution: Early Industrial Capitalism in Three English Towns* (London, Weidenfeld & Nicolson, 1974).

M. D. George, *English Political Caricature, 1792–1832* (London, Oxford University Press, 1959).

E. Glasgow, 'The establishment of the *Northern Star* newspaper', *History*, xxxix (1954).

B. Harrison, 'A world of which we had no conception: liberalism and the temperance press, 1830–72', *Victorian Studies*, xiii (December 1969).

J. Hatton, *Journalistic London* (London, Sampson Low, 1882).

A. F. Havighurst, *Radical Journalist: H. W. Massingham* (Cambridge, Cambridge University Press, 1974).

P. Hollis, *The Pauper Press* (London, Oxford University Press, 1970).

D. Hopkin, 'The socialist press in Britain 1890–1910', in G. Boyce, J. Curran and P. Wingate (eds), *Newspaper History* (London, Constable, 1978).

D. Hudson, *Thomas Barnes of The Times* (Cambridge, Cambridge University Press, 1943).

L. James (ed.), *Print and the People, 1819–1851* (London, Allen Lane, 1976).

E. E. Kellett, 'The press', in G. M. Young (ed.), *Early Victorian England* (London, Oxford University Press, 1934).

C. Kent, 'Higher journalism and the mid-Victorian clerisy', *Victorian Studies*, xiii (December 1969).

S. Koss, *Fleet Street Radical: A. G. Gardiner and the Daily News* (London, Allen Lane, 1973).

A. J. Lee, 'The management of a Victorian local newspaper: the *Manchester City News*, 1864–1900', *Business History*, xv (1973).

——'The radical press', in A. Morris (ed.), *Edwardian Radicalism, 1900–1914* (London, Routledge & Kegan Paul, 1974).

——*The Origins of the Popular Press, 1855–1914* (London, Croom Helm, 1976).

J. R. McCulloch, *Dictionary of Commerce and Commercial Navigation* (London, Longman, Brown & Green, 1854).

Mitchell's Newspaper Press Directory (Mitchell).

P. Mountjoy, 'The working-class press and working-class conservatism', in G. Boyce, J. Curran and P. Wingate (eds), *Newspaper History* (London, Constable, 1978).

A. E. Musson, 'Newspaper printing in the Industrial Revolution', *Economic History Review*, x, 2nd series (1957–58).

V. Neuberg, 'The literature of the streets', in H. J. Dyos and M. Wolff (eds), *The Victorian City* (London, Routledge & Kegan Paul, 1973).

T. Nevett, 'Advertising and editorial integrity in the nineteenth century', in M. Harris and A. Lee, *The Press in English Society from the Seventeenth to Nineteenth Centuries* (London and Toronto, Associated University Presses, 1986).

L. O'Boyle, 'The image of the journalist in England, France and Germany, 1815–48', *Comparative Studies in Society and History*, x (1968).

P. O'Malley, 'Capital accumulation and press freedom, 1800–850', *Media, Culture and Society*, 3, 1 (1981).

H. J. Perkin, 'The origins of the popular press', *History Today*, vii (1957).

R. Pound and G. Harmsworth, *Northcliffe* (London, Cassell, 1959).

R. Price, *An Imperial War and the British Working Class: Working-class Attitudes and Reactions to the Boer War 1899–1902* (London, Routledge & Kegan Paul, 1972).

D. Read, *Press and People 1790–1850* (London, Edward Arnold, 1961).

J. Roach, 'Education and public opinion', in C. Crawley (ed.), *War and Peace in an Age of Upheaval* (Cambridge, Cambridge University Press, 1965).

F. G. Salmon, 'What the working class read', *Nineteenth Century*, cxiii (1886).

M. Sanderson, 'Literacy and social mobility in the Industrial Revolution', *Past and Present*, 5, 6 (1972).

A. R. Schoyen, *The Chartist Challenge: A Portrait of George Julian Harney* (London, Heinemann, 1956).

J. Shattock and M. Wolff (eds), *The Victorian Periodical Press: Samplings and Soundings* (Leicester, University of Leicester Press, 1982).

H. Simonis, *The Street of Ink* (London, Cassell, 1917).

J. A. Spender, *Life, Journalism and Politics*, 2 vols (London, Cassell, 1927).

J. F. Stephen, 'Journalism', *Cornhill Magazine*, 6 (1862).

L. Stone, 'Literacy and education in England 1640–1900', *Past and Present*, 42 (1969).

J. D. Symon, *The Press and its Story* (London, Seeley Service, 1914).

T. Tholfsen, *Working-Class Radicalism in Mid-Victorian Britain* (London, Croom Helm, 1976).

D. Thompson, *The Chartists* (London, Maurice Temple Smith, 1984).

E. P. Thompson, *The Making of the English Working Class* (London, Gollancz, 1963).

R. K. Webb, *The British Working-Class Reader, 1790–1848* (London, Allen & Unwin, 1955).

W. H. Wickwar, *The Struggle for the Freedom of the Press, 1819–1832* (London, Allen & Unwin, 1928).

J. Wiener (ed.), *Millions for the Millions* (New York, Greenwood, 1992).
J. H. Wiener, *The War of the Unstamped* (New York, Cornell University Press, 1969).

Twentieth-century press history

J. R. Adams, *Media Planning* (London, Business Books, 1971).
A. Angell, *The Press and the Organisation of Society* (London, Labour Publishing Co, 1922).
D. Ayerst, *Garvin of the Observer* (London, Croom Helm, 1985).
Lord Beaverbrook, *Men and Power* (London, Hutchinson, 1956).
W. Belson, *The British Press* (London, London Press Exchange, 1959).
A. Bingham, *Gender, Modernity and the Popular Press in Inter-war Britain* (Oxford, Clarendon, 2004).
T. Bower, *Maxwell: The Outsider* (London, Aurum, 1989).
O. Boyd-Barrett, C. Seymour-Ure and J. Tunstall, *Studies on the Press*, Royal Commission on the Press, Working Paper 3 (London, HMSO, 1977).
R. Braddon, *Roy Thomson* (London, Fontana, 1968).
P. Brendon, *Eminent Edwardians* (London, Secker & Warburg, 1979).
T. B. Browne, *Advertisers' ABC* (London, Browne, 1927).
A. Calder, *The People's War* (London, Panther, 1971).
S. Chibnall, *Law-and-Order News* (London, Tavistock, 1977).
C. Chisholm, *Marketing and Merchandising* (London, Modern Business Institute, 1924).
A. Chisolm and M. Davie, *Beaverbrook* (London, Hutchinson, 1992).
H. Christian (ed.), *The Sociology of Journalism and the Press*, Sociological Review Monograph 29 (Keele, University of Keele, 1980).
A. Christiansen, *Headlines All My Life* (London, Heinemann, 1961).
T. Clarke, *My Northcliffe Diary* (London, Gollancz, 1931).
——*Northcliffe in History* (London, Hutchinson, 1950).
G. Cleverley, *The Fleet Street Disaster* (London, Constable, 1976).
C. Cockburn, *Brothers: Male Dominance and Technological Change* (London, Pluto, 1983).
M. Cockerell, P. Hennessy and D. Walker, *Sources Close to the Prime Minister* (London, Macmillan, 1984).
R. Cockett, *Twilight of Truth* (London, Weidenfeld & Nicolson, 1989).
S. Cohen and J. Young, *The Manufacture of News* (London, Constable, 1973).
H. Cox and D. Morgan, *City Politics and the Press* (Cambridge, Cambridge University Press, 1973).
R. A. Critchley, *UK Advertising Statistics* (London, Advertising Association, n.d.).
H. Cudlipp, *At Your Peril* (London, Weidenfeld & Nicolson, 1962).
——*Walking on the Water* (London, Bodley Head, 1976).
J. Curran, 'The impact of TV on the audience for national newspapers, 1945–68', in J. Tunstall (ed.), *Media Sociology* (London, Constable, 1970).
——(ed.), *The British Press: A Manifesto* (London, Macmillan, 1978).
——'Advertising and the press', in J. Curran (ed.), *The British Press: A Manifesto* (London, Macmillan, 1978).
T. Driberg, *Beaverbrook* (London, Weidenfeld & Nicolson, 1956).
H. W. Eley, *Advertising Media* (London, Butterworth, 1932).
H. Evans, *Good Times, Bad Times* (London, Weidenfeld & Nicolson, 1983).
B. Falk, *He Laughed in Fleet Street* (London, Hutchinson, 1933).
M. Ferguson, *Forever Feminine* (London, Heinemann Educational, 1983).
P. Ferris, *The House of Northcliffe* (London, Weidenfeld & Nicolson, 1971).

C. Freer, *The Inner Side of Advertising: A Practical Handbook for Advertisers* (London, Library Press, 1921).

H. Fyfe, *Sixty Years of Fleet Street* (London, W. H. Allen, 1949).

F. R. Gannon, *The British Press and Germany, 1936–1939* (London, Oxford University Press, 1971).

N. Garland, *Not Many Dead* (London, Hutchinson, 1990).

J. E. Gerald, *The British Press under Government Economic Controls* (Minneapolis, University of Minnesota Press, 1956).

P. Gibbs, *Adventures in Journalism* (London, Harper, 1923).

F. Giles, *Sundry Times* (London, Murray, 1986).

G. Glenton and William Pattinson, *The Last Chronicle of Bouverie Street* (London, Allen & Unwin, 1963).

P. Golding and S. Middleton, *Images of Welfare* (Oxford, Martin Robertson, 1982).

D. Goodhart and P. Wintour, *Eddie Shah and the Newspaper Revolution* (London, Coronet, 1986).

R. Greenslade, *Press Gang* (Basingstoke, Macmillan, 2003).

J. Haines, *Maxwell* (London, Macdonald, 1989).

S. Hall, 'The social eye of *Picture Post*', *Cultural Studies*, ii (1971).

——'Deviancy, politics and the media', in M. McIntosh and P. Rock (eds), *Deviancy and Social Control* (London, Tavistock, 1973).

S. Hall, C. Critcher, T. Jefferson, J. Clarke and B. Roberts, *Policing the Crisis: Mugging, the State, and Law and Order* (London, Macmillan, 1978).

J. Halloran, P. Elliott and G. Murdock (eds), *Demonstrations and Communication* (Harmondsworth, Penguin, 1970).

D. Hamilton, *Who is to Own the British Press?* (London, Birkbeck College, 1976).

R. Harris, *Gotcha: The Media, The Government and The Falklands War* (London, Faber, 1983).

W. Harris, *J. A. Spender* (London, Cassell, 1946).

G. Harrison and F. C. Mitchell, *The Home Market: A Handbook of Statistics* (London, Allen & Unwin, 1936).

N. Hartley, P. Gudgeon and R. Crafts, *Concentration of Ownership in the Provincial Press*, Royal Commission on the Press 1974–77, Research Series 5 (London, HMSO, 1977).

P. Hartmann, 'Industrial relations in the news media', *Industrial Relations Journal*, 6, 4 (London, HMSO, 1977).

——'News and public perceptions of industrial relations', *Media, Culture and Society*, 1, 3 (1979).

P. Hartmann and C. Husband, *Racism and the Mass Media* (London, Davis-Poynter, 1974).

Lord Hartwell, *William Camrose* (London, Weidenfeld & Nicolson, 1992).

J. Harvey (ed.), *The War Diaries of Oliver Harvey 1941–5* (London, Collins, 1978).

M. Hastings, *Editor* (Basingstoke, Macmillan, 2002).

H. Henry (ed.), *Behind the Headlines* (London, Associated Business Press, 1978).

——*The Dynamics of the British Press 1961–1984* (London, Advertising Association, 1986).

A. Hetherington, *News, Newspapers and Television* (London, Macmillan, 1985).

C. Higham, *Advertising* (London, Williams & Norgate, 1925).

F. Hirsch and D. Gordon, *Newspaper Money: Fleet Street and the Search for the Affluent Reader* (London, Hutchinson, 1975).

P. Hoch, *The Newspaper Game* (London, Calder & Boyars, 1974).

R. Hoggart (ed.), *Your Sunday Paper* (London, University of London Press, 1967).

M. Hollingsworth, *The Press and Political Dissent* (London, Pluto Press, 1986).

D. Hubback, *No Ordinary Press Baron* (London, Weidenfeld & Nicolson, 1985).

Hulton Readership Surveys (London, Hulton, 1947–55).

N. Hunter, *Advertising Through the Press* (London, Pitman, 1925).

Institute of Incorporated Practitioners in Advertising, *An Analysis of Press Circulations 1934* (London, IIPA, 1934).

——*Survey of Press Readership* (London, IIPA, 1939).

——*National Readership Surveys* (London, IIPA, 1956–67).

——*Joint Industry Committee for National Readership Surveys* (London, IIPA, 1968–84).

S. Inwood, 'The press in the First World War, 1914–16', unpublished Ph.D. thesis (University of Oxford, 1971).

I. Jackson, *The Provincial Press and the Community* (Manchester, Manchester University Press, 1971).

S. Jenkins, *Market for Glory* (London, Faber, 1986).

N. Kaldor and R. Silverman, *A Statistical Analysis of Advertising Expenditure and of the Revenue of the Press* (Cambridge, Cambridge University Press, 1948).

P. Kimble, *Newspaper Reading in the Third Year of the War* (London, Allen & Unwin, 1942).

C. King, *The Future of the Press* (London, MacGibbon & Kee, 1967).

——*Strictly Personal* (London, Weidenfeld & Nicolson, 1969).

——*With Malice Towards None: A War Diary* (ed. W. Armstrong) (London, Sidgwick & Jackson, 1970).

——*Without Fear or Favour* (London, Sidgwick & Jackson, 1971).

——*The Cecil King Diary 1965–70* (London, Cape, 1972).

S. Koss, *Fleet Street Radical: A. G. Gardiner and the Daily News* (London, Allen Lane, 1973).

G. Lansbury, *The Miracle of Fleet Street* (London, Victoria House, 1925).

M. Leapman, *Barefaced Cheek* (London, Hodder & Stoughton, 1983).

H. P. Levy, *The Press Council* (London, Macmillan, 1967).

L. London, *Whitehall and the Jews, 1933–48* (Cambridge, Cambridge University Press, 2000).

London Research Bureau, *Press Circulations Analysed 1928* (London Research Bureau, 1928).

A. G. Lyall, *Market Research: A Practical Handbook* (London Research Bureau 1933).

D. McLachlan, *In the Chair, Barrington-Ward of The Times, 1927–48* (London, Weidenfeld & Nicolson, 1971).

S. McLachlan and P. Golding, 'Tabloidization in the British press: a quantitative investigation into changes in British newspapers, 1952–97', in C. Sparks and J. Tulloch, *Tabloid Tales* (Lanham, Rowman & Littlefield, 2000).

I. McLaine, *Ministry of Morale* (London, Allen & Unwin, 1979).

D. McQuail, *Analysis of Newspaper Content*, Royal Commission on the Press 1974–77, Research Series 4 (London, HMSO, 1977).

Mass Observation, *The Press and its Readers* (London, Art & Technics, 1949).

T. S. Mathews, *The Sugar Pill: An Essay on Newspapers* (London, Gollancz, 1957).

R. J. Minney, *Viscount Southwood* (London, Odhams Press, 1954).

S. Mulvern, *The End of the Street* (London, Methuen, 1986).

G. Munster, *Rupert Murdoch* (Victoria, Viking Press, 1985).

G. Murdock, 'Class, power and the press: problems of conceptualisation and evidence', in H. Christian (ed.), *The Sociology of Journalism and the Press*, Sociological Review Monograph 29 (Keele, University of Keele, 1981).

D. Murphy, *The Silent Watchdog: The Press in Local Politics* (London, Constable, 1976).

——*The Stalker Affair and the Press* (London, Unwin Hyman, 1991).

A. Neil, *Full Disclosure* (London, Macmillan, 1996).

News Chronicle, *A Survey of Reader Interest* (1934).

H. Nicolson, *Diaries and Letters* (London, Collins, 1967).

Lord Northcliffe, *Newspapers and their Millionaires* (London, Associated Newspapers, 1922).

L. Owen, *Northcliffe: The Facts* (privately published, 1931).

B. Page, *The Murdoch Archipelago* (London, Simon and Schuster, 2003).

W. Parsons, *The Power of the Financial Press* (Aldershot, Elgar, 1989).

Periodicals and the Alternative Press, Royal Commission on the Press 1974–77, Research Series 6 (London, HMSO, 1977).

F. Pethick-Lawrence, *Fate Has Been Kind* (London, Hutchinson, 1943).

H. Porter, *Lies, Damned Lies and Some Exclusives* (London, Chatto & Windus, 1984).

R. Pound and G. Harmsworth, *Northcliffe* (London, Cassell, 1959).

A. Rappaport, *The British Press and Wilsonian Neutrality* (London, Oxford University Press, 1951).

Report on the British Press (London, Political & Economic Planning, 1938).

G. Robertson, *People Against the Press* (London, Quartet, 1983).

D. Rooney, 'Thirty years of competition in the British tabloid press: the *Mirror* and the *Sun* 1968–98', in C. Sparks and J. Tulloch, *Tabloid Tales* (Lanham, Rowman & Littlefield, 2000).

T. Russell, *Commercial Advertising* (London, Putnam, 1919).

A. P. Ryan, *Lord Northcliffe* (London, Collins, 1953).

M. Scammell and M. Harrop, The press: still for Labour, despite Blair , in D. Kavanagh and D. Butler (eds), *The British General Election of 2005* (Basingstoke, Palgrave Macmillan, 2005).

C. Seymour-Ure, *The Press, Politics and the Public* (London, Methuen, 1968).

——'Policy-making in the press', *Government and Opposition*, iv, 4 (1969).

——*The Political Impact of the Mass Media* (London, Constable, 1974).

——'The press and the party system between the wars', in G. Peele and C. Cook (eds), *The Politics of Reappraisal, 1918–1939* (London, Macmillan, 1976).

——*The British Press and Broadcasting Since 1945* (2nd edn) (Oxford, Blackwell, 1996).

R. Shannon, *A Press Free and Responsible* (London, John Murray, 2001).

A. Sharf, *The British Press and Jews Under Nazi Rule* (London, Oxford University Press, 1964).

W. Shawcross, *Rupert Murdoch* (London, Chatto & Windus, 1992).

K. Sisson, *Industrial Relations in Fleet Street* (Oxford, Blackwell, 1975).

A. Smith, *The British Press Since the War* (Newton Abbot, David & Charles, 1974).

A. C. H. Smith, E. Immirzi and T. Blackwell, *Paper Voices: The Popular Press and Social Change, 1933–1965* (London, Chatto & Windus, 1975).

Social and Community Planning, *Attitudes to the Press*, Royal Commission on the Press 1974–77, Research Series 3 (London, HMSO, 1977).

J. A. Spender, *Life, Journalism and Politics* (London, Cassell, 1927).

R. Stannard, *With the Dictators of Fleet Street* (London, Hutchinson, 1934).

Survey of the National Newspaper Industry (London, Economist Intelligence Unit, 1965).

A. J. P. Taylor, *English History 1914–1945* (Harmondsworth, Pelican, 1970).

——*Beaverbrook* (London, Hamish Hamilton, 1972).

——(ed.), *Off the Record: W. P. Crozier, Political Interviews 1933–1943* (London, Hutchinson, 1973).

S. J. Taylor, *Shock! Horror! The Tabloids in Action* (London, Bantam, 1991).

Lord Thomson of Fleet, *After I Was Sixty* (London, Hamish Hamilton, 1975).

The Times, *The History of The Times, iv: The 150th Anniversary and Beyond, 1912–1948*, 2 vols (London, The Times Publishing Co, 1952).

J. Tunstall, *The Westminster Lobby Correspondents* (London, Routledge & Kegan Paul, 1970).

——*Journalists at Work* (London, Constable, 1971).

J. Tunstall, 'The problem of industrial relations news in the press', in *Studies on the Press*, Royal Commission on the Press 1974–77, Working Paper 3 (London, HMSO, 1977).

——*The Media in Britain* (London, Constable, 1983).

——*Newspaper Power* (Oxford, Oxford University Press, 1996).

J. Whale, *Journalism and Government* (London, Macmillan, 1972).

C. White, *The Women's Periodical Press in Britain 1946–1976*, Royal Commission on the Press, Working Paper 4 (London, HMSO, 1977).

H. Wickham Steed, *The Press* (Harmondsworth, Penguin, 1938).

T. Wilson (ed.), *The Political Diaries of C. P. Scott* (London, Collins, 1970).

R. Winsbury, *New Technology and the Press*, Royal Commission on the Press and Acton Society Press Group (London, HMSO, 1975).

C. Wintour, *Pressures on the Press: An Editor looks at Fleet Street* (London, Deutsch, 1972).

J. E. Wrench, *Geoffrey Dawson and our Times* (London, Hutchinson, 1955).

Broadcasting

Memoirs and biographies

R. Baker, *Here is the News* (London, Leslie Frewin, 1966).

G. Beadle, *Television, A Critical Review* (London, Allen & Unwin, 1963).

M. Bell, *In Harm's Way: Reflection of a War Zone* (London, Hamish Hamilton, 1994).

M. Bhose, *Michael Grade: Screening the Image* (London, Virgin, 1992).

J. Birt, *John Birt the Autobiography* (London, Little, Brown, 2002).

A. Boyle, *Only the Wind Will Listen: Reith of the BBC* (London, Hutchinson, 1972).

C. Brewer, *The Spice of Variety* (London, Muller, 1948).

D. G. Bridson, *Prospero and Ariel: The Rise and Fall of Radio* (London, Gollancz, 1971).

H. Brittain, *The ABC of the BBC* (London, Pearson, 1932).

J. C. Cassell, *In Town Tonight* (London, Harrap, 1935).

S. Chesmore, *Behind the Microphone* (London, Nelson, 1935).

Sir Kenneth Clark, *The Other Half: A Self-Portrait* (London, Murray, 1977).

Sir Alfred D. Cooper, *Old Men Forget* (London, Hart-Davis, 1953).

N. Davenport, *Memoirs of a City Radical* (London, Methuen, 1959).

R. Day, *Television – A Personal Report* (London, Hutchinson, 1961).

——*Day by Day* (London, William Kimber, 1975).

B. Deane, *Seven Ages, An Autobiography, 1927–72* (London, Hutchinson, 1973).

J. Dimbleby, *Richard Dimbleby: A Biography* (London, Hodder & Stoughton, 1975).

R. Dimbleby, *The Waiting Year* (London, Hodder & Stoughton, 1944).

P. P. Eckersley, *The Power Behind the Microphone* (London, Cape, 1941).

R. Eckersley, *The BBC and All That* (London, Sampson, Low, Marston, 1946).

L. Fielden, *The Natural Bent* (London, Deutsch, 1960).

V. Gielgud, *Years of the Locust* (London, Nicholson & Watson, 1947).

G. W. Goldie, *Facing the Nation: Television and Politics, 1936–76* (London, Bodley Head, 1977).

M. Gorham, *Sound and Fury* (London, Percival-Maskell, 1948).

F. Grisewood, *The World Goes By* (London, Secker & Warburg, 1952).

——*Years in the Mirror* (London, Gollancz, 1967).

H. Grisewood, *One Thing at a Time* (London, Hutchinson, 1968).

H. Hall, *Here's to the Next Time* (London, Deutsch, 1935).

L. Henry, *My Laugh Story* (Edinburgh, Simon Paul, 1937).

A. S. Hibberd, *This is London* (Plymouth, Macdonald & Evans, 1950).

Lord Hill of Luton (C. Hill), *Both Sides of the Hill* (London, Heinemann, 1967).

——*Behind the Screen* (London, Sidgwick & Jackson, 1974).

J. Hilton, *This and That* (London, Allen & Unwin, 1938).

J. Isaacs, *Storm over Four: A Personal Account* (London, Weidenfeld & Nicolson, 1989).

P. J. Kavanagh, *The Itma Years* (London, Heinemann, 1974).

T. Kavanagh, *Tommy Handley* (London, Hodder & Stoughton, 1949).

F. Keane, *Rivers of Blood; Reporting Rwanda* (London, Hamish Hamilton, 1995).

L. Kennedy, *Ludo: A Life* (London, Macmillan, 1989).

R. S. Lambert, *Ariel and All His Quality* (London, Gollancz, 1940).

C. A. Lewis, *Broadcasting from Within* (London, George Newnes, 1924).

E. Maschwitz, *No Chip on My Shoulder* (London, Jenkins, 1957).

A. Milne, *D. G. The Memoirs of a British Broadcaster* (London, Hodder & Stoughton, 1988).

S. A. Mosely, *Broadcasting in my Time* (London, Rich & Cowan, 1935).

——*Private Diaries* (London, Parrish, 1960).

E. Nixon, *John Hilton* (London, Allen & Unwin, 1946).

J. Payne, *This is Jack Payne* (London, Marston, 1932).

——*Signature Tune* (Edinburgh, Simon Paul, 1947).

W. Pickles, *Between You and Me* (London, Heinemann, 1949).

J. B. Priestley, *Margin Released* (London, Mercury, 1966).

J. C. W. Reith, *Into the Wind* (London, Hodder & Stoughton, 1949).

R. Silvey, *Who's Listening?* (London, Allen & Unwin, 1974).

C. Stuart, *The Reith Diaries* (London, Collins, 1975).

Sir Stephen Tallents, *Man and Boy* (London, Faber, 1943).

H. Thomas, *With an Independent Air* (London, Weidenfeld & Nicolson, 1977).

M. Tracey, *A Variety of Lives: A Biography of Sir Hugh Greene* (London, Bodley Head, 1982).

M. Whitehouse, *Who Does She Think She Is?* (London, New English Library, 1971).

The history of broadcasting

M. Abrams, *Granada Viewership Survey* (1959).

R. Alston, *Taking the Air* (London, Hodder & Stoughton, 1951).

G. L. Archer, *A History of Broadcasting to 1926* (London, Allen & Unwin, 1938).

J. Bakewell and N. Garnham, *The New Priesthood: British Television Today* (Harmondsworth, Allen Lane, 1970).

S. Barnett (ed.), *Funding the BBC's Future* (London, BFI, 1988).

S. Barnett and A. Curry, *The Battle for the BBC* (London, Aurum Press, 1993).

S. Barnett and E. Seymour, '*A Shrinking Iceberg Travelling South*' (London, Campaign for Quality Television, 1999).

E. Barnouw, *A Tower in Babel: The History of Broadcasting in the United States* (London, Oxford University Press, 1966).

BBC Handbook (London, BBC, annually).

BBC, 'Comparative European programming', *BBC Handbook* (London, BBC, 1934).

——*The Third Programme: Plans for October–December 1944* (London, BBC, 1944).

——*The Public and their Programmes* (London, BBC, 1959).

J. Bennett, *British Broadcasting and the Danish Resistance Movement 1940–1945* (Cambridge, Cambridge University Press, 1965).

P. Black, *The Biggest Aspidistra in the World* (London, BBC, 1972).

——*The Mirror in the Corner* (London, Hutchinson, 1972).

P. Bloomfield, *BBC* (London, Eyre & Spottiswoode, 1941).

G. Brandt (ed.), *Television Drama* (Cambridge, Cambridge University Press, 1981).

A. Briggs, *The History of Broadcasting in the United Kingdom*: Vol. I, *The Birth of Broadcasting*; Vol. II, *The Golden Age of Wireless*; Vol. III, *The War of Words*; Vol. IV, *Sound and Vision* (London, Oxford University Press, 1961, 1965, 1970 and 1979).

——'The rise of the mass entertainment industry' (Fisher Lecture, 1961).

——*The BBC Governors* (London, BBC, 1979).

——*The BBC: The First Fifty Years* (Oxford, Oxford University Press, 1985).

P. J. Brown, 'Broadcasting in Britain', *London Quarterly Review*, 145, 1 (January 1926).

A. R. Burrows, *The Story of Broadcasting* (London, Cassell, 1924).

Sir Cyril Burt, 'The psychology of listeners', *BBC Quarterly*, 4, 2 (April 1949).

H. L. Childs and J. B. Whitton (eds), *Propaganda by Shortwave* (London, Oxford University Press, 1943).

J. A Cole, *Lord Haw Haw – and William Joyce* (London, Collins, 1964).

C. A. R. Crosland, 'The mass media', *Encounter* (November 1962).

R. H. S. Crossman, 'The politics of viewing', *New Statesman* (25 October 1968).

——'The BBC, Labour and the public', *New Statesman* (17 July 1971).

C. Curran, *Code or Conscience* (London, BBC, 1970).

——*A Maturing Democracy* (London, BBC, 1973).

——*The Seamless Robe* (London, Bodley Head, 1979).

——'Television journalism: theory and practice, the case of *Newsnight*', in P. Holland, *Television Handbook* (London, Routledge, 2nd edn, 2000).

R. Day, 'Troubled reflections of a TV journalist', *Encounter* (May 1970).

B. Deane, *The Theatre At War* (London, Harrap, 1956).

S. Delmer, *Black Boomerang* (London, Secker & Warburg, 1962).

D. Docherty, D. E. Morrison and M. Tracey, *Keeping Faith? Channel Four and its Audience* (London, Libbey, 1988).

L. W. Doob, 'Goebbels' principles of propaganda', *Public Opinion Quarterly*, 21, 2 (1950).

P. P. Eckersley, *Captain Eckersley Explains* (London, Hodder & Stoughton, 1924).

——*All About your Microphone* (London, BBC Broadcast Library, 1925).

——*The Power Behind the Microphone* (London, Cape, 1941).

H. Fairlie, 'TV, idiot box', *Encounter* (August 1959).

——'The BBC', in H. S. Thomas (ed.), *The Establishment: A Symposium* (London, New English Library, 1962).

Sir Robert Fraser, *The Coming of Independent Television* (London, Hutchinson, 1955).

——*ITA Notes* (October 1970).

V. Gielgud, *British Radio Drama 1922–1956* (London, Harrap, 1957).

P. Goodwin, *Television Under the Tories* (London, British Film Institute, 1998).

G. W. Goldie, 'The new attraction', *Listener* (26 December 1940).

——'TV report', *Listener* (23 October 1968).

——*Facing the Nation: Television and Politics 1936–1976* (London, The Bodley Head, 1977).

M. Gorham, *Broadcasting and Television Since 1900* (London, Collins, 1952).

T. Green, *The Universal Eye: World Television in the Seventies* (London, The Bodley Head, 1972).

——'The future of broadcasting in Britain', Granada Guildhall Lecture (1972).

H. C. Greene, 'The BBC since 1958', *BBC Handbook* (1969).

——*The Third Floor Front: A View of Broadcasting in the Sixties* (London, The Bodley Head, 1969).

T. Harrisson, 'War books', *Horizon* (December 1941).

D. Hawkins and D. Boyd (eds), *BBC War Report* (London, Oxford University Press, 1946).

Sir William Hayley, *The Central Problem of Broadcasting* (London, BBC, 1948).

C. Horrie and S. Clarke, *Fear and Loathing at the BBC* (London, Heinemann, 1993).

IBA, *Annual Reports*.

ITV, *The Annan Report: An ITV View* (London, ITV, 1977).

E. T. Lean, *Voices in the Darkness* (London, Allen & Unwin, 1943).

M. Leapman, *The Last Days of the Beeb* (London, Coronet, 1987).

D. McLachlan, *Room 39* (London, Weidenfeld & Nicolson, 1968).

Mass Observation, *The War Begins at Home* (London, Chatto & Windus, 1940).

H. Matheson, *Broadcasting* (London, Butterworth, 1933).

——'Listener research in broadcasting', *Sociological Review*, 27, 3 (1935).

A. Mitchell, 'The decline of current affairs television', *Political Quarterly*, 44, 1 (1973).

S. Nicholas, *The Echo of War: Home Front Propaganda 1939–45* (Manchester, Manchester University Press, 1995).

H. Nicolson, *The Third Programme: A Symposium of Opinions and Plans* (London, BBC, 1947).

S. Orwell and I. Angus (eds), *The Collected Essays, Letters and Journalism of George Orwell* (Harmondsworth, Penguin, 1971).

B. Paulu, *British Broadcasting: Radio and Television in the United Kingdom* (Oxford, Oxford University Press, 1957).

G. Pedrich, *Battledress Broadcasters* (London, Marston, 1964).

R. Postgate, *What to Do with the BBC?* (London, Hogarth, 1935).

J. B. Priestley, *Postscripts* (London, Heinemann, 1940).

J. C. W. Reith, *Broadcast over Britain* (London, Hodder & Stoughton, 1924).

N. Riley, *999* (London, Gollancz, 1943).

C. J. Rolo, *Radio Goes to War* (London, Hutchinson, 1943).

G. Ross, *T.V. Jubilee* (London, W. H. Allen, 1961).

P. Rotha (ed.), *Television in the Making* (London, The Bodley Head, 1956).

P. Scannell, 'The social eye of television, 1946–55', *Media, Culture, and Society*, 1, 1 (1979).

——*Radio, Television and Modern Life* (Oxford, Blackwell, 1996).

P. Scannell and D. Cardiff, 'The social foundations of British broadcasting', in J. Curran, M. Gurevitch and J. Woollacott (eds), *Mass Communication and Society* (London, Edward Arnold/Open University Press, 1977).

J. Seaton, 'The BBC and the Holocaust', *European Journal of Communication*, 2, 1 (1987).

——'Reporting atrocities', in J. Seaton and B. Pimlott, *The Media in British Politics* (Aldershot, Gower, 1987).

——*The Media and the Constitution* (London, Charter 88, 1993).

——'Broadcasting in the 1980s: is it possible to under-estimate public taste?', *Political Quarterly*, Special issue on broadcasting, 47, 1 (1993), pp. 50–76.

——'Yesterday's men: deception or mistake?', together with edited transcript of 1994 ICBH Witness Seminar, *Contemporary British History*, 10, 3 (1996).

——'Misery and the media: the media and ethnic violence', *Contemporary Politics*, 2, 2 (1996).

G. Seldes, *The Great Audience* (London, Oxford University Press, 1950).

T. Shaw, *Eden, Suez and the Mass Media* (Birmingham, I.B. Tauris, 1995).

R. Silvey, 'Some recent trends in listening', *BBC Handbook* (London, BBC, 1946).

——'TV viewing in Britain', *Public Opinion Quarterly*, 25, 2 (1950).

——*Whose Listening?* (London, The Bodley Head, 1974).

Lord Simon of Wythenshawe, *The BBC from Within* (London, Gollancz, 1953).

A. Smith, *The Shadow in the Cave* (London, Allen & Unwin, 1973).

——*British Broadcasting* (Newton Abbot, David & Charles, 1974).

S. W. Smithers, *Broadcasting from Within* (London, Pitmans, 1938).

N. Swallow, *Factual Television* (London, Focal Press, 1966).

J. Swift, *Adventures in Vision* (London, Lehmann, 1950).

I. Thomas, *Warfare By Words* (London, Gollancz, 1942).

The Times, special broadcasting number (14 August 1934).

P. Todd, 'Scarcity of TV time', *Campaign* (26 January 1979).

M. Tracey, *Whitehouse* (London, Constable, 1979).

R. West, *The Meaning of Treason* (London, Macmillan, 1948).

H. Wheldon, 'Competition in television', Address to the Royal Society of Arts (1971).

——*Tastes and Standards in BBC Programmes* (London, BBC, 1973).

H. H. Wilson, *Pressure Group* (London, Secker & Warburg, 1961).

F. Worsley, *ITMA* (London, Collins, 1948).

The background to broadcasting

M. Abrams, 'Advertising', *Listener* (15 December 1956).

——'Motivation research', *Advertising Quarterly* (November 1959).

P. Addison, *The Road to 1945* (London, Cape, 1975).

K. Allsop, *The Angry Decade* (London, Owen, 1958).

N. Annan, 'Love among the moralists', *Encounter* (February 1960).

E. Barendt and L. Hitchens, *Media Law* (Harlow, Longman, 2000).

D. Bell, 'Advertising: is it worth it?', *Listener* (13 December 1956).

W. H. Beveridge, *Unemployment: A Problem of Industry* (London, Longman Green, 1910).

——*Public Service in War and Peace* (London, Constable, 1920).

——*Constructive Democracy* (London, Allen & Unwin, 1937).

——*Power and Influence* (London, Hodder & Stoughton, 1953).

V. Bogdanor and R. Skidelsky, *The Age of Affluence* (Harmondsworth, Penguin, 1970).

E. Bowen, *The Heart of the Matter* (London, Faber, 1944).

V. Brittain, *Testament of Friendship* (London, Macmillan, 1940).

G. Bruntz, *Allied Propaganda and the Collapse of the German Empire in 1918* (Stanford, Calif., Stanford University Press, 1938).

Sir Cyril Burt, *The Distribution and Relations of Educational Abilities* (London, London County Council, 1917).

——'The measurement of mental capacities', Henderson Trust Lecture 7, Edinburgh (1927).

——(ed.), *How The Mind Works* (London, Allen & Unwin, 1933).

——*Intelligence and Fertility* (London, Cassell, 1952).

D. Butler and R. Rose, *The British General Election of 1959* (London, Macmillan, 1960).

Lord Butler, *The Education Act of 1944 and After*, First Noel Buxton Lecture, University of Essex (Harlow, Longman, 1965).

——*The Art of the Possible* (London, Hamish Hamilton, 1971).

A. Calder, *The People's War: Britain 1939–45* (London, Cape, 1969).

H. Cantril, *Public Opinion 1935–46* (Princeton, NJ, Princeton University Press, 1951).

C. Cockburn, *I Claud* (Harmondsworth, Penguin, 1967).

C. A. R. Crosland, *The Future of Socialism* (London, Cape, 1956).

R. H. S. Crossman, 'Psychological warfare', *Journal of the Royal United Services Institution* (August 1952).

——'The lessons of 1945', in P. Anderson and R. Blackburn (eds), *Towards Socialism* (London, Fontana, 1965).

H. Dalton, 'The "popular front"', *Political Quarterly*, 4, 7 (1936).

M. E. Dimmock, *British Public Utilities and National Development* (London, Allen & Unwin, 1933).

C. H. Dobinson (ed.), *Education in a Changing World* (Oxford, Oxford University Press, 1951).

T. Driberg, *The Best of Both Worlds* (Phoenix House, 1958).

M. R. D. Foot, *Resistance: An Analysis of European Resistance to Fascism* (London, Methuen, 1976).

P. Foot, *The Politics of Harold Wilson* (Harmondsworth, Penguin, 1968).

Fougasse (pseud. C. K. Bird), *The Changing Face of Britain* (London, Methuen, 1950).

B. Gates, *The Road Ahead* (Boston, Viking, 1995).

M. Gilbert, *Churchill*, Vol. 5 (London, Heinemann, 1976).

M. Gilbert and R. Gott, *The Appeasers* (London, Weidenfeld & Nicolson, 1963).

D. Gordan, 'Ten points about the crisis in the British film industry', *Sight and Sound*, 43, 2 (1974).

L. Gorden, *The Public Corporation in Great Britain* (Oxford, Oxford University Press, 1938).

P. H. J. H. Gosden, *Education in the Second World War* (London, Methuen, 1972).

C. Handy, *The Age of Unreason* (Boston, Mass., Harvard University Press, 1989).

——'The New Federalist Papers', *Harvard University Business Review*, 3 (Autumn 1992).

——*The Empty Raincoat* (London, HarperCollins, 1993).

J. Harris, *William Beveridge* (Oxford, Clarendon Press, 1977).

N. Harris, *Competition and the Corporate State* (London, Methuen, 1972).

R. Harris, *Politics Without Prejudice* (Tonbridge, Staples, 1956).

T. Harrisson, 'Who'll win?', *Political Quarterly*, 15, 4 (1944).

——*Living Through the Blitz* (Harmondsworth, Penguin, 1978).

J. Harvey-Jones, *Making it Happen* (London, BBC Books, 1994).

E. Hobsbawm, *Nations and Nationalism since 1780* (Cambridge, Cambridge University Press, 1992).

——*The Age of Extremities* (London, Allen Lane, 1994).

J. A. Hodson, *Somewhere in France … B.E.F.* (London, Whithey Grove, 1940).

——*War Diary* (London, Gollancz, 1941).

——*The Home Front* (London, Gollancz, 1944).

W. Hutton, *The State We Are In* (London, Cape, 1996).

L. J. Kamin, *The Science and Politics of IQ* (Harmondsworth, Penguin, 1977).

P. Kennedy, *Preparing for the 21st Century* (London, HarperCollins, 1993).

Labour Party, *Twelve Wasted Years* (London, Labour Party, 1963).

D. Low, *Low's Autobiography* (London, Michael Joseph, 1956).

R. Low, *The History of the British Film*, Vol. 1 (London, Allen & Unwin, 1948).

I. McLaine, 'The Ministry of Information', unpublished D.Phil. thesis (University of Oxford, 1976).

——*The Ministry of Morale* (London, Allen & Unwin, 1978).

F. Marquis (ed.), *The Memoirs of the Rt Hon. the Earl of Woolton* (London, Cassell, 1959).

A. Marr, *Ruling Britannia* (London, Penguin, 1996).

A. Marwick, 'Middle opinion in the thirties', *English Historical Review*, 79, 2 (1964).

Mass Observation, *The War Begins at Home* (London, Chatto & Windus, 1940).

——*Home Propaganda* (London, Chatto & Windus, 1941).

——*War Factory* (London, Gollancz, 1943).

——*The Journey Home* (London, Murray, 1944).

——*The Press and Its Readers* (London, Art & Technics, 1949).

Ministry of Pensions, *Neuroses in War Time* (London, HMSO, 1940).

J. Montgomery, *The Fifties* (London, Collins, 1965).

H. Morrison, *Socialization and Transport* (London, Constable, 1933).

G. Mulgan, *Politics in an Anti-Political Age* (Cambridge, Polity Press, 1995).

H. Nicolson, *Diaries and Letters 1930–45* (London, Collins, 1967).

T. H. O'Brien, *British Experiments in Public Ownership and Control* (London, Allen & Unwin, 1937).

F. Owen, 'This war', *Horizon* (February 1940).

V. Packard, *The Hidden Persuaders* (London, Longman, 1957).

S. Papathanassopoulos, *European Television in the Digital Age* (London, Sage, 2002).

H. Pelling, *Britain and the Second World War* (London, Collins, 1970).

B. Pimlott, *Labour and the Left in the 1930s* (Cambridge, Cambridge University Press, 1977).

——*Hugh Dalton* (London, Cape, 1985).

——*Harold Wilson* (London, HarperCollins, 1993).

——*The Queen: A Biography of Queen Elizabeth II* (London, HarperCollins, 1996).

J. W. C. Reith, *Personality and Career* (London, George Newnes, 1925).

——*Winning Spurs* (London, Hutchinson, 1966).

P. Renshaw, *The General Strike* (London, Methuen, 1975).

W. A. Robson, *Public Enterprise* (London, New Fabian Research Bureau, 1937).

——*Nationalized Industry and Public Ownership* (London, Allen & Unwin, 1960).

R. J. W. Selleck, 'The scientific educationalist', *British Journal of Educational Studies*, 15, 3 (June 1967).

B. Simon, *Education and the Labour Movement, 1870–1920* (London, Lawrence & Wishart, 1965).

——*The Politics of Educational Reform, 1920–1940* (London, Lawrence & Wishart, 1971).

——*Intelligence, Psychology and Education* (London, Lawrence & Wishart, 1978).

P. Sissons and R. French (eds), *The Age of Austerity* (Harmondsworth, Penguin, 1962).

R. Skidelsky, *Politicians and the Slump* (London, Macmillan, 1967).

——'Keynes and the reconstruction of liberalism', *Encounter* (April 1979).

——*Maynard Keynes: A Biography– The World After Communism* (London, Macmillan, 1995).

J. Strachey, *Post D* (London, Gollancz, 1940).

B. Sweet-Escott, *Baker Street Irregular* (London, Collins, 1966).

J. Symons, *The General Strike* (London, Cressett, 1957).

S. Tallents, *The Projection of England* (London, Empire Marketing Board, 1932).

A. J. P. Taylor, *English History 1914–1945* (London, Allen & Unwin, 1965).

——*Beaverbrook* (London, Hamish Hamilton, 1972).

M. Thatcher, *The Downing Street Years* (London, HarperCollins, 1995).

R. Titmuss, *Problems of Social Policy* (London, Longman/HMSO, 1950).

Sir Robert Vansittart, *Black Record: Germans Past and Present* (London, Hamish Hamilton, 1941).

P. E. Vernon and J. B. Barry, *Personnel Selection in the British Forces* (London, University of London Press, 1949).

Beatrice Webb's Diaries, 1924–32, ed. M. Cole (London, Longman Green, 1956).

W. Whitelaw, *The Whitelaw Memoirs* (London, Aurum Press, 1989).

N. S. Wilson, *Education in the Forces, 1939–1946: The Civilian Contribution* (London, Allen & Unwin, 1949).

S. W. L. Woodward, *British Foreign Policy in the Second World War* (London, HMSO, 1970/1).

H. Young, *One of Us: A Biography of Margaret Thatcher* (London, Cape, 1993).

Sociology

T. W. Adorno, *Prisms* (Sudbury, Spearman, 1967).

——*The Jargon of Authenticity* (London, Routledge & Kegan Paul, 1973).

T. W. Adorno, E. F. Brunswick, D. J. Levinson and R. N. Sandford, *The Authoritarian Personality* (London, Harper & Row, 1950).

M. Alvarado and E. Buscombe, *Hazell: The Making of a Television Series* (London, British Film Institute, 1978).

H. Arendt, *The Burden of Our Time* (London, Secker & Warburg, 1950).

——*The Life of the Mind,* Vol. 2, *Thinking* (London, Secker & Warburg, 1978).

U. Beck, *The Risk Society* (London, Sage, 1995).

P. Becker and M. McCombs, 'The development of political cognition', in S. H. Chaffee (ed.), *Political Communication: Issues and Strategies* (Beverly Hills, Calif., Sage, 1975).

B. Berelson, 'The state of communication research', *Public Opinion Quarterly*, 31, 2 (1959).

S. Blanchard, *What's This Channel Four?* (London, Comedia, 1983).

J. G. Blumler, 'The audience', in *The Political Effects of Mass Communication* (Milton Keynes, Open University Press, DE 353, 1977).

——'The intervention of television in British politics', *Report of the Committee on the Future of Broadcasting* (Annan Report) (1977) [Cmnd 6753, Appendix E].

——'An overview of recent research into the impact of broadcasting in democratic politics', in M. J. Clark (ed.), *Politics and the Media* (Oxford, Pergamon Press, 1979).

J. G. Blumler and M. Gurevitch, 'Towards a comparative framework for political communication', in S. H. Chaffee (ed.), *Political Communication: Issues and Strategies* (London, Sage, 1975).

J. G. Blumler and D. McQuail, *Television in Politics: Its Uses and Influences* (London, Faber, 1968).

J. G. Blumler and J. Madge, *Citizenship and Television* (London, Political & Economic Planning, 1965).

D. Boorstin, *The Image, Or What Happened to the American Dream* (Harmondsworth, Penguin, 1963).

P. Bourdieu, *Outline of a Theory of Practice* (Cambridge, Cambridge University Press, 1977).

T. Boyce, *Health, Risk and News* (New York, Lang, 2007).

O. Boyd-Barrett, D. Seymour-Ure and J. Tunstall, *Studies on the Press*, Royal Commission on the Press 1974–77, Working Paper 3 (London, HMSO, 1977).

B. Brown, 'An interview with the film censor', *Screen*, 23, 5 (1982).

——'Pornography: some modest proposals', *M/F* (January 1982).

S. Bryant, *The Television Heritage* (London, British Film Institute, 1990).

M. Bulmer, *Working-Class Images of Society* (London, Routledge & Kegan Paul, 1975).

T. Burns, *The BBC, Public Institutions and Private World* (London, Macmillan, 1977).

H. Cantril, *The Invasion From Mars: A Study in the Psychology of Panic* (Princeton, NJ, Princeton University Press, 1940).

D. Chaney, *Processes of Mass Communication* (London, Macmillan, 1972).

M. Cockerell, P. Hennessy and D. Walker, *Sources Close to the Prime Minister* (London, Macmillan, 1984).

S. Cohen, *Images of Deviance* (Harmondsworth, Penguin, 1971).

S. Cohen and J. Young (eds), *The Manufacture of News* (London, Constable, 1973).

Conference of Socialist Economics Microelectronics Group, *Microelectronics: Capitalist Technology and the Working Class* (CSE Books, 1980).

I. Connell, 'Commercial broadcasting and the British left', *Screen*, 24, 6 (1983).

G. Cumberbatch and D. Howitt, *A Measure of Uncertainty: The Effects of the Mass Media* (London, Libbey, 1989).

J. Curran, 'The boomerang effect: the press and the battle for London 1981–86', in J. Curran and A. Smith (eds), *Impacts and Influences* (London, Methuen, 1986).

——'Culturalist perspectives of news organizations: a reappraisal and a case study', in M. Ferguson (ed.), *Public Communication* (London, Sage, 1990).

——'The new revisionism in mass communication research: a reappraisal', *European Journal of Communications*, 5, 2–3 (1990).

J. Curran, I. Gaber, and J. Petley, *Culture Wars* (Edinburgh, Edinburgh University Press, 2005).

J. H. Dunning, *Multinational Corporations and the Global Economy* (Wokingham, Addison-Wesley, 1993).

R. Dyer, *Light Entertainment*, BFI Television Monograph 2 (London, British Film Institute, 1973).

M. Edelmann, *The Symbolic Uses of Politics* (Urbana, Ill., University of Illinois Press, 1964).

P. Elliot, *The Making of a Television Series* (London, Constable, 1972)

——'Intellectuals and "The information society" and the disappearance of the public sphere', *Media, Culture and Society*, 6, 4 (1982).

P. Elliot, G. Murdock and P. Schlesinger, 'Terrorism and the state: a case study in the discourse of television', *Media, Culture and Society*, 5, 2 (1983).

J. Ellis, *Visible Fiction: Cinema, TV, Video* (London, Routledge & Kegan Paul, 1982).

E. J. Epstein, *News from Nowhere* (New York, Random House, 1973).

R. Ericson, P. Baranec and J. Chan, *Visualizing Deviance* (Milton Keynes, Open University Press, 1987).

J. Fiske, *Television Culture* (London, Methuen, 1987).

S. Frith, *The Sociology of Rock* (London, Constable, 1979).

——*The Aesthetics of Rock* (London, Macmillan, 1997).

P. Fussell, *The Great War in Modern Memory* (London, Oxford University Press, 1975).

N. Garnham, *Structures of Television*, BFI Television Monograph 1 (London, British Film Institute, 1973).

——'Contribution to a political economy of mass communications', *Media, Culture and Society*, 1, 2 (April 1979).

——'Public service versus the market', *Screen*, 24, 1 (1983).

E. Gellner, *Nations and Nation Building* (Cambridge, Cambridge University Press, 1984).

A. Giddens, *The Transformations of Intimacy: Sexuality, Love and Eroticism in Modern Societies* (Cambridge, Polity Press, 1992).

——*Post-Modernity* (Cambridge, Polity Press, 1994).

——*Beyond Left and Right* (Cambridge, Polity Press, 1995).

T. Gitlin, *The Whole World is Watching* (Berkeley, Calif., University of California Press, 1982).

Glasgow University Media Group, *Bad News* (London, Routledge & Kegan Paul, 1976).

——'Prime time ideology: the hegemonic process in television entertainment', *Social Problems*, 25, 3 (1979).

——*More Bad News* (London, Routledge & Kegan Paul, 1980).

P. Golding, *The Mass Media* (Harlow, Longman, 1974).

P. Golding and P. Elliot, *Making the News* (Harlow, Longman, 1979).

P. Golding and S. Middleton, *Images of Welfare* (London, Macmillan, 1980).

J. H. Goldthorpe and D. Lockwood, *The Affluent Worker: Political Attitudes and Behaviour* (Cambridge, Cambridge University Press, 1968).

K. Hafez, *The Myth of Media Globalization* (Cambridge, Polity, 2007).

S. Hall, 'The external/internal dialectic on broadcasting', *4th Symposium on British Broadcasting Policy*, February 1972.

——'The determination of news photographs', in S. Cohen and J. Young (eds), *The Manufacture of News* (London, Constable, 1973).

——'The hinterland of science: ideology', in Centre for Contemporary Cultural Studies, *On Ideology* (London, Hutchinson, 1977).

——'Culture, the media and the ideological effect', in J. Curran, M. Gurevitch and J. Woollacott (eds), *Mass Communication and Society* (London, Edward Arnold/Open University, 1977).

——'Newspapers, parties and classes', in J. Curran (ed.), *The British Press: A Manifesto* (London, Macmillan, 1978).

S. Hall, C. Critcher, T. Jefferson, J. Clarke and B. Roberts, *Policing the Crisis: Mugging, the State, and Law and Order* (London, Macmillan, 1978).

S. Hall, C. Curtis and I. Connell, 'The unity of current events TV', in Centre for Contemporary Cultural Studies, *Working Papers in Cultural Studies*, 9 (Spring 1976).

J. D. Halloran and G. Murdoch, *Demonstrations and Communications* (Harmondsworth, Penguin, 1970).

P. Halmos (ed.), *Sociology of Mass Media Communicators*, Sociological Review Monograph 13 (Keele, University of Keele, 1969).

R. Harris, *Gotcha! The Media and the Falklands War* (London, Faber, 1983).

M. Harrop, 'Voters and the media', in J. Seaton and B. Pimlott (eds), *The Media in British Politics* (Aldershot, Gower, 1987).

M. Harrop and R. Worcester (eds), *Political Communication: The 1979 General Election* (London, Macmillan, 1981).

P. Hartmann and C. Husband, *Racism and the Mass Media* (London, Davis-Poynter, 1973).

B. Harvey, *The Condition of Post-Modernity* (Oxford, Oxford University Press, 1992).

F. Hayek, *The Road to Serfdom* (London, Routledge & Kegan Paul, 1944).

D. Held, *Democracy and the New International Order* (Cambridge, Polity Press, 1993).

——(ed.), *Prospects for Democracy* (Cambridge, Polity Press, 1994).

C. Heller, *Broadcasters and Accountability*, BFI Television Monograph 3 (London, British Film Institute, 1978).

E. Herman and N. Chomsky, *Manufacturing Consent* (New York, Pantheon, 1988).

P. M. Hirsch, 'Processing fads and fashions', *American Journal of Sociology*, 46, 1 (1977).

P. Hirst, *After Thatcher* (London, Hutchinson, 1991).

P. Hirst and S. Khilnani, *Re-Inventing Democracy* (London, Political Quarterly, 1996).

P. Hirst and G. Thompson, *Globalisation in Question* (Cambridge, Polity Press, 1996).

D. Hobson, *Crossroads* (London, Methuen, 1983).

P. Hoch, *The Newspaper Game* (London, Calder & Boyars, 1974).

R. Hoggart, *The Uses of Literacy* (London, Chatto & Windus, 1957).

A. Hooper, *The Military and the Media* (London, Routledge & Kegan Paul, 1981).

M. Horkheimer, *The Eclipse of Reason* (Oxford, Oxford University Press, 1947).

C. I. Hovland, *Experiments in Mass Communication* (Princeton, NJ, Princeton University Press, 1949).

——'Reconciling conflicting results derived from experimental and survey studies of attitude change', *American Psychologist*, 14, 3 (1959).

J. Howkins, *New Technologies, New Policies* (London, British Film Institute, 1982).

G. A. Huaco, *The Sociology of Film Art* (New York, Basic Books, 1965).

C. Husband (ed.), *White Media and Black Britain* (London, Routledge & Kegan Paul, 1962).

B. Jackson and D. Marsden, *Education and the Working Class* (London, Routledge & Kegan Paul, 1962).

M. Jay, *The Dialectical Imagination* (London, Heinemann, 1973).

E. Katz and P. Lazarsfeld, *Personal Influence: The Part Played by People in the Flow of Mass Communication* (West Drayton, Free Press, 1955).

T. Klapper, *The Effects of Mass Communication* (West Drayton, Free Press, 1960).

F. G. Kline and P. J. Tichenor, *Current Perspectives in Mass Communications Research* (London, Sage, 1972).

W. Kornhauser, *The Politics of Mass Society* (London, Routledge & Kegan Paul, 1959).

R. Kuhn, 'Government broadcasting in the 1980s: cross channel perspective', *Political Quarterly*, 53, 4 (1982).

——'Ballot box', *Stills* (May–June 1983).

K. Kumar, 'Holding the middle ground: the BBC, the public and the professional broadcaster', in J. Curran, M. Gurevitch and J. Woollacott (eds), *Mass Communication and Society* (London, Edward Arnold/Open University Press, 1977).

——*Policy and Progress* (Harmondsworth, Penguin, 1978).

——*Utopia and Anti-Utopianism in Modern Times* (Oxford, Blackwell, 1991).

S. Lambert, *Channel 4* (London, British Film Institute, 1982).

K. Lang, 'Images of society, media research in Germany', *Public Opinion Quarterly*, 22, 3 (1974).

K. Lang and G. Lang, *Politics and Television* (New York, Quadrangle, 1968).

——*The Battle For Public Opinion: Watergate and the Media* (Westport, Conn., Greenwood Press, 1982).

S. Lasch and J. Urry, *The End of Organised Capital* (Cambridge, Polity Press, 1990).

H. D. Lasswell, *Psychopathology and Politics* (Chicago, Ill., University of Chicago Press, 1930).

——'The garrison state', *American Journal of Sociology*, 46, 2 (1941).

P. Lazarsfeld and R. Merton, 'Mass communication, popular taste and organised social action', in B. Rosenberg and D. White (eds), *Mass Culture* (West Drayton, Free Press, 1957).

P. Lazarsfeld and F. Stanton, *Radio Research 1942–3* (Boston, Mass., Duell Sloan Pearce, 1944).

P. Lazarsfeld, B. Berelson and H. Gaudet, *The People's Choice* (New York, Columbia University Press, 1944).

M. Leapman, *Treachery? The Power Struggle at TVAM* (London, Allen & Unwin, 1984).

F. R. Leavis, *Mass Civilisation and Minority Culture* (London, Minority Press, 1930).

——*The Common Pursuit* (London, Chatto & Windus, 1952).

——*Scrutiny: A Retrospect* (Cambridge, Cambridge University Press, 1962).

——*A Selection From Scrutiny*, 2 vols (Cambridge, Cambridge University Press, 1968).

F. R. Leavis and D. Thompson, *Culture and Environment* (London, Chatto & Windus, 1933).

Q. D. Leavis, *Fiction and the Reading Public* (London, Chatto & Windus, 1932).

T. Lovell, 'Sociology of aesthetic structures', in D. McQuail (ed.), *Sociology of Mass Communications* (Harmondsworth, Penguin, 1972).

L. Lowenthal, *Prophets of Deceit* (New York, Harper & Row, 1949).

R. S. Lynd and H. M. Lynd, *Middletown: A Study on Contemporary American Culture* (London, Constable, 1929).

——*Middletown: In Transition* (London, Constable, 1935).

A. McBarnett, 'The North Sea oil story', *Scottish Journal of Sociology*, 3, 1 (1977).

D. McQuail, *Towards a Sociology of Mass Communication* (West Drayton, Collier Macmillan, 1969).

——*Sociology of Mass Communications* (Harmondsworth, Penguin, 1972).

——'Review of sociological writings on the press', Royal Commission on the Press 1974–77, Working Paper 2 (London, HMSO, 1977).

——*Mass Communication Theory: An Introduction* (2nd edn) (London, Sage, 1987).

H. Marcuse, *'The End of Utopia', Five Lectures* (Harmondsworth, Allen Lane, 1970).

——*One Dimensional Man* (London, Routledge & Kegan Paul, 1974).

M. Mendelsohn and I. Crespi, *Polls, Television and the New Politics* (New York, Harper & Row, 1970).

R. K. Merton, *Social Theory and Social Structure* (West Drayton, Free Press, 1957).

F. Mulhearn, *The Moment of Scrutiny* (London, New Left Books, 1979).

K. Ohmae, *The Borderless World* (London, Collins, 1993).

——*The End of the Nation State* (London, HarperCollins, 1996).

E. Ostrom, *Governing the Commons* (Oxford, Oxford University Press, 1994).

T. Pateman, *Language, Truth and Politics* (Brighton, Southern Books, 1974).

——*Television and the February 1974 General Election* (London, British Film Institute, 1976).

J. A. R. Pimlott, *Public Relations and American Democracy* (Princeton, NJ, Princeton University Press, 1951; repr. 1974).

A. Ray and K. Rowan (eds), *Inside Information: British Government and the Media* (London, Constable, 1982).

D. Reisman, *The Lonely Crowd* (New Haven, Conn., Yale University Press, 1950).

J. P. Robinson, 'The press as king-maker', *Journalism Quarterly*, 41, 4 (1974).

B. Rosenberg and D. White (eds), *Mass Culture* (West Drayton, Free Press, 1957).

P. Schlesinger, *Putting 'Reality' Together* (London, Constable, 1974).

——'Rethinking the sociology of journalism: source strategies and the limits of media-centrism', in M. Ferguson (ed.), *Public Communication* (London, Sage, 1990).

P. Schlesinger, G. Murdoch and P. Elliot, *Televising Terrorism* (London, Comedia, 1984).

J. Seaton, 'The image of trade unions in the media', in B. Pimlott and C. Cook (eds), *Trade Unions in British Politics* (Harlow, Longman, 1982).

——'The media and the politics of unemployment', in S. Allen, S. Waton and S. Wood (eds), *Unemployment* (London, Macmillan, 1985).

——'Politics and the media in Britain', *Journal of Western European Politics*, special broadcasting issue (London, Summer 1985).

J. Seaton and B. Pimlott, 'The role of the media in the Portuguese Revolution', in A. Smith (ed.), *Newspapers and Democracy* (Cambridge, Mass., MIT Press, 1980).

——'The Portuguese media in transition', in K. Maxwell (ed.), *The Press and the Rebirth of Iberian Democracy* (Westport, Conn., Greenwood Press, 1983).

——'Political power and the Portuguese media', in L. Graham (ed.), *In Search of Modern Portugal: The Revolution and its Consequences* (Madison, University of Wisconsin Press, 1983).

C. Seymour-Ure, *The Press, Politics and Public* (London, Methuen, 1968).

——*The Political Impact of the Mass Media* (London, Constable, 1974).

——*The American President: Power and Communication* (London, Macmillan, 1982).

——'The SDP and the media', *Political Quarterly*, 53, 4 (1982).

E. Shils, *The Intellectuals and the Powers* (Chicago, Ill., University of Chicago Press, 1972).

E. Shils and M. Janowitz, 'Cohesion and disintegration in the Wehrmacht in World War II', *Public Opinion Quarterly*, 12, 3 (London, 1948).

P. Siegelhart (ed.), *Chips with Everything* (London, Comedia, 1982).

P. Slater, *The Origin and Significance of the Frankfurt School* (London, Routledge & Kegan Paul, 1977).

A. Smith, *The Politics of Information* (London, Macmillan, 1968).

A. Smith, *The Shadow in the Cave* (London, Allen & Unwin, 1973).

——(ed.), *Television and Political Life* (London, Macmillan, 1979).

——'The fading of the industrial age', *Political Quarterly*, 53, 3 (June 1983).

——*From Books to Bytes* (London, BFI, 1993).

B. L. Smith, H. D. Lasswell and R. Casey, *Propaganda Communication and Public Opinion* (Princeton, NJ, Princeton University Press, 1946).

A. Swingewood, *The Myth of Mass Culture* (London, Macmillan, 1977).

M. Tracey, *The Production of Political Television* (London, Routledge & Kegan Paul, 1978).

J. Trenaman, *Communications and Comprehension* (London, Collins, 1967).

J. Trenaman and D. McQuail, *Television and the Political Image* (London, Methuen, 1961).

G. Tuchman, 'Making news by doing work', *American Journal of Sociology*, 79, 1 (1973).

——(ed.), *The TV Establishment* (New York, Random House, 1975).

J. Tulloch, *Watching Television Audiences* (London, Arnold, 2000).

J. Tunstall, *Advertising Man* (London, Constable, 1969).

——*The Westminster Lobby Correspondents* (London, Routledge & Kegan Paul, 1970).

——*Journalists at Work* (London, Constable, 1971).

——*The Media in Britain* (London, Constable, 1983).

F. Webster, *The Information Society* (Cambridge, Polity Press, 1996).

E. G. Wedell, *Broadcasting and Public Policy* (London, Michael Joseph, 1968).

——*Structures of Broadcasting* (Manchester, Manchester University Press, 1970).

J. Whale, *The Half Shut Eye* (London, Macmillan, 1969).

——*The Politics of the Media* (London, Fontana, 1977).

R. Williams, *The Long Revolution* (Harmondsworth, Pelican, 1965).

——*Communications* (London, Chatto & Windus, 1966).

——*Television: Technology and Cultural Form* (London, Fontana, 1974).

——*Drama from Ibsen to Brecht* (Harmondsworth, Penguin, 1976).

——*Keywords* (London, Fontana, 1976).

——*Marxism and Literature* (Oxford, Oxford University Press, 1977).

——*Politics and Letters: Interviews with the New Left Review* (London, New Left Books, 1979).

J. Willis and T. Wollen (eds), *The Neglected Audience* (London, British Film Institute, 1990).

P. Willis, *Learning to Labour* (Farnborough, Saxon House, 1977).

——*Sacred and Profane Culture* (London, Routledge & Kegan Paul, 1978).

P. Willmott and M. D. Young, *Family and Class in a London Suburb* (London, Routledge & Kegan Paul, 1960).

——*The Symmetrical Family* (London, Routledge & Kegan Paul, 1973).

Mass communications readers

O. Boyd Barrett and C. Newbold (eds), *Approaches to Media* (London, Arnold, 1995).

R. Collins, J. Curran, N. Garnham, P. Scannell, P. Schlesinger and C. Sparks (eds), *Media, Culture and Society: A Critical Reader* (London, Sage, 1986).

J. Curran and M. Gurevitch (eds), *Mass Media and Society* (4th edn) (London, Arnold, 2005).

J. Curran and A. Smith (eds), *Impacts and Influences* (London, Methuen, 1987).

J. Curran, M. Gurevitch and J. Woollacott (eds), *Mass Communication and Society* (London, Edward Arnold/Open University, 1977).

J. Curran, D. Morley and V. Walkerdine (eds), *Cultural Studies and Communications* (London, Arnold, 1996).

J. Downing, A. Mohammadi and A. Sreberny-Mohammadi (eds), *Questioning the Media* (2nd edn) (London, Sage, 1995).

J. Eldridge (ed.), *Getting the Message* (London, Routledge, 1993).

M. Ferguson (ed.), *Public Communication* (London, Sage, 1990).

M. Gurevitch, T. Bennett, J. Curran and J. Woollacott (eds), *Culture, Society and the Media* (London, Methuen, 1982).

M. Levy and M. Gurevitch (eds), *Defining Media Studies* (New York, Oxford University Press, 1994).

D. McQuail (ed.), *Sociology of Mass Communication: Selected Reading* (Harmondsworth, Penguin, 1972).

R. Manoff and M. Schudson (ed.), *Reading the News* (New York, Pantheon, 1987).

P. Marris and S. Thornham (eds), *Media Studies* (Edinburgh, Edinburgh University Press, 1996).

J. Munns, *A Cultural Studies Reader* (London, Longman, 1996).

E. Seiter, H. Borchers, G. Kreutzner and E.-M. Warth (eds), *Remote Control* (London, Routledge, 1989).

Economic approaches to the media

T. P. Barwise, A. S. C. Ehrenberg and G. J. Goodhart, 'Audience appreciation and audience size', *Journal of the Market Research Society*, 21, 4 (October 1979).

L. Brown, *Television: The Business Behind the Box* (New York, Harcourt Brace Jovanovich, 1971).

M. Cave, 'The conduct of auctions for broadcasting franchises', *Fiscal Studies*, 10, 1 (February 1989).

R. H. Coase, *British Broadcasting: A Study in Monopoly* (London, Longman Green, 1950).

——'The market for goods and the market for ideas', *American Economic Review* (1974), p. 384.

R. Collins, N. Garnham and G. Locksley, *The Economics of Television: The UK Case* (London, Sage, 1987).

——, ——and——, *The Economics of Television* (London, Sage, 1988).

T. Congdon, B. Sturgess, W. Shaw, A. Graham and G. Davies, *Paying for Broadcasting* (London, Routledge, 1992).

J. Curran, 'Advertising and the press', in J. Curran (ed.), *The British Press: A Manifesto* (London, Macmillan, 1978).

——'Press freedom as a property right', *Media, Culture and Society*, 1, 1 (1979).

——'Advertising as a patronage system', *Sociological Review Monograph*, 29 (1980).

——'The impact of advertising on the British mass media', in R. Collins *et al.* (eds), *Media Culture and Society: A Critical Reader* (London, Sage, 1986).

J. Curran, A. Douglas and G. Whannel, 'The political economy of the human interest story', in A. Smith (ed.), *Newspapers and Democracy* (Cambridge, Mass., MIT Press, 1981).

R. Darlington, 'Telecoms: the broadband revolution', *Information Technology and Public Policy*, 8, 1 (winter 1989).

E. Epstein, *Broadcast Journalism. The Ratings Game* (London and New York, Vintage, 1975).

D.Freedman, The political economy of the new news environment , in N. Fenton (ed.), *New Media, Old News* (London, Sage, 2009).

J. E. Gerald, *The British Press under Government Economic Controls* (Minneapolis, University of Minnesota Press, 1956).

T. Gitlin, *Inside Prime Time* (New York, Pantheon, 1983).

P. Golding and G. Murdoch, 'Culture, communications and political economy', in J. Curran and M. Gurevitch (eds), *Mass Media and Society* (2nd edn) (London, Arnold, 1996).

G. J. Goodhart, A. S. C. Ehrenberg and M. A. Collins, *The Television Audience: Patterns of Viewing* (Farnborough, Saxon House, 1975)

N. Gowing, 'Real time television and political crises' (Shorenstein Centre Paper, Kennedy School of Government, 1994).

T. H. Gubach, *The International Film Industry* (Indiana, University of Indiana Press, 1971).

A. Henney, 'Regulating public and privatized monopolies: a radical approach', *Policy Journal for the Public Finance Corporation* (February 1986).

F. Hirsch and D. Gordan, *Newspaper Money* (London, Hutchinson, 1975).

P. M. Hirsch, 'Processing fads and fashions', *American Journal of Sociology*, 77 (1972).

S. Hoyer, S. Hadenius and I. Weibull, *The Politics and Economics of the Press: A Developmental Perspective* (Beverly Hills, Calif., Sage, 1975).

R. E. Jackson, 'Satellite business systems and the concept of the dispersed enterprise', *Media, Culture and Society*, 1, 3 (1979).

F. D. Klingender and S. Legg, *Money Behind the Screen* (London, Lawrence & Wishart, 1937).

M. Matson, 'Telecoms: the broadband revolution', Parliamentary Information Technology Committee 2 (22 November 1989).

A. Mattelart (trans. M. Chanan), *Multinational Corporations and the Control of Culture* (Brighton, Harvester Press, 1979).

K. Morgan and A. Sayer, *Microcircuits of Capital: Sunrise Industry and Uneven Development* (London, Polity Press, 1987).

V. Mosco, *The Political Economy of Information* (Madison, Wisconsin University Press, 1988).

G. Mulgan, *Communication and Control* (London, Polity Press, 1990).

G. Murdock, 'Redrawing the map of the communications industries: concentration and ownership in the era of privatization', in M. Ferguson (ed.), *Public Communication* (London, Sage, 1990).

G. Murdock and P. Golding, 'For a political economy of mass communication', in J. Saville and R. Miliband (eds), *The Socialist Register 1973* (London, Merlin, 1974).

——'Capitalism, communication and class relations', in J. Curran, M. Gurevitch and J. Woollacott (eds), *Mass Communication and Society* (London, Edward Arnold/Open University Press, 1977).

Political and Economic Planning, *The British Press* (London, PEP, 1938).

——*The Factual Film* (London, Arts Enquiry, PEP, 1947).

——*The British Film Industry* (London, PEP, 1952).

R. Putnam, *Hanging Together: Cooperation and Conflict in Seven Power Summits* (Cambridge, Mass., Harvard University Press, 1987).

K. Robins and F. Webster, 'Mass communications and information technology', in R. Miliband and J. Saville (eds), *The Socialist Register 1979* (London, Merlin, 1979).

H. Schiller, *Who Knows: Information in the Age of Fortune 500* (New Jersey, Ablex, 1981).

——*Mass Communications and the American Empire* (Boulder, Col., Westview Press, 1993).

M. Sharp (ed.), *Europe and New Technologies* (London, Pinter, 1989).

A. Smith, 'Subsidies and the press in Europe', *Political and Economic Planning*, 43, 569 (1977).

——*The Geopolitics of Information* (London, Faber, 1980).

——*Goodbye Gutenburg: The Newspaper Revolution of the 1980s* (London, Oxford University Press, 1980).

S. G. Sturmey, *The Economic Development of Radio* (London, Duckworth, 1958).

J. Taylor, 'The broadband revolution: implications for major networks', *Information Technology and Public Policy*, 8, 1 (Winter 1990).

J. Tunstall, *The Media are American* (London, Constable, 1977).

T. Varis, 'The international flow of television programmes', *Journal of Communication*, 34 (1984).

F. Wolf, *Television Programming for News and Current Affairs* (New York, Praeger, 1972).

Politics of mass media

Adam Smith Institute, *Omega Report: Communications Policy* (London, Adam Smith Institute, 1984).

——*Funding the BBC* (London, Adam Smith Institute, 1985).

M. Aldridge and N. Hewitt (eds), *Controlling Broadcasting* (Manchester, Manchester University Press, 1994).

N. Ascherson, 'Newspapers and internal democracy', in J. Curran (ed.), *The British Press: A Manifesto* (London, Macmillan, 1978).

T. Austin and T. Haines (eds), *The Times Guide to the House of Commons June 2001* (London, Times Books, 2001).

R. Avery (ed.), *Public Service Broadcasting in a Multichannel Environment* (New York, Longman, 1993).

T. Baistow, *Fourth-Rate Estate* (London, Comedia, 1985).

E. Barendt, *Broadcasting Law* (Oxford, Oxford University Press, 1993).

J. Barron, *Freedom of the Press for Whom?* (Ontario, Midland, 1975).

D. Berry, L. Cooper and C. Landry, *Where is the Other News?* (London, Comedia, 1980).

J. Blumler and M. Gurevitch, *The Crisis of Public Communication* (London, Routledge, 1995).

S. Brittan, 'The fight for freedom in broadcasting', *Political Quarterly*, 58 (1987).

——'The case for the consumer market', in C. Veljanovski (ed.), *Freedom in Broadcasting* (London, Institute of Economic Affairs, 1989).

Broadcasting Research Unit, *The Public Service Idea* (London, Broadcasting Research Unit, 1985).

D. Butler and G. Butler, *Twentieth-Century British Political Facts, 1900–2000* (8th edn) (Basingstoke, Macmillan, 2000).

V. Cable, *The World's New Fissure* (London, Demos, 1994).

M. Cockerell, *Live from No. 10* (London, Faber and Faber, 1988).

R. Collins, *Television: Culture and Policy* (London, Unwin Hyman, 1990).

——*Satellite Television in Western Europe* (revised edn) (London, Libbey, 1992).

——*Broadcasting and Audio-visual Policy in the European Single Market* (London, Libbey, 1994).

R. Collins and C. Murroni, *New Media, New Policies* (Cambridge, Polity Press, 1996).

L. Cooper, C. Landry and D. Berry, *The Other Secret Service* (London, Comedia, 1980).

G. Cumberbatch and D. Howitt, *A Measure of Uncertainty* (London, Libbey, 1989).

J. Curran (ed.), *The British Press: A Manifesto* (London, Macmillan, 1978).

——'Rethinking the media as a public sphere', in P. Dahlgren and C. Sparks (eds), *Communication and Citizenship* (London, Routledge, 1991).

——'Regulation and deregulation of the British media', in K. E. Gustafsson (ed.) *Media Structure and the State* (Gothenburg, University of Gothenburg, 1995).

——'Mass media and democracy revisited', in J. Curran and M. Gurevitch (eds), *Mass Media and Democracy* (2nd edn) (London, Arnold, 1996).

——'Media and democracy: the third route', in M. Andersen (ed.), *Media and Democracy* (Oslo, University of Oslo, 1996).

——'Television journalism: theory and practice. The case of *Newsnight*', in P. Holland, *Television Handbook* (London, Routledge, 1997).

——'Press reformism 1918–98: a study of failure', in H. Tumber (ed.), *Media Power, Professionals and Policies* (London, Routlege, 2000).

——*Media and Power* (London, Routledge, 2002).

J. Curran (ed.), 'Global journalism: a case study of the internet', in Nick Couldry and James Curran (eds), *Contesting Media Power* (Boulder, Col., Rowman & Littlefield, 2003).

J. Curran, J. Ecclestone, G. Oakley and A. Richardson (eds), *Bending Reality: The State of the Media* (London, Pluto Press, 1986).

J. Curran, S. Iyengar, A.B. Lund and A. Salovaara-Moring, 'Media system, public knowledge and democracy: A comparative study', *European Journal of Communication*, 24, 1 (2009).

P. Dahlgren, *Television and the Public Sphere* (London, Sage, 1995).

P. Dahlgren and C. Sparks (eds), *Communication and Citizenship* (London, Routledge, 1991).

——and——(eds), *Journalism and Popular Culture* (London, Sage, 1992).

M. Dickinson and S. Street (eds), *Cinema and the State* (London, British Film Institute, 1985).

B. Franklin, *Packaging Politics* (London, Arnold, 1994).

C. Frost, 'The Press Complaints Commission: a study of ten years of adjudications on press complaints', *Journalism Studies*, 5, 1 (2004).

C. Gardiner and J. Sheppard, 'Transforming TV: the limits of left policy', *Screen*, 25, 2 (1984).

N. Garnham, 'Public service versus the market', *Screen*, 24, 1 (1983).

——'Telecommunications policy in the United Kingdom', *Media, Culture and Society*, 7, 1 (1985).

——*Communications and Capitalism* (London, Sage, 1990).

T. Gitlin, 'Public sphere or sphericules?', in T. Liebes and J. Curran (eds), *Media, Ritual and Identity* (London, Routledge, 1998).

Glasgow University Media Group, *Really Bad News* (London, Writers & Readers, 1982).

D. Goldberg, T. Prosser and S. Verhulst, *Regulating the Changing Media* (Oxford, Clarendon Press, 1998).

P. Golding and G. Murdock, 'Confronting the market: public intervention and press diversity', in J. Curran (ed.), *The British Press: A Manifesto* (London, Macmillan, 1978).

——and——, 'The new communications revolution', in J. Curran, J. Ecclestone, G. Oakley and A. Richardson (eds), *Bending Reality: The State of the Media* (London, Pluto Press, 1986).

A. Graham and G. Davies, *Broadcasting, Society and Policy in the Multimedia Age* (Luton, University of Luton Press, 1997).

J. Gray, *After Social Democracy* (London, Demos, 1996).

K. E. Gustafsson, 'Government policies to reduce newspaper entry barriers', *Journal of Economics*, 6, 1 (1993).

A. Harcourt, 'Institution-driven competition: the regulation of cross-border broadcasting in the EU', *Journal of Public Policy*, 27, 3 (2007).

I. Hargreaves, *A Sharper Vision: The BBC and the Communication Revolution* (London, Demos, 1993).

S. Harvey (ed.), *The Regions, the Nation, the BBC* (London, BFI, 1993).

S. Harvey and K. Robins, 'Voices and places: the BBC and regional policy', *Political Quarterly*, 65, 1 (1994).

S. Hearst, 'The development of cable systems and services', *Political Quarterly*, 54, 3 (1983).

P. Hennessy, D. Walker and M. Cockerell, *Sources Close to the Prime Minister* (London, Macmillan, 1985).

D. Hesmondhaulgh, *The Cultural Industries* (London, Sage, 2002).

S. Holland, 'Countervailing press power', in J. Curran (ed.), *The British Press: A Manifesto* (London, Macmillan, 1978).

S. Hood (ed.), *Behind the Scenes* (London, Lawrence & Wishart, 1994).

S. Hood and G. O'Leary, *Questions of Broadcasting* (London, Methuen, 1990).

R. Horwitz, 'The First Amendment meets some new technologies: broadcasting, common carriers and free speech in the 1990s', *Theory and Society*, 20 (1991).

P. Humphreys, *Mass Media and Media Policy in Western Europe* (Manchester, Manchester University Press, 1996).

P. Humphreys, 'The EU, communications liberalization and the future of public service broadcasting', in K. Sarikakis (ed.), *Media and Cultural Policy in the European Union*, (Amsterdam, Rodopi, 2007).

N. Jones, *Soundbites and Spin Doctors* (London, Cassell, 1995).

E. Katz, 'And deliver us from segmentation', *Annals of the American Academy of Political and Social Science*, 546 (1996).

J. Keane, *The Media and Democracy* (Cambridge, Polity Press, 1991).

S. K. Kent, *Gender and Power in Britain, 1640–1990* (London, Routledge, 1999).

A. Knight, *A British Success Story* (London, News International, 1993).

R. Kuhn, *Politics and the Media in Britain*, (Basingstoke, Palgrave Macmillan, 2007).

Labour Party, *People and the Media* (London, Labour Party, 1974).

C. Landry, D. Morley, R. Southwood and P. Write, *What a Way to Run a Railroad* (London, Comedia, 1985).

C. Leys, *Market-Driven Politics* (London, Verso, 2001).

L. Lichtenberg, 'The Dutch model of press policy', in K. E. Gustafsson (ed.), *Media Structure and the State* (Gothenberg, University of Gothenberg, 1995).

S. Livingstone and P. Lunt, *Talk on Television* (London, Routledge, 1994).

C. MacCabe and O. Stewart (eds), *The BBC and Public Service Broadcasting* (Manchester, Manchester University Press, 1986).

P. McDonald, 'The music industry', in J. Stokes and A. Reading (eds), *The Media in Britain* (Basingstoke, Macmillan, 1999).

B. McNair, *Mediated Sex* (London, Arnold, 1996).

——*News and Journalism in the UK* (5th edn) (London, Routledge, 2009)

D. McQuail and K. Siane (eds), *New Media Politics* (London, Sage, 1986).

T. Madge, *Beyond the BBC* (London, Macmillan, 1989).

W. Melody, 'Communication policy in the global information economy: whither the public interest', in M. Ferguson (ed.), *Public Communication* (London, Sage, 1990).

Militant, *What We Stand For* (London, Militant, 1985).

T. Miller, N. Govil, J. McMurria, R. Maxwell and T. Wang, *Global Hollywood 2* (London, British Film Institute, 2004).

E. Moonman (ed.), *The Press: A Case for Commitment* (London, Fabian Society Trust, 391, 1969).

G. Mulgan and K. Worpole, *Saturday Night or Sunday Morning* (London, Comedia, 1986).

R. Murdoch, 'Freedom in broadcasting', *MacTaggart Lecture 1989* (London, News International, 1989).

P. Murschetz, 'State support for the daily press in Europe: a critical appraisal', *European Journal of Communication*, 13, 3 (1998).

R. Negrine, *Politics and the Mass Media in Britain* (2nd edn) (London, Routledge, 1994).

T. O'Malley and C. Soley, *Regulating the Press* (London, Pluto Press, 2000).

R. Picard, *Ravens of Odin* (Ames, Iowa State University Press, 1988).

V. Porter, 'The Janus character of television', in G. Locksley (ed.), *Integration: The Single European Market and the Information Communication Technologies* (London, Pinter, 1990).

M. Puppis, 'National media regulation in the era of free trade: the role of global media governance', *European Journal of Communication*, 23, 4 (2008).

G. Robertson, *People Against the Press* (London, Quartet, 1983).

G. Robertson and A. Nicol, *Media Law* (3rd edn) (Harmondsworth, Penguin, 1992).

J. Rowbottom, 'Media freedom and political debate in the digital era', *Modern Law Review*, 69 (4), 2006.

L. Sabato, *Feeding Frenzy: Attack Journalism and Politics* (New York, Free Press, 1995).

P. Scannell, 'Public service broadcasting and modern public life', in P. Scannell, P. Schlesinger and C. Sparks (eds), *Culture and Power* (London, Sage, 1992).

P. Schlesinger, 'From public service to commodity: the political economy of teletext in the UK', *Media, Culture and Society*, 7, 4 (1984).

J. Seaton, 'Government policy and the mass media', in J. Curran (ed.), *The British Press: A Manifesto* (London, Macmillan, 1978).

——'Broadcasting and politics in Britain', in R. Kuhn (ed.), *Broadcasting and Politics in Western Europe* (London, Sage, 1985).

——'The media and politics in Britain', *Journal of Western European Politics*, 6,3 (June 1985).

——'Pornography annoys', in J. Curran (ed.), *Bending Reality: The State of the Media* (London, Pluto Press, 1986).

——'The media and the politics of unemployment', in S. Allen (ed.), *The Experience of Unemployment* (London, Macmillan, 1986).

——'Atrocities and the media', *European Journal of Communications*, 2, 1 (January 1987).

——'The Holocaust: a case study of atrocities and the media', in J. Seaton and B. Pimlott (eds), *The Media in British Politics* (Aldershot, Gower, 1987).

——'Down with Aunt Tabitha: a modest media proposal', in B. Pimlott and T. Wright (eds), *The Alternative: Politics for a Change* (London, W. H. Allen, 1990).

——(ed.) *The Media of Conflict* (London, Zed Books, 1998).

——*Politics and the Media in the New Millennium* (Blackwell, 1998).

J. Seaton and B. Pimlott, 'The struggle for balance: the BBC and the politicians 1926–45', in J. Seaton and B. Pimlott (eds), *The Media in British Politics* (Aldershot, Gower, 1987).

C. Seymour-Ure, 'Leaders and the media', in J. Seaton and B. Pimlott (eds), *The Media in British Politics* (Aldershot, Gower, 1987).

J. Sinclair, E. Jacka and S. Cunningham (eds), *New Patterns in Global Television* (Oxford, Oxford University Press, 1996).

E. Skogerbo, 'The press subsidy system in Norway', *European Journal of Communication*, 12, 1, (1997).

A. Smith, *Subsidies and the Press in Europe* (London, Political & Economic Planning, 1977).

R. Sparks and I. Taylor, 'Mass communications', in P. Brown and R. Sparks (eds), *Beyond Thatcherism* (Milton Keynes, Open University Press, 1989).

W. Stevenson (ed.), *All our Futures* (London, BFI, 1993).

S. Tunney, *Labour and the Press* (Brighton, Sussex University Press, 2007).

C. Veljanovski (ed.), *Freedom in Broadcasting* (London, Institute of Economic Affairs, 1989).

J. Whale, *The Politics of the Media* (London, Fontana, 1980).

P. Whitehead, 'Reconstructing broadcasting', in J. Curran, J. Ecclestone, G. Oakley and A. Richardson (eds), *Bending Reality: The State of the Media* (London, Pluto Press, 1986).

R. Worcester, 'Demographics and values: what the British public reads and what it thinks about its newspapers', in H. Stephenson and M. Bromley (eds), *Sex, Lies and Democracy* (London, Longman, 1998).

New media

J. Abbate, *Inventing the Internet* (Cambridge, Mass., MIT Press, 2000).

Advertising Statistics Yearbook 2002 (London, Advertising Association, 2002).

N. Baym, 'Interpersonal life online', in L. Lievrouw and S. Livingstone (eds), *The Handbook of New Media* (London, Sage, 2002).

D. Bell and B. Kennedy (eds), *The Cybercultures Reader* (London, Routledge, 2000).

C. Bellamy and J. Taylor, *Governing in the Information Age* (Milton Keynes, Open University Press, 1998).

T. Berners-Lee, *Weaving the Web* (London, Orion, 2000).

A. Briggs and P. Burke, *A Social History of the Media* (Cambridge, Polity Press, 2002).

M. Cassells, *The Internet Galaxy* (Oxford, Oxford University Press, 2001).

J. Cassidy, *Dot.Con* (London, Penguin Books, 2003).

N. Chenoweth, *Virtual Murdoch* (London, Secker Warburg, 2001).

S. Coleman, 'New media and democratic politics', *New Media and Society*, 1, 1 (1999).

J. Cornford and K. Robins, 'New media', in J. Stokes and A. Reading (eds), *The Media in Britain* (Basingstoke, Macmillan, 1999).

J. Curran, 'Global journalism: a case study of the internet', in N. Couldry and J. Curran (eds), *Contesting Media Power* (New York, Rowman & Littlefield, 2003.

J. Curran and T. Witschge, 'Liberal dreams and the internet', in N. Fenton (ed.), *New Media, Old News* (London, Sage, 2009).

D. Elstein, 'The politics of digital TV', www.openDemocracy.net/forum, 2002.

P. Evans and T. Wurster, *Blown to Bits* (Boston, Mass., Harvard Business School Press, 2000).

N. Fenton (ed.), *New Media, Old News* (London, Sage, 2009).

P. Flichy, 'New media history', in L. Lievrouw and S. Livingstone (eds), *The Handbook of New Media* (London, Sage, 2002).

C. George, 'The Internet's political impact and the penetration/participation paradox in Malaysia and Singapore', *Media, Culture and Society*, 27, 6, 2005.

J. Gillies and R.Cailliau, *How the Web Was Born* (Oxford, Oxford University Press, 2000).

G. Goggin, 'Pay per browse? The Web's commercial future', in D. Gauntlett (ed.), *Web Studies* (London, Arnold, 2000).

L. Gross, 'The gay global village in cyberspace', in N. Couldry and J. Curran (eds), *Contesting Media Power* (Boulder, Col., Rowman & Littlefield, 2003.

D. Held, A. McGrew, D. Goldblatt and J. Perraton, *Global Transformations* (Cambridge, Polity Press, 1999).

K. Hill and J. Hughes, *Cyberpolitics* (Lanham, MD, Rowman & Littlefield, 1998).

M. Hindman, *The Myth of Digital Democracy* (Princeton, Princeton University Press, 2009).

M. Ito, 'Virtually embodied: the reality of fantasy in a multi-user dungeon', in D. Porter (ed.), *Internet Culture* (New York, Routledge, 1997).

N. Klein, *No Logo* (London, Flamingo, 2001).

C. Kramarae, 'The language and the nature of the Internet: the meaning of global', *New Media and Society*, 1, 1 (1999).

S. Lax, 'The Internet and democracy', in D. Gauntlet (ed.), *Web Studies* (London, Arnold, 2000).

T. Lennon, 'Digital TV: a phoenix risen from the ashes', *Free Press*, 129, 2002.

L. Lessig, *Code and Other Laws of Cyberspace* (New York, Basic Books, 1999).

——*The Future of Ideas* (New York, Random House, 2001).

S. Levy, *Hackers* (London, Penguin, 1994).

M. Lim, 'The internet, social networks and reform in Indonesia', in N. Couldry and J. Curran (eds), *Contesting Media Power* (Boulder, Col., Rowman & Littlefield, 2003).

S. Ling, 'The alternative media in Malaysia: their potential and limitations', in N. Couldry and J. Curran (eds), *Contesting Media Power* (Boulder, Col., Rowman & Littlefield, 2003).

S. Livingstone and M. Bovill, *Young People: New Media* (London, London School of Economics and Political Science, 1999).

P. Lovelock and J. Ure, 'The new economy: internet, telecommunications and electronic commerce?', in L. Lievrouw and S. Livingstone (eds), *The Handbook of New Media* (London, Sage, 2002).

R. McChesney, *Rich Media, Poor Democracy* (Urbana, University of Illinois Press, 1999).

M. Mallapragada, 'The Indian diaspora in the USA and around the world', in D. Gauntlett (ed.), *Web Studies* (London, Arnold, 2000).

R. Mansell, 'New media and the power of networks' (London, London School of Economics and Political Science, Inaugural Professorial Lecture, 2001).

D. Miller and D. Slater, *The Internet: An Ethnographic Approach* (Oxford, Berg, 2000).

V. Miller, 'Search engines, portals and global capitalism', in D. Gauntlett (ed.), *Web Studies* (London, Arnold, 2000).

G. Murdock and P. Golding, 'Digital possibilities, market realities: the contradictions of communications convergence', in L. Panitch and C. Leys (eds), *A World of Contradictions: Socialist Register 2002* (London, Merlin Press, 2001).

J. Naughton, *A Brief History of the Future* (London, Phoenix, 2000)

N. Negroponte, *Being Digital* (London, Hodder & Stoughton, 1996 [1995]).

K. Patelis, 'The political economy of the Internet', in J. Curran (ed.), *Media Organisations in Society* (London, Arnold, 2000).

M. Poster, *The Second Media Age* (Cambridge, Polity Press, 1995).

——'Cyberdemocracy: Internet and the public sphere', in D. Porter (ed.), *Internet Culture* (New York, Routledge, 1997).

M. Price, *Media and Sovereignty* (Cambridge, Mass., MIT Press, 2002).

H. Rheingold, *The Virtual Community* (rev. edn) (Cambridge, Mass., MIT Press, 2000).

G. Rodan, *Transparency and Authoritarian Rule in Southeast Asia* (London: CurzonRoutledge, 2004).

D. Schiller, *Digital Capitalism* (Cambridge, Mass., MIT Press, 2000).

D. Slater, 'Social relationships and identity online and offline', in L. Lievrouw and S. Livingstone (eds), *The Handbook of New Media* (London, Sage, 2002).

J. Slevin, *The Internet and Society* (Cambridge, Polity Press, 2000).

C. Sparks, 'From dead trees to live wires: the Internet's challenge to the traditional newspaper', in J. Curran and M. Gurevitch (eds), *Mass Media and Society* (3rd edn) (London, Arnold, 2000).

——'The internet and the global public sphere', in W. Lance Bennett and R. Entman (eds), *Mediated Politics* (New York, Cambridge University Press, 2001).

L. Stein and N. Sinha, 'New global media and communication policy: the role of the state in the twenty-first century', in L. Lievrouw and S. Livingstone (eds), *The Handbook of New Media* (London, Sage, 2001).

J. Stratton, 'Cyberspace and the globalisation of culture', in D. Porter (ed.), *Internet Culture* (New York, Routledge, 1997).

T. Streeter, 'Romanticism in business culture: the Internet, the 1990s, and the origins of irrational exuberance', in A. Calabrese and C. Sparks (eds), *Toward a Political Economy of Culture* (Boulder, Col., Rowman & Littlefield, 2003).

F. Turner, *From Counterculture to Cyberculture* (Chicago, University of Chicago Press, 2006).

A. Willheim, *Democracy and the Digital Age* (New York, Routledge, 2000)

S. Williams, *Free as in Freedom* (Sebastopol, Calif., O'Reilly, 2002).

B. Winston, *Media Technology and Society* (London, Routledge, 1998).

Y. Zhao, 'Falun Gong, identity, the struggle over meaning in and out of reformed China', in N. Couldry and J. Curran (eds), *Contesting Media Power* (Boulder, Col., Rowman & Littlefield, 2003).

Index

eBooks

eBooks – at www.eBookstore.tandf.co.uk

A library at your fingertips!

eBooks are electronic versions of printed books. You can store them on your PC/laptop or browse them online.

They have advantages for anyone needing rapid access to a wide variety of published, copyright information.

eBooks can help your research by enabling you to bookmark chapters, annotate text and use instant searches to find specific words or phrases. Several eBook files would fit on even a small laptop or PDA.

NEW: Save money by eSubscribing: cheap, online access to any eBook for as long as you need it.

Annual subscription packages

We now offer special low-cost bulk subscriptions to packages of eBooks in certain subject areas. These are available to libraries or to individuals.

For more information please contact webmaster.ebooks@tandf.co.uk

We're continually developing the eBook concept, so keep up to date by visiting the website.

www.eBookstore.tandf.co.uk